NON-CIRCULATING

10·95

BRITISH FILM INSTITUTE

bfi

FILM AND TELEVISION HANDBOOK 1990

Editor: David Leafe
Assistant Editor: Susan Oates
Consultant Editor: Wayne Drew
Editorial assistance: Allen Eyles, Jane
Ivey, Jilly Marsh, Brian Robinson, Linda
Wood
Cover: Catherine Denvir
Design: Bobbett Design Ltd, Penshurst,
Kent
Production: Landmark Production
Consultants Ltd
Advertisement Managers: Jackson-Rudd
and Associates

**With a special thanks for their assistance
and advice to BFI staff, and to former
editor Patience Coster**

Many thanks also to all those who assisted
with illustrations: Artificial Eye Film Co,
BBC Photographic Library, BSB, Blue
Dolphin, Brent Walker Group, British
Telecom International, Broadcasting
Standards Council, CNN, Central
Independent TV, Channel 4, The Children's
Channel, Contemporary Films, Corbett and
Keene, DDA, Deutscher Bundestag,
Enigma Productions, Enterprise Pictures,
Entertainment Film Distributors, FR3,
Lynne Franks PR, Glinwood Films, The
Grade Company, Granada Television, Gus
Gregory, Guild Film Distributors, HTV,
HandMade Films, Henson International
Television, Richard Holliss, IBA, ICA
Projects, Carolyn Jardine Publicity, MTV
Europe, Mainline Pictures, Marble Arch
Productions, Medusa Communications,
Metro Pictures, National Amusements
(UK), New World, PSA Public Relations,
Palace Pictures, Pas Paschali, Pathé
Releasing, Recorded Releasing Co, Sky
Television, Super Channel, Touchstone/
Amblin, Twentieth Century Fox Film Co,
UCI (UK), United International Pictures,
Vestron Pictures, Warner Bros, Working
Title, Zakiya and Associates, Zenith
Productions

The articles in this book are an expression
of the authors' views, and do not necessarily
reflect BFI policy in any given area

All reasonable measures have been taken
to ensure the accuracy of the information in
this handbook, but the publisher cannot
accept any responsibility for any errors or
omissions or any liability resulting from
the use or misuse of any such information

© British Film Institute 1989
21 Stephen Street, London W1P 1PL
Tel: 01 255 1444

Typeset by Florencetype Ltd, Kewstoke,
Avon

Made and printed in Great Britain by
Hazell, Watson and Viney Ltd, Aylesbury

British Library
Cataloguing in Publication Data
BFI film and television handbook 1990
    1. Great Britain. Cinema Industries.
Serials. 2. Great Britain. Television
Services. Serials. I. British Film Institute.
348'.8'0941

ISBN 0 85170 246 5
ISSN 0956 8409

Price £10.95

CONTENTS

Foreword

by BFI Chairman Sir Richard Attenborough

*E*ach year the British Film Institute publishes this directory which explains and illuminates the many areas of its work. Now, in this new and expanded edition for 1990, the BFI has also set out to examine some of the major issues which currently confront the United Kingdom's film and television industries.

Cinema attendances, for example, are rising yet British filmmakers benefit little from this seemingly encouraging state of affairs. In a series of interviews with some of our major producers and directors, we look at possible solutions.

As BFI Director Wilf Stevenson explains in his article on the approach of 1992, one solution may be to look to our cultural links with Europe rather than, as has been traditional, to the USA.

A sustained upturn at the box office, allied to the popularity of videocassettes and the burgeoning of additional television channels has resulted in the British public enjoying more films more often than ever before. But how much of the original picture do we actually see? Richard Holliss pans and scans some of the mysteries of the screen, from Academy ratio to 70mm, in his guide to film formats.

Now that we are faced with an imminent explosion in the available number of television channels, the cable versus satellite debate will undoubtedly take on new connotations. Peter Elman unscrambles the finance and technology, granting us a glimpse of what may yet be in store.

Our review of the past year, with a commentary by Sean Day-Lewis, includes an examination of major events which will shape the future of British film and television for years to come. Television in particular, with the introduction of new legislation, may have to pit quality programming and true choice against the race for ratings and the domination of market forces. Either way, current developments will have far reaching implications for the broadcasters and viewers of tomorrow.

The review, together with the other features I have described, can be found in the pages which follow. We hope that they, together with the listings, will give the reader a comprehensive overview of events taking place today and tomorrow.

But yesterday is also important to our understanding of film and television in this country. And nowhere is yesterday more potently evoked, nor more lovingly chronicled, than at the Institute's newly opened Museum of the Moving Image.

Thanks to the remarkable vision of its principal creators, Leslie Hardcastle and David Francis, and the brilliance of its designer, Neal Potter, MOMI is already proving immensely successful on London's South Bank.

Those who work so devotedly at the BFI are possessed of a vast range of skills which, thanks to the unparalleled generosity of J Paul Getty Jnr, they are now able to exercise in up-to-date and purpose-built surroundings – be they in the field of restoration, preservation or information. But no organisation of such diversity and such complexity can function at its best without superb leadership.

And that is what our new and tireless Director, Wilf Stevenson, has provided so admirably, so calmly and so wisely during his first year of tenure. On behalf of the Board of Governors, I should like to thank him and his staff for taking the Institute forward into the 1990s with energy, efficiency and unbounded confidence.

Richard
Attenborough

About the BFI

This Handbook is published by the British Film Institute whose task is to promote the 20th century's major new art form, the moving image.

The BFI was originally founded in 1933 to "foster the art of film". With the invention of television and video, the Institute's role has expanded and we now aim to stimulate public interest in all moving image art forms.

Gaining public and government recognition of film and television as arts has been difficult. One expects that theatre, music, painting and sculpture will have generous and continuing public support. But film and television have not been well provided for in the past, although it may be that we are winning the battle to convince people that our ideas are worthy of support.

Approximately half our funding comes from the Office of Arts and Libraries, the Government Department with responsibility for funding the arts and the heritage. We raise the rest from

Guarding the moving image: the BFI's headquarters at 21 Stephen Street

our 40,000 members, our commercial activities, sponsorship and donations.

Where possible we provide funds for others to undertake tasks similar to our own. However, as the following outline shows, we are ourselves actively involved in ensuring that the cultural value of the moving image is recognised and enhanced.

BFI South Bank

*T*he BFI plays an important role in cultural life at the South Bank arts complex through the National Film Theatre and the Museum of the Moving Image.

Museum of the Moving Image

Since MOMI opened in September 1988, over a million visitors have passed through its turnstiles and set out on the fascinating journey through the history of cinema and television which unfolds in over 1,000 film and television extracts.

Award-winning MOMI

MOMI's actors guide the museum's visitors from one century to the next in period style through 50 different 'hands-on' exhibit areas where they are able to witness an 18th century Phantasmagoria, board a Russian agit-prop train to view Eisenstein's first attempts at political filmmaking, climb atop an authentic Movietone van to watch 1930s newsreels, or get close to Chaplin's original 'Tramp' costume.

MOMI's entrance, the start of a journey through cinema and television history

In its first year, MOMI and its co-ordinators, Leslie Hardcastle and David Francis, have won several awards – from BAFTA, the Critics Circle, and the English Tourist Board. Most importantly, MOMI has won the approval of the public and the industries to which it is dedicated.

National Film Theatre

The NFT is one of the world's leading cinematheques, screening over 2,000 films a year and boasting some 40,000 members. It aims to provide the best of world cinema from the early silent era to the present day and its three theatres, together with MOMI's Image Workshop, are superbly equipped to show every kind of film format.

A series of live interviews with leading film and television personalities has been sponsored by The Guardian newspaper since 1981. Recent appearances include Dustin Hoffman, Sir David Lean, Yves Montand and Walter Matthau.

The NFT is also home to the London Film Festival in November each year which continues to expand with the Festival on the Square featuring screenings in the cinemas around Leicester Square, sponsored by the Evening Standard.

Funding and Development

*A*lthough based in London, the BFI is very much a *national* body and most of its regional activities are looked after by the Funding and Development Division. To make sure that films can be seen in the regions, it finds sites for a growing network of Media Centres and Regional Film Theatres, and promotes their development.

In production, workshops offer under-represented groups the chance to make films and tapes which add variety to our film and video culture. Most of this work is funded via Regional Arts Associations, but funding is also given direct to organisations whose work is deemed nationally

Chapter Arts: once a school, now one of the BFI-funded Regional Film Theatres showing the best of world cinema across the country

important. A separate budget uses incentive funding to encourage investment from the private sector which in turn can help film and video projects to earn their own income.

Working in partnership with a large number of local organisations from television companies to local authorities, F & D's officers travel extensively to get an accurate overview of what is happening in the regions, checking on how projects are going and advising on finance and management.

Training is increasingly important and the BFI's training co-ordinator provides short training courses for Regional Film Theatre staff, produces 'Directions', a guide to short production courses, writes articles on training and represents the BFI on a number of national training initiatives, including the Independent Media Training Federation.

Research and Information

Library Services

The largest collection of documentation on film and television in the world is held by the BFI's Library Services which hold both published and unpublished material, including books, periodicals, news cuttings, press releases, scripts and theses. Special collections of private papers from such major figures as Carol Reed, Michael Balcon and Joseph Losey are housed in the Paper Store of the J Paul Getty Jnr Conservation Centre at Berkhamsted.

The library has moved into the computer age with the arrival of the Summary of Information on Film and Television (SIFT), an on-line database of information dating back to the beginning of film production which includes details of over 300,000 films, videos and television programmes, as well as details of individuals and organisations.

TV Unit

The television industry is changing rapidly and so the work of the Television Unit is ever more

Manchester's Cornerhouse – the most recent media centre opened with the support of the BFI

One Day in the Life of Television: Alan Jungarrayi Dixon and family of Australia's Northern Territory. Taken by Nick Lockett, chief stills photographer for Central TV who was photographing the Aboriginal people for the 'Beaming the Dreamtime' exhibition

important. 1988 and 1989 were dominated by the massive 'One Day in the Life of Television' project which will culminate in the publication of the book, transmission of the network ITV documentary and opening of a MOMI exhibit on November 1 1989. The Unit works with agencies and institutions at the forefront of the television culture as the BFI takes a prominent position in its exciting development.

Publishing

BFI Publishing produces a range of topical, scholarly and popularising books on all aspects of film and television, either under its own imprint or in association with other publishers.

Besides books produced under the BFI Publishing imprint, the department also provides a sales and distribution service for all the BFI's other publications.

Education

BFI Education's aim is to enable as many people as possible to discover new ways of thinking about, producing and enjoying the media, particularly film, video and television. Working with people in formal education, from primary to university level, in the community at large and in many other institutions, the department exists to develop knowledge and ideas about the media and through research, teaching, producing materials and lobbying, it sets agendas and provokes debate.

Periodicals

Periodicals publishes the quarterly 'Sight and Sound' which is international in scope and features articles covering a wide spectrum of critical writing and the gamut of film history. Economic and technical developments are also covered as are interviews, news and current production information. Periodicals also publishes the 'Monthly Film Bulletin' which provides detailed information on feature films released in London each month and other films such as those from the early sound and silent eras which have not been previously reviewed.

Starting them young, BFI Education

Production

BFI Production is committed to innovative work, whether in form, content, production method or use of film or video technology and deals with a very broad range of projects on film and video, from £5,000 projects to low-budget features. The Production Board is a successor to the Experimental Film Fund, set up in 1953 and administered by the BFI which since the late 1960s has received direct government grant aid to make films of significant artistic quality which couldn't be financed commercially. Since 1985 the

Controversial: Veronico Cruz (1988), a BFI co-production, was denounced by the popular press as Argentinian propaganda but won praise from the critics

Production Board has also been supported by a grant from Channel 4 and a small sum from the Independent Television Association.

A production agency rather than a funding institution the Production Board's main criteria for making a film is not whether it will make money but it is always concerned that its films should find audiences. BFI Production undertakes its own distribution and world sales, and its better-known releases over the last few years include *The Draughtsman's Contract, Caravaggio, On The Black Hill* and *Distant Voices, Still Lives.*

National Film Archive

*T*he National Film Archive was founded in 1935 and now includes 146,000 titles from 1895 to the present day, covering features and shorts, newreels, amateur films and television programmes, on an extensive range of gauges and formats, both obsolete and current.

Mainly financed through the BFI's annual grant, the Archive also receives a grant for the archiving of Independent Television and Channel 4. The National Heritage Memorial Fund, and business and private sponsors also contribute to the hard-pressed nitrate preservation programme.

No law of statutory deposit for film, TV and video production exists yet in the UK, and the archive's acquisitions are mostly donated. Three acquisition sections: Fiction, Non-Fiction and

Television are responsible for establishing and maintaining goodwill with potential donors in order to satisfy the Archive's brief which includes not only all British productions, but also foreign material exhibited in the UK.

The Archive makes the collection accessible in many ways ranging from the provision of viewings for researchers to the organising of retrospectives of British Cinema, at home and abroad.

The J Paul Getty Jnr Conservation Centre, opened in June 1987 and named after its generous sponsor, is the technical centre and store for safety film and video, where the principal work of preservation and restoration is performed. It also administers the storage of some 140 million feet of nitrate film in a specially equipped site some 50 miles away from the Centre.

Stills, Posters and Designs

More than 4 million photographs from film and television, 500,000 colour transparencies, 15,000 posters and 2,000 original set and costume designs and animation cels are held by BFI Stills, Posters and Designs. The collection illustrates the development of world cinema and television via 60,000 title files, which include production photographs of actors and crews at work on location and in the studio, and a further 15,000 portrait files of film and television personalities

and other related subjects such as studios, equipment, cinemas, newsreels and awards.

This unique source of visual information is much in demand from teachers, students, researchers, publishers, television, film and video companies worldwide. Researching and mounting exhibitions at the National Film Theatre and throughout Britain, BFI Stills, Posters and Designs also advises, and lends items from the collection to, recognised museums and galleries.

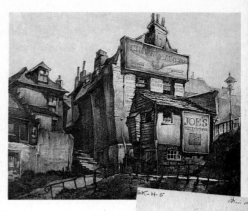

Distribution

*B*FI Distribution facilitates access to film, television and video by putting copies of historic, innovative and newly discovered material into circulation for screening and study, as well as providing programming advice and publicity services to a wide variety of clients.

The Acquisitions Unit monitors overall UK availability of world cinema and increasingly 'works on video', negotiating new distribution agreements whenever possible. Launching and hiring these to exhibitors – worldwide in the case of rare prints specially made by BFI Distribution – is the responsibility of the Library Unit, which also publishes and updates a catalogue. The Despatch Unit services general Institute film handling and shipping needs, as well as those of Distribution.

(Top) Set design for **Temptation Harbour** *(1946) by C Dawe; (above) costume design for* **High Treason** *(1929)*

The Programming and Publicity Units support a network of nearly 40 UK Regional Film Theatres by liaising with distributors and producers to make available the distinctive programme mix which is offered by these cinemas. Temporary sub-distribution arrangements are often made for the mutual convenience of distributors and exhibitors, and special touring programmes and events are regularly organised by the officers of the units.

The Thin Blue Line *(1988), distributed by the BFI, highlighted the case of Randall Adams, wrongly imprisoned for the murder of a policeman. The film secured Adams' eventual release*

Film Society Unit

The Film Society Unit is the link between the independent British Federation of Film Societies, run by thousands of volunteers around the country, and the British Film Institute. The FSU responds to existing societies' needs, provides services and information for them, organises national events, publishes a journal 'Film', a Handbook, and programmes for the viewing sessions it sets up each year.

It also speaks actively to trade organisations on behalf of societies; ensures that a wide range of 16mm film material is available through its intervention procedure; has 16mm and 35mm equipment available for special film society screenings, and through its Field Officer can give practical advice in the setting up of film societies throughout the country. Special film packages are arranged from abroad and, through its close involvement with the International Federation of Film Societies, the FSU keeps abreast of activities worldwide.

Contacts at the BFI

British Film Institute
21 Stephen Street, London W1P 1PL
Tel: 01 255 1444
Director: Wilf Stevenson

Head of Press and Promotions: Wayne Drew
Press Officer: Brian Robinson

Funding and Development:
Acting Head Funding and Development: Irene
  Whitehead
Regional Funding Advisor: Steve Brookes

National Film Archive
Curator: David Francis
Deputy Curator: Michelle Aubert
Head of Stills, Posters and Designs: Bridget
  Kinally

Research and Information
Head of Research and Information: Colin
  MacCabe
Head of Library Services: Gillian Hartnoll
Head of BFI Education: Manuel Alvarado
Head of TV Unit: Richard Paterson
Head of Periodicals: Penelope Houston
Head of BFI Production: Ben Gibson
Sales: Sue Bruce-Smith

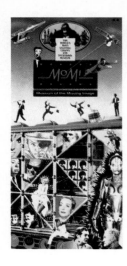

Press and Publicity: Liz Reddish
29 Rathbone Street, London W1P 1AG
Tel: 01 636 5587/4736
Head of BFI Publishing: Geoffrey Nowell-Smith
(Sales enquiries) 29 Rathbone St,
London W1P 1AG (01 636 3289)

Distribution
Head of Distribution: Ian Christie
Head of Acquisitions and Contracts: Barry Edson
Head of Sales and Marketing: Nigel Algar
Head of Programming Services: Jayne Pilling
Head of Film Society Unit: Tom Brownlie
Film Society Unit Information Officer: Peter
Cargin

National Film Theatre and Museum of the Moving Image
South Bank London SE1 8XT, Tel: 01 928 3535
Controller: Leslie Hardcastle
Deputy Controller: Paul Collard
Head of Programming: Sheila Whitaker
Head of Marketing: Helen Mackintosh
Press Officer: Susan Santini

The atmosphere of the nineteenth century magic lantern show, the Phantasmagoria, recreated at MOMI

BFI Facilities for the Disabled
The British Film Institute is working
to improve access to its buildings
for disabled visitors.

Facilities include:

21 Stephen Street: toilet for disabled on ground floor, limited access by lifts to all areas, car parking, ramp into building at the rear, full access via main reception (no steps into building).

Museum of the Moving Image: Ramp access to ground and first floor levels. Two scissor lifts and one stair lift between the ground and first floor, one stair lift between the first and second floor. MOMI's cinema, the Image Workshop, has 3 wheelchair positions and an induction loop system for those wearing aids incorporating a T switch. Disabled toilet facilities in every public toilet.

National Film Theatre: NFT1 has 6 wheelchair positions at the rear of the auditorium which must be booked in advance. NFT1 has an induction loop system for those wearing aids with a T switch and both NFT1 and NFT2 have certain seats with a special earphone facility. Earpieces are available from the manager before the performance. There are no wheelchair facilities in NFT2. There are lavatories adapted for use by those in wheelchairs to the right of the restaurant entrance near NFT1 and off the main foyer towards the National Theatre.

National Film Archive: Ramps into main building, electronically operated doors, disabled toilet, lift to main building, no steps anywhere in the main building. Main conference room in house has ramp.

The Year in Review

Will 1988–89 be seen by posterity as a watershed in the history of British film and television? Writer and critic Sean Day-Lewis asks whether much has really changed.

Licence to Kill: *a sad first for British film*

*L*ooking back, events suggest that, for better or worse, major change was taking place. The much discussed 'third age of broadcasting' seemed to be drawing close. Yet our nation's homes have yet to be festooned with dishes and squarials. There came the good news that cinema admissions rose from 74.8m in 1987 to 78.4m in 1988. But early in 1988 it was announced that, as an economy measure, the 17th James Bond picture would be made at a studio in Mexico City, the first of the series not to be produced at Pinewood.

Wishful thinking about a European film industry, strong enough to marginalise Hollywood and able to take advantage of Glasnost, wherever it might appear in the East, was very seductive. Meanwhile the reality of language and our unbreakable cultural tie with other English speaking peoples, was not diminished. It was still the Oscars which attracted attention and excitement here. And if the Channel 4-sparked mini-revival of 'the British film industry' began to lose impetus, the main reason was the age old resistance of the United States box office to our parochially focused movies.

When juxtaposed, these facts do not give an appearance of a new era, of a time better or worse than other recent years.

January – March 1988

*T*he Government asked the Monopolies and Mergers Commission to investigate labour practices in television and any film industry that was going at the time. It was pointed out that the jibe about ITV being "the last bastion of restrictive practice" was already out of date and that, by definition, there could be no restrictive practices elsewhere. Such objections were brushed aside and the Commission duly went to work finding out that there was little or nothing to find out.

In a different attempt to "secure a more competitive environment," the Government introduced a draft order, under the Fair Trading Act, restricting the cinema practice of exclusive runs to four weeks. At the same time Cannon UK introduced a new restrictive, and exclusive, practice by barring Alexander Walker from its facility screenings for film critics.

Granada announced a feature film division to make four to six low budget pictures a year, in addition to its television filmmaking. "We are not just interested in good financial investments. The attraction of a screenplay is the important thing," said production head Mike Wooller. Fifteen months later, it was announced that Granada Film Productions would be subsumed into Granada Television. "People found it strange and confusing that Granada had two film arms and the merger is an absolutely logical and expected step," said former production head Mike Wooller.

In the same period, Granada got into bed with Home Box Office with the expectation of producing quads, four £1 million drama documentaries. Central Independent Television, having deserted the bed it shared with its offspring Zenith, announced a relationship with a new, more manageable, less independent film subsidiary.

The BBC reached agreement with independent producers on their terms of trade. TV-am dismissed its ACTT technicians, locked out over a manning dispute, and turned to non-union labour. London Weekend Television announced job cuts and "reformed" labour practices. After a 22 year gap away from feature films, 77 year old Charles Crichton received a new lease of life directing John Cleese and others in *A Fish Called Wanda*. Trevor Howard, John Clements, Kenneth Williams, Emeric Pressburger and Nat Cohen died.

Charles Crichton, back in action with the Oscar-winning A Fish Called Wanda

April – June 1988

*T*he Department of Trade and Industry floated the idea of transmitting BBC2 and Channel 4 on spare satellite frequencies. When it was pointed out that this would render both channels unavailable to most of their present audience, the idea was dropped as quietly as possible. The Department was also silent as Cannon failed to keep its promise to initiate film production, neglected its cinema circuit and followed the sale of the Thorn-EMI film library with that of Elstree studios. When Cannon undertook to keep Thorn-EMI Screen Entertainment as a going concern, the DTI had chosen to ignore advice and allow the takeover to proceed.

The Treasury was less silent as it announced plans to levy the net advertising revenue of the ITV companies. The existing levy on profits allowed the companies to deduct production costs before calculating what should be paid. The tax bill was now expected to rise from £120 million to £200 million a year.

Still more noisy was the criticism by Government, and its Fleet Street allies, of a Thames *This Week* documentary called *Death on the Rock*. This investigated the Gibraltar shooting of three IRA terrorists by SAS soldiers and did not conform in all particulars to the official Ministry of Defence account. Prime Ministerial displeasure was con-

Chris Oxley, producer of the controversial BAFTA winner Death On The Rock

veyed to the IBA which permitted the ITV transmission, as well as Thames.

The BBC and Equity announced an electronic casting directory known as Lasercast, in the hope of ending the general tendency towards lazy casting. The BBC also promised to inject an extra £200 million into television and radio programmes over the next five years as a response to fresh competition – both terrestrial and satellite.

The Cable Authority invited applications for six new cable franchises covering 1.39m homes. A gala dinner at the Cannes Film Festival honoured Sir David Lean who had lately achieved his 80th birthday, for his contribution to the British film industry. Wilf Stevenson was appointed Director of the British Film Institute to succeed Anthony Smith. Justin Dukes declared an end to his term as the first managing director of Channel 4. Russell Harty and actor Andrew Cruickshank died.

July – September 1988

*L*eaks about the impending Government White Paper on the future of broadcasting became a torrent matching the prevailing wet weather. A Cabinet committee chaired by Mrs Thatcher was said to have endorsed competitive tendering for ITV franchises, the creation of a fifth terrestrial television channel and the replacement of the Independent Broadcasting Authority with a new quango to regulate de-regulated television.

The more we heard in detail about the Government plans, the more it became clear that the public service ethic, which has previously moderated the mix on the television screen, would no longer be officially cherished. Already, the signs are that ITV has become more commercial, whether by necessity or choice, and has begun eliminating programme strands which advertisers find unhelpful. And commercial competition has already made it much harder for mainstream channels to buy, for instance, packages of films successfully trailed for them in the cinema.

Prince Charles at the opening of MOMI

The House of Commons Home Affairs Committee published a report suggesting that television "should be about making programmes and not simply delivering audiences to advertisers". Sir Richard Attenborough, wearing his hat as chairman of Channel 4, suggested that Channel 4 should receive a percentage of the Channel 5 advertising revenue. The existing ITV companies took a largely gloomy view of their chances in a franchise auction. Television South became a £300 million international conglomerate following its takeover of the American MTM company. Limehouse Studios sold its Docklands site to developers for around £25 million, looked around for a new home and decided on Elstree. Channel 4 decided to go in for breakfast television. Mark Shivas, the new head of BBC drama, said that "while BBC drama must not seek any safe or bland routes" it must be "responsible and defendable".

The Prince of Wales opened the Museum of the Moving Image and registered his disapproval of screen violence. Graham Greene, Vanessa Redgrave and Anthony Smith were created British Film Institute fellows. Robert Atkins became the seventh junior Trade and Industry minister in nine years to have "special responsibility" for films. Jimmy Edwards, Roy Kinnear and Charles Hawtrey died.

October – December 1988

he Government published its White Paper on the future of broadcasting delivered very much as leaked. An Independent Television Commission would replace both the IBA and the Cable Authority and, in commercial matters, would be expected to apply a light touch. Channel 5 would start in 1993. Also in this year ITV would become Channel 3. It would be separated from Channel 4 and run by companies licensed for ten years, after winning their place by competitive tender.

The BBC would remain "the cornerstone of British broadcasting", threatened with a diminishing licence fee and finance by subscription during the 1990s. The Broadcasting Standards Council, imposing an official view of "taste and decency", would become statutory. In case this offered insufficient regulation in the deregulated era, broadcasting would also be made subject to the Obscene Publications Act.

Lord Thomson of Monifieth, the retiring chairman of the IBA, said that British broadcasting faced "near anarchy" in the 1990s as a result of the Government proposals. Other television industry leaders were more muted in their objections, seemingly worried that any display of passion or anger would further provoke She Who Must Be Obeyed.

The industry was favourably surprised when George Russell, a businessman who confessed to knowing and caring about television, was announced as last chairman of the IBA and first chairman of the ITC. There was a less ecstatic response when Lord Chalfont, noted for heavy disapproval of television journalism challenging his view of the world, was appointed vice-chairman. John Whitney, director general of the IBA since 1982, resigned.

Lord Chalfont: an unenthusiastic response met his appointment as vice-chairman of the newly-formed ITC

George Russell: last chairman of the IBA, first chairman of the ITC

Sir William Rees-Mogg, soon to be elevated to the House of Lords and already chairman of the Broadcasting Standards Council, talked about sex on television. "There are erotic scenes which are perfectly clearly all right to show. What I would call, broadly speaking, Romeo and Juliet scenes, romantic scenes," he told viewers of Channel 4's *Signals*. "But there are erotic scenes which seem to me to raise very serious questions – what I would call pornographic scenes – where there is very explicit sex and a very explicit view of the sex act. There are then (pause) gropings which appear in the middle. And these gropings are found to be very offensive by large numbers of viewers."

Later respected regulator Colin Shaw was appointed director of the Council and it began looking around for a constructive role. Its draft code of practice on sex, violence and "bad language" proved to be no more draconian than the codes already operated by the BBC and the IBA. A round Britain tour testing public opinion in the early months of 1989 convinced Lord Rees-Mogg that television audiences were rather less offended by such "gropings" than he had expected.

Lord Rees-Mogg's definition of the acceptably erotic includes Romeo and Juliet *(above) but almost certainly not films like* Sebastiane *(top)*

Colin Shaw: influencing the bounds of taste and decency on TV as director of the Broadcasting Standards Council
Photo: Zooom

The Government introduced a ban on television and radio interviews with people speaking on behalf of Irish political extremism. Violent objection by journalists was not supported by public opinion.

Tuesday November 1 was chosen by the BFI's Television Unit for its 'One Day in the Life of Television' project. Some 18,000 viewers and television professionals kept a diary of the day and, in providing a snapshot of television present, demonstrated a widespread concern for television future.

Whether or not anybody noticed it at the time 1988 was designated European Year of Cinema and Television, a year intended to culminate in November with the conferring of European Oscars at a suitably portentous Berlin ceremony. Hands up anybody who can name one of the winners or, come to that, anybody who knows whether the epoch making occasion happened at all.

In that same month of November film guru David Puttnam was in the City of London giving the Financial Times Arts Lecture. He was still licking those honourable Californian wounds, received while attempting to persuade Columbia and their Coca-Cola owners that he was a prophet who could deliver profit. He had since come round to the idea that "our best hope lies, probably, I think, in Europe. I believe that Europe is slowly re-asserting itself as the creative and moral leader of the industrial world." Quite apart from which did not Europe constitute 56 per cent of the world film market?

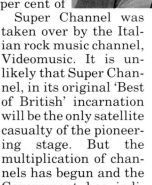

David Puttnam: "our best hope lies . . . in Europe"

Super Channel was taken over by the Italian rock music channel, Videomusic. It is unlikely that Super Channel, in its original 'Best of British' incarnation will be the only satellite casualty of the pioneering stage. But the multiplication of channels has begun and the Government has indicated that, in case liberated market forces prove less potent than expected, it will join enthusiastically in the demolition of the BBC and IBA status quo.

Once "Best of British", now Italian owned, Super Channel was an early casualty of the satellite boom

Brent Walker, new owner of Elstree Studios, announced that its Goldcrest subsidiary would run the site and retain seven of the ten sound stages and post production units. British Screen shareholders agreed to wait an extra two years before the film finance company must start to repay their loans.

The satellite film channel scramble ended with

Record-breaker: **Who Framed Roger Rabbit?**

BSB in alliance with Columbia, MCA/Universal, Paramount, MGM/UA, Cannon, Warner and Nelson. Sky got Fox, Disney, Touchstone and Orion and (with some film exceptions) Warners. *Who Framed Roger Rabbit?* broke the opening weekend record set earlier in the year by *Fatal Attraction* and broken by *"Crocodile" Dundee*. Total box office revenue from the top United Kingdom earners was £101,293,540, constituting a 22.5 per cent rise on the previous year.

Into 1989

*I*n early 1989 Sky began broadcasting on four channels, the shortage of satellite dishes ensuring that the audience was largely restricted to cable users. Meanwhile, BSB (British Satellite Broadcasting) embarked on a £20 million advertising campaign for its autumn launch and claimed to have signed up over 2,000 first-run features for transmission. At this point the potential audience remained unimpressed.

Lord Windlesham's Thames initiated independent inquiry into the *Death on the Rock* documentary cleared the company of all major criticism arising out of the programme. The Government dismissed the report out of hand and were labelled as "bad losers" by the former IBA chairman, Lord Thomson. There were many awards from both BAFTA (British Academy of Film and Television Arts) and the BPG (Broadcasting Press Guild) celebrating this and the other 1988 television programmes of which the Government disapproved.

As if in response to this, the Home Office dug in its heels over some of the more questionable aspects of its broadcasting White Paper. There would be competitive tendering and no requirement on Channels 3 or 5 to transmit children's or educational programmes. George Russell emerged from his first months as IBA chairman to say he would resign unless the Channel 3 tendering process had a proper quality requirement.

European Community ministers backed away from stringent quotas on imported film and television. The Association of Independent Producers and the British Film and Television Producers Association proposed that the investment of "substantial" sums of money for film and video drama by television broadcasters should be made mandatory. Not a new call and not made with more than the usual hope of success.

On top from down under:"Crocodile" **Dundee II**

British Film — Where Now?

What hope is there for British cinema as television faces a huge shake-up, the American market turns cool, our major talents disappear to Hollywood, and the Government keeps its distance. Six of our leading producers and directors discuss the future.

Stephen Frears' directing career covers films for both television and cinema including Gumshoe, My Beautiful Launderette, Sammy and Rosie Get Laid, The Hit, *and* Prick Up Your Ears. *His most recent success is* Dangerous Liaisons.

Stephen Frears: identifying with the emigrés

"*T*ake four films which have opened this year – *High Hopes, Baron Munchausen, Scandal* and *Dangerous Liaisons.* The fact that the British are involved with four such different and eccentric films with such diversity and scope suggests a picture of health, a fertile industry.

"But how you are supposed to run an industry on that basis alone, I don't know. There is no economic basis for film in this country and filmmakers here are faced with impossible circumstances. It really is a triumph of hope over experience.

"My next film, I guess, will be American. That's not to say I never want to make another film in, or about, Britain. That would be ridiculous but the most invigorating work I am being offered is in America. I'm not sure where the material is at the moment in this country, the people I work with aren't writing scripts at the moment. So I suppose you could say I do identify with the emigrés.

"The British haven't got an eye for a commercial film. I certainly don't think I have. If you look at some of the films which have made money recently, I wouldn't have been the one to put the money up for them. I still have no idea why *Launderette* was a success. When I made it I thought 'this is for television'. I had no idea that people in America or France or Australia would want to see it.

"When I do want to make another film about Britain with recognisably British people and a high level of social realism then I will go straight to television. I imagine that the office Mark Shivas is sitting in is one of the most interesting rooms in London at the moment.

"I don't see why there has to be this monolithic view of cinema and involvement with television doesn't have to make a film less cinematic. Television puts perhaps more emphasis on dialogue but then so do the films of Billy Wilder or Mankiewicz or Lubitsch. If I could make a film as well as Mankiewicz I would be very happy.

"The future of television looks catastrophic. My heart soars every time I read stories about dishes not selling but I don't know if satellite will fail. I don't think the money it plans to put into films will help much, at least not until they start writing cheques for the kind of amount you need to make *Tumbledown*, or *Jewel in the Crown*. It all comes down to pounds per hour.

Prick Up Your Ears

"The Government's changes have got very little to do with commercialising television, it's a straightforward attack on the unions. There was quite a funny period a few years ago when we were marketing anti-Thatcher films paid for by Thatcher and I remember thinking that in a way that we were model Thatcherites. We were practising thrift and economy and turning ourselves into exports. But she doesn't like us, what she wants is Murdoch and game shows."

As head of drama at Channel 4, David Rose is one of Britain's most prolific post-war British producers and has overseen the commissioning and support of more than 150 low-budget films by Film Four International.

"*T*here has traditionally been a gulf between cinema and television and right through until the 1980s they had never really opened a dialogue. It would have been sensible because there were a lot of things happening in writing and directing which would have benefited both. Since Film on Four started and since companies like Euston Films, Granada Films and Zenith were set-up, I think it is true that this television backed activity means there has been what some people call, and it's not an entirely appropriate word, a renaissance in British cinema.

"But I'm only talking about low-budget features, not high budget. The only chink in the armour seems to have been the change of the National Film Finance Corporation to become British Screen although Simon Relph has a derisively small amount of money to disperse.

"Today, I think we have an enriched cinema. Enriched by new talent coming from film schools and quite a lot crossing over from TV like David Hare and Stephen Frears, and also through routes such as the BFI, for example Derek Jarman and Peter Greenaway.

"So something interesting has happened creatively but we are in a precarious position. The future is uncertain for Channel 4, a question mark related not only to our funding but also to the new TV channels and how competitive we will have to be to satisfy advertisers. If things become extremely tight, we may find we can't do all the things we set out to do in 1982 which may include supporting fewer feature films. The only two constant funders of film in Britain are Channel 4 and British Screen and I regret that. As I have said to Simon Relph, "Wouldn't it be great if we never had to support the same film?" But we can't do that, we need each other and the few other financiers there are.

"One problem is that we haven't had a very strong team of producers, simply because there hasn't been the experience for them, but some have now emerged. Beyond that, I can't think of another European country which gets less help from its Government than we do. There is a potential for export which could be even stronger. The glamorous side of the business as seen at awards ceremonies gives a wrong impression of what goes on down in the boiler house and that makes it harder to raise public funds.

"Within Britain, I think British films are highly regarded by a few but don't reach a large audience. As far as I can make out, it is the Americans who control the cineplexes. From the outset, the Americans approach a film as a highly marketable piece of work and we simply haven't enough money to do that.

The Belly of an Architect

David Rose: "we are in a precarious position"

"However, I don't think we can talk about British cinema in isolation within the UK, we have to look at how it is seen in Europe too and our cinema certainly has a high profile today. I can only reflect that I was the one board member of the European film prize asked to sit on the executive committee of the European Film Academy with directors like Wenders, Chabrol, Bertolucci and Szabo. Ten years ago, it would have been unheard of for a British TV executive to be invited to be among those filmmakers and I think that says something for the regard in which we are held.

"Opportunities are definitely arising with Europe. I was delighted when I sat down with the European directors and realised that though we had come together tentatively and nervously, we represent an extraordinary body of work, either because of individual talent or because we reflect our nation's style and culture.

"So there are financial opportunities and ways ahead but I must admit that within the British cinema scene itself, the situation is not very encouraging."

Tim Bevan is one of Britain's most successful independent producers. His company Working Title, run with partner Sarah Radclyffe, produced My Beautiful Launderette *which proved that a film can be British, low-budget and still a success. Their other films include* Personal Services, Sammy and Rosie Get Laid, A World Apart, *and* The Tall Guy.

"*I* think there are three main areas that British film will have to consider for the future and we will be looking to each of those areas with our productions.

"First there will be product aimed at TV, probably with budgets under £1m and shot on 16mm. These will run first on TV, then move on to video and perhaps ultimately onto BSB and the other satellite channels when they come about. I think it's in that area that the experimental filmmakers will probably do best.

"I don't think that will hamper their creativity, there's such a range of television and most of the British films over the last four or five years have used TV money.

"A second opportunity lies in the chance of a commercial strand for a series of comedies which could appeal in a number of different English speaking territories, the kind of film we are doing with *The Tall Guy*.

"And then there is potential for films which might hit the wider American market. They would need to be something like *A World Apart* or *Scandal* but with an extra element, something that will really appeal to that market. We just haven't got a big enough market here.

Tim Bevan: three main markets in mind

The Tall Guy

"There is a lot of British talent around. We have some great directors – the only problem is that they do one good thing here and then get tempted abroad. There are a lot of excellent writers around too but I think we still tend to think in terms of literature. In America, script-writing is a service industry and they think nothing of revising a script and going through five or six writers.

"I think the Government should be doing more to help the industry but it's hard to know exactly what. If they gave tax incentives to investors that would mean we would run up against other industries saying 'Why should they get special treatment?'.

"Perhaps some kind of special fund should be set up, maybe raising money by a levy on blank tapes. Something should be done because the film industry reflects our culture, it is our profile abroad."

John Schlesinger is one of the foremost British directors and his films include the Oscar-winning **Midnight Cowboy, Marathon Man, Yanks, Madame Sousatzka, Sunday Bloody Sunday** *and* **The Falcon and the Snowman.** *Yet few of his films have been made in Britain or financed here and he spends much of his time as a film exile in Hollywood.*

"*I* wish I could be more optimistic. I feel like a cracked gramophone record but my opinions haven't changed, the British film industry always seems to be in financial trouble. There is a vast untapped pool of talent. Our writers are better than a lot of the Americans, we have very good lighting men and cameramen. And the unions seem to be realising that they need to be flexible, a difference I noticed when making *Madame Sousatzka* here which was a lot easier than making *Yanks* a few years ago. But because of the pound/dollar situation we are not even being used as a service industry.

"We also lack entrepreneurial talent, we are no good at selling. In my American contracts, I have a consultation clause written in which gives me the right to discuss trailers, promotion, advertising etc and I'm very actively involved with those discussions. Over here, the industry does not encourage that.

"The British are not a cinema nation, they would far rather stay in and watch TV. That's partly the fault of the cinema duopoly. I hate going to the cinema in this country, it's not

Publicity poster

a pleasant experience. As a result, our film industry is dominated by TV.

"But while Channel 4 has been an extraordinary innovator, you can't have an industry based on low budget alone. You must also have high budget, people need to be able to spread their wings.

"And TV is not a very satisfactory medium for directors because it's watched with half an eye. I don't want to make films for TV because of the way it is perceived. People are constantly switching channels and saying 'Oh yes, I caught the end of that piece you did'.

"One encouraging development I suppose is the move for more television companies like the BBC and Granada to offer filmmakers the chance to make films for both a television showing and theatrical release. I think most established directors might be attracted by that if they were allowed to work on 35mm and are guaranteed a theatrical release. I have just turned down a TV project because they wouldn't guarantee that I could do it on 35mm.

"You have to think differently for TV to some extent but a film is a film and you just can't work constantly on such low budgets and short schedules.

John Schlesinger: "astounded" by lack of government support

"I'm not sure how the European film industry might help. We are only an hour away from France but we are such different cultures. People abroad aren't that interested in our culture, in Thatcherite Britain. The Americans certainly aren't. I think a film like *My Beautiful Launderette* was a success because it was a good raunchy story, not just because of the political content.

"I'm astounded by the lack of support this government gives. Self-confidence is important for an industry and it's important that the government should give some sign that it cares what happens. It's depressing to go down to Pinewood and find you are the only stage working down there. I love working here, this is staunchly my home, and I find the whole situation extremely sad."

Variously described as "Britain's No 1 movie brat" and "a young lion of British film", Stephen Woolley runs Palace with partner Nik Powell. Originally distributors of art films and cult movies, they have successfully moved into both mainstream and alternative production with films including Scandal, High Spirits, Mona Lisa, Company of Wolves *and* Shag.

"British films will never really crack the American market because it wants American actors and easily identifiable American situations. Certain films succeed there. *Room with a View* and *Chariots of Fire* are the kind of films that middle class Americans will watch to see men valiantly upholding the Empire and women struggling to keep their breasts inside their dresses.

"Then there are gritty, gutsy movies which younger Americans will go to and they have a certain cache because people want to see today's Thatcherite Britain in films like *My Beautiful Launderette,* and *Sammy and Rosie get laid.* There are also performance films: when *Mona Lisa* was honoured at Cannes, people in the States wanted to see Bob Hoskins, and Emily Lloyd was a great hit in *Wish You Were Here.* But for all of those we are talking about a small percentage of the American market.

"However, there is other potential for British films which is why we should encourage the Government to think about ways of subsidising British production. What is happening in the UK with the multiplexes is fantastic, people are rushing to go back to the cinema. The deterioration of TV through the envisioned White Paper changes means they will want to go to the cinema even more. But the films they are seeing are American, the multiplexes are owned by Americans and because there is no kind of levy, there is no money going back into British cinema.

"So there is an upsurge in attendance without an upsurge in UK production. That's a shame because if you really push a British film, then British audiences do respond. A successful British film needs to be about subjects that our audiences know first hand and they have to know and understand who the actors are. I would love to re-invent the *Carry Ons* for example, not as *Carry Ons,* but as a series with eight or nine modern comedians in recognisable situations.

"With our distribution, we have had a varied balance of releases which kept us going while

Stephen Woolley: "British films will never really crack the American market"
Photo: Mike Laye

Company of Wolves

other companies bit the dust.

"We have survived by ducking and weaving between the majors, releasing when we know they are not. It is getting more difficult to get the theatres, they have just got too many films lined up and we have had to fight tooth and nail to keep our cinemas. Even some of the independent cinemas are forced by declining audiences for foreign and subtitled films to put themselves increasingly at the call of the majors by taking more American product.

"For the future, we will continue to tailor our production to very distinct markets. We will make a film every year or so in the USA for the American market. We'll continue with lower budget dramas like *Mona Lisa* and *Scandal* and we'll also make bigger budget films like *The Pope Must Die* for the international market. We will also go in for much smaller budget films too and will use our muscle to get theatres for films that people have said no to.

"Films like *A World Apart* and *High Hopes* aren't ever going to wow the box office but we will use the high profile *Scandal* side of the business to continue to give films like those a proper release and backing."

Producer Lynda Myles' career has included work as director of the Edinburgh Film Festival, European production chief at Columbia during David Puttnam's reign, and an advisor on film production for satellite company BSB. As the BBC prepares to invest in cinema production, she has joined as its first commissioning editor for independent drama.

"**B**ecause of the success of a couple of British films in the States, there was an over-reaction and at one point the Americans were paying over the odds for British films. Unfortunately, the batch of films which followed the original successes didn't perform well. At the same time there seems to have been a collapse in the American video market which has hit a cluster of smaller American companies, the companies who initially welcomed British product.

"I think things might pick up again in another couple years, it's a cycle, but we are slightly in the doldrums at the moment. The tradition has been to look to the USA for money but now I think our filmmakers will have to look more to Europe. That brings with it its own problems, for example our budgets tend to be higher than those in

Lynda Myles

Defence of the Realm

Europe and I'm not sure how the difference can be met, but something is going to have to shift.

"Another source of finance will obviously be television. My experience with BSB has left me with the view that any source of money for independents is a good thing. BSB want films with a commercial edge but they are aiming at a broad market so though they are more mainstream than Film Four, they are looking for quality movies.

"At the BBC, we are investing in six theatrical films to begin with and that will be a straightforward investment so I don't think you can say that the creative content of the films will be affected because they will ultimately be shown on television. Films do work differently on television, but we are going for smaller budget movies so they won't be epics, and within those boundaries I can't see there will be any problems.

"I am looking for British talent, for example writers and directors, but not necessarily for British stories. I couldn't work bounded by the notion of having to find a British subject. I have always looked at cinema internationally and I am more concerned that the story should be compelling and original than that it should be British.

"It's such a joy when you do get a script that is purely a movie script because we are not a cinema culture and our writers tend to think in terms of the theatrical and literary tradition where the emphasis is on the word. We aren't a visual culture and we don't have a strong painting tradition. We are learning, but it isn't in our genes.

"Nobody has really thought about how to teach writing here. There are criticisms of the American attitude to scriptwriting, that it's too formulaic, but I admire the way they are prepared to work at a script. There are a lot of British films that would have benefited from one more draft.

"We are also somewhat in the shadow of America in sharing a common language. One of the reasons other European countries have poured money into film is to preserve their national culture and we don't have that sense of preserving a national linguistic barrier. I'm not saying we should have a completely subsidised industry here but there is so much more the Government could do which would help the industry more. It's hard to know exactly how money could be raised but I do know there is a lot of talent in this country and I wish it could find more of an outlet."

FFILM CYMRU

Reflecting the South West

TSW—Television South West

Lights! Camera! Action?

Parliament has witnessed some startling events including demonstrators throwing manure at ducking politicians, an MP brandishing the mace and protesting lesbians abseiling into the Lords. But the proposals to bring TV cameras to the Commons are no guarantee of exciting viewing as BFI Governor Tom Clarke MP, explains.

*M*Ps are acutely aware that the televising of the House of Commons might become excruciatingly boring if not carefully handled. So there was much debate in May when the Select Committee on Televising the House produced what many politicians saw as unduly restrictive proposals on the editorial freedom of television directors covering the Commons.

Coverage of the Lords is far from top of the TV ratings but broadcasters knew it would eventually lead to a greater prize – the Commons

The House voted by 293 to 69 to go ahead with an experimental nine month broadcast period, starting with the State Opening of Parliament in Autumn 1989. However, an amendment proposed by Conservative Roger Sims to give the cameras more freedom won strong support. Although this was defeated, it won a sizeable minority of 109 votes compared to 243, and there was strong feeling that the House would return to this issue.

Until that happens, wide angle shots of the House will be banned and cutaway shots and other editorial devices will not normally be allowed, neither will close-ups of MPs and coverage of any disorder.

This cautious start to Commons broadcasting reflects concern that the cameras might encourage unseemly behaviour from MPs, and visitors in the public gallery. (There is little doubt that MPs are aware of the power of television – a Manchester charm school reported earlier this year that 50 MPs had signed up for a £300 a day course to learn body language, colour coordination, camera skills and hair care.) And wary of this, the Select Committee published a report late in 1988 entitled 'Implications for procedure of the experiment in televising the proceedings of the House'.

Its main conclusion was that it would not be appropriate at this stage to suggest changes in procedure just because of television, though these could not be ruled out for the future. The questions of members standards of conduct and related issues which had been raised with the Committee were held over for later consideration. The Committee believed them, though undoubtedly potentially relevant to the issue of televising the House, to have a wider importance deserving of separate consideration. This report appeared in April – 'Conduct of Members in the Chamber and the alleged abuse of parliamentary privilege' – and came down heavily on the side of self regulation based on the need for greater discipline by the Party whips.

Those are just some of the issues considered by the Committee which was set up in the summer of 1988 after the House of Commons decided on 9 February 1988 to consider experimenting with broadcasting.

It was originally assumed that the Committee would report before the end of the summer recess of that year and televising begin with the opening of the new session. This proved a vain hope, however, and the Committee was widely accused of dragging its feet. A second projected deadline of Budget Day was missed but now at last faster progress has been made. Now that the report has finally been debated and approved, preparatory arrangements can be made.

Costume drama on a Hollywood scale

It was always thought unlikely that the Commons would do its own 'in house' broadcasting and the report recommended that a broadcasting unit should be set up between the Commons, the IBA and the BBC which could recover its running costs by selling the signal from the proceedings to the broadcasters 'at a fair price'.

This arrangement was criticised by some MPs who called for a satellite or terrestrial channel dedicated to continuous televising of the Commons. Among them was Labour MP Tony Banks who criticised the 'commercialism' of setting up a limited company to provide the signal.

'It would be the thin end of the sponsorship wedge,' he suggested,

French politicians are put on the spot twice weekly in their Question Time which is televised live

'and before long we will end up as the John Player Parliament with Mr Speaker's wig being sponsored by Vidal Sassoon and Geoffrey Dickens sponsored by Harrod's food hall!'

Although the House of Lords experiment is thought to have been highly successful with viewing ratings well above what many had anticipated, opinion is not unanimous about its impact in terms of the status of the Chamber. Anyway, it was always thought on both sides of the argument, that this was simply the broadcasters keeping their foot in the door, mindful of the far greater opportunities of televising the Commons itself. Worries, though, that people would play up to the cameras were largely, if not totally, dispelled. The Earl of Stockton's brilliant speech (what a capture for the archives!) appropriately confirmed that a wind of change was in the air and that comprehensive parliamentary television was on its way.

Technical problems appear to be less intimidating than was originally thought. There are still concerns about the chamber becoming overheated – not just in a metaphorical sense – and it is felt that the Chandelier-style lighting in the Lords is softer in its impact than the new strip lighting effects in the Commons Chamber which is of course of post-war reconstruction.

Although television is unlikely to replace the written Hansard, it will become increasingly important as an audio-visual record of events. Apart from live coverage on Budget Day and during other major events including Prime Minister's Question Time, viewers can look forward to a summary of proceedings and clips being seen on bulletins. TV's historical potential is enormous. Just imagine how helpful it would be to have Churchill's war time speeches, or the Falklands saga, or even Sidney Silverman's contributions when hanging was abolished. The oratory of Michael Foot – far better from the back-benches than at the despatch box – and the wit and wisdom of the then Speaker Thomas would have been well worth pursuing.

Alas, much excellent material has already been lost. But because the Westminster Parliament has lagged behind other nations in introducing the cameras, we can learn from their experience.

Televising of the Commons has lagged far behind other countries – the German Bundestag admitted cameras in 1953

Although many Parliaments have some live television coverage, only the Canadian House of Commons and the United States House of Representatives – recently joined by both Australian Houses – have blanket 'gavel to gavel' coverage under the strict control of a Broadcasting Unit. In other Parliaments, regulation of television coverage varies a great deal but broadly speaking most of them are able to select the items they want to broadcast.

Most Western European Parliaments have been televised for many years. Indeed, the French National Assembly was included on newsreels before the war. The German Bundestag admitted cameras in 1953, The Netherlands in 1955 and Sweden in 1957.

The amount of coverage varies a great deal but verbatim broadcasts in Western Europe seem to be fairly rare and reserved for really important debates, particularly budgets and major international debates. Notable exceptions are the two French Chambers where Question Time (two hours once a week) is televised live.

Almost all the countries have summary reports edited by the broadcasting authorities on a daily or weekly basis although in Italy a weekly summary is produced by the House authorities themselves. In all countries, brief extracts are included in general and regional news reports. In Europe, unlike the USA, many committees remain private and their proceedings are not therefore televised.

So in Britain, comprehensive televising of Parliament has been a very long time in coming. Although Richard Crossman, as leader of the House, made a brave attempt to introduce it in 1966, he committed the fundamental error of combining the votes on

radio and TV broadcasting, thus both fell together when very possibly sound broadcasting alone might have been approved: as it was the combination was only defeated by 131 votes to 130.

An experiment in sound broadcasting was agreed to in the following year but the real landmarks for broadcasting were to be on 24 February 1975 when the House agreed to an

Power, intrigue, and drama – the Commons has them all. But might restrictions on the editorial freedom of the broadcasters turn coverage into **The Big Sleep?**

experiment on sound broadcasting but rejected a parallel motion on television and the debate of 8 and 9 March 1976 in which the House agreed in principle to permanent sound broadcasting.

This began in April 1978. Since then, there had been a number of attempts by backbenchers to move towards televised proceedings. None of these private members bills got anywhere until very recently although some had more success than others.

Then on 2 November 1983, Austin Mitchell succeeded in getting leave to introduce his Ten Minute Rule Bill to this end by 164 votes to 159 – the first ever vote in favour of televising the commons. This immediately gave rise to much speculation both inside and outside the House, but prematurely as it turned out – the Government soon made it clear that they would not offer the bill any support, any more than they would support Mr Mitchell's bill to introduce the televising of select committees as favoured by the liaison committee in its report 'The Select Committee system'.

Parliament's buildings will soon be more than just a scenic backdrop for television news reports

No further debating time was offered by the Government at that stage although some effort was made to keep the issue before the House.

The House of Lords had meanwhile grasped the initiative. After toying with the proposal for many years, they adopted Lord Soames motion, put forward on 8 December 1983 "that this House endorses its decision of 15 June 1966 in favour of the public televising of some of its proceedings for an experimental period." The motion was carried by 74 votes to 24.

The Lords decided on 12 May 1986 to continue the televising of their proceedings until the House should decide otherwise. They have not looked back since. Will the Commons experiment be equally successful? We shall see.

USE **K**NOWLEDGE

Since its launch in 1986, THE KNOWLEDGE has become the daily source book of professional film-makers – *the* most comprehensive annual directory, researched and published by people who actually work in film.

As well as supplying contact numbers for crew and facilities companies, THE KNOWLEDGE has a vast amount of additional information within its 600 pages – all in an easy alphabetical format. THE KNOWLEDGE is invaluable for the busy film maker; it has quick reference charts for Studios and Video Post-production, many coding systems comprising at-a-glance information as to which facility company is the most suitable for a particular project, as well as giving credits for key film personnel.

Many unions involved in film-making have their own sections outlining working practices for Actors, Technicians and Musicians. Also many professionals in the film business have contributed to this book, supplying specialist information on complex film making requirements; aerial filming guidelines, carnets, shipping information – to name but a few.

THE KNOWLEDGE is a phone directory and a reference book so informative it ensures daily use. This directory does NOT remain on the shelf.

THE KNOWLEDGE is available from Cyclone Couriers 01-636 4811 (free delivery in the Central London area). For mail order or your local stockist please call The PA Publishing Co 01-969 5777. Price £50.

Next edition available in April 1990.

Watching the dishes

Is satellite television here to stay? Peter Elman, co-editor of the Financial Times newsletters New Media Markets and Screen, examines the uncertainty surrounding the satellite revolution.

Satellite TV brings with it two possibly competing ways of transmitting channels to the home. In both, television channels are carried on a satellite. But in one technology – the newest – the viewer buys or rents a small satellite dish in order to receive the channels directly in the home. This has been possible only since this year, with the launch of the higher power Astra satellite.

In the other technology, the viewer subscribes to a cable television system, the cable company having itself picked up the channels from the satellite before sending them down the cable. This satellite to cable delivery has been possible for a long time because the operators

Dawn of a new era? (Aerial at British Telecom International's Goonhilly satellite earth station at Helston in Cornwall)

use bigger, and more expensive, dishes to pick up the signals from low-power, old-fashioned telecommunications satellites.

Neither is of much use unless there is a strong demand for more channels. So will enough of the public want to watch the channels, thereby attracting advertising revenue? How much advertising revenue is there, anyway, for the channels to tap? And will enough people be prepared to pay a direct subscription in order to see 'premium' channels, such as Rupert Murdoch's Sky Movies or BSB's The Movie Channel, or the mini-pay channels of some of the independent companies.

In the United States, far more channels survive than are now even contemplated in this country. Most are delivered via cable, which has nearly 49 million subscribers – or 54% of all TV homes. There is little direct-to-home business to talk about. The growth of cable – and the decision of the channels to charge a small subscription as well as to carry advertising – means that most have climbed out of the red.

But Britain is not the USA. It is a much smaller country, with a much smaller advertising and subscription potential. Some would argue also that the quality of the broadcast channels here is better than in the USA, so that the incentive to view new channels is not nearly so great.

The satellite and cable lobby argue that every time a new channel has been mooted in Britain, the established broadcasters and their supporters have claimed that there is already enough television choice and quality without more channels being added. And the demand has always turned out to be there. The point is a good one, but one can't go on using that argument forever to support the case for more channels. There comes a time when enough really is enough.

Has that time come? To answer that we have to look at satellite TV in the context of terrestrial television. For the viewer, it is really all the same, except perhaps for the glamour that may be attached to having a satellite dish. This question of context is far more important than all the problems over reception equipment, most of which can be regarded as hiccups.

The wider environment will become a more difficult one for the satellite channels in 1993 when a fifth terrestrial channel will be launched – supported by advertising revenue or subscription or both, depending on what the eventual licence holder or holders prefer.

With 70% of the country in its coverage area, the new channel could siphon off a good deal of the viewer and advertising demand. It is true that most people will need a new aerial to receive the channel. But the fifth channel should still do better than the satellite channels: BSB's original forecasts were that only half the country's homes would buy its dishes after 15 years. The satellite channel's big advantage is that they have a four year head start.

There is, according to the X25 Media Partnership Consultancy, a 'law' of satellite-TV success which relates the potential viability of satellite television to the availability of terrestrial

The fight for popular films like Alien *(which* Sky *won) will play an important part in the satellite battle*

channels. If they are to have a chance of success, satellite channels require the presence of particular conditions.

The first part of the law says that a subscription channel has no chance of being viable unless there are insufficient terrestrial frequencies made available by the government to meet viewers' appetites for channels (ie, are four British channels enough to meet viewer demand?).

The second part of the law states that an advertising supported channel has no chance of being viable unless there are insufficient outlets for advertising on those terrestrial frequencies (in other words, are the two existing British advertising channels enough?).

Neither Sky nor BSB believes that there is room for both of them. That means that the competition is a fight to the death. But not only are the Sky and BSB channels at stake. Since Sky is on the Astra satellite, the other channels are likely to live or die by Sky's fate. As the pop music channel MTV puts it, it will for the moment hang on to Murdoch's coat-tails.

The losses of the satellite channels could be very great. The BSB project will cost about £700 million which includes the cost of the company's own satellites. The Astra channels do not have to pay for satellite (which is owned by the Luxembourg company, Société Européenne des Satellites, with several bankers as shareholders as well as Thames Television). But they still have heavy costs: for instance, it costs over £3.5 million a year to lease an Astra transponder before a channel even looks at the programming and marketing. Murdoch got his first four transponders at a knock-down price: he paid under £90 million for 10 years use.

In the first year alone, Murdoch is spending about £170 million, of which £120 million will go on programming. With no subscription revenue for the first few months, Sky's income (from advertising) might be no more than £15 million. It is likely that Murdoch will lose at least £500 million before the tide begins to move.

When or if that will happen is not clear from the early experiences with satellite TV which have proved little about long-term viewer demand, one way or another. But it is not difficult to accept that there could be a long-lasting demand for more channels.

The Number 1 'need' is probably a good film channel: indeed, both Sky and BSB believe a film channel is the driving force behind their programme packages and have paid over the odds to ensure that they have a respectable run of newish (post video window) releases. The prices were high enough to drive the Premiere channel, which was already running on cable and had every reason to be a front-runner in the direct-to-home stakes, out of business.

Is the sun about to set on terrestrial television? (Aerial at British Telecom International's Goonhilly satellite earth station at Helston in Cornwall)

Arguably, too, there could be demand for the other major specialist channels being shown by both big players and the independents: on sport, music, news and children's programming. Yet is the demand for such programming as insatiable as it appears to be for top Hollywood films? One could argue that the existing broadcast channels provide enough in terms of quantity and quality on each theme. Sky and BSB do not believe so.

Anthony Simonds-Gooding, chief executive of BSB which has delayed the start of its battle with Sky until spring 1990

The demand for films is vitally important for both Murdoch and BSB because, with the relative slowness of dish sales and, consequently, of advertiser interest, subscription revenue is likely to be their main source of revenue in the early years. But can there really be enough to make up for what would appear to be a huge shortfall in advertising revenue?

Analysts Booz Allen and Hamilton predict that by the end of 1993 – or after four full years of service – Sky and BSB will be bringing in a combined total of £200 million subscription and only £62 million in advertising. John Clemens, who quit earlier this year as director of AGB International Research,

The launch of Sky: Rupert Murdoch (left) and Andrew Neil

takes a view which is rather more optimistic, suggesting that by 1993 the satellite channels could take £265 million, or 12% of total television advertising revenue.

Compare those figures with the advertising revenue being taken by ITV and Channel Four. ITV took £1.3 billion in advertising revenue last year, Channel Four £220 million.

Neither Sky nor BSB believes that more than a handful of people will install two dishes – and two sets of the associated electronics – in order to watch the channels from both satellites. The alternative of buying a mechanised dish that turns from one satellite to another is too expensive and is likely to be so for a long time. So, ironically, the more satellites there are, the better it is for cable.

One of cable's strongest selling points is that it can deliver the channels from any number of satellites – usually up to 30 channels and sometimes 50 channels. It can overcome technological confusion in the shops caused by different satellites and different transmission standards. It can also overcome the need for consumers to make a choice between one satellite and another.

The cable operators argue that they offer not only the same channels as the viewer can receive on his or her individual dish but also those channels that are delivered to the operator by low-power satellite (where only the operators tend to have big enough dishes) and by video-cassette. The main cable-only offering at the moment is the Discovery Channel, which carries science and nature programmes.

Technically, cable can be two-way or interactive. It can provide an alternative telephony service, which some operators have started already, and a range of data-transmission services such as electronic-mail, home-shopping and home-banking.

That is the promise. But in the five and a half years since the government's first franchise awards at the end of 1983, cable has failed to get off the ground. The first setback was the 1984 budget, which removed capital allowances – and a good deal of investor confidence. The remaining confidence was removed by the fact that only a small percentage of people who had cable passing the front door were able to sign up.

Finally, however, cable's day may be approaching. Little British money is coming forward. But North American cable companies, flush with cash from their own operations and with nowhere at home to put it, are promising to invest in Britain and are getting the Cable Authority to award them a string of franchises across the country.

The moves are opportune because the cable operators have long argued that the arrival of Astra and BSB is a challenge as much as it is a threat. First the satellite companies would stimulate viewer interest with better programming than has existed in the past and with a massive amount of advertising. Then, the cable operators would cash in on the satellite companies' work, using their publicity to channel that interest towards cable.

One key ingredient is essential to this scenario: the availability of cable. Viewers wanting more channels have little choice but to install a dish if there is no cable running past their front door. The industry's problem is that there is little cable in the ground, it is painfully slow to install it here – say 3,000 homes in one franchise of 100,000 can be passed in a month – and there appears, surprisingly, to be little rush to quicken the pace.

For little evidence has been seen of the Americans and Canadians actually putting their hands in their pockets. There is a feeling that they may be merely collecting franchises – and putting off the big decisions until later: until they have seen how direct-to-home satellite is going and, where there is cable in the ground, whether prospects are picking up as a result of possible new interest.

The approach may be the most prudent. But it will force the viewers who are most keen to watch more channels to buy or rent their own dishes. And it will mean that cable will succeed only by subsequently weaning viewers off their dishes.

Television is just one of satellite's uses: one of the Goonhilly aerials, for example, is being used to pioneer a trial telephone service for aeroplane passengers, Skyphone

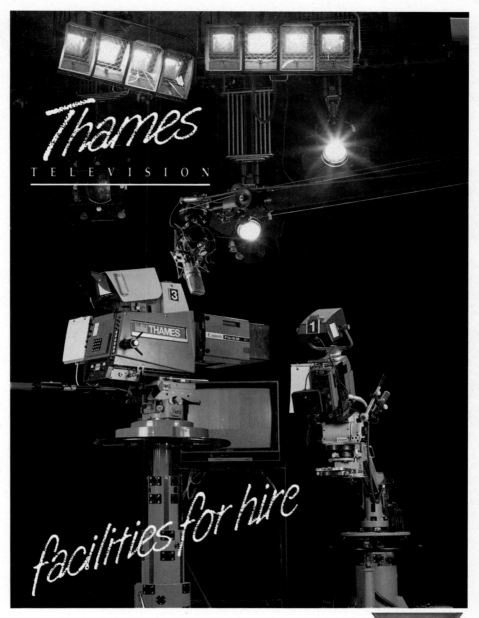

Thames
T E L E V I S I O N

facilities for hire

THE FACILITIES OF BRITAIN'S FLAGSHIP
INDEPENDENT TELEVISION COMPANY
ARE ALL AVAILABLE FOR HIRE BY
INDEPENDENT PRODUCERS.
FROM SINGLE CAMERA TO MULTI CAMERA,
WE CAN PROVIDE ALL THE EQUIPMENT YOU
NEED - IN THE STUDIO OR OUT ON LOCATION.

THAMES TELEVISION PLC, 306 EUSTON ROAD, LONDON NW1 3BB

FOR DETAILS
CONTACT PETER KEW
☎ 01-387 9494

THAMES
TELEVISION

Reel Hopes From Europe

Public funding of UK production, distribution and exhibition has had a chequered history, and faces an uncertain future. BFI director Wilf Stevenson looks at how that might change as our links with Europe are strengthened.

European Cinema and Television Year promised to bring together Europe's film and television industries. What will that mean in practice?

I was amused to note that at a recent conference, organised in Italy as a part of European Cinema and Television Year, one session was called "Public Funding in the Cinema: Abolish it or Reform it?". Amused, because if the conference had been organised for a British audience such a title simply could not have appeared. There is virtually no public funding in the UK Cinema, so we could hardly debate the issues proposed by the Italians. However given that we are approaching 1992 and the European Market, I began to speculate on how things are at the moment, and whether they might change.

First, how do we stand at the moment and how does our cinema look to other Europeans? UK cinema attendances have been increasing since 1984. That this may be as much to do with a general growth in the population as an increase in interest is a moot point, but the fact is that we are back to where we were in 1981 in terms of attendances. What has changed in that period?

In the first place there is a lot more film about. According to the 'Cultural Trends 1989' report from the Policy Studies Institute, there are on average four or five feature films on British television each day. There is evidence to show that most people who have video-recorders use them to record feature films to watch later. Each day 1 million pre-recorded video tapes are hired, and some 20,000 tapes are purchased. These are mainly feature films. So a lot of people watch films on the small screen, and yet, according to a recent survey, published in 'The Last Picture Show?' (BFI 1987) over a third of them say they prefer to watch feature films in the cinema.

So do they go to the cinema? Well yes it seems so, since the incidence in cinema going is also on

the rise according to 'The Last Picture Show?'
with 82% of 15-24 year olds now going (compared
to 59% in 1983), and 65% of the 25-34 year olds
going (compared to 49% in 1983). But population
studies show that the birth rate peaked in the
1960s, resulting in a high number of 16-24 year
olds in the late 1980s, and that between now and
1995 the number of 16-24 year olds is expected to
fall by some 20%.

Given all this, it is clear that if the exhibition
industry is to sustain the present growth it
must encourage those who are entering
the higher age groups to keep
coming to the cinema, and to
encourage those older
people to return to
the viewing
habits

which they had in the past. One way in which this
might happen is through the multiplexes. These
are offering a new environment for British filmgoers, with multi-screen centres; on-site restaur-
ants and bars; adequate and secure on-site car
parking; flexible scheduling and pricing; and
attractive marketing. The choice of films is
perhaps no greater than that available from the
current chains (Rank and Pathé/Cannon), but the
environment is certainly different, and they may
well be able to hold on to their audiences.

So is there a
need for subsidy
in the exhibition
sector of the
industry? The BFI
has argued for a
number of years
that, particularly
away from the
main urban cen-
tres, there is a
need to support
the culturally
valuable, and
particularly for-
eign language,

*Cheesecake smiles,
but multiplex chains
like UCI (UK) Ltd are
serious about the UK
market*

films which might otherwise not get shown in this country.

However this is not the only argument for subsidy of our cinema. Another is that the simple exhibition of a film does not necessarily satisfy audience needs. Experience in the Regional Film Theatres has shown that audiences want not only to see the treasures from the past, and foreign material, they also want programme notes. They want people on hand to provide educational and contextual events around screening activities. And they also want good quality prints which they want to be shown on the best available equipment.

Duke's Playhouse, Lancaster: to satisfy their audiences, the Regional Film Theatres have to do more than simply show films

All this is an add-on to operations showing simply popular films, and it has to happen in small independent cinemas, which have little or no opportunity of finding economies of scale or of scope. This means that it is a more expensive operation, and one which is worthy of support from Government. They do it slightly differently in other European countries, particularly in France and Germany, where there are support mechanisms to provide extra prints for the small independent cinemas in these countries, but despite these variations, the end result is probably much the same as in Britain.

It is with British film production that most commentators adopt a gloomy tone. It is sad that, despite growing cinema attendances, producers in this country rarely can get back more than 30% of the cost of a medium budget British-produced film, even including TV and video sales. There are many factors in play here.

Although the unit costs of film-making are high, they are not so much more than our competitors', and are probably offset by the high quality of the technical support for film making in this country. The producers share of the cinema box-office take is lower here than for many other countries. TV companies do not seem to pay a high enough price for screening films. And the video market is dominated by successful American product, which has often fully recovered its costs in the USA domestic market.

Indeed the growth in foreign material – almost exclusively from the USA – is shown by the growth in royalties paid by UK cinema and TV exhibitors to foreign rights-holders. In 1985 this was £49m but it had risen to £94m by 1988. And the foreign interest in the financing of UK production can be deduced by looking at figures quoted in 'The Last Picture Show?' which show that while £264m was earned through exhibition of UK produced material abroad and the foreign use of UK facilities in 1988, £100m went to UK subsidiaries of USA companies.

Until 1985, the UK government went along with the concept of support for UK film production, through the Eady Levy, a 12.5% take on cinema admissions, which raised £3.4m in its last full year of operation. From 1985 it has been replaced by a £1.5m a year grant to British Screen Finance (due to expire in 1990) and £0.5m a year to the National Film Development Fund. It is perhaps too late to go back over that decision, but it is sad that these grants, together with the £1m available for experimental films through the BFI Production Board, represent the sum total of all Government support for film production. In this we are far worse off than our European colleagues.

Various schemes have recently been put up to the Treasury both in terms of absolute grant aid, but also in such ways as re-classifying the negative out of the category of plant and machinery, so as to be able to write off its full cost

What will 1992 mean for the funding of films like Venus Peter, *a BFI production, which probably couldn't be financed commercially*

against tax instead of 25% as of now; of making film production better able to benefit from Business Expansion Scheme funding, as the present £500,000 limit is clearly a problem; and introducing a levy on blank video tapes (which has happened in Sweden to great effect).

It is a curious fact that British films rarely do well in the USA – the notable exceptions like *A Fish Called Wanda* prove the rule. Perhaps the language affiliation to the USA is a snare and a delusion, and we should be thinking more of our cultural associations with Europe. Europe certainly seems to be thinking along potentially useful lines, with the development of the Media 92 programme. This has been largely opposed by the UK Government, but details of what is available are now beginning to emerge. Some £30m is being provided annually by the EEC and funding partners to: support cinema distribution of low-budget feature films; provide assistance and training for independent producers in European markets; support efforts to improve subtitling and dubbing; support the development of new scripts; invest in the new technologies; and to support production, distribution and training in animation. We shall see how it works in due course, but it is clear that there are already benefits in terms of new co-production deals and in the wider distribution of foreign films.

A Fish Called Wanda *was a success in America but, for the future, British film may do better to look to other markets*

It may be, then, that the future hopes for public funding of UK cinema will lie increasingly with Europe. In the meantime, we shall continue to press for positive reforms at home, while at the same time pressing the Government not to leave the question of the future viability of the British Film Industry exclusively to our European partners.

BRITISH Screen

On Release 1990

THE BEARSKIN
THE BIG MAN
DANCIN' THROUGH THE DARK
DECEMBER BRIDE
DIAMOND SKULLS
THE DIVE
HARDWARE
HUSH-A-BYE BABY
KILLING DAD
LADDER OF SWORDS
LOSER TAKES ALL
PAPER MASK
THE REFLECTING SKIN
VENUS PETER

British Screen Finance Limited
37-39 Oxford Street, London W1R 1RE
Telephone 01-434 0291. Telex 888694 BRISCR G. FAX 434 9933

A Walk on the Wide Side

Bigger is better. That's the message from the cinema as it fights to keep audiences from television. Richard Holliss looks at some of the twists that message has taken and describes the sometimes bizarre results when big screen meets small.

*A*udiences screamed and gripped the armrests of their seats back in 1952 when to their amazement they found themselves lurching to and fro on a harrowing rollercoaster ride – courtesy of the inventors of Cinerama. That reaction was just what the Hollywood studios were hoping for as they used ever wider formats to thrill audiences and fight off the threat of television.

Today that battle is ever more relevant as satellite and cable add to the armoury of the electronic enemy. The cinema's tactics have changed somewhat – ranging from offering the comfort of the multiplexes to blatant advertising. The recent 'The first place to see films is at the cinema' campaign, for example, featured two decorators painting a cinema screen black and then chalking onto it a television set on which a ridiculously small fragment of *The Last Emperor* could be seen.

But the basic message is the same: bigger is better and the cinema can offer an experience which television can't rival.

Cinerama was just one of the formats used to ram that message home in the 50s. In their desperate battle for supremacy over television the major Hollywood studios bombarded their audiences with a number of popular, if short-lived, gimmicks including 3-D and Smell-O-Vision. But none could rival the outstanding

The Decorators: *stills from an advertising campaign run in British cinemas, telling audiences what they miss when they see films on television*

success of epic films in Cinerama and the other equally impressive wide screen cinematic formats; CinemaScope, Technirama 70mm, Panavision, VistaVision etc.

Wide screen was not new however and first appeared in the late twenties. Prints for a 1930 MGM film called *Billy the Kid,* shot in a process known as 70mm Realife, still exist today. Like the Grandeur format used by the William Fox Studio, Realife started as a result of technological advances in cinematography by the Mitchell Camera Corporation.

A problem facing both those early systems in the 1930s was the failure of the major studios to interest exhibitors in the idea. It could prove extremely expensive to convert theatres to accommodate wide screen formats. The Mitchell equipment was put in storage and the idea would have been almost forgotten had not that ground breaking roller-coaster ride been shown in 1952 at the Broadway Theatre in New York.

A specially invited audience were witness to this and other hair-raising scenes in *This Is Cinerama,* the first film to be shot using the format. After a brief prologue in black and white on an average sized screen featuring Lowell Thomas, the famed explorer, the curtains opened to a full 146° and wide screen burst upon the cinema world.

Like the other wide screen formats, Cinerama had to overcome a number of technical problems. A movie screen built to extend to the periphery of the human eye can totally engulf the audience. The problem, however, was to achieve the correct perspective. Fred Waller, the man who devised the Cinerama process, used three 35mm cameras, each set up to cover one third of the complete image. But to further complicate matters the cameras were designed to film across each other's field of view. Therefore the left hand camera shot the right hand side of the completed picture and vice versa. Three cinema projectors electronically locked with selsyn motors and placed across the back of the auditorium ensured a perfectly synchronised panorama on screen. There was a marginal overlap where the images combined and these are sometimes noticeable in films such as *The Wonderful World of the Brothers Grimm* or *How the West was Won* owing to a slight difference in colourisation of film stock. In order to solve the problem of overlap, film directors would try to frame the edge of the picture against a vertical object such as a tree or post.

This is Cinerama was an enormous success, grossing nearly $5m on its initial release. Yet there was a limit to the number of cinemas that were equipped to show it and despite being the most impressive of the deep curved systems (a reference to the shape of the cinema screen) it was overtaken by rival formats. Not before it had been used for a number of experimental films however including *Cinerama Holiday*, and *Seven Wonders of the World* (both 1955). And not before its backers had tried every attempt to make it succeed. As late as 1963 *The Best Of Cinerama* in a supposedly improved format called Super Cinerama was shown on an even larger screen.

One of the last Cinerama releases was in 1972 and was a reissue of *This is Cinerama*. By then it had caught up with other formats by abandoning the unwieldy three projector set-up and using one 70mm strip of film via an anamorphic lens.

The anamorphic process first entered the cinema in 1952 when 20th Century Fox purchased the rights to the Hyper-Gonar system. Quite simply, the anamorphic lens can optically squeeze a wide screen image to fit within the width of a regular 35mm frame and then reverse the image back to its original proportions during cinema projection. Studio head Darryl F Zanuck saw this wide screen method as Fox's answer to the threat of television and launched Cinema-Scope with a clever series of advertisements and a beautifully designed colour and sound extension to their famous fanfare opening. The first two features to be filmed in CinemaScope were *How to Marry a Millionaire* and *The Robe*. The latter was a spectacular biblical epic that made full use of the new screen size. Shot in

Fox's CinemaScope system was so important to the studio that it appears more dominant than the film title on this advertising hoarding for The Robe *at Grauman's Chinese Theatre in Hollywood*

The Robe

the anamorphic process on 35mm film stock, CinemaScope, unlike Cinerama, could be shown in all types of theatres equipped with a wide screen. All a projectionist had to do was place a Hyper-Gonar lens on the projector for instant scope.

Fox also scored over its competitors, and after the success of *The Robe* there were quite a few, by hiring out the process to any studio that wanted to make wide screen films. Walt Disney, for example, used CinemaScope for the first cartoon short in the new format, *Toot, Whistle, Plunk and Boom* (1953) and the features *20,000 Leagues Under the Sea* (1954) and *Lady and the Tramp* (1955).

When the film *Oklahoma* (1955) made a hit with audiences thanks to a new system called Todd-AO named after veteran showman Michael Todd and the innovations of the American Optical Company, Fox decided to increase the size of its film to 55mm from 35mm. Their first production was *Carousel* (1956) which, as usual, was backed up by a tremendous advertising campaign. But CinemaScope 55 was to have a short life as other widescreen formats vied for top position.

Cecil B DeMille directs a sequence from The Ten Commandments, *flanked by the enormous VistaVision camera*

Paramount Pictures introduced VistaVision which had the advantage of a much larger screen than conventional scope or the standard Academy cinema format. (The Academy ratio was the name given to a system of masking optical sound film frames and was standardised by the Academy of Motion Picture Arts and Sciences). Cecil B.

Like other tall actors, Charlton Heston suffered "decapitation" when wide screen formats like VistaVision were converted to 70mm

DeMille's *The Ten Commandments* (1956) was a perfect example of the use of VistaVision particularly in its recreation of the parting of the Red Sea. VistaVision equipment is still in use today because its large frame area is suitable for certain optical and special visual processes.

RKO Radio Pictures set up a cheaper system called SuperScope. Here films were shot on conventional 35mm with a standard lens. The frames were then cropped and subsequently squeezed with an anamorphic attachment giving the false impression of having been filmed in scope.

Television uses a similar method to crop wide screen films except they achieve their results in the horizontal field not vertical.

SuperScope also allowed existing films to be reprocessed into widescreen at the laboratory. Walt Disney's *Fantasia* (1941) fell victim to this process during the mid-fifties by being re-released with cropped frames that played havoc with some of the exquisite animation. Even *The Ten Commandments* was converted from VistaVision to 70mm in the seventies. Very tall actors (Charlton Heston being one of them) suffered, on occasions, from visual decapitation.

Films shown in the cinemas on 70mm wide film carried the Super Technirama logo. Although shot on 35mm, the film moved horizontally through the camera as opposed to vertically which meant that twice the amount of film stock was used, a very expensive system. Roadshow releases at higher admission prices were used in an effort to retrieve some of the astronomical costs. Only 27 features were made in Super Technirama 70mm, landmarks for the process being *Sleeping Beauty* (1959), *El Cid* (1961), *King of Kings* (1961) and *Zulu* (1964). Disney's *The Black Cauldron* (1985) was the last film to be made incorporating this system.

Other 70mm formats, such as Ultra Panavision and Super Panavision 70mm were used in films such as *West Side Story* (1961), *Lawrence of Arabia* (1962 and recently restored in a new scope print with additional sequences), *My Fair Lady* (1964) and under the advertising banner of 70mm Super Cinerama, Stanley Kubrick's *2001 A Space Odyssey* (1968).

Today most modern cinema screens are designed for a widescreen process which means that new films are deliberately shot to make full use of these new ratios, usually with Panavision equip-

Action sequences from films like Lawrence of Arabia lose a lot of their grandeur when cropped to fit the television screen

ment. Sadly re-issues of classic films suffer unless projection boxes are geared up to show them such as those installed at the National Film Theatre. *Fantasia*, for example, in its recently restored digital version shows the cropping of the Academy ratio to fit the new cinema screens.

It was inevitable that wide screen films would be bought for television. Ironically the flat squarer tubes have been a perfect medium for the classic Academy format and the small screen has often betrayed the filmmakers art by showing the microphone in shot, something that's usually hidden by the black masking around the edge of a cinema screen. But wide screen formats have

Bus Stop, *starring Marilyn Monroe, suffered disastrously when converted for television*

had a long and tedious battle with television engineers. Adaptation to the medium has ranged from mildly irritating to catastrophic.

The Marilyn Monroe film *Bus Stop* (1956) was a recent example of how CinemaScope can suffer on television. As most television viewers insist on watching a picture that fills the screen (some have even written letters of complaint to television companies over credits sequences to wide screen films) left and right sections of the frame are missing. Aware that action or dialogue vital to the plot of *Bus Stop* may be taking place at the side of the screen the print is scanned prior to showing and various sections of one camera angle are reshot. To better understand this, imagine two actors standing apart at the full width of the CinemaScope screen. Television can only show one at a time. Consequently, the idea is to re-edit the scene and, therefore, show the actors separately. Unfortunately in *Bus Stop,* certain background objects and people could be seen in both shots and appeared to leap back and forth most disconcertingly. Television scanning can also be a problem if it coincides with a camera pan resulting in a blurred image on screen.

Occasionally a major studio will prepare a version of a wide screen film especially for television. Fox did with *The Robe,* which also proved useful for cinemas in Europe, many of which were unequipped to show CinemaScope. This is a more satisfactory solution to scanning but, unfortunately, with the exception of 16mm releases intended for private hire, few 35mm prints exist in this format.

After the disastrous television premiere of *2001 A Space Odyssey,* technicians at the BBC decided to present Kubrick's film in a letterbox style, a scope format across the centre of the screen with masking at the top and bottom. The image is

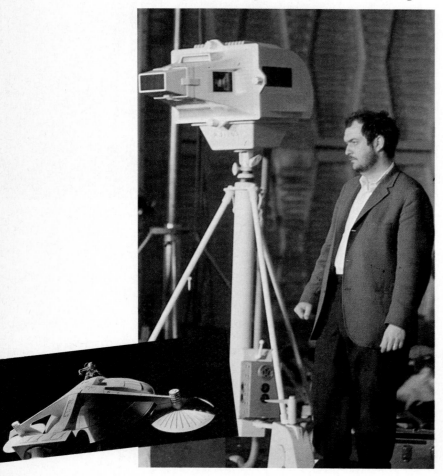

2001 A Space Odyssey made spectacular use of the wide screen format. However director Stanley Kubrick's work presented problems for any television station trying to do justice to the film

greatly reduced but at least none of the film is lost. Channel 4 did likewise with its screening of the sequel *2010* (1984), which was originally released in Panavision via the 35mm anamorphic process.

The debate on the screening of scope films on television will no doubt continue until the introduction of 1000 line television, combined with recent experiments in liquid crystal screens breaks away from the standard size altogether.

Lowell Thomas, the explorer, introduces unsuspecting audiences to Cinerama

In the meantime, viewers will have to put up with the disappointing compromise between film studios and television companies. It will be a long time before the likes of *This is Cinerama* ever finds a place in the living room alongside the home computer and compact disc player.

Sound Formats

by Dolby Laboratories

Established worldwide

DolbyⓇ A-type Over 120,000 tracks of professional noise reduction in use in music, broadcast and film recording studios around the world.

DOLBY B·C NR More than 245 million cassette recorders and players with B or C-type noise reduction manufactured by over 138 licensees. More than 450 licensed producers of pre-recorded cassettes.

DOLBY STEREOⓇ Over 2,200 feature films using Dolby Stereo optical soundtracks, plus foreign language versions, produced by 90 studios in 20 countries. Four channels reproduced in the cinema.

New but proven

DolbyⓇ SR More than 28,000 tracks already in use worldwide. Dolby spectral recording offers sound quality superior to that of 16-bit PCM, with the practicality and economy of analogue recording. Available to anyone with a professional analogue recorder – everywhere.

DolbyⓇ ADM High quality digital stereo sound for television and radio broadcasting, distribution, DBS and teleconferencing. Over 50,000 decoding channels currently employed. Users include ABC (Australia), A L Williams, AT&T, Aussat, Australian Dept of Communications, Australian Telecom, Bonneville, British Telecom, California Racing Commission, Coca Cola, Computerland, Federal Express, Ford, Ford Aerospace, General Motors, Golden West Network, Hewlett Packard, HI-NET, IBM, Kodak, K-Mart, Mayo Clinic, Merrill Lynch, MicroAge, MTV (USA), New York Gaming Commission, Satellite Leisure Services, SBS, Swan 9, TV Globo.

DOLBY SURROUND™ Stereo sound programmes for television and video, with centre and surround channels encoded in the two conventional channels. Many stereo TV broadcasts and pre-recorded videos draw on the library of over 2,200 Dolby Stereo films. Successfully used with original television drama and live broadcasts. About 2,000,000 decoders already in use and now becoming available in TV sets, video control centres and video cassette recorders.

Dolby Laboratories Inc
100 Potrero Avenue, San Francisco CA 94103-4813   346 Clapham Road London SW9 9AP
tel 415-558-0200   tlx 34409   tel 01-720-1111   tlx 919109
Dolby, Dolby Stereo, Dolby SR and Dolby Surround are trademarks of Dolby Laboratories Licensing Corp.

L89/054

Quality + Practicality + Economy

DIRECTORY

CONTENTS

ARCHIVES AND LIBRARIES

International Federation of Film Archives (FIAF)

Coudenberg 70
1000 Brussels
Belgium
Tel: 511 13 90
Though not itself an archive, FIAF, which has over 50 member archives and many observers from 58 countries, exists to develop and maintain the highest standards of film preservation and access. It also publishes handbooks on film archiving practice which can be obtained from the above address

International Federation of Television Archives (FIAT)

c/o Vittorio Sette
RAI Radiotelevisione
Italiana
Direzione
Amministrativa/GSA
Via Cernaia 33
10121 Turino
Italy
Tel: 11 88 00 x2626

NATIONAL ARCHIVES

There are two national archives in the UK that are recognised by FIAF:

Imperial War Museum

Department of Film
Lambeth Road
London SE1 6HZ
Tel: 01 735 8922

National Film Archive

21 Stephen Street
London W1P 1PL
Tel: 01 255 1444
See also p 11

REGIONAL COLLECTIONS

East Anglian Film Archive

Centre of East Anglian Studies
University of East Anglia
Norwich
Norfolk NR4 7TJ
Tel: 0603 56161 x2664

David Cleveland
Cathryn Terry

North West Film Archive

Manchester Polytechnic
Minshull House
47–49 Chorlton Street
Manchester M1 3EU
Tel: 061 228 6171 x2590
Maryann Gomes
Marion Hewitt

Northern Film and Television Archive

36 Bottle Bank
Gateshead
Tyne and Wear NE8 2AR
Tel: 091 477 3601
Kevin Brown

Scottish Film Archive

74 Victoria Crescent Road
Dowanhill
Glasgow G12 9JN
Scotland
Tel: 041 334 9314
Janet McBain

South East Regional Film Archive

c/o Film Archive
Management and Entertainment
Lansdowne Vaults
Imperial Studios
Maxwell Road
Borehamwood
Herts WD6 1WE
Tel: 01 207 6446
Barry Coward

Wessex Film and Sound Archive

Hampshire Archives
Trust
20 Southgate Street
Winchester SO23 9EF
Tel: 0962 847742
David Lee

NEWSREEL, PRODUCTION AND STOCK SHOT LIBRARIES

These are film and television libraries which specialise in locating material on a particular subject. For other, sometimes more specialised, film libraries consult the

'Researcher's Guide to British Film and Television Collections' and the 'Researcher's Guide to British Newsreels', published by the BUFVC

Archive Film Agency

21 Lidgett Park Avenue
Roundhay
Leeds LS8 1EU
Tel: 0532 662454
Agnese Geoghegan
Newsreel, documentary and feature material from 1900

Boulton-Hawker Films

Hadleigh
Ipswich
Suffolk IP7 5BG
Tel: 0473 822235
Peter Boulton
Educational films produced over 44 years. Subjects include: health, biology, botany, geography, history, archaeology, and the arts

British Movietone News Film Library

North Orbital Road
Denham
Uxbridge
Middx UB9 5HQ
Tel: 0895 833071
London Office
71 Dean Street
London W1V 6DE
Tel: 01 437 7766 x206
Newsreel (1929 – 1979), b/w, some colour, 35mm

Chameleon Film and Stockshot Library

The Magistretti Building
Harcourt Place
Leeds LS1 4RB
Tel: 0532 434017
Linda Woodhouse
16mm material from 1970s onwards includes climbing and caving films for use as stockshots. Also output from Trident Television, including *Whicker's World* and Channel 4 programme trims

Educational and Television Films (ETV)

247a Upper Street
London N1 1RU
Tel: 01 226 2298

Documentaries on Eastern Europe, USSR, China, British Labour movement, b/w and colour, 16mm and 35mm, 1896 to present day

Film Research and Production Services
73 Newman Street
London W1P 3LA
Tel: 01 580 4882/3
Amanda Dunne
David Collier
Gerard Wilkinson
Film holdings, with comprehensive film research and copyright clearance facilities

GB Associates
80 Montalt Road
Woodford Green
Essex IG8 9SS
Tel: 01 505 1850
Malcolm Billingsley
An extensive collection of fact and fiction film from 1896 onwards, 35mm and 16mm

Huntley Archive
22 Islington Green
The Angel
London N1 8DU
Tel: 01 226 9260
John Huntley
Amanda Huntley
Documentary and newsreel film, 16mm/35mm specialist collections in transport, street scenes, industrial history, music etc from 1895

Index Stock Shots
12 Charlotte Mews
London W1P 1LN
Tel: 01 631 0134
Stock footage on film and video, including international locations, aircraft, natural phenomena and wildlife

Kobal Archive Films
28–32 Shelton Street
London WC2H 9HP
Tel: 01 240 9565
Footage and stills from silent films, features, newsreels, industrial films, documentaries; b/w and colour

Oxford Scientific Films
Long Hanborough
Oxford OX7 2LD
Tel: 0993 881881
Stock footage and stills library; 16mm, 35mm film and transparencies covering wide range of wildlife and special effects subjects

Visnews Library
Cumberland Avenue
London NW10 7EH
Tel: 01 965 7733
Pam Turner
Newsreel, TV news, special collections. Colour and b/w, 16mm, 35mm, 1896 to present day and all material pre 1951 and post July 1981 on 1″ video

Weintraub Feature Film Library
Goldcrest Elstree Studios
Shenley Road
Borehamwood
Herts WD6 1JG
Tel: 01 953 1600
John Herron
Feature, b/w and colour, 35mm, 1925 to present day

Weintraub/Pathé Library
Goldcrest Elstree Studios
Shenley Road
Borehamwood
Herts WD6 1JG
Tel: 01 953 1600
George Marshall
Index and London Office
167–169 Wardour Street
London W1V 3TA
Tel: 01 439 1790
Larry McKinna
Newsreel, b/w and colour, 35mm, 1896 to 1970

World Backgrounds Film Production Library
Imperial Studios
Maxwell Road
Borehamwood
Herts
Tel: 01 207 4747
Ralph Rogers
Ron Saunders
Worldwide establishing shots, colour, 35mm and back projection plates, 1964 to present day, supplied to TV series, commercials, features, documentaries and sports programmes

AWARDS

BAFTA FILM AWARDS – BRITISH ACADEMY OF FILM AND TELEVISION ARTS

Awarded March 1988 for 1987 Films

Best film: *Jean de Florette* (France/Italy) Dir Claude Berri
Best achievement in direction: Oliver Stone for *Platoon* (USA)
Best actress: Anne Bancroft for *84 Charing Cross Road* (USA)
Best actor: Sean Connery for *The Name of the Rose* (W Germany/Italy/France)
Best supporting actress: Susan Wooldridge for *Hope and Glory* (GB)
Best supporting actor: Daniel Auteuil for *Jean de Florette*
Best original screenplay: David Leland for *Wish You Were Here* (GB)

Best adapted screenplay: Claude Berri and Gerard Brach for *Jean de Florette*
Best cinematography: Bruno Nuytten for *Jean de Florette*
Best editing: Claire Simpson for *Platoon* (USA)
Best sound: Jonathan Bates, Simon Kaye and Gerry Humphreys for *Cry Freedom* (GB)
Best production design: Santo Loquasto for *Radio Days* (USA)
Best costume design: Jeffrey Kurland for *Radio Days*
Best achievement in special effects: Michael Owens, Edward L Jones, Bruce Walters and Michael Lanteri for *The Witches of Eastwick* (USA)
Best film score: Ennio Morricone for *The Untouchables* (USA)
Best foreign language film: *Sacrificio (The Sacrifice)* (Sweden/France) Dir Andrei Tarkovsky
Best make-up: Hasso von Hugo for *The Name of The Rose*

Best short film: *Artisten*
Dir Jonas Grimas
BAFTA fellowship:
Ingmar Bergman
Michael Balcon award for
outstanding British
contribution to cinema:
The Monty Python team
BAFTA special tribute:
Sir John Mills

Awarded March 1989 for 1988 Films

Best film: *The Last
Emperor* (Italy/China) Dir
Bernardo Bertolucci
Best achievement in
direction: Louis Malle
for *Au Revoir Les Enfants*
(France/W Germany)
Best actress: Maggie
Smith for *The Lonely
Passion of Judith Hearne*
(GB)
Best actor: John Cleese
for *A Fish Called Wanda*
(GB)
Best supporting actress:
Judi Dench for *A Handful
of Dust* (GB)
Best supporting actor:
Michael Palin for *A Fish
Called Wanda*
Best original
screenplay: Shawn Slovo
for *A World Apart* (GB)
Best adapted
screenplay: Jean-Claude
Carriere and Philip
Kaufman for *The
Unbearable Lightness of
Being* (USA)
Best cinematography:
Allan Daviau for *Empire
of the Sun* (USA)
Best editing: Michael
Kahn and Peter E Berger
for *Fatal Attraction* (USA)
Best sound: Charles L
Campbell, Lou Edeman,
Colin Charles and Robert
Knudson for *Empire of the
Sun*
Best production design:
Dean Tavoularis for
*Tucker – The Man and
His Dream* (USA)
Best costume design:
James Acheson for *The
Last Emperor*
Best achievement in
special effects: Richard
Williams, Ken Ralston,
George Gibbs and Edward
Jones for *Who Framed
Roger Rabbit* (USA)
Best film score: John
Williams for *Empire of the
Sun*
Best foreign language

The Name of the Rose

film: *Babettes Gaestebud
(Babette's Feast)*
(Denmark) Dir Gabriel
Axel
Best make-up: Fabrizio
Sforza for *The Last
Emperor*
Best short film: *Defence
Counsel Sedov* (USSR)
Dir Evgeny Tsymbal
BAFTA fellowship: Alec
Guinness
Michael Balcon award for
outstanding British
contribution to cinema:
Charles Crichton
BAFTA special awards:
Richard Williams for *Who
Framed Roger Rabbit;*
Leslie Hardcastle for
MOMI
BAFTA scholarship
awarded by the Post
Office: Gillian Wilkinson

BAFTA TELEVISION AWARDS

Awarded March 1988

Best single drama: *Life
Story* (BBC/Arts and
Entertainment Channel)
Prod/Dir Mick Jackson
Best drama series/
serial: *Tutti Frutti* (BBC)
Prod Andy Park Dir Tony
Smith
Flaherty documentary
award: *Baka – People of
the Rain Forest* (Dja River

Films) Prod Phil Agland
Best factual series: *The
Duty Men* (BBC) Prod
Paul Hamann
Best light
entertainment
programme: *Victoria
Wood as Seen on TV*
(BBC) Prod/Dir Geoff
Posner
Best comedy series:
Blackadder the Third
(BBC) Prod John Lloyd
Best children's
programme

Louis Malle's **Au revoir
les enfants**

(entertainment/drama):
A Little Princess (LWT)
Prod Colin Shindler Dir
Carol Wiseman
Best children's
programme
(documentary/
educational): *The Really
Wild Show* (BBC) Prod
Mike Beynon

Blackadder the Third

Best news/OB coverage: *Special edition of Channel 4 news – coverage of the Zeebrugge disaster* (ITN) Ed Stewart Purvis
Best actress: Emma Thompson for *Tutti Frutti* and *Fortunes of War* (BBC)
Best actor: David Jason for *Porterhouse Blue* (Picture Partnership Prods/Channel 4)
Best light entertainment performance: Nigel Hawthorne for *Yes, Prime Minister* (BBC)
Best animation: *The Reluctant Dragon* (Thames TV) Dir Bridget Appleby
Best original TV music: Christopher Gunning, Rick Lloyd for *Porterhouse Blue*
Writer's award: Antony Jay and Jonathan Lynn
Richard Dimbleby award (for factual television): Esther Rantzen
Desmond Davis award for outstanding creative contribution to television: Julia Smith
Television award for originality: *Network 7*
Huw Wheldon award (best arts programme): *A Simple Man – LS Lowry* (BBC) Prod Ian Squires Dir Gillian Lynne
Best foreign television programme: *Günter Walraff – Ganz Unten* (W Germany) Dir Jörg Gförer

Awarded March 1989

Best single drama: *Tumbledown* (BBC) Prod Richard Broke Dir Richard Eyre
Best drama series/serial: *A Very British Coup* (Skreba Films/Parallax Pictures/Channel 4) Prods Ann Skinner, Sally Hibbin Dir Mick Jackson
Flaherty documentary award: *This Week: Death On the Rock* (Thames TV) Prod Chris Oxley
Best factual series: *Arena* (BBC) Eds Anthony Wall, Nigel Finch
Best light entertainment programme: *An Audience with Victoria Wood* (LWT) Prod David G Hillier
Best comedy series: *Only Fools and Horses: Christmas Special* (BBC) Prod Gareth Gwenlan
Best children's programme (entertainment/drama): *The Storyteller* (TVS/Jim Henson Organisation) Prod Duncan Kenworthy
Best children's programme (documentary/educational): *Going to School: Near and Far, Now and Then* Prod Nicholas Whines
Best news/OB coverage: *Channel 4*

The Storyteller

News Production Team (ITN)
Best actress: Thora Hird for *Talking Heads: A Cream Cracker Under the Settee* (BBC)
Best actor: Ray McAnally for *A Very British Coup*
Best light entertainment performance: Victoria Wood for *An Audience With Victoria Wood*
Best animation: *The Hill Farm* (National Film and Television School) Dir Mark Baker
Best original TV music: Frank Ricotti for *The Beiderbecke Connection* (Yorkshire TV)
Writer's award: Alan Plater
Richard Dimbleby award: Ludovic Kennedy
Desmond Davis award for outstanding creative contribution to television: Stuart Burge
Television award for originality: Adrian Cowell
Huw Wheldon award (best arts programme): *The South Bank Show: Bertolucci and The Last Emperor* (LWT) Prod David Hinton
Best foreign television programme: *Tanner '88* (Zenith Prods/Darkhorse Prods, USA) Prods Garry Trudeau, Robert Altman

Tumbledown

BFI AWARDS 1988

Grierson award: Paul Hamann for *Fourteen Days in May*
Technical achievement: *Cry Freedom* (GB) Dir Richard Attenborough
Archival achievement: *Struggles for Poland* (David Naden Associates/Channel 4/WNET/NDR) Exec Prod/Dir Martin Smith
A career in the industry: Eva Monley
Commercial film and television award: *40 Minutes* (BBC) Ed Edward Mirzoeff
Independent film and television award: Retake Film and Video Collective
Book award: Leonard J Leff for 'Hitchcock and Selznick: The Rich and Strange Collaboration of Alfred Hitchcock and David O Selznick in Hollywood'
Anthony Asquith young composer award: Rachel Portman
Anthony Asquith film music award: Howard Blake for *A Month in the Country*
Kodak newcomer of the year: Molly Dineen for *40 Minutes: My African Farm* (Allegra Film/BBC)
1988 BFI fellowships: Vanessa Redgrave, Graham Greene, Anthony Smith

BFI Fellows 1988, with BFI Chairman Sir Richard Attenborough

BERLIN FESTIVAL

Awarded February 1988

Golden Bear: *Hong Gaoliang (Red Sorghum)* (People's Republic of China) Dir Zhang Yimou

Hong Gaoliang (Red Sorghum)

SILVER BEARS
Best film: *La Deuda Interna (The Debt/Veronico Cruž)* (Argentina/UK) Dir Miguel Pereira
Best director: Norman Jewison for *Moonstruck* (USA)
Best actress: Holly Hunter for *Broadcast News* (USA)
Best actor: Jörg Posse and Manfred Möck for *Einer Trage des Anderen Last (Bear Ye One Another's Burdens)* (E Germany)
Special jury prize: *Komissar (Commissar)* (USSR) Dir Alexander

SHORT FILMS
Golden Bear: *Oblast (The Power)* (Yugoslavia) Dir Zdravko Barisio
Silver Bear: *Laska Na Prvni Pohled (Love at First Sight)* (Czechoslovakia) Dir Pavel Koutsky
FIPRESCI (international critics') awards:
Best film in competition: *Komissar (Commissar)*
Best film in forum: *Dani, Michi, Renato & Max* (Switzerland) Dir Richard Dindo
Askoldov
Outstanding single achievement: *Matka Krolow (Mother of Kings)* (Poland) Dir/Writer Janusz Zaorski

Awarded February 1989

GOLDEN BEARS
Rain Man (USA) Dir Barry Levinson

Honorary Golden Bear: Dustin Hoffman
Alfred Bauer prize: *Sluga (The Servant)* (USSR) Dir Vadim Abdrashitov
SILVER BEARS
Hakayitz Shel Aviya (Aviya's Summer) (Israel) Dir Eli Cohen
Best director: Dusan Hanak for *Ja Milujem, Ty Milujes (I Love, You Love)* (Czechoslovakia)
Best actress: Isabelle Adjani for *Camille Claudel* (France)
Best actor: Gene Hackman for *Mississippi Burning* (USA)
Special jury prize: *Wan*

Isabelle Adjani as Camille Claudel

Zhong (Evening Bells) (People's Republic of China) Dir Wu Ziniu
Outstanding single achievement: Eric

Bogosian (writer/actor) for *Talk Radio* (USA)
Special mention: Jacques Rivette

SHORT FILMS
Golden Bear: *Pas A Deux (Film Dansant)* (Netherlands) Dirs Monique Renault, Gerrit Van Dijk
Silver Bear: *Udel (Fate)* (Czechoslovakia) Dir Jaroslava Havettova
FIPRESCI (international critics') award *La Bande des Quatre (The Gang of Four)* (France) Dir Jacques Rivette

BROADCASTING PRESS GUILD AWARDS

Presented March 1988

Best drama series: *Fortunes of War* (BBC) Prod Betty Willingale
Best actor: David Jason for *Porterhouse Blue* (Picture Partnership Prods/Channel 4)
Best actress: Emma Thompson for *Fortunes of War* and *Tutti Frutti* (BBC)
Best single drama: *Life*

Story (BBC/Arts and Entertainment Channel) Prod Mick Jackson
Best documentary series: *The Duty Men* (BBC) Prod Paul Hamann
Best single documentary: *The Falklands War: The Untold Story* (Yorkshire TV) Exec Prod John Willis Prods Peter Kosminsky, Michael Bilton
Best light entertainment: *The Dame Edna Experience* (LWT) Prod Judith Holder
Most original drama: *Tutti Frutti* Prod Andy Park
Best arts programme: *The RKO Story: Tales from Hollywood* (BBC/RKO) Exec Prod Leslie Megahey Prods Rosemary Wilton, Charles Chabot
Special awards: Jeremy Isaacs for his contribution to television; Ray Moore for his contribution to radio as a Radio 2 presenter
Best imported

Emma Thompson as Suzi Kettles in **Tutti Frutti**

programme: *Shoah* (France/Switzerland) Dir Claude Lanzmann
Outstanding programme contribution: *After Henry* written by Simon Brett

CANNES FESTIVAL 1988

Golden Palm: *Pelle Erobreren (Pelle The Conqueror)* (Denmark) Dir Bille August
Best director: Fernando Solanas for *Sur (South)* (Argentina)
Special jury prize: *A World Apart* (GB) Dir Chris Menges
Jury prize: *Krotki Film O Zabijaniu (A Short Film About Killing)* (Poland) Dir Krysztof Kieslowski
Best actress: Barbara Hershey, Jodhi May, Linda Mvusi for *A World Apart*
Best actor: Forest Whitaker for *Bird* (US)
Best artistic contribution: *Drowning By Numbers* (GB) Dir Peter Greenaway

The Duty Men

Golden Camera (best first feature): *Salaam Bombay* (India) Dir Mira Nair
Grand prize for superior technical achievement: *Bird*
Short film Golden Palm: *Bukpytacy (Fioritures)* (USSR) Dir Gary Bardine
Short film prize (animation): *Ab Ovo/ Homoknyomok* (Hungary) Dir Ferenc Cako
Short film prize (fiction): *Sculpture Physique* (France) Dirs Yann Piquer, Jean-Marie Maddedu
FIPRESCI (international critics') awards
Best film in official selection: shared by *Krotki Film O Zabijaniu (A Short Film about Killing)* and *Hotel Terminus: Klaus Barbie, His Life and Times* (France) Dir Marcel Ophuls
Best film outside official selection: *Distant Voices, Still Lives* (GB) Dir Terence Davies
Prix Jeunesse: *Herseye Ragmen (Despite Everything)* (Turkey) Dir Orhan Oguz

40TH EMMY AWARDS FOR TELEVISION – NATIONAL ACADEMY FOR TELEVISION ARTS AND SCIENCES

DRAMA
Lead actor: Joe Gardner for *A Year in the Life* (NBC)
Lead actress: Tyne Daly for *Cagney and Lacey* (CBS)
Supporting actor: Larry Drake for *LA Law* (NBC)
Supporting actress: Patricia Wettig for *thirtysomething* (ABC)
Director: Mark Tinker for *St Elsewhere: Weigh In, Way Out* (NBC)
Outstanding series: *thirtysomething*

Outstanding special (drama/comedy): *Inherit the Wind* (AT&T Presents) (NBC)
Writing: Paul Haggis and Marshall Herskovitz for *thirtysomething: Business as Usual*
MINI-SERIES/SPECIALS
Lead actor: Jason Robards for *Inherit the Wind*
Lead actress: Jessica Tandy for *Foxfire* (CBS)
Supporting actor: John Shea for *Baby M* (ABC)
Supporting actress: Jane Seymour for *Onassis: The Richest Man in the World* (ABC)
Outstanding mini-series: *The Murder of Mary Phagan* (NBC) Prod George Stevens Jnr
Director: Lamont Johnson for *Gore Vidal's Lincoln* (NBC)
Writing: William Hanley for *The Attic: The Hiding*

thirtysomething

Individual performance (variety/music): Robin Williams for *ABC Presents a Royal Gala* (ABC)
Writing (comedy): Hugh Wilson for *Frank's Place: The Bridge* (CBS)
Writing (variety/music): Jackie Mason for *Jackie Mason on Broadway* (HBO)
Best animation: *A Claymation Christmas Celebration* (CBS)
Governor's award: *of Anne Frank* (CBS)
COMEDY/VARIETY/MUSIC
Lead actor: Michael J Fox for *Family Ties* (NBC)
Lead actress: Beatrice Arthur for *The Golden Girls* (NBC)
Supporting actor: John Larroquette for *Night Court* (NBC)
Supporting actress: Estelle Getty for *The Golden Girls*
Directing (comedy): Gregory Hoblit for *Hooperman* (pilot episode) (ABC)
Directing (variety/music): Patricia Birch and Humphrey Burton for *Celebrating Gershwin* (PBS)
Outstanding series (comedy): *The Wonder Years* (ABC)
Outstanding programme (variety/music/comedy): *Irving Berlin's 100th Birthday Celebration* (CBS)
William Hanna and Joseph Barbera

Beatrice Arthur (centre) in The Golden Girls

INTERNATIONAL EMMYS 1988

Awarded November 1988
Best drama: *A Very British Coup* (Skreba Films/Parallax Pictures/Channel 4) Prods Ann Skinner, Sally Hibbin
Best documentary: *The Last Seven Months of Anne Frank* (TROS Television/BRT/AVA, Belgium/Netherlands)
Best performing arts programme: *The South Bank Show: Ken Russell's ABC of British Music* (LWT) Prod/Dir Ken Russell
Best popular arts programme: *The New Statesman* (Yorkshire TV) Prod David Reynolds
Children's and young people award: *Touch the Sun – Captain Johnno* (Australian Children's Television Foundation, Australia) Prod Jane Ballantyne
Directorate award: Vittorio Boni
Founder's award: Goar Mestre

EUROPEAN FILM AWARDS 1988

Best film: *Krotki Film o Zabijaniu (A Short Film*

about Killing) (Poland)
Dir Krzysztof Kieslowski
Best young film: *Mujeres al Borde de un Ataque de Nervios (Women on the Verge of a Nervous Breakdown)* (Spain) Dir Pedro Almódovar
Best director: Wim Wenders for *Der Himmel uber Berlin (Wings of Desire)* (W Germany/France)
Best actor: Max Von Sydow for *Pelle Erobreren (Pelle the Conqueror)* (Denmark)
Best actress: Carmen Maura for *Mujeres al Borde de un Ataque de Nervios*
Best supporting actor: Curt Bois for *Der Himmel uber Berlin*
Best supporting actress: Johanna ter Steege for *Spoorloos (The Vanishing)* (Netherlands)
Best young actor/actress: Pelle Hvenegaard for *Pelle Erobreren*
Best script: Louis Malle for *Au Revoir Les Enfants* (France/W Germany)
Special aspect award: G Aleksi-Meschischiwili, N Sandukeli and Sch Gogolaschwili for art direction on *Asik Kerib* (USSR)
Special awards: Bernardo Bertolucci; Mikis Theodorakis
Award of merit: Sir Richard Attenborough
Life achievement awards: Marcello Mastroianni; Ingmar Bergman

KARLOVY VARY FILM FESTIVAL 1988

Alternates with Moscow

Grand Prix: *Fuzhung Cheng (Hibiscus Town)* (People's Republic of China) Dir Xie Jin
Rose of Lidice Prize: *The Dressmaker* (GB) Dir Jim O'Brien
Main prizes: *Weeds* (US) Dir John Hancock, *Tuske A Korom Alatt (Thorn Under the Fingernail)* (Hungary) Dir Sandor Sara
Best actor: Les Seruk for *Solomennie Kolokova*

(Straw Bells) (USSR)
Best actress: Corinna Harfouch for *Die Schauspielerin (The Actress)* (E Germany)
Special jury prize: *Ofelas (Pathfinder)* (Norway) Dir Nils Gaup
Opera Prima: *Lo Que Vendra (What Will Come)* (Argentina) Dir Gustavo Mosquera
Special mention: *The Raggedy Rawney* (GB) Dir Bob Hoskins
Opera Prima Prize: *Nabljudatel (Bird Watcher)* (USSR) Dir Arvo Ikho
FIPRESCI (international critics') jury prize – unofficial: *Anataram*

Atom Egoyan's Family Viewing

The Raggedy Rawney

(Monologue) (India) Dir Adoor Gopalakrishnan

LOCARNO FILM FESTIVAL 1988

Gold Leopard: shared by *Distant Voices, Still Lives* (GB) Dir Terence Davies and *Schmetterlinge (Butterflies)* (W Germany) Dir Wolfgang Becker
Silver Leopard: *Halodhia Choraye, Boodhan Khai (The Catastrophe)* (India) Dir Jahny Barua
Bronze Leopards: *Nakhoda Khorshid (Captain Khorshid)* (Iran) Dir Nasser Taghuai and *Schlaflose Nächte (Sleepless Nights)* (Switzerland/W Germany) Dir Marcel Gisler
Best actress: Indra Bania for *Halodhia Choraye, Boodhan Khai (The Catastrophe)*
Special mentions: *Family Viewing* (Canada) Dir Atom Egoyan and *Kyoshu (Memory)* (Japan) Dir Takehiro Nakajima
FIPRESCI (international critics') prize: *Family Viewing* (Canada) Dir Atom Egoyan
Special mention: *Schmetterlinge (Butterflies)*
Ecumenical jury prize: *Family Viewing*
Art cinemas jury prize

(CICAE): *Distant Voices, Still Lives*
Youth jury prizes:
First: *Family Viewing*
Second: *Schmetterlinge*
Third: *Eden Miseria (France)* Dir Christine Laurent

MONTE CARLO TV FESTIVAL 1988

GOLD NYMPH AWARDS
Fiction: *Road* (BBC) Prods Andree Molyneux, David Thompson
News features: *Panorama: The Private Wars of Colonel North* (BBC) Dir Jana Bennett
SILVER NYMPH AWARDS (FICTION)
Screenplay: Gert Steinheimer for *Zweikampf (Single Combat)* (ARD/Sudwestfunk, W Germany)
Direction: Lars Molin for *Saxophonhalliken (The Saxophone Pimp)* (SVT, Sweden)
Best actor: Tetsuda Sugimoto for *Ugetsu No Shisba (The Moon in the Rainy Night)* (NHK, Japan)
Best actress: Ellen Burstyn for *Pack of Lies* (Robert Halmi, USA)
Special jury mention: *Die Bombe (The Bomb)* (ZDF, W Germany)
SILVER NYMPH AWARDS (NEWS)

Ellen Burstyn (left) in Pack of Lies

News features: *Temps Present: USSR – Camarades, Encore Un Effort (USSR – Comrades, Another Effort)* (TSR, Switzerland)
News reports: *Miharayama Daifunka (Mount Mihara Erupts)* (NHK, Japan)
Special jury mention: *Siege of Bourj Al Barajneh Camp, West Beirut* (ITN)

MONTREUX FESTIVAL OF LIGHT ENTERTAIN-MENT 1988

Golden Rose: *The Strike* (Comic Strip Prods/Channel 4) Exec Prod Michael White
Silver Rose: *The Island of Lost Ships* (Gostelradio, USSR)
Bronze Rose: *Children For Children* (VARA/NOS, Netherlands)
City of Montreux prize: *Tres Estrelles (Three Stars)* (Catalonia TV3, Spain)
Press jury prize: *The Strike*
Special mentions:
Independent category: *Grand Illusions* (Philippa Walker Prods UK) Prod/Dir Philippa Walker
Official category: *Disturbance at the Post Office* (MTV, Finland) and *Swissmad – The Most Democratic Show on Earth* (DRS Zurich, Switzerland)

OSCARS – ACADEMY OF MOTION PICTURE ARTS AND SCIENCES

Awarded March 1988 for 1987 Films
Best film: *The Last Emperor* (Italy/China) Dir Bernardo Bertolucci
Best foreign language film: *Babettes Gaestebud (Babette's Feast)* (Denmark) Dir Gabriel Axel
Best director: Bernardo Bertolucci for *The Last Emperor*
Best actor: Michael Douglas for *Wall Street* (USA)
Best actress: Cher for *Moonstruck* (USA)
Best supporting actor: Sean Connery for *The Untouchables* (USA)

The Strike

Best supporting actress: Olympia Dukakis for *Moonstruck*
Best original screenplay: John Patrick Shanley for *Moonstruck*
Best screenplay adaptation: Mark Peploe and Bernardo Bertolucci for *The Last Emperor*
Best cinematography: Vittorio Storaro for *The Last Emperor*
Best film editing: Gabriella Cristiani for *The Last Emperor*
Best original music score: Ryuichi Sakamoto, David Byrne and Cong Su for *The Last Emperor*
Best original song: '(I've Had) The Time of My Life' by Franke Previte, John DeNicola and Donald Markowitz from *Dirty Dancing* (USA)
Best art direction: Ferdinando Scarfiotti for *The Last Emperor*
Best set decoration: Bruno Cesari for *The Last Emperor*
Best costume design: James Acheson for *The Last Emperor*
Best sound: Bill Rowe and

Ivan Sharrock for *The Last Emperor*
Best make-up: Rick Baker for *Harry and the Hendersons* (USA)
Best visual effects: Dennis Muren, William George, Harley Jessup and Kenneth Smith for *Innerspace* (USA)
Best sound effects editing: not awarded
Best short film (animated): *L'Homme Qui Plantait Des Arbres (The Man Who Planted Trees)* (Canada) Prod Frederic Back
Best short film (live action): *Ray's Male Heterosexual Dance Hall* (USA) Prods Jonathan Sanger, Jana Sue Memel
Best documentary (feature): *The Ten Year Lunch: The Wit and Legend of the Algonquin Round Table* (USA) Prod Aviva Slesin
Best documentary (short): *Young at Heart* (USA) Prods Sue Marx, Pamela Conn
Honorary award: Ralph Bellamy
Irving G Thalberg memorial award: Billy Wilder

Awarded March 1989 for 1988 Films
Best film: *Rain Man*

(USA) Dir Barry Levinson
Best foreign language film: *Pelle Erobreren (Pelle the Conqueror)* (Denmark) Dir Bille August
Best director: Barry Levinson for *Rain Man*
Best actor: Dustin Hoffman for *Rain Man*
Best actress: Jodie Foster for *The Accused* (USA)
Best supporting actor: Kevin Kline for *A Fish Called Wanda* (GB)
Best supporting actress: Geena Davis for *The Accidental Tourist* (USA)
Best original screenplay: Ronald Bass and Barry Morrow for *Rain Man*

Best screenplay adaptation: Christopher Hampton for *Dangerous Liaisons* (USA)
Best cinematography: Peter Biziou for *Mississippi Burning* (USA)
Best film editing: Arthur Schmidt for *Who Framed Roger Rabbit* (USA)
Best original music score: Dave Grusin for *The Milagro Beanfield War* (USA)
Best original song: 'Let the River Run' by Carly Simon from *Working Girl* (USA)
Best art direction: Stuart Craig for *Dangerous Liaisons*

Beetlejuice *with Michael Keaton*

Best set decoration: Gerard James for *Dangerous Liaisons*
Best costume design: James Acheson for *Dangerous Liaisons*
Best sound: Les Presholtz, Dick Alexander, Vern Poore and Willie D Burton for *Bird* (USA)
Best make-up: Ve Neill, Steve La Porte and Robert Short for *Beetlejuice* (USA)

Geena Davis in The Accidental Tourist, *with William Hurt*

Best visual effects: Ken Ralston, Richard Williams, Edward Jones and George Gibbs for *Who Framed Roger Rabbit*
Best sound effects editing: Charles L Campbell and Louis L Edemann for *Who Framed Roger Rabbit*
Best short film (animated): *Tin Toy* Prod John Lasseter
Best short film (live action): *The Appointments of Dennis Jennings* (GB) Prods Dean Parisot, Steven Wright
Best documentary (feature): *Hotel Terminus: Klaus Barbie, His Life and Times* (France) Prod Marcel Ophuls
Best documentary (short): *You Don't Have to Die* Prods William Guttentag, Malcolm Clarke
Academy honorary award: National Film Board of Canada in recognition of its 50th anniversary to originate artistic, creative and technological activity and excellence in every area of filmmaking
Special achievement award: Richard Williams

ROYAL TELEVISION SOCIETY AWARDS 1988

News Awards March 1988

Regional daily news magazine: *Reporting Scotland* (BBC Scotland)
Regional current affairs: *East on Two: Scientology* (BBC South and East – Norwich)
Television journalist of the year: Desmond Hamill – ITN
Special commendation for reporting: Luke Casey – Tyne Tees TV
Current affairs, home: *Panorama: Brent Schools Hard Left Rules* (BBC)
Current affairs, international: *Dispatches: AIDS – The Unheard Voices* (Channel 4)
Television cameraman of the year: Phillip Bye – ITN

News, home: *Channel 4 News: King's Cross Fire* (ITN)
News, international: *Inside the Bourj Al-Barajneh Camps* (ITN)
Topical feature: *Newsnight: Aleutians* (BBC)
Judges' award: Charles Stewart and Malcolm Hirst (Central TV) for their coverage of Ethiopia

Ray McAnally (right) in A Perfect Spy, with Peter Egan

Programme and Performance Awards May 1988

Original programme: *V* (produced by LWT, transmitted by Channel 4) Prod Sue Birtwistle
Writer's award: Bill Nicholson for *Life Story* (BBC/Arts and Entertainment Channel) and *Sweet As You Are* (BBC)
Best actor: Ray McAnally for *A Perfect Spy* (BBC/Arts and Entertainment Channel/ABC, Australia)

Best actress: Miranda Richardson for *Sweet As You Are* (BBC)
Regional programme award: *Paper Kisses* (BBC North East – Leeds) Prod Patrick Hargreaves
Technique award: *Cariani and the Courtesans* (BBC) Cameraman John Hooper
Children's programme award: *Bad Boyes* (BBC) Prod Pa il Stone
Cyril Bennett award: Charles Denton
Judges' award: Betty Willingale
Silver medal: John Willis

Gold medal: David Rose
Popular arts award: Cilla
Black
Geoffrey Parr award:
Philips Research
Laboratories for research
and development work on
the frame transfer solid
state image sensor, as
used in portable and
studio CCD colour
cameras

News Awards March 1989

Regional daily news
magazine: *Midlands
Today* (BBC Midlands)
Regional current affairs:
*The London Programme:
Wall of Silence* (LWT)
Television journalist of
the year: Charles Wheeler
(BBC)
Special commendations:
BBC for coverage of the

Clapham rail crash and
ITN for its special report
from Lockerbie
Current affairs, home:
Crying in the Dark (Tyne
Tees TV)
Current affairs,
international: *Afghantsi*
(Yorkshire TV)
Television cameraman of
the year: Eric Thirer
(BBC)
News, home: ITN for the
filming of the lynching of
British soldiers at a
Belfast funeral procession
News, international: BBC
for coverage of the Israeli
armed forces attack on
the Temple Mount
Mosque in Jerusalem
Topical feature: *Channel
4 News: The Bush Tapes*
(ITN)
Judges' award: Channel 4
News – Peter Sissons

VENICE FESTIVAL 1988

Golden Lion: *La Leggenda
del Santo Bevitore (The
Legend of the Holy
Drinker)* (Italy) Dir
Ermanno Olmi
Special grand prix: *Camp
de Thiaroye (Camp
Thiaroye)* (Senegal/
Algeria/Tunisia) Dirs
Ousmane Sembene,
Thierno Faty Sow
Silver Lion: *Topio Stin
Omihli (Landscape in the
Mist)* (Greece) Dir Theo
Angelopoulos
Best direction: Theo
Angelopoulos for *Topio
Stin Omihli*
Best actor: shared by
Don Ameche and Joe
Mantegna for *Things

Change (USA)
Best actress: shared by
Isabelle Huppert for *Une
Affaire de Femmes
(Women's Affair)* (France)
and Shirley MacLaine for
Madame Sousatzka (GB)
Special mention: David
Eberts, young actor in
Burning Secret (GB/USA/
W Germany)
Italian senate prize: Carlo
Lizzani for *Caro
Gorbaciov (Dear
Gorbachev)* (Italy)
Italian critics' prize: *Let's
Get Lost* (USA) Dir Bruce
Weber
FIPRESCI (international
critics') prize: shared by
*Malenkaya Vera (Little
Vera)* (USSR) Dir Vassili
Pitchul and *High Hopes*
(GB) Dir Mike Leigh
Special mention: *Tempos
Dificeis (Hard Times)*
(Portugal) Dir João
Botelho

David Eberts in **Burning Secret**

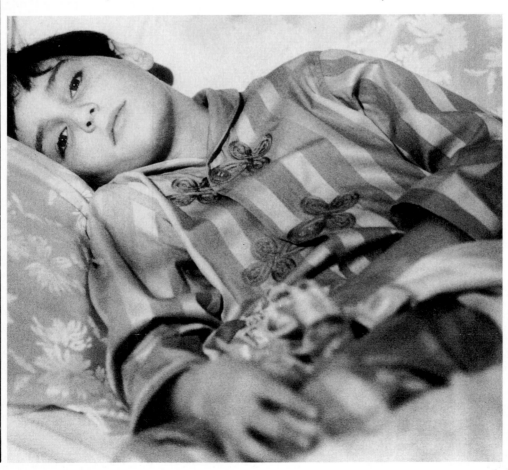

'*They* consist largely of calcium carbonate, which is secreted by glands contained in a fleshy part of the mantle ...'[1]

This story or the like is shown as a series of images projected consecutively to create the impression of a continuously moving subject usually accompanied by a soundtrack.[2]

Together with or in addition,[3] a laser beam is used to sense variations in height on the surface and convert them into electronic pulses for playback[4] by a group regarded as a distinct entity within a larger group performing a usually specified function.[5]

[1]SHELL [2]FILM [3]AND [4]VIDEO [5]UNIT

The Shell Film and Video Unit is responsible for producing a variety of films and videos covering a wide variety of subjects and events. For further details, contact your local Shell company or Shell International Petroleum Co. Ltd. PAC/231, Shell Centre, London, SE1 7NA.

BOOKSHOPS

Most bookshops stock film and cinema books and, if they don't have the book you want, they are usually happy to order it for you direct from the publisher. However, if the book you are looking for proves elusive or if you are looking for magazines, posters or memorabilia, you might try the specialist mail order services offered by the following bookshops

Arnolfini Bookshop
First Floor
16 Narrow Quay
Bristol BS1 4QA
Tel: 0272 299191
Stock: A, B, C, E, F
Opening hours: 10.00–
19.00 Monday–Saturday,
12.30–18.30 Sunday
Based in the Arnolfini
Gallery. No catalogues
are issued. Send requests
for specific material with
SAE

B H Blackwell
50 Broad Street
Oxford OX1 3BQ
Tel: 0865 792792
Stock: A
Opening hours: 09.00–
18.00 Monday–Saturday
There is a section of
cinema books in
Blackwell's monthly
catalogue, all of which are
available by mail order.
Contact the Marketing
Department for further
details

The Cinema Bookshop
13–14 Great Russell
Street
London WC1B 3NH
Tel: 01 637 0206
Stock: A, B, C, D
Opening hours: 10.30–
17.30 Monday–Saturday
No catalogues are issued.
Send requests for specific
material with SAE

The Cinema Shop
45 Summer Row
Birmingham B3 1JJ
Tel: 021 236 9879
Stock: B, C, D, F
Opening hours: 11.30–
17.30 Tuesday–Saturday,
closed Sunday, Monday
Shop rather than mail
order service, but will
accept telephone queries

Geoffrey Clifton
Performing Arts
Bookstore
44 Brazennose Street
Manchester M2 5EA
Tel: 061 831 7118
Stock: A, B, C, D, F
Opening hours: 10.00–
17.30 Monday–Saturday
Stock mainly new books
but a search service is
available for out-of-print
titles. Send SAE for
details

Cornerhouse Books
70 Oxford Street
Manchester M1 5NH
Tel: 061 228 7621 x165
Stock: A, B, C, F
Opening hours: 10.30–
18.00 Monday–Saturday
No catalogues are issued.
Send requests for specific
material with SAE

A E Cox
21 Cecil Road
Itchen
Southampton SO2 7HX
Tel: 0703 447989
Stock: A, B, C, D
Telephone enquiries and
orders are accepted at any
time. Mail order only. A
catalogue, 'Stage and
Screen', is published
every six weeks. Send two
first-class stamps or three
international reply
vouchers overseas to
receive the current issue

Richard Dalby
4 Westbourne Park
Scarborough
North Yorks YO12 4AT
Tel: 0723 377049
Stock: A, B
Mail order only. Send
SAE for specific rare, out-
of-print and secondhand
cinema books. Free search
service for titles not in
stock

Dress Circle
57–59 Monmouth Street
Upper St Martin's Lane
London WC2H 9DG
Tel: 01 836 8279
Stock: A, B, C, D, E, F
Opening hours: 10.00–
19.00 Monday–Saturday
Specialists in music and
soundtracks. A catalogue
of the entire stock is
issued annually. Send
SAE for details

58 Dean Street Records
58 Dean Street
London W1V 5HH
Tel: 01 437 4500/734 8777
Stock: E
Opening hours: 10.00–
18.30 Monday–Thursday,
10.00–19.00 Friday,
Saturday
Retail shop with recorded
mail order service. Over
7,000 titles including
soundtracks, original cast
shows, musicals and
nostalgia. Telephone for
information

Film Magic
18 Garsmouth Way
Watford
Herts
Stock: A, B, C, D, E, F
Opening hours: 11.00–
19.00 Monday–Friday
Comprehensive catalogue
costing £1.00 available on
request

Filmworld
De Courcy's Arcade
5 Cresswell Lane
Glasgow G12
Tel: 041 339 5373
Stock: A, B, C, D, F
Opening hours: 10.00–
17.30 Monday–Saturday,
12.00–17.00 Sunday
Catalogues of posters and
postcards are issued free
of charge. Send SAE for
details

Anne FitzSimons
62 Scotby Road
Scotby
Carlisle
Cumbria CA4 8BD
Tel: 0228 513815
Stock: A, B, C, D, F
Mail order only.
Antiquarian and out-of-print titles on cinema, broadcasting and performing arts. A catalogue is issued three times a year. Send three first-class postage stamps for current issue

Flashbacks
6 Silver Place
Beak Street
London W1R 3LJ
Tel: 01 437 8562
Stock: C, D
Opening hours: 10.30–19.00 Monday–Saturday
Shop and mail order service. Send SAE and 'wanted' list for stock details

Forbidden Planet
71 New Oxford Street
London WC1A 1DG
Tel: 01 836 4179/379 6042
Stock: A, B, C, D, E
Opening hours: 10.00–19.00 Monday–Wednesday, Friday, 10.00–20.00 Thursday, 10.00–18.00 Saturday
Science fiction, horror, fantasy and comics specialists

Heffers Booksellers
20 Trinity Street
Cambridge CB2 3NG
Tel: 0223 358351
Stock: A
Opening hours: 09.00–17.30 Monday–Saturday
A cinema and theatre catalogue is issued. Copies are available free on request

David Henry
36 Meon Road
London W3 8AN
Tel: 01 993 2859
Stock: A, B
Mail order only. A catalogue of out-of-print and secondhand books is issued two or three times a year and there is a search service for titles not in stock

MOMI Bookshop
South Bank
London SE1 8XT
Tel: 01 928 3535
Stock: A, B, C, D, F
Opening hours: 10.00–21.00 Tuesday–Saturday, 10.00–19.00 Sunday, 12.00–19.00 Monday
Based in the Museum of the Moving Image. Mail order available with special orders on request

The Media Bookshop
Book Base
PO Box 1057
Quinton
Birmingham B17 8EZ
Tel: 021 429 2606
Stock: A
Mail order only. A complete catalogue of books is produced once a year. Send request for catalogue with A4 SAE

Movie Finds
4 Ravenslea Road
London SW12 8SB
Stock: C, D
Mail order only. Two catalogues are available: one for posters, one for portraits. Both cost £1.00 and are updated every three months

National Museum of Photography, Film and Television
Princes View
Bradford BD5 0TR
Tel: 0274 727488
Stock: A, B, C, F
Opening hours: 11.00–18.00 Tuesday–Sunday
Mail order available. Send SAE with requests for information

Offstage
37 Chalk Farm Road
London NW1 8AJ
Tel: 01 485 4996
Stock: A, B, D, F
Opening hours: 10.00–17.30 Tuesday–Saturday, 11.00–17.30 Sundays, closed Mondays
A cinema and television catalogue is planned. Send SAE for details.

Tyneside Cinema Bookshop
10 Pilgrim Street
Newcastle upon Tyne
NE1 6QG
Tel: 091 232 5592
Stock: A, B, C, D, F
Opening hours: 10.00–17.00 Monday–Saturday
Based in Tyneside Cinema. Send requests for specific material with SAE

Vintage Magazine Co
39–41 Brewer Street
London W1R 3FD
Tel: 01 439 8525
Stock: B, C, D, F
Opening hours: 10.00–19.00 Monday–Saturday, 14.00–19.00 Sunday
247 Camden High Street
London NW1
Tel: 01 482 0587
Opening hours: 10.00–18.00 Monday–Friday, 10.00–19.00 Saturday, Sunday
Picture library and research service
Tel: 01 482 5083
No catalogues are issued. Send requests for specific material with SAE

Peter Wood
20 Stonehill Road
Great Shelford
Cambridge CB2 5JL
Tel: 0223 842419
Stock: A, B, C, D

Mail order only. Only back issues of magazines are held in stock. Visitors are welcome by appointment. A free catalogue is available of all new and secondhand books in stock

A Zwemmer
80 Charing Cross Road
London WC2
Tel: 01 836 4710 x21
Stock: A, B
Opening hours: 09.30–18.00 Monday–Friday, 10.00–17.30 Saturday
A catalogue of new and forthcoming cinema, television and video titles is issued as well as a catalogue of out-of-print titles still available. All books are available by mail order. Contact John Nichol for more information

A – Books
B – Magazines
C – Posters
D – Memorabilia (eg stills)
E – Records and cassettes
F – Postcards and greetings cards

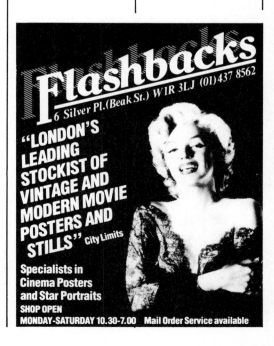

CABLE AND SATELLITE

Listed below is a range of cable and satellite channels currently on offer, together with cable operators offering a service within the UK and owners of European satellites

UK CABLE AND SATELLITE CHANNELS

British Satellite Broadcasting (BSB)
Marco Polo Building
Queenstown Road
London SW8
Tel: 01 581 1166
Service: Launching with three channels in early 1990. Two further channels planned
1. Now: Sport and news, 18 hours; advertising-supported, free to viewers
2. Movie Channel: Free matinee service (classic films), evening subscription service (£9.99) including new productions
3. Galaxy: 'Pure entertainment', soaps, game shows, serials, classic TV repeats, contemporary theatre; advertising-supported, free to viewers
Ownership: Bond Corporation, Anglia Television, Granada Group, S Pearson

Bravo
Communications House
Blue Riband Estate
Roman Way
Croydon
Surrey CR9 3RA
Tel: 01 680 1444
Contact: Fiona McFadzean
Type of service: Classic movies
Language: English
Start date: September 1985
Programming hours: Daily, 24 hours
Delivery: U-Matic and VHS cassettes
Systems: Aberdeen, Clyde, Coventry, Croydon, Ealing, East London, Swindon, Westminster, Windsor
Upgrades: BT Vision (Bracknell and Milton Keynes)
Ownership: Cablevision UK Partnership

The Cable Jukebox
The Quadrangle
180 Wardour Street
London W1V 4AE
Tel: 01 439 1177
Contact: Peter Brice
Type of service: Interactive broadband video jukebox service; 75–85 clips a month
Start date: November 1987
Programming hours: Daily, 24 hours
Delivery: Six computer-controlled laser disc players programmed to respond to viewer requests made via a keypad. On-screen message tells viewer when selection will be played
Systems: Cabletel, Coventry, Toulouse, Windsor
Ownership: W H Smith Television Services

Cable News Network
25–28 Old Burlington Street
London W1X 1LB
Tel: 01 434 9323
Contact: Harriet Stopher
Type of service: Live worldwide news plus features on business and financial news, health, entertainment and fashion; from CNN Atlanta, Georgia
Language: English
Start date: 1 June 1980 in US; 30 September 1985 in Europe
Programming hours: Daily, 24 hours
Delivery: Intelsat VA-F11, transponder 2E
Systems: Aberdeen, Cabletel, Camden, Clyde, Coventry, Croydon, Eastside, Swindon, Westminster
Upgrades/SMATV: BT (Barbican, Bracknell), Cablecom, IVS, A Thomson
Ownership: CNN International Sales, subsidiary of Turner Broadcasting System

The Children's Channel
9–13 Grape Street
London WC2H 8DR
Tel: 01 240 3422
Contact: Dan Maddicott Richard Wolfe
Type of service: Children's entertainment
Language: English, with some Dutch, Norwegian and Swedish subtitles
Start date: 1 September 1984
Programming hours: Intelsat V: daily, 05.00–15.00
Astra: weekdays, 05.00–10.00; weekends: 05.00–12.00
Delivery: Intelsat VA-F11, transponder 1; Astra, transponder 5
Systems: Aberdeen, Bedfordshire, Cabletel, Camden, Clyde, Coventry, Croydon, Eastside, Swindon, Westminster, Windsor
Upgrades/SMATV: BCS, Cablecom, CST, Greenwich, A Thomson, Wellingborough
Also in Denmark, Finland, Ireland, Netherlands, Norway, Sweden
Subscribers: 135,820 (end 1987)
Ownership: Starstream (British Telecom, Central Independent Television, Thames Television, D C Thomson)

Home Video Channel
PO Box 2AD
5 D'Arblay Street
London W1A 2AD
Tel: 01 434 0611
Type of service: Movies etc. Ownership merger with Premiere March 1987 but continues as separate channel

Start date: 1 September 1985
Programming hours: Daily 19.00–07.00
Delivery: Videotape
Systems: Aberdeen, Cabletel, Clyde, Coventry, Croydon, Eastside, Swindon, Westminster, Windsor
Upgrades: Greenwich
Ownership: Premiere Partnership

Indra Dhnush
Unit K1/K2
Fieldway
Bristol Road
Greenford
Middx UB8 8UM
Tel: 01 575 9000
Type of service: Indian movies, general entertainment
Language: Indian languages
Programming hours: Daily, 09.00–24.00
Delivery: Videotape
Distribution: UK only
Systems: Croydon, Ealing, Eastside, Windsor
Subscribers: Over 40% take-up of cable among Asian families
Ownership: Ealing Cabletel

Lifestyle
The Quadrangle
180 Wardour Street
London W1V 4AE
Tel: 01 439 1177
Contact: Francis Baron
Type of service: General domestic and family interest, health, chat shows, soap operas
Language: English
Start date: October 1985
Programming hours: Weekdays, 10.00–15.00; weekends 12.00–15.00 to be extended
Delivery: Astra, transponder V UK systems: Aberdeen, BCS, Barbican, Beith, Bracknell, Coventry, Croydon, ELT, Ealing, Glasgow, Greenwich, Llandeilo, Medway, Milton Keynes, Neath, Northampton, Perth, Swindon, Washington, Wellingborough, Westminster, Windsor
Also on Dutch cable networks
Subscribers: 80,020 (Apr 1989)

Ownership: W H Smith (75%), Yorkshire Television, TVS, D C Thompson

MTV Europe
Centro House
20–23 Mandela Street
London NW1 0DU
Tel: 01 383 4250
Contact: William Roedy
Type of service: Pop music, using format developed by MTV in US
Language: English
Start date: 1 August 1987
Programming hours: Daily, 24 hours
Delivery: Intelsat VA-F11 transponder 4H
Systems: Aberdeen, Cabletel, Camden, Croydon, Eastside, Westminster, Windsor
Upgrades: Bedfordshire, BCS, BT Vision Also in Belgium, Finland, France, Germany, Greece, Ireland, Italy, Netherlands, Sweden and Switzerland
Subscribers: 8.373 million in Europe, incl. UK (May 1989)
Ownership: Consortium of Mirror Group Newspapers (owned by Robert Maxwell), British Telecom and Viacom (US owner of MTV)

Music Box
19–22 Rathbone Place
London W1P 1DS
Tel: 01 636 7888
Contact: Kate Mundle
Type of service: Music programmes, concerts etc. Weekly production of 7–10 hours of programming plus catalogue of over 500 hours of music programming
Start date: 1 June 1984
Programming hours: Daily, 3–4 hours on daytime Super Channel (qv) Ownership: Virgin Group, Yorkshire Television, Granada Television

Satellite Information Services
Satellite House
17 Corsham Street
London N1 6DR
Tel: 01 253 2232
Contact: Julia King

Type of service: Racing/ sport
Language: English
Start date: 5 May 1987
Programming hours: Daily, 10.30–06.30
Delivery: Intelsat VA-F11 Direct broadcast to UK private subscriber network of 10,000 – principally licensed betting offices
Also in Ireland, Netherlands, West Germany
Ownership: Bass, Grand Metropolitan, Ladbroke, Racecourse Association, Sears, Tote. Balance of shares in process of being placed with financial institutions

Screen Sport
The Quadrangle
180 Wardour Street
London W1V 4AE
Tel: 01 439 1177
Contact: Francis Baron
Type of service: European sport; sponsorship, subscription, advertising-supported
Start date: March 1984
Programming hours: Daily, 24 hours
Delivery: Astra, transponder I
Systems: Aberdeen, BCS, Barbican, Beith, Bracknell, Cablevision Bedfordshire, Coventry, Croydon, ELT, Ealing, Glasgow, Greenwich, Irvine, Llandeilo, Medway, Milton Keynes, Neath, Northampton, Perth, Swindon, Washington, Wellingborough, Westminster, Windsor
Also on cable systems in Finland, Ireland, Netherlands, Norway and Sweden
UK Subscribers: 120,690 (Apr 1989)
Ownership: W H Smith (75%), Ladbroke Group, ESPN

Sky Channel
6 Centaurs Business Park
Grant Way
off Syon Lane
Isleworth
Middx TW7 5QD
Tel: 01 782 3000
Type of service: Sky Channel (entertainment), Sky News (24 hour news

service), Sky Movies (film channel), Eurosport (European sports channel), The Disney Channel (a family programming service offered jointly with the Walt Disney Co) and Sky Arts (arts programming)
Start date: 5 February 1989 (Sky Channel, Sky News, Eurosport, Sky Movies); 1 August 1989 (The Disney Channel), late 1989 (Sky Arts)
Programming hours: Weekdays, 06.30–00.30; weekends 07.00–00.30
Delivery: ASTRA (six transponders via British Telecom)
Systems: Aberdeen, BCS, Bedfordshire, Cabletel, Camden, Clyde, Coventry, Croydon, Eastside, Swindon, Westminster, Windsor
Upgrades/SMATV: BCS, British Telecom, Cablecom, Cable Television, CST, Greenwich, Harris of Saltcoats, IVS, Teleline, A Thomson
Also in Austria, Belgium, Denmark, Finland, France, Germany, Greece, Hungary, Iceland, Ireland, Luxembourg, Netherlands, Norway, Portugal, Spain, Sweden, Switzerland and Yugoslavia
Subscribers: 221,748 in UK (Oct 1987); 10 million in Europe (Dec 1987)
Ownership: News International, Sky Television and The Walt Disney Co (Sky Movies and The Disney Channel), and EBU members (Eurosport)

Super Channel
19–21 Rathbone Place
London W1P 1DS
Tel: 01 631 5050
Contact: Marialina Marcucci
Type of service: Programmes acquired and commissioned in UK from Music Box and from independent producers in Australia, EEC and USA; news from Visnews; advertising-supported
Language: English, multi-lingual
Start date: 30 January 1987

Programming hours:
Daily, 06:00–01:00
Delivery: Eutelsat
ECS1-F4, transponder 12
Total: 15,332,600 (Apr 1989)
Systems: Aberdeen, BCS, Bedfordshire, Cabletel, Camden, Clyde, Coventry, Croydon, Eastside, Swindon, Westminster, Windsor
Upgrades/SMATV: BCS, Cablecom, Cable Television, CST, Greenwich, IVS, Teleline, A Thomson, West Wales Aerials
Also in Austria, Belgium, Denmark, Finland, France, Germany, Ireland, Luxembourg, Netherlands, Norway, Spain, Sweden and Switzerland
Subscribers: 171,000 in UK (Apr 1989), 15,332,600 in Europe (Apr 1989)
Ownership: Beta Television (53.21%), Virgin Group (45.72%), and 2 others

UK CABLE OPERATORS

Three types of cable service are provided in the UK. The most important are those established from scratch on franchises from the Cable Authority (the first 11 were awarded on an interim basis by the Government). These provide up to 30 channels of television plus other radio, text, data, interactive and telephony channels. These programme services are usually packaged either as 'tiers', which incrementally add more channels for higher charges, or 'a la carte', in which individual channels are added to a basic package.

Upgrade systems are based on old – sometimes primitive – existing installations and are capable of only limited services.

SMATV (satellite master antenna television) systems are a halfway stage to full franchises, bringing satellite channels to networks limited in size and geographical spread.

Charges quoted are per month unless otherwise stated.

FULL FRANCHISE NEW-BUILD SYSTEMS

Aberdeen Cable Services
303 King Street
Aberdeen AB2 3AP
Scotland
Tel: 0224 649444
Contact: John Miller
Area: Aberdeen (91,000 homes)
Licensing: Interim franchise (Nov 1983); 15-year licence from May 1985
System: Tree and branch, 29 channels, to be upgraded to switched system Construction: Completed March 1989. Final cabling cost of £25–30 million to be carried by British Telecom, which charges ACS just under £6.00 per subscriber connected
Connection charge: £20
Service: From September 1988. Initial service (£6.95–£8.95): broadcast channels – Eurosport, Moskva, RAI, SAT1, Sky, Sky News, Superchannel, TV5, Worldnet.
Additional channels: CNN, Children's Channel, Lifestyle, MTV, Screensport (+£1.50 each); Bravo, HVC (+£3.00 each); Sky Movies (+£6.95)
BSB, Discovery and Disney to be added in late 1989.
Ownership: British Telecom, Legal and General Assurance, Time Life International, Standard Life Assurance, Investors In Industry, North of Scotland Investment Company, Clydesdale Bank and a

number of smaller investment funds

Andover Cablevision
PO Box 77
Andover
Hants SP10 1YB
Tel: 0264 332300
Contact: Peter C Funk/Alan Burgess
Area: Andover, Hampshire (12,500 homes)
Construction: Expected to commence in June 1989, due for completion 1991/92
Connection charge: Not yet determined
Ownership: Wholly owned subsidiary of IVS Cable Holdings

Bolton Telecable
c/o National Telecable
Tenison House
159–165 Great Portland Street
London W1N 5FD
Tel: 01 493 8388
Contact: Malcolm Matson
Area: Metropolitan Borough of Bolton and district (135,000 homes)
Licensing: First round franchise (Aug 1985)
System: Switched system intended
Ownership: Not fixed

British Cable Services
Southern House
1–4 Cambridge Terrace
Oxford OX1 1UD
Tel: 0865 250110
Area 1: Guildford (22,000 homes). Contiguous with separate west Surrey/east Hampshire franchise, with which it is now combined
Licensing: Interim franchise (Nov 1983)
Area 2: West Surrey/east Hampshire, including Aldershot, Camberley, Farnborough, Farnham, Godalming, Fleet and Woking (115,000 homes)
Licensing: First round franchise (Aug 1985)
Areas 1 and 2 being contiguous, are treated as a single area System: Rediffusion System 8 switched system to be installed by BCS
Construction: Phase 1

(HP 2,400) started cabling Spring 1987; HP 1,290 achieved by Oct 1987
Service: Started July 1987 Area 3: Cardiff and Penarth (103,000 homes)
Licensing: Second round franchise (Feb 1986).
Licences not granted
System: Rediffusion System 8
Ownership: Wholly owned subsidiary of Metromode (Pergamon Press 50%, Robert Maxwell 50%)

Cable Camden
The Elephant House
Hawley Crescent
London NW1 8NP
Tel: 01 528 0555
Contact: Jerrold Nathan
Area: London Borough of Camden (70,000 homes)
Licensing: Second round franchise (Feb 1986).
Interim licence (Jan 1987)
System: Five-phase development planned between 1989 and 1993.
First phase used Cabletime switch
Construction: Pilot phase (HP 104 flats) started Jan 1987
Service: From March 1987 (pilot)
Darwin (£13.80): 9 channels; 4 broadcast, Lifestyle, MTV, SC, Sky SS; teletext
Darwin Plus (£23.00): 11 channels
Additional channels: CC, CNN, Children's Channel (+£7.50 each)
Will include option of direct Mercury telephone connections
Ownership: Wholly owned subsidiary of Cable London – US WEST (15%), Rosehaugh (12%), Mercury (7%), McNicholas Construction (6%), Jerrold Nathan (6%), Logica UK (6%).
Cable London is bidding for Haringey and Waltham Forest. See also Westminster

Cabletel Communications
Unit K1/K2
Fieldway
Bristol Road
Greenford
Middx UB8 8UN
Tel: 01 575 9000

Contact: J Haftke
Area: London Borough of Ealing (100,000 homes)
Licensing: Interim franchise (Nov 1983); 23-year licence from Nov 1986
System: Cabletime 28-channel switched system
Construction: Phase 1 in Southall and Greenford (HP 16,500). HP 7,000 (end Jan 1987), 18,000 (Jan 1988)
Connection charge: £25–£30
Service: From Nov 1986 Basic (£12.95): 18 channels; 4 broadcast, Bravo, Cable Jukebox, CNN, Discovery, Lifestyle, MTV, SC, Sky, TV5, WN, community channel, multiplex channel guide, teletext programme guide
Additional channels: CC (+£1.75), HVC (+£4.50), Indra Dhnush (Asian movie channel +£7.00), SS (+£1.75)
Subscribers: 13% penetration
First operator to use audience research facility of Cabletime 16 system
Ownership: Wholly owned subsidiary of City Centre Communications

Cablevision Bedfordshire

Camp Drive
Houghton Regis
Dunstable
Bedfordshire LU5 5HE
Tel: 0582 865095
Contact: Phillip Morgan
Area: Luton, Dunstable, Leighton Buzzard (104,000 homes)
Licensing: Second round franchise (July 1986). Interim licence (Nov 1986)
System: Star-configured tree-and-branch
Connection charge: £25
Service: From Nov 1986 on existing installations in Luton (HP 5,000) and Houghton Regis (HP 2,500)
Service: Interim package (£4.95–£13.95): 12 channels; 4 broadcast, CC, MTV, SC, Sky, SS, WN
Ownership: Private company

Cablevision (Scotland)

4 Melville Street
Edinburgh EH3 7NS
Tel: 031 453 1919
Contact: Eric Sanderson
Area: City of Edinburgh (183,000 homes)
Licensing: Second round franchise (Feb 1986). Licences not granted
Ownership: British Linen Bank, Christian Salvesen, Cox Cable, Ferranti, Grampian Television, F Johnston and Co, Radio Forth, Radio Rentals, D C Thomson (10.47% each), Press Construction (5.77%)

Clyde Cablevision

40 Anderston Quay
Glasgow G3 8DA
Tel: 041 221 7040
Area: Central/north-west Glasgow and Clydebank (112,000 homes); applied for North and South Glasgow (357,000), Cumbernauld (60,000), Motherwell and East Kilbride (125,000), and Dumbarton (19,000)
Licensing: Interim franchise (Nov 1983); 15-year licence from Nov 1985
Construction: Started July 1985. Phase 1 (HP 300) in Drumchapel area; 420km of cable laid and HP 8,729 (July 86); plans to pass 3,000 homes a month
Connection charge: Rates on application
Service: Started 9 October 1985
Full a la carte menu
Special senior citizens package
Ownership: GEC, Cable and Wireless, Scottish Daily Record and Sunday Mail, British Cable Service, Balfour Kilpatrick, Investors in Industry, and 42 others

Coventry Cable Television

London Road
Coventry
West Midlands CV3 4HL
Tel: 0203 505345
Contact: Roy Emerson
Area: City of Coventry (119,000 homes)
Licensing: Interim franchise (Nov 1983); 15-year licence from Sept 1985
System: 32-channel tree-and-branch installed by British Telecom between March 1985 and end 1988; to be upgraded to switched system in due course. Many of final drops to subscribers made from BT telegraph poles
Construction: Cabling in 10 phases from autumn 1986. HP 75,000 (Mar 1989)
Connection charge: £30
Service: Started Sept 1985
First Choice (basic service) £9.95, plus optional channels
Ownership: British Telecom (74%), Courier Press (15%), Equity and Law (11%)

Eastside Cable

East London Telecommunicatons
ELT House
2 Millharbour
London E14 9TE
Tel: 01 538 4838
Contact: Roger Marchall
Area: London Boroughs of Tower Hamlets and Newham, including London Docklands Enterprise Zone, Redbridge, Barking, Dagenham, Bexley (400,000 homes)
Licensing: First round franchise (Aug 1985); 23-year licence from July 1986

Jersey Cable

c/o IVS Enterprises
54 Warwick Square
London SW1V 2AJ
Tel: 01 834 6012
Contact: Peter C Funk, Carol Dukes
Area: Jersey, Channel Islands (HP 7,000)
Licensing: Special licence from the States of Jersey
System: HF
Service: Relay of off-air channels (BBC1, BBC2, ITV – Channel Television – and Channel 4) (£1.90)
Additional channels: Sky and Children's Channel (+£7.85 each)
Ownership: Private company

Lancashire Cable Television

c/o Oyston Cable
Oyston Mill
Strand Road
Preston
Lancashire PR1 8UR
Tel: 0772 721505
Contact: R M Nixon
Area: Central Lancashire, including Chorley, Preston, Leyland (114,000 homes)
Licensing: Second round franchise (Feb 1986). Licences not granted. Won franchise against competitive bid
System: 30-channel network
Construction: Due to start late 1989
Ownership: Still being negotiated

Merseyside Cablevision

c/o Oyston Cable
Oyston Mill
Strand Road
Preston
Lancashire PR1 8UR
Tel: 0772 721505
Contact: R M Nixon
Area: South Liverpool (125,000 homes)
Licensing: Interim franchise (Nov 1983). Licences not granted
System: 30-channel switched system
Construction: Due to start 1989/90
Ownership: Oyston Cable (see Lancashire Cable Television) took 75%+ of shares (Dec 1985). Original shareholders: Pilkington Brothers, Virgin Records, Marchwiel, Searidge Properties, Lord Derby, Tysons (Contractors), Whitbread, BICC, British Telecom, Plessey, Littlewoods, Liverpool Daily Post, Richard Starkey (Ringo Starr)

Southampton Cable

87 Jermyn Street
London SW1Y 6JD
Tel: 01 839 7106
Contact: Peter Alden
Area: Southampton and urban Eastleigh (HP 97,000)
Licensing: Licence from Jan 1989
Construction: Started early 1989

CABLE AND SATELLITE

Service to commence
autumn 1989
Ownership: Videotron
(45%), Compagnie
Générale des Eaux (45%)
and others

Swindon Cable
Newcome Drive
Hawkesworth Estate
Swindon
Wiltshire SN2 1TU
Tel: 0793 615601
Area: Swindon (75,000
homes) part covered by
upgrade system (HP
48,000)
Licensing: Interim
franchise (Nov 1983); 15-
year licence from Sept
1984
System: Initially 16-
channel tree-and-branch
being installed by
Swindon Cable, now
upgraded to 32 channels
by British Telecom
Construction: Cabling
started mid 1984. The
majority of homes passed
are to be overbuilt during
1989/90. Plans for a
further 6,000 homes
passed during 1989
Connection charge: £25
Service: Started Sept
1984
Basic (£6.95): 14
channels; 6 broadcast (4
West of England and
Central), SAT1, SC, Sky,
TCC, TV5, local, cabletext
Additional channels:
MTV (+£1.95), CNN (+
£2.95), HVC (+£3.00),
Bravo (+£3.95), Sky
Movies (+£5.95)
Subscribers: Penetration
rate at March 88 –
narrowband 17%,
broadband 40% expected
to rise to 25% and 45%
respectively by 1989
Ownership: Wholly
owned by British Telecom
(bought from Thorn EMI
Feb 1986)

Ulster Cablevision
40 Victoria Square
Belfast BT1 4QB
Tel: 0232 249141
Contact: George F Alton
Area: City of Belfast and
district (136,000 homes)
Licensing: Interim
franchise (Nov 1983)
Ownership: British
Telecom, Ulster
Television

United Cable Television (Cotswolds)
The Quadrangle
Imperial Square
Cheltenham
Gloucestershire
GL50 1YX
Tel: 0242 224992
Contact: John McCarren
Area: Cheltenham and
Gloucester (90,000
homes)
Licensing: First round
franchise (Aug 1985).
Licence from Aug 1988
System: Jerrold system
Service: Originally
intended by end 1986,
now due late 1989
Ownership: United Cable
Television

United Cable Television (London South)
Communications House
Blue Riband Estate
Roman Way
Croydon
Surrey CR9 3RA
Tel: 01 760 0222
Contact: George Stewart
Area: London Borough of
Croydon (114,000 homes)
Licensing: Interim
franchise (Nov 1983); 15-
year licence from Oct
1985
System: 27-channel tree-
and-branch system in star
configuration installed
from June 1985 using
Jerrold Starcom 450
decoders
Construction: By Peter
Birse Ltd. HP 30,000 (Dec
1987); completion by 1989
Connection charge: £10
plus £15 deposit
Service: Started Sept
1985
Spectrum (basic service)
£9.95: 22 channels; 5
broadcast (4 London plus
TVS), Bravo, CC, CNN,
Lifestyle, MTV, SS, Sky,
SC, TV5, Channel 15
(local), multiplex preview,
Arcade (news, business,
weather, jobs, classified)
Premium (£7.25 each):
HVC
Ownership: United Cable
Television

Wandsworth Cable
c/o Southampton Cable
87 Jermyn Street
London SW1Y 6JD
Tel: 01 839 7106
Area: London Borough of

Wandsworth (HP
100,000)
Licensing: First round
franchise awarded (Aug
1985); licences not
granted
Ownership: Wandsworth
Cable
Management: Richard
Tripp

Westminster Cable Television
87–89 Baker Street
London W1M 1AJ
Tel: 01 935 6699
Contact: Samantha Gates
Area: City of Westminster
(96,000 homes, 23,000
businesses, 500 hotels
with 60,000 beds)
Licensing: Interim
franchise (Nov 1983); 15-
year licence from Oct
1985
System: British Telecom
30-channel switched star
system (optical fibre with
co-axial for final drop)
Construction: By BT from
Feb 1985 – pilot
installation (HP 600) in
St John's Wood – to 1988.
HP 10,000 (Feb 1986);
HP 26,000 (Jan 1988); HP
40,000 (Jan 1989)
Connection charge:
£25.00 during trunk cable
laying in the vicinity,
otherwise £50.00
Service: Started Sept
1985
Equipment rental £11.90
Sat 1 Welcome Package
(free): 6 channels; 4
broadcast, SC, Westscan
(13-image multiplex), text
services*
Sky Package (free):
Eurosport, Sky, Sky News
Add-on packages:
Sat 2 Package (+£3.95): 3
channels; CC, HVC, MTV
Sat 3 Package (+£3.95): 3
channels; HVC, MTV, SS
Sat 4 Package (+£6.95): 5
channels; CC, HVC,
Lifestyle, MTV, SS
Sat 5 Package (+£6.95): 3
channels; CNN,
European, Lifestyle
Additional channels:
Arabic channel (+
£11.50), Bravo (+£5.95)
*Text services: Books,
Cable News, Community
Information, Fireline,
Health, Home Shopping
– Records, Prestel
Connection, Sports,
Theatre Showcase,
Weather, Wine, etc.

Subscribers: 11,500 (Jan
1989)
Ownership: BRIT, British
Telecom, City Centre
Cable, ECI
Communications AG,
Prudential-Bache
Interfunding
Experimenting with
interactive video disc
system in collaboration
with British Telecom (60
discs remotely controlled,
available on demand)

Westside Cable
Parkways
179–181 The Vale
London W3 7QS
Tel: 01 740 4848
Contact: Frank Bateson
Area: London Borough of
Barnet (117,497); London
Borough of Brent
(93,350); London Borough
of Hammersmith and
Fulham (70,365); London
Borough of Kensington
and Chelsea (76,498
homes)
Licensing: North West
(Barnet, Brent,
Hammersmith and
Fulham): Interim
franchise (Jan 1989);
licence under negotiation;
Kensington and Chelsea:
Interim franchise (May
1988); DTI licence
awarded July 1988, Cable
Authority licence
awarded Jan 1989
System: 860MHz tree-
and-branch
Connection charge:
£35.00
Service: basic (£6.95): 14
channels; plus full a la
carte menu, available by
Aug/Sept 1989
Ownership: Company
name – City Centre
Communications

Windsor Television
Cable House
Waterside Drive
Langley
Berks SL3 3EZ
Tel: 0753 44144
Contact: Tim Halfhead
Area: East Berkshire/
north Surrey, including
Ashford, Maidenhead,
Slough, Staines, Stanwell
and Windsor (100,000
homes)
Licensing: Interim
franchise (Nov 1983) with
subsequently expanded
area: 15-year licence
from Dec 1985
System: 28-channel

Cabletime switched star system (replacing GEC-modified Delta Kabel switches)
Construction: Own installation started Oct 1985, after taking some months to decide on go-ahead. Phase 1 (HP 2,500). HP 30,000 (end 1987), 50,000 (end 1988), 88,000 (end 1989), 100,000 completion by mid-1990
Connection charge: £35
Service: Started December 1985
Basic service: Cablescene (£9.95): 18 channels: 4 broadcast, Bravo, Cable Jukebox, Discovery, Eurosport, Landscape, Lifestyle, SC, Sky, Sky Arts, Sky News, TVS, Arcade, screen sampler
Extra channels offered on Cable Choice: SAT1/TV5 (free); RAI (free); CC (+ £1.99); Disney Channel (price not set); HVC (+ £2.75); Indra Dhnush (Asian movie channel + £4.95; MTV (+75p); SS (+£1.99); Sky Movies (+ £6.99)
Subscribers: 2,500 (April 1987), 6,000 (end 1987), 11,700 (end 1988), forecast 28,000 (end 1989)
Ownership: Standard Life Assurance (33%), CIN Industrial Investments (20.3%), Drayton Consolidated Trust (19%), Investors in Industry (12%), McNicholas Construction (6%), Sharp Technology Fund, Kleinwort Grieveson Investment Management, County Development Capital, Grosvenor Technology Fund, Fountain Development Capital Fund. In Nov 1986 Compagnie Générale de Chauffe acquired 20% stake for £2.6 million. Further investment from US and French sources to be set up during 1989
Telephone service with fibre optic link to Mercury network started on trial basis on a Slough industrial estate (Dec 1987); full service in operation from end 1988. Domestic telephony trial now completed. Full service available in specific areas. FM hook-up (provides 10 FM stereo radio stations and 6 synchronised soundtracks)

UPGRADED CABLE SYSTEMS

British Cable Services
Southern House
1–4 Cambridge Terrace
Oxford OX1 1UD
Tel: 0865 250110
Operating as Maxwell Cable Television (formerly Rediffusion Cablevision)
Areas: Regional offices at locations marked *
Northern Region
Barrow-in-Furness
                  HP 11,200
Burnley*   HP 18,360
Hull   HP 73,040
Lancaster   HP 6,936
Leicester   HP 7,654
Mansfield   HP 19,603
Nottingham*   HP 71,976
Rotherham   HP 18,102
Stoke-on-Trent*/
  Newcastle-under-Lyne
                  HP 46,400
Teeside: Hartlepool/
  Stockton/Billingham*/
  Middlesborough
                  HP 25,032
Tyneside   HP 23,427
Wirral MBC
  (Birkenhead*)
                  HP 23,000
Worcester   HP 9,964
Southern Region
Ashford   HP 11,000
Basildon*   HP 26,100
Brighton/Hove
                  HP 20,000
Bristol*   HP 47,000
Canterbury*   11,000
Deal/Dover/Folkestone
                  HP 23,000
Eastbourne*   HP 20,250
Exeter*   HP 16,087
Guildford (see also
  Franchises)   HP 2,236
Hastings   HP 30,000
Heads of Valley   HP 3,500
Maidstone*   HP 15,000
Merthyr Tydfil   HP 13,000
Newbridge/Bargoed
                  HP 42,900
Norwich*   HP 7,120
Oxford*   HP 8,100
Reading   HP 14,600
Plymouth   HP 21,000
Rhondda*   HP 35,000
Southampton*   HP 21,000
Swansea*   HP 16,140
Thanet   HP 30,000

Welwyn Garden City*/
  Hatfield   HP 13,100
West Wales   HP 9,200
Subscribers: Total BC 75,000 at Jan 1986; 66,000 at Jan 1988
Connection charge: £25
Service:
Tier 1 (Silver £5.95): 4 channels; CC (day), SS, MTV, Sky
Ownership: Wholly owned subsidiary of Metromode

British Telecom Vision
Room 26/07, Euston Tower
286 Euston Road
London NW1 3DG
Tel: 01 728 3405
Areas:
Barbican, London*
          HP 2,016/BC 2,016
Bracknell*
          HP 10,000/BC 8,800
Irvine+   HP 8,000
Milton Keynes
          HP 24,500/BC 24,000
Washington   HP 13,000
New systems established in Aberdeen, Coventry, Swindon, Thames Valley. Also relay systems at Brackla, Irvine, Martlesham Heath and Walderslade
Systems: Co-axial
Connection charge: £10
Service: 'Range of satellite-delivered programme services'
Ownership: Wholly owned subsidiary of British Telecom
+Irvine is operated by Broadband Ventures, wholly owned subsidiary of British Telecom

Cable and Satellite Television Holdings
Unit 2
Dorcan Business Village
Murdock Road
Swindon SN3 5HY
Tel: 0793 611176
Contact: Michael O'Brien
Area 1: Medway (Chatham, Gillingham, Rochester, Strood; HP 16,000)
Connection charge: Varies
Service: Started late 1985
Basic (£5.95): 9 channels; 5 broadcast (4 south-east England plus ITV London), Eurosport, Sky, Sky News, SC
Premium (£11.95): 14 channels; Basic plus CC,

Lifestyle, SS
Subscribers: 9,000
Area 2: Neath/Port Talbot (HP 28,000)
Connection charge: Varies
Service: Started Sept 1985
Bronze (£5.95): 8 channels; 5 broadcast (4 Wales plus Channel 4–S4C is local fourth channel), Sky, Sky News, SC
Silver (£7.95): 10 channels; Bronze plus CC, Sport
Gold (£12.95): 13 channels: Silver + Lifestyle
Subscribers: 5,000
Area 3: Herne Bay and Faversham (HP 3,000)
Connection charge: Varies
Service: Started late 1987
Basic (£4.95): 8 channels; 5 broadcast (4 south-east England plus ITV London), Eurosport, Sky, SC
Subscribers: 2,000
Area 4: Sittingbourne (HP 7,000)
Connection charge: Varies
Service: Started late 1987
Basic (£5.95): 9 channels; 5 broadcast (4 south-east England plus ITV London), Eurosport, Sky, Sky News, SC
Premium (£11.95): 12 channels; Basic plus CC, MTV
Subscribers: 4,000

Cablevision (Wellingborough)
c/o Mobile Radio Services
Central Hall Buildings
Wellingborough
Northants NN8 4HT
Tel: 0993 222078
Contact: P W Elson
Area: Wellingborough (HP 8,800, BC 4,000)
System: 8-channel VHF, constructed c1960
Ownership: Private company

Greenwich Cablescene
Tex House
62–64 Beresford Street
London SE18 6BG
Tel: 01 316 1200
Contact: John Braund
Area: Plumstead/Woolwich/Abbey Wood/Belvedere/Charlton (HP c20,000)

System: 10-channel VHF co-axial
Connection charge: None
Service:
Basic (£8.25): 13 channels; 4 broadcast, CC, Eurosport, Lifestyle, MTV, SC, Sky, Sky News, SS, local teletext service plus enhanced service with extra channels
Subscribers: 1,370
Ownership: Under negotiation

Gwent Cablevision

88 Commercial Street
Tredegar
Gwent NP2 3DN
Tel: 0495 252600
Contact: Tom White
Area: Tredegar (HP 5,200)
Ownership: Private company, formerly Philips Cablevision

Harris of Saltcoats

22 Green Street
Saltcoats
Strathclyde KA21 5HQ
Scotland
Tel: 0294 63541
Contact: Hugh Mackay
Area: Saltcoats (HP 3,675), Largs (HP 3,300)
Subscribers: 4,200 (Nov 1985)

Teleline

3–5 High Street
Princes Risborough
Buckinghamshire
HP17 0AE
Tel: 08444 3196
Contact: Roy Boughton
Area: Princes Risborough (HP 650; BC 175)
System: VHF
Connection charge: £10
Service: Basic: 7 channels; 6 broadcast (4 London plus Central, TVS), Sky
Subscribers: 187
Ownership: Teleline Ltd

West Wales Aerials

97 Rhosnan Street
Llandeilo
Dyfed SA19 6HA
Wales
Tel: 0558 823278
Contact: A J E Jones
Area: Llandeilo and district (HP 1,500; BC 1,400)
System: 4 channel twisted pair
Service: 4 broadcast; Sky, Sky Movies, Sky News, SS

SMATV OPERATORS

Cablecom Investments

PO Box 31 Ampthill Road
Kempston
Beds MK42 9QQ
Tel: 0234 55233 x4335
Contact: Charles H Tompkins
Areas: Chicksands (HP 800), Lakenheath (HP 2,500), Mildenhall (HP 1,202), USAF military installations – total HP 12,838 (Dec 1987)
Service: CC, CNN, Lifestyle, SS, Sky, SC
Subscribers: 6,200 (end 1988)

Davis Cable TV

34a Church Street
Eastbourne
Sussex BN21 1HS
Tel: 0323 33279
Contact: A V Davis
Area: East Dean area of Sussex (HP 1,000)

IVS Enterprises

54 Warwick Square
London SW1V 2AJ
Tel: 01 834 6012
Contact: Peter C Funk/ Gill Dales
Areas: Chelsea Cloisters, London (HP 560), various UK/European hotels, including some in Hilton, Hyatt and Inter-Continental chains
System: Varies according to installation; Cabletime switched star at Chelsea Cloisters
Connection charge: None
Service: Varies; 'all satellite-delivered channels offered'
Ownership: Private company
See also Andover Cablevision

G Lal

50 Grove Lane
Handsworth
Birmingham B20 9EP
Area: Handsworth (HP 1,000)

Baldev Singh

7 Pippens Way
Randley
Telford
Shropshire
Area: Randley district of Telford (HP 50)

Telefusion Communications

Unit 10
Barsfold Close
Wingate Industrial Estate
Westhoughton
Lancashire BL5 3XH
Tel: 0942 817788
Contact: Peter Collins
Area: Runcorn, Cheshire (HP 10,000)

A Thomson (Relay)

1 Park Lane
Beith
Strathclyde KA15 2FG
Scotland
Tel: 05055 3441
Contact: D Biggar
Area: Beith (HP 1,700), Dalry (HP 800), Kilbirnie (HP 1,700), extending in 1989/90 to Lochwinnoch (HP 600)
System: VHF co-axial
Connection charge: None
Service: 9 channels; 4 broadcast, CC, CNN, SS, Sky, SC
Subscribers: 450

EUROPEAN SATELLITE OPERATORS

Astra

Société Européenne des Satellites
Château de Betzdorf
L-6832 Betzdorf
Luxembourg
Tel: 010 352 717 251

BSB

Marco Polo Building
Queenstown Road
London SW8
Tel: 01 581 1166

Eutelsat

Tour Maine
Montparnasse
33 Avenue du Maine
F-75755 Paris
France
Tel: 45 38 47 47

Intelsat

3400 International Drive
Northwest
Washington
DC 20008
USA
Tel: 202 944 6800

Abbreviations

BC – Basic Cable Homes (subscribers)
CC – Children's Channel
CNN – Cable News Network
HP – Homes Passed by Cable
HVC – Home Video Channel
MB – Music Box
RAI – RAI Uno Satellite Channel SC – Super Channel
Sky – Sky Channel
SS – Screen Sport
TV5 – TV Cinq

Isn't TV supposed to be killing off the British film industry?

That's the current opinion.

Fortunately, at BSB, we've taken an interest in the British film industry by funding four new, major British films.

These films will use British producers, British crews, British locations and British stars including Lenny Henry, Joanne Whalley and Emily Lloyd.

After all, if we didn't support the British film industry, we know our channels wouldn't be half as entertaining.

BSB. 5 Channel TV.

CINEMAS

CINEMA CIRCUITS

CAC Leisure
PO Box 21
23–25 Huntly Street
Inverness IV1 1LA
Tel: 0463 237611
Operates 21 screens on 10
sites, all in Scotland

Hutchinson Leisure Group (Apollo Leisure UK)
PO Box 251
Oxford OX1 1HH
Tel: 0865 248262
Operates 14 screens on 6
sites

National Amusements (UK)
200 Elm Street
Dedham
Massachusetts 02026-9126
USA
Tel: 0101 617 461 1600
Operators of three
Showcase multiplexes at
the end of 1988 with
several more scheduled to
open during 1989

Panton Films
Coronet Cinema
Notting Hill Gate
London W11
Tel: 01 221 0123
Operates the Coronet
circuit of 13 screens on 6
sites, comprising former
circuit cinemas of Rank
and Cannon

Pathé House
76 Hammersmith Road
London W14 8YR
Tel: 01 603 4555
Operates 387 screens on
144 sites, comprising the
Cannon and former
Granada circuits

Rank Theatres
439–445 Godstone Road
Whyteleafe
Surrey CR3 0YG
Tel: 08832 3355
Operates the Odeon chain
of 218 screens on 74 sites
in early 1989, with many
additional screens under
construction

Tatton Group
Davenport Theatre
Buxton Road
Stockport
Greater Manchester
Tel: 061 483 3801
Operates 8 screens on 4
sites in the Manchester
area

UCI (UK)
Parkside House
51–53 Brick Street
London W1Y 7DU
Tel: 01 409 1346
Formerly CIC/UA
Operators of 9 purpose-
built multiplexes with 86
screens at the end of 1988,
with 6 more scheduled to
open during 1989

Unit Four Cinemas
56 Bank Parade
Burnley
Lancs
Tel: 0282 28221
Operates 28 screens on 8
sites in the Manchester
area

LONDON WEST END – PREMIERE RUN

Astral
Brewer Street
Tel: 01 734 6387
Seats: 1:89, 2:159

Barbican
Silk Street
Tel: 01 628 8795/638 8891
Seats: 1:280, *2:255,
*3:153

Camden Plaza
Camden High Street
Tel: 01 485 2443
Seats: 340

Cannon Baker Street
Marylebone Road
Tel: 01 935 9772
Seats: 1:176, 2:169

Cannon Chelsea
King's Road
Tel: 01 352 5096/351 1026
Seats: 1:254, 2:227, 3:163,
4:130

Cannon Fulham Road
Tel: 01 370 0265/2636/
2110
Seats: 1:416, 2:374, 3:223,
4:223, 5:222

Cannon Haymarket
Tel: 01 839 1527/1528
Seats: 1:455, 2:200, 3:201

Cannon Moulin Complex
Great Windmill Street
Tel: 01 437 1653
Seats::1:200, 2:200, 3:100,
4:100, 5:80, 6:200

Cannon Oxford Street
Tel: 01 636 0310/3851
Seats: 1:325, 2:225, 3:195,
4:225, 5:48

Cannon Panton Street
Tel: 01 930 0631/2
Seats: 1:127, 2:148, 3:140,
4:136

Cannon Piccadilly Circus
Tel: 01 437 3561
Seats: 1:125, 2:118

Cannon Premiere
Swiss Centre
Tel: 01 439 4470/437 2096
Seats: 1:97, 2:101, 3:93,
4:108

Cannon Shaftesbury Avenue
Tel: 01 836 8606/6279
Seats: 1:616, 2:581

Cannon Tottenham Court Road
Tel: 01 636 6148/6749
Seats: 1:328, 2:145, 3:137

Centre Charles Peguy*
Leicester Square
Tel: 01 437 8339
Seats: 100

Chelsea Cinema
King's Road
Tel: 01 351 3742
Seats: 713

Coronet
Notting Hill Gate
Tel: 01 727 6705
Seats: 396

Curzon Mayfair
Curzon Street
Tel: 01 499 3737
Seats: 542

Curzon Phoenix
Phoenix Street
Tel: 01 240 9661
Seats: 212

Curzon West End
Shaftesbury Avenue
Tel: 01 439 4805
Seats: 624

Dominion*
Tottenham Court Road
Tel: 01 580 9562/3
Seats: 2000

Empire Leicester Square
Tel: 01 200 0200
Seats: 1:1330, 2:353, 3:80

Everyman
Holly Bush Vale,
Hampstead
Tel: 01 435 1525
Seats: 285

French Institute*
Queensberry Place SW7
Tel: 01 589 6211
Seats: 350

Gate
Notting Hill Gate
Tel: 01 727 4043
Seats: 241

Goethe Institute*
Princes Gate SW7
Tel: 01 581 3344
Seats: 170

 ICA Cinema
The Mall
Tel: 01 930 0493
Seats: 208, C'thèque: 50

Imperial War Museum*
Lambeth Road
Tel: 01 735 8922
Seats: 216

 **London Filmmakers' Co-op***
Gloucester Avenue NW1
Tel: 01 586 8516
Seats: 100

Lumière
St Martin's Lane
Tel: 01 836 0691/379 3014
Seats: 737

Metro
Rupert Street
Tel: 01 437 0757
Seats: 1:195, 2:85

Minema
Knightsbridge
Tel: 01 235 4225
Seats: 68

Museum of London*
London Wall EC2
Tel: 01 600 3699/1058
Seats: 270

National Film Theatre/ Museum of the Moving Image
South Bank, Waterloo
Tel: 01 928 3232
Seats: 1:466, 2:162,
MOMI:130

Odeon Haymarket
Tel: 01 839 7697
Seats: 600

Odeon High Street Kensington
Tel: 01 602 6644/5
Seats: 1:657, 2:301, 3:193,
4:234

Odeon Leicester Square
Tel: 01 930 6111/4250/
4259
Seats: 1983

Odeon Marble Arch
Tel: 01 723 2011
Seats: 1360

Odeon Swiss Cottage
Finchley Road
Tel: 01 586 3057
Seats: 1:736, 2:152, 3:155

Odeon West End
Leicester Square
Tel: 01 930 5252/3
Seats: 1402

Plaza Piccadilly Circus
Lower Regent Street
Tel: 01 200 0200
Seats: 1:732, 2:367, 3:161,
4:187

Prince Charles
Leicester Square
Tel: 01 437 8181
Seats: 487

Queen Elizabeth Hall*
South Bank, Waterloo
Tel: 01 928 3002
Seats: 906

Renoir
Russell Square
Tel: 01 837 8402
Seats: 1:251, 2:251

Royal Festival Hall*
South Bank, Waterloo
Tel: 01 928 3002
Seats: 2419

Scala Kings Cross
Pentonville Road
Tel: 01 278 8052/0051
Seats: 350

Screen on Baker Street
Tel: 01 935 2772
Seats: 1:95, 2:100

Screen on the Green
Upper Street
Tel: 01 226 3520
Seats: 300

Screen on the Hill
Haverstock Hill
Tel: 01 435 3366/9787
Seats: 339

Warner West End
Leicester Square
Tel: 01 439 0791
Seats: 1:150, 2:900, 3:272,
4:434, 5:108

OUTER LONDON

Acton
Acton Screen
High Street
Tel: 01 993 2558
Seats: 100(V)

Barking
Odeon Longbridge
Road
Tel: 01 594 2900
Seats: 1:846, 2:149, 3:144

Barnet
Odeon Great North
Road
Tel: 01 449 4147
Seats: 1:543, 2:140, 3:140

Battersea
Arts Centre Old Town
Hall*
Lavender Hill
Tel: 01 223 2223
Seats: 180

Beckenham
Cannon High Street
Tel: 01 650 1171/658 7114
Seats: 1:478, 2:228, 3:127

Borehamwood
Hertsmere Hall*
Elstree Way
Tel: 01 953 2223
Seats: 664

Brentford
Watermans Arts Centre
High Street
Tel: 01 568 1176
Seats: 240

Brixton
Ritzy Brixton Oval
Tel: 01 737 2121
Seats: 420

Bromley
Odeon High Street
Tel: 01 460 4425
Seats: 1:402, 2:125, 3:98,
4:273

Catford
Cannon Central Parade
Tel: 01 698 3306/697 6579
Seats: 1:519, 2:259

Croydon
Cannon London Road
Tel: 01 688 0486/5775
Seats: 1:650, 2:399, 3:187
Fairfield Hall Park
Lane*
Tel: 01 688 9291/0821
Seats: 1552

Dalston
Rio Kingsland High
Street
Tel: 01 254 6677/249 2722
Seats: 400

Ealing
Cannon Northfields
Avenue
Tel: 01 567 1075
Seats: 1:155, 2:155
Cannon Uxbridge Road
Tel: 01 567 1333/579 4851
Seats: 1:764, 2:414, 3:210

East Finchley
Phoenix High Road
Tel: 01 883 2233
Seats: 300

Edgware
Cannon Station Road
Tel: 01 952 2164/951 0299
Seats: 1:705, 2:207, 3:146

Elephant & Castle
Coronet Film Centre
New Kent Road
Tel: 01 703 4968/708 0066
Seats: 1:546, 2:271, 3:211

Enfield
Cannon Southbury
Road
Tel: 01 363 4411/367 4909
Seats: 1:700, 2:356, 3:217,
4:140

Golders Green
Cannon Ionic Finchley
Road
Tel: 01 455 1724/4134

Hammersmith
Cannon King Street
Tel: 01 748 0557/2388
Seats: 1:955, 2:455, 3:326
Odeon Queen Caroline
Street*
Tel: 01 748 4081/2
Seats: 3485

Riverside Studios
Crisp Road
Tel: 01 748 3354
Seats: 200

Hampstead
Cannon Pond Street
Tel: 01 794 4000/435 3307
Seats: 1:474 2:193, 3:186

Harrow
Cannon Station Road
Tel: 01 427 1743/863 4137
Seats: 1:612, 2:133
Cannon Sheepcote
Road
Tel: 01 863 7261
Seats: 1:627, 2:204, 3:205

Hayes
Beck Theatre*
Grange Road
Tel: 01 561 8371
Seats: 484

Hendon
Cannon Central Circus
Tel: 01 202 7137/4644
Three screens

Highgate
Jackson's Lane*
Community Centre
Tel: 01 340 5226

Holloway
Odeon Holloway Road
Tel: 01 272 6331
Seats: 1:388, 2:198, 3:270,
4:391, 5:361

Ilford
Odeon Gants Hill
Tel: 01 554 2500
Seats: 1:768, 2:253, 3:315

Kilburn
Odeon Willesden Lane
Tel: 01 328 6225
Seats: 245

Kingston
Options Richmond
Road
Tel: 01 546 0404
Three screens. Owned by
Pathé

Mile End
Coronet Mile End Road
Tel: 01 790 2041/5517
Seats: 1:694, 2:226, 3:225

Muswell Hill
Odeon Fortis Green
Road
Tel: 01 883 1001
Seats: 1:610, 2:134, 3:130

Purley
Cannon High Street
Tel: 01 660 1212/668 5592
Seats: 1:438, 2:135, 3:120

Putney
Cannon High Street
Tel: 01 788 2263/3003
Seats: 1:434, 2:312, 3:147

Richmond
Odeon Hill Street
Tel: 01 940 5759
Seats: 1:478, 2:201, 3:201

Romford
Cannon South Street
Tel: 0708 43848/47671
Seats: 1:652, 2:494, 3:246
Odeon South Street
Tel: 0708 40300
Seats: 1:694, 2:127, 3:358

Sidcup
Cannon High Street
Tel: 01 300 2539/309 0770
Seats: 1:516, 2:303

Streatham
Cannon High Road
Tel: 01 769 1928/6262
Seats: 1:630, 2:432, 3:231
Odeon High Road
Tel: 01 769 3346
Seats: 1:1095, 2:267,
3:267

Sutton
Cannon Cheam Road
Tel: 01 642 8927/0855
Seats: 1:260, 2:120, 3:120

Turnpike Lane
Coronet Turnpike
Parade
Tel: 01 888 2519/3734
Seats: 1:624, 2:417, 3:269

Walthamstow
Cannon Hoe Street
Tel: 01 520 7092
Seats: 1:944, 2:181, 3:181

Well Hall
Coronet Well Hall Road
Tel: 01 850 3351
Seats: 1:450, 2:131

West Norwood
Cinema Nettlefold
Hall*
High Street
Tel: 01 670 6212
Seats: 213

Wimbledon
Odeon The Broadway
Tel: 01 542 2277
Seats: 1:702, 2:218, 3:190

Woodford
Cannon High Road
Tel: 01 989 3463/4066
Seats: 1:562, 2:199, 3:131

Woolwich
Coronet John Wilson
Street
Tel: 01 854 2255
Seats: 1600

ENGLAND

Abingdon Oxon
Regal Picture Palace
The Square
Tel: 0235 20322
Seats: 340

Accrington Lancs
Unit Four Broadway
Tel: 0254 33231
Seats: 1:315, 2:195, 3:100

Aldeburgh Suffolk
Aldeburgh Cinema
High Street
Tel: 072 885 2996
Seats: 286

Aldershot Hants
Cannon High Street
Tel: 0252 317223/20355
Seats: 1:313, 2:183, 3:150

Alton Hants
Palace Normandy
Street*
Tel: 0420 82303
Seats: 654

Ambleside Cumbria
Zeffirelli's Compston
Road
Tel: 0966 33845
Seats: 200

Andover Hants
Savoy London Street
Tel: 0264 52624
Seats: 350

Ardwick Greater
Manchester
Apollo Ardwick Green*
Tel: 061 273 6921
Seats: 2641

Ashford Kent
Picture House Beaver
Road
Tel: 0233 20124
Three screens

Ashton-under-Lyne
Greater Manchester
Metro Old Street
Tel: 061 330 1993
Seats: 979

Atherstone Warwicks
Regal Long Street*
Tel: 08277 2220
Seats: 326

Aylesbury Bucks
Odeon Cambridge
Street
Tel: 0296 82660
Seats: 1:450, 2:108, 3:113

Banbury Oxon
Cannon The Horsefair
Tel: 0295 62071
Seats: 1:432, 2:225

Barnsley South Yorks
Odeon Eldon Street
Tel: 0226 205494
Seats: 1:419, 2:636

Barnstaple Devon
Astor Boutport Street
Tel: 0271 42550
Seats: 360

Barrow Cumbria
Astra Abbey Road
Tel: 0229 25354
Seats: 1:640, 2:260, 3:260

Basildon Essex
Cannon Great Oaks
Tel: 0268 27421/27431
Seats: 1:644, 2:435,
3:101(V)
Towngate*
Tel: 0268 23953
Seats: 459

Basingstoke Hants
Cannon Wote Street
Tel: 0256 22257/59446
Seats: 1:407, 2:218

Bath Avon
Cannon
Westgate Street
Tel: 0225 61730/62959
Seats: 737
Gemini St John's Place
Tel: 0225 61506
Seats: 1:126, 2:151, 3:49
Little Theatre
St Michaels Place
Tel: 0225 66822
Seats: 1:222, 2:78

Beaconsfield Bucks
Chiltern Station Road
Tel: 049 46 3248
Seats: 277

Bedford Beds
Civic Theatre*
Tel: 0234 44813
Seats: 266
Cannon St Peter Street
Tel: 0234 53848
Seats: 1:1476, 2:209

Belper Derbys
Screen

Berwick
Northumberland
Playhouse Sandgate
Tel: 0289 307769
Seats: 650

Beverley East Yorks
**Playhouse The Market
Place**
Tel: 0482 881315
Seats: 310

Bexhill-on-Sea East
Sussex
Curzon Western Road
Tel: 0424 210078
Seats: 200

Billingham Cleveland
Forum Theatre*
Town Centre
Tel: 0642 552663
Seats: 494

Birkenhead
Merseyside
Cannon Conway Street
Tel: 051 647 6509

Birmingham West
Mids
**Cannon John Bright
Street**
Tel: 021 643 0292/2128
Seats: 1:699, 2:242
**Capitol Alum Rock
Road**
Ward End
Tel: 021 327 0528
Seats: 1:340, 2:250, 3:130
**Midlands Arts Centre
Cannon Hill Park**
Tel: 021 440 3838
Seats: 1:202, 2:144
Odeon New Street
Tel: 021 643 6101
Seats: 1:330, 2:387; 3: 308;
4:239, 5:210; 6:190
Tivoli Station Street
Tel: 021 643 1556
Two screens
bfi **Triangle Gosta
Green**
Tel: 021 359 4192/2403
Seats: 180
Warwick Westley Road
Acocks Green
Tel: 021 706 0766
Seats: 462

Blackburn Lancs
**Unit Four King William
Street**
Tel: 0254 51774
Three screens

Blackpool Lancs
Cannon Church Street
Tel: 0253 27207/24233
Seats: 1:717, 2:330, 3:231
Odeon Dickson Road
Tel: 0253 23565
Seats: 1:1404, 2:190,
3:190
**Royal Pavilion Rigby
Road**
Tel: 0253 25313
Seats: 347

Blyth Northumberland
Wallaw Union Street
Tel: 0670 352504
Seats: 1:850, 2:150, 3:80

Bognor Regis West
Sussex
Cannon Canada Grove
Tel: 0243 823138
Two screens

Bolton Greater
Manchester
Cannon Bradshawgate
Tel: 0204 25597
Seats: 1:274, 2:324, 3:100

Boston Lincs
Regal West Street
Tel: 0205 50553
Seats: 182

Bourne Lincs
**Film Theatre North
Street**
Seats: 55

Bournemouth Dorset
Cannon Westover Road
Tel: 0202 28433/290345
Seats: 1:652, 2:585, 3:223
**Continental Wimborne
Road**
Winton
Tel: 0202 529779
Seats: 368
Odeon Westover Road
Tel: 0202 22402
Seats: 1:757, 2:1168

Bovington Dorset
Globe Bovington Camp
Wool
Tel: 0929 462666
Seats: 396

**Bowness-on-
Windermere** Cumbria
Royalty Lake Road
Tel: 09662 3364
Seats: 399

Bracknell Berks
**South Hill Park Arts
Centre**
Tel: 03444 27272
Seats: 1:60, 2:200

Bradford West Yorks
bfi **National Museum
of Photography,
Film and TV**
Princes' View
Tel: 0274 732277/727488
Seats: 340
Odeon Prince's Way
Tel: 0274 726716
Seats: 1:467, 2:1190,
3:244
bfi **Playhouse and
Film Theatre**
Chapel Street
Tel: 0274 720329
Seats: 1:295, 2:45

Braintree Essex
Studio Fairfield Road*
Tel: 0376 20378
Seats: 812

Brentwood Essex
Cannon Chapel High
Tel: 0277 212931/227574
Two screens

Bridgnorth Salop
**Majestic Whitburn
Street**
Tel: 0746 761815
Seats: 1:500, 2:200

Bridgwater Somerset
**Film Centre Penel
Orlieu**
Tel: 0278 422383
Seats: 1:230, 2:240

Bridport Dorset
Palace South Street
Tel: 0308 22167
Seats: 420

Brierfield Lancs
**Unit Four Burnley
Road**
Tel: 0282 63932
Seats: 1:70, 2:70, 3:61,
4:66

Brierley Hill West
Mids
Merry Hill 10
Tel: 0384 78244
Seats: 1:175, 2:254, 3:226,
4:254, 5:350, 6:350, 7:254,
8:226, 9:254, 10:175

Brighton East Sussex
Cannon East Street
Tel: 0273 27010/202095
Seats: 1:835, 2:345, 3:271,
4:194
**Duke of York's Preston
Circus**
Tel: 0273 602503
Seats: 359
Odeon West Street
Tel: 0273 25890
Seats: 1:390, 2:885, 3:504,
4:273, 5:242

Bristol Avon
bfi **Arnolfini Narrow
Quay**
Tel: 0272 299191
Seats: 176
**Cannon Frogmore
Street**
Tel: 0272 262848/9
Seats: 1:427, 2:311
**Cannon Northumbria
Drive**
Henleaze
Tel: 0272 621644
Seats: 1:186, 2:129, 3:126
**Cannon Whiteladies
Road**
Tel: 0272 730679/733640

Seats: 1:372, 2:253, 3:135
**Concorde Stapleton
Road**
Tel: 0272 510377
Seats: 1:166, 2:183
Gaiety Wells Road
Tel: 0272 776224
Seats: 650
Odeon Union Street
Tel: 0272 290882
Seats: 1:399, 2:224, 3:215
bfi **Watershed**
Tel: 0272 276444
Seats: 1:200, 2:50

Broadstairs Kent
**Windsor Harbour
Street**
Seats: 100

Bungay Suffolk
Mayfair Broad Street
Tel: 0986 2397
Seats: 400

Burgess Hill West
Sussex
Cinema Cyprus Road
Tel: 04416 2137
Seats: 400

**Burnham-on-
Crouch** Essex
Rio Station Road
Tel: 0621 782027
Seats: 200

Burnham-on-Sea
Somerset
Ritz Victoria Street
Tel: 0278 782871
Seats: 260

Burnley Lancs
Unit Four Rosegrove
Tel: 0282 22876

Burton-on-Trent
Staffs
Odeon Guild Street
Tel: 0283 63200
Seats: 1:502, 2:110, 3:110

Bury St Edmunds
Suffolk
Cannon Halter Street
Tel: 0284 754477
Seats: 1:196, 2:117

Camberley Surrey
Cannon London Road
Tel: 0276 63909/26768
Seats: 1:441, 2:116, 3:92
Globe Hawley*
Tel: 0252 876769
Seats: 200

Camborne Cornwall
Palace Roskear
Tel: 0209 712020
Seats: 212

Cambridge Cambs
bfi **Arts Market Passage**
Tel: 0223 352001/462666
Seats: 275
Cannon St Andrews Street
Tel: 0223 354572/645378
Seats: 1:736, 2:452

Cannock Staffs
Cannon Walsall Road
Tel: 05435 2226
Two screens

Canterbury Kent
Cannon St Georges Place
Tel: 0227 462022/453577
Seats: 1:536, 2:400
bfi **Cinema 3***
University of Kent
Tel: 0227 764000
Seats: 300

Carlisle Cumbria
Lonsdale Warwick Road
Tel: 0228 25586
Seats: 1:410, 2:220, 3:50

Chatham Kent
Cannon High Street
Tel: 0634 42522/46756
Seats: 1:520, 2:360, 3:170

Chelmsford Essex
Select
New Whittle Street
Tel: 0245 352724
Seats: 400

Cheltenham Glos
Odeon Winchcombe Street
Tel: 0242 524081
Seats: 1:756, 2:130, 3:130, 4:90

Chester Cheshire
Cannon Foregate Street
Tel: 0224 22931
Seats: 1:468, 2:248
Odeon Northgate Street
Tel: 0224 24930
Seats: 1:798, 2:122, 3:122

Chesterfield Derbys
Regal Cavendish Street
Tel: 0246 73333
Seats: 484

Chippenham Wilts
Cannon Marshfield Road
Tel: 0249 652498
Seats: 1:215, 2:215

Chipping Norton Oxon
The Theatre Spring Street*

Tel: 0608 2349/2350
Seats: 195

Christchurch Hants
Regent Centre*
High Street
Tel: 0202 499148

Cirencester Glos
Regal Lewis Lane
Tel: 0285 2358
Seats: 1:100, 2:100
Video only

Clacton Essex
Coronet Pier Avenue
Tel: 0255 429627
Seats: 1:600, 2:187

Clevedon Avon
Curzon Old Church Road
Tel: 0272 872158
Seats: 425

Clitheroe Lancs
Civic Hall York Street
Tel: 0200 23278
Seats: 400

Colchester Essex
Odeon Crouch Street
Tel: 0206 572294
Seats: 1:482, 2:208, 3:120, 4:135

Coleford Glos
Studio High Street
Tel: 0594 333331
Seats: 1:200, 2:80

Corby Northants
Forum Queens Square
Tel: 0536 203974
Seats: 1:339, 2:339

Cosford Staffs
Astra RAF Cosford*
Tel: 090 722 2393
Seats: 460

Cosham Hants
Cannon High Street
Tel: 0705 376635
Three screens

Coventry West Mids
bfi **Arts Centre***
University of Warwick
Tel: 0203 417417/417314
Seats: 1:250, 2:500, 3:150
Odeon Jordan Well
Tel: 0203 22042
Seats: 1:716, 2:170, 3:172
Theatre One Ford Street
Tel: 0203 24301
Seats: 1:230, 2:140, 3:153

Cranleigh Surrey
Regal High Street
Tel: 0483 272373
Seats: 268

Crawley West Sussex
Cannon High Street
Tel: 0293 27497/541296
Seats: 1:297, 2:214, 3:110

Crewe Cheshire
Lyceum Theatre*
Heath Street
Tel: 0270 215523
Seats: 750
Victoria Film Theatre
West Street
Tel: 0270 211422
Seats: 180

Cromer Norfolk
Regal Hans Place
Tel: 0263 513735
Seats: 326

Crookham Hants
Globe
Queen Elizabeth Barracks
Tel: 0252 876769
Seats: 340

Crosby Merseyside
Cannon Crosby Road North
Tel: 051 928 2108
Three screens

Darlington Co Durham
Arts Centre Vane Terrace*
Tel: 0325 483168/483271
Seats: 100
Cannon Northgate
Tel: 0325 62745/484994
Seats: 1:590, 2:218, 3:148

Dartington Devon
bfi **Barn Theatre***
Tel: 0803 862224
Seats: 208

Deal Kent
Flicks Queen Street
Tel: 0304 361165
Seats: 173

Derby Derbys
Assembly Rooms*
Market Place
Tel: 0332 369311
Seats: 998
Meteor Centre 10
Tel: 0332 295010
Seats: 1:192, 2:189, 3:189, 4:192, 5:278, 6:278, 7:192, 8:189, 9:189, 10:192
bfi **Metro Green Lane**
Tel: 0332 40170
Seats: 126
Showcase Cinemas
Outer Ring Road
Osmarton Park Road at
Sinfin Lane
Tel: 0332 270300
Eleven screens

Dereham Norfolk
CBA Dereham Entertainment Centre
Market Place
Tel: 0362 3261
Seats: 210

Devizes Wilts
Palace Market Place
Tel: 0380 2971
Seats: 253

Dewsbury West Yorks
Cannon Market Place
Tel: 0924 464949
Two screens

Didcot Oxon
New Coronet The Broadway*
Tel: 0235 812038
Seats: 490

Doncaster South Yorks
Cannon Cleveland Street
Tel: 0302 67934/66241
Seats: 1:477, 2:201, 3:135
Civic Theatre Waterdale*
Tel: 0302 62349
Seats: 547
Odeon Hallgate
Tel: 0302 344626
Seats: 1:1003, 2:155, 3:155

Dorchester Dorset
Plaza Trinity Street
Tel: 0305 3488
Seats: 1:100, 2:320

Dorking Surrey
Grand Hall*
Dorking Halls
Tel: 0306 889694
Seats: 851

Dudley West Mids
Odeon Castle Hill
Tel: 0384 55518
Seats: 1:540, 2:215

Durham Co Durham
Cannon North Road
Tel: 091 384 8184
Two screens

Eastbourne East Sussex
Cannon Pevensey Road
Tel: 0323 23612/642443
Seats: 1:585, 2:160
Curzon Langley Road
Tel: 0323 31441
Seats: 1:530, 2:236, 3:236

Elland Yorks
Rex
Tel: 0422 72140

Ely Cambs
The Maltings*
Tel: 0353 2633
Seats 212

Esher Surrey
Cannon High Street
Tel: 0372 65639/63362
Seats: 1:918, 2:117

Evesham Hereford &
Worcs
Regal Port Street
Tel: 0386 6002
Seats: 540

Ewell Surrey
Cannon Kingston Road
Tel: 01 393 2211/0760
Seats: 1:606, 2:152

Exeter Devon
Northcott Theatre*
Stocker Road
Tel: 0392 54853
Seats: 433
Odeon Sidwell Street
Tel: 0392 54057
Seats: 1:744, 2:119, 3:105, 4:344

Exmouth Devon
Savoy Market Street
Seats: 1:230, 2:110

Fawley Hants
Waterside Long Lane
Tel: 0703 891335
Seats: 355

Felixstowe Suffolk
Top Rank Crescent
Road
Tel: 0394 282787
Seats: 1:150, 2:90

Filey Yorks
Grand Union Street†
Tel: 072381 2373

Frome Somerset
Westway Cork Street
Tel: 0373 65685
Seats: 304

Gainsborough Lincs
Trinity Arts Centre*
Trinity Street
Tel: 0427 617 242
Seats: 210

Gateshead Tyne &
Wear
AMC Metro 10 Metro
Centre
Tel: 091 493 2022/3
Seats: 1:196, 2:196, 3:227, 4:252, 5:364, 6:364, 7:252, 8:227, 9:196, 10:196

Gatley Greater
Manchester
Tatton Gatley Road
Tel: 061 491 0711
Seats: 1:648, 2:247, 3:111

Gerrards Cross
Bucks

Cannon Ethorpe
Crescent
Tel: 0753 882516/883024
Two screens

Gloucester Glos
Cannon St Aldate
Street
Tel: 0452 22399/415215
Seats: 1:658, 2:348, 3:294
Guildhall Arts Centre*
Eastgate Street
Seats: 125

Godalming Surrey
Borough Hall

Gosport Hants
Ritz Walpole Road
Tel: 0705 501231
Seats: 1136

Grantham Lincs
Paragon St Catherine's
Road
Tel: 0476 70046
Seats: 270

Gravesend Kent
Cannon King Street
Tel: 0474 356947/352470
Seats: 1:576, 2:320, 3:107

Grays Essex
State George Street
Tel: 0375 372799
Seats: 2200
Thameside Orsett
Road*
Tel: 0375 382555
Seats: 303

Great Yarmouth
Norfolk
Cinema Royal
Aquarium
Tel: 0493 842043/842707
Seats: 1:1180, 2:264
Empire Marine
Parade*
Tel: 0493 843147
Seats: 967
Windmill Theatre
Marine Parade*
Tel: 0493 843504
Seats: 892

Grimsby Humberside
Cannon Freeman
Street
Tel: 0472 42878/49368
Seats: 1:419, 2:251, 3:130
bfi **Whitgift Crosland**
Road*
Tel: 0472 887117
Seats: 206

Guildford Surrey
Odeon Epsom Road
Tel: 0483 504990
Seats: 1:452, 2:135, 3:144, 4:250

Halifax West Yorks
Cannon Ward's End
Tel: 0422 52000/46429
Seats: 1:670, 2:199, 3:172

Halstead Essex
Empire Butler Road
Tel: 078 7477001
Seats: 320

Halton Bucks
Astra RAF Halton
Tel: 0296 623535
Seats: 570

Hanley Staffs
Cannon Broad Street
Tel: 0782 22320/268970
Seats: 1:573, 2:233, 3:162
Odeon Piccadilly
Tel: 0782 25311
Seats: 1:1298, 2:177, 3:177

Harlow Essex
Odeon The High
Tel: 0279 26989
Seats: 1:450, 2:243, 3:201
Playhouse The High*
Tel: 0279 24391
Seats: 435

Harrogate North
Yorks
Odeon East Parade
Tel: 0423 503626
Seats: 1:532, 2:108, 3:108

Harwich Essex
Electric Palace*
King's Quay
Tel: 0255 553333
Seats: 204

Hastings East Sussex
Cannon Queens Road
Tel: 0424 420517
Three screens

Hatfield Herts
Forum*
Tel: 07072 71217
Seats: 210

Haywards Heath
Sussex
Clair Hall*
Perrymount Road
Tel: 0444 455440/454394

Heaton Moor Greater
Manchester
Savoy Heaton Manor
Road
Tel: 061 432 2114
Seats: 496

Hebden Bridge West
Yorks
Cinema New Road
Tel: 0422 842807
Seats: 498

Hemel Hempstead
Herts
Odeon Marlowes*
Tel: 0442 64013
Seats: 785

Hereford Hereford &
Worcs
Cannon Commercial
Road
Tel: 0432 272554

Hexham
Northumberland
Forum Market Place
Tel: 0434 602896
Seats: 207

High Wycombe
Bucks
Wycombe 6 Crest Road
Cressex
Tel: 0494 463333/464309/
465565
Seats: 1:390, 2:390, 3:285, 4:285, 5:200, 6:200

Hinckley Leics
Cannon Trinity Lane
Tel: 0455 637523
Three screens

Hoddesdon Herts
Broxbourne Civic Hall*
High Road
Tel: 0992 441946/31
Seats: 564

Holbury Hants
Waterside Long Lane
Tel: 0703 891335
Seats: 355

Hordern Co Durham
Fairworld Sunderland
Road
Tel: 0783 864344
Seats: 1:156, 2:96

Horsham Sussex
Arts Centre (Ritz
Cinema and Capitol
Theatre)
North Street
Tel: 0403 68689
Seats: 1:126, *2:450

Horwich Lancs
Leisure Centre Victoria
Road*
Tel: 0204 692211
Seats: 400

Hoylake Merseyside
Cannon Alderley Road
Tel: 051 632 1345

Hucknall Notts
Byron High Street
Tel: 0602 636377
Seats: 430

Huddersfield West
Yorks
**Cannon Queensgate
Zetland Street**
Tel: 0484 530874
Two screens

Hull Humberside
Cannon Anlaby Road
Tel: 0482 224981
Three screens
Cannon Ferensway
Tel: 0482 26518/23530
Seats: 1:569, 2:346, 3:261,
4:166, 5:96
bfi **Film Theatre***
Central Library
Albion Street
Tel: 0482 224040 x30
Seats: 247

Hulme Greater
Manchester
**Aaben Jackson
Crescent**
Tel: 061 226 5749
Seats: 1:100, 2:100, 3:100

Huntingdon Cambs
**Cromwell Cinema
Centre
Princes Street**
Tel: 0480 411575
Seats: 300

Hyde Greater
Manchester
**Royal Corporation
Street**
Tel: 061 368 2206
Seats: 1:800, 2:224

Ilfracombe Devon
**Pendle Stairway High
Street**
Tel: 0271 63484
Seats: 460

Ilkeston Derbys
Scala Market Place
Tel: 0602 324612
Seats: 500

Ipswich Suffolk
bfi **Film Theatre Corn
Exchange**
Tel: 0473 55851
Seats: 1:221, 2:40
Odeon St Helens Street
Tel: 0473 53641
Seats: *1:1813, 2:186

Keighley West
Yorkshire
**Picture House North
Street**
Tel: 0535 602561
Seats: 1:376, 2:95

Kendal Cumbria
Brewery Arts Centre
Highgate
Tel: 0539 25133
Seats: 148

Keswick Cumbria
**Alhambra St John
Street**
Tel: 0596 72195
Seats: 313

Kettering Northants
Ohio Russell Street
Tel: 0536 515130
Seats: 1:145, 2:206

King's Lynn Norfolk
**Fermoy Centre King
Street***
Tel: 0553 4725/3578
Seats: 359
Majestic Tower Street
Tel: 0553 2603
Seats: 1:847, 2:136

Kirkby-in-Ashfield
Notts
Regent
Tel: 0623 753866

Kirkham Lancs
Empire Birley Street
Tel: 07722 684817
Seats: 256

Knutsford Cheshire
Civic Hall Toft Road*
Tel: 0565 3005
Seats: 400

Lancaster Lancs
Cannon King Street
Tel: 0524 64141/841149
Seats: 1:250, 2:250
bfi **Duke's
Playhouse***
Moor Lane
Tel: 0524 66645/67461
Seats: 307

Leamington Spa
Warwicks
Regal Portland Place
Tel: 0926 26106/27448
Seats: 904
Royal Spa Centre*
Newbold Terrace
Tel: 0926 34418
Seats: 1:799, 2:208

Leatherhead Surrey
Thorndike Theatre*
Church Street
Tel: 0372 376211/377677
Seats: 526

Leeds West Yorks
Cannon Vicar Lane
Tel: 0532 451013/452665
Seats: 1:670, 2:483, 3:227
**Cottage Road Cinema
Headingley**
Tel: 0532 751606
Seats: 468
**Hyde Park Brudenell
Road**
Tel: 0532 752045
Seats: 360

**Lounge North Lane
Headingley**
Tel: 0532 751061/58932
Seats: 691
Odeon The Headrow
Tel: 0532 430031
Seats: 1:982, 2:441, 3:200,
4:174, 5:126

Leicester Leics
Cannon Belgrave Gate
Tel: 0533 24346/24903
Seats: 1:616, 2:408, 3:232
Odeon Queen Street
Tel: 0533 22892
Seats: 1:872, 2:401, 3:111,
4:142
bfi **Phoenix Arts***
Newarke Street
Tel: 0533 559711/555627
Seats: 270

Leigh Greater
Manchester
Cannon Leigh Road
Tel: 0942 673728
Two screens

Leiston Suffolk
**Film Theatre High
Street**
Tel: 0728 830 549
Seats: 350

Letchworth Herts
Broadway Eastcheap
Tel: 0462 684721
Seats: 1410

Lichfield Staffs
Civic Hall Castle Dyke*
Tel: 054 32 54021
Seats: 278

Lincoln Lincs
Ritz High Street
Tel: 0522 46313
Seats: 1400

Littlehampton West
Sussex
Windmill Church Street
Tel: 09064 6644
Seats 650

Liverpool Merseyside
Cannon Allerton Road
Tel: 051 709 6277/708
7629
Cannon Lime Street
Tel: 051 709 6277/708
7629
Seats: 1:697, 2:274, 3:217
Odeon London Road
Tel: 051 709 0717
Seats: 1:976, 2:597, 3:167,
4:148, 5:148
Woolton Mason Street
Tel: 051 428 1919
Seats: 256

Long Eaton Notts
Screen Market Place
Tel: 060 732185
Seats: 253

Longridge Lancs
Palace Market Place
Tel: 07747 85600
Seats: 212

Loughborough Leics
Curzon Cattle Market
Tel: 0509 212261
Seats: 1:407, 2:199, 3:185,
4:135, 5:80

Louth Lincs
**Playhouse Cannon
Street**
Tel: 0507 603333
Seats: 218

Lowestoft Suffolk
Marina*
Seats: 900

Luton Beds
Cannon George Street
Tel: 0582 27311/22537
Seats: 1:615, 2:458, 3:272
St George's Theatre*
Central Library
Tel: 0582 21628
Seats: 256

Lyme Regis Dorset
Regent Broad Street
Tel: 0297 42053
Seats: 400

Lymington Hants
Community Centre*
New Street
Tel: 05907 2337
Seats: 110

Mablethorpe Lincs
Bijou Quebec Road
Tel: 0521 77040
Seats: 264

Macclesfield Ches
Majestic Mill Street
Tel: 0625 22412
Seats: 687

Maghull Merseyside
Astra Northway
Tel: 051 526 1943
Seats: 1:200, 2:200, 3:300,
4:300

Maidstone Kent
**Cannon
Lower Stone Street**
Tel: 0622 52628
Seats: 1:260, 2:90, 3:260

Malton Yorks
Palace Yorkersgate*
Seats 140

Malvern Hereford &
Worcs
Cinema Grange Road
Tel: 0684 892279/892710
Seats: 407

Manchester Greater Manchester
Cannon 1 and 2 Deansgate
Tel: 061 832 5252/2112
Seats: 1:639, 2:167
bfi **Cornerhouse Oxford Street**
Tel: 061 228 7621
Seats: 1:300, 2:170, 3:58
Odeon Oxford Street
Tel: 061 236 8264

Mansfield Notts
Cannon Leeming Street
Tel: 0623 23138/652236
Seats: 1:367, 2:359, 3:171
Studio Leeming Street
Tel: 0623 653309
Seats: 75

March Cambs
Hippodrome Dartford Road*
Tel: 0354 53178
Seats: 150

Margate Kent
Dreamland Marine Parade
Tel: 0843 227822
Seats: 1:378, 2:376, 3:66(V)

Marple Greater Manchester
Regent Stockport Road
Tel: 061 427 5951
Seats: 285

Matlock Derbys
Ritz Causeway Lane
Tel: 0629 2121
Seats: 1:176, 2:100

Melton Mowbray Leics
Regal King Street
Tel: 0664 62251
Seats: 226

Middlesbrough Cleveland
Odeon Corporation Road
Tel: 0642 242888
Seats: 1:654, 2:120, 3:120

Middleton Greater Manchester
Palace Manchester Middleton Gardens
Tel: 061 643 2852
Seats: 234

Midsomer Norton Somerset
Palladium High Street
Tel: 0761 413266
Seats: 482

Millom Cumbria
Palladium Horn Hill
Tel: 0657 2441
Seats: 400

Milton Keynes Bucks
AMC The Point 10 Midsummer Boulevard
Tel: 0908 661662
Seats: 1:156, 2:169, 3:248, 4:220, 5:220, 6:220, 7:220, 8:248, 9:169, 10:156

Minehead Somerset
Regal The Avenue
Tel: 0683 2439

Mirfield West Yorks
Vale Centre Huddersfield Road
Tel: 0924 493240
Seats: 1:98, 2:96

Monkseaton Tyne & Wear
Cannon Caldwell Lane
Tel: 091 252 5540
Two screens

Monton Greater Manchester
Princess Monton Road
Tel: 061 789 3426
Seats: 580

Morpeth Northumberland
New Coliseum New Market
Tel: 0670 516834
Seats: 1:132, 2:132

Nantwich Cheshire
Civic Hall Market Street*
Tel: 0270 628633
Seats: 300

Nelson Lancs
Grand Market Street
Tel: 0282 692860
Seats: 391

Newark Notts
Palace Theatre Appleton Gate*
Tel: 0636 71636
Seats: 351

Newbury Berks
Cannon Park Way
Tel: 0635 41291/49913
Seats: 484

Newcastle-under-Lyme Staffs
Savoy High Street
Tel: 0782 616565
Seats: 200

Newcastle upon Tyne Tyne & Wear
Cannon Westgate Road
Tel: 091 261 0618
Seats: 1:600, 2:373
Jesmond Cinema Lyndhurst Avenue
Tel: 091 281 0526/2248
Seats: 626

Odeon Pilgrim Street
Tel: 091 232 3248
Seats: 1:1228, 2:159, 3:250, 4:361
bfi **Tyneside Pilgrim Street**
Tel: 091 232 8289/5592
Seats: 1:400, 2:155

Newport Isle of Wight
Cannon High Street
Tel: 0983 527169
Seats: 377

Newport Pagnell Bucks
Electra St John Street
Tel: 0908 611146
Seats: 400

Newquay Cornwall
Camelot The Crescent
Tel: 063 73 874222
Seats: 812

Newton Abbot Devon
Alexandra Market Street
Tel: 0626 65368
Seats: 360

Northallerton North Yorks
Lyric Northend
Tel: 0609 2019
Seats: 305

Northampton Northants
Cannon Abingdon Square
Tel: 0604 35839/32862
Seats: 1:1018, 2:275, 3:210
bfi **Forum, Weston Favell Centre**
Tel: 0604 401006/407544
Seats: 250

Northwich Ches
Regal London Road
Tel: 0606 3130
Seats: 1:797, 2:200

Norwich Norfolk
Cannon Prince of Wales Road
Tel: 0603 624677/623312
Seats: 1:524, 2:343, 3:186
bfi **Cinema City St Andrews Street**
Tel: 0603 625145
Seats: 230
Noverre Theatre Street
Tel: 0603 626402
Seats: 272
Odeon Anglia Square
Tel: 0603 621903
Seats: 1016

Nottingham Notts
Cannon Chapel Bar
Tel: 0602 45260/418483
Seats: 1:764, 2:437, 3:280

bfi **Media Centre Broad Street**
Due to open 1990
Odeon Angel Row
Tel: 0602 417766
Seats: 1:924, 2:581, 3:141, 4:153, 5:114, 6:96
Savoy Derby Road
Tel: 0602 472580
Seats: 1:386, 2:128, 3:168
Showcase Redfield Way Lenton
Tel: 0602 866766
Seats: 2650 (11 screens)

Nuneaton Warwicks
Nuneaton Arts Centre Abbey Theatre Pool Bank Street
Tel: 0203 382706

Okehampton Devon
Carlton St James Street
Tel: 0822 2425
Seats: 380

Oldham Greater Manchester
Roxy Hollins Road
Tel: 061 681 1441
Seats: 1:400, 2:300, 3:128

Oswestry Salop
Regal Salop Road
Tel: 0691 654043
Seats: 1:261, 2:261, 3:66

Oxford Oxon
Cannon George Street
Tel: 0865 244607/723911
Seats: 1:626, 2:326, 3:140
Cannon Magdalen Street
Tel: 0865 243067
Seats: 866
Not the Moulin Rouge New High Street Headington
Tel: 0865 63666
Seats: 350
Penultimate Picture Palace Jeune Street
Tel: 0865 723837
Seats: 185

Phoenix Walton Street
Tel: 0865 54909/512526
Seats: 1:234, 2:95

Oxted Surrey
Plaza Station Road West
Tel: 0883 712567
Seats: 442

Padstow Cornwall
Capitol Lanadwell Street
Tel: 0841 532344
Seats: 210

Paignton Devon
Palladium Torquay
Road*
Tel: 0803 550369
Seats: 461
Torbay, Torbay Road
Tel: 0803 559544
Seats: 484

Penistone South
Yorkshire
Town Hall
Tel: 0226 767532/205128
Seats: 450

Penrith Cumbria
Alhambra Middlegate
Tel: 0768 62400
Seats: 202

Penzance Cornwall
Savoy Causeway Head
Tel: 0736 3330
Seats: 450

Peterborough Cambs
Cannon Broadway
Tel: 0733 43461/43504
Seats: 1:656, 2:284, 3:147
Odeon Broadway
Tel: 0733 43319
Seats: 1:544, 2:110, 3:110
Showcase Mallory
Road
Boongate
Tel: 0733 558498
Eleven screens

Pickering North Yorks
Castle Burgate
Tel: 0751 72622
Seats: 386

Plymouth Devon
bfi Arts Centre Looe
Street
Tel: 0752 660060
Seats: 73
Cannon Derry's Cross
Tel: 0752 63300/25553
Seats: 1:583, 2:340, 3:115
Odeon Derry's Cross
Tel: 0752 668825/227074
Seats: 1:946, 2:168, 3:168

Pocklington East
Yorks
Ritz Market Place
Tel: 0759 303420
Seats: 250

Pontefract West Yorks
Crescent Ropergate
Tel: 0977 703788
Seats: 412

Poole Dorset
Ashley Arts Centre*
Kingsland Road
Seats: 143

Portsmouth Hants
Cannon Commercial
Road
Tel: 0705 823538/839719
Seats: 1:542, 2:255, 3:203
Odeon London Road
Tel: 0705 661539
Seats: 1:640, 2:225, 3:225
Rendezvous
The Hornpipe
Kingston Road
Tel: 0705 833854
Seats: 90

Potters Bar Herts
Oakmere House*
Tel: 0707 45005
Seats: 165

Preston Lancs
Odeon Church Street
Tel: 0722 23298
Seats: 1:1166, 2:112

Quinton West Midlands
Cannon Hagley Road
West
Tel: 021 422 2562/2252
Four screens

Ramsgate Kent
Granville Victoria
Parade*
Tel: 0843 591750
Seats: 861

Rawtenstall Lancs
Picture House
Tel: 0706 226774
Seats: 120
Unit Four Bacup Road
Tel: 070 62 3123
Seats: 1:121, 2:118, 3:165,
4:118

Reading Berks
Cannon Friar Street
Tel: 0734 573907
Seats: 1:532, 2:226, 3:118
Film Theatre
Whiteknights*
Tel: 0734 868497/875123
Seats: 409
Odeon Cheapside
Tel: 0734 507887
Seats: 1:400, 2:640

Redcar Cleveland
Regent The Esplanade
Tel: 0642 482094
Seats: 381

Redditch Hereford &
Worcs
Cannon Unicorn Hill
Tel: 0527 62572
Three screens

Redruth Cornwall
Regal Film Centre
Fore Street
Tel: 0209 216278
Seats: 1:200, 2:128, 3:600,
4:95

Reigate Surrey
Screen Bancroft Road
Tel: 0737 223213
Seats: 1:139, 2:142

Rickmansworth
Herts
Watersmeet Theatre*
High Street
Tel: 0923 771542
Seats: 390

Ripley Derbys
Hippodrome High
Street
Tel: 0773 46559
Seats: 350

Rochdale Greater
Manchester
Cannon The Butts
Tel: 0706 524362/45954
Seats: 1:538, 2:276, 3:197

Rotherham South
Yorks
Cannon High Street
Tel: 0709 382402
Two screens

Royston Herts
Priory, Priory Lane
Tel: 0763 43133
Seats: 305

Rugeley Staffs
Plaza Horsefair
Tel: 08894 2099
Seats: 621

Rushden Northants
Ritz College Street
Tel: 0933 312468
Seats: 822

Ryde Isle of Wight
Cannon Star Street
Tel: 0983 64930
Seats: 1:184, 2:184, 3:176

St Albans Herts
City Hall Civic Centre*
Tel: 0727 61078
Seats: 800
Odeon London Road
Tel: 0727 53888
Seats: 1:452, 2:115, 3:128,
4:145

St Austell Cornwall
Film Centre Chandos
Place
Tel: 0726 73750
Seats: 1:605, 2:125, 3:138

St Helens Merseyside
Cannon Bridge Street
Tel: 0744 51947/23392
Seats: 1:494, 2:284, 3:179

St Ives Cornwall
Royal, Royal Square
Tel: 0736 796843
Seats: 682

Salford Quays Lancs
Cannon Quebec Drive
Trafford Road
Tel: 061 873 7155/7279
1:265, 2:265, 3:249, 4:249,
5:213, 6:213, 7:177, 8:177

Salisbury Wilts
Odeon New Canal
Tel: 0722 22080
Seats: 1:471, 2:120, 3:120

Scarborough North
Yorks
Futurist Foreshore
Road*
Tel: 0723 365789
Seats: 2155
Hollywood Plaza
North Marine Road
Tel: 0723 365119
Seats: 275
Opera House*
St Thomas Street
Tel: 0723 369999
Seats: 225

Scunthorpe
Humberside
Majestic Oswald
Road
Tel: 0724 842352
Seats: 1:177, 2:162, 3:193
bfi Film Theatre*
Central Library
Carlton Street
Tel: 0724 860161 x30
Seats: 249

Sevenoaks Kent
Ace London Road
Tel: 0732 460576
Seats: 1:104, 2:106

Sheffield South Yorks
bfi Anvil Charter
Square
Tel: 0742 701920/760778
Seats: 1:110, 2:76, 3:65
Crystal Peaks 10
Mosbrough
Tel: 0742 480064
Seats: 1:200, 2:200, 3:228,
4:224, 5:312, 6:312, 7:224,
8:228, 9:200, 10:200
Odeon Barker's Pool
Tel: 0742 767962
Seats: 1:500, 2:324

Sheringham Norfolk
Little Theatre
Station Road
Tel: 0263 822347
Seats: 198

Shipley West Yorks
Unit Four Bradford
Road
Tel: 0274 583429
Seats: 1:89, 2:72, 3:121,
4:94

Shrewsbury Shrops
Cannon Empire Mardal
Tel: 0743 62257
Seats: 573
Cinema in the Square,
The Music Hall
Tel: 0743 50763
Seats: 100

Sidmouth Devon
Radway, Radway Place
Tel: 039 55 3085
Seats: 400

Sittingbourne Kent
Cannon High Street
Tel: 0795 23984
Two screens

Skegness Lincs
Tower Lumley Road
Tel: 0754 3938
Seats: 401

Skelmersdale Lancs
Premiere Film Centre
Tel: 0695 25041
Seats: 1:230, 2:248

Skipton North Yorks
Plaza Sackville Street
Tel: 0756 3417
Seats: 320

Sleaford Lincs
Sleaford Cinema
Southgate
Tel: 0529 30 3187
Seats: 60

Slough Berks
Maybox Movie Centre
High Street
Tel: 0753 692233/692492
Seats: 2058

Solihull West Midlands
Cinema High Street
Tel: 021 705 0398
Seats: 650
Metropole Hotel*
National Exhibition
Centre
Tel: 021 780 4242
Seats: 200

Southampton Hants
Cannon Above Bar
Street
Tel: 0703 223536/221026
Seats: 1:688, 2:433,
3:85(V)
Cannon Cinema
Five screens. Opening
July 1989
Mountbatten Theatre*
East Park Terrace
Tel: 0703 221991
Seats: 515
Odeon Above Bar
Street
Tel: 0703 333243
Seats: 1:476, 2:756, 3:127

Southend Essex
Cannon Alexandra
Street
Tel: 0702 344580
Seats: 1:665, 2:498
Odeon Elmer Approach
Tel: 0702 344434
Seats: 1:455, 2:1235

Southport Merseyside
Arts Centre Lord
Street*
Tel: 0704 40004/40011
Seats: 400
Cannon Lord Street
Tel: 0704 30627
Two screens

Spilsby Lincs
Phoenix Reynard
Street
Tel: 0790 53675/53621
Seats: 264

Stafford Staffs
Apollo New Port Road
Tel: 0785 51277
Seats: 1:170, 2:170
Picture House Bridge
Street
Tel: 0785 58291
Seats: 483

Staines Surrey
Cannon Clarence
Street
Tel: 0784 53316/59140
Seats: 1:586, 2:361, 3:173

Stalybridge Greater
Manchester
New Palace Market
Street
Tel: 061 338 2156
Seats: 414

Stanley Co Durham
Civic Hall*
Tel: 0207 32164
Seats: 632

Stevenage Herts
Cannon St Georges
Way
Tel: 0438 313267/316396
Seats: 1:340, 2:182
Gordon Craig Theatre*
Lytton Way
Tel: 0438 354568/316291
Seats: 507

Stockport Greater
Manchester
Cannon
Wellington Road South
Tel: 061 480 0779/2244
Two screens
Davenport Buxton
Road
Tel: 061 483 3801/2
Seats: 1:1794, 2:170

Stockton Cleveland
Cannon Dovecot Street
Tel: 0642 676048
Three screens
bfi Dovecot Film
Centre
Bishop Street
Tel: 0642 605506/611626
Seats: 100

Stoke-on-Trent
Staffs
bfi Film Theatre
College Road
Tel: 0782 411188
Seats: 212

Stowmarket Suffolk
Movieland Church
Walk
Tel: 0449 672890
Seats: 234
Regal Ipswich Street*
Tel: 0449 612825
Seats: 234

Street Somerset
Maxime Leigh Road
Tel: 0458 42028
Seats: 470
bfi Strode Theatre*
Church Road
Tel: 0458 42846
Seats: 400

Sudbury Suffolk
The Quay Theatre
Quay Lane
Tel: 0787 74745
Seats: 129

Sunderland Tyne &
Wear
Cannon Holmeside
Tel: 091 567 4148
Seats: 1:550, 2:209
Empire High Street
West*
Tel: 0783 42517
Seats: 1000
Studio High Street West
Tel: 0783 42517
Seats: 150

Sunninghill Berks
Novello Theatre*
High Street
Tel: 0990 20881
Seats: 160

Sutton Coldfield
West Midlands
Odeon Birmingham
Road
Tel: 021 354 2714
Seats: 1:598, 2:132, 3:118,
4:307

Swanage Dorset
Mowlem Shore Road
Tel: 0929 422229
Seats: 400

Swindon Wilts
Cannon Regent Street
Tel: 0793 22838/40733
Seats: 1:604, 2:402, 3:151
Wyvern Theatre
Square*
Tel: 0793 24481
Seats: 617

Tadley Hants
Cinema Royal*
Boundary Road
Tel: 073 56 4617
Seats: 296

Tamworth Staffs
Palace Lower Gungate
Tel: 0827 57100
Seats: 325

Taunton Somerset
Cannon Station Road
Tel: 0823 72291
Two screens

Telford Shrops
Telford Centre 10
Tel: 0952 290126
Seats: 1:192, 2:189, 3:189,
4:192, 5:278, 6:278, 7:192,
8:189, 9:189, 10:192

Tenbury Wells
Hereford & Worcs
Regal Teme Street
Tel: 0584 810235
Seats: 260

Tewkesbury Glos
Roses Theatre
Tel: 0684 295074
Seats: 375

Thirsk North Yorks
Studio One
Tel: 0845 24559
Seats: 238

Tiverton Devon
Tivoli Fore Street
Tel: 0884 252157
Seats: 364

Toftwood Norfolk
CBA Shipham Road
Tel: 0362 3261
Seats: 30

Tonbridge Kent
Angel Centre Angel
Lane*
Tel: 0732 359588
Seats: 306

Torquay Devon
Odeon Abbey Road
Tel: 0803 22324
Seats: 1:309, 2:346

Torrington Devon
Plough Fore Street
Tel: 0805 22552/3
Seats: 108

CINEMAS

Truro Cornwall
Plaza Lemon Street
Tel: 0872 72894
Seats: 1:849, 2:102, 3:160

Tunbridge Wells
Kent
Cannon Mount
Pleasant
Tel: 0892 41141/23135
Three screens

Uckfield East Sussex
Picture House High
Street
Tel: 0825 3822
Seats: 1:150, 2:100

Ulverston Cumbria
Laurel & Hardy
Museum*
Upper Brook Street
Tel: 0229 52292/86614
Seats: 50 (free)
Roxy Brogdon Street
Tel: 0229 52340
Seats: 310

Urmston Greater
Manchester
Curzon Princess Road
Tel: 061 748 2929
Seats: 1:400, 2:134

Uttoxeter Staffs
Elite High Street
Tel: 08893 3348
Seats: 120

Wadebridge Cornwall
Regal The Platt
Tel: 020 881 2791
Seats: 1:250, 2:120

Wakefield West Yorks
Cannon Kirkgate
Tel: 0924 373400/365236
Seats: 1:532, 2:233, 3:181

Walkden
Greater Manchester
Unit Four Bolton Road
Tel: 061 790 9432
Seats: 1:118, 2:108, 3:86,
4:94

Wallasey Merseyside
Unit Four Egremont
Tel: 051 639 2833
Seats: 1:181, 2:126, 3:176,
4:102

Wallingford Oxon
Corn Exchange*
Tel: 0491 39336
Seats: 187

Walsall West Mids
Cannon Townend Bank
Tel: 0922 22444/644330
Seats: 1:506, 2:247, 3:143

Waltham Cross
Herts
Cannon High Street
Tel: 092 761160
Seats: 1:460, 2:284, 3:103,
4:83

Wantage Oxon
Regent Newbury Street
Tel: 02357 67878
Seats: 228

Wareham Dorset
Rex West Street
Tel: 092 95 2778
Seats: 239

Warrington Ches
Odeon Buttermarket
Street
Tel: 0925 32825
Seats: 1:576, 2:291, 3:196
Westbrook 10
Tel: 0925 416677
Seats: 1:192, 2:189, 3:189,
4:192, 5:278, 6:278, 7:192,
8:189, 9:189, 10:192

Washington Tyne &
Wear
Fairworld Victoria
Road
Tel: 091 4162711
Seats: 1:227, 2:177

Watford Herts
Cannon Merton Road
Tel: 0923 24088/33259
Seats: 1:356, 2:195

Wellingborough
Northants
Palace Gloucester
Place
Tel: 0933 222184
Seats: 200

Wellington Somerset
Wellesley Mantle Street
Tel: 082 347 2135
Seats: 429

Wells Somerset
Regal Priory Road*
Tel: 0749 73195
Seats: 498

**Welwyn Garden
City** Herts
Campus West*
Tel: 0707 332880
Seats: 365

West Bromwich
West Midlands
Kings Paradise Street
Tel: 021 553 0192
Seats: 1:326, 2:287, 3:462

Westcliff-on-Sea
Essex
Cannon London Road
Tel: 0702 332436/342773
Two screens

Westgate-on-Sea
Kent
Carlton St Mildreds
Road
Tel: 0843 32019
Seats: 303

West Thurrock Essex
Retail Park 10
(open from summer 1989)

**Weston-super-
Mare** Avon
Odeon The Centre
Tel: 0934 21784
Seats: 1:875, 2:110, 3:133
Playhouse High Street*
Tel: 0934 23521/31701
Seats: 658

Weymouth Dorset
Cannon Gloucester
Street
Tel: 0305 785847

Whitby North Yorks
Coliseum Victoria
Square*
Tel: 0947 604641
Seats: 226

Whitefield Lancs
Mayfair Bury Old Road
Tel: 061 766 2369
Seats: 1:578, 2:232

Whitehaven Cumbria
Gaiety Tangier Street
Tel: 0946 3012
Seats: 330

Whitley Bay Tyne &
Wear
Playhouse Park Road
Tel: 0632 523505
Seats: 860

Wigan Greater
Manchester
Ritz Station Road
Tel: 0942 323632
Seats: 1:485, 2:321, 3:106
Unit Four Ormskirk
Road
Tel: 0942 214336
Seats: 1:99, 2:117, 3:88

Wilmslow Ches
Rex Alderley Road*
Tel: 0625 522145
Seats: 838

Wincanton Som
Plaza South Street
Seats: 346

Winchester Hants
Theatre Royal Jewry
Street*
Tel: 0962 843434
Seats: 405

Wisbech Cambs
Unit One Hill Street
Tel: 0945 61224
Seats: 238

Withington Greater
Manchester
Cine-City Wilmslow
Road
Tel: 061 445 3301
Seats: 1:150, 2:150, 3:150

Wokingham Berks
Ritz Easthampstead
Road
Tel: 0734 781888
Seats: 1:200, 2:200

Wolverhampton
West Midlands
Cannon Garrick Street
Tel: 0902 22917/11244
Seats: 1:590, 2:127, 3:94
Light House Lichfield
Street
0902 312032/3/4
Seats: 40

Woodbridge Suffolk
Riverside Theatre
Quay Street
Tel: 039 43 2174
Seats: 280

Woodhall Spa Lincs
Kinema in the Woods
Coronation Road
Tel: 0526 52166
Seats: 365

Worcester Hereford &
Worcs
Odeon Foregate Street
Tel: 0905 24733
Seats: 1:650, 2:109, 3:109

Worksop Notts
Regal Carlton Road
Tel: 0909 482896
Seats:: *1:326, 2:154

Worsley Greater
Manchester
Unit Four Bolton Road
Tel: 061 790 9432
Seats: 1:118, 2:108, 3:86,
4:94

Worthing West Sussex
Connaught Theatre
Union Place*
Tel: 0903 31799/35333
Seats: 400
Dome Marine Parade
Tel: 0903 200461
Seats: 650

Wymondham
Norfolk
Regal Friarscroft Lane
Tel: 0953 602025
Seats: 300

98

Yeovil Somerset
Cannon Court Ash Terrace
Tel: 0935 23663
Three screens

York North Yorks
City Screen Tempert Anderson Hall
Yorkshire Museum
Tel: 0904 627129
🄱 **Film Theatre***
Central Hall,
University
Tel: 0904 59861
Seats: 750
Odeon Blossom Street
Tel: 0904 23040
Seats: 1:834, 2:111, 3:111

CHANNEL ISLANDS AND ISLE OF MAN

Douglas Isle of Man
Summerland Cinema
Seats: 200

St Helier Jersey
Odeon Bath Street
Tel: 0534 24166
Seats: 1:719, 2:171, 3:213

St Peter Port
Guernsey
Beau Sejour Centre
Tel: 0481 26964
Seats: 398

St Saviour Jersey
Cine de France
St Saviour's Road
Tel: 0534 71611
Seats: 291

SCOTLAND

A number of BFI-supported cinemas in Scotland also receive substantial central funding and programming/management support via the Scottish Film Council

Aberdeen Grampian
Cannon Union Street
Tel: 0224 591477/587458
Seats: 1:566, 2:153, 3:146
Capitol Union Street
Tel: 0224 583141
Seats: 2010
Odeon Justice Mill Lane
Tel: 0224 586050
Seats: 1:793, 2:123, 3:123

Annan Dumfries & Gall
Ladystreet, Lady Street
Tel: 046 12 2796
Seats: 450

Arbroath Tayside
Palace James Street
Tel: 0241 73069
Seats: 900

Aviemore Highland
Speyside Aviemore Centre
Tel: 0479 810627
Seats: 721

Ayr Strathclyde
Odeon Burns Statue Square
Tel: 0292 264049
Seats: 1:433, 1:138, 3:138

Bathgate Lothian
Regal North Bridge Street
Tel: 0506 630869
Seats: 467

Brechin Tayside
Kings High Street
Tel: 035 62 2140
Seats: 754

Campbeltown
Strathclyde
Picture House Hall Street
Tel: 0586 2264
Seats: 430

Castle Douglas
Dumfries & Gall
Palace St Andrews Street
Tel: 0556 2141
Seats: 400

Clydebank
Strathclyde
Clydebank 10
Kilbowie Road
Tel: 041 951 1949
Seats: 1:200, 2:200, 3:228, 4:252, 5:385, 6:385, 7:252, 8:228, 9:200, 10:200

Cumnock Strathclyde
Picture House
Glaisnock Street
Tel: 0290 20160
Seats: 652

Dumbarton
Strathclyde
Rialto College Street
Mill Road
Tel: 0389 62763
Seats: 1:175, 2:143

Dumfries Dumfries & Gall
Cannon Shakespeare Street
Tel: 0387 53578
Seats: 532
Robert Burns Centre Film Theatre*
Mill Road
Tel: 0387 64808
Seats: 67

Dundee Tayside
Cannon Seagate
Tel: 0382 26865/25247
Seats: 1:618, 2:319
🄱 **Steps Theatre***
The Wellgate
Tel: 0382 24938/23141
Seats: 250
Victoria, Victoria Road
Tel: 0382 26186
Seats: 350

Dunfermline Fife
Orient Express East Port
Tel: 0383 721934
Seats: 1:209, 2:156, 3:93(V)

Dunoon Strathclyde
Studio John Street
Tel: 0369 4545
Seats: 1:188, 2:70

Edinburgh Lothian
Calton Studio Calton Street
Tel: 031 5567066
Seats: 183
Cameo Home Street
Tollcross
Tel: 031 2284141
Seats: 398
Cannon Lothian Road
Tel: 031 228 1638/299 3030
Three screens
Dominion Newbattle Terrace
Tel: 031 447 2660
Seats: 1:584, 2:296, 3:50
🄱 **Filmhouse**
Lothian Road
Tel: 031 228 2688/6382
Seats: 1:285, 2:90
Metro Nicholson Street
Tel: 031 667 1839
Odeon Clerk Street
Tel: 031 667 7331/2
Seats: 1:695, 2:293, 3:201
Playhouse Leith Walk*
Tel: 031 557 2692
Seats: 3131

Elgin Grampian
Moray Playhouse High Street
Tel: 0343 2680
Seats: 1:330, 2:220

Eyemouth Berwicks
Cinema Church Street
Tel: 0390 50490
Seats: 220

Falkirk Central
Cannon Princess Street
Tel: 0324 31713/23805
Seats: 1:704, 2:128, 3:128

Fort William
Highlands
Studios 1 and 2
Tel: 0397 5095

Galashiels Borders
Kingsway Market Street
Tel: 0896 2767
Seats: 395

Girvan Strathclyde
Vogue Dalrymple Street
Tel: 0465 2101
Seats: 500

Glasgow Strathclyde
Cannon Clarkston Road
Muirend
Tel: 041 637 2641
Seats: 1:482, 2:208, 3:90
Cannon Grand Jamaica Street
Tel: 041 248 4620
Cannon Sauchiehall Street
Tel: 041 332 1592/9513
Seats: 1:970, 2:872, 3:384, 4:206, 5:194
🄱 **Film Theatre Rose Street**
Tel: 041 332 6535
Seats: 404
Grosvenor Ashton Lane
Hillhead
Tel: 041 339 4298
Seats: 1:277, 2:253
Odeon Renfield Street
Tel: 041 332 8701/3413
Seats: 1:1138, 2:852, 3:288, 4:222
Parkhead Forge
Seven screens
Salon Vinicombe Street
Hillhead
Tel: 041 339 4256
Seats: 406

Glenrothes Fife
Kingsway Church Street
Tel: 0592 750980
Seats: 1:294, 2:223

Hamilton Strathclyde
Odeon Townhead Street
Tel: 0698 283802/422384
Seats: 1:466, 2:224, 3:310

Inverness Highland
🄱 **Eden Court**
Bishops Road
Tel: 0463 221718/239841

Seats: 1:797, 2:70
La Scala Strothers Lane
Tel: 0463 233302
Seats: 1:438, 2:255

Inverurie Grampian
Victoria West High Street
Tel: 0467 21436
Seats: 473

Irvine Strathclyde
Magnum Harbour Street
Tel: 0294 78381
Seats: 323
WMR Film Centre Bank Street
Tel: 0294 79900/76817
Seats: 252

Kelso Borders
Roxy
Tel: 0573 24609
Seats: 260

Kilmarnock
Strathclyde
Cannon Titchfield Street
Tel: 0563 25234/37288
Seats: 1:602, 2:193, 3:149

Kirkcaldy Fife
bfi **Adam Smith Theatre***
Bennochy Road
Tel: 0592 260498/202855
Seats: 475
Cannon High Street
Tel: 0592 260143/201520

Kirkwall Orkney
Phoenix Junction Road
Tel: 0856 4407
Seats: 500

Lerwick Shetland
North Star Harbour Street
Tel: 0595 3501
Seats: 200

Livingston Lothian
The Cinema Almondvale Centre
Tel: 0506 33163
Seats: 1:168, 2:165

Lockerbie Dumfries & Gall
Rex Bridge Street
Tel: 05762 2547
Seats: 195

Millport Strathclyde
The Cinema (Town Hall)
Clifton Street
Tel: 0475 530741
Seats: 250

Motherwell
Lanarkshire
Civic Theatre*

Newton Stewart
Dumfries & Gall
Cinema Victoria Street
Tel: 0671 2058
Seats: 412

Oban Strathclyde
Highland Theatre George Street*
Tel: 0631 62444
Seats: 420

Paisley Strathclyde
Kelburne Glasgow Road
Tel: 041 889 3612
Seats: 1:275, 2:275

Perth Tayside
Playhouse Murray Street
Tel: 0738 23126
Seats: 1:590, 2:227, 3:196

Peterhead Grampian
Playhouse Queen Street
Tel: 0779 71052
Seats: 731

Pitlochry Tayside
Regal Athal Road
Tel: 0796 2560
Seats: 400

St Andrews Fife
New Picture House North Street
Tel: 0334 73509
Seats: 1:739, 2:94

Saltcoats Strathclyde
La Scala Hamilton Street
Tel: 0294 63345/68999
Seats: 1:301, 2:142

Stirling Central
Allanpark, Allanpark Road
Tel: 0786 74173
Seats: 1:321, 2:287
bfi **MacRobert Centre***
University of Stirling
Tel: 0786 73171
Seats: 500

WALES

Aberaman Aberdare
Grand Theatre*
Cardiff Road
Tel: 0685 872310
Seats: 950

Aberystwyth Dyfed
Commodore Bath Street
Tel: 0970 612421
Seats: 410

Bala Gwynedd
Neuadd Buddig*
Tel: 0678 520 800
Seats: 372

Bangor Gwynedd
Plaza High Street
Tel: 0248 362059
Two screens
Theatr Gwynedd Deiniol Road
Tel: 0248 351707/351708
Seats: 343

Bargoed Mid Glam
Cameo High Street
Tel: 0443 831172
Seats: 302

Barry South Glam
Theatre Royal Broad Street
Tel: 0446 735019
Seats: 496

Brecon Powys
Coliseum Film Centre
Wheat Street
Tel: 0874 2501
Seats: 1:164, 2:164

Brynamman Dyfed
Public Hall Station Road
Tel: 0269 823232
Seats: 838

Brynmawr Gwent
Market Hall Market Square
Tel: 0495 310576
Seats: 320

Builth Wells Powys
Wyeside Arts Centre Castle Street
Tel: 0982 552555
Seats: 210

Caerphilly Mid Glam
Castle Market Street
Tel: 0222 868083
Seats: 1:375, 2:130

Cardiff South Glam
Cannon Queen Street
Tel: 0222 31715
Seats: 1:616, 2:313, 3:152
bfi **Chapter Market Road**
Tel: 0222 396061
Seats: 1:195, 2:78
Monico Pantbach Road
Tel: 0222 691505
Seats: 1:500, 2:156
Monroe, Globe Centre
Albany Road
Seats: 216

Odeon Queen Street
Tel: 0222 27058
Seats: 1:448, 2:643
bfi **Sherman Theatre***
Senghennydd Road
Tel: 0222 30451/396844
Seats: 474
St David's Hall*
The Hayes
Tel: 0222 371236/42611
Seats: 1600

Carmarthen Dyfed
Lyric King's Street
Seats: 800

Cwmbran Gwent
Scene The Mall
Tel: 063 33 66621
Seats: 1:115, 2:78, 3:130

Denbigh Powys
Futura
Tel: 0745 715210

Fishguard Dyfed
Studio West Street
Tel: 0348 873421/874051
Seats: 252

Gilfach Goch Mid Glam
Workmen's Hall Glenarvon Terrace
Tel: 044 386 231
Seats: 400

Haverfordwest
Dyfed
Palace Upper Market Street
Tel: 0437 2426
Seats: 538

Holyhead Gwynedd
Empire Stanley Street
Tel: 0407 2093
Seats: 1:350, 2:159

Llandudno Gwynedd
Palladium Gladdheath Street
Tel: 0492 76244
Seats: 355

Llanelli Dyfed
Entertainment Centre Station Road
Tel: 0554 774057/752659
Seats: 1:516, 2:310, 3:122

Merthyr Tydfil Mid Glam
Studio Castle Street
Tel: 0685 3877
Seats: 1:98, 2:198

Milford Haven Dyfed
Torch Theatre St Peters Road
Tel: 064 62 4192/5267
Seats: 297

Mold Clwyd
(bfi) Theatr Clwyd Civic Centre
Tel: 0352 56331
Seats: 1:530, 2:129

Monmouth Gwent
Magic Lantern
Church Street
Tel: 0600 3146
Seats: 124

Newport Gwent
Cannon Bridge Street
Tel: 0633 54326
Seats: 1:572, 2:190, 3:126

Newtown Powys
Regent Broad Street
Tel: 0686 25917
Seats: 210

Pontypool Gwent
Scala Osborne Road
Tel: 049 55 56038
Seats: 197

Porthcawl Mid Glam
Regent Trecco Bay
Tel: 065 671 2103
Seats: 168

Portmadoc Gwynedd
Coliseum Avenue Road
Tel: 0766 2108
Seats: 582

Port Talbot West Glam
Plaza Theatre Talbot Road
Tel: 0639 882856
Seats: 1000

Prestatyn Clwyd
Scala High Street
Tel: O7456 4365
Seats: 314

Pwllheli Gwynedd
Town Hall Cinema
Tel: 0758 613371
Seats: 450

Resolven West Glam
Welfare Hall
Tel: 063 710410
Seats: 600
Seats: 541

Rhyl Clwyd
Apollo High Street
Tel: 0745 53856
Seats: 1:250, 2:225

St Athan South Glam
Astra Llantwit Major RAF St Athan
Tel: 04465 3131 x 4124
Seats: 350

Swansea West Glam
Filmcenta Worcester Place
Tel: 0792 53433
Seats: 650
Odeon Kingsway
Tel: 0792 52351
Seats: 1:708, 2:242, 3:172
Parc Tawe 10
(open from summer 1989)
Studio St Helen's Road
Tel: 0792 460996
Seats: 1:294, 2:190, 3:52

Taibach West Glam
Entertainment Taibach
Seats: 200

Tenby Dyfed
Royal Playhouse White Lion Street
Tel: 0834 4809
Seats: 479

Treorchy Mid Glam
Parc and Dare Hall Station Road
Tel: 0443 773112
Seats: 794

Tywyn Gwynedd
The Cinema
Tel: 0654 710260
Seats: 368

Welshpool Powys
Pola Berriew Street*
Tel: 0938 2145
Seats: 500
Regent Broad Street
Tel: 0686 25917
Seats: 200

Wrexham Clwyd
Hippodrome Henblas Street
Tel: 0978 364479
Seats: 613

NORTHERN IRELAND

Antrim Antrim
Cinema Castle Street
Tel: 084 94 3136
Seats: 400
Coltworthy House Arts Centre
Louth Road

Ballymena Antrim
State Ballymoney Road
Tel: 0266 2306
Seats: 1:215, 2:166

Banbridge Down
Iveagh Huntley Road
Tel: 082 06 22423
Seats: 930

Belfast Antrim
Cannon Fisherwick Place
Tel: 0223 222484/248110
Seats: 1:551, 2:444, 3:281, 4:215
Curzon 300 Ormeau Road
Tel: 0232 491071/641373
Seats: 1:453, 2:360, 3:200
(bfi) Queen's Film Theatre
University Square Mews
Tel: 0232 244857/667687
Seats: 252
The Strand Hollywood Road
Tel: 0232 673500
Four screens

Coleraine Londonderry
Palladium Society Street
Tel: 0265 2948
Seats: 538

Cookstown Tyrone
Ritz Studio Burn Road
Tel: 06487 65182
Seats: 1:192, 2:128

Downpatrick Down
Grand Market Street
Tel: 0396 2104
Seats: 450

Dungannon Tyrone
Astor George's Street
Tel: 08687 23662

Dungiven Derry
St Canice Hall Main Street

Enniskillen Fermanagh
Ritz Forthill Street
Tel: 0365 22096

Seats: 450
Ardhowen Centre Dublin Road
Tel: 0365 23233
Seats: 296

Keady Armagh
Scala Cinema Granemore Road
Tel: 0861 531547
Seats: 200

Kilkeel Down
Vogue Newry Street
Seats: 413

Londonderry Londonderry
Strand, Strand Road
Tel: 0504 262084
Seats: 1:293, 2:178

Magherafelt Londonderry
Cinema Queen Street
Tel: 0648 33172
Seats: 230

Newry Down
Savoy 2 Merchant's Quay
Tel: 0693 67549
Seats: 1:197, 2:58

Portrush Antrim
Playhouse
Tel: 0265 823917

(bfi) – Supported by the BFI through finance, programming assistance or occasional programming/publicity services
* – Part-time or occasional screenings
† – Cinema open seasonally
V – Video

COURSES

Film and TV study courses generally fall into two categories: academic and practical. Listed here are the educational establishments which offer film and television as part of a course or courses. Where a course is mainly practical, this is indicated with a 🅿 next to the course title. In the remaining courses, the emphasis is usually on theoretical study; some of these courses include a minor practical component as described. The information here is drawn from two BFI education booklets – 'Film and television training: A guide to courses' and 'Studying film and tv: A list of courses in higher education'. More information about listed courses can be found in these booklets, along with information on certain further education courses not included here

University of Bath
School of Modern Languages and International Studies
Claverton Down
Bath BA2 7AY
Tel: 0225 826826
BA (Hons) Modern Languages and European Studies
First year lectures and seminars on the language and theory of film, whilst the second and fourth years offer a wide range of options on French films between the wars, the films of the Nouvelle Vague, film and television in German speaking countries and film in Italy. There is a final year option dealing with European cinema in the 70s and 80s. No practical component
MPhil and PhD
Part-time or full-time research degrees in French cinema

Bedford College of Higher Education
Polhill Avenue
Bedford
Tel: 0234 51671
BA (Hons) Combined Studies
Two-year option, Drama in Camera (3 hours per week) involving critical work on image formation, film and television, and practical work involving photography and video or 8mm filmmaking. Facilities include 3-camera TV studio

University of Birmingham
Department of Cultural Studies
Faculty of Commerce and Social Sciences
PO Box 363
Birmingham B15 2TT
Tel: 021 414 6060/6061
BA (Combined Hons) Media and Cultural Studies
A half degree, either combined with another Arts subject or as base for a General degree. Course (brochure available) includes media history; year's course on contemporary media, particularly press and TV; option of specialist dissertation on media; some practical SLR photography (Year 1), video (Year 2), plus short period of placement in local media organisations. This new department will also be offering a full honours degree in Media, Culture and Society for a first intake in October 1989

Department of French Language and Literature
BA (Hons) French
Four-year course which includes options on French cinema (Year 1), documentary film (Year 2) and the practice of transposing works of fiction to the screen (Year 4)

Bournemouth and Poole
College of Art and Design
School of Film, Television and Audio Visual Production
Wallisdown Road
Poole
Dorset BH12 5HH
Tel: 0202 595281

🅿 **BTEC ND in Audio Visual Production**
A new course, offering initial experience of tape slide, video production and audio recording at a practical level. Facilities include 9 projector Multivision rig, 4 track and 8 track music studios, VHS cameras and edit suite and full photographic rostrum. Supported by design studies, creative writing, music and word processing

🅿 B/TEC Higher National Diploma in Design (Film and Television)
An extensive two-year course based around the production process. All areas of film and television production are covered, with an emphasis on drama and documentary. The majority of work is student originated, with an equal emphasis on film and tape. The course has a substantial input from, and contact with, working professionals within the industry
The course has full ACTT accreditation. Facilities include: Arriflex SR and BL Film cameras, Nagra 4.2 recorders, Steenbeck, pic-syncs, PAG dubbing suite, 2 TV studios, 2 Hitachi FP60 cameras, 2 FP21 and 1 FP40 cameras, Sony 4800 recorders, Sony 5 series edit suites, Quantel paintbox, video and film rostra, 4 and 8 track music studios etc

🅿 Advanced Diploma in Media Production
Film/television option. One-year production opportunity for post B/TEC, postgraduate and mid-career students. Application through personal statement of intent and interview. Equipment as HND, above

University of Bristol
Department of Drama
29 Park Row
Bristol BS1 5LT
Tel: 0272 303030
BA Drama
Three-year course, includes an element of film/TV studies plus optional practical courses in Years 2 and 3

🅿 Postgraduate Certificate in Radio, Film and Television
One-year practical course. Possibility of making fictional or documentary films, a radio play and videotapes. Film and TV activities include both location and studio work. Facilities include 4-

camera colour studio of full broadcast standard; colour portapacks; Arriflex cameras; Nagra tape-recorders; film and video editing facilities: rostrum camera; props, furniture, scenery and costumes, stores and workshops. Close links with the industry

Brunel University
Department of Human Sciences
Uxbridge
Middx UB8 3PH
Tel: 0895 56461
BSc Communication and Information Studies
Four-year interdisciplinary course which aims to give an understanding of the social, intellectual and practical dimensions of the new technologies. Includes practical courses in computing and in video production and technology. All students undertake three periods (five months) of work placement

College of Cardiff
University of Wales
PO Box 908
French Section
EUROS
Cardiff Tel: 0222 875000
BA French
Study of French cinema included as part of optional courses. Small practical component
BA German
Study of contemporary German cinema forms part of both compulsory and optional courses

Polytechnic of Central London
Faculty of Communication
18-22 Riding House Street
London W1P 7PD
Tel: 01 486 5811

🅿 BA (Hons) Film, Video and Photographic Arts
Gives equal emphasis to filmmaking and to film theory and criticism. After a general introductory year, students choose either a Film Option or a Photography Option. Film Option students

combine theoretical study with filmmaking in years 2 and 3. The film course is ACTT-accredited. Facilities include: TV studio with 3 Pye LDK 2 colour cameras; Cox chromakey and central Dynamics extended effects units; Pye colour telecine/teleslide unit; Sony Mark 5 video tape recorders; 2 VTR edit suites; 3 sound studios, one with Syncon 12 channel/12 group multi-track mixing console, Scully 8 track, Sony PCM digital unit, Studer mastering and reduction machines, etc

🅿 BA (Hons) Media Studies
This course studies the history, sociology and aesthetics of all the mass media, including film and TV, and teaches the practice of print journalism, radio and TV production. Students devote half their time to theory and half to practice. From the second year there are practical options in video, radio or journalism. The video course is ACTT-accredited. Facilities as above.

Linked MA and Postgraduate Diploma in Film and Television Studies
Part-time evening course over 10 terms with study weekends. Exemption from first three terms for students with substantial undergraduate experience of film studies, postgraduate diploma awarded after seven terms. An academic course with the study of film/TV fiction and the institutions of cinema and television as its principal concerns. No practical component
BSc and BSc (Hons) in Photographic and Electronic Imaging Sciences
Aims to give students a thorough grounding in scientific method and to develop ability in relating principles to applications in theoretical situations and in practice. Students are encouraged to gain knowledge and

understanding of imaging science and technology. Third year modules allow students to specialise in photography, image science or electronic and computer imaging or to select a mix of these
MPhil and PhD Film Studies (CNAA)
Part-time or full-time research degrees in film and television history, theory and criticism

Central Manchester College
East Manchester Centre
Taylor Street
Gorton
Manchester M18 8DF
Tel: 061 223 8282 x476
🅿 B/TEC National Diploma in Audio Visual Design
Multi-disciplinary integrated, group-based course working between graphics, video, film/animation, sound recording, photography and tape/slide production. Assessment is continuous, based on practical projects linked to theoretical studies. Equipment includes 4 VHS portapacks and cameras, VHS Camcorder, 2 JVC KY1900 cameras, VHS and low-band U-Matic edit suites, 16mm Bolex camera, VHS effects generator plus supporting studio/portable sound, lighting equipment and computer graphics

Christ Church College
North Holmes Road
Canterbury
Kent CT1 1QU
Tel: 0227 762444
🅿 BA (Hons)/BSc (Hons)
Combined Studies
Radio, film and television can be studied along with one other subject. Course introduces students to an understanding of radio, film and TV as media of communication and creative expression, and the practice of production skills in each of the three media. Where possible, industrial attachments are arranged. Production facilities include: Super 8mm and 16mm film

equipment; fully colourised 3-camera TV studio with two editing suites, portapacks and supporting sound and lighting equipment

Coventry (Lanchester) Polytechnic

Faculty of Art and Design
Department of Graphic Design and Communication
Gosford Street
Coventry CV1 5RZ
Tel: 0203 224166

BA (Hons) Communication Studies

Three-year course which includes optional modules in Film Studies and Media Institutions in Year 2 and an optional module in Film Studies in Year 3. Includes a practical component

P BA (Hons) Fine Art

BA (Hons) Graphic Design

Students may specialise in film and video within the Fine Art and Graphic Design degrees

P MA/PgD Electronic Graphics

The course offers full-time students the choice of a three-term postgraduate diploma, or four-term MA. All students register initially for the postgraduate diploma and may, on successful completion, progress to the MA. Most of the time is spent using the computing equipment for the generation of electronic images, although a theoretical component supports this. Facilities include a computer studio containing a network of computer graphics workstations, video suite and video editing facilities

Derbyshire College of Higher Education

Faculty of Art and Design
Kedleston Road
Derby DE3 1GB
Tel: 0332 47181

P BA (Hons) Photographic Studies

Three-year course divided

into two parts of five and four terms. The course offers students the ability to specialise in film/video practice in addition to the normal photographic and academic routes. Part 1 concentrates on development of ideas and investigation of ways they may be carried out. In Part 2 students are expected to assume considerable responsibility for their own work programmes. Academic studies form 30% of the course. Creative and inventive use of the media is encouraged from conception to projection. Facilities include: Super 8mm sound and silent cameras, editing and projection; 16mm Bolex, Pathe, Auricon, Beaulieu, Eclair NPR, time lapse and rostrum cameras; Uhers, Nagra, Revox and 4-track Teac recorders; 6-plate flat-bed and pic sync editing; animation stand for 16mm and QAR video animation; VHS and U-Matic portable video recorders; U-Matic edit suite; studio; cinema with 35mm, 16mm and video projection

Postgraduate Diploma in Film Studies

Part-time evening course over two years, with study weekends. An academic course having the study of film and the institution of cinema as its principal concerns. No practical component

Dewsbury College

School of Art and Design
Cambridge Street
Batley
West Yorkshire
WF17 5JB
Tel: 0924 474401

P B/TEC National Diploma in Design (Communications) Video Production and Related Studies

Two-year course in video production in which some role specialisation is possible in the second year. Students are placed in industry for a minimum of four weeks during Year 2. Facilities include: VHS and U-Matic Portapacs; 2 U-

Matic low-band edit suites with TBCs and FX generator; 2-camera studio with full mixing and Chromakey; computer graphics with animation, frame grab and video interface; computer tapeslide production; 16mm cameras; animation rostrum; still photography studios and darkrooms. Yearly intake: 16 students

Dorset Institute of Higher Education

Department of Communication and Media
Wallisdown Road
Poole
Dorset BH1 5BB
Tel: 0202 524111

P BA (Hons) Production

A three-year course covering the academic, practical, aesthetic, technical and professional aspects of work in the media. The course is equally divided between practical and theoretical studies. After Year 1 students can specialise in audio, video or computer graphics, leading to a major production project in Year 3. In addition students complete a piece of individual research in the area of Communication Processes. Facilities include 4-colour CCTV studio with DVE equipment, 6 U-Matic edit suites, 6 U-Matic O/B units, 5 sound studios (including a radio studio linked directly to BBC Radio Solent), 21 computer graphics workstations including Iris 2400 Turbo, DG MV400 and 3 Sony SMC 70s

Ealing College of Higher Education

School of Humanities
St Mary's Road
Ealing W5 5RF
Tel: 01 579 4111

BA (Hons) Humanities
Students take 12 units as part of degree, of which two may be in film studies. No practical component

University of East Anglia

School of English and American Studies
Norwich NR4 7TJ
Tel: 0603 56161

BA (Hons) Film and English Studies
A Joint Major programme which integrates Film and Television study with Literature, History and Cultural Studies. Course includes either a practical project on film or video or an independent dissertation on a film or television topic.

BA (Hons) in Literature, History, Linguistics, Drama or American Studies
Film can be taken as a substantial Minor programme (up to 45% of degree work) in combination with any of these Major subjects
There is no formal practical element in these programmes, but students have access to instruction in the use of 8mm, 16mm and video equipment, and have the option of submitting practical work

MA Film Studies
One-year full-time taught programme. MA is awarded 50% on coursework, 50% on individual dissertation. Courses include: Early Cinema, Film Industry/ Film History, Structuralist and Post-structuralist Film Theory, British Cinema. There is scope for work on television as well as on other aspects of cinema

MPhil and PhD
Students are accepted for research degrees

Edinburgh College of Art

Visual Communications Department
School of Design and Crafts
Lauriston Place
Edinburgh EH3 9DF
Tel: 031 229 9311

P BA (Hons) in Design

Following a Foundation course in Art and Design this course offers an intensive introduction to film, television, and still photography. Practical production techniques, with a complementary series of critical and historical talks and screenings. Years 3 and 4 involve group and individual projects allowing students to develop their own creative styles in the media of photography, audio, tape-slide, video, film, and animation. Strong links exist with the other elements of the Visual Communications Department, which covers illustration, graphic design and computer graphics. Facilities include 8-track sound recording and mixing, Super 8mm, 16mm cameras, 16mm rostrum camera for animation, VHS and U-Matic video equipment and edit suites

University of Exeter
American and Commonwealth Arts School of English Queen's Building The Queen's Drive Exeter EX4 4QH Tel: 0392 264263
BA (Hons) American and Commonwealth Arts
BA (Combined Hons) American and Commonwealth Arts and English
BA (Combined Hons) American and Commonwealth Arts and Music
BA (Combined Hons) American and Commonwealth Arts and Italian
Students can take up to a third of their degree in Film Studies, with the emphasis on American film. Combined Hons with Italian also include a course on Italian cinema and culture. No practical component
MA, MPhil and PhD
Students wishing to take an MA degree by coursework and dissertation or an MPhil or PhD by thesis alone can be accommodated and candidates with proposals in any aspect of American or Commonwealth cinema will be considered. Applications for postgraduate study in

American Film History will be particularly welcome

School of Modern Languages Italian Department
BA (Combined Hons) Italian
Italian combined with another subject. One of the six courses that students take is Italian cinema and culture. In general, Neo-realism to the present day
School of Education St Luke's Exeter EX1 2LU Tel: 0392 76311
MEd/BPhil
Film/TV occupies 50% of this postgraduate course. Some practical work in portable video, CCTV and 8mm. Colour TV studio with editing facilities
PGCE
Includes a unit of media studies. Some practical work

Glasgow College
Department of Communication Cowcaddens Road Glasgow G4 0BA Tel: 041 332 7090
BA Communication Studies
Three-year course examining the place of mass communication in contemporary society. Includes practical studies in print, television, advertising and public relations

University of Glasgow
Department of Theatre, Film and TV Studies Glasgow G12 8QQ Tel: 041 339 8855
MA Joint Honours in Film and Television Studies
Four-year undergraduate course. Film/TV Studies represents 50% of an Honours degree or 30% of an Ordinary degree. Year 1 is concerned with Film and TV as 'languages', the institutional structures of British TV, and the implications of recent developments in technology and programming. Year 2 is structured under two headings: Genre in Film

and Television and Film, Television and British National Culture. Years 3 and 4 consist of eight Honours courses, four to be taken in each year. There is also a compulsory practical course, involving the production of a video

Department of French Glasgow G12 8QQ Tel: 041 339 8855
BA (Hons) French
Study of French Cinema is a one-year special subject comprising one two-hour seminar per fortnight plus weekly screenings. No practical component

Goldsmiths' College, University of London
Lewisham Way London SE14 6NW Tel: 01 692 7171
P BA Communication Studies
This new course brings together theoretical analyses in social sciences and cultural studies with practical work in TV, film, photography, journalism, radio and electronic graphics. The practical element contitutes 50% of the total degree course. The theoretical element includes media history and sociology, textual and cultural studies, personal and interpersonal contexts of communication and media management
BA Anthropology and Communication Studies
Half of this course constitutes Communication Studies and is split equally between practice and theory. Practical options include TV, film, journalism, photography, radio and electronic graphics. The theory component of the Communications is concerned with media history, sociology, textual and cultural studies
BA Communication Studies/Sociology

Communication studies constitutes half of this course and is split equally between theoretical studies and practice. Practical options include TV, film, photography, journalism, radio and electronic graphics. The theory component of communications is concerned with psychology, media sociology, cultural studies, semiotics and media history
P Diploma in Communications
One-year full-time course with practical work in one of the following: TV and video, film, radio, photography, electronic graphics and creative writing. Students complete 10,000-word dissertation (or three 3,000-word essays) which counts for 30% at final assessment. Equipment includes 8mm, 16mm, VHS and U-Matic editing facilities, multi-camera TV studio, Paintbox, computer graphics laboratory and video animator, photographic studio, colour and black and white darkrooms
Department of Continuing and Community Education
A programme of evening courses are offered which include video production and editing

Gwent College of Higher Education
Faculty of Art and Design Clarence Place Newport Gwent NP9 0UW Tel: 0633 259984
P B/TEC Higher National Diploma in Film and Video Production: Live Action and Animation
Two-year intensive vocational course. Two strands: Live Action: lighting camera operating, sound recording, film and video editing, scriptwriting, directing and art directing, and producing; and Animation: scripting and storyboarding, 2 and 3D animation techniques and theory, and post production skills. All

students go on placement with BBC, ITV or other production companies. Facilities include: Arriflex, Eclair and Bolex cameras, Nagra tape recorders, Steenbeck editors, Nielson Hordell rostrum camera, and VHS and low band U-Matic production and editing

Harrogate College of Arts and Technology
Hornbeam Park
Hookstone Road
Harrogate HG1 8QT
Tel: 0423 879466

P B/TEC Diploma in Design (Communications)
Two-year course providing training in a range of high tech arts subjects. Options include video production, TV graphics, computer imaging and animation, DTP, basic design, animation and model-making, sound creation, radio and tape/slide. Research and scripting are included in all areas. Course is 80% practical and vocationally based. Entry requirements: four GCSE or equivalent plus folder of relevant work. Equipment includes: 3 U-Matic edit benches, 3 portable packs, TV studio with 6 colour cameras, TV graphics, Chromakey and SEG/TBC computer graphics, 15 Amigas/Macs with laser and colour printers, purpose-built sound, radio and TV rooms and portable recorders. Also available for course use: 16mm film and darkrooms

Harrow College of Higher Education
Faculty of Art and Design
Northwick Park
Harrow
Middlesex HA1 3TP
Tel: 01 864 5422

P BA (Hons) in Photography, Film and Video
A practical course with integrated theoretical, historical and critical studies. After a first year which is both fundamental and experimental, students may specialise or

continue using a variety of media. 70% practical, 30% theoretical. Equipment includes Arriflex, Eclair and Bolex 16mm cameras; Bolex, Nalcom, Canon and Eumig Super 8mm cameras; three studio colour video cameras; colour portapacks; Nagra, Uher, Philips, Revox, Tanberg, Ferrograph and Teac tape-recorders; 8mm, 16mm, VHS and U-Matic editing facilities; specialist AV facility; computer image generators with video interface

P BA (Hons) in Photographic Media Studies
Three-year part-time course designed to enable professionally qualified photographers to strengthen an interest in the contemporary scope and limitations of photographic media. Mainly theoretical but with a practical composition in the third year

Hatfield Polytechnic
School of Humanities
PO Box 109
College Lane
Hatfield
Herts AL10 9AB
Tel: 07072 79403

BA (Hons) Contemporary Studies
Full-time and part-time course for mature students. Media Studies is a one-year optional course for second year students and introduces study of media practices and institutions/apparatuses. No practical component

University of Hull
Department of Drama
Cottingham Road
Hull HU6 7RX
Tel: 0482 46311

BA Joint and Special Honours
Introduction to film and TV studies in Year 1. Honours students may opt for practical courses in TV and radio in subsequent years. Special Honours students may also opt for practical course in either filmmaking or TV directing (five hours per

week for two terms). Equipment includes 16mm cameras, TV and radio studios, film and U-Matic editing

MA in Theatre and Media Production
One-year course with options in filmmaking and TV directing

Humberside College of Higher Education
School of Visual Communication Design
Queens Gardens
Hull HU1 3DH
Tel: 0482 224121

P BA (Hons) Graphic Design
Students may specialise in film/video, photography, graphic design or illustration. After a common first term, film primers are introduced in the second term, and specialisation may begin at the start of term 3. The course is essentially practical, with a strong theoretical/critical back-up and a programme of visiting animators and filmmakers. Most work is in documentary, animation and public information film, but an increasing amount of work is being carried out using video formats. Computer graphics is a new major component. Equipment includes Bolex and Eclair cameras, Uher, Nagra and Tandberg recorders, VHS and U-Matic video portapacks; 16mm editing tables and U-Matic editing suites; film/video studio; three animation stands (16mm); video line-test rostrum; optical printer; computer animation systems including Picaso; post-production/dubbing sound rooms; TV and sound studios
School of Fine Art

P BA (Hons) Fine Art
Time-based media: 8mm and 16mm film; VHS and U-Matic video; sound; photography; and related live work. Course is essentially practical (80%), projects being student-initiated

following the first general introductory term. Work frequently crosses disciplines including printmaking, painting and sculpture. Supported by a programme of visiting tutors, artists, film/videomakers, screenings and critical/theoretical studies (20%). Equipment as for BA (Hons) Graphic Design

Institute of Education, University of London
Joint Department of English and Media Studies
20 Bedford Way
London WC1H 0AL
Tel: 01 636 1500

PGCE English and Media Studies
One-year full-time teacher training course, including practical component. Additional course options in TV, Film and Media Studies

PGCE Curriculum Options in Film Studies and in Media/Television Studies
Options are open to PGCE students from any specialisation (equivalent to approximately 20% of overall commitment)

MA Film and TV Studies for Education
One-year full-time or two-year part-time. Core courses on the Theory and Practice of Film and TV Education, and Film and TV History and Theory. Options on Realist and Anti-Realist Theory and Practice in Film and TV, or Children, Education and TV (including practical component). Plus dissertation

MA Media Studies/MA Media Education
(awaiting approval; one year full-time, two years part-time)

Associateship
Individualised courses for mature academics who wish to spend one year studying and considering the latest pedagogical and intellectual developments in their field

MPhil and PhD
Supervision of theses in the area of Film, TV and Media Education

Kent Institute of Art and Design

Rochester upon Medway College
(formerly Medway College of Design)
Fort Pitt
Rochester
Kent ME1 1DZ
Tel: 0634 44815

P B/TEC Higher National Diploma in Advertising and Editorial Photography
Two-year course which includes the possibility of specialising in film/TV

Kent Institute of Art and Design at Maidstone
(formerly Maidstone College of Art)
Oakwood Park
Oakwood Road
Maidstone
Kent ME16 8AG
Tel: 0622 57286/9

P BA (Hons) Communication Media Pathway in Time-Based Studies
Full-time production and theory centred and mainly video based, seeking to explore new creative developments in moving imagery as well as linking to other pathways through such areas as animation and computer generated imagery

University of Kent

Rutherford College
Canterbury
Kent CT2 7NX
Tel: 0227 764000
BA Combined Hons
A Part 1 course on Narrative Cinema is available to all Humanities students in Year 1. The Part 2 component in Film Studies in Years 2 and 3 can vary from 25% to 75% of a student's programme. Courses include Film Theory, British Cinema, Early Film Form, and Sexual Difference and Cinema. The rest of a student's programme consists of courses from any other Humanities subject. No practical component
MA and PhD
There are no courses at postgraduate level but students are accepted for MA or PhD by thesis

King Alfred's College of Higher Education

Sparkford Road
Winchester SO22 4NR
Tel: 0962 841515 x231
P BA (Hons) (CNAA) in Drama, Theatre and TV
Three-year practical course. Well-equipped studios

Kingston Polytechnic

School of Three Dimensional Design
Knights Park
Kingston-upon-Thames
Surrey KT1 2QJ
Tel: 01 549 6151
Post-Graduate Diploma in Film and Television Design
One-year course leading to Polytechnic Diploma

Department of History of Art and Design and Contextual Studies
BA (Hons) Architecture
Options in History of Film. No practical component
BA (Hons) Fine Art
Two-year Complementary Studies course. First year is an 18-week introductory course. Second year is a 12-week course on Modernism in the cinema. No practical component
BA (Hons) Three Dimensional Design
Second year Complementary Studies: one-term option on scenography
BA (Hons) Graphic Design
First year Complementary Studies: History of Animation and History of Documentary. No practical component
School of Graphic Design
P BA (Hons) Graphic Design
Includes some practical filmmaking (animation)

School of Languages
Penrhyn Road
Kingston-upon-Thames
Surrey
BA (Hons) Modern Arts
Two-term option course in Year 2 on French Cinema since 1930. No practical component

Kingsway College

Grays Inn Centre
Sidmouth Street
Grays Inn Road
London WC1H 8JB
Tel: 01 837 8185
P B/TEC National Diploma
Two-year full-time course in photography and photographic laboratory skills
P B/TEC National Diploma in Media
Two-year full-time course primarily in lens media
P GCE A Level
Two-year full-time media studies course, including practical filmmaking, video and photography
P Super 8 Live Action Class/Workshop
One evening per week
P Super 8 Animation Class/Workshop
One evening per week
Equipment includes 3-camera monochrome TV studio, Betamax and VHS portapacks, Betamax and VHS editing facilities, Super 8mm cameras and editing facilities, portable lighting, animation rostrum, and b/w and colour photography processing and printing facilities

Leicester Polytechnic

Department of Art History
PO Box 143
Leicester LE1 9BH
Tel: 0533 551551
BA (Hons) History of Art and Design in the Modern Period
Introduction to film studies is a compulsory one-term element of Year 1. Film and TV studies is one of four options in Years 2 and 3. No practical component
BA Art and Design Courses
Introduction to film and TV studies is a three-term course for second year students. No practical component
BA Graphic Design
Introduction to film and TV studies is a two-term course for second year students

University of Leicester

Centre for Mass Communication Research
104 Regent Road
Leicester LE1 7LT
Tel: 0533 523863
MA Mass Communications
One-year taught course studying the organisation and impact of the mass media both nationally and internationally and providing practical training in research methods

Liverpool Polytechnic

Faculty of Art and Design
Department of Graphic Design
2a Myrtle Street
Liverpool L7 7DN
Tel: 051 207 3581
P BA (Hons) Graphic Design
Film/Animation is a specialised option within the Graphic Design degree. After a general first year a number of students may specialise in Film/Animation in their second and third years

University of Liverpool

Department of Communication Studies
Chatham Street
Liverpool L69 3BX
Tel: 051 794 2653/6
BA Combined Hons (Arts)
BA Combined Hons (Social Studies)
BA Joint Hons (English and Communication Studies)
Film and television studies form a substantial component within the above degrees. In Year 1 there is an introductory course on Communication, involving work on photography and television; in Year 2, courses on Broadcasting, Film Studies and Drama; and in Year 3, a course on Documentary and a course on Persuasion which includes an element of media analysis. No practical component

London College of Printing

Department of Photography, Film and Television
Elephant and Castle
London SE1 6SB
Tel: 01 735 9100

P BA (Hons) Film and Video

The first autonomous course in Film and Video leading to the award of BA (Hons) degree. Main concerns are Women's Cinema, Third World Cinema, Popular Culture and Film. Stress on experimentation and innovation, education, independent filmmakers rather than specialised technicians. Practice/Theory ratio is 70:30. Course stresses integration of theory and practice. As from 1988 the course will include an option in Animation. Facilities include 8mm, 16mm film and VHS, U-Matic video, production and postproduction facilities. This course is accredited by ACTT

London International Film School

Department F15
24 Shelton Street
London WC2H 9HP
Tel: 01 836 9642

P Two-year Diploma course in the Art and Technique of Filmmaking

A practical course teaching skills necessary for professional employment in the industry, recognised by LEAs and the ACTT. Courses commence in January, April and September. Each student works on one or more films in every term. Approximately half of each term is spent in filmmaking, half in practical tuition, lectures, tutorials, film analysis and scriptwriting. Facilities include two viewing theatres, two fully-equipped studios, a video rehearsal studio, and comprehensive editing and sound departments. Equipment includes 35mm Mitchell, 16mm and 35mm Arriflex cameras, Nagra sound recorders and Steenbeck and Prevost editing tables

University College London

Department of Spanish and Latin American Studies
Gower Street
London WC1 6BT
Tel: 01 380 7121

BA (Hons) Spanish

Two courses are available on Images of Women in Latin American Film and Narrative: one at MA level, the other at undergraduate level. No practical component

Manchester Polytechnic

Department of Communication Arts and Design
Capitol Building
School Lane
Didsbury
Manchester M20 0HT
Tel: 061 434 3331

P BA (Hons) Design for Communication Media

Film and television is a main area of study offering a three-year full-time course with options in film and TV production, or TV production design (set design). The Film and TV course is chiefly practical and includes research and scriptwriting, directing for film and TV, film production, TV and sound operations, scenic design, animation, photography and TV graphics. Facilities include two colour TV studios, record and edit suite, 3 sound studios, scenic workshops, rostrum camera room, video portapacks, 16mm cameras, cutting rooms and cinema. Equipment includes 16mm Arriflex and CP16 cameras, Nagra and Uher sound recorders, Intercine and Prevost editing tables, Hi-band U-Matic video recorders, VHS portable camera units with JVC KY1900 cameras

Department of English and History
Aytoun Street
Manchester M1
Tel: 061 228 6171

BA (Hons) Humanities/Social Studies

Film/TV small component. A mixed course of English, Film and Current TV News

BA (Hons) English Studies/Historical Studies

Film/TV small component. A mixed course including documentary film, TV soap opera and TV news. No practical component

Department of General Studies
Chester Street
Manchester M1 5GD
Tel: 061 228 6171

BA (Hons) General Arts

One-year course for students with Dip HE or equivalent. Mass Media: a multi-disciplinary course which applies the methodologies of the social sciences and the humanities to the mass media. No practical component

Dip HE

Two-year course which includes an introduction to film and film theory in Year 1 and a course on film as propaganda in Year 2. No practical component

University of Manchester

Department of Drama
Oxford Road
Manchester M13 9PL
Tel: 061 273 3333

BA Single and Joint Honours in Drama

Normally an optional course in film studies in Year 3 with a compulsory course for Single Honours in Year 2 (optional for Joint). No practical component

MLitt

Possibility for research theses on aspects of film and TV drama

Department of Education
Oxford Road
Manchester M13 9PL
Tel: 061 275 3463

MEd in Education and the Mass Media

Course offered on a full- or part-time basis, which enables teachers and youth and community workers to explore effective communication techniques within their fields of work. Some practical work. Visits to media organisations and contributions from media specialists are arranged

Diploma in Advanced Study in Education and the Mass Media

Designed for educators from the UK and overseas, this full- or part-time course provides an introduction to the study of mass media systems and the use of audiovisual material for teaching and learning

Middlesex Polytechnic

Modular Scheme
Combined Studies
Trent Park
Cockfosters Road
Barnet
Herts EN4 0PT
Tel: 01 368 1299

BA (Hons) Combined Studies

Modular system degree. In years 2 and 3 students take twelve modules. From the range on offer a student may take four on film or TV

BA (Hons) History of Art, Design and Film

Modular system degree. First two years as combined studies. Third year allows greater specialisation and includes dissertation which could be in film or TV studies. The modules are: British Cinema; History of the Cinema; Hollywood, Authorship and Genre; Art and the Mass Media; Realisms; Independent Film. No practical component

Faculty of Art and Design
Cat Hill
Barnet
Herts EN4 8HT
Tel: 01 440 5181

BA (Hons) Contemporary Cultural Studies

One-year course (or 2/3 years part-time) designed for students who possess a Dip HE or equivalent (2 years full-time degree-level work). Film and television are studied as aspects of cultural practice. No practical component

P MA in Video

A one year full-time

course (48 weeks) emphasising the creative aspects of professional video production in the independent sector. Intended for graduate students with considerable low-band video experience. The course covers all aspects of the production cycle, with an emphasis on scriptwriting. 50% practical; 50% theoretical.

Napier Polytechnic
Photography Department
61 Marchment Road
Marchment
Edinburgh EH9 1HU
Tel: 031 444 2266
BA Photographic Studies
Three years full-time with option of specialising in film and television production in third year
HNC (Scottish Vocational Educational Council) Audio Visual Techniques
One year full-time or two years part-time. Students should have previously done an ONC or similar course

National Film and Television School
Beaconsfield Studios
Station Road
Beaconsfield
Bucks HP9 1LG
Tel: 0494 671234
P The School offers a three-year, full-time professional course leading to an Associateship (ANFTS) with specialisation in the training of producers, directors, writers, lighting camera operators, editors, animators, art directors, sound recordists, documentary and film composition. Students are encouraged to interchange roles in any practical activity. Approximately 30 students are admitted annually, with five or six places reserved for overseas students. Average age is 26 years. Previous experience in film or a related field is expected. Facilities include three studios, fully equipped to professional standards,

hi-band and low-band U-Matic video editing suites, 20 film editing rooms, professional cameras and tape recorders, lighting equipment for studio and location work, 35mm/16mm Oxberry rostrum camera with 3-D facility, viewing facilities. The school is funded by a partnership of Government and industry (film and TV). Its graduates occupy leading roles in all aspects of film and TV production. It is a full member of CILECT (Centre International de Liaison des Ecoles de Cinéma et de Télévision) and actively co-operates with professional bodies in the UK and abroad

Newcastle upon Tyne Polytechnic
Faculty of Art and Design
Squires Building
Sandyford Road
Newcastle upon Tyne
NE1 8ST
Tel: 091 232 6002
P **BA (Hons) Media Production**
Three-year course, started in September 1986. Practical course with fully integrated theoretical and critical components in which students are offered the opportunity to specialise in individual programmes of work. Organised into three stages with the Media Theory programme continuing throughout. Facilities include nine new computer workstations, a sound studio, U-Matic 3-camera studio with mixing and effects facility, edit suite, U-Matic portapack, Super 8mm and 16mm cameras and Rostra
BA (Hons) History of Modern Art, Design and Film
Offered as a three-year full-time course or as a five-year part-time course (over two evenings a week). Film Studies is given equal weighting with painting and architecture/design in the first two years of both the full- and part-time courses. Thereafter a student can spend up to

75% of his or her time involved with the study of film
MPhil
There are possibilities for research degrees in either film theory or practice

University of Newcastle upon Tyne
Department of English Language and Literature
Newcastle upon Tyne
NE1 7RU
Tel: 0632 328511
BA (Hons) English
Third year optional course: Introduction to Film (mainly Hollywood interests). No practical component
BA (Hons) Modern Languages
Optional final year course: studies in European film
MA English and American Literature of the 20th Century
Optional course in contemporary film narrative. Optional course in TV studies

Department of Spanish and Latin-American Studies
Claremont Bridge
Newcastle upon Tyne
NE1 8ST
Tel: 0632 328511
BA (Hons) Spanish
Undergraduate special subject Hispanic Drama and Film
MA Hispanic Drama and Film
MA in film is in two parts: Bunuel and post-50s Spanish Film. No practical component

North Cheshire College
Padgate Campus
Fearnhead Lane
Fearnhead
Warrington WA2 0DB
Tel: 0925 814343
BA (Joint Hons) Media with Business Management and Information Technology
A modular system degree. The media component combines practical production work in video, sound recording, photography, graphics and print media, with academic analysis of the

media through modules on Forms, Representations, Institutions and Audiences. The course structure enables students to relate their business and information technology studies to their work in media. Year 3 calls for specialisation in one medium of production, combined with a choice of options in the theory course. The programme includes one term in Year 2 devoted to work experience in the media industry and institutions. Facilities include well-equipped graphics and photography studios, multi-track sound studio and desk-top publishing. There is a three colour-camera TV studio with extensive post-production facilities, chromakey, U-Matic and VHS edit suites, U-Matic and VHS location cameras and equipment
BA (Hons) Mature Student Programme
A modular system degree, designed specifically for mature student entry. A broad range of modules is available, and students can choose some or all of the media modules, theoretical and practical
Diploma in Media Education
A part-time postgraduate Diploma designed for serving teachers in the primary, secondary and further education sectors who are, or who wish to be, involved in teaching some aspect of media education. The course calls for analysis of key theoretical issues, consideration of issues of curriculum and pedagogy, together with practical work in video, sound and photography. Attendance is either one evening a week over two years or day release over one year

North East London Polytechnic
School of Art and Design
Greengate Street
London E13
Tel: 01 590 7722
P **BA (Hons) Fine Art**
During the first year of

the course students can experiment with each of the disciplines that are available but can also specialise in film and video throughout the three years. Facilities include studio, U-Matic colour cameras and edit suite, Sony portapacks, 16mm and Super 8mm film cameras, Revox and Teac tape-recorders

Department of Cultural Studies
Livingstone House
Livingstone Road
Stratford
London E15 2LL
BA (Hons) Cultural Studies
Three-year course offering options on media, film and photography in Years 2 and 3. Also includes a practical component (20%) in video, slide-tape and photography over all three years
BSc (Hons) New Technology (Interdisciplinary Studies)
This new degree examines the development, applications and implications of new technologies. Options will involve the study and practice of video, computer graphics and newspaper production

Polytechnic of North London

School of Literary and Media Studies
Prince of Wales Road
London NW5 3LB
Tel: 01 607 2789
BA (Hons) Humanities
Three-year course. Film Studies is one of ten subject components and may be taken as a two-year Minor or as a three-year Joint. No practical component
MA Modern Drama Studies
Two-year part-time evening course with optional one-year Film Studies unit in Year 2. No practical component
Evening Degree Scheme
Five-year part-time course as a Combined Study. No practical component

Nottingham University

School of Education
Nottingham
Tel: 0602 506101
BEd/BPhil Specialist Options in Mass Media Communication
Particular emphasis on TV and media studies in schools. Opportunities are provided for a good deal of practical work, though the major emphasis is upon analysis and criticism
Specialist Diploma in Mass Media Education
Postgraduate course with emphasis on TV and media studies in schools
PGCE
Second area option in media studies
MPhil and PhD
Research can be supervised for higher degrees by thesis

Portsmouth Polytechnic

School of Social and Historical Studies/School of Languages and Area Studies
Kings Rooms
Bellevue Terrace
Southsea PO5 3AT
Tel: 0705 827681
BA (Hons) Cultural Studies
Year 1: 10 one-hour introductory lectures, five seminars. Year 2 options: Mass Media Texts; Power, Gender, Genre I and II. Year 3 options: British Cinema 1939-49; British Cinema 1950-65; Feminist Film and the Avant-Garde; British TV Plays
Department of Fine Art
Lion Terrace
Portsmouth PO1 3HF
Tel: 0705 827681
P BA (Hons) in Multi-Area Design
Three-year course.
In the first year students experience working in four main resource areas, one of which is film and video. By the second year, students concentrate on two areas, so film may become a major preoccupation.
Equipment includes 16mm and 8mm sound cameras, editing facilities, animation rostrum, U-Matic

portapack and edit suite, VHS portapack and edit suite

Ravensbourne College of Design and Communication

School of Television
Walden Road
Chislehurst
Bromley
Kent BR7 5SN
Tel: 01 464 3090
P B/TEC Higher National Diploma in Engineering Communications (for Television and Broadcasting)
Two-year full-time vocational course designed in consultation with the TV broadcasting industry leading to employment opportunities as technician-engineers
B/TEC Higher National Diploma in Design Communication (Television Programme Operations)
Two-year full-time vocational course designed in consultation with the TV broadcasting industry leading to employment opportunities as programme operators in lighting, camera operators, sound, video recording and editing, vision-mixing, telecine, and audio-recording. Facilities include two TV studios each with production, lighting and sound control rooms. Each studio has its own vision apparatus room and shares a central apparatus room, telecine and video recording and editing facilities

University of Reading

Faculty of Letters and Social Sciences
Whiteknights
Reading RG6 2AA
Tel: 0734 875123
BA Film and Drama (Single Subject)
After the first two terms in which three subjects are studied, students work wholly in film and drama. The course is critical but with

significant practical elements which are designed to extend critical understanding. It does not provide professional training
BA Film and Drama with English, French, German, Italian or Sociology
Students in general share the same teaching as Single Subject students but the course does not include practical work

Department of English
BA (Hons) English
Third year optional course in media semiotics
PhD
Research can be supervised on the history of the British Broadcasting Corporation

Department of German
BA (Hons) German
Two-term Finals option: The German Mass Media. Involves study of mass media in East and West Germany. No practical component. Two-year core course: German Literature and Civilisation 1900 to the Present

Department of Italian Studies
BA (Hons) Italian/French and Italian with Film Studies
First year introductory course: Post-War Italian Cinema (one half-term). Second year course: Italian Cinema (three terms). Final year course: European Cinema (two terms). Dissertation on an aspect of Italian cinema. These courses available to students reading other subjects in the Faculty. No practical component
MA Italian Cinema
One-year full-time or two-year part-time course on Italian Cinema: compulsory theory course, options on film and literature, Bertolucci, Italian industry and genre – the Spaghetti Western. No practical component
MPhil and PhD
Research can be supervised on Italian cinema for degree by thesis

Graduate School of European and International Studies
MA European Media Studies
One year full-time or two years part-time. The course covers the mass media of Great Britain, France, Italy, East and West Germany. Two compulsory courses: Theory, Institutions and Forms of the Mass Media; and The European Media. Two options to be chosen from: Press and Broadcasting in the Two Germanies; The Sociology of Popular Culture; Representations of Women in the Mass Media; French Film; Genre and Industry in the Italian Cinema; and Literature and Film

College of Ripon and York St John
Lord Mayor's Walk
York YO3 7EX
Tel: 0904 56771
BA Combined Hons
Honours degree students take 16 courses in four years. Of these, five may be film/TV courses including three practical TV courses. The practical component includes some off-campus work and experience in related industries

Royal College of Art
School of Film and Television
Kensington Gore
London SW7 2EU
Tel: 01 584 5020
P MA in Film
Two-year course. Three postgraduate courses offered:
1 Filmmaking – Year 1 advertising and pop promos, Year 2 narrative and documentary making;
2 Production – a training in the business and entrepreneurial skills of low budget film production;
3 3D design for the moving image – concentrates on art direction and design for film and television. Course units include costume, set design, location dressing. Entries

to the filmmaking course must submit up to 30 minutes of film or video. Entries to design course must submit a relevant portfolio of design material. Entries to the production course should demonstrate some knowledge of film production methods. Equipment includes 16mm cameras and editing equipment, studio and cutting rooms
Department of Animation
P MA in Animation
Two-year full-time course with work divided roughly into 80% practical and 20% theoretical. Equipment includes 2 16mm cameras, 2 video scanners and video edit suite. Also 16mm Steenbeck, editing and sound recording equipment

Royal Holloway and Bedford College, University of London
Department of Drama and Theatre Studies
Egham Hill
Egham
Surrey TW20 0EX
Tel: 0784 34455
BA (Hons) Drama and Theatre Studies
History of Film: a two-year course for second and third-year students, constituting one paper at Finals. Principally a historical and critical account of the development of cinema and the use of film for entertainment and art. Film – mainly film theory – is also taught as a special subject. Examination includes a dissertation. No practical component
P Television Drama
A two-year studio production course for second and third-year students. Largely practical with some critical analysis of television and television drama. By the end of the course all students direct their own short production

Saint Martin's School of Art
Film, Video and

Photography Department
27-29 Long Acre
London WC2E 9LA
Tel: 01 437 0611
P BA (Hons) Fine Art
Three years full-time. After a first year during which students undertake a number of projects related to film and video (with one project carried out in another area of Fine Art), the second and third years can be spent exclusively in film and video. 75% practical; 25% theoretical
P BA (Hons) Graphic Design
Three years full-time. All students undertake two or three practical film production projects in first year. Up to 10 students can opt for a film/AV specialist option in second and third years. Work is project-based in the field of 16mm live-action and animation film, tape-slide and video. 80% practical; 20% theoretical
P MA Independent Film and Video
Two years part-time. Aimed at students working (or who intend to work) in the independent sector of film and video production. It offers a lecture/seminar-based directed study programme and a Workshop Attachment Scheme. Students should have access to production facilities outside St Martin's. Equipment includes 16mm facilities (3 Arriflex, 2 Bolex, Beaulieu cameras; 3 Steenbecks; 5 pic syncs); U-Matic video recorders, cameras and edit suites; 2 sound rooms; 3 16mm animation rostra; computerised tape/slide equipment

University of Salford
Department of Modern Languages
Salford M5 4WT
Tel: 061 736 5843
BA (Hons) Modern Languages
One of three Final Year options is in French Cinema. One hour per week out of a total of 15 hours of language work.

No practical component
MA Modular (Part-time) Degree Includes two modules on French Cinema

Sandwell College of Further and Higher Education
Department of Design/ Creative Arts
Wednesbury Campus
Woden Road South
Wednesbury
Sandwell
West Midlands WS10 0PE
Tel: 021 556 6000 x8736/ 8001
P B/TEC National Diploma in Electronics and Television Studio Operations
Two-year course for those seeking a career in the broadcast media and associated industries. Offers a sound foundation in electronics and computer awareness. Course consists of the following components: vision and sound principles and operations; micro-electronics systems; computer graphics and assignments; transmission principles; radio and TV systems; programme production; communications and media studies; electrical and electronic principles; electronics; mathematics; industry and society

Sheffield City Polytechnic
Department of Communication Studies
36 Collegiate Crescent
Sheffield S10 2BP
Tel: 0742 665274
BA (Hons) Communication Studies
Course covers all aspects of communications, one area being Mass Communication. Option course in TV Fictions and Applied Media Studies in Year 3. Some practical work
MA Communication Studies
Part-time course over six terms, followed by the completion of a dissertation by the end of term eight. Aims to develop theoretical

understandings and analytical skills in relation to the processes and practices of communication in modern society. Students attend for two sessions of 2+ hours each week

Faculty of Art and Design
Psalter Lane
Sheffield S11 8UZ
Tel: 0742 556101
BA (Hons) History of Art, Design and Film
Film studies is a major component of this course. Year 1: introduction to film analysis and history. Year 2: special study on Hollywood. Year 3: critical and theoretical studies in Art, Design and Film and Contemporary Film Theory and Practice. No practical component
P BA (Hons) Fine Art (Communication Arts)
After initial work with a range of media, students can specialise in film and/or video. Film productions can range from short 8mm films, through 16mm documentaries or widescreen features, to small 35mm productions. There are professional facilities for shooting, processing, editing, recording and dubbing 16mm films, and good animation equipment. Also well-equipped video and sound studios, with studio cameras, portable units, automatic colour edit suite, multi-track sound recording and mixing, disc tape-cassette transfer and synthesisers
MA Film Studies
Two-year part-time course; two evenings per week, plus dissertation to be written over two terms in a third year. Main areas of study: Problems of Method; The Classical Narrative Tradition; British Cinema 1927-45; British Independent Cinema 1966-84. No practical component

University of Sheffield
Department of English Literature
Shearwood Mount
Shearwood Road
Sheffield S10 2TD

Tel: 0742 768555 x6043/6276
MA Theatre and Film
One-year course on elements of both theatre and film studies. Work on all topics is assessed at the conclusion of the course

South Thames College
Wandsworth High Street
London SW18 2PP
Tel: 01 870 2241
P B/TEC Higher National Certificate in Design (Communication) – Television Production
Two-year part-time course aimed to equip students with the knowledge, skills and experience required for work in the professional or corporate field of TV production. Students make both single camera and studio television programmes. Facilities include: 3-colour studio with telecine, caption camera, caption generator, source and record VCRs and a microprocessor controlled lighting rig, plus 8-channel sound mixing with usual sources. Further facilities are bookable by arrangement including Nimbus computers with Pluto graphics packages and an audio laboratory with 16 into 4 into 2 audio mixer, and 4-track recording

University of Southampton
Faculty of Educational Studies
Southampton SO9 5NH
Tel: 0703 595000
MA Education
Television/Media/Video and Education comprise two of six modules in this full- or part-time taught course. Theoretical work and the viewing of specific programmes is complemented by practical experience
PGCE
The use of educational film and TV is a major component of a half-term course for all students on Educational Media, with one 1-hour session per week. A one-term option

course, of one 2-hour session per week on Educational Technology is offered, in which the students have the opportunity to acquire a practical working knowledge of the production processes of film and TV

Staffordshire Polytechnic
Department of History of Art and Design
College Road
Stoke on Trent ST4 2DE
Tel: 0782 744531
BA (Hons) History of Design and the Visual Arts
Film studies is a compulsory option in Year 1 and a special option in Years 2 and 3, comprising 30% of study time. 5-6 week professional/industrial placement opportunities offered in Year 2. Dissertation in Year 3. Minor practical component

Department of Design
P BA (Hons) Multi-disciplinary Design
Audiovisual Communication is a major design specialisation within the course, engaging in film, video, slide-tape programmes and sound recording. In the third year students engage in practical projects for clients from the local community. Facilities include two U-Matic edit suites, two colour video rostrum-animation suites, 16mm production facilities and an 8-track sound recording studio

University of Stirling
Stirling FK9 4LA
Scotland
Tel: 0786 73171
BA (Hons) in Film and Media Studies (Single and Joint Honours)
Four-year degree in which students follow courses in the theory and analysis of all the principal media. All students take courses on the theory of mass communication and on

problems of textual analysis and then select from a range of options, including practical courses in the problems of news reporting in radio and TV. As a joint honours degree Film and Media Studies can be combined with a variety of other subjects
BA General Degree
Students can build a component of their degree in film and media studies ranging from as much as eight units (approximately 50% of their degree) if they take a major in the subject, down to as little as three if they wish merely to complete a Part 1 major. For the most part students follow the same units as do Film and Media Studies Honours students
MLitt and PhD
Applications are considered for research in a number of areas of film and media studies

Suffolk College of Higher and Further Education
School of Art and Design
Rope Walk
Ipswich
Suffolk IP4 1LT
Tel: 0473 55885
P B/TEC Higher National Diploma in Design Communication
A two-year course with options in film/TV graphics, animation, film/video production. Students complete a period of work experience with employers in film and TV companies. Facilities include two colour TV studios, post-production facilities for film and video, and a film animation unit

Sunderland Polytechnic
School of Humanities
Forster Building
Chester Road
Sunderland SR1 3R
Tel: 091 515 2188/9
BA (Hons) Communication Studies
Study of linguistics, psychology and sociology

in relation to interpersonal communications and mass communication. The course is primarily academic, but includes practical study of radio, video and computing. Options include: Perspectives on Visual Communications, The Languages of Film and Representations of Women in Painting and Film

MA/Postgraduate Diploma in Film and Television Studies
Two-year part-time course. Sociologically based, with the main emphasis on the British context. One evening a week, with a second evening for screenings. MA by thesis in year 3. Next intake September 1990

MA/Postgraduate Diploma in Communication Studies
Two-years part-time. Year 1 concentrates on interpersonal communication

(linguistics, social psychology, sociology); Year 2 deals with mass communication (with units on new communications technologies and the representation of history in film and television). One evening per week for two years; followed by a year-long research project. Next intake September 1991

University of Sussex
Arts Building
Brighton BN1 9QN
Tel: 0273 606755
BA English with Media Studies
A three-year full-time degree course which includes analysis of television, film and the press, together with some opportunity (unassessed) to be involved in practical television and video production

Educational Development Building
Brighton BN1 9RG
Tel: 0273 606755

MA Language, the Arts and Education
A one-year full-time and two-year part-time course, primarily for teachers in schools, FE and HE. Though work on film/TV forms only a small part of the taught seminar courses, students can specialise in the film/TV area for all written and practical work

Trent Polytechnic
School of Art & Design
Department of Fine Art
Burton Street
Nottingham NG1 4BU
Tel: 0602 418248
P BA (Hons) Fine Art
Filmmaking and video are available as options within the Fine Art degree. These options, separately or in combination, can be taken as the main area of study. At present up to eight students in each year do this. Equipment includes Arriflex, Bolex and Beaulieu cameras, Oxberry Animation Rostrum, Nagra, Revox

and Bauer tape-recorders, sound desk and 16mm editing facilities

Trinity and All Saints College
Faculty of Academic Studies
Brownberrie Lane
Horsforth
Leeds LS18 5HD
Tel: 0532 584341
BA (Hons) Communications and Cultural Studies
Three-year course in combination with a professional study in either Public Media or Business Management and Administration. Film and TV Studies is a major component within the course, which includes some practical work

University of Ulster
Coleraine
Co Londonderry
Northern Ireland BT52 1SA
Tel: 0265 44141
BA (Hons) Media Studies
Three-year course integrating theoretical,

critical and practical approaches to film, TV, radio and the press. Film and TV Studies constitutes over 60% of the course. Important practical component. Facilities include: colour TV studio; portable VHS, Hi-band and low-band; post-production COX 58; Gemini 2; Hi-band video animation suite; 16mm Frezzolini; 4-plate Steenbeck; Super 8; professional 8-track sound studio; Uher and Marantz portables; Apple Mac computer lab; Amiga graphics generator.

Faculty of Art and Design
BA (Hons) Fine Art
BA (Hons) Design
BA (Hons) Combined Studies in Art and Design
B/TEC Higher National Diploma in Design Communication
Minor component units in theoretical and some practical elements of film, video and media studies as part of the core studies of all BA courses. Combined Studies students undertake a greater Media Studies input. Fine Art students may specialise in Fine Art video as part of their final studio work. Design students may take video production as part of their graphic design studio work. Design Communication students all take video production project work in Year 1.

University of Warwick
Joint School of Film and Literature
Faculty of Arts
Coventry CV4 7AL
Tel: 0203 523523
BA Joint Degree in Film and Literature
Four courses offered each year, two in film and two in literature. Mainly film studies but some TV included. No practical component
BA French with Film Studies
This degree puts a particular emphasis on film within and alongside its studies of French language, literature and

society. No practical component
Various Degrees
Options in film studies can be taken as part of undergraduate degrees in other departments. No practical component
MA, MPhil and PhD
Students are accepted for research degrees

West Glamorgan Institute of Higher Education
Townhill Road
Swansea SA2 0UT
Tel: 0792 203482
P BA (Hons) Combined Studies
Three year degree with several options. The Art in Society option includes a substantial amount of practical work, of which video and tape-slide form a major element. Facilities include: a Sony Series 5 animation unit, a sound studio based on a Tascam Portastudio, a Fairlight Computer Video Instrument. U-Matic editing suite and portable U-Matic unit dedicated to the course. Additional facilities include U-Matic and VHS editing suites and 3-camera studio. The Modern English Studies option includes Film and TV Studies (no practical component)
BEd Primary
This course includes a Literature and Media Studies main subject option.

West Surrey College of Art and Design
Department of Fine Art and Audio-Visual Studies
Falkner Road
The Hart
Farnham
Surrey GU9 7DS
Tel: 0252 722441
P BA (Hons) Photography, Film and Video, Animation
Students are enrolled in one of the three chief study areas of the course title. The approach is essentially practical, structured to encourage a direct and fundamental appraisal of photography, film, video and animation

through practice and by theoretical study. 70% practical, 30% theoretical. Equipment includes 16mm Arriflex, Bolex, Canon Scopic and CP16 cameras; sound studio with Neve 12 channel mixer; 10 edit rooms; 4-camera TV studio; Ikegami 3-tube camera; portable 3-tube video camera; U-Matic record and edit suites; range of VHS equipment; three animation rostra; aerial image faculty; NAC quick action recorder; Image Artist and Picaso computer graphics systems

Wimbledon School of Art
Merton Hall Road
London SW19 3QA
Tel: 01 540 0231
P BA (Hons) Fine Art
Students enrol in either Painting or Sculpture. It is more usual for Painting students to study Film and/or Video. Equipment includes Super 8mm sync sound and editing facilities; 16mm Bolex with post-sync sound; ½" b/w video and colour U-Matic with editing
P BA (Hons) Theatre Design
There are substantial opportunities for Super 8 filmmaking within the course of Theatre Design. Equipment include Beaulieu and Nizo cameras; Schmidt 4-plate sound mixing/editing suite; Uher, Revox, Teac, Soundcraft, MXR, Lexicon, Greengate and Casio sound facilities

The Polytechnic, Wolverhampton
School of Humanities and Cultural Studies
Wulfruna Street
Wolverhampton
WV1 1DT
Tel: 0902 313001
Diploma in Higher Education
Two-year course. Film and TV studies form part of four Cultural Studies units which may constitute 25% of the course. Students may also take a significant

proportion of independent study on film/media/cultural studies. No practical component
BA (Hons) Theme Studies
One-year degree programme open to those with a relevant Diploma in Higher Education. Film and TV emphasis dependent upon subject of the Independent Study paper (40% of the final assessment). No practical component

School of Humanities and Cultural Studies
Castle View
Dudley DY1 3HR
Tel: 0384 59741
BA Humanities
A three-year modular degree programme offering a Cultural Studies theme in Years 2 and 3. Film and TV are also components of complementary modules in History, French and Drama. No practical component
BA and BA (Hons) Combined Studies
TV and film components as for BA Humanities

Working Men's College
Crowndale Road
London NW1 1TR
Tel: 01 387 2037/8208
In association with the Charitable Trust for the Advancement of Film Education
P One year (part-time) adult education course in practical 16mm filmmaking
The course leads, after a series of joint mute exercises in black and white, to a short colour film with added (not shot-synchronous) sound, made by each student individually. All stages are in 16mm
Attendance is one whole day or two half-days or evenings each week

THE LONDON
•INTERNATIONAL•
FILM SCHOOL

• Training film makers for over 30 years •
• Graduates now working worldwide •
• Located in Covent Garden in the heart of London •
• Recognised by A.C.T.T. •
• 16mm documentary & 35mm studio filming •
• Two year Diploma course in film making
commences three times a year: January, April, September •

**London International Film School, Department FI9, 24 Shelton Street, London WC2H 9HP
01-836 9642**

DISTRIBUTORS

These are companies which acquire the UK rights to films for distribution to cinemas and, in many cases, also for sale to network TV, satellite, cable and video media. Listed is a selection of features certificated by the censor for those companies in 1988 and the first quarter of 1989. Some of the films mentioned were not released during the period

Albany Video
The Albany
Douglas Way
London SE8 4AG
Tel: 01 692 6322
Films and video art

Apollo Film Distributors
14 Ensbury Park Road
Bournemouth BH9 2SJ
Tel: 0202 520962/533577

Artificial Eye Film Co
211 Camden High Street
London NW1 7BT
Tel: 01 267 6036/482 3981
Commissar, The
Daughter of the Nile
Death of a Salesman
Diary for my Loves
Hard Times
Long Live the Lady!
My Girlfriend's Boyfriend
Taxing Woman, A
Vincent
Yeelen

Arts Council of Great Britain
See under Organisations

Atlantic Film Distributors
1st Floor
Paramount House
162 Wardour Street
London W1V 3AT
Tel: 01 437 4415/9513
French Massage Parlour
Luscious
Slip into Silk

BFI Distribution
21 Stephen Street
London W1P 1PL
Tel: 01 255 1444
See also p13

BFI Film + Video Library
21 Stephen Street
London W1P 1PL
Tel: 01 255 1444
See also p13

Alice in the Cities
American Friend
8½
Kings of the Road
Thin Blue Line, The

BFI Production
29 Rathbone Street
London W1P 1AG
Tel: 01 636 5783
See also p10
Circle of Gold
Deep Red Instant Love
Degrees of Blindness
Distant Voices/Still Lives
On the Black Hill
Out of Order
Venetian Ghost

Blue Dolphin Films
15–17 Old Compton Street
London W1V 6JR
Tel: 01 439 9511
Backlash
Cactus
Explorers
Fantasist, The
Holy Innocents, The
Hustler, The
Kamikaze
Last of England, The
PI Private Investigations
What Happened to Kerouac?

Bordeaux Films International
22 Soho Square
London W1V 5FJ
Tel: 01 434 3459
See under Production Companies for list of films

BratPack Programme Distribution Co
Canalot Studios
222 Kensal Road
London W10 5BN
Tel: 01 969 7609

Brent Walker Film Distributors
36–44 Brewer Street
London W14 3HP
Tel: 01 437 3696

John Burder Films
7 Saltcoats Road
London W4 1AR
Tel: 01 995 0547
Handles product from Sorel Films

Cavalcade Films
(formerly Stratford Films)
Regent House
235–241 Regent Street
London W1R 8JU
Tel: 01 734 3147

Cinema of Women
Unit 313
31 Clerkenwell Close
London EC1R 0AT
Tel: 01 251 4978
Booked through Glenbuck Films

Circles (Women's Film and Video Distribution)
113 Roman Road
London E2 0HU
Tel: 01 981 6828

Columbia Tri-Star Films (UK)
19–23 Wells Street
London W1P 3FP
Tel: 01 580 2090
Feature releases from the Columbia and Tri–Star companies, and Weintraub Screen Entertainment
Adventures of Baron Munchausen, The
Last Emperor, The
My Stepmother is an Alien
Punchline
Rambo 3
Red Heat
Short Circuit 2
Things Change
True Believers
Vice Versa

Contemporary Films
24 Southwood Lawn Road
Highgate
London N6 5SF
Tel: 01 340 5715

Distribute product on
behalf of Electric Pictures

Crawford Films
15–17 Old Compton
Street
London W1V 6JR
Tel: 01 734 5298

Curzon Film
Distributors
38 Curzon Street
London W1Y 8EY
Tel: 01 499 7571
Au Revoir Les Enfants
Dark Eyes
La Lectrice
Pelle the Conqueror

Darvill Associates
280 Chartridge Lane
Chesham
Bucks HP5 2SG
Tel: 0494 783643

Dee and Co
Suite 204
Canalot
222 Kensal Road
London W10 5BN
Tel: 01 960 2712
See under International
Sales

Walt Disney
See Warner Bros

Electric Pictures
22 Carol Street
London NW1 0HU
Tel: 01 267 8418/
284 0524/0583
Bohème, La
Chocolat
Death Japanese Style
*Ghosts . . . of the Civil
  Dead*
Life is a Long Quiet River
Mapantsula
Parents Terribles, Les
Runner, The
Tampopo
Virgin

Elephant
Entertainments
15–17 Old Compton
Street
London W1V 5PJ
Tel: 01 437 9541

English Film Co
6 Woodland Way
Petts Wood
Kent BR5 1ND
Tel: 0689 71535/71519

Enterprise Pictures
113 Wardour Street
London W1V 3TD
Tel: 01 734 3372
Dawning, The

Deceivers, The
Fatal Beauty
Jimmy Reardon
Matewan
Perfect Murder, The
Testimony

Entertainment Film
Distributors
27 Soho Square
London W1V 5FL
Tel: 01 439 1606
Cop
18 Again
*Elvira, Mistress of the
  Dark*
Flowers in the Attic
Full Moon in Blue Water
Hellraiser
Kansas
Near Dark
Patty Hearst
Slipstream

Film and Video
Umbrella
7 Denmark Street
London WC2H 8LS
Tel: 01 497 2236

Glenbuck Films
Glenbuck House
Glenbuck Road
Surbiton
Surrey KT6 6BT
Tel: 01 399 0022/5266

The Samuel
Goldwyn Company
St George's House
14–17 Wells Street
London W1P 3FP
Tel: 01 436 5105
Heart of Midnight
Lady in White
Mr North
Mystic Pizza
Prayer for the Dying, A
Two Moon Junction

Guild Film
Distribution
Evelyn House
62 Oxford Street
London W1N 6LD
Tel: 01 631 0240
Bat – 21
Deepstar Six
Iron Eagle II
Mac and Me
Pathfinder
Phantasm II
*Return of the Living Dead
  Part II*
They Live
Watchers

HandMade Films
(Distributors)
26 Cadogan Square
London SW1X 0JP
Tel: 01 584 8345

Hobo Film
Enterprises
9 St Martin's Court
London WC2N 4AJ
Tel: 01 895 0328
Little Dorrit
Madame Sousatzka
Soursweet
Souvenir

ICA Projects
12 Carlton House Terrace
London SW1Y 5AH
Tel: 01 930 0493
Alice
Big Parade, The
Hibiscus Town
Horse Thief
King of the Children
Rouge
Senyora, La
Someone to Love
Swan Song
Terrorisers, The

Kruger Leisure
Organisation
PO Box 130
Hove
East Sussex BN3 6QU
Tel: 0273 550088
Gallivant

MGM/UA
See UIP

Mainline Pictures
37 Museum Street
London WC1A 1LP
Tel: 01 242 5523
Bagdad Cafe
Broken Noses
Crazy Love
*Dona Herlinda and Her
  Son*
Flame in My Heart, A
Little Vera
Salaam Bombay

Medusa Pictures
41–42 Berners Street
London W1P 3AA
Tel: 01 255 2200
Fair Game
Ghost Chase
Iron Triangle
Lighthorsemen, The
Maniac Cop
Out of the Dark
Warlock
See also Medusa
Communications under
Video Labels

Metro Pictures
(formerly The Other
Cinema)
79 Wardour Street
London W1V 3TH
Tel: 01 734 8508/9
Able
Camp Thiaroye

Family Viewing
Law of Desire
Shame
*She Must Be Seeing
  Things*

Miracle
Communications
69 New Oxford Street
London WC1A 1DG
Tel: 01 379 5006

Nelson
Entertainment
International
8 Queen Street
London W1X 7PH
Tel: 01 493 3362
Brothers in Arms
Lord of the Flies
Pentagram
Queen of Hearts
Tennessee Waltz
When Harry Met Sally

New Realm
Entertainments
Hammer House
113–117 Wardour Street
London W1V 3TD
Tel: 01 437 9143/4

Orbit Films
14 Campden Hill Gardens
London W8
Tel: 01 221 5548
*Adventures of Buckaroo
  Banzai, The*
Mean Streets

Palace Pictures
16–17 Wardour Mews
London W1V 3FF
Tel: 01 734 7060
High Hopes
High Spirits
*Nightmare on Elm Street
  4, A: The Dream Master*
Prince of Pennsylvania
Red Sorghum
Scandal
Shag
Torch Song Trilogy
World Apart, A
Year My Voice Broke, The

Paramount
See UIP

Pathé Releasing
76 Hammersmith Road
London W14 8YR
Tel: 01 603 4555
Camille Claudel
Cry in the Dark, A
Haunted Summer, The
Jean de Florette
Manon des Sources
Petite Voleuse, La
Revolving Doors, The
*Short Film About Killing,
  A*
Short Film About Love, A
Sur

Poseidon Film Distributors
Hammer House
113 Wardour Street
London W1V 3TD
Tel: 01 734 4441
Ashik Kerib
Life, Love and Tears
Lonely Woman is Looking
for a Life Companion
My English Grandfather
Rape of Aphrodite, The
Return, The
Solovetskaya Power
Theme, The
Tomorrow There Was a
War

Premier Releasing
360 Oxford Street
London W1N 9HA
Tel: 01 493 0440/409 1984
Backfire
Carmen
Da
Handful of Dust, A
Hellbound: Hellraiser II
Hollywood Shuffle
Naked Cell, The
Night Zoo
Shooting Party
Sticky Fingers

Rank Film Distributors
127 Wardour Street
London W1V 4AD
Tel: 01 437 9020
Releases own titles as
well as all Orion product
Bull Durham
Dead Ringers
Dirty Rotten Scoundrels
Dressmaker, The
Eight Men Out
Married to the Mob
Mississippi Burning
Moderns, The
Without a Clue
Women on the Verge of a
Nervous Breakdown

Recorded Releasing
66–68 Margaret Street
London W1N 7FL
Tel: 01 734 7477
A Bout de Souffle
Drowning by Numbers
Manhunter
Navigator
Track 29
Veronico Cruz
We Think the World of
You
Withnail and I
Wings of Desire

Respectable Films
6 Silver Place
Beak Street
London W1R 3LJ
Tel: 01 437 8562

Bleak Moments
Last Night at the Alamo
Mala Noche

Sony Video Software Europe
41–42 Berners Street
London W1P 3AA
Tel: 01 631 4000
For Queen and Country
Jimmy Reardon
Also handle television
sales. See also under
Video Labels

Supreme Film Distributors
Paramount House
162 Wardour Street
London W1V 3AT
Tel: 01 437 4415/9513

TCB Releasing
Stone House
Rudge
Frome
Somerset BA11 2QQ
Tel: 0373 830769

Touchstone Pictures
See Warner Bros

Twentieth Century Fox Film Co
20th Century House
31–32 Soho Square
London W1V 6AP
Tel: 01 437 7766
Alien Nation
Big
Big Blue, The
Broadcast News
Cocoon: The Return
Die Hard
Predator
Saigon
Wall Street
Working Girl

UA (United Artists)
See UIP

UIP (UK) (United International Pictures)
Mortimer House
37–41 Mortimer Street
London W1A 2JL
Tel: 01 636 1655
Releases product from
Paramount, Universal,
and MGM/UA
Accused, The
Betrayed
Child's Play
Indiana Jones and the
Last Crusade
Licence to Kill
Naked Gun, The
Rain Man

Tucker: The Man and His
Dream
Serpent and the Rainbow,
The
Twins

Vestron Pictures
69 New Oxford Street
London WC1A 1DG
Tel: 01 379 0406
Amsterdamned
Burning Secret
Buster
Heart of Midnight
Lair of the White Worm
Paperhouse
Promised Land
Unholy, The
Young Guns

Virgin Vision
5 Great Chapel Street
London W1V 3AG
Tel: 01 494 3756
Lonely Passion of Judith
Hearne, The
Man in Love, A
Pascali's Island
Tall Guy, The

Warner Bros Distributors
135 Wardour Street
London W1V 4AP
Tel: 01 734 8400
Feature releases from
Warner Bros and Disney/
Touchstone
Accidental Tourist, The
Batman
Cocktail
Crossing Delancey
Dangerous Liaisons
Good Mother, The
Gorillas in the Mist
Grand Chemin, Le
Tequila Sunrise
Who Framed Roger
Rabbit?

Weintraub Screen Entertainment
Distributed through Hobo
Film Enterprises

Winstone Film Distributors
84 Wardour Street
London W1
Tel: 01 439 4525

NON-THEATRICAL DISTRIBUTORS

Companies here
control UK rights for
non-theatrical
distribution (for
domestic and group

viewing in schools,
hospitals, airlines and
so on); they also control
certain video rights, as
non-theatrical
exhibitors increasingly
use video. For other
sources of film and
video, see Archives and
Libraries (p64) and
Workshops (p260). To
find the distributors of
feature films released
in 1988–89 see Releases
(p208).

ABC Films
via Glenbuck Films

Albany Video
The Albany
Douglas Way
London SE8 4AG
Tel: 01 692 6322
Val Martin
Julia Knight
Education videos

Amber Films
5 Side
Newcastle upon Tyne
NE1 3JE
Tel: 091 232 2000

Apollo Films
See under Distributors

Argus Film Library
15 Beaconsfield Road
London NW10 2LE
Tel: 01 451 1127

Artificial Eye Film Co
See under Distributors

Arts Council of Great Britain
via Concord Films
Council

Audience Planners
4 Beadles Lane
Oxted
Surrey RH8 9JJ
Tel: 0883 717194

Australia Tourist Commission
via Audience Planners

Austrian Tourist Office
via Audience Planners

Avon Distributors
Everyman Cinema
Holly Bush Vale
London NW3 6TX
Tel: 01 485 4326

BBC Enterprises Video Sales
via Guild Sound and Vision

BP Film Library
15 Beaconsfield Road
London NW10 2LE
Tel: 01 451 1129

Bahamas Tourist Office
via Audience Planners

Banking Information Service
via Multilink Film Library

Barclays Bank Film Library
via Multilink Film Library

Belgian National Tourist Office
38 Dover Street
London W1X 3RB
Tel: 01 499 5379
and via Audience Planners

Big Bear Records
PO Box 944
Birmingham B16 8UT
Tel: 021 454 7020

Birmingham Film and Video Workshop
2nd Floor
Pitman Buildings
161 Corporation Street
Birmingham B4 6PH
Tel: 021 233 3423

Blue Dolphin Films
via Glenbuck Films

Boulton-Hawker Films
Hadleigh
near Ipswich
Suffolk IP7 5BG
Tel: 0473 822235

Brent Walker Films
See under Distributors

British Film Institute
Film + Video Library
21 Stephen Street
London W1P 1PL
Tel: 01 255 1444

British Film Institute
BFI Production
via BFI Film + Video Library

British Gas Film Library
via Viscom

British Steel Films
via Viscom

British Telecom Film Library
via Random Film Library

British Transport Films
via CFL Vision, Film Archive Management and Entertainment, and SCFVL

British Universities Film and Video Council
via SCFVL

Bryanston Films
via Filmbank

Bulgarian Tourist Office
via Audience Planners

CFL Vision
PO Box 35
Wetherby
Yorks LS23 7EX
Tel: 0937 541010

CSIRO Australia
via Darvill Associates

CTVC
Beeson's Yard
Bury Lane
Rickmansworth
Herts WD3 1DS
Tel: 0923 777933

Caledonian MacBrayne
via Audience Planners

Canada House Film and Video Library
Canada House
Trafalgar Square
London SW1Y 5BJ
Tel: 01 629 9492 x284

Castrol Film and Video Library
Athena Avenue
Swindon
Wiltshire SN2 6EQ
Tel: 0793 693402

Cayman Islands Tourist Office
via Audience Planners

Central Electricity Generating Board Film and Video Library
via Viscom

Central Film Library
See CFL Vision

Central Office of Information
See CFL Vision

Central Television Films
via Concord Films

Children's Film and Television Foundation
via Glenbuck Films

Cinema Action
27 Winchester Road
London NW3 3NR
Tel: 01 586 2762

Cinema of Women
See under Distributors

Circles (Women's Film and Video Distribution)
See under Distributors

Civic Trust
via Viscom

Columbia Tri-Star Films (UK)
via Filmbank

Concord Video and Film Council
201 Felixstowe Road
Ipswich
Suffolk IP3 9BJ
Tel: 0473 715754/726012

Connoisseur Films
via Glenbuck Films

Contemporary Films
via Glenbuck Films

Costain Film Library
via Viscom

Curzon Film Distributors
See under Distributors

Dandelion Film Distributors
49 St Peters Street
London N1 8JP
Tel: 01 354 2472

Danish Embassy
55 Sloane Street
London SW1X 9SR
Tel: 01 235 1255

Darvill Associates
280 Chartridge Lane
Chesham
Bucks HP5 2SG
Tel: 0494 783643

Fergus Davidson Associates
via NAVAL and SCFVL

Derann Film Services
99 High Street
Dudley
W Midlands DY1 1QP
Tel: 0384 233191
8mm package movie distributors
16mm via Glenbuck Films

Walt Disney Productions
via Filmbank
See also under Distributors

Dutch Embassy Films
via NAVAL

EMI Films
via Viscom

East Anglian Film Archive
Centre of East Anglian Studies
University of East Anglia
Norwich NR4 7TJ
Tel: 0603 592664

Eastern Arts Association
Cherry Hinton Hall
Cherry Hinton Road
Cambridge CB1 4DW
Tel: 0223 215355

Educational and Television Films
247a Upper Street
London N1 1RU
Tel: 01 226 2298

Educational Foundation for Visual Aids
via NAVAL

Electric Pictures
via Glenbuck Films and BFI Film + Video Library
See also under Distributors

Electricity Council Film Library
30 Millbank
London SW1P 4RD
Tel: 01 834 2333

Enterprise Pictures
via Glenbuck Films

Essential (16mm) Films
via Concord Films

Esso Film & Video Library
via Viscom

Eyelash Flutter Enterprises
18 West Parade
Norwich NR2 3DW
Tel: 0603 663966

Film Archive Management and Entertainment
Lansdowne Vaults
Imperial Studios
Maxwell Road
Borehamwood
Herts WD6 1WE
Tel: 01 207 6446
Manages the British
Transport Films archive
and library

Film Australia
via Darvill Associates

Filmbank
135 Wardour Street
London W1V 4AP
Tel: 01 734 8400
Handles 16mm film on
behalf of major, and some
other, UK distributors

Films of Israel
via Viscom

Films of Poland
Polish Cultural Institute
34 Portland Place
London W1N 4HQ
Tel: 01 636 6032/3/4

Films of Scotland
via SCFVL

Finnish Embassy
via Audience Planners

Flamingo Pictures
47 Lonsdale Square
London N1 1EW
Tel: 01 607 9958

Ford Film and Video Library
via Guild Sound and
Vision

French Institute
See Institut Français du
Royaume-Uni

French Scientific Film Library
via SCFVL

David Furnham Films
39 Hove Park Road
Hove
Sussex BN3 6LH
Tel: 0273 559731

GTO (Mike Ewin Films)
via Glenbuck Films

Gas Council
See British Gas Film
Library

German Film and Video Library
via Viscom

Glenbuck Films
Glenbuck House
Glenbuck Road
Surbiton
Surrey KT6 6BT
Tel: 01 399 0022/5266
Handles non-theatrical
16mm and video
See also under
Distributors

Sheila Graber Animation
50 Meldon Avenue
South Shields
Tyne and Wear
NE34 0EL
Tel: 091 455 4985

Granada Television Film Library
via Concord Films
Council

Greece National Tourist Office
via Audience Planners

Colin Gregg Films
via BFI Film + Video
Library

Guild Sound and Vision
6 Royce Road
Peterborough PE1 5YB
Tel: 0733 315315

HandMade Films
via Glenbuck Films
See also under
Distributors

IAC (Institute of Amateur Cinematographers)
63 Woodfield Lane
Ashstead
Surrey KT21 2BT
Tel: 03722 76358

ICA Projects
See under Distributors

India Government Tourist Office
via Audience Planners

India House Information Service
India House
Aldwych
London WC2B 4NA
Tel: 01 836 8484 x147

Institut Français du Royaume-Uni
17 Queensberry Place
London SW7 2DT
Tel: 01 589 6211

Intercontinental Films
via Glenbuck Films

Irish Tourist Board
via Viscom

Jamaica Tourist Board
via Audience Planners

Japan Tourist Organisation
via Viscom

Japanese Embassy Films
via Viscom

Robert Kingston Films
via Glenbuck Films

Leeds Animation Workshop
(A Women's Collective)
45 Bayswater Row
Leeds LS8 5LF
Tel: 0532 484997

London Filmmakers' Co-operative
42 Gloucester Avenue
London NW1 8JD
Tel: 01 586 4806

London International Film School
24 Shelton Street
London WC2H 9HP
Tel: 01 836 9642

Luxembourg National Tourist Office
via Audience Planners

Mainline Pictures
via Glenbuck Films and
BFI Film + Video Library
See also under
Distributors

Metro Pictures
See under Distributors

Multilink Film Library
12 The Square
Vicarage Farm Road
Peterborough PE1 5TS
Tel: 0733 67622

National Audio Visual Aids Film Library (NAVAL)
George Building
Normal College
Holyhead Road
Bangor
Gwynedd LL57 2PZ
Tel: 0248 370144

National Film and Television School
Beaconsfield Studios
Beaconsfield
Bucks HP9 1LG
Tel: 04946 71234

National Society for the Prevention of Cruelty to Children
67 Saffron Hill
London EC1N 8RS
Tel: 01 242 1626

Netherlands Information Service
via Darvill Film
Associates

Netherlands PD Films
via Darvill Film
Associates

New Zealand House Film Library
via Viscom

Northern Arts
via Amber Films

Open University
via Guild Sound and
Vision

Palace Pictures
via Glenbuck Films

See also under
Distributors

Palladium Media
via Glenbuck Films

Peru Tourist Board
via Audience Planners

**PlayBack
Communications**
25A Saffron Hill
Farringdon Road
London EC1N 8RA
Tel: 01 430 1785

**Polytechnic of
Central London
(Film Section)**
18–22 Riding House
Street
London W1P 7PD
Tel: 01 486 5811 x6531

RSPCA
Causeway
Horsham
West Sussex RH12 1HG
Tel: 0403 64181

**Radio Sweden
International**
via Darvill Associates

**Random Film
Library**
Unit 2 Cornwall Works
Cornwall Avenue
Finchley
London N3 1LD
Tel: 01 349 0008

**Rank Film
Distributors**
via Filmbank
See also under
Distributors

Rank Training Films
Cullum House
North Orbital Road
Denham
Uxbridge
Middx
Tel: 0895 834142

Recorded Releasing
via Blue Dolphin and
Filmbank
See also under
Distributors

**Retake Film and
Video Collective**
19 Liddell Road
London NW6 2EW
Tel: 01 328 4676

Royal College of Art
Department of Film
Queensgate

London SW7 5LD
Tel: 01 584 5020 x337

**Royal Mail Film and
Video Library**
London Road Trading
Estate
Sittingbourne
Kent ME10 1NQ
Tel: 0795 26465

**Royal Society for
the Protection of
Birds**
Film Hire Library
15 Beaconsfield Road
London NW10 2LE
Tel: 01 451 1127

**Scottish Central
Film and Video
Library (SCFVL)**
74 Victoria Crescent Road
Dowanhill
Glasgow G12 9JN
Tel: 041 334 9314

**Scottish Tourist
Board Films**
via SCFVL

Shell Film Library
via Random Film Library

Sorel Films
via John Burder Films
under Distributors

**South West Arts
Association**
Bradninch Place
Gandy Street
Exeter EX4 3LS
Tel: 0392 218188

**Steel Bank Film
Co-op**
Albreda House
Lydgate Lane
Sheffield S10 5FH
Tel: 0742 662583

Supreme Films
via Glenbuck Films

**Swedish Embassy
(Cultural Dept)**
via Darvill Associates

**Swiss National
Tourist Office and
Swiss Federal
Railways**
Swiss Centre
10th Floor
New Coventry Street
London W1V 8EE
Tel: 01 734 1921

TCB Releasing
See under Distributors

**Television History
Centre**
42 Queen Square
London WC1N 3AJ
Tel: 01 405 6627/8
See also under Production
Companies

Texaco Film Library
via Guild Sound and
Vision

**Thames Television
Video Sales**
via Guild Sound and
Vision

Transatlantic Films
Blythe Hall
100 Blythe Road
London W14 0HE
Tel: 01 727 0132

**Twentieth Century
Fox** via Filmbank
See also under
Distributors

UIP (UK)
via Filmbank
See also under
Distributors

**UK Atomic Energy
Authority Film
Library**
via Viscom

Video Arts
Dumbarton House
68 Oxford Street

London W1N 9LA
Tel: 01 637 7288

Virgin Films
via Glenbuck Films
See also under
Distributors

Viscom
Unit B11
Park Hall Road Trading
Estate
London SE21 8EL
Tel: 01 761 3035

Welsh Arts Council
Museum Place
Cardiff CF1 3NX
Tel: 0222 394711

**Welsh Office Film
Library**
Crown Building
Cathays Park
Cardiff CF1 3NQ
Tel: 0222 825639/41

**Workers Film
Association**
9 Lucy Street
Manchester M15 4BX
Tel: 061 848 9782

Yorkshire Arts
Glyde House
Glydegate
Bradford BD5 0BQ
Tel: 0274 723051

**Yugoslavian
Tourist Board**
via Audience Planners

AIRtv Facilities
Hawley Crescent
London NW1 8NP
Tel: 01 485 4121
Video formats: C, BVU,
Betacam
Editing: Paltex Esprit
controller in two suites,
Paltex ES1 controller in
third suite
Vision effects: ADO,
2-channel Quantel with
rotate, Aston 3, colour
caption cameras
Graphics: SuperNova 24
and two computer paint
systems
Telecine: Rank Cintel
Mk3

AKA
60 Farringdon Road
London EC1R 3BP
Tel: 01 251 3885
Editing: Three machine
Betacam SP Componant
with 1", Zeno, Aston 3,
Nagra T¼", and colour
caption camera
Offline editing, 16mm
film cutting room
Sound transfer
Equipment hire incl.
Aaton 16mm, Betacam SP
Studios: 2 sound proofed
stages, 180° Cyc,
overhead rigging
Full crewing and
production management
Equipment hire

Abbey Road Studios
3 Abbey Road
London NW8 9AY
Tel: 01 286 1161
Four studios
Music to picture
Film sound transfer
facilities
Audio post-production
Audio sweetening for
video and TV

Abbey Video
Five Lamps Studio
West Avenue
Derby DE1 3HR
Tel: 0332 40693
Editing: two/three-
machine hi/low-band edit
suite
Vision effects: KM2000,
caption camera, FOR-A
DVE
Camera: Single camera
unit
Sound: voiceover studio
Drive-in studio with cyc

Acricius
86 Albert Street
London NW1 7NR
Tel: 01 387 2183
Special effects
cinematography
Live action, stop-
motion, time-lapse and
programmable camera
equipment
Matte and process

Activision Studios
Unit 20
St James Wharf
All Saints Street
London N1 9RL
Tel: 01 833 4488
Full M3A Sony camera
kit
Video format editing:
Sony Series 5, TBC, DVE,
caption camera, three-
machine

Advision Studios
23 Gosfield Street
London W1P 7HB
Tel: 01 580 5707
Three sound recording
studios, digital/analogue
24/48-track, studio 1 for
around 60 musicians,
with large video screen,
Lynx synchronisation
Digital editing suite
Advision mobile for
location recording,
62-input desk,
24/48-track digital/
analogue recording, full
complement of mics,
outboard, 2-track

After Image
32 Acre Lane
London SW2 5SG
Tel: 01 737 7300
Video formats: C, Beta SP
Cameras: Sony 330P, M3
Studio: 2000 sq ft

Air Recording Studio
214 Oxford Street
London W1N 9DF
Tel: 01 637 2758
Five studios: large studio
65 musicians; small
studio 30 musicians; 72
channel mixing desk
Pre-production MIDI
suite
24/48 analogue 32TK
digital U-Matic video lock
up using Timeline lynx
synchronisers in all rooms
Mixing to 16/35mm mag
film

Angel Recording Studios
311 Upper Street
London N1 2TU
Tel: 01 354 2525
2 x 100-musician studio
complex with mixing to
35mm and 16mm film
Customised Neve desks

Anner Communications
Stillorgan Industrial
Park
Blackrock
Co Dublin
Tel: 0001 952221
Two studios, one 3,000 sq
ft, with drive-in
Ultimatte facilities
Two CMX edit suites,
DVE, Abekas,
Steadycam, Aston 3
character generator,
computerised graphics,
Neve sound, Dolby, 1"B
and C, BVU 500 and Beta
edit play/record
200 PAL slaves mastering
from Sony 1180

Anvil Film and Recording Group
Denham Studios
North Orbital Road
Denham
Uxbridge
Middx UB9 5HH
Tel: 0895 833522
35/16mm film and video
production
Studio re-recording, ADR,
post-sync FX recording,
transfers, foreign version
dubbing
Cutting rooms, neg
cutting

Any Effects
43 Farlton Road
London SW18 3BJ
Tel: 01 874 0927/870 9201
Mechanical (front of
camera) special effects
Pyrotechnics: simulated
explosions, bullet hits
Weather: rain, wind, fog,
snow
Breakaways: shatterglass
windows, bottles, glasses,
collapsing furniture,
walls, floors
Mechanical effects and
prop-making service

Ariada Film Productions
Goldcrest Elstree Studios
Shenley Road
Borehamwood
Herts
Tel: 01 953 1600

Aspen Spafax Television
6 Portland Place
Pritchard Street
Bristol BS2 8RH
Tel: 0272 232880
Graphics, Quantel
Paintbox, editing formats,
BVU SP, Betacam SP,
1″C, ADO Digital Effects,
Sony 9000 Edit
Controller, GBG 200
Vision Mixer, sound
dubbing, AMS Audio File

Atmosphere Recording Studios
6–10 Lexington Street
London W1R 3HS
Tel: 01 734 7443
24-track studio,
Q-lock synchroniser
Voiceover studio
Copying room

Avalon Video
27 Lexington Street
London W1
Tel: 01 437 6625
Time code transfer
facilities
ENG equipment hire
Crews

Avolites Production Co
184 Park Avenue
London NW10 7XL
Tel: 01 965 8522
Manufacture, sale and
hire
of dimming systems,
memory and manual
lighting control consoles
and chain hoist control
systems
Sales of relevant cabling
and connectors
Distributors for SL series
Socapex connectors in UK

Geoff Axtell Associates
16a Newman Street
London W1P 3HD
Tel: 01 637 9321
Digital video and film
opticals and effects
Harry/Paintbox digital
suite, film opticals, film
and video computerised
rostrum cameras
3D video motion graphics

BBRK
Shepperton Studio Centre
Studios Road
Shepperton
Middx TW17 0QB
Tel: 0932 564922
Art direction and
construction

Building services
Prop hire
Catering services
Three stages

BTS Television
Television House
221 Ordsall Lane
Salford
Manchester M5 4TH
Tel: 061 848 9033
Video formats: Beta,
BVU, 1″, VHS, 'U' Studio,
edit suites available
Studio: 1200 sq metres

BUFVC
55 Greek Street
London W1V 5LR
Tel: 01 734 3687
16mm cutting room and
viewing facilities

Jim Bambrick and Associates
10 Frith Street
London W1V 5TZ
Tel: 01 434 2351
16mm, 35mm cutting
rooms
Off-line video edit suite

Barcud
Cibyn
Caernarfon
Gwynedd
Tel: 0286 3458
Video formats: 1″C,
Betacam
Cameras: 3/4/5-camera
unit, single EFP unit,
Betacam unit
Editing: Beta and 1″ Sony
5000 suite, Sony 3000
suite, Quantel, Aston 3
Sound: post-production
with Audiofile, voiceover
booth, effects library
VHS off-line editing

Boulton–Hawker Films
Hadleigh
Ipswich
Suffolk IP7 5BG
Tel: 0473 822235
Time-lapse,
cinemicrography and
other specialised
scientific filming
techniques

CTS Studios
The Music Centre
Engineers Way
Wembley
Middlesex HA9 0DR
Tel: 01 903 4611
Largest of 4 studios holds
130 musicians with three
alternatives between 10
and 40

Synchronised film
projection available with
Telecine or video facilities
for recording music to
picture
Digital or analog
available, restaurant,
large car park

CTV
18 Oak End Way
Gerrards Cross
Bucks SL9 8BT
Tel: 0753 885554
Cassette duplication
Telecine
VHS, low-band U-Matic
and hi-band editing
Production facilities with
OB unit

CTVC
Hillside
Merry Hill Road
Bushey
Herts WD2 1DR
Tel: 01 950 4426
Video formats: 1″C,
Betacam, cassette formats
Cameras: Hitachi SK970,
Sony 330 and Betacam
Hitachi FPZ31
Studios: 120 sq metres,
32 sq metres and two
sound studios
Location units: C, BVU,
Betacam
Editing: 4 x Marconi 1″C
machines, Betacam, BVU
controlled by Datatron
Esprit, Cox T16 vision
mixer, Amek audio mixer,
O-Flex with E-Flex
digital effects, Ryley Cap
Gen, 2 colour caption
camera, VHS off-line edit
suite
Sound: Studer 16-track
machine with Q-lock
synchroniser and full
range of ancillary
equipment, timecode-
locked ¼″ machines

Capital Television Facilities
22 Newman Street
London W1P 4AJ
Tel: 01 636 3663
Video formats: Quad, 1″C,
BVU, Betacam, U-Matic
Cameras: Ikegami
Editing: Datatron
Vision effects: Ampex
ADO, Gemini 3
Standards conversion
Cassette duplication

Carlton Television
St Johns Wood Studios
St Johns Wood Terrace
London NW8
Tel: 01 722 8111/9255

ENG/Multi Camera OB
Units: 4-10 camera OB
unit, 1-4 camera OB
unit, 3-8 VTR/editing truck,
2-4 VTR recording truck,
single and multi-camera
units
Post production: two 4 x 1″
edit suites with Abekas
A64, ADO and Abekas
1530 digital effects, colour
caption camera, Aston 4
and Aston 3 character
generator, Beta and BVU
play-in machines, vertical
interval time code and
disc conform editing

Cell Animation
48 Charlotte Street
London W1P 1LX
Tel: 01 636 1392
28–30 Osnaburgh Street
London NW1 3ND
Two Harry/Paintbox
suites
Motion control rig, video/
film rostrum (aerial
image), six computerised
film rostrums (one with
aerial image)

Chamberlain Film Studio
16–20 Wharfdale Road
London N1 9RY
Tel: 01 837 3855
Stage: 80 sq metres
Construction facilities

Chatsworth Television
97–99 Dean Street
London W1V 5RA
Tel: 01 734 4302/3/4
Transportable Sony edit
suite with RM440
controller

Colin Cherrill Editing
82 Wardour Street
London W1V 3LF
Tel: 01 434 1265
35mm, 16mm film editing
Music library
VHS and U-Matic
viewing facilities

Roger Cherrill
65–66 Dean Street
London W1V 6PL
Tel: 01 437 7972
25 cutting rooms for
35mm and 16mm
ADR (Automatic
Dialogue Replacement)
16mm, 35mm dubbing
theatre
Effects recording
Dolby 'A' system sound
department
Telecine

Film opticals and titles
Trailers

Cherry Video
65–66 Dean Street
London W1V 6PL
Tel: 01 437 7972
Video formats: 1″C,
U-Matic, VHS, Betamax
Telecine: Rank Cintel
Mark 3C with Digiscan,
X-Y Zoom, Scope Pan and
Scan for 35mm and 16mm
Amigo with Kameleon,
secondary colour
correction, autoshot,
vari-speed 16-30fps

Chess Valley Films and Video
Film House
Little Chalfont
Bucks HP7 9PY
Tel: 02404 2222
Video formats: BVU hi-band
16mm film editing,
off-line editing
16mm Arri, crystal-synch
Nagra
Lighting
Viewing theatre

Chromacolour
Cartoon House
27–29 Whitfield Street
London W1P 5RB
Tel: 01 636 2103
Animation supplies and
equipment

Chrysalis Television
Granville House
St Peter Street
Winchester
Hants SO23 9AF
Tel: 0962 63449
Video formats: 1″C,
Betacam SP
Studio: 300 sq metres
Editing: Betacam SP to
1″, VHS off-line
Vision effects: Grass
Valley 1600, Gemini 2,
Aston 3

Cinecontact
175 Wardour Street
London W1V 3AB
Tel: 01 434 1745
Editing: 16mm cutting
rooms with 1901s, VHS
off-line with or without
editor
Cameras and crews: Arri
SR, Sony Betacam, Sony
M3A with low-band
recorder Sony 6800
Transfer: Betacam to
VHS with BITC, ¼″
sound to 16mm mag

Cine-Europe
7 Silver Road
Wood Lane
London W12 7SG
Tel: 01 743 6762
16mm, 35mm and full
range of grip equipment
hire

Cinefocus
1 Pavilion Parade
Wood Lane
London W12 0HQ
Tel: 01 743 2552
Unit 9, Orchard Street
Industrial Estate
Salford
Manchester M6 6FL
Tel: 061 745 8146
16mm, 35mm equipment
hire, Moviecam, Arriflex
35BL4, Tulip, Peewee

Cine-Lingual Sound Studios
27–29 Berwick Street
London W1V 3RF
Tel: 01 437 0136
3 sound studios
35mm and 16mm high
speed
ADR
Dolby Stereo 4-track
recording
Two 16mm, 35mm sound
transfer bays

Cinequip Lighting Co
Units 6–8 Orchard
Street
Industrial Estate
Salford
Manchester M6 6FL
Tel: 061 736 8034
Lighting equipment hire

Cinevideo
Broadcast Television
Equipment Hire
7 Silver Road
White City Industrial
Park
Wood Lane
London W12 7SG
Tel: 01 743 3839
Video formats: C, BVU,
Betacam
Cameras: Ikegami
HL79D, HL79EK,
HL95K, Sony 330AP,
Hitachi SK91

Colosseum Production Centre
Portland Gate
Leeds LS2 3AW
Tel: 0532 461311
6,000 sq ft television
studio theatre. Full
broadcast production and
technical facilities,

technical and workshop
crews, British Telecom
sound and vision links
250 permanent audience
seating
Licensed catering
facilities

Colour Video Services
22–25 Portman Close
Baker Street
London W1A 4BE
Tel: 01 486 2881/998 2731
Videotape to film transfer
specialists, direct from
broadcast video to 35mm
and 16mm negative
Telecine mastering and
tape dubbing all formats
16mm sound dubbing
studios
Bulk cassette duplication
Full film laboratory
services

Compass Production Associates
3rd Floor
18–19 Warwick Street
London W1R 5RB
Tel: 01 439 2581
Production offices
16mm cutting rooms
U-Matic off-line edit
suite

Complete Video Facilities
3 Slingsby Place
London WC2E 9AB
Tel: 01 379 7739
Telecom lines
Video formats: 1″C,
DVTR, D2, BVU,
U-Matic, SP Betacam
Editing: Sony DVE 9000,
Harry, Abekas A64,
Aston 3
Vision effects: Grass
Valley DVE, Quantel
Mirage, Encore, Paintbox,
Abekas A60
Sound: 32 channel and 16
channel solid state logic
console, voiceover and
sound library
Telecine: 35mm/16mm
Cintel Mk3, Colourist
colour corrector, Pin
registration cameras

Corinthian and Synchro-Sonics
5 Richmond Mews
Richmond Buildings
London W1V 5AG
16mm and 35mm cutting
rooms
Sound transfer, video
transfer

Equipment hire
16mm or video
commentary to picture
studio

Crow Film and Television Services
12 Wendell Road
London W12 9RT
Tel: 01 749 6071
Video formats: BVU,
Betacam, Betacam SP, 1″,
Arriflex SR
Cameras: BVP50P,
Arriflex SR, CCD
Editing: BVU, Betacam,
Betacam SP and 1″ to 1″
Colour caption camera,
commentary booth, Aston
3, Questech special
effects, Grass Valley 1600
vision mixer, Quantel
digital effects

Crystal Film and Video
Church Studios
50 Church Road
London NW10 9PY
Tel: 01 965 0769
Film facilities include
Aatons, Arriflex, Nagras,
radio mics, lights and
transport
Video formats: 1″C, BVU,
Betacam
Cameras: Ikegami, Sony

Cullen Television
83 Goswell Road
London EC1
Tel: 01 253 2660
3 machine low-band edit
suite

Cygnet
Bilton Centre Studios
Coronation Road
High Wycombe
Bucks HP12 3TA
Tel: 0494 450541
Full production facilities
for 16mm and video
Editing suites
Sound department
16mm preview and
dubbing theatre

DATS Video
80–86 Bridge Street
Warrington WA1 2RQ
Tel: 0925 35243
Video format: U-Matic
Cameras: Ikegami 2400,
Sony DXC M3A
Editing: Cox vision mixer
with Chromakey,
downstream keyer, IVC
time base corrector, 3M
character generator
Studio: 500 sq metres

DBA Television
21 Ormeau Avenue
Belfast BT2 8HD
Tel: 0232 231197
Crews and editing on
16mm, BVU, Betacam
and 1″, off-line and sound
transfer
Aaton, Steenbeck
Studio: 600 sq ft

Dateline Productions
79 Dean Street
London W1V 5HA
Tel: 01 437 4510
16mm, 35mm film
editing, off-line editing,
negative cutting

De Lane Lea Sound Centre
75 Dean Street
London W1V 6PU
Tel: 01 439 1721
2 high speed 16/35mm
Dolby stereo dubbing
theatres, high speed ADR
and FX theatre
Video dubbing/audio
recording with time code
synchroniser, sound
transfers and rushes
15 film cutting rooms
Preview theatre

De Wolfe
80–88 Wardour Street
London W1V 3LF
Tel: 01 439 8481
24-track studio
18 composers on contract
Offices in Tokyo, Paris,
Holland, Italy, Brussels
Controls 26,000 titles as
publisher
Film cutting rooms
Effects department

Delta Sound Services
Lee Shepperton Studios
Centre
Squires Bridge Road
Shepperton
Middx
Tel: 0932 562045
35mm dubbing theatre
Post-sync Effects work
In-house sound
transfers

Denman Productions
60 Mallard Place
Strawberry Vale
Twickenham TW1 4SR
Tel: 01 891 3461
Video and film
production, ENG crews
and equipment

Diverse Production
6 Gorleston Street
London W14 8SX
Tel: 01 603 4567
VHS, low-band, Hi-band,
Beta and 1″ editing,
Abekas DVE, image
processing and computer
graphics

Document Films
8–12 Broadwick Street
London W1V 1FH
Tel: 01 437 4526
16mm Aaton/Nagra
equipped crews, 16mm
cutting rooms
16mm, 35mm sound
transfer bay, mono and
stereo
Production offices

Dolby Laboratories
346 Clapham Road
London SW9 9AP
Tel: 01 720 1111
Cinema processors for
replay of Dolby Stereo
and Dolby Stereo SR
encoded soundtracks
Audio noise reduction
equipment

Joe Dunton Cameras
Wycombe Road
Wembley
Middx HA0 1QN
Tel: 01 903 7933
Camera equipment hire
Services many major
feature productions

ECO
The Exchange Building
Mount Stuart Square
Cardiff CF1 6EA
Tel: 0222 493321
Studio 1: 16-track Dolby
U-Matic video sound
dubbing; Studio 2: film
dubbing; Studio 3: Otari
8-track U-Matic with
AMS audiofile; Studio 5:
Otary 8-track U-Matic;
transfer suite

ENG Video
3 Nimrod Way
Elgar Road South
Reading
Berks RG2 0EB
Tel: 0734 751555
Video formats: 1″, SP
Betacam, SP BVU
Cameras: SP Betacam 507
Facilities: Fully
component mixed format
broadcast editing facility
with 2 channels DVE
duplication, standards
conversion
Equipment hire, technical
support

EOS Electronics AV
EOS House
Weston Square
Barry CF6 7YF
Tel: 0445 741212
Lo- and hi-band editing,
standards conversion
Broadcast video
animation controller
Neilson Hordell Camera
Rostrum and Sony
DXCM7
Frame by frame video
recording

Edinburgh Film and Video Productions
Edinburgh Film and TV
Studios
Nine Mile Burn
by Penicuik
Midlothian EH26 9LT
Tel: 0968 72131
Stage: 50 sq metres
16mm, 35mm cutting
rooms
16mm, 35mm transfer
facilities
Preview theatre
Sound transfer
Edge numbering
Lighting grip equipment
hire
Scenery workshops

Edinburgh Film Workshop Trust
29 Albany Street
Edinburgh EH1 3QN
Tel: 031 557 5242
Facilities include
low-band edit suite,
rostrum camera
VHS off-line suite

Edit 142
142 Wardour Street
London W1V 4AE
Tel: 01 439 7934
16mm and 35mm cutting
rooms

Ewart Television
Wandsworth Plain
London SW18 1ET
Tel: 01 874 0131
Video formats: D2, C,
Quad
Editing: Ampex Ace
Vision Effects: Charisma
(2 inputs)
Studios: 270 sq metres,
180 sq metres
Sound: 24/16/8/4/2 track
to picture

Eye Film and Television
The Guildhall
Church Street
Eye
Suffolk IP23 7BD

Tel: 0379 870083
Betacam SP production
crew
Component Betacam SP
editing suite

FTS (Freight Forwarders)
Unit 2b
Northumberland Close
Stanwell
Staines
Middx TW19 7LN
Tel: 0784 243901
International air-freight
with full bonded
warehouse and freight
forwarding

Fantasy Factory Video
42 Theobalds Road
London WC1X 8NW
Tel: 01 405 6862
Video formats: U-Matic,
hi-band SP, hi-band and
low-band, VHS, S-VHS
Editing: three machine
hi-band SP and low-band
with listing, automated
vision mixer, EDIS DVE,
with full timecode system
using VITC and LTC and
Quanta Cap Gen
2-Machine low-band with
a caption camera, CEL
DVE, for a Cap Gen and
timecode reader/
generator, 6-channel
audio mixer; 2-machine
VHS Panasonic with
caption camera and
coloriser, 6-channel audio
mixer

SG Fenner Lighting
Unit 5a
1–5 Standard Road
London NW10 6EX
Tel: 01 961 1935
Lighting equipment hire

Fidelity Films
34–36 Oak End Way
Gerrards Cross
Bucks SL9 8BR
Tel: 0753 884646
Audiovisual and video
production facilities

Film Clinic
8–14 Meard Street
London W1V 3HR
Tel: 01 734 9235
Restoration, cleaning and
reconditioning of film

The Film Company
14 Brownlow Street
London WC1V 6JD
Tel: 01 405 2734
Film and video production

and post-production Studio: 40′ x 22′ x 14′ ceiling height 35mm equipment-dry hire available

The Film Stock Centre
68–70 Wardour Street
London W1V 3HP
Tel: 01 734 0038
Film stock supplies: Kodak, Agfa, Ilford and Fuji 16mm, 35mm Videotape supplies

Filmwrights
73 Newman Street
London W1P 3LA
Tel: 01 637 5052
Film production and post-production

FinePoint Broadcast
The Red Lodge
Brighton Road
Tadworth
Surrey KT20 6UQ
Tel: 0737 833099
Broadcast equipment hire in PAL and NTSC
Video formats: 1″C, Beta SP, Beta, BVU
Cameras: Sony 330A, BVP-50, BVP-30, BVP-200, BVP-7, Ikegami HL-79E
6 camera 4 VTR outside broadcast production vehicle
Edit suites, dubbing and standards conversions
DVE: Paintbox, DLS, Charisma, Abekas A53

Flintdown – Channel Five Television
339 Clifton Drive South
St Annes on Sea
Lancashire FY8 1LP
Tel: 0253 725499
Video formats: C, BVU, U-Matic
Cameras: IVC

Fox Television
10–12 Fitzroy Mews
London W1P 5DQ
Tel: 01 387 3308
Video formats: BVU, 1″C, Beta
Cameras: Ikegami HL79 and HL95
Editing: Three-machine BVU and Beta

Mike Fraser
225 Goldhawk Road
London W12 8ER
Tel: 01 749 6911

Neg cutting, rubber numbering, Profilm EFC logging
Tape erasing, cleaning, evaluation

Frontline Video
44 Earlham Street
London WC2H 9LA
Tel: 01 836 0411
2 x Betacam/BVU to 1″ and three-machine computerised editing with Abekas Zeno, Gemini 3 digital FX, Z6000 edit controller and Aston 4 graphics generator
Tape duplication, standards conversion, all formats, telecine and studio

Fundamental Films
15 Wardour Mews
D'Arblay Street
London W1V 3FF
Tel: 01 437 9475
Film and video production
Editing: 16mm/35mm, low-band U-Matic

GBS Film Lighting
169 Talgarth Road
London W14
Tel: 01 748 0316
Lighting equipment hire

General Screen Enterprises
97 Oxford Road
Uxbridge
Middx UB8 1LU
Tel: 0895 31931
Studio: 100 sq metres
16mm, 35mm opticals including matting, aerial image work, titling
Editing, trailers, promos, special effects, graphics, VistaVision
Computerised rostrum animation
Computerised video suite
Preview theatres

Gibson Guards
Gibson Building
19–20 Pentonville
Newport
Gwent NP9 5HB
Tel: 0633 56746
Film and OB location security

Goldcrest Elstree Studios
Borehamwood
Herts
Tel: 01 953 1600
Viewing and dubbing theatres
Cutting rooms

Complete Dolby installation
Post-production department with a re-recording theatre providing 16mm, 35mm and 70mm facilities
Dialogue and sound effects theatre, ADR (Automatic Dialogue Replacement) plus standard looping system 16mm and 35mm

Grip House Studios
5–11 Taunton Road
Metropolitan Centre
Greenford
Middx UB6 8UQ
Tel: 01 578 2382
Equipment hire

Hammonds Audio Visual and Video Services
Presentation Division
60–62 Queens Road
Watford
Herts WD1 2LA
Tel: 0923 39733
ENG crews
Betacam SP, BVU, BVP 7 DXC M7
Editing
Multiformat, DVE, computer graphics (animation), audio and studio facilities. S-VHS off-line
Duplication and STDS conversion via AVS systems

Hedley Griffin Films
4 Cowcross Street
London EC1M 6DR
Tel: 01 608 0301
Cartoon and special effects animation
Rotascope machine

Jim Henson's Creature Shop
1b Downshire Hill
Hampstead
London NW3 1NR
Tel: 01 431 2818
Animatronics, puppets and prosthetics

Hirearchy Classic and Contemporary Costume
45 Palmerston Road
Boscombe
Bournemouth
Dorset BH1 4HW
Tel: 0202 34465
Specialise in twentieth century costume hire

Holborn Studios
Herbal House
10 Back Hill
London EC1
Tel: 01 278 4311
Three film stages, set building

Howell Optical Printers
25 Lexington Street
London W1R 3HQ
Tel: 01 734 2323
Graphics, titles, opticals

Humphries Video Services
Unit 2, The Willows
Business Centre
17 Willow Lane
Mitcham
Surrey CR4 4NX
Tel: 01 648 6111
62–66 Whitfield Street
London W1
Tel: 01 636 3636
Videocassette duplication, standards conversion, mastering, dubbing facilities
Full packaging and distribution service

ITN House
48 Wells Street
London W1P 4DE
Tel: 01 580 8333
Video formats: Quad, 1″C, BVU
Cameras: 4 Marconi Mk9
Studio: 45 sq metres
Vision effects: Quantel
Standards conversion via ACE
OB unit three cameras, C format VTR, Grass Valley mixer, Links

Image Transfer
16–18 Grape Street
London WC2H 8DY
Tel: 01 379 3435
Telecine onto 1″ C, hi-band, low-band, VHS, Beta, with Topsy controlled grading

Image Transform
140 Wollaton Vale
Nottingham NG8 2PL
Tel: 0602 287777
Specialist tape to film and film to tape transforms with computerised control
Video signal processing and noise reduction

In Camera/ Chromavideo
13 Abbey Road
Abbey Mills
Kirkstall

Leeds LS5 3HP
Tel: 0532 740349
Video formats: Betacam
SP, BVU
Shooting and editing
facilities

In Video Broadcast

16 York Place
Edinburgh EH1 3EP
Tel: 031 557 2151
Four Sony 1″ VTRs, Sony
5000 edit controller,
Grass Valley 300
switcher, Grass Valley
Kaleidoscope digital
effects unit, Quantel
digital effects unit, Aston
caption generator
Cameras: Sony 330, Link
110
Video studio, 8-track
sound studio, voice-over
booth

Chris James and Co

19 New Wharf Road
London N1 9RT
Tel: 01 837 3062
Lighting filters

Jenkinson Film and TV Productions

32 Heaton Road
Newcastle upon Tyne
NE6 1SD
Tel: 091 276 1970
Three-machine BVU
editing
Eight-track sound
studio

Terry Jones Post Productions

9 Greek Street
London W1V 5LE
Tel: 01 434 1173
16mm, 35mm post-
production facilities

Kodak

Motion Picture Sales
Division
PO Box 66
Hemel Hempstead
Herts
Tel: 0442 62331
Film stock

LTM (UK) Cinebuild

Studio House
Rita Road
London SW8 1JU
Tel: 01 582 8750
Special effects: rain,
snow, fog, mist, smoke,
fire, explosions
Lighting and equipment
hire
Studio: 200 sq metres

Ladbroke Films (Dubbing)

4 Kensington Park
Gardens
London W11 3HB
Tel: 01 727 3541
16mm/35mm Steenbeck
editing
16mm/35mm dubbing up
to 6 tk
70mm Dolby stereo
(12 tk)
ADR, footsteps, sound
transfer

Lane End Productions

63 Riding House Street
London W1P 7PP
Tel: 01 637 2794/5
Video formats: 1″C,
Betacam, SP, BVU,
U-Matic, VHS
Vision effects: Grass
Valley mixer, Gemini 2,
colour camera, Aston 3,
Abacus A53D, THRV,
CAR
Transfer and standards
conversion

F Larner Film and TV Lighting

155 Vauxhall Street
London SE11 5RH
Tel: 01 582 0834
Location lighting

Lazer F.I.L.M.S.

Building No 1
GEC Estate
East Lane
Wembley
Middx Tel: 01 904 1448
Editing and other
post-production facilities

Lee Lighting

Wycombe Road
Off Beresford Avenue
Wembley
Middx HA0 1QN
Tel: 01 903 7933
Lighting equipment hire

Lee International Studios

Studios Road
Shepperton
Middx TW17 0QD
Tel: 0932 562611
128 Wembley Park Drive
Wembley
Middx HA9 8JE
Tel: 01 902 1262
Manchester Road
Kearsley
Bolton BL4 8RL
Tel: 0204 73373
Cutting rooms
16mm, 35mm viewing
theatres

Light House Media Centre

Art Gallery
Lichfield Street
Wolverhampton WV1
1DU
Tel: 0902 312032/3/4
Video production with
three-machine edit,
computer graphics/
animation

Limehouse Studios

3rd Floor, Trocadero
Centre
19 Rupert Street
London W1
Tel: 01 287 3333
Two studios with
post-production facilities

London Fields Film and Video

10 Martello Street
London E8 3PE
Tel: 01 241 2997
Low-band production
and editing facilities.
Special rates for artists/
community use

London Filmmakers' Co-operative

42 Gloucester Avenue
London NW1 8JD
Tel: 01 722 1728
Equipment hire, editing
facilities (16mm and
Super 8mm)
16mm b/w processing

London Video Access

23 Frith Street
London W1V 5TS
Tel: 01 734 7410/437 2786
Video Access workshop
with production and
editing facilities up to 3-
machine U-Matic with
digital effects. Training
workshops from basic to
advanced editing. Archive
of over 700 'VideoArt'
tapes and active
distribution catalogue

Lynx Video

Lynx House
7 High Road
Ickenham
Uxbridge
Middx UB10 8LE
Tel: 0895 676221
Video formats: 1″C,
Betacam SP, BVU
Cameras: Ikegami
HL79Es, H195s
Vision effects: Questech
digital effects

MAC Sound Hire

1–2 Attenburys Park
Park Road
Altrincham
Cheshire WA14 5QE
Tel: 061 969 8311
Hire of professional sound
equipment

Austin Martin Film Services

61 Frith Street
London W1
Tel: 01 439 4397
Editing rooms

Mayflower Sound Studios

3 Audley Square
Mayfair
London W1Y 5DR
Tel: 01 493 0016
High-speed
computerised film and
video recording studio
specialising in Automated
Dialogue Replacement
(ADR) and sound effects
including digital sound
effects library

Media Arts

Town Hall Studios
Regent Circus
Swindon SN1 1QF
Tel: 0793 26161 x3140
Video cameras: F10s,
KY1900s, M3
Video editing: VHS
two-machine, Series 5
two-machine, hi-band and
effects
Sound studio and effects,
interview studio
8mm/16mm cutting
rooms
B/W and colour
photography
Lighting: Reds and
2000W
Dry hire, crews, training

The Media Centre

South Hill Park
Bracknell
Berkshire RG12 4PA
Tel: 0344 427272
Cameras: Sony M3A,
6000, 1820, VHS
camcorder
Editing: three-machine
Sony 5850s with Merlin
DVE, convergence editing
with list management,
two-machine Sony 5850,
two-machine Nat-Pan
with caption cameras and
video typewriters
Digital recording studio,
interview studio, preview
theatre

Media Communications
Park Gate Industrial
Estate
Knutsford
Cheshire
Tel: 0565 52871
Five-machine edit suite
Two-channel Quantel
CDL mixer
Purpose-built studio

Mercury Studio Sound
84–88 Wardour Street
London W1
Tel: 01 734 0263
Dubbing and sound
transfer facilities, cutting
rooms, production offices

MetroVideo
The Old Bacon Factory
57–59 Great Suffolk
Street
London SE1 0BS
Tel: 01 928 2088
The Old Fish Shop
14 Livonia Street
London W1
Tel: 01 439 3494
Video formats: Betacam
SP, MII, BVU SP,
Low-band
Cameras: BVP5/7/50,
BVW 507/550, DXC-M7,
DXC3000/325
OB unit, standards
conversion, duplication,
Telecine, videowalls,
video projectors, large
screen monitors

Metropolis Video
8–10 Neal's Yard
London WC2H 9DP
Tel: 01 240 8423
Editing: Two-machine,
low-band, two-machine
VHS, three-machine
low-band with computer
controller and feature
film video mastering
Video duplication
Film and video production

PMPP (Paul Miller Post-Production)
69 Dean Street
London W1V 5HB
Tel: 01 437 0979
Editing: On-line 1″,
Betacam, Component
Betacam SP with
Charisma and ADO
digital effects with
Aston 3
Off-line: 3 machine
computerised low-band,
2 machine low-band and
VHS
Matisse computer

graphics
24 track sound dubbing
studio with Q lock and
voice over
Duplication, standards
conversion, camera studio
and camera crew

Molinare
34 Fouberts Place
London W1V 2BH
Tel: 01 439 2244
Video formats: Quad, C,
BCN, BVU SP, Beta SP,
D1, D2
Video studios: Studio 1 –
33′ x 45′, broadcast TV
studio with drive-in
access, Soft Cyc, black
drapes on track,
'Ultimatte', 4 Ikegami
HL79 cameras on Vinten
Peds, GVG 300 24-input
3-M/E vision mixer, TV
grid, computer-controlled
lighting console, 16 Ch
audio mixer
Studio 2 – 25′ x 15′.
3 Ikegami HL79 cameras,
soft cyc, black drapes on
track
Editing: computer edit
suites, Grass Valley
vision mixers, 3-channel
ADO with concentrator,
digimatte and infinity
options, 4-channel DVE,
Aston character
generators, colour caption
cameras
Standards conversion;
graphics – Quantel
Paintbox, digital library
store, Harry; Telecine
Audio: 2 multitrack
dubbing studios with
Eclipse edit controllers
and Mastermix
4 OB units available; land
lines; direct reception via
satellite

Morgan Laboratories
Unit 4.16
Wembley Commercial
Centre
East Lane
Wembley
Middx HA9 7XD
Tel: 01 908 3856
Post-production facilities

Tom Morrish Films
171 Wardour Street
London W1V 3TA
Tel: 01 437 2136
16mm, 35mm post-
production

Motion Control Studio
Vision House
19–22 Rathbone Place

London W1P 1DF
Tel: 01 436 5544
Studio with overhead
motion control rig

The Moving Picture Company
25 Noel Street
London W1
Tel: 01 434 3100
Video formats: 1″C, DI,
DII, MII, Beta SP,
Betacam, hi-band,
low-band, A64 digital disc
recorder
Cameras: Sony BVP 330
portable and Sony DXC
3000 CCD video cameras
Editing: five editing
suites (one fully digital),
using CMX editors
Vision effects: ADO,
Mirage, Abekas, A53-D
Telecine: two 4.2.2 Digital
Rank Cintel MK IIIC
enhanced 16mm/35mm
machines with Digigrade
and da Vinci colour
correctors with Register
Pin and steadyguide
gates. Digital noise
reductions and Match Box
Graphics: 2 x Paintbox/
Harrys, Alias and Bosch
FGS 4500 3-D computer
animated graphics, Aston
3 and 4 character
generators
Studios: motion control
studio for special effects.
Main studio: 50′ x 35′,
with a 45′ cyclorama.
Insert studio
Cutting rooms and
off-line editing suite

Mr Lighting
19 New Wharf Road
London N1 9RX
Tel: 01 278 3321
Lighting equipment hire

Nant Films
Moreia
Penrallt Isaf
Caernarfon
Gwynedd L55 1NS
Tel: 0286 5722
Production company with
two 16mm cutting rooms

National Screen Productions
2nd Floor
2 Wedgwood Mews
12–13 Greek Street
London W1V 5LW
Tel: 01 437 2783
Creative and technical
services for production of
promos, documentaries,
trailers, teasers and TV

spots. Logo and main title
design and animation. All
aspects of on-screen
promotion and
presentation for feature
films, TV, cable and
video. In-house film/video
editing, design and art
studio

Northern Light
39–41 Assembly Street
Leith
Edinburgh EH6 7RG
Tel: 031 553 2383
Lighting equipment hire

Numo Productions
8–11 Bateman Street
London W1V 5TD
Tel: 01 439 4017
Stop-frame, live-action
special effects
Mitchell S35R with colour
video assist

Odyssey Studios
26–27 Castlereagh Street
London W1H 5YR
Tel: 01 402 2191
Sound-dubbing to video,
Q-lock system, SSL
6000E, Calrec U8000,
48-channel desks
Barco projection, Sony
U-Matic machines

Omnititles
37 Ripplevale Grove
London N1 1HS
Tel: 01 607 9047
Spotting and subtitling
services for film, telecine,
video, satellite and cable.
Subtitling in most world
languages and for the
deaf

Open Eye
90–92 Whitechapel
Liverpool L1 6EN
Tel: 051 709 9460
U-Matic three-machine
editing, VHS editing,
16mm rostrum, 16mm
editing, 3:1 dubbing

Roger Owen and Associates
8–18 Smith's Court
off Great Windmill Street
London W1V 9PF
Tel: 01 439 3772
Video formats: all
cassette formats
Editing: three-machine
low-band offline editing
suite
Mk2 telecine

Owen Beston Enterprises
8–18 Smith's Court
off Great Windmill Street

London W1V 9PF
Tel: 01 439 3772
Film editing

Oxford Film and Video Makers

The Stables
North Place
Headington
Oxford OX3 9HY
Tel: 0865 60074
Editing: Low-band
U-Matic
Camera: VHS portapack
Super 8mm and 16mm
equipment
Cutting rooms
Animation rostrum

Oxford Scientific Films (OSF)

Long Hanborough
Oxford OX7 2LD
Tel: 0993 881881
7 Poland Street
London W1V 3DG
Tel: 01 437 8865
Specialists in macro,
micro, time-lapse,
high-speed and snorkel
optic photography for
natural history
programmes,
commercials, features,
corporate videos and
videodiscs

PAC Video Productions

Rosehill
Erbistock
Bangor on Dee
Wrexham
North Wales
Tel: 0978 780181
Low-band edit suite

The Palace (Video Editing Centre)

8 Poland Street
London W1V 3DG
Tel: 01 439 8241
Video formats: 1″, Beta
SP, Beta, BVU
Editing: three five-
machine suites
Digital effects: 3 ADO
3000 with infinity and
digimatte, Quantel
digital effects
Offline editing:
multimachine U-Matic
and VHS
Graphics: Spaceward
Matisse system

Picardy Television

Picardy House
4 Picardy Place
Edinburgh C111 3JT
Tel: 031 558 1551
Facilities include: dry/
crewed camera hire; multi
format editing with
effects/graphics; full
broadcast standard studio
for single/multi shoots
and casting; EVS Video
Paint System

Picture Post

55 Greek Street
London W1V 5LR
Tel: 01 439 1661
4 edit suites, 1″, Betacam
SP, BVU, low-band,
computer graphics,
computerised rostrum
camera. 16mm and 35mm
cutting rooms

Pinewood Studios

Iver
Buckinghamshire
SL0 0NH
Tel: 0753 656301
Two large high-speed
stereo dubbing theatres
Small general purpose
recording theatre
Large ADR and sound
effects theatre
Preview theatre: 115
seats, 70/35/16mm; all
formats stereo sound
Four-bay sound transfer
area
Mono/stereo sound
negative transfer
60 fully-serviced cutting
rooms

Platypus

Craven House
34 Fouberts Place
London W1V 1HF
Tel: 01 734 2148
Film and video equipment
hire
Crewing facility

Provideo

29–35 Lexington Street
London W1R 3HQ
Tel: 01 439 8901
Video formats: 1″C, 2″
Quad, Betacam, Betacam
SP
Standards conversion:
ADAC, Quantel Silk,
AVS6500, Aston 3,
2D and 3D computer
animation
Transmission facilities

Q Studios

1487 Melton Road
Queniborough
Leicester
Tel: 0533 608813
Video formats: Betacam
SP, BVU
Component editing with
Charisma DVE, off-line
edit, 24 track sound,
original music production

Two drive-in studios
(1,350 and 754 sq ft),
black and chromakey
drapes, computer
controlled lighting. Full
production services
available including crews,
set construction, on-line
and off-line editing

Rank Video Services

Phoenix Park
Great West Road
Brentford
Middx TW8 9PL
Tel: 01 568 4311
3000 slaves, hi-fi capable
Specialist corporate
duplication department
including standards
conversion

Recording and Production Services

10 Giltway
Giltbrook
Nottingham NG16 2GN
Tel: 0602 384103
Video formats: Betacam,
1″C
Cameras: Sony 330
Studio: 176 sq metres
6-camera OB unit, Sony
350/360

Redapple

214 Epsom Road
Merrow
Guildford
Surrey
Tel: 0483 575655
Video formats: 1″C, Beta,
Beta SP, BVU, NTSC/
PAL
Cameras: Sony 330, Sony
BVP50, Sony BVP700D,
ENG/EFP units
Film: 16mm Arriflex unit
Transport: 5 estate cars,
pressurised twin engine
aircraft
Two lighting vehicles

Rockall Data Services

320 Western Road
London SW19 2QA
Tel: 01 640 6626
Safe storage of film, video
and audio material

Rushes

66 Old Compton Street
London W1V 5PA
Tel: 01 437 8676
Television
post-production, graphics,
special effects
1″ on-line, off-line, Harry,
Paintbox, FGS 4500,
studio

SVC Television

142 Wardour Street
London W1V 3AU
Tel: 01 734 1600
4 x 1″ edit suites with A64
digital disk recorder,
Mirage, Encore, four
channel DVE, 1 x digital
suite with A84 digital
vision mixer, 2 x Betacam
SP component suites with
A53 digital effects,
3 x telecine suite and
MASTERGRADE colour
grading suite with da
Vinci colour corrector
Quantel Paintbox,
Symbolics computer
animation, motion control
rig, rostrum camera

SVP Communications

70 Maltings Place
Bagleys Lane
London SW6 2BY
Tel: 01 731 3017
Video production and
post-production

Salon Post-Productions

13–14 Archer Street
London W1V 7HG
Tel: 01 437 0516
35/16mm Steenbecks and
editing equipment hire
Cutting rooms
35/16mm Steenbeck,
telecine, VHS edit suite

Samuelson Film Service London

21 Derby Road
Metropolitan Centre
Greenford
Middx UB6 8UJ
Tel: 01 578 7887
35mm/16mm rental
equipment
Sound/video assist
Sole agent for Panavision

Michael Samuelson Lighting

Dudden Hill Lane
London NW10 1DS
Tel: 01 452 6400
Milford Place
Lennox Road
Leeds LS4 2BL
Tel: 0532 310770
Pinewood Studios
Iver
Bucks SL0 0NH
Tel: 0753 658253
Lighting equipment hire

Stephen Saunders Films

32 Selwood Road
Addiscombe

Croydon
Surrey CR0 7JR
Tel: 01 654 4495
Post-production facilities

Screenworks
Portsmouth Media Trust
The Hornpipe
143 Kingston Road
Portsmouth PO2 7EB
Tel: 0705 861851/833854
16mm and video hire and
post-production
90-seat auditorium with
35mm and 16mm, video
and slide projection
VHS edit suite
U-Matic to VHS

Security Archives
Saref House
135 Shepherdess Walk
London W1 7PZ
Tel: 01 253 0027
Film and video storage
and retrieval services

Sheffield Independent Film
Avec
Brown Street
Sheffield S1 2BS
Tel: 0742 720304
16mm Aaton LTR,
Arriflex BL, Beaulieu
R16, 6-plate Steenbeck
and Picsyncs, Nagra IS,
Nagra 3, Revox B77,
Fostex 350 mixer
Sony U-Matic type 5
including TBC mixer and
captions, National
Panasonic VHS, M5 VHS
camcorder, Sony
portapaks VO 4800 and
VO 6800, Sony DXC 1640
and BVP 110 cameras
Lighting equipment hire

Sound House
87 Wardour Street
London W1V 3TF
Tel: 01 434 2928
Sound transfer base,
magnetic and DAT as
well as a comprehensive
sound effects library

Brian Stevens Animated Films
21 Newman Street
London W1P 3HB
Tel: 01 637 0535/7
Rostrum cameras
Studio animation
facilities

Studio Film and Video
Video Facilities
Royalty House
72–73 Dean Street

London W1V 6DE
Tel: 01 437 4161
Video formats: 1″C,
Betacam SP, BVU SP,
BVU, U-Matic, VHS,
Betamax, Video 8
Telecine: 35mm, 16mm
and Super 8, Rank Cintel
MkIII with Digigrade.
Also 8mm and 9.5mm
Editing: U-Matic suite,
standards conversion,
NTSC, PAL, Secam

Studio Operation SW
The Old Chapel
Abbey Hill
Lelant
Cornwall TR26 3EG
Tel: 0736 753538/01 379
6724
1500 sq ft studio with
production office, cam,
lighting, sound, special
effects, pyrotechnics, post
production film/video and
digital sound suite

Swanlind
Stafford Road
Fordhouses
Wolverhampton
WV10 7EL
Tel: 0902 784848
Video formats: 1″C,
Betacam
Cameras: Hitachi SK91/
97
Vision effects: Aston 3,
Questech, DVE,
Supernova graphics
Voiceover studio and full
digital audio effects

TSFX
Unit 6
Portland Business Centre
Manor House Lane
Datchet
Berkshire SL3 9EG
Tel: 0753 584667
Film and television
effects

TSI Video
10 Grape Street
London WC2H 8DY
Tel: 01 379 3435
Video formats: 1″C, BVU,
Betacam
Editing: Sony BVE 5000
edit controller with any
combination of above,
Grass Valley vision
mixer, Quantel Encore,
NEC E-Flex DVE, caption
camera, Aston 3 character
generators
Computer graphics:
Quantel Paintbox unit
with latest Pro 4 software
and digital library store,

Dubner 3D, Chyron
Telecine: Rank Cintel
Mk3 with XY zoom,
Digigrade 3, Autoshot,
VTR remote, secondary
colour correction
Sound: Q-Lock dubbing,
16-track, 24-track,
voiceover recording
Four BT lines (vision and
sound), BT control lines
(two in, two out), colour
caption camera, Sony
BVH 2500 single frame
recorder, Honeywell
Matrix camera

TV Broadcast Facilities
41 Paddington Street
London W1V 5DE
Tel: 01 437 5407
3-tube Betacam,
camera and editing
facilities

TVi
Film House
142 Wardour Street
London W1V 3AU
Tel: 01 434 2141/2
Video formats: 1″B, 1″C,
2″ Quad, Betacam,
Betacam SP, Betacam
NTSC, BVU hi-band and
low-band, BVU SP, VHS,
Beta, multi-standard
VHS and U-Matic, D1 and
MII
Editing: Six Paltex
computer edit suites with
1″ C, BVU hi-band and
Betacam VTRs Abacus
A53D with warp and
dimension. A64 digital
disc recorder for
multi-layering
Digital effects, colour and
b/w caption cameras,
Aston 3 character
generator, A72 character
generator, video colour
correction ¼″ sound
replay, vision and audio
mixing (stereo
capability). Off-line VHS
and U-Matic
Digital effects: ADO
digital effects rotate,
perspective and
Digimatte. Single
channel NEC E-Flex
O-Flex. Quantel
two-channel rotate and
dimension. Quantel
single-channel rotate and
dimension. Quantel
single-channel
Sound: post-production
dubbing to picture (1″
VTR, BVU or U-Matic),
Q-Lock, 24-track Otari,
PCM 701 on U-Matic, film
sound follow, 8-track

Studer A80; TS24 mixer
with A4 master mix
computer, voiceover
booth; Digital Audio
Research (DAR) for hard-
disc digital recorder;
music and effects library;
PAL/NTSC operation plus
time-link for code
conversions; CD
equipment
Telecine: 16mm/35mm to
625 PAL/Secam or 525
NTSC; Rank Cintel Mk3
with Digiscan or
jumpscan; Amigo
computer control and
secondary colour
correction; Varispeed,
Pan and Scan, S Pan
Curve facility and X-Y
zoom
Graphics: Matisse
Studios: 900 sq ft
2-camera sync studio; two
1-camera interview
studios; insert studio with
Hitachi FPZ 31 colour
camera

TWTV
20 Kingly Street
London W1R 5LD
Tel: 01 437 4706
Video editing and
post-production,
standards conversion,
video duplication,
computer graphics

Tattooist International
3 Centre House
20 Mandela Street
London NW1 0DU
Tel: 01 380 0488
16mm cutting room,
Super 16 and stereo
options, low-band
U-Matic off-line, Aaton
camera hire specialists,
Steadicam, time lapse
equipment, production
offices

Team Television
The Exchange Buildings
Mount Stuart Square
Cardiff CF1 6EA
Tel: 0222 484080
Edit 1 Multiformat
1″ Beta, Beta SP, BVU
Edit 2: Fully Component
Beta, Beta SP
T/K 16mm/35mm
Pos/Neg Prefix Grading

Tele–cine
48 Charlotte Street
London W1P 1LX
Tel: 01 637 3253
Specialists in film and
video transfers

Telecine with da Vinci, 35mm, 16mm, super 8, all VTR formats, broadcast standards conversion Multi-format on-line editing, and off-line editing

Tiny Epic Video Co
138–140 Wardour Street
London W1V 3AU
Tel: 01 437 2854/5
Seven computerised
off-line edit suites

Transworld TV Productions
Whitecrook Centre
Whitecrook Street
Clydebank
Glasgow G81 1QS
Tel: 041 952 4816
Production facilities
Location camera crews
Three-machine hi-band
and low-band editing

Troubleshooters (Shepperton)
PO Box 53
Lee International Studios
Studios Road
Shepperton
Middx TW17 0QD
Tel: 0932 562611
Script and production

services
ADR sheets, music cue sheets, transcribing audio and video cassettes, bio's, schedules, etc

Roy Turk Opticals
57 Rupert Street
London W1
Tel: 01 437 8884
Titles and opticals

Twickenham Studios
St Margaret's
Twickenham
Middlesex TW1 2AW
Tel: 01 892 4477
Two dubbing theatres,
ADR effects theatre, 41
cutting rooms, Dolby
installation

Mike Uden Opticals
21a Kingly Court
Kingly Street
London W1R 5LE
Tel: 01 439 1982
Opticals
Special effects

The Video Duplicating Co
Unit 8
Banbury Avenue
Slough

Berkshire SL1 4LH
Tel: 01 0753 25142
Comprehensive video services in all formats, tape to tape, film to tape mastering, bulk cassette duplication

Video London Sound Studios
16–18 Ramillies Street
London W1V 1DL
Tel: 01 734 4811
Sophisticated sound recording studio with overhead TV projection system, 16mm and 35mm post-synch recording and mixing. All sound facilities for film or video post-production

Video Time
22–24 Greek Street
London W1V 5LG
Tel: 01 439 1211
Video formats: 1″C, 1″B, BVU, BVU SP, Betacam, Betacam SP, MII, VHS, Betamax, V8, S-VHS (all PAL/NTSC/Secam)
Video disc cutting, audio layback, full 3M/C edit suite BVU/SP/U-Matic
Standards conversion:
ACE, 2 x ADAC, AVS
Telecine: 2 x Cintel MKIII
Video duplication

Videola
171 Wardour Street
London W1V 3TA
Tel: 01 437 9693
Video formats: 1″, BVU,
U-Matic
Cameras: Sony, Ikegami
Computer rostrum
camera
Editing: hi-band to 1″,
BVU

Videoscope
Cattwg Cottage
Llancarfan
Barry
South Glamorgan
CF6 9AG
Tel: 0446 710963
Video format: hi-band
U-Matic, Betacam, 1″
Cameras: Sony M3A,
Sony 330, Sony BVP3
APC/N
Timecode transfer,
3-machine, hi-band
editing

VisCentre
66–67 Newman Street
London W1P 3LA
Tel: 01 436 5692
Two-camera broadcast
interview studio
ENG crews worldwide
2-machine BVU Pal/
NTSC
2-machine Betacam PAL

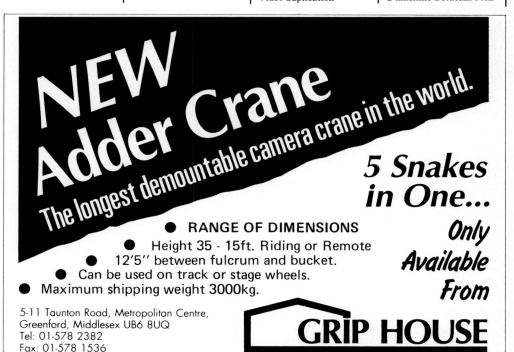

NEW Adder Crane
The longest demountable camera crane in the world.

5 Snakes in One...
Only Available From

● **RANGE OF DIMENSIONS**
● Height 35 - 15ft. Riding or Remote
● 12'5″ between fulcrum and bucket.
● Can be used on track or stage wheels.
● Maximum shipping weight 3000kg.

5-11 Taunton Road, Metropolitan Centre,
Greenford, Middlesex UB6 8UQ
Tel: 01-578 2382
Fax: 01-578 1536

GRIP HOUSE

Video formats: 1",
Betacam, BVU
Editing: Betacam SP
PAL, Betacam PAL,
BVU, PAL/NTSC
Standards conversion:
AVS
Telecine: Rank Cintel
enhanced MkIIIC 4:2:2
digital telecine 35/16 and
8mm with Da Vinci colour
corrector
Satellite transmissions

Visions
8 Dean Street
London W1V 5RL
Tel: 01 734 5231
Video formats: 1"C,
Betacam SP, BVU,
D-VTR
Editing: two 1" suites,
1 x multiformat Beta SP
and 1"
Special effects: 2 x
Channels ADO, 2
Channels Abekas A53
with warp. 1 Abekas A64
digital disc recorder
Graphics: Paintbox with
Abekas A64 digital disc
recorder
Telecine: Digital Rank
Cintel with Steadigate
Post office lines to Tower

Visions Mobiles
34 Fouberts Place
London W1V 2BH
Tel: 01 439 4536
Unit 1: 10 cameras, 3 x 1"
VTRs, Grass Valley 1600
vision mixer, Neve 24
channel audio mixer, full
monitoring and talk back,
Aston character

generator, full range of
lenses
Unit 2: 3 cameras, 2 x 1"
VTRs, 8 input vision
mixer, 12 channel audio
mixer, full monitoring
and talk back
Unit 3: 4/5 cameras, 2 x 1"
VTRs, GVG 1600 vision
mixer, 12 channel audio
mixer, Aston character
generator, full monitoring
and talk back
Unit 4: Up to 12 cameras,
6 x 1" VTRs, GVG 200
vision mixer, Neve 24
channel audio mixer,
32x16 routing matrix,
Aston character
generator, full monitoring
and talk back
VTR Unit: 4 x 1" VTRs,
Cox 16x8 vision/audio
matrix, full monitoring
and talk back

Visnews
Cumberland Avenue
London NW10 7EH
Tel: 01 965 7733
Video formats: 1"C, 1"B,
2", MII, Betacam SP, BVU
SP, Betacam, BVU, Video
8, U-Matic, VHS,
Betamax
Standards conversion:
Ace, Quantel and AVS
Transcoding: PAL-
SECAM-PAL
Post production: BVE
3000, Grass Valley,
Quantel 5001, Aston 3
Telecine: Rank Cintel
Enhanced MkIIIC 4:2:2
digital telecine, 35/16 and

8mm with da Vinci colour
corrector
Satellite transmissions
Complete 16mm film
laboratory

Wardour Studios
11 Wardour Mews
London W1
Tel: 01 439 4313

Warwick Dubbing Theatre
WFS (Film Facilities)
151–153 Wardour Street
London W1V 3TB
Tel: 01 437 5532
Sound transfer
Dubbing facilities

Wembley Studios
10 Northfield Industrial
Estate
Beresford Avenue
Wembley
Middlesex HA0 1RT
Tel: 01 903 4296
Studios: 3640 sq ft,
production offices,
dressing rooms

Barry Westwood Productions
231 West Street
Fareham
Hants PO16 0HZ
Tel: 0329 285941
Video format: U-Matic
Cameras: Sony DXC 1640
Mobile studio

Whitelion Facilities
Bradley Close
White Lion Street
London N1 9PN
Tel: 01 837 4836
Location units: Sony
BVP7 cameras recording
onto Betacam SP
Graphics: Quantel
Paintbox
Editing: main suite
equipped with 1", Beta
SP, Abekas A53-D,
caption camera and
Aston, plus two computer
controlled off-line 3
machine edit suites

David Williams Special Effects
Hendafarn
Pontrobert
Meifod
N Powys
Tel: 0938 84595
Special effects

Windmill Lane Pictures
4 Windmill Lane
Dublin 2

Tel: 0001 713444
Film, video, news and
recording
facilities

Wolff Productions
6a Noel Street
London W1V 3RB
Tel: 01 439 1838/734 4286
35mm/16mm rostrum
camera work
Animation production

John Wood Studios
Colquhoun House
27–37 Broadwick Street
London W1V 1FR
Tel: 01 439 9031
7 post-production
recording studios to
handle 35mm and 16mm.
Video and ¼" tape for TV
and radio advertising,
documentaries, TV
programmes and AVs,
plus full transfer suite
facilities

World Wide Sound
21–25 St Annes's Court
London W1V 3AW
Tel: 01 434 1121
ADR facility
High-speed rock'n'roll
dubbing theatres
Effects recording
Post synchronisation
Translation facilities

Worldwide Television News Corporation
31–36 Foley Street
London W1P 7LB
Tel: 01 323 3255
BVU editing (PAL and
NTSC); multi-machine
editing with digital
effects and colour
captioning; Betacam
record/replay; 1"C editing;
digital standards
conversion; PAL/SECAM
transcoding; duplication;
local and international
feeds

Yorkshire Film and Video Centre
Hall Place Studios
4 Hall Place
Leeds LS9 8JD
Tel: 0532 405553
16mm/U-Matic/VHS
production units,
lighting, cutting rooms,
edit suite with TBC,
rostrum camera, film/
video studio, sound
studio, 4-track 16mm
dubbing, sound transfer,
sound effects library

FILMED WITH

CAMERAS & LENSES

Panavision Europe
2 Wycombe Road, Stonebridge Park, Wembley,
Middlesex HAO 1QN, England
Tel: 01-902-3473, Telex: 291843 JDCG, FAX: 01-902-3273

FESTIVALS

Listed below by country of origin are the main international film, TV and video festivals with contact addresses and brief synopses

AUSTRALIA

Australian Video Festival (Sept)
PO Box 316
NSW 2021
Australia
Tel: (02) 339 9555
Competitive for video –
art, graphics, music,
documentary and drama/
narrative. Also includes a
student section

Melbourne Film Festival (June)
41-45 A'Beckett Street
Victoria 300
GOP Box 2760
Melbourne 3001
Australia
Tel: (3) 663 2953/2954
Non-competitive section
for feature films (60 mins
and over) and a
competitive section for
short films (less than 60
mins). Films should not
previously have been
shown in Melbourne

Sydney Film Festival (June)
Box 25
PO Glebe
NSW 2037
Australia
Tel: (2) 660 3844
Non-competitive for
feature films and shorts
not previously shown in
Australia

AUSTRIA

Viennale (March)
Turmstiege
Uraniastrasse 1
1010 Vienna
Austria
Tel: (222) 75 32 84
Non-competitive for
features and
documentaries

BELGIUM

Antwerp International Film Festival (March)
Antwerpse Film Stichting
Theatercentrum
Theaterplein 1
B-Antwerp
Belgium

Tel: (3) 232 66 77
Non-competitive for
documentary, fiction and
animation. Films must
have been completed in
three years prior to
festival and not
previously screened in
Belgium, the Netherlands
and Luxembourg

Brussels International Film Festival (Jan)
Palais des Congrès
32 avenue de
l'Astronomie
1030 Brussels
Belgium
Tel: (02) 538 7067
Competitive for feature
films

Brussels International Fantasy Film Festival (Sept)
Passage 44 Auditorium
Boulevard du Jardin
Botanique
1000 Brussels
Belgium
Competitive for features
and shorts (less than 50
mins), including
animation, produced in
the previous two-and-a-
half years

BRAZIL

Rio de Janeiro International Festival of Film, TV and Video (+ Market) (Nov)
Direcao Geral
Hotel Nacional
Av Niemeyer 769
São-Conrado
Brazil CEP 22450
Tel: (21) 322 2860/2855/
1064/1000
Competitive for films –
features and shorts, TV
and video – including
music, educational,
drama and news
programmes,
experimental video,
produced in previous year

BULGARIA

Varna World Animated Film Festival (Oct odd years)
Bulgariafilm
96 Rakovsky Street
Sofia 1000
Bulgaria
Tel: (2) 59 50 61/88 41 83
Competitive for animated
films produced in previous
two years, including
children's animation,
animation for TV, student
films, first films. (NB
Films awarded prizes at
Annecy or Zagreb not
accepted)

CANADA

Atlantic Film Festival (Oct–Nov)
Suite 24
5211 Blowers Street
Halifax
Nova Scotia
Canada
Tel: (902) 422 3429
Competitive for feature
films, animation,
experimental,
documentary, educational
and industrial. Also
includes student section,
first film/video, short
drama, news/current
affairs, TV variety and
commercials. All work
must have been made
during two years
preceding festival

Banff Television Festival (May–June)
St Julien Road
PO Box 1020
Banff
Alberta
Canada TOL OCO
Tel: (403) 762 3060
Competitive for films
made for television,
including features, drama
special, limited series,
continuing series,
documentary, children's
programmes and comedy
which were broadcast for
the first time in the
previous year

Canadian International Animation Festival
(Sept–Oct even years only)
217 George Street
Toronto
Ontario
Canada
Tel: (416) 367 0088
Competitive for animation

International Festival of New Cinema and Video
(Oct)
3724 Boulevard Saint-Laurent
Montreal
Quebec
Canada H2X 2V8
Tel: (514) 843 4725
Non-competitive for innovative films produced during previous two years which have not been screened in Canada

Montreal World Film Festival (+ Market) (Aug)
1455 de Maisonneuve Blvd West
Montreal
Quebec
Canada H3G IM8
Tel: (514) 848 3883
Competitive for feature films and shorts (up to 30 mins), produced in previous year, which have not been screened outside country of origin or been entered in other competitive festivals

Toronto Annual International Festival of Festivals
(Sept)
69 Yorkville Avenue
Suite 205
Toronto
Ontario M5R 1B8
Canada
Tel: (416) 967 7371
Non-competitive for feature films and shorts not previously shown in Canada. Also includes some American premieres, retrospectives and national cinema programmes. Films must have been completed within the year prior to the festival to be eligible

Vancouver International Film

Festival (Sept)
788 Beatty Street
Suite 303
Vancouver
BCV6B 2M1
Canada
Tel: (604) 685 0260

COLOMBIA
Cartagena International Film Festival (June)
Apartado Aereo 1834
Cartagena
Colombia
Tel: (58) 40 003
Competitive for films produced in Colombia and Latin America. Also non-competitive section for feature films, shorts and documentaries. Films must be subtitled in Spanish and not previously screened in Colombia

CZECHO-SLOVAKIA
Golden Prague International TV Festival (June)
Czechoslovakia
Television
Gorkeho nam 29
111 50 Prague 1
Czechoslovakia
Tel: (2) 220158

Karlovy Vary International Film Festival (+ Market)
(June–July even years, alternates with Moscow)
Vaclavské Nám 28
11145 Prague 1
Czechoslovakia
Tel: (2) 24 67 41
Competitive for feature films and shorts, including first films and documentaries, produced in previous 14 months and not shown in competition at other festivals

EGYPT
Cairo International Film Festival (Dec)
11 Oraby St
Cairo
Egypt
Tel: (2) 753988/758979
Non-competitive for feature films and shorts (up to 30 mins) in festival of festivals section.

Entries must have been produced in preceding four years

EIRE
Cork Film Festival
(Sept–Oct)
5 Tuckey Street
Cork
Eire
Tel: (2) 271711
Non-competitive for features, documentaries, animation, video, and student films. Also competitive for short films (up to 35 mins) produced in the previous year

FINLAND
Tampere International Short Film Festival (Feb–March)
PO Box 305
SF 33101 Tampere 10
Finland
Tel: (32) 35681
Competitive for short films (up to 35 mins), including fiction, animation, documentary, experimental and children's fiction, produced in the previous year

FRANCE
Annecy International Festival of Animation (+ Market) (May–June odd years)
4 Passage des Clercs
BP 399
74013 Annecy Cedex
France
Tel: (50) 51 78 14
Competitive for animated short films, non-competitive for animated feature-length films, produced in the previous 26 months

Avoriaz International Fantasy Film Festival (Jan)
33 Avenue Mac-Mahon
75017 Paris
France
Tel: (1) 47 55 71 40
Competitive for science fiction, horror, supernatural and fantasy

feature films, which have not been commercially shown in France or participated in festivals in Europe

Cannes International Film Festival (May)
71 Rue du Faubourg St Honoré
75008 Paris
France
Tel: (1) 42 66 92 20
Directors Fortnight
215 Rue du Faubourg St Honoré
75008 Paris
France
Tel: (1) 45 61 01 66
Semaine de la Critique
90 Rue d'Amsterdam
75009 Paris
France
Tel: (1) 40 16 98 30/(1) 45 74 53 53
Competitive section for feature films and shorts (up to 15 mins) produced in the previous year, which have not screened outside country of origin nor been entered in other competitive festivals. Plus non-competitive events – Director's Fortnight, Critic's Week and programme of French cinema

Creteil International Festival of Women's Films (+ Market) (March)
Maison des Arts
Place Salvador Allende
94000 Creteil
France
Tel: (1) 48 99 90 50/ (1) 42 07 38 98
Competitive for feature films, shorts, retrospectives directed by women and produced in the previous 23 months and not previously shown in France

Deauville European Festival of American Film (Sept)
33 Avenue Mac-Mahon
75017 Paris
France
Tel: 755 71 40
Non-competitive festival of American feature films, not yet released in Europe (except UK), or shown in other French film festivals

MIP-TV International TV Programme Market
(April)
179 Avenue Victor Hugo
75116 Paris
France
Tel: 505 14 03
Market for television programmes, TV films and video. Non-competitive

Montbéliard International Video and TV Festival
(May)
Centre d'Action Culturelle
12 rue du College
25204 Montbéliard
France
Tel: (81) 91 37 11/
91 49 67/91 09 23
Competitive for documentaries, news, fiction, art, animation, music, computer graphics produced during 18 months preceding festival

Paris Festival of Science Fiction and Fantasy Films (+ Market) (Nov)
9 Rue du Midi
92200 Neuilly
France
Tel: 624 04 71/745 62 31
Competitive for features and shorts

GERMANY (EAST)

Leipzig International Documentary, Short Film and TV Festival (Nov)
DDR 1055 Berlin
Chodowieckistrasse 32
E Germany
Tel: (4) 30 0617

GERMANY (WEST)

Berlin International Film Festival (Feb)
Budapester Strasse 50
D-1000 Berlin 30
W Germany
Tel: (30) 254 89 0
Competitive for feature films and shorts (up to 15 mins), plus a separate competition for children's

films – feature length and shorts – produced in the previous year and not entered for other festivals. Also has non-competitive programme consisting of Forum of Young Cinema, Film Market and an Information Show

Mannheim International Filmweek (Oct)
Stadt Mannheim
Rathaus E5
D-6800 Mannheim 1
W Germany
Tel: (621) 192 27 45
Competitive for first features, documentaries, short films, animation and TV films, released in the previous year not previously shown in W Germany

Munich Film Festival (June–July)
München Filmwochen
Turkenstrasse 93
8000 München 40
W Germany
Tel: (89) 39 30 11/12
Non-competitive for feature films, shorts and documentaries which have not previously been shown in W Germany

Oberhausen International Short Film Festival
(March–April)
Westdeutsche Kurzfilmtage
Grillostrasse 34
4200 Oberhausen 1
W Germany
Tel: (208) 825 2651
Competitive for social documentaries (up to 60 mins), animation, experimental and short features (up to 35 mins), student films, which have been produced in the previous 16 months and not previously shown in W Germany

Prix Futura International Radio and TV Contest
(April odd years)
Sender Freies Berlin
Masurenallee 8-14
D-1000 Berlin 19
W Germany
Tel: (030) 308 2302
Competition for TV

programmes (documentary and drama) and radio (documentary and drama) which were first broadcast in the preceding two years. Only two entries per organisation are accepted

Prix Jeunesse International Television Competition (May–June even years only)
Bayerischer Rundfunk
Rundfunkplatz 1
D-8000 Munich 2
W Germany
Tel: (089) 5900 2058
Competitive for TV drama, documentaries and music programmes, produced in the previous two years. Only two entries per organisation are accepted

Stuttgart International Animated Film Festival (Jan–Feb even years only)
Stuttgarter Trickfilmtage
Kernerstrasse 65
D-7000 Stuttgart 1
W Germany
Competitive for animated short films of an artistic and experimental nature, which have been produced in the previous five years

HONG KONG

Hong Kong International Film Festival (March–April)
Hong Kong Coliseum
Annex Building
Parking Deck Floor
KCR Kowloon Station
8 Cheong Wan Road
Kowloon
Hong Kong
Tel: (3) 642217
Non-competitive for feature films, documentaries and invited short films, which have been produced in the previous two years

INDIA

International Film Festival of India (+ Market)/Filmotsav
(Jan)
Directorate of Film Festivals

Lok Nayak Bhawan
Fourth Floor
Khan Market
New Delhi 110 002
India
Tel: (9) 694 920/
(9) 615 953
Pamela Cullen
National Film Development Corporation
42 Hertford Street
London W1Y 7TF
Held in New Delhi in odd years when it is competitive for feature films and shorts which have not been shown in competition elsewhere. In even numbered years it is non-competitive and held in Bombay

ITALY

Cattolica International Mystery Festival – Mystfest (June–July)
Direzione Mystfest
Via dei Coronari 44
00186 Rome
Italy
Tel: (6) 6567 902
Competitive for television thrillers between 30-180 mins length, which have been produced in the previous year and not broadcast in Italy

Florence International Festival of Independent Cinema (May)
Via Martiri del Popolo 27
50122 Florence
Italy
Tel: (055) 245869/243651
Non-competitive for recent quality feature-length fiction films

Florence International Festival of Social Documentary Films – Festival dei Popoli (Nov–Dec)
Via Fiume 14
14-50123 Florence
Italy
Tel: (055) 294353
Competitive for documentaries on sociological, political, anthropological, economic, folklore and ethnographic subjects.

Plus a non-competitive information section. Entries must not have been released previously in Italy

MIFED (Milan) (April)
Largo Domodossola 1
CP 1270
20145 Milan
Italy
Tel: (39) 24678
Competitive for films and television programmes on aspects of maritime activities, including technical, scientific, tourism, sports, energy research subjects. Entries must have been produced during three years preceding festival

Pesaro International Festival of New Cinema (+ Market)
(June)
Via Yser 8
00198 Rome
Italy
Tel: (06) 369524
Non-competitive for films from new directors, film groups and national cinemas

Pordenone Le Giornate del Cinema Muto (Sept–Oct)
Segretaria
Viale Grigoletti 20
33170 Pordenone
Italy
Non-competitive silent film festival. Annual award for restoration and preservation of the silent film heritage

Prix Italia (Sept–Oct)
RAI Radiotelevisione Italiana
Viale Mazzini 14
00195 Rome
Italy
Tel: 3878 4118
Competitive for television and radio productions (up to 90 mins) from national broadcasting organisations. Only two productions per country accepted

Salerno International Film Festival (Oct)
Casella Postale 137
Salerno 84100
Italy

Tel: (89) 223 19 53
Competitive for scientific, medical, educational, animation, sponsored feature and documentary films

Taormina International Film Festival (July)
Via Belsiana 100
Rome 00187
Italy
Tel: (6) 679197
Competitive for directors of first and second feature films. Emphasis on new directors and cinema from developing countries

Turin International Youth Film Festival
(Oct)
Via Cavour 19
10123 Turin
Italy
Tel: (011) 540 037/531 733
Non-competitive for films by and for young people made during the preceding 21 months and not screened commercially in Italy

La Biennale di Venezia (Aug–Sept)
Settore Cinema and Spettacolo Televisivo
Ca' Giustinian
San Marco
30124 Venice
Italy
Competitive for feature films which have not been shown at other festivals or released outside the country of origin. By invitation only

JAPAN
Hiroshima International Animation Festival
(Aug)
1-1 Nakajima-cho
Naka-ku
Hiroshima 730
Tel: (82) 245 0145/46
Non-competitive for promotional material (up to 5 mins), student debut and work by independent filmmakers intended for public exhibition. Also includes works for children and educational purposes

Tokyo Video Festival (Sept)
c/o Victor Co of Japan
1 Nihombashi-Honcho 4 Chome
Chuo-ku
Tokyo
103 Japan
Michael Whyman
Video Information Centre
82 Piccadilly
London W1
Tel: 01 491 3909
Competitive for videos up to 20 mins in length

Tokyo International Film Festival (Sept odd years only)
Organizing Committee
Asano Building No 3
2-14-19 Ginza Chuo-Ku
Tokyo 104
Japan
Tel: (03) 563 6305
Competitive international festival. Young cinema section for first films by young directors born in or after 1952. Films must have been produced during the 18 months prior to the festival, and not have won any award at events recognised by the IFFPA

MONACO
Monte Carlo International TV Festival (Feb)
Palais des Congrès
Avenue d'Ostende
Monte Carlo
Monaco
78 Avenue des Champs Elysées
75008 Paris
France
Tel: (1) 43 59 70 28/
45 62 31 00
Competitive for television productions in drama, news reports and documentary sections

THE NETHERLANDS
Stichting Film Festival Rotterdam
(Jan–Feb)
Kruishofkade 36b
3012 EJ Rotterdam
The Netherlands
Tel: (10) 411 80 80
Non-competitive for feature films. Retrospective programmes

NEW ZEALAND
Auckland International Film Festival (July)
PO Box 1411
Auckland
New Zealand
Tel: 33 629
Non-competitive for shorts (up to 45 mins) and feature films (up to 180 mins)

Wellington Film Festival (July)
PO Box 9544
Courtenay Place
Wellington
New Zealand
Tel: 850 162
Non-competitive for feature and short films not screened at festivals outside New Zealand. By invitation only

POLAND
Cracow International Festival of Short Films (May–June)
Pl Zwyciestwa 9
PO Box 127
00950 Warsaw
Poland
Tel: (22) 26 40 51
Competitive for short films (up to 30 mins), including documentaries, fiction, animation, popular science and experimental subjects, produced in the previous 15 months and not awarded prizes in other international festivals

PORTUGAL
Espinho International Animated Film Festival (Nov)
Organizing Committee 'Cinanima'
Apartado 43
4501 Espinho Codex
Portugal
Tel: (2) 721621/724611
Competitive for features, advertising, children, youth and experimental films. Also includes work by student-directors. Entries must have been completed in the two years preceding festival

Oporto Fantasporto (Feb)
Rua Diogo Brandao 87
4000 Oporto
Portugal
Tel: (2) 32 07 59
Competitive section for feature films and shorts, produced in the previous three years. Also holds retrospectives, an information section and a programme of Portuguese cinema

SPAIN

Bilbao International Festival of Documentary and Short Films (Nov)
Colón de Larreátegui 37-40
48009 Bilbao
Spain
Tel: (4) 24 8698/16 5429/24 7860
Competitive for documentary, animation, drama and experimental short films (up to 60 mins, except documentaries), produced in the previous two years, which have not won awards at other European festivals

Costa Brava International Festival of Cinema (June)
San Feliu de Guixols
Gerona
Spain
Competitive for features and shorts produced 3½ years preceding festival

Huesca International Short Film Festival (Nov)
Cortos – Ciudad de Huesca
Ricado de Arco 6
22003 Huesca
Spain
Tel: (974) 22 70 58
Competitive for short films (up to 30 mins) on any theme except tourism and promotion. Films which have won awards at other festivals are not elegible. Entries must have been produced in the previous two years

Madrid International Film Festival – Imagfic (March)
Gran Via 62-8
Madrid 28013
Spain
Competitive for science fiction and fantasy films

Murcia International Festival of Short Films (March)
Centro Cultural Salzillo 7
30001 Murcia
Spain
Tel: (968) 21 77 52/71 23 02
Competitive for fiction, animation and documentaries

Oviedo International Video-Film Festival (July)
Nueve de Mayo 2-1 A
Oviedo 1
Spain
Tel: (985) 22 20 96/7/8 ext 30
Competitive for programmes made on video (up to 30 mins), defence of nature programmes (up to 45 mins) and feature films recorded on video. Non-competitive information section

San Sebastián International Film and Video Festival (Sept)
Apartado Correos 397
Reina Regenta s/n
20080 San Sebastian
Spain
Tel: (43) 42 96 25
Competitive for feature films and shorts (up to 15 mins), produced in the previous year and not released in Spain or shown in any other festivals. Also section for new directors

Seville International Film Festival (Oct)
Paseo de Colón II
Seville
Spain
Non-competitive for features and shorts (up to 35 mins). Also holds information and official screenings and an Andalusian film competition

Sitges International Festival of Fantastic Cinema (Oct)
Rambla Catalunya 81
Barcelona 08008
Spain
Tel: (3) 215 74 91/215 73 17
Competitive for fantasy and horror films and shorts. Plus information section and retrospective programmes

SWEDEN

Gothenburg Film Festival (Jan–Feb)
Box 7079
S-402 32 Gothenburg
Sweden
Tel: (31) 41 05 46/41 05 47
Non-competitive for independent feature films which have not been released in Sweden

Uppsala International Film Festival (Oct)
Kulturforeningen for Filmfestival i Uppsala
Box 1746
75147 Uppsala
Sweden
Tel: (46) 18 10 18 30
Competitive for shorts, features and children's films, fiction, documentaries, animation and experimental (up to 60 mins). No advertising or tourist films

SWITZERLAND

Geneva International Video Week (Nov)
Maison des Jeunes et de la Culture
5 rue du Temple
1201 Geneva
Switzerland
Competitive for original work displaying an individual approach (up to 13 mins in length) and made less than a year before festival

Locarno International Film Festival (+ Market) (Aug)
Via della Posta G
CP 465
CH 6600 Locarno
Switzerland
Tel: (093) 32 02 32
Competitive for fiction films by new directors and TV movies, produced in the previous year, which have not won prizes at other festivals. Plus information and retrospective programmes

Golden Rose of Montreux TV Festival (May)
Case Postale 97
1820 Montreux
Switzerland
Secretariat de la Rose d'Or de Montreux
Direction Generale de la SSR
Giacomettistrasse 1-3
CH 3000 Berne 15
Switzerland
Tel: (32) 43 92 11
Competitive for TV productions (24-60 mins) of light-entertainment, music and variety, first broadcast in the previous 14 months

TUNISIA

International Film Festival of Carthage (Oct even years only)
The JCC Managing Committee
PO Box 1029-1045
Tunis RP
Tunisia
Tel: 262 034
Competitive for short and full-length films by, or concerned with, African and Arab societies. Also children's film section and international film market. Entries must have been made within two years before festival and not have been awarded a prize at any previous festival in an African or Arab country

UNITED KINGDOM

Birmingham Film and Television Festival (Oct–Nov)
Film Festival Office
Midlands Arts Centre
Cannon Hill Park
Birmingham B12 9QH
Tel: (021) 440 2543/4221

The Bristol Animation Festival (formerly the Cambridge Animation Festival)
(Oct–Nov odd years only)
41b Hornsey Lane Gardens
London N6 5NY
Tel: (01) 341 5015
Non-competitive thematic festival. Entry by invitation only

Cambridge Film Festival (July)
Arts Cinema
Market Passage
Cambridge CB2 3PF
Tel: (0233) 351263/316914
Non-competitive for feature films; some selected from other festivals, original choices, short retrospectives and revived classics

Edinburgh International Film Festival (Aug–Sept)
Filmhouse
88 Lothian Road
Edinburgh EH3 9BZ
Scotland
Tel: (031) 228 6382/3
Non-competitive for feature films and shorts produced in the previous year. Plus retrospective programmes

Edinburgh International Television Festival
(Aug–Sept)
c/o EITF
5 Betterton Street
London WC2H 9BU
Conference discussing current issues in television, accompanied by screenings of television programmes grouped according to the themes/topics under discussion

Guildford Independent Video Festival (March–April)
13 Litchfield Way
Onslow Village
Guildford
Surrey
Non-competitive for video (max 20 mins) produced in and around West Surrey. Work originated on other media is accepted, but final product must be on video

International Festival of Film and TV in the Celtic Countries (Scotland, Wales, Ireland, Brittany – March peripatetic)
The Library
Farraline Park
Inverness IV1 1LS
Scotland
Tel: (0463) 226189
Competitive for films whose subject matter has particular relevance to the Celtic nations

IVCA Film and Video Festival (June)
International Visual Communications Association
(incorporating BISFA and ITVA)
Bolsover House
5/6 Clipstone Street
London W1P 7EB
Tel: (01) 580 0962
Competitive for industrial/training films and videos, covering all aspects of the manufacturing and commercial world, plus categories for educational, environmental, leisure and communications subjects. Entries to have been produced or sponsored by a British company in the preceding 18 months

Leicester Super 8 Festival (Nov)
Leicester Film and Video Association
11 Newark Street
Leicester LE1 5SS
Tel: (0533) 559711 ext 294
Non-competitive for Super 8 films, includes international retrospective and programmes of new work

London International Film Festival (Nov–Dec)

National Film Theatre
South Bank
London SE1 8XT
Tel: (01) 928 0536
Non-competitive festival for feature films and shorts, by invitation only, which have not previously been released in Great Britain. Films are selected from other festivals, plus some original choices

National Festival of Independent Video (Oct–Nov)

The Media Centre
South Hill Park
Bracknell
Berkshire RG12 4PA
Tel: (0344) 427272
Non-competitive for educational, political, community and arts video. Entries must have been produced during previous 12 months

Southampton Film Festival (Feb–March)

Room 342
Civic Centre
Southampton SO9 4XF
Tel: (0703) 223855
Non-competitive festival open to all categories

Tyneside Film Festival (Oct)

Tyneside Cinema
10-12 Pilgrim Street
Newcastle-upon-Tyne
Tel: (091) 232 8298/9
Competitive for independent cinema from around the world, covering feature films, shorts and documentary productions which have not had general cinema distribution

USA

American Film Festival (May–June)

Educational Film Library Association
45 John Street
New York
NY 10038
USA
Competitive for films on all subjects, intended for non-theatrical use in educational institutions. Films must have been

two years and be available for hire or sale in USA.

American Film Market – AFM (Feb–March)

9000 Sunset Boulevard
Suite 516
Los Angeles
California 90069
USA
Tel: (213) 275 3400
Market for international film, TV and video

Athens Video Festival (Nov)

PO Box 388
Athens
Ohio 45701
USA
Tel: (614) 594 6888/
593 1330
Competitive for video including art, narrative, documentary, education and video record. Entries must have been produced in two years preceding festival

Chicago International Film Festival (Nov)

415 North Dearborn Street
Chicago
Illinois 60610
USA
Tel: (312) 644 3400
Competitive for feature films, shorts, animation, TV productions, student films and commercials

Cleveland International Film Festival (March–April)

1501 Euclid Avenue
Suite 510
Cleveland
Ohio 44115
USA
Competitive for feature, narrative, documentary, animation and experimental films

Denver International Film Festival (Oct)

999 Eighteenth Street
Suite 247
PO Box 17508
Denver
Colorado 80217
USA
Tel: (303) 298 8223
Non-competitive mainly for independent material – features, shorts,

documentary, animation and children's films. Entry by invitation only

Los Angeles International Film Exposition – Filmex (April)

Berwin Entertainment Complex
6525 Sunset Boulevard
Hollywood
USA 90028 7275
Tel: (213) 856 7707
Non-competitive for feature films, shorts, animation, documentary and experimental films - mostly by invitation

New York Film Festival (Sept–Oct)

140 West 65th Street
New York
NY 10023
USA
Tel: (212) 877 1800
Non-competitive for feature films, shorts (up to 30 mins), including drama, documentary, animation and experimental films. Films must have been produced in the 15 months prior to festival

New York International Film and TV Festival (Nov)

IFTF of New York Inc
246 West 38th Street
New York
NY 10018
USA
Tel: (914) 238 4481
Competitive for industrial and educational films, filmstrips, shorts and commercials which have been produced in the previous year

San Francisco International Film Festival (March)

1560 Fillmore
San Francisco
CA 94115
USA
Tel: (415) 567 4641
Primarily non-competitive for features by invitation only. Also includes a competitive section for shorts, documentaries, animation, experimental works, and TV productions

US Film and Video Festival (April)

841 North Addison Avenue
Elmhurst
Illinois 60126
USA
Tel: (312) 834 7773
Competitive for films and videos produced during previous year

USSR

Moscow International Film Festival (July odd years)

Sovinterfest
State Committee for Cinematography of the USSR
10 Khokhlovsky per
Moscow 109028
USSR
Tel: (95) 297 7645
Competitive for feature films (up to 150 mins), shorts, children's films (up to 35 mins), produced in the previous two years. Plus a non-competitive section and an information programme

YUGOSLAVIA

Zagreb World Festival of Animated Films (June even years)

Nova Ves 18
41000 Zagreb
Yugoslavia
Tel: (41) 276 636
Competitive for animated films (up to 30 mins), educational children's films and first films categories. Films must have been completed in two years prior to festival and not have been awarded prizes at Annecy or Varna in the previous year

**We are pleased
to continue our support
for the BFI Film
and Television Handbook.**

FILM SOCIETIES

Listed below are UK film societies which are open to the public. Addresses are grouped in broad geographical areas, along with the regional officers who can offer specific local information. There is a constant turnover of society officers, so if your enquiry goes astray, you should contact the Film Society Unit at the BFI (see p14). The Film Society Unit can also provide addresses of film societies based in educational establishments, which are not included in these listings

BFFS CONSTITUENT GROUPS

The Film Society Unit exists to service the British Federation of Film Societies.
The BFFS is divided into Constituent Groups which usually follow the borders of Regional Arts Associations, but sometimes include more than one RAA area

London
Greater London Arts Association area

Southern
Berkshire, Buckinghamshire, Hampshire, Isle of Wight, Kent, Oxfordshire, Surrey, Sussex

South West
Channel Islands, Cornwall, Devon, Dorset, Gloucestershire, Somerset, Wiltshire

Eastern
Bedfordshire, Cambridgeshire, Ely, Essex, Hertfordshire, Huntingdon, Norfolk, Peterborough, Suffolk

Lincolnshire and Humberside
East Riding, Lincolnshire

Midlands
Derby, Herefordshire, Leicestershire, Northamptonshire, Nottinghamshire, Shropshire, Staffordshire, Warwickshire, Worcestershire

Northern
Cumberland, Durham, Northumberland, Westmoreland

Yorkshire
North and West Ridings

North West
Cheshire, Lancashire, Northern Ireland

Wales

Scotland

LONDON

BFFS London Group
Mr M Sullivan
7 Contour House
663 London Road
North Cheam
Surrey SM3 9DF

Aquila Film Society
Mr M A Lever
Block 4, DGDQA
'Aquila' Golf Road
Bromley
Kent BR1 2JB

Australian Film Society
Mr S C Hughes
'Eagle'
33 Delius Way
Stanford-Le-Hope
Essex SS17 8RG

Avant-Garde Film Society
Mr C J White
9 Elmbridge Drive
Ruislip
Middlesex HA4 7XD

Barbican Film Society
Christine Freetham
348 Henley Road
Ilford Essex IG1 2TJ

Battersea Arts Centre Film Society
Mr D Hughes
The Old Town Hall
Lavender Hill
London SW11 5TF

Belvedere Film Society
Mr O Moore
c/o RB/PA/ADA Room 1B4W
County Hall
London SE1 7PB

Bowring Film Society
Ms D Woods
58 Beehive Lane
Redbridge
Ilford Essex IG1 3RS

Camberwell Film Appreciation Society
Richard Mason
Camberwell School of Art
Peckham Road
London SE5

Education Through Art
Mr S Barnham
98 High Street
Croydon
Surrey
CR0 1ND

Environment and Transport Film Society
Ms Clare Shaw
Room 260 Lambeth
Bridge House
Embankment
London SE1 7SB

Four Corners Film Club
Ms Sylvia Hines
113 Roman Road
London E2

Gothique Film Society
Mr R James
75 Burns Avenue
Feltham
Middlesex TW14 9LX

Greenwich Film Society
Mr Stan Slaughter
11 Campana Road
Fulham
London SW6 4AS

Holborn Film Society
Mr A Sykes
90 Church Road
Richmond
Surrey TW10 6LW

Hounslow Film Society
Mr B R Walkinshaw
Civic Centre
Lampton Road
Hounslow
Middx TW3 4DN

Institut Français du Royaume-Uni Film Society
The Secretary
17 Queensberry Place
London SW7 2DT

Lambeth Film Society
Mrs J Abbott
22 Hoadly Road
London SW16 1AR

Lensbury Film Society
Mrs A Catto
Shell Centre
Room Y1085, York Road
Waterloo
London SE1 7NA

Lewisham Film Society
Mr N Binstead
125 Thornsbeach Road
London SE6 1HB

London Film-Makers Co-Op
Mr M Maziere
The Cinema
42 Gloucester Avenue
London NW1

Mullard House Film Society
Mr R Howells
Mullard House
Torrington Place
London WC1E 7HD

North London Film Theatre
Miss B Underwood
19 Norman Way
Southgate
London N14 6LY

Polish Social and Cultural Association
Mr A Ostaszewski
238–246 King Street
London W6 0RF

Richmond Film Society
Mr N Wilson
94 Fifth Cross Road
Twickenham
Middx TW2 5LB

South London Film Society
Dr M Essex-Lopresti
14 Oakwood Park Road
Southgate
London N14 6QG

UDT Film Society
Mr M A Finlay
1 Lyonsdown Road
New Barnet
Herts EN5 1HU

Visionaries
Mr John Beech
1 Norfolk Road
Thornton Heath
Surrey CR4 8ND

Waltham Forest (Libs) Film Society
Mrs V Bates
William Morris Gallery
Lloyd Park
Forest Road
Walthamstow E17 4PP

Washouse Film Society
Debbie Leistnter
Oak Tree Community Centre
Osborne Road
Acton
London W3

Woolwich and District Co-op Film Society
Mr P Graham
10 Harden Court
Tamar Street
Charlton
London SE7 8DQ

SOUTHERN

BFFS Southern Group
Mr D Smithers
1 Vanstone Cottages
Bagshot Road
Egham
Surrey TW20 0RS

Abingdon College and District Film Society
Mr M Bloom
Abingdon College of FE
Northcourt Road
Abingdon
Oxon 0X14 1NN

Amersham and Chesham Film Society
Mr D Goddard
9 Hospital Hill
Chesham
Bucks

Arundel Festival Film Society
Mrs J Beard
18 Tarrant Street
Arundel
West Sussex

Aylesbury Vale Film Society
Mr A Brockington
3 Kings Road
Aylesbury
Bucks HP21 7RR

Bracknell Film Society
Mrs Shelagh Barnett
35 Spinis
Roman Wood
Bracknell
Berks RG12 4XA

Burford Feature Film Society
Mr N Wallen
Lane End
Cheyne Lane
Bampton
Oxon OX8 2HB

Chertsey Film Society
Mr H Lawes
29 Sayes Court

Addlestone
Surrey KT15 1NA

Chichester City Film Society
Mr R Gibson
Westlands
Main Road Hunston
Chichester
West Sussex PO20 6AL

Cranbrook Film Society
Mrs C Williams
1 Aurania Villas
Cranbrook Road
Hawkhurst
Kent

Cranleigh Film Society
Mr H B Hemingway
9 Hitherwood
Cranleigh
Surrey GU6 8BN

Ditchling Film Society
Mr G Hinckley
11 The Fieldway
Lewes Road
Ditchling
Hassocks
West Sussex BN6 8UA

Dover Film Society
Miss M A Potts
8 Chevalier Road
Dover
Kent CT17 9PG

Eastbourne Film Society
Miss B A E Wilson
2 Chalk Farm Close
Willingdon
Eastbourne
East Sussex BN20 9HY

Fareham Film Society
Mr Finch, Director
Fareham and Gosport
Drama Centre
Osborn Road
Fareham
Hants PO16 7DX

Farnham Film Society
Mrs P M Woodroffe
c/o The Maltings
Bridge Square
Farnham
Surrey GU9 7QR

Faversham Film Society
Mrs V Cackett
15 South Road
Faversham
Kent ME13 7LR

Harwell Film Society
Ms J Allan
B150 AERE
Harwell
Didcot
Oxon OX11 0RA

Havant Film Society
Mrs P Stallworthy
The Old Town Hall
East Street
Havant
Hants PO9 1BS

Henley-on-Thames Film Society
Mr P Whitaker
10 St Andrews Road
Henley-on-Thames
Oxon RG9 1HP

Horsham Film Society
Mr R J Alderton
The Round House
Brighton Road
Woodmancote
Henfield
West Sussex BN5 9ST

Isle of Wight Film Society
Mr D Havis
52 Victoria Avenue
Shanklin
Isle of Wight PO37 6LY

Jersey Film Society
Ms Fiona Emmett
7 Grouvill Park
Grouvill
Jersey
Channel Islands

Lewes Film Society
Ms V Craver
58a Grange Road
Lewes
East Sussex BN7 1TN

Maidstone Film Society
Ms C Herrmann
60 Church Road
Tovil
Maidstone
Kent ME15 6QY

Newbury Film Society
Mrs J Markham
19 Gloucester Road
Newbury
Berks RG14 5JF

Old Market Arts Centre Film Society
Mr J Marsh
54 Tivoli Crescent

Brighton
Sussex BN1 5ND

Portsmouth PO Area Film Society
Mr D Stubbington
72 Newcomen Road
Stamshaw
Portsmouth
Hants PO2 8LB

Reigate and Redhill Film Society
Mrs A Spice
17 Parkgate Road
Reigate
Surrey RH2 7JL

Rewley House Film Theatre Club
M J Shallis
Rewley House (Dept Ext Studies)
1 Wellington Square
Oxford OX1 2JA

Salisbury Film Society
Mrs S Collier
45 St Ann Street
Salisbury
Wiltshire

Slough Co-Operative Film Society
Mr C A Sissons
39 Hardy Close
Cippenham
Slough
Berks SL1 9AH

Stables Film Society
Mr Ivor Hopkins
2 Stanhope Place
St Leonards on Sea
East Sussex TN38 0ED

Steyning Film Society
Mr W Martin
6 Elm Terrace
Elm Grove Lane
Steyning
West Sussex BN4 3RB

Walton and Weybridge Film Society
Mrs P Davidoff
13 Woodlands Park
Spinney Hill
Addlestone
Surrey KT15 1AG

West End Centre (Aldershot) Film Society
Ms J Bowden
West End Centre

Queens Road
Aldershot
Hants GU11 3JD

West Oxfordshire Arts Association
Mr J Bliss
4 Broad Street
Bampton
Oxford OX8 2LS

Winchester Film Society
Ms A Rushworth
1 Lower Farm Cottages
Owslebury
Winchester
Hants SO21 1JJ

Windsor Arts Centre Film Society
Mr C Brooker
61 Sheet Street
Windsor
Berks SL4 1BY

Woking's New Cinema Club
Mr A E Rozelaar
67 Lansdown Close
St Johns
Woking
Surrey GU21 1TG

Worthing Film Society
Fiona Heselgrave
Connaught Theatre
Union Place
Worthing

SOUTH WEST

BFFS South West Group
Mr B Clay
1 Arbutus Close
Dorchester
Dorset DT1 1PZ

Bath Film Society
Ms Carole Sartain
c/o Royal Photographic Society
Milsom Street
Bath
Avon BA1 1DN

Bideford Film Club
Mr A Whittaker
Factory Cottage
Rope Walk
Bideford
Devon EX39 2NA

Blandford Forum Film Society
Mr J E England
6 Kings Road
Blandford Forum
Dorset DT11 7LD

Bournemouth and Poole Film Society
Mrs C Stevenson
15 Milestone Road
Oakdale
Poole
Dorset BH15 3DR

Bridport Film Society
Mrs M Wood
Greenways
9 Bowhayes
Bridport
Dorset DT6 4EB

Cheltenham Film Society
Mrs N Weir
Orchard Cottage
Whitminster Lane
Frampton on Severn
Glos GL2 7PR

Dartington Arts Film Society
The Arts Officer
College of Arts
Dartington Hall
Totnes
Devon TQ9 6EJ

Dorchester Film Society
Mr N Holt
Stallen
621 Dorchester Road
Broadway
Weymouth
Dorset DT3 5BX

Exeter Film Society
Ms H James
16 Pavilion Place
Exeter
Devon EX2 4HR

Gloucester Film Society
Mr C Toomey
8 Garden Way
Longlevens
Gloucester GL2 9JL

Holsworthy Film Society
Ms C Wade
Olympia Bungalow
The Green
Chilsworthy
Holsworthy
Devon EX22 7BQ

Lyme Regis Film Society
Ms Selina Hill
Sundial House
Marine Parade
Lyme Regis
Dorset DT7 3JQ

Merlin Theatre Film Society
Mr M Golder
c/o Merlin Theatre
Bath Road
Frome
Somerset BA11 2HQ

'Projection' Penwith's Film Society
Mrs G Little
5 Alma Terrace
Penzance
Cornwall TR18 2BY

Rolle College Community Arts Group Film Society
Mr J Collins
Rolle College
2 Douglas Avenue
Exmouth
Devon EXB 2AT

Shaftesbury Arts Centre Film Society
Mr P Schilling
Sheepwash Cottage
Barton
Mere
Warminster
Wilts BA12 6BR

Stroud and District Film Society
Mrs M G Allington
'Camelot'
East Drive
Ebley
Stroud
Glos GL5 4QF

Swindon Film Society
Mrs S Suchopar
The Limes
22 Oxford Street
Ramsbury
Marlborough
Wilts SN8 2PS

Tavistock Film Society
Mr C Taylor
19 St Maryhaye
Treetops
Tavistock
Devon PL19 8LR

Thornbury Film Society
Mr A J Gullick
9 Meadowside
Thornbury
Bristol BS12 2EN

Yeovil Cinematheque
Mr P Walkley
Yeovil College
Ilchester Road
Yeovil
Somerset BA21 3BA

EASTERN

BFFS Eastern Group
Mr C Jeffries
78 Fieldside
Ely
Cambridgeshire CB6 3AR

Bedford Film Society
Ms C Taylor
35 Putnoe Lane
Bedford
Beds MK41 9AD

Berkhamsted Film Society
Dr C J S Davies
Seasons
Gardenfield Lane
Berkhamsted
Herts HP4 2NN

Bury St Edmunds Film Society
Mr J W Garbutt
Sharon Livermere Road
Conyers Green
Bury St Edmunds
Suffolk IP31 2QG

Epping Film Society
Mr A R Carr
58 Centre Drive
Epping
Essex CM16 4JE

Fermoy Centre Film Society
Mr A Wilkinson
27 King Street
King's Lynn
Norfolk PE30 1HA

Great Yarmouth Film Society
Mr E C Hunt
21 Park Lane
Norwich
Norfolk NR2 3EE

International University Film Society
Mr D B Rogalski
The Avenue
Bushey
Herts WD2 2LN

Ipswich Film Society
Mr Terry Cloke
4 Burlington Road
Ipswich
Suffolk IP1 2EU

Leighton Buzzard Library and Arts Centre
Mr H Mennie
Lake Street
Leighton Buzzard
Beds LU7 8RX

Letchworth Film Society
Sean Boughton
27 Norton Road
Letchworth
Herts SG6 1AA

Minerva Film Society
Ms C Sack
c/o N de Berry
115 Manson Road
Cambridge CB1 2DZ

Old Town Hall Film Society
Mr R A Adams
Old Town Hall Arts Centre
High Street
Hemel Hempstead
Herts HP1 3AE

Peterborough Film Society
Mr A J Bunch
196 Lincoln Road
Peterbough
Cambs PE1 2NQ

Playhouse Co-operative Film Society (Harlow)
Mrs S Herbert
72 Broadfields
Harlow
Essex CM20 3PT

Thameside Film Society
Mr J Kent
14 Palmers Avenue
Grays
Essex RM17 5UB

Welwyn Garden City Film Society
Mr R P Head
3 Marsden Close
Welwyn Garden City
Herts AL8 6YE

LINCOLNSHIRE AND HUMBERSIDE

BFFS Lincolnshire and Humberside Group
Mr G Dobson
Kennel Cottage
Burton
Nr Lincoln
Lincs

Alford Film Society
Ms J Kirby
22 East Street
Alford
Lincs LN13 9EQ

Lincoln Film Society
Mr M Bingham
27 Breedon Drive
Lincoln LN1 3XA

Market Rasen Film Society
Mr H B Proctor
3 Church Lane
Tealby
Lincoln

MIDLANDS

BFFS Midlands Group
Mr P Collins
Beech Haven
Cobden Street
Wollaston
Stourbridge
Worcs

Bishops Castle Film Society
Ms J Parker
4 Lavender Bank
Bishops Castle
Shropshire SY9 5BD

Brierley Hill Film Society
Mr N S Robins
43 Clark Street
Stourbridge
W Midlands DY8 3UF

Castle Film Society
Mr A Forbes
Castle Hall
Rouncil Lane
Kenilworth
Warwickshire CV8 1FN

Hook Norton Film Society
Mrs E Simpson
Holmesdale
Whichford
Shipston-on-Stour
Warwickshire

Light House Media Centre
Mr F Challenger
Art Gallery
Lichfield Street
Wolverhampton
WV1 1DV

Ludlow and District Film Society
Mrs K Taylor
7 Castle View Terrace
Ludlow
Shropshire SY8 2NG

New Kettering Film Society
Mr C J E Owen
4 Church Street
Cottingham
Market Harborough
Leics

Northampton Arts Centre Film Society
Mr A Smith
College of F/E
Booth Lane South
Northampton NN3 4JR

Open Film Society
Gaynor Arrowsmith
c/o Maths Department
Open University
Walton Hall
Milton Keynes
Bucks MK7 6AA

Redditch Film Society
Paul Tucker
Alcester Street
Redditch
Worcestershire B98

Shrewsbury Film Society
Mr B Mason
Pulley Lodge
Lower Pulley Lane
Bayston Hill
Shrewsbury
Shropshire

Solihull Film Society
Mr S Sharam
2 Coppice Road
Solihull
W Midlands B92 9JY

Stafford Film Society
Mrs A Paterson
22 Peel Street
Stafford
Staffs ST16 2DZ

Stourbridge Film Society
Ms R Holt

6 Bernwall Close
Stourbridge
West Midlands DY8 1SD

Weston Coyney and Caverswall Film Society
Ms D Brassington
13 Green Lane
Blythe Bridge
Stoke-on-Trent ST11 9LZ

Wolverhampton Film Society
Mr G Hewitt
51 Reansway Square
Wolverhampton
WV6 0EY

NORTHERN

BFFS Northern Group
Mr Peter Swan
48 Brackenway
Albany Village
Washington
Tyne and Wear

Alnwick Film Society
Mr J McMeeking
20 Riverside Road
Alnmouth
Alnwick
Northumberland

Arts Centre Darlington
Ian Hague
Vane Terrace
Darlington
Co Durham DL3 7AX

Centre Film Club
Mr R A Smith
20 Stanhope Grove
Acklam
Middlesbrough
Cleveland TS5 9SG

Hartlepool Film Society
Mr A Gowing
6 Warkworth Drive
Hartlepool
Cleveland TS26 0EW

Sunderland Film Society
Mr P G Swan
48 Brackenway
Albany Village
Washington
Tyne and Wear
NE37 1AP

YORKSHIRE

BFFS Yorkshire Group
Mr Richard Fort
Yorkshire Group
8 Bradley Grove
Silsden
Keighley
West Yorkshire
BD20 9LX

Anvil Civic Cinema
Dr D Godin
Senior Film Officer
21 Charter Square
Sheffield S1 4HS

Friends of the Grange Film Society for the Disabled
Ms S Tate
50 Manor Park Road
Rawcliffe
York YO3 6UL

Halifax Playhouse Film Club
Mr R Spruce
32 Athol Green
Halifax
West Yorks HX3 5RN

Harrogate Film Society
Mr P Caunt
19 Keats Walk
Harrogate
North Yorks HG1 3LN

Hebden Bridge Film Society
Ms S Bower
Windyroyd
3 Stile Road
Todmorden
Lancs OL14 5NU

Huddersfield and District Film Society
Mr J E Cooper
43 St Helen's Gate
Almondbury
Huddersfield HD4 6SD

Ilkley Film Society
Mr R J Fort
8 Bradley Grove
Silsden
Keighley
West Yorks BD20 9LX

Scarborough Film Society
Mr A E Davison
29 Peasholm Drive
Scarborough
North Yorks Y012 7NA

NORTH WEST

BFFS North West Group
Mr A Payne
18 Cecil Street
Lytham St Annes
Lancs FY8 5NN

Armagh Film Society
Mr P Bell
26 Charlemont Gardens
Armagh
Northern Ireland

Birkenhead Library Film Society
Mr H G Mortimer
Music Dept
Borough Road
Birkenhead
Merseyside L41 2XB

Blackburn and District Film Society
Mr I Ibbotson
15 Gorse Road
Blackburn
Lancs BB2 6LY

Carver Theatre Film Society
Mr M R Baguley
16 Marsland Road
Marple
Stockport
Cheshire SK6 6HD

Chester Film Society
Mr G Mayled
19 Crofters Way
Saughall
Chester
Cheshire CH1 6AA

Chorley Film Society
Richard Riley
65 Charter Lane
Charnock Richard
Chorley
Lancs PR7 5LY

Daneside Film Society
Mr P Lilley
85 Lower Heath
Congleton
Cheshire CW12 1NJ

Deeside Film Society
Mr C Ramsey Hewson
44 Albion Street
Wallasey
Merseyside L45 9JG

Ellesmere Port Library Film Society
Mr J G Fisher
Chester Library
Town Hall Square
Chester CH1 2EF

Forum Film Society
Mrs M Holleran
Central Library
Wythenshawe
Manchester M22 5RT

Frodsham Film Society
Mr M F Donovan
58 The Willows
Frodsham
Cheshire WA6 7QS

Golden Oldies Film Club
Mr D Lomax
26 Lodge Court
Hollyhedge Road
Manchester M22 4QW

Heswall Film Society
Mr P Reed
90 Irby Road
Heswall
Wirral
Merseyside L61 6XG

Lytham St Annes Film Society
Mr A Payne
18 Cecil Street
Lytham St Annes
Lancs FY8 5NN

Manchester and Salford Film Society
Mr H T Ainsworth
64 Egerton Road
Fallowfield
Manchester M14 6RA

Manchester Women's Film Group
Ms N Pattison
4 Bury Avenue
Whalley Range
Manchester M16 0AT

Merseyside Film Institute
Mr G Donaldson
45 Bluecoat Chambers
School Lane
Liverpool L1 3BX

Nantwich Film Society
Mrs J Curtis
108 Rope Lane
Wistaston Crewe Cheshire

Padgate Film Society
Mr Christopher Taylor
276 Redshank Lane
Oakwood
Warrington
Cheshire WA3 6RE

The Picture Place (Leigh)
Ms C Dahl
Media Education Centre
Leigh College
Railway Road
Leigh WN7 7AH

Preston Film Society
Mr M Lockwood
14 Croftgate
Highgate Park
Fulwood
Preston
Lancs PR2 4LS

Runcorn Library Film Society
Mrs S Davies
Runcorn Library
Shopping City
Runcorn
Cheshire WA7 2PF

Saddleworth Film Society
Ms Sheila Watts

45 Oldham Road
Delph
Oldham
O13 5EB

Southport Film Guild
Mr A Naylor
20 Greengate
Hutton
Preston PR4 5FH

Winnington Hall Club Film Society
Mr C Riemer
15 Hadrian Way
Sandiway
Northwich
Cheshire CW8 2JR

Workers' Film Association
Mr F Coker
9 Lucy Street
Old Trafford
Manchester M15 4BX

WALES

BFFS Welsh Group
Mr A Fisher
43 Atlantic Drive
Broadhaven
Dyfed

Abergavenny Film Society
Mrs C Philips
Ty-Bryn
Tal-y-Doed
Monmouth
Gwent

Bridgend Cinema Club
Ms A R Jones
56 Park Court Road
Bridgend
Mid Glamorgan
CF31 4BP

Canton Film Appreciation Group
Mr F Sharpe
c/o 235 Cowbridge Road
East
Canton
Cardiff CF1 9AL

Fishguard Film Society
Ms J Worsley
Church Hill House
Treffgarne
Haverfordwest
Dyfed

Haverfordwest Film Society
Mrs J Evans
Dyfed County Library
Dew Street
Haverfordwest
Dyfed SA16 1SU

Lleyn Film Society
Mr D K Mills
Lodge Cottage
Bodfean/Pwllheli
Gwynedd LL53 7DR

Monmouth Film Society
Mrs J M Waters
The Mount
83 Hereford Road
Monmouth
Gwent NP5 4JZ

Mostyn Film Society
Ms Nathalie Camus
Mostyn Gallery
12 Vaughan Street
Llandudno
Gwynedd LL30 1AB

Phoenix Film club
Ms S Hallam
48 Barrack Hill
Newport
Gwent NP9 5FY

Presteigne Film Society
Mr R Scadding
Sunrise Cottage
Green Lane
Pembridge
Leominster HR6 9EL

Swansea Film Society
Mrs K Burrell
Cilhendre Cottage
Wernddu
Alltwen
Pontardawe
Swansea SA8 3HY

Theatr Mwldan Film Society
Ms Helen Steel
Theatr Mwldan
Cardigan
Dyfed

SCOTLAND
BFFS Scottish Group
Ms Helene Telford
43 Thistle Street
Edinburgh EH2 1DY

Alternative Screen Film Society
Ms C Gratton
c/o Moira Architects
6 Queensgate
Inverness IV1 1LA

Avondale Film Society
Mr Tom Goodwillie
3 Kirkhill Road
Strathaven
Lanarkshire ML10 6HN

Ayr Film Society
Mrs P Allison
15 Ronaldshaw Park
Ayr KA7 2TJ

Banff Film Club
Mr E Ellington
30 Crouie
Gardenstown
Banffshire AB4 3JQ

The Barony Film Society
Ms M Macivor
Top Flat
1 Lower Granton Road
Edinburgh EH5 3RS

Berwickshire Film Society
Mr E B Sykes
c/o Balfour
7 Langtongate
Duns
Berwickshire TD11 3AF

Crieff Film Society
Ms M Thomson
Glenshira
Drummond Terrace
Crieff
Perthshire PH7 4AF

East Kilbride Film Society
Mrs Barbara Perry
67 Cantieslaw Drive
Calderwood
East Kilbride G74 3AH

Edinburgh Film Guild
Mr C Butler
The Filmhouse
88 Lothian Road
Edinburgh EH3 9BZ

Fort Film Theatre
J Bissell
Heathbank
25 Springfield Road
Bishopbriggs
Glasgow G64 1PJ

Haldane Film Society
Mr A S Davis
12 Wylie Avenue
Burnbrae
Alexandria
Strathclyde G83 0AX

Lewis Film Society
Mr K Kennedy
9 Goathill Road
Stornoway
Outer Hebrides PA87 2NJ

Linlithgow Film Society
Mr G Shinwell
90 Deanfield Road
Bo'ness
West Lothian EH51 0ER

Moray Film Society
Mrs I Sinclair
Northbank
7 Lesmurdie Place
Lossiemouth
Moray IV31 6AH

North Ayrshire Arts Centre
Mrs N Yuill
Sannox
Ardrossan Road
Seamill
W Kilbride
Ayrshire KA23 9LX

Robert Burns Centre – Film Theatre
Kenneth Eggo
Dumfries Museum
The Observatory
Dumfries

Shetland Film Club
Mr R Tait
Flat 3
The Old School
Cunningsburgh
Shetland Isles ZE2 9HB

Traquair Film Society
Mr P Maxwell Stuart
Traquair House
Innerleithen
Peebles EH44 6PW

Tweeddale Film Club
Mrs Jeanette Carlyle
23 Marchmont Road
Edinburgh EH9 1HX

We're piling success on success.

Following the successes with *Codename Kyril*, *Grand Larceny*, *The Woman He Loved*, *Wall of Tyranny*, *Maigret*, *Voice of the Heart*, *We are Seven* and *Better Days*, HTV have produced an exciting new line-up of dramas for the months ahead.

Attracting big audiences nationally will be *Indiscreet* starring Lesley Anne Down and Robert Wagner, *Pursuit* starring Ben Cross, *The Diamond Trap* starring Brooke Shields and Twiggy, *A Time to Dance* starring Judi Trott and Patrick Ryecart, and *Some Other Spring* starring Jenny Seagrove and Dinsdale Landen.

It's a programme of major productions unequalled for entertainment and sheer star quality. And it's going to boost HTV's reputation as the pace-setting ITV company even higher.

These companies acquire the rights to audiovisual product for sale to foreign distributors in all media (see also Distributors p116)

Allied Vision
Avon House
360 Oxford Street
London W1N 9HA
Tel: 01 409 1984
Ed Simons

Arts Council of Great Britain
105 Piccadilly
London W1V 0AU
Tel: 01 629 9495
Distributes Arts Council funded films such as *Jessye Norman – Singer, Ballet Black, The Mark of the Hand – Aubrey Williams*. Also Channel 4 funded arts programmes such as *Looking into Paintings* and *State of the Art*. See also under Organisations

Australian Film Commission
2nd Floor
Victory House
99–101 Regent Street
London W1R 7HB
Tel: 01 734 9383

BBC Enterprises
Woodlands
80 Wood Lane
London W12 0TT
Tel: 01 576 0254
Commercial exploitation and export of BBC product, including books, records and programmes edited as videogrammes for consumer and educational markets. Also responsible for BBC television co-productions and BBC journals publication ('Radio Times', 'The Listener' and 'BBC Wildlife')

BFI Production
See p10 and under Distributors

Jane Balfour Films
110 Gloucester Avenue
London NW1 8JA
Tel: 01 586 3443/8762/3
Jane Balfour
Mary Barlow
Helen Loveridge
Distribution agent for

Channel 4 and independent producers, handling drama, documentaries and specialised feature films

The Box Office
3 Market Mews
London W1Y 7HH
Tel: 01 499 3968
Paul Shields
TV product. Australian agents for Central Television

Brent Walker
Knightsbridge House
197 Knightsbridge
London SW7 1RB
Tel: 01 225 1941
John Quested
Tony Murphy
Televisual material includes *Mounbatten, The Last Viceroy* and ongoing drama *Worlds Beyond*. Feature film *American Gothic* starring Rod Steiger

British Home Entertainment
26 D'Arblay Street
London W1
Tel: 01 734 3573

CBC Enterprises
43–51 Great Titchfield Street
London W1P 8DD
Tel: 01 580 0336
Rosemary Krupa
Wendy Hallam
Susan Jolley
The marketing division of Canadian Broadcasting Corporation and Société Radio-Canada

CBS Broadcast International Europe
1 Red Place
London W1Y 3RE
Tel: 01 355 4422
Greg Phillips
Sonja Mendes
Wide range of US TV product

CTVC
Beeson's Yard
Bury Lane

Rickmansworth
Herts WD3 1DS
Tel: 0923 777933
Peter Leeming
Programmes that explore areas of social concern and Christian themes, including dramas, documentaries and children's programming

Central Independent Television
35–38 Portman Square
London W1A 2HZ
Tel: 01 486 6688
Philip Jones
David Llewellyn-Jones
Evi Nicoupolis
Sale of all Central TV-produced films and TV programmes, amounting currently to a 650-hour catalogue

Channel 4 International
60 Charlotte Street
London W1P 2AX
Tel: 01 631 4444
Jane Small
Where Channel 4 retains sales rights in its programmes, they are handled either through this in-house programme sales operation or through its approved distributors and sales agents. For film sales, see Film Four International

Chatsworth Television
97–99 Dean Street
London W1V 5RA
Tel: 01 734 4302
Halina Stratton
Extensive library of documentary and special interest films. Also Chatsworth-produced light entertainment, drama and adventure series

Colstar Communications and Entertainment
1 Wardour Mews
D'Arblay Street
London W1V 3FF

Tel: 01 437 5725
International distributors of broadcast programming for all media; documentaries, short films, drama, programme specials and series. Library includes films and series on art, the sciences, history, sport and nature. Titles include *The National Gallery – A Private View* series, *Kenneth Clark's Romantic Classic Art* series, *The Wandering Company* (50 mins), *The Life and Times of Lord Mountbatten* series, *The Monkey's Paw* (30 mins), *The Man Who Loves Giants* (70 mins) and *The Most Dangerous Animal* (50 mins)

Columbia Pictures Television
19 Wells Street
London W1P 3FP
Tel: 01 637 8444
Nick Bingham
Production and co-production of TV product and international distribution of Columbia's feature films

Consolidated Distribution
5 Jubilee Place
London SW3 3TD
Tel: 01 376 5151/8
Worldwide distributor of films and television programming

Cori Film Distributors
19 Albemarle Street
London W1X 3HA
Tel: 01 493 7920
Marie Hoy
Keith Howe
Patricia Brown
Louise Rimoldi
Elizabeth Cook
With offices in London, Tokyo and Los Angeles, Cori handles features, mini-series, family films and documentaries and arranges international co-production funding. Recent acquisitions include the features *The Perfect Murder*, *Distortions*, *Girl from the South* and *My Little Girl*, documentaries *Conquest* and *Frozen in Time*, TV series *The Boy Who Lost His Laugh* and children's series *Dot and Koala*

Dee and Co
Suite 204
Canalot
222 Kensal Road
London W10 5BN
Tel: 01 960 2712
Drew Ellicott
Distributes film and television programmes. Catalogue contains selected award-winning titles under the headings wildlife, documentary and animation

Film Four International
60 Charlotte Street
London W1P 2AX
Tel: 01 631 4444
Bill Stephens
Heather Denman
Film sales arm of Channel 4, set up in 1984 to sell feature films which it finances or part-finances. Recent titles include *The Dressmaker*, *Drowning by Numbers*, *Ladder of Swords*, *Diamond Skulls*, *High Hopes* and *The Cook, The Thief, His Wife and Her Lover*

Glinwood Films
8–12 Broadwick Street
London W1V 1AH
Tel: 01 437 1181
Terry Glinwood
Marie Vine
Sale of feature films such as *Insignificance*, *Merry Christmas Mr Lawrence*, *The Last Emperor*, *When The Wind Blows*, *Erik the Viking* and *Everybody Wins*

Global Television Services
1 Duke of York Street
St James's
London SW1Y 6JE
Tel: 01 839 5644
Lucy Brodie
Long-established TV and video distribution company

Goldcrest Films and Television
36–44 Brewer Street
London W1R 3HP
Tel: 01 437 8696
Thierry Wase-Bailey
Acquisition, sales, distribution and marketing of Goldcrest's film productions in all media worldwide

Golden Communications (Overseas)
47 Greek Street
London W1V 5LQ
Tel: 01 439 1431
David Shepperd
Gina Foster
Part of the Golden Harvest Group responsible for selling the company's features: *High Road to China*, *Cannonball Run II*, *Lassiter, The Protector*, *Flying* and other projects

The Samuel Goldwyn Co
St George's House
14–17 Wells Street
London W1P 3FP
Tel: 01 439 5105
Diana Hawkins
Liz Elton
Lynden Parry
Jessica Rockley
Offices in Los Angeles, London, New York. Acquisition, sales, distribution and marketing of films and television product worldwide. Recent titles include *Breaking in* and *Stella*. Television product includes Goldwyn Classics Library and the Rodgers and Hammerstein Film Library

Grampian Television
Queen's Cross
Aberdeen AB9 2XJ
Tel: 0224 646464
Michael McLintock
North Scotland ITV station producing a wide range of product including documentaries *OIL, The Blood is Strong*, *Sea Farmers* (on the development of fish farming), and *Home at Last*, telling the story of a shipwreck which devastated an island community. Extensive footage available on the world's oil industry with large library of offshore material. Represented by Richard Price Television

Granada Television International
36 Golden Square
London W1R 4AH
Tel: 01 734 8080
Vivien Wallace

HTV
99 Baker Street
London W1M 2AJ
Tel: 01 486 4311/0662

Henson International Television
2 Old Brewery Mews
Hampstead High Street
London NW3 1PZ
Tel: 01 435 7121
Peter Orton
Sophie Turner Laing
Jane Smith
Adam Shaw
David Ferguson
Distributors of *The Storyteller, The Jim Henson Show, The Ghost of Faffner Hall, Rarg, Charlie Chalk, The Metronome HIT! Collection, The Muppet Show, Fraggle Rock*

ITC Entertainment
45 Seymour Street
London W1A 1AG
Tel: 01 262 3262
Joshua Elbaum
Vickie Gubby
Distributors of *Poor Little Rich Girl* – The Barbara Hutton story, *Billionaire Boys Club, Windmills of the Gods, Without a Clue, At Mother's Request, Detective Sadie and Son, Secret Passions, Christmas Comes to Willow Creek, Baby Girl Scott, The Father Clements Story* and many other titles

International Television Enterprises (ITEL)
48 Leicester Square
London WC2H 7FB
Tel: 01 491 1441
Andrew MacBean
Distribution and production development company representing Anglia TV, Anglia Films, Action Time, ITN, Home Box Office, and Little Bird among others. Interested in co-production and the acquisition of programming for distribution. Representation in US through two full-time offices, and worldwide through a network of representatives. Works closely with producers at all stages of production

and subsequent distribution

J & M Film Sales

2 Dorset Square
London NW1 6PU
Tel: 01 723 6544
Julia Palau
Michael Ryan
Michael Brawley
Anthony Miller
Specialise in sales of all media, distribution and marketing of independent feature films. Recent films are *Running Man* starring Arnold Schwarzenegger, *Ironweed* starring Jack Nicholson and Meryl Streep, *Miles From Home* starring Richard Gere, *Skin Deep* starring John Ritter, and *Major League* starring Tom Berenger and Charlie Sheen

Liberty Films

222 Regent Street
London W1R 5DE
Tel: 01 434 9571
John Kelleher
International sales for films such as *The Whistleblower, War Zone, Wherever You Are, Savage Justice, Whiteforce, The Bulldance* and *War Requiem*

Link Licensing

United Newspaper Buildings
23–27 Tudor Street
London EC4Y 0HR
Tel: 01 353 7305
Claire Derry
David Hamilton
Gillian Akester
Specialists in children's programmes for worldwide distribution and character licensing. New properties include: *Barney, Count Duckula, Silentnight's Hippo & Duck, What a Mess*

London Film Productions

44a Floral Street
London WC2E 9DA
Tel: 01 379 3366
Mark Shelmerdine
Rosie Bunting
Sheila Berry
Independent production and distribution company, with offices in London and LA. London Films offers a distribution and sales service to independent producers as

well as selling its own productions

London Television Service

Hercules Road
London SE1 7DU
Tel: 01 928 2345
Sally Barrett
Distributes documentaries made by the Central Office of Information including the series *Perspective* and *A Woman's Place*

London Weekend Television International

19th Floor
c/o London Weekend Television
South Bank Television Centre
London SE1 9LT
Tel: 01 928 8473
Karine Cullen
Overseas sales representative for LWT programmes

MCA TV

139 Piccadilly
London W1V 9FH
Tel: 01 629 7211
Roger Cordjohn
Bernadette Vacher
UK operation for the major US corporation which owns Universal Pictures

MGM/UA Television

see **Turner International**

MPC Television

(formerly Moving Picture Co)
20 St Anne's Court
London W1V 3AW
Tel: 01 494 2967/8/9
Avie Littler
Producers and distributors of factual programmes, natural history specials, children's TV and light entertainment

McCann International Programme Marketing

68 Gloucester Place
London W1H 3HL
Tel: 01 224 4748
Andrew Luff
Jean Thompson
International distributors

of drama series, TV movies, music, light entertainment, documentaries and children's programmes to broadcasters, cable and satellite operators and home-video distributors worldwide

Movie House Sales Co

Regal Chambers
51 Bancroft
Hitchin
Herts SG5 1LL
Tel: 0462 421818
Film sales division of Medusa Communications. For list of product, see Medusa Pictures in Distributors

NBD Pictures

Remo House
310–312 Regent Street
London W1R 5AJ
Tel: 01 499 9701
Nicky Davies
Maria Anderton
Company specialising in music-based and light entertainment programming, but broadening into features and drama. Clients include The Elvis Presley Estate, Polygram Music Video, Lightyear, CBS Records International and Island Visual Arts

NVC Arts

Liberty House
222 Regent Street
London W1R 5DE
Tel: 01 434 9571
Helen Asquith
Hazel Wright
Paul Hembury
Distributes an extensive catalogue of music, dance and arts-related programmes, including *Opera Stories* narrated by Charlton Heston, *La Sylphide* from the Royal Danish Ballet, *La Corsaire* from the Kirov Ballet, and Derek Jarman's film *War Requiem* set to the Benjamin Britten's music

National Film Board of Canada

1 Grosvenor Square
London W1X 0AB
Tel: 01 629 9492 x3482
Hannah Kelson
European agent for documentary, drama and animation productions

from Canada's National Film Board

O G International

Pinewood Studios
Pinewood Road
Iver Heath
Bucks SL0 0NH
Tel: 0753 651700
Oliver Gamgee
Production, packaging and distribution company for feature films and TV, representing Alpine Pictures
and Western Pacific Films

Orbit Films

14 Campden Hill Gardens
London W8
Tel: 01 221 5548
Specialises in vintage product from the first decade of American TV, including features and serials

Overview Films

7th Floor
Hammer House
113–117 Wardour Street
London W1V 3TD
Tel: 01 439 7491
International sales for films such as *Empire State, American Gothic, Devil's Paradise, Afraid to Dance, Streets of Yesterday,* and *Going Undercover*

Palan Entertainment Corporation

Prestwich House
Brunswick Industrial Park
Brunswick Way
New Southgate
London N11 1HX
Tel: 01 368 5545
Nick Moncrieff

Palladium International Television

6 Goodwins Court
St Martin's Lane
London WC2N 4LL
Tel: 01 836 0576
Gary Dartnall
June Morrow
Adrian Caddy
Full range of TV: light entertainment, features, documentary and sport

Paramount Television

23 Berkeley House
Hay Hill

London W1X 8JB
Tel: 01 629 1150
Peter Cary

Pathé House
76 Hammersmith Road
London W14 8YR
Tel: 01 607 4555
Sells films previously
produced by Cannon (now
Pathé) in the UK and US,
as well as pick-ups from
other production
companies, through its
international network of
offices

Picture Music International
20 Manchester Square
London W1A 1ES
Tel: 01 486 4488
Dawn M Stevenson
Big World Café, a series of
10 one-hour shows
presenting exciting
sounds from around the
world

Richard Price Television Associates (RPTA)
Seymour Mews House
Seymour Mews
Wigmore Street
London W1H 9PE

Tel: 01 935 9000
Richard Price
RPTA distributes for over
40 companies, including
Channel 4, ABC Sports,
ABC Pictures
International and
Grampian TV

Radiovision International
Avon House
360 Oxford Street
London W1N 9HA
Tel: 01 493 0439
Leading comtemporary
music distributors,
specialising in live and
recorded concerts
including: Go Global,
Nelson Mandela,
Amnesty, Moscow, Elton
John, Genesis, Pink
Floyd, Sting, Bowie,
Eurythmics and many
others

Rank Film Distributors
127 Wardour Street
London W1V 4AD
Tel: 01 437 9020
Chris Towle
A library of 500 feature
films plus TV series. Also
200 hours of colour

programming from the
Children's Film and
Television Foundation.
New product includes *The
Big Town, Switching
Channels, Physical
Evidence, Dead Ringers,
Gleaming the Cube,
Millennium, Dealers* and
*Scenes From the Class
Struggle in Beverly Hills*

Red Rooster Films
11–13 Macklin Street
London WC2B 5NH
Tel: 01 405 8147
Linda James
Feature film production
and producers and
distributors of quality
television fiction and
documentaries: *Joni
Jones, And Pigs Might
Fly, The Works, The Flea
and the Giant, Hazel's
Children, Coming Up
Roses, Equinox:
Earthquake Country* and
Just Ask for Diamond

S4C Enterprises
Sophia Close
Cardiff CF1 9XY
Tel: 0222 343421
Chris Grace
Teleri Roberts

Sales of programmes
commissioned by S4C
from independent
producers

Safir Films
22 Soho Square
London W1V 5FJ
Tel: 01 734 5085
Lawrence Safir
Sidney Safir
Holds rights to a number
of Australian, US and
British pictures,
including Sam Spiegel's
Betrayal, Steve Jodrell's
Shame, and the Romulus
Classics comprising more
than 30 titles such as *The
African Queen, Moulin
Rouge, Room at the Top*
and *Beat the Devil*

The Sales Company
62 Shaftesbury Avenue
London W1V 7AA
Tel: 01 434 9061
Carole Myer
John Durie
Alison Thompson
Formed October 1986 by
British Screen, Palace
and Zenith to represent
their theatrical
productions worldwide in
all media. Now also

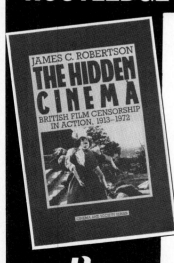

represent Working Title. Recent films include *Scandal, The Tall Guy, Diamond Skulls, Killing Dad*

Scottish Television International
Cowcaddens
Glasgow G2 3PR
Tel: 041 332 9999
Michael Trotter
Sales of all programmes from Scottish Television

Screen Ventures
49 Goodge Street
London W1P 1FB
Tel: 01 580 7448
Dominic Saville
Specialise in international TV and video licensing of music specials such as: *Sweet Toronto, John Lennon, Remembering Otis, Otis Redding, Pointer Sisters, B B King and Jimi Hendrix.* Sales agents for international independent producers, handling documentaries, current affairs and drama programmes

Silverbach-Lazarus
South Bank Television Centre
Upper Ground
London SE1 9LT
Tel: 01 261 1284
George Blaug
UK base of SLG, Los Angeles. Documentaries, children's series, feature films, musical specials

Sony Video Software Europe
41–42 Berners Street
London W1P 3AA
Tel: 01 631 4000
Recent films include: *Women's Club, Square Dance, Jimmy Reardon* and *Sweet Lies*

D L Taffner (UK)
10 Bedford Square
London WC1B 3RA
Tel: 01 631 1184
Don Taffner
UK base of D L Taffner, New York (US representative of Thames TV International). International distributors of all types of TV material

Talbot Television
Greendon House
7c/d Bayham Street
London NW1 0EY
Tel: 01 380 1189
Anthony S Gruner

London arm of NY-based Fremantle Int. Produces and distributes game shows and light entertainment

Target International Pictures
Avon House
360 Oxford Street
London W1N 9HA
Tel: 01 491 4421/493 0440
An international sales company working with the following films: *White Roses, Dragon Under the Hill, The Naked Cell, Sweet Toronto, Innocent Prey, Prime Suspect, Night of Retribution*

Televentures
19–23 Wells Street
London W1P 3FP
Tel: 01 436 5720/5729
Ray Lewis
Representing: Stephen J Cannell Productions, Witt/Thomas/Harris Productions, Tri-Star Pictures

Telso International
84 Buckingham Gate
London SW1E 6PD
Tel: 01 976 7188
Ann Harris
Nick Witkowski
Properties include: *Murderers Among Us – The Story of Simon Wiesenthal* starring Ben Kingsley, about the life of a Nazi hunter, and *The Heroes*, a mini-series about the true story of the 1943 Allied sabotage bombing raid on Singapore Harbour

Thames Television International
149 Tottenham Court Road
London W1P 9LL
Tel: 01 387 9494
Mike Phillips
Roger Miron
Represents largest programme producer in ITV network and its subsidiaries Euston Films and Cosgrove Hall Productions in programme sales, co-productions, the non-theatrical and home video markets, publishing and merchandising

Trans World International
The Pier House
Strand on the Green

Chiswick
London W4 3NN
Tel: 01 994 1444
Buzz Hornett
UK wing of the Mark McCormack Organisation, specialising in sport programming

Turner International
25 Old Burlington Street
London W1X 1LB
Tel: 01 434 4341
Howard Karshan
US production amd distribution company. Distributor of MGM, pre-1950 Warner Bros features and Turner series

Twentieth Century Fox Television
31–32 Soho Square
London W1
Tel: 01 437 7766
Malcolm Vaughan
Sales of all Twentieth Century Fox product to TV worldwide

Tyne Tees Enterprises
15 Bloomsbury Square
London WC1A 2LJ
Tel: 01 405 8474
Ann Gillham
International sales division of Tyne Tees TV. Also represents the catalogues of Border TV and others. Distributing Catherine Cookson dramas including *The Fifteen Streets*, and *The Moth*

VATV
3rd Floor
17–19 Foley Street
London W1P 7LB
Tel: 01 636 9421
Jane Lighting
As well as distributing its own product, the company represents other independent companies in the international market. Approved distributor for Channel 4 documentary and factual programmes

Viacom International
40 Conduit Street
London W1R 9FB
Tel: 01 434 4483
Peter Press
UK-based distribution operation for the US independent company. Current product includes *The Cosby Show* (fifth year), *Different World* (second year), *Roseanne,*

Garry Shandling (third year), *Matlock* (third year), *Jake and the Fatman* (second year), Perry Mason TV movie specials, *Father Dowling Mysteries, New Adventures of Mighty Mouse,* mini-series, plus an extensive library of theatrical and made-for-TV movies

Virgin Vision
328 Kensal Road
London W10 5XJ
Tel: 01 968 8888
Mary Glanville

Visnews
Cumberland Avenue
London NW10 7EH
Tel: 01 965 7733
Syndication of international TV news sport, library footage and complete programmes

Warner Bros Television
49 Berkeley Square
London W1X 5DB
Tel: 01 409 1190
Stuart B Graber
Taken over Lorimar Telepictures product

Weintraub Screen Entertainment
167–169 Wardour Street
London W1V 3TA
Tel: 01 439 1790
Gary Phillips
A library of over 1500 titles from classic to contemporary: *Highlander, The Hitcher, Link, Clockwise, Sweet Dreams* and *Deadly Game*

Worldwide Television News Corporation
WTN House
31–36 Foley Street
London W1P 7LB
Tel: 01 323 3255
Keith Reynolds
Gerry O'Reilly
International TV news, features, sport, documentary programmes, *Earthfile* (an environmental programme series), archives resources. Camera crews in major global locations, plus in-house broadcasting and production facilities; and a commercial productions division which undertakes sponsored documentary, industrial and corporate video production.

LABORATORIES

Bucks Motion Picture Laboratories
714 Banbury Avenue
Slough
Berks SL1 4LH
Tel: 0753 76611
Full motion picture laboratory services, 35mm, 16mm, 8mm, filmstrips, photogard protective coating, Chromascan (tape to film). Specialist archive/ nitrate stock restoration services. Colour dubbing prints

Colour Film Services Group
22–25 Portman Close
Baker Street
London W1A 4BE
Tel: 01 486 2881
(Laboratories)
10 Wadsworth Road
Perivale
Greenford
Middx
Tel: 01 998 2731
Full 35mm, 16mm and Super 16mm 24-hour laboratory services, handling all aspects of film work from feature films and TV programming to industrial shorts. In-house sound transfer and telecine mastering. Tape to film transfer to 35mm and 16mm. Bulk cassette duplication. Conference centre, equipment hire

Colour Tone Film Laboratories
18 Oak End Way
Gerrards Cross
Bucks
Tel: 0753 885554
Film duplication for specialised distributors

Filmatic Laboratories/ Filmatic Television
16 Colville Road
London W11 2BS
Tel: 01 221 6081
Complete film processing laboratory and sound transfer service with full video post production facility including Digital Telecines, 1″ VTRs, Betacam SP and other video formats. On-line editing, duplication and standard conversion. Electronic Film Conforming (EFC), the system that produces the highest quality video masters from any original source, with frame accurate editing

Henderson Film Laboratories
18–20 St Dunstan's Road
South Norwood
London SE25 6EU
Tel: 01 653 2255
Full b/w laboratory service in 35mm and 16mm including b/w reversal processing in 16mm and Super 8. Blow-up to 16mm from 9.5mm and Std 8mm. Specialists in the handling of archive material, especially shrunken and nitrate film

London Filmmakers' Co-operative
42 Gloucester Avenue
London NW1 8JD
Tel: 01 722 1728
16mm b/w processing

Metrocolor London
91–95 Gillespie Road
London N5 1LS
Tel: 01 226 4422
Full 16mm, Super 16mm and 35mm processing services, handling a range from 16mm short films through pop promos, commercials, BBC and ITV programmes to feature films, video mastering, sound transfer and stereo-optical camera

Rank Film Laboratories
North Orbital Road
Denham
Uxbridge
Middx UB9 5HQ
Tel: 0895 832323
The largest film laboratory outside the USA combining satellite laboratories in Manchester, Leeds and Glasgow. The main laboratory at Denham features in-house optical and sound departments, with a large experienced sales and contact team capable of servicing the theatrical, television, documentary and commercial markets. Received two American Academy Awards and Queen's Award for Technological Achievement

Studio Film and Video Group
8–14 Meard Street
London W1V 3HR
Tel: 01 437 0831
Full film processing facilities plus telecine transfer, mastering and video duplication. Film restoration and preservation (Film Clinic)

Technicolor
PO Box 7
Bath Road
West Drayton
Middx UB7 0DB
Tel: 01 759 5432
24-hour laboratory service, adjacent to London Heathrow Airport. Modern high speed plant caters for all formats: 16mm, 35mm, 70mm. Laboratories in Rome, Hollywood and NY

Universal Film and Video
Braintree Road
Ruislip
Middx HA4 0XP
Tel: 01 841 5101
Specialist 16mm film laboratory with overnight rushes service and full video and film sound dubbing facilities in two theatres. Film to tape transfer suites with four Rank Cintel Mark 3 telecines with Amigo, two in tandem with wet gates for video mastering direct from A and B roll negative. 'C' format 3-hour capability. Video cassetting service for all formats. Wet gate telecines for 35mm and 16mm negative or positive transfer to video

Visnews Laboratories
Cumberland Avenue
London NW10 7EH
Tel: 01 965 7733
Round-the-clock full 16mm laboratory service, day and night rushes service, full sound, transfer facilities, commercial reductions, video to film transfer, 16mm colour neg reversal and b/w. Telecine mastering and a full range of supporting video services, including video format on any broadcast standard with burnt-in timecode if required on film and tape

LEGISLATION

The principal acts affecting the operation of the film and television industries in the UK are listed chronologically below with a brief explanation of their provisions. The list does not include statutory instruments by which the measures may be modified or implemented. All the items listed are published by HMSO and available in public reference libraries or through BFI Library Services (see p9). The more important measures are marked by ☆

CINEMA LEGISLATION

☆ Cinematograph Act, 1909
Provisions for licensing of exhibition premises and the safety of audiences. (The first Act of Parliament relating to cinema)

Celluloid and Cinematograph Film Act, 1922
Provisions for the prevention of fire in premises where raw celluloid or cinematograph film is stored or used

☆ Cinematograph Films Act, 1927
(repealed by Cinematograph Films Act, 1948)
Restrictions on blind booking and advance booking of films. Registration of films exhibited to the public. Provisions for securing a 'quota' of British films for renting by exhibitors

Sunday Entertainment Act, 1932
(amended by Sunday Cinema Act 1972)
Permits and regulates the opening and use of premises on Sundays for certain entertainments. Establishment of the Sunday Cinematograph Fund for 'encouraging the use and development of the cinematograph as a means of entertainment and instruction'. (This is the means by which the BFI was originally funded)

The Cinematograph Films (Animals) Act, 1937
Designed to prevent exhibition or distribution of films in which suffering may have been caused to animals

Cinematograph Films Act, 1938
(repealed by and consolidated in Films Act, 1960)
Renters' and exhibitors' quotas. Restrictions on blind and advance booking. Registration of films for public exhibition. Wages and conditions of people employed in production

Cinematograph Films Act, 1948
(repealed and consolidated in Films Act, 1960)
Provisions on quotas. Composition of Cinematograph Films Council

☆ Cinematograph Film Production (Special Loans) Act, 1949
Establishment of the National Film Finance Corporation

☆ British Film Institute Act, 1949
Provides for payment of grants to BFI from the Treasury as well as from the (Sunday) Cinematograph Fund (see also Sunday Cinema Act, 1972)

Cinematograph Film Production (Special Loans) Act, 1950
(repealed by Films Act, 1970)
Amends the 1949 Act

Cinematograph Film Production (Special Loans) Act, 1952
(repealed by Films Act, 1980)
Empowers the NFFC to borrow otherwise than from the Board of Trade

☆ Cinematograph Act, 1952
Extends the 1909 Act to cover exhibition premises using non-flam film and television. Control of cinema exhibition for children. Exemptions for non-commercial exhibition. Music and dancing licences not required for cinematograph exhibitions

Cinematograph Film Production (Special Loans) Act, 1954
Extended the period during which loans and advances may be made under The Cinematograph Film Productions (Special Loans) Acts, 1949 and 1952 and authorised the NFFC to enter into special arrangements on certain loans

157

★ Cinematograph Films Act, 1957

(amended by Films Act, 1960)
Provides for a statutory levy on exhibitors to be collected by Customs and Excise and paid to the British Film Fund Agency (to be established by Statutory Instrument). The BFFA to pay the resulting funds to makers of British films and to the Children's Film Foundation. This put the formerly voluntary levy, known as 'Eady Money' on a statutory footing. Amends law relating to National Film Finance Corporation, laying down its duty to pay its way and providing for its eventual dissolution under certain specified conditions

Cinematograph Films Act, 1960

(repealed by and consolidated in Films Act, 1960)
Extension of existing legislation with minor variations

★ Films Act, 1960

(consolidates The Cinematograph Film Acts, 1938–1960)
Includes the up-to-date legislation on: quota; registration: conditions for registration as British or foreign, renters' and exhibitors' licences; restrictions on blind and advance booking; registration of newsreels; wages and conditions of employment; powers of Board of Trade; constitution of The Cinematograph Films Council, amends the Copyright Act, 1956 as it relates to film; amends references to previous legislation in Cinematograph Films Act, 1957

Films Act, 1964

Amends The Films Act, 1960 in its relation to newsreels

Films Act, 1966

Extends and adjusts provisions of previous measures. Much of it subsequently repealed by Films Act, 1970

Films Act, 1970

Extends functions of the National Film Finance Corporation. Imposes time limit of 1980 on all loan arrangements. Repeals various provisions of previous Acts

Sunday Cinema Act, 1972

Repeals certain sections of The Sunday Entertainments Act, 1932 and The British Film Institute Act, 1949. Winds up the Cinematograph Fund. Ends restrictions on Sunday opening of cinemas

European Communities Act, 1972

Community films not to be classed as foreign but as quota films under The Films Acts, 1960–1970

Cinematograph Films Act, 1975

(repealed by Films Act, 1980)

Films Act, 1979

Amends Films Act, 1960 in relation to foreign films shown for at least eight weeks

★ Films Act, 1980

Extends functions of NFFC. Provides for Government grant of £1 million and write-off of accumulated outstanding capital and interest repayments. NFFC may borrow up to £5 million at any time. Extends levy and quota periods. Provides for aggregation of screen time for quota when more than one cinema in a building. Provides power to suspend quota by Statutory Instrument. (Note: Quota ended 1982)

National Film Finance Corporation Act, 1981

Consolidates The Cinematograph Film Production (Special Loans) Acts, 1949–1980 and makes certain changes in the operation of the NFFC

Film Levy Finance Act, 1981

Consolidates The Cinematograph Films Acts, 1957–1980. Contains provisions for a certain proportion of Eady Levy to be paid to the NFFC

Cinematograph (Amendment) Acts 1982

Extends the provisions of the 1909 Act to 'all exhibitions of moving pictures for private gain'. This brings pornographic cinema and video 'clubs' within the licensing requirements. Bona fide film societies and 'demonstrations' such as those used in video shops are excluded. Also excluded are exhibitions to provide information, education or instruction

Cinema Act, 1985

This consolidates the Cinematograph Acts 1909 to 1982. Licences are required for exhibition, and the Act lays down the procedure for application for and renewal of licences. Exempted exhibition includes exhibition in private dwelling houses, non-commercial shows and premises used only occasionally. The Act also specifies the conditions for Sunday opening

Films Act, 1985

This Act repeals the Films Acts 1960 to 1980, abolishes the Cinematograph Films Council, ends Eady Levy and dissolves the National Film Finance Corporation. It makes provision for future Government financial assistance to the film industry – should Government decide to provide such assistance. (In fact, the Government has agreed to provide £1.5 million for five years to the loan fund of the British Screen Finance Consortium which takes over from the NFFC and whose members include Screen Entertainment, Rank and Channel 4). The Register of Films, started

by the Board of Trade in 1928, is to be discontinued

TELEVISION LEGISLATION

The rapid development of the new medium was foreseen in the Wireless Telegraphy Act, 1904 which reserved wide powers to the State for the regulation of wireless telegraphy. It was the first Wireless Act in the world and gave the Postmaster General the duty to license all wireless-telegraphy apparatus. The BBC was originally registered as a company (The British Broadcasting Co Ltd) in 1922 and received a licence from the Post Office in 1923. The present Corporation has never been a statutory body but has operated under a Royal Charter since 1926. The present Charter came into force on August 1, 1981 for 15 years. Subsequently developments in television have been covered by statutory measures and the principal ones are listed below

Television Act, 1954

Provides for a commercial television service from companies supervised by the Independent Television Authority (the ITA, later the IBA). Advertising was to be separated from programming, and requirements were laid down on the content of programmes

Copyright Act, 1956

Provides for copyright protection of broadcasting for the first time

Television Act, 1963

Extends the period for which the ITA should provide services until 1976

Television Act, 1964

Consolidates the 1954 and 1963 Acts

Sound Broadcasting Act, 1972

Extends the functions of the Independent Television Authority (ITA) to cover provision of local sound broadcasting services and renames it the Independent Broadcasting Authority (IBA)

Independent Broadcasting Authority Act, 1973

Consolidates the Television and Sound Broadcasting Acts, 1964 and 1972. Its provisions are essentially the same as those two Acts

Independent Broadcasting Authority Act, 1974

Makes further provision on payments to be made to the IBA by television programme contractors.

The 'Exchequer Levy' payments are changed to a tax on profits instead of advertising revenue only

Independent Broadcasting Authority (No 2) Act, 1974

Extends the date until which IBA provides television and sound broadcasting services to July 31, 1979

Independent Broadcasting Authority Act, 1978

Extends the above functions to December 31, 1981. Removes prohibition on certain specified people from broadcasting opinions where opinion is expressed in proceedings of parliament or local authorities

Independent Broadcasting Authority Act, 1979

Confers power on IBA to transmit a fourth channel

Broadcasting Act, 1980

Extends IBA's functions to provision of programmes, but not advertisements, for the fourth channel. Extends IBA's function to December 31, 1996. Establishes a Broadcasting Complaints Commission

Broadcasting Act, 1981

Consolidates the Independent Broadcasting Authority Acts, 1973, 1974 and 1978 and the Broadcasting Act, 1980

Copyright (Amendment) Act, 1983

This act increases significantly the penalties for trading in and making pirate videocassettes, with heavier fines and possible prison sentences

Video Recordings Act, 1984

This Act requires the certification of all new video releases. In view of the large number of titles to be classified, the work is to be done in six phases, beginning on 1 September 1985 – from which date any new release on video has to have a certificate – and finishing on 1 September 1988, by which time the backlog of titles should have been classified

Cable and Broadcasting Act, 1984

This Act set up the new Cable Authority, following a second reading of the Cable and Broadcasting Bill, introduced in 1983. The Cable Authority has the job of selecting operators for particular areas on the basis of the range of services which they intend to offer, and of seeing that they then live up to their promises

ORGANISATIONS

Listed below are the main trade/government organisations and bodies relevant to the film and television industry. A separate list of Regional Arts Associations is included at the end of this section

Advertising Association
Abford House
15 Wilton Road
London SW1V 1NJ
Tel: 01 828 2771
Contact: Information Officer
The Advertising Association is a federation of 29 trade associations and professional bodies representing advertisers, agencies, the media and support services. It is the lobbying organisation for the UK advertising business, on British and European legislative proposals and other issues of common concern, both at national and international levels, and as such campaigns actively to maintain the freedom to advertise and to improve public attitudes to advertising. It publishes UK and European statistics on advertising expenditure, instigates research on advertising issues and organises seminars and courses for people in the communications business. Its Information Centre is one of the country's leading sources for advertising and associated subjects

Advertising Film Rights Society (AFRS)
26 Noel Street
London W1V 3RD
Tel: 01 434 2651
Contact: Wayne Fitzgerald
Negotiates on behalf of producer members to collect royalties for further uses of members' material, such as overseas cable and satellite usage, and any other media

Advertising Film and Videotape Producers' Association (AFVPA)
26 Noel Street
London W1V 3RD
Tel: 01 434 2651
Contact: Cecilia Garnett
The Association represents most producers of TV commercials. It negotiates with recognised trade unions, with the advertisers and agencies and also supplies a range of member services

Arts Council of Great Britain
Film, Video and Broadcasting
105 Piccadilly
London W1V 0AU
Tel: 01 629 9495
Director: Rodney Wilson
Film and Video Officer: David Curtis
Film Education Services Officer: Will Bell
Film Sales Executive: Angie Mulhall
The Arts Council is funded by the Office of Arts and Libraries to encourage and support the arts. One of the means of achieving its objectives is the funding of documentary films on the arts intended for broad public use, particularly television and education. As an extension of its support for the visual arts, funds are available for the production, distribution and exhibition of artists' film and video

Arts Council of Northern Ireland
181a Stranmillis Road
Belfast BT9 5DU
Tel: 0232 667687
Contact: Michael Open
The Northern Irish Arts Council is funded from the Department of Education for Northern Ireland and promotes film culture in the region by supporting Queen's Film Theatre, assisting film societies and occasionally commissioning films on arts subjects

Association of Black Film and Video Workshops
Unit 215
22 Highbury Grove
London N5 2EA
Tel: 01 359 0302
Contact: Stephen Philip
The Association aims to represent and advance the interests of the black grant-aided sector in all areas of film and video production, distribution, training and exhibition, to initiate discussion and where relevant, policies on film culture, training and matters related to the grant-aided sector

Association of Cinematograph, Television and Allied Technicians (ACTT)
111 Wardour Street
London W1
Tel: 01 437 8506
General Secretary: Alan Sapper
The Association of Cine Technicians was formed in 1933 and in 1956 TV and allied technicians were included. ACTT is a union which represents the interests of people employed in many aspects of film and TV. It negotiates agreements with bodies such as BFTPA, ITCA, IPPA, AFVPA and MFVPA on behalf of its members, and is involved in lobbying for the film and broadcasting industries. Membership of the ACTT in either the freelance or the fully-employed sector is a useful credential for employment within the film and TV industries

Association of Independent Cinemas (AIC)

Theatre One
Ford Street
Coventry
Tel: 0203 220446
AIC was formed in 1953 to safeguard the interests of independent cinema owners against those exhibitors who are also involved in production or distribution. It is active on behalf of its 200 members on questions of barring and product allocation and, with the BFTPA, on copyright issues

Association of Independent Producers (AIP)

17 Great Pulteney Street
London W1R 3DG
Tel: 01 434 0181
Contact: Jane Williams
AIP was formed in 1976 by British producers 'to encourage production of films and to broaden the base of finance and exhibition'. Anyone involved in film, television and video production, or whose livelihood is dependent on the film and television industries, may apply for membership. AIP is a pressure group that campaigns for its members at government and industry level. It promotes and markets the work of independent film and television producers and provides a wide range of services that includes information, research, seminars, training courses, production and legal surgeries. It publishes handbooks and a widely read magazine. AIP is an associate member of the Independent Features Project (IFP) in New York and Los Angeles. AIP is also the UK representative for Euro Aim, an EEC marketing initiative for European independent producers. Merged with the British Film and Television Producers' Association (BFTPA) in 1989

Association of Professional Composers

34 Hanway Street
London W1P 9DE
Tel: 01 436 0919
Contact: Rosemary Dixson
APC represents composers from all sides of the profession – serious music, film, television, radio, theatre, electronic media, library music, jazz and so on. Its aims are to further the collective interests of its members and to inform and advise them on professional and artistic matters

Association of Professional Recording Studios

163a High Street
Rickmansworth
Herts WD3 1AY
Tel: 0923 772907
Represents the interests of the professional recording industry, including radio, TV and video studios and companies providing equipment and services in the field. It runs the international APRS Exhibition held at Olympia, London each year

Association of Professional Video Distributors

PO Box 25
Godalming
Surrey GU7 1PL
Tel: 04868 23429
Contact: Charles Potter MBE
Formed to improve the standards of the video industry with regard to the hardware by imposing professional discipline and controlling quality

British Academy of Film and Television Arts (BAFTA)

195 Piccadilly
London W1V 9LG
Tel: 01 734 0022
BAFTA was formed in 1946 by Britain's most eminent filmmakers as a non-profit making company. It aims to advance the art and technique of film and television and encourage experiment and research.

Membership is restricted to those who have made a creative contribution to the industry. BAFTA has facilities for screenings and discussion meetings, and makes representations to parliamentary committees. Its awards to the industries (Craft Awards and Production and Performance Awards) are annual televised events. The Academy has branches in Manchester, Glasgow, Cardiff and Los Angeles. Also see under Awards

British Academy of Songwriters, Composers and Authors (BASCA)

34 Hanway Street
London W1
Tel: 01 436 2261/2
Aims to assist both established and aspiring British songwriters with advice, guidance and encouragement. It issues standard contracts between publisher and songwriter

British Amateur Television Club (BATC)

Grenehurst
Pinewood Road
High Wycombe
Bucks HP12 4DD
The BATC exists to inform, instruct and co-ordinate members in amateur TV transmission, closed circuit, slow scan, special effects, new techniques and construction projects. It publishes TV handbooks and printed circuit boards for members to construct TV equipment

British Board of Film Classification (BBFC)

3 Soho Square
London W1V 5DE
Tel: 01 439 7961
The 1909 Cinematograph Films Act forced public cinemas to be licensed by their local authority. Originally this was a safety precaution against fire risk but was soon interpreted by the local authorities as a way of censoring cinema owners' choice of films. In 1912, the British Board of Film Classification was established to impose a conformity of viewpoint: films cannot be shown in public in Britain unless they have the BBFC's certificate or the relevant local authorisation. The Board finances itself by charging a fee for the films it views. When viewing a film, the Board attempts to judge whether a film is liable to break the law, for example by depraving and corrupting a significant proportion of its likely audience. It then assesses whether there is material greatly and gratuitously offensive to a large number of people. The Board seeks to reflect contemporary public attitudes. There are no written rules but films are considered in the light of the above criteria, previous decisions and the examiners' personal judgement. It is the policy of the Board not to censor anything on political grounds. Five film categories came into effect in 1982, with the introduction of a '12' category in August 1989:

Universal:
Suitable for all

Parental
Guidance:
Some scenes
may be
unsuitable for
young
children

Passed only
for persons of
12 years and
over

Passed only
for persons of
15 years and
over

Passed only
for persons of
18 years and
over

For Restricted
Distribution
only, through
segregated
premises to
which no one
under 18 years
is admitted

The final decision, however, still lies with the local authority. In 1986 the GLC ceased to be the licensing authority for London cinemas, and these powers devolved to the Borough Councils. Sometimes films are passed by the BBFC and then banned by local authorities (*Straw Dogs, Caligula*). Others may have their categories altered (*Monty Python's Life of Brian, 9½ Weeks*). Current newsreels are exempt from censorship. In 1985 the BBFC was designated by the Home Secretary as the authority responsible for classifying video works under the Video Recordings Act 1984. The film categories listed above are also used for video

British Broadcasting Corporation (BBC)
Portland Place
London W1A 1AA
Tel: 01 580 4468
The BBC provides its radio and TV services under the auspices of the Home Office, which deals with legislative and constitutional aspects of broadcasting. See also pp251-255

British Copyright Council
29–33 Berners Street
London W1P 4AA
Provides liaison between societies which represent the interest of those who own copyright in literature, music, drama and works of art, making representation to Government on behalf of its member societies

British Council
10 Spring Gardens
London SW1A 2BN
Tel: 01 930 8466
Contact: Brian Humphreys
11 Portland Place
London W1N 4EJ
Tel: 01 930 8466
As part of its work of promoting understanding of Britain in other countries, the British Council purchases films for showing by its offices in around 80 countries. It

also selects the films for British film weeks and film festivals overseas. The British Council has a Film, TV and Video Advisory Committee chaired by Lord Brabourne. The British Council receives funds from the Foreign and Commonwealth Office and from the Overseas Development Administration

British Equity
8 Harley Street
London W1N 2AB
Tel: 01 636 6367/637 9311
Equity was formed in 1930 by professional performers to achieve solutions to the problems of casual employment and short-term engagements. Equity has over 40,000 members, an increase by 30,000 since the 1950s. It represents performers (other than musicians), stage managers, stage directors, stage designers and choreographers in all spheres of work from variety and circus to television. It negotiates agreements on behalf of its members with producers' associations and other employers. In certain areas of work it has agreements with employers which regulate entry into the profession. In some fields of work only artists with previous professional experience are normally eligible for work. Membership of Equity is treated as evidence of professional experience under these agreements. It publishes a quarterly Equity Journal

British Federation of Film Societies (BFFS)
21 Stephen Street
London W1P 1PL
Tel: 01 255 1444
The BFFS exists to promote the work of some 350 film societies in the UK. In 1982 the BFI set up the Film Society Unit to service the BFFS. See also p14

British Film Fund Agency (BFFA)
St Martins House

16 St Martins Le Grand
London EC1A 4EP
Tel: 01 600 0818
The BFFA, under the jurisdiction of the Department of Trade and Industry, administered the Eady Levy, by which cinema exhibitors were required to contribute a twelfth of the price of every ticket they sold to a fund aimed at promoting indigenous British film production. Grants from the Fund went to the National Film School, BFI Production Board and – until 1981 – the Children's Film Foundation. The remaining money was divided amongst commercial productions which complied with certain regulations (British or co-produced films that employed over a certain percentage of British labour, a certain percentage of which was shot in Britain, etc). In 1982 the system came under the critical scrutiny of two government agencies: the Select Committee for Education, Science and the Arts, which recommended levying the Fund from video as well as cinema exhibition; and an enquiry at the Department of Trade on whether the levy should be abolished altogether. In 1985 Parliament passed a Films Bill that dispensed with the levy and meant that the BFFA would cease operation as soon as the final distribution of levy had been made

British Film Industry in Cannes (BFIC)
162–170 Wardour Street
London W1V 4LA
Tel: 01 437 7700
Contact: David G Watson
BFIC is organised by the Cannes Action Committee to oversee the British presence at the Cannes Film Festival and acts as an information base for all things connected with the festival

British Film Institute (BFI)
21 Stephen Street
London W1P 1PL
Tel: 01 255 1444
The BFI was set up in 1933 and has as its aim 'to encourage the development of the art of film and TV'. It is funded largely by a grant from the OAL. Among its activities are the preservation, exhibition and distribution of film and television as well as funding film theatres in the regions, film and video workshops, experimental productions and documenting film history. In 1988 the BFI opened its new Museum of the Moving Image on London's South Bank. For full description of BFI activities see pp6–15

The British Film and Television Producers' Association (BFTPA)
Paramount House
162–170 Wardour Street
London W1V 4LA
Tel: 01 437 7700
Contact: Andrew Patrick
The present BFTPA consists of the old British Film Producers' Association (formed in 1941) and the Federation of British Filmmakers (formed in 1957). BFTPA represents principally the interests of the production side of the industry. Its membership includes major production companies, studios, facility houses, production financing companies, specialised producers and British production subsidiaries of the American companies. As an employers' association, industrial relations are an important part of its activities. It is in constant contact with all the unions within the industry. It runs an Industrial Relations Service with IPPA. The BFTPA has an international marketing committee to represent British production abroad especially at film

festivals. All producers of cinema and TV films may become members. Merged with the Association of Independent Producers (AIP) in 1989

British Kinematograph Sound and Television Society (BKSTS)

547–549 Victoria House
Vernon Place
London WC1B 4DJ
Tel: 01 242 8400
Contact: Ray Mobsby
British technicians formed this society in 1931 to keep in touch with major technical developments. The Society arranges regular meetings, where new equipment and techniques are demonstrated and discussions held. It organises a biennial International Conference and Exhibition attended by delegates from all over the world. The monthly BKSTS journal, 'Image Technology', includes technical articles and reviews. Corporate members must hold responsible positions in film or TV. There is also an Associate membership and a third membership for students

British Radio and Electronic Equipment Manufacturers' Association

Landseer House
19 Charing Cross Road
London WC2H 0ES
Tel: 01 930 3206
Trade association for British consumer electronics industry

British Screen Advisory Council

13 Bateman Street
London W1V 6EB
Tel: 01 437 9617/8
The BSAC is a non-statutory advisory body set up to replace the statutory-based Cinematograph Films Council and the non-statutory Interim Action Committee which were respectively abolished and wound up on the passing of the Films Act 1985. Lord Wilson, Honorary President of the BSAC, has determined the Council's membership, taking into account the view expressed in the 1984 White Paper on film policy that it should be a broadly based industry body. The Council now embraces film, television and video, meeting every month under the Chairmanship of Sir Richard Attenborough to consider a number of industry questions

British Screen Finance (British Screen)

37–39 Oxford Street
London W1R 1RE
Tel: 01 434 0291
Since January 1986, British Screen, a private company aided by Government grant, has taken over the role and the business of the National Film Finance Corporation which was dissolved following the Films Act 1985. The Department of Trade and Industry, Channel 4 and Granada TV have pledged support until the end of 1990. British Screen aims to support new talent in commercially viable productions which might find difficulty in attracting mainstream commercial funding. Since 1986 it has supported 37 productions, 14 of them in 1988

British Tape Industry Association

Carolyn House
22-26 Dingwall Road
Croydon CR0 9XF
Tel: 01 681 1680
Trade association for the manufacturers of audio and videotape

British Universities Film and Video Council (BUFVC)

55 Greek Street
London W1V 5LR
Tel: 01 734 3687
Contact: Elizabeth Oliver
The BUFVC is an organisation with members in many institutions of higher education. It provides a number of services in the general area of production and use of audiovisual materials for teaching and research and receives a grant from the Department of Education and Science for its work in the higher education sector. It operates a comprehensive Information Service, produces catalogues and other publications, such as the 'Researchers' Guide to British Film and Television Collections', organises conferences and seminars and distributes specialised film and video material. It maintains a preview service called the Audiovisual Reference Centre where visitors may see a wide range of items, mainly on videocassette. Researchers in history come to the Council's offices to use the Slade Film History Register, with its information on British newsreels

British Videogram Association (BVA)

22 Poland Street
London W1V 3DD
Tel: 01 437 5722
Contact: N C B Abbott
The BVA represents the interests – with particular regard to copyright – of British producers and distributors of prerecorded videocassettes and videodiscs

Broadcasters' Audience Research Board (BARB)

5th Floor, North Wing
Glenthorne House
Hammersmith Grove
London W6
Tel: 01 741 9110
Succeeding the Joint Industries' Committee on Television Audience Research (JICTAR), BARB commissions audience research on behalf of the BBC and ITV

Broadcasting Complaints Commission (BCC)

Grosvenor Gardens House
35–37 Grosvenor Gardens
London SW1W 0BS
Tel: 01 630 1966
A statutory body set up by the Home Secretary under the Broadcasting Act 1981 to consider complaints of unjust or unfair treatment or unwarranted infringement of privacy in programmes broadcast by the BBC, IBA or included in a licensed cable programme service

Broadcasting and Entertainment Trades Alliance (BETA)

181–185 Wardour Street
London W1V 4BE
Tel: 01 439 7585
Contacts: D A Hearn
BETA is the general trade union for the broadcasting and entertainment industry. It was formed in early 1984 by the merger of the Association of Broadcasting Staff (ABS), and the National Association of Theatrical Television and Kine Employees (NATTKE). The origins of the latter go back to 1890, so BETA is celebrating its centenary this year. Its 30,000 members include staff in the BBC, independent broadcasting, film and video production (craft and general grades), cinema exhibition and theatre

Broadcasting Press Guild

c/o Harvey Lee
25 Courthouse Gardens
Finchley
London N3 1PU
Tel: 01 346 0643
An association of journalists who write about TV and radio in national, regional and trade press. Membership by invitation

Broadcasting Research Unit

39c Highbury Place
London N5 1QP

Tel: 01 226 9903
The Broadcasting Research Unit was set up in 1980 to initiate and implement research into issues related to broadcasting policy. The aim of BRU is to clarify complex issues and inform the decisions of broadcasters and policy-makers. In February 1988 BRU became an independent company with charitable status. BRU is funded by a combination of core grants, currently provided by the BBC, IBA, BFI and the Markle Foundation of New York, and individual project funding. BRU has developed a tradition of large-scale empirical investigation, particularly in the field of attitudinal surveys and cross-cultural studies. Recent and current topics of study include: Channel 4, radio usage in the UK, images of disability on television, the use of schools' broadcasting, funding structures for broadcasters in several countries, standards of taste and decency on television and the effects of deregulation on European broadcasting. A list of publications is available from the above address. Articles by BRU researchers appear regularly in newspapers and specialist press

Broadcasting Standards Council
5–8 The Sanctuary
London SW1P 3JS
Tel: 01 233 0544
In May 1988, the Home Secretary announced the establishment of BSC and appointed Lord Rees-Mogg as its Chairman. The Council's aim is to strengthen programme standards and reinforce the work of individual regulatory bodies. In addition, the Council is consulted by the Government on the implications, for the matters within its remit, of the negotiations under way in Europe and for the regulation of transfrontier

broadcasting, and on the implementation of the results of those negotiations

CFL Vision
PO Box 35
Wetherby
Yorkshire LS23 7EX
Tel: 0937 541010
CFL Vision began in 1927 as part of the Imperial Institute and is reputedly the oldest non-theatrical film library in the world. It is part of the COI and is the UK distributor for their audiovisual productions as well as for a large number of programmes acquired from both public and private sectors. Over 2,000 titles are available for hire or purchase by schools, film societies and by industry

Cable Authority
Gillingham House
38–44 Gillingham Street
London SW1V 1HU
Tel: 01 821 6161
The Cable Authority was established under the Cable and Broadcasting Act 1984 to license and regulate the UK cable industry. The Authority awards franchises for the operation of large wide-band cable systems and shorter licences for smaller systems. It also draws up a number of codes of practice, dealing with programming issues and the conduct of advertising and sponsorship

The Cable Television Association
50 Frith Street
London W1V 5TE
Tel: 01 437 0549/0983
Represents the interests of cable operators, installers, programme providers and equipment suppliers. For further information on cable, see under Cable and Satellite

Campaign for Press and Broadcasting Freedom
9 Poland Street
London W1V 3DG
Tel: 01 437 2795
A broad-based

membership organisation campaigning for more diverse, accessible and accountable media in Britain, backed by the media unions. Established in 1979, it now incorporates the Campaign Against Racism in the Media (CARM), the Television Users Group (TUG) and is developing regional structures. Specialist groups deal with Women's issues and Media Studies. CPBF publications cover all aspects of the media from broadcasting policy to sexism; its bi-monthly journal 'Free Press' watches ethical, industrial and political developments, with regular supplements on topical issues; its video library includes Open Door films *It Ain't Half Racist, Mum, Why Their News is Bad News, Making News* and *Wapping Lies*. CPBF organises conferences, offering the public assistance in obtaining a right of reply against media bias or misrepresentation. It helped set up the educational project, Media Research Trust and is promoting a Media Manifesto

Central Office of Information (COI)
Films and Television Division
Hercules Road
London SE1 7DU
Tel: 01 261 8500
Contact: Charles Skinner
COI Films and Television Division is responsible for government filmmaking on informational themes as well as the projection of Britain overseas. The COI organises the production of a wide range of documentary films, television programmes, video programmes and audio visual presentations including video disc production. It uses staff producers and draws on the film and video industry for production facilities. It provides help to visiting overseas television teams

Centre for the Study of Communication and Culture
221 Goldhurst Terrace
London NW6 3EP
Tel: 01 328 2868
A Jesuit-founded centre which promotes inter-disciplinary applied research on the problems of modern communication. Particular attention is paid to issues affecting the Third World and to the field of religious communication

Children's Film and Television Foundation
Goldcrest Elstree Studios
Borehamwood
Herts WD6 1JG
Tel: 01 953 0844
In 1944 Lord Rank founded the Children's Entertainment Film Division to make films specifically for children. In 1951 this resulted in the setting up of the Children's Film Foundation (now CFTF), a non-profit-making organisation which, up to 1981, was funded by an annual grant from the BFFA (Eady money). The CFTF no longer makes films from its own resources but, for suitable children's/family cinema/ television projects, is prepared to consider financing script development for eventual production by commercial companies. Films from the Foundation's extensive library are available for hiring at nominal charge in 35mm, 16mm and video format. Overseas sales are handled by Rank Film Distributors

Church of England Broadcasting Department
Church House
Great Smith Street
London SW1P 3NZ
Tel: 01 222 9011 x 260/ 261
(Out of office hours: 01 222 6672)
Contact: Rev John Barton
Responsible for liaison between the Church of

England and the broadcasting and film industries. Advises the C of E on all matters relating to broadcasting

Cinema and Television Benevolent Fund (CTBF)
Royalty House
72 Dean Street
London W1V 6LT
Tel: 01 437 6567
The CTBF helps those in need who have worked in cinema and/or ITV industries

Cinema and Television Veterans
Pinewood Studios
Iver
Bucks SL0 0NH
Tel: 0753 651700
An association open to anyone with 35 years or more service in cinema and/or television

Cinema Theatre Association
40 Winchester Street
London SW1V 4NF
Tel: 01 834 0549
Contact: Richard Gray
The Cinema Theatre Association was formed in 1967 to promote interest in Britain's cinema building legacy, in particular the magnificent movie palaces of the 1920s and 1930s. It is the only major organisation committed to cinema preservation in the UK. It campaigns for the protection of architecturally important cinemas and runs a comprehensive archive. The CTA publishes a bi-monthly bulletin and the magazine 'Picture House'

Cinematograph Exhibitors' Association of Great Britain and Ireland (CEA)
1st Floor
Royalty House
72–73 Dean Street
London W1V 5HB
Tel: 01 734 9551
The first branch of the industry to organise itself was the cinema owners, who formed the CEA in 1912. CEA members account for the vast

majority of all UK public cinemas. The Association represents members' interests both within the industry and to Government departments concerned with exhibition. It has been closely involved with such recent legislation as the Video Recordings Act 1984, the Cinemas Act 1985 and the Films Act 1985

Commonwealth Broadcasting Association
Broadcasting House
London W1A 1AA
Tel: 01 927 5022
An association of 56 public service broadcasting organisations in 51 Commonwealth countries

Composers' Guild of Great Britain
34 Hanway Street
London W1P 9DE
Tel: 01 436 0007
The Guild represents composers of serious music, covering the stylistic spectrum from jazz to electronics. Although its main function is to safeguard and assist the professional interests of its members, it also provides information for those wishing to commission music and will put performers or societies in touch with composers

Confederation of Entertainment Unions (CEU)
Contact: John Morton via Musicians' Union
A confederation made up of the Federation of Broadcasting Unions (FBU), Federation of Film Unions (FFU) and Federation of Theatre Unions

Critics' Circle
Film Section
31 Hampstead Lane
London N6
Tel: 01 340 7862
Chairman: William Hall
Vice-Chairman: George Perry
Honorary Sec: Alan Frank

Assistant Sec: Virginia Dignam
The film section of the Critics' Circle brings together most national and regional critics for meetings, functions and the presentation of annual awards

Deaf Broadcasting Council (DBC)
592 Kenilworth Road
Balsall Common
Coventry CV7 7DQ
Tel: 0203 832076
Contact: Austin Reeves
An umbrella group of organisations for the deaf which campaigns to ensure that TV services are accessible to deaf and hard of hearing viewers

Defence Press and Broadcasting Committee
Room 2235
Ministry of Defence
Main Building
Whitehall
London SW1A 2HB
Tel: 01 218 2206
This committee is responsible for D notices. These give guidance on the publication of information which it regards as sensitive for reasons of national security

Department of Education and Science (DES)
Elizabeth House
York Road
London SE1 7PH
Tel: 01 934 9000
The DES is responsible for: policies for education in England; the Government's relations with universities in England, Scotland and Wales; fostering civil science

Department of Trade and Industry (DTI)
Kingsgate House
66–74 Victoria Street
London SW1E 6SW
Tel: 01 215 7877
The DTI is responsible for carrying out Government policy concerning the commercial and business aspects of the film, video and cinema industries including the film

facilities sector; UK and EEC films legislation; OECD (Organisation for Economic Co-operation and Development) and GATT (General Agreement on Tariff and Trade) films interest. It is also responsible for the administration of co-production agreements and the certification of British films

Designers and Art Directors' Association
Nash House
12 Carlton House Terrace
London SW1Y 5AH
Tel: 01 839 2964
A professional association, registered as a charity, which publishes an annual of the best of British design, advertising, television commercials, pop promos/videos and organises travelling exhibitions. Membership is selected and only those who have had work accepted are eligible

Directors' Guild of Great Britain
125 Tottenham Court Road
London W1P 9HN
Tel: 01 387 7131
Contact: Suzan Dormer, Moira Stirling, Marisa Keating
Represents interests and concerns of directors in all media

Educational Broadcasting Services, BBC
Villiers House
The Broadway
Ealing
London W5 2PA
Tel: 01 991 8037
Contact: Jim Stevenson
EBS supports the work of BBC Education radio and television production departments. It services the Educational Broadcasting Council representing professional users

Educational Television Association
The King's Manor
Exhibition Square
York Y01 2EP

ORGANISATIONS

Tel: 0904 433929
Contact: Josie Key
An umbrella organisation of institutions and individuals using TV for education and training. Award scheme and conference held annually. Membership enquiries welcome

Electrical Electronic Telecommunication and Plumbing Union (EETPU)

Hayes Court
West Common Road
Bromley BR2 7AU
Tel: 01 462 7755
A trade union representing – among others – people employed in film and TV lighting/electrical/electronic work

The Federation Against Copyright Theft (FACT)

7 Victory Business Centre
Worton Road
Isleworth
Middlesex TW7 6ER
Tel: 01 568 6646
An organisation founded in 1982 by the legitimate film and video industry, dedicated to stamping out copyright piracy in the UK

Federation of Broadcasting Unions (FBU)

Contact: Paddy Leech, BETA
The FBU comprises Broadcasting and Entertainment Trades Alliance (BETA), Association of Cinematograph, Television and allied Technicians (ACTT), Musicians' Union (MU), British Actors' Equity, Electrical Electronic Telecommunication and Plumbing Union (EETPU), the NUJ and the Writers' Guild

Federation of Commercial Audio-Visual Libraries (FOCAL)

37 Stanmore Hill
Stanmore
Middx HA7 3DS
President: Jill Haskins
This newly-formed federation published its first directory in 1988,

listing its 23 members in three categories: corporate, associate, and affiliated

Federation of Film Unions (FFU)

111 Wardour Street
London W1V 4AY
Tel: 01 437 8506
Secretary: Alan Sapper
Represents a group of unions in the entertainment industry devoted to film production. Each union is an independent and autonomous body coming together under the Federation. The unions are: ACTT, BETA, British Actors' Equity, Electrical, Electronics Telecommunication and Plumbing Union, Film Artistes' Association, Musicians' Union and Writers' Guild of Great Britain

Feminist Library (formerly WRRC)

5 Westminster Bridge Road
London SE1
Tel: 01 928 7789
Feminist Lending Library keeps an index of research by and on women and women's issues, and information on women's study courses as well as having both fiction and non-fiction for loan. Holds a wide selection of journals and newsletters and publishes its own newsletter four times a year. Open Tuesday (11.00–20.00) and Saturday and Sunday (14.00–17.00)

Ffilm Cymru

33 Castle Arcade
Cardiff CF1 2BW
Tel: 0222 340868
Artistic Director: John Hefin
Director, Business Affairs: Richard J Staniforth
An organisation founded in 1982 by S4C and BBC Cymru to fund low budget feature films in Welsh, English and other European languages

Film and Television Lighting Contractors Association

20 Darwin Close
New Southgate
London N11
Tel: 01 361 2122
Contact: A W Jacques
Set up in 1983 to negotiate with the EETPU on behalf of individual lighting contractors

Film and Video Press Group

c/o Adam Cook
IVCA
Bolsover House
5/6 Clipstone Street
London W1P 7EB
Tel: 01 580 0962
UK professional association for editors, journalists and freelance writers in the audiovisual media

Film Artistes' Association (FAA)

61 Marloes Road
London W8 6LF
Tel: 01 937 4567
The FAA represents extras, doubles, stand-ins and small parts. Under an agreement with the BFTPA any crowd scenes within 40 miles of Charing Cross Road must use FAA members

Film Industry Council

c/o BFTPA
Paramount House
162–170 Wardour Street
London W1V 4LA
Tel: 01 434 7700
Contact: Andrew Patrick
Membership of FIC is open to recognised industry bodies only. Its purpose is to create a forum for industry discussion, to explore common interests, to achieve wherever possible a collective policy on key issues and problems and to represent the film industry with an effective political voice

Guild of Animation

26 Noel Street
London W1V 3RD
Tel: 01 434 2651
Contact: Cecilia Garnett
Represents interests of producers of animated

films. The AFVPA acts as secretariat for this association

Guild of British Camera Technicians

5–11 Taunton Road
Metropolitan Centre
Greenford
Middlesex UB6 8UQ
Tel: 01 578 9243
Contact: Julie Curran
ADUTG Consultant: Ron Bowyer (Eyepiece)
The Guild exists to further the professional interests of technicians working with motion picture cameras. Membership is restricted to those whose work brings them into direct contact with motion picture cameras and who can demonstrate competence in their particular field of work. They must also be members of the appropriate union. By setting certain minimum standards of skill for membership, the Guild seeks to encourage its members, especially newer entrants, to strive to improve their art. Through its publication, 'Eyepiece', GBCT disseminates information about latest developments in equipment and techniques

Guild of British Film Editors

c/o Alfred E Cox
Travair
Spurlands End Road
Great Kingshill
High Wycombe
Bucks
Tel: 0494 712313
To ensure that the true value of film and sound editing is recognised as an important part of the creative and artistic aspects of film production

Guild of Television Cameramen

'Whiteacres'
1 Churchill Road
Whitchurch
Tavistock
Devon PL19 9BU
The Guild was formed in 1972 'to ensure and preserve the professional status of the television

cameramen and to establish, uphold and advance the standards of qualification and competence of cameramen'. The Guild is not a union and seeks to avoid political involvement

Home Office
50 Queen Anne's Gate
London SW1H 9AT
Tel: 01 273 3000
The Home Office deals with questions of policy on broadcasting, classification of videos, cinema licensing and obscenity, and issues exemption certificates under the Cinemas Act 1985. It also sponsors publicity and training films through the COI

Imperial War Museum
Department of Film
Lambeth Road
London SE1 6HZ
Tel: 01 735 8922
Contact: Anne Fleming
The Imperial War Museum illustrates and records all aspects of the two World Wars and other military operations involving Britain and the Commonwealth since 1914. It maintains an extensive archive of film and video material on a broad range of topics. The Museum offers research and viewing facilities which are extensively used by film and television companies. It also promotes activities to do with film history and holds special seminars and conferences

Incorporated Society of British Advertisers (ISBA)
44 Hertford Street
London W1Y 8AE
Tel: 01 499 7502
Contact: Trudy Gordon
The ISBA was founded in 1900 as an association for advertisers, both regional and national. Subscriptions are based on advertisers' expenditure and the main objective is the protection and advancement of the advertising interests of member firms. This involves organised

representation, co-operation, action and exchange of information and experience, together with conferences, workshops and publications

Incorporated Society of Musicians
10 Stratford Place
London W1N 9AE
Tel: 01 629 4413/4302
Contact: David Padgett-Chandler
The professional association for all musicians: music teachers, performers and conductors. The society produces the monthly 'Music Journal'

Independent Broadcasting Authority (IBA)
70 Brompton Road
London SW3 1EY
Tel: 01 584 7011
The IBA operates under the Broadcasting Act 1981 and is the controlling body for Independent Local Radio, ITV and Channel 4. Its four main functions are to select and appoint the programme companies, supervise the programme planning, control the advertising and to own and operate the transmitters

Independent Film Distributors' Association (IFDA)
c/o Contemporary Films
24 Southwood Lawn Road
London N6 5SF
Tel: 01 340 5715
Contact: Charles Cooper
The IFDA was formed in 1973, and its 18 members are mainly specialised film distributors who deal in both 16mm and 35mm from 'art' to 'popular music' films. They supply to many sources including schools

Independent Film, Video and Photography Association (IFVPA)
79 Wardour Street
London W1V 3PH
Tel: 01 439 0460
Contact: Simon Blanchard

The IFVA was formed in 1974 to represent the views and interests of independent filmmakers. In 1983 video was added to the title and the brief, followed by photography in 1986. The IFVPA aims to develop the practices, knowledge and understanding of independent photography, film and video making, distribution and exhibition. It runs a legal advisory service for members on contracts, copyright and so on. It also publishes a regular newsletter and a discussion journal

Independent Programme Producers' Association (IPPA)
50–51 Berwick Street
London W1V 4RD
Tel: 01 439 7034
IPPA is the trade association for British independent television producers, representing more than 600 production companies based throughout the UK. Services to members include a specialist industrial relations unit and advice on all matters relating to independent production for television. Having led the campaign for 25% of all new British TV programmes to be made by independents, IPPA maintains an active lobby to ensure that the needs of the sector are heard and understood by Government in Britain and Europe

Independent Television Association (ITV Ass'n)
Knighton House
56 Mortimer Street
London W1N 8AN
Tel: 01 636 6866
Contact: Margaret Bassett
Incorporated as a company limited by guarantee, the ITV Ass'n is the organisation which provides a Central Secretariat to service those needs of the industry requiring a co-

ordinated and centralised approach. The governing body is the Council, comprising all the Managing Directors, and its main task is to determine the joint policy of the companies over a wide range of industry matters. Several committees – Network Programme, Industrial Relations, Marketing, Finance and General Purposes, Rights and Technical, supported by specialised sub-committees and working groups – undertake the detailed work

Indian Videogram Association
PO Box 230
London W2 1BN
Represents concerns of producers and distributors of Indian videos

Institute of Practitioners in Advertising (IPA)
44 Belgrave Square
London SW1X 8QS
Tel: 01 235 7020
The IPA is the representative body for UK advertising agencies and the people who work in them. It represents the collective views of its member agencies in liaison with Government departments, the media and industry and consumer organisations

International Association of Broadcasting Manufacturers (IABM)
Triumph House
1096 Uxbridge Road
Hayes
Middlesex UB4 8QH
Tel: 01 573 8333
Administrator: Alan Hirst
IABM aims to foster the interests of manufacturers of broadcast equipment from all countries. Areas of interest include liaison with broadcasters, standardisation and exhibitions. All companies active in the field of broadcast equipment

manufacturing are welcome to join

International Federation of Producers of Phonograms and Videograms (IFPI)

IFPI Secretariat
54 Regent Street
London W1R 5PJ
Tel: 01 434 3521
An international association of over 880 members in 62 countries, representing the copyright interests of the sound recording and music video industries

International Institute of Communications

Tavistock House South
Tavistock Square
London WC1H 9LF
Tel: 01 388 0671
Contact: John Howkins
The IIC provides a centre for the analysis of social, economic, political, cultural and legal issues related to media and electronic communication. It carries out research projects and consultancy, holds conferences and seminars and publishes books. UK members include BBC, IBA, C4 and many individuals. Its journal is 'InterMedia' which appears bi-monthly

International Songwriters' Association (ISA)

22 Sullane Crescent
Raheen Heights
Limerick
Ireland
Tel: 010 353 61 28837
Contact: James Liddane
Founded in 1967, the ISA represents songwriters in more than 40 countries and publishes 'Songwriter' magazine

International Visual Communications Association (IVCA)

IVCA
Bolsover House
5/6 Clipstone Street
London W1P 7EB
Tel: 01 580 0962
Contact: Stuart Appleton
IVCA is the professional association providing a voice and a network for the promotion and use of screen communications. Among its membership services IVCA publishes a monthly magazine and runs the industry's premier festival

London Screenwriters' Workshop

64 Church Crescent
London N10 3NE
Tel: 01 883 7218
Formed in 1983 to create a forum for contact, discussion and practical criticism, the London Screenwriters' Workshop campaigns on behalf of writers in film and TV, and organises seminars and workshops on all aspects of the screenwriting process. Membership is open to anyone interested in writing for film and television, and to anyone in these and related media

Mechanical Copyright Protection Society (MCPS)

Elgar House
41 Streatham High Road
London SW16 1ER
Tel: 01 769 4400
Contact: Alasdair Blaazer
Music copyright society whose functions include the clearance of music and record copyrights for film, video, and TV programme makers. Production companies who want to use music in their films should contact the Licensing Department

Media Project

The Volunteer Centre
29 Lower Kings Road
Berkhamsted
Herts HP4 2AB
Tel: 0442 873311
Contact: Moyra Tourlamain, Andrew Taylor, Liz Schofield
Media Project provides an information, advisory and monitoring service for broadcasters and voluntary/statutory organisations working in the area of social action broadcasting. The Project encourages and undertakes research, runs local radio training courses and organises a national social action broadcasting conference. 'On Air/Off Air', a bi-monthly magazine, case studies, information papers and 'Action Stations', the directory of social action programmes are available on annual subscription (£15.00)

Media Studies Association

c/o Jim Brennan
Brennan Publications
148 Birchover Way
Allestree
Derby
Tel: 0332 551884
Promotes the exchange of ideas between teachers and practitioners of broadcasting and journalism

Mental Health Film Council

380 Harrow Road
London W9 2HU
Tel: 01 286 2346
Contact: Elizabeth Garrett
An independent charity founded in 1965, the MHFC provides information, advice and consultancy on film/video use and production relevant to mental health education. Newsletter, bi-monthly screenings, resource lists, videography available on annual subscription

Music Film and Video Producers' Association (MFVPA)

26 Noel Street
London W1V 3RD
Tel: 01 434 2651
Contact: Cecilia Garnett
The MFVPA was formed in 1985 to represent the interests of pop/music promo production companies. It negotiates agreements with bodies such as the BPI and ACTT on behalf of its members. Secretariat support is run through AFVPA

Music Publishers' Association

7th Floor
Kingsway House
103 Kingsway
London WC2B 6QX
Tel: 01 831 7591
The only trade association in this country which represents music publishers. List of members available at £2.50

Musicians' Union (MU)

60–62 Clapham Road
London SW9 0JJ
Tel: 01 582 5566
Contact: Don Smith
The MU represents the interests of performing musicians in all areas

National Association for Higher Education in Film and Video

c/o West Surrey College of Art and Design
Falkner Road
Farnham
Surrey GU9 7DS
Tel: 0252 722441
Contact: Claire Mussell
The Association's main aims are to act as a forum for debate on all aspects of film, video and TV education and to foster links with industry, the professions and Government bodies. It was established in 1983 to represent all courses in the UK which offer a major practical study in film, video or TV at the higher educational level. Some 40 courses are currently in membership

National Audiovisual Aids Centre and Library (NAVAC)

The George Building
Normal College
Bangor
Gwynedd LL57 2PZ
Tel: 0248 370144
NAVAC gives advice and information on the application of audiovisual resources, mainly in education. Offers films and videos for sale and hire

National Council for Educational Technology (NCET)

3 Devonshire Street
London W1N 2BA
Tel: 01 580 7553

A government-funded development agency for promoting the application of educational technology (including new information technology) in all sectors of education and training. Merged in 1988 with the Microelectronics Education Support Unit

National Film Development Fund (NFDF)

37–39 Oxford Street
London W1R 1RE
Tel: 01 434 0291
Administrator: Adrian Hodges
The NFDF was set up in 1976 to make loans for the development of British cinema feature films. Funded originally from the Eady Levy, it has helped to develop such films as *Defence of the Realm*, *Dance with a Stranger*, *A Room with a View*, *Tree of Hands*, *Joyriders*, *A Very British Coup* and *Soursweet*. Under the 1985 Films Act, the fund receives £500,000 annually from the Department of Trade and Industry – £350,000 for the development of scripts and £150,000 for the production of short films. The NFDF is managed by British Screen Finance (the semi-privatised successor of the NFFC), but has a separate administrator and panel of independent consultants

National Film and Television School

Beaconsfield Studios
Station Road
Beaconsfield
Bucks HP9 1LG
Tel: 0494 671234
Director: Colin Young
The National Film and Television School provides advanced training and retraining in all major disciplines to professional standards. Graduates are entitled to ACTT membership on gaining employment. It is an autonomous non-profit-making organisation funded by the Office of Arts and Libraries and the film and television industries. See also p109

National Union of Journalists

314 Grays Inn Road
London WC1X 8DP
Tel: 01 278 7916
Contact: John Foster
NUJ represents all journalists working in broadcasting in the areas of news, sport, current affairs and features. It has agreements with all of the broadcasting companies and the BBC. It also has agreements with the main broadcasting agencies, WTN and Visnews with approximately 5,000 members in broadcasting

National Viewers' and Listeners' Association (NVALA)

Ardleigh
Colchester
Essex C07 7RH
Tel: 0206 230123
Contact: Mary Whitehouse
General Sec: John Beyer
Concerned with moral standards in the media, particularly the role of TV in the creation of social and cultural values

National Youth Film Foundation

52 Canalot Studios
222 Kensal Road
London W10 5BN
Tel: 01 969 5195
Launches in April 1989, partly sponsored by S4C and Tyne Tees TV

Office of Arts and Libraries (OAL)

Horse Guards Road
London SW1P 3AL
Tel: 01 270 5865/6326
Within its wider concern with matters affecting the arts, museums and libraries, the OAL is the major source of government finance for film. It funds – among other bodies – the BFI and the Arts Council

Office of Fair Trading

Field House
Bream's Buildings
London EC4A 1PR
Tel: 01 242 2858
The Office of Fair Trading has an interest in the film industry following two

reports on the supply of films for exhibition in cinemas – by the Monopolies Commission in October 1966 and by the Monopolies and Mergers Commission in 1983

Performers' Alliance

Consists of British Equity, Musicians' Union, Writers' Guild of Great Britain. Contact through member organisations above

Performing Right Society (PRS)

29–33 Berners Street
London W1P 4AA
Tel: 01 580 5544
The PRS is a non-profit-making association of composers, authors and publishers of musical works. It collects and distributes royalties for the use, in public performances, broadcasts and cable programmes, of its members' copyright music and has links with other performing right societies throughout the world. Explanatory literature and/or a film explaining the Society's operations is available from the Public Relations Department

Phonographic Performance

Ganton House
14–22 Ganton Street
London W1V ILB
Tel: 01 437 0311
Formed by the British recording industry for the collection and distribution of revenue in respect of the UK public performance and broadcasting of sound recordings

Radio, Electrical and Television Retailers' Association (RETRA)

Retra House
St John's Terrace
1 Ampthill Street
Bedford MK42 9EY
Tel: 0234 269110
Contact: Josie Matthews
The Association was founded in 1942 to represent the interests of

independent electrical dealers to all those who make decisions likely to affect the selling and servicing of electrical and electronic products

Royal Television Society (RTS)

Tavistock House East
Tavistock Square
London WC1H 9HR
Tel: 01 387 1970
Contact: Tracey Dyer
The Royal Television Society, founded in 1927, has over 3,000 members in the UK and overseas, half of which are serviced by the Society's 14 regional centres. The Society aims to bring together all the disciplines of television by providing a forum for debate on the technical, cultural and social implications of the medium. This is achieved through the many lectures, conferences, symposia and training courses organised each year. A bi-monthly journal 'Television' and a monthly publication 'Talkback' are published by the RTS as well as monographs, television engineering textbooks, career broadsheets and a number of topical papers relating to Society events. The RTS Television Journalism Awards are presented every year in February and the Programme Awards in May also Design and Educational Television Awards. See also under Awards

Scottish Film Council

Dowanhill
74 Victoria Crescent Road
Glasgow G12 9JN
Tel: 041 334 9314
Sisterbody to the BFI, the SFC receives funds from the Scottish Education Department for the promotion of film culture in Scotland. See also under Cinemas – Scotland

Scottish Film Production Fund

74 Victoria Crescent Road
Glasgow G12 9JN
Tel: 041 337 2526

Director: Penny Thomson
The Fund was set up in 1982 with a brief to foster and promote film and video production in Scotland. The Production Fund committee meets quarterly to consider applications for finance for projects which must have a particular connection with and relevance to Scotland. The Fund's annual budget now stands at £200,000

Scottish Film Training Trust
74 Victoria Crescent Road
Glasgow G12 9JN
Tel: 041 337 2526/334 4445
Contact: Penny Thomson, Kevin Cowle
A charitable trust set up in 1982 and financed by the Scottish Film Council, the European Social Fund, Scottish Television plc and BAFTA/Shell. It aims to assist in the training of young Scots entering the film and TV industries.

Society of Authors' Broadcasting Committee
84 Drayton Gardens
London SW10 9SB
Tel: 01 373 6642
Specialities: Radio, television
and film scriptwriters

Society of Cable Television Engineers (SCTE)
10 Avenue Road
Dorridge
Solihull
West Midlands B93 8LD
Tel: 0564 774058
Contact: T H Hall
Aims to raise the standard of cable TV engineering to the highest technical level and to elevate and improve the status and efficiency of those engaged in cable TV engineering

Society of Film Distributors (SFD)
Royalty House
72–73 Dean Street
London W1V 5HB
Tel: 01 437 4383
SFD was founded in 1915 and membership includes

all the major distribution companies and several independent companies. It promotes and protects its members' interests and co-operates with all other film organisations and Government agencies where distribution interests are involved

Society of Television Lighting Directors
46 Batchworth Lane
Northwood
Middlesex HA6 3HG
The Society provides a forum for the exchange of ideas in all aspects of the TV profession including techniques and equipment. Meetings are organised throughout the UK and abroad. Technical information and news of members' activities are published in the Society's magazine. The Society has no union or political affiliations

Variety Artistes Ladies and Childrens Guild
Bon Marche House
Unit 131
44 Brixton Road
London SW9 8EJ
Tel: 01 978 8776
Contact: June Groves
Founded in 1906 for the purpose of assisting members of the entertainment professions and their children. Funds are raised by the organisation of an annual dinner and dance, stars bazaar, theatre collections and contributions

Variety Club of Great Britain
32 Welbeck Street
London W1M 7PG
Tel: 01 935 4466
The greatest children's charity in the world

Video Trade Association
54d High Street
Northwood
Middlesex HA6 1BL
Tel: 09274 29122
Trade association set up to improve trading standards and customer service offered by the video software retailer

Voice of the Listener
101 King's Drive
Gravesend
Kent DA12 5BQ
Tel: 0474 564676
An independent non-profit-making association working to ensure high standards in broadcasting. Membership is open to all concerned for the future quality and range of British radio and television services

Welsh Arts Council
9 Museum Place
Cardiff CF1 3NX
Tel: 0222 394711
Director: T A Owen
Film Services Organiser: Martyn Howells
Advises the Arts Council on matters in Wales. Like the Regional Arts Associations, it is eligible to receive funds from the BFI

Wider Television Access (WTVA)
c/o Illuminations
3rd Floor
16 Newman Passage
London W1P 3PE
Tel: 01 580 7877
A pressure group and publisher of 'Primetime' magazine, seeking to stimulate interest in old UK and US TV programmes and promote greater use of TV archives

Women's Media Action Group
c/o London Women's Centre
Wesley House
4 Wild Court
London WC2B 5AU
Feminist group campaigning to promote positive and representative images of women and to eliminate sexist stereotyping in all areas of the media. With Women's Monitoring Network, it has published seven reports on various aspects of sexism in the media. Publishes bi-monthly bulletin

Writers' Guild of Great Britain
430 Edgware Road
London W2 1EH
Tel: 01 723 8074

Contact: Walter J Jeffrey
The Writers' Guild is the recognised TUC-affiliated trade union for writers working in film, television, radio, theatre and publishing. It has negotiated industrial agreements in all the areas mentioned above. These agreements set the minimum rates and conditions for each field of writing

REGIONAL ARTS ASSOCIATIONS

Council of Regional Arts Associations
13a Clifton Road
Winchester SO22 5BP
Tel: 0962 51063
Executive Officer: Christopher Gordon
Administrator: Nicola Gunn

East Midlands Arts
Mountfields House
Forest Road
Loughborough
Leicestershire LE11 3HU
Tel: 0509 218292
Director: John Buston
Film Officer: Caroline Pick
Derbyshire (excluding High Peak District), Leicestershire, Northamptonshire, Nottinghamshire, Milton Keynes DC

Eastern Arts
Cherry Hinton Hall
Cherry Hinton Road
Cambridge CB1 4DW
Tel: 0223 215355
Director: Jeremy Newton
Film Officer: Martin Ayres
Bedfordshire, Cambridgeshire, Essex, Hertfordshire, Norfolk and Suffolk

Greater London Arts
9 White Lion Street
London N1 9PD
Tel: 01 837 8808
Director: Trevor Vibert
Film Officer: Felicity Sparrow
The area of the 32 London Boroughs and the City of London

Lincolnshire and Humberside Arts
St Hugh's
23 Newport
Lincoln LN1 3DN
Tel: 0522 533555
Director: Clive Fox
Film and Media Officer:
Geoff Swallow
Lincolnshire and
Humberside

Merseyside Arts
Graphic House
Duke Street
Liverpool L1 4JR
Tel: 051 709 0671
Director: Peter Booth
Liverpool, Sefton,
Knowsley, St Helens,
Wirral, West Lancashire,
Ellesmere Port and
Neston, Halton

North West Arts
12 Harter Street
Manchester M1 6HY
Tel: 061 228 3062
Director: Josephine Burns
Film Officer: Laura
Hollins
Greater Manchester,
Lancashire (except West
Lancashire DC), High
Peak DC, Cheshire

(except Ellesmere Port
and Neston, Halton DCs)

Northern Arts
9-10 Osborne Terrace
Jesmond
Newcastle upon Tyne
NE2 1NZ
Tel: 091 281 6334
Director: Peter Stark
Film Officer: John
Bradshaw
Cleveland, Cumbria,
Durham,
Northumberland, Tyne
and Wear

South East Arts
10 Mount Ephraim
Tunbridge Wells
Kent TN4 8AS
Tel: 0892 515210
Director: Chris Cooper
Film Officer: Tim Cornish
East Sussex, Kent and
Surrey

South West Arts
Bradninch Place
Gandy Street
Exeter EX4 3LS
Tel: 0392 218188
Director: Martin
Rewcastle
Film and TV Officer:

Judith Higginbottom
Avon, Cornwall, Devon,
Dorset (except
Bournemouth,
Christchurch and Poole
DCs), Gloucestershire and
Somerset

Southern Arts
19 Southgate Street
Winchester
Hampshire SO23 9DQ
Tel: 0962 55099
Director: Bill Dufton
Film Officer: David
Browne
Berkshire, Hampshire,
Isle of Wight,
Oxfordshire, West Sussex,
Wiltshire; Bournemouth,
Christchurch and Poole
DCs

West Midlands Arts
82 Granville Street
Birmingham B1 2LH
Tel: 021 631 3121
Director: Mick Elliot
Film Officer: Helen
Doherty
Hereford and Worcester,
Shropshire, Staffordshire,
Warwickshire, West
Midlands

Yorkshire Arts
Glyde House
Glydegate
Bradford BD5 0BQ
Tel: 0274 723051
Director: Roger Lancaster
Film Officer: Paul
Brookes, Sara Worrall
North, South and West
Yorkshire

PRESS CONTACTS

Below are magazine and newspaper critics and journalists who write about film, TV and video. Also listed are the news and photo agencies which handle media news syndication and TV and radio programmes concerned with the visual media

African Times
(weekly)
139–149 Fonthill Road
London N4 3HF
Tel: 01 281 1191
Editor: Arif Ali
Tabloid dealing with issues pertinent to community it serves. Also at this address are 'Caribbean Times' and 'Asian Times'
Press day: Mon

Arena (bi-monthly)
The Old Laundry
Ossington Buildings
London W1
Tel: 01 935 8232
Editor: Nick Logan
Film: Dylan Jones, Ian Penman
Magazine for men covering general interest, avant-garde, film, music and fashion
Lead time: 4–5 weeks
Circulation: 62,302 (UK); 95,151 (worldwide)

Art Monthly
36 Great Russell Street
London WC1B 3PP
Tel: 01 580 4168
Editors: Jack Wendler, Peter Townsend
Aimed at artists, arts administrators, teachers, collectors, amateurs directly connected with the visual arts
Lead time: 4 weeks
Circulation: 4,000

Blitz Magazine
(monthly)
40–42 Newman Street
London W1P 3TP
Tel: 01 436 5211
Editor: Simon Tesler
Publisher: Carey Labovitch
Media, entertainments and style monthly
Lead time: 6 weeks
Circulation: 60,000

Broadcast (weekly, Fri)
100 Avenue Road
London NW3 3TP
Tel: 01 935 6611
Publisher: Martin Jackson
Editor: Marta Worhle
Broadcasting industry news magazine with coverage of TV, radio, cable and satellite, corporate production and international programming and distribution in a monthly section 'Worldwatch'. Also publishes a monthly supplement 'Videographic' which covers applications of technology in video production
Press day: Wed
Lead time: 2 weeks
Circulation: 9,645

The Business of Film (monthly)
24 Charlotte Street
London W1P 1HJ
Tel: 01 580 0141
Publisher/executive editor: Elspeth Tavares
Editor: Ruth Picardie
Aimed at film industry professionals – producers, distributors, exhibitors, investors, financiers
Lead time: 2 weeks

City Limits (weekly, Thur)
8–15 Aylesbury Street
London EC1R 0LR
Tel: 01 250 1299
Film: John Wrathall
TV: John Lyttle
Video: Stephen Bode
London listings magazine with cinema and TV sections
Press day: Mon
Lead time: 8-11 days
Circulation: 31,000

Company (monthly)
National Magazine House
72 Broadwick Street
London W1V 2BP
Tel: 01 439 5372
Arts/style editor: Dee Pilgrim
Glossy magazine for women aged 18-30
Lead time: 10 weeks
Circulation: 182,000

Cosmopolitan
(monthly)
National Magazine House
72 Broadwick Street
London W1V 2BP
Tel: 01 439 7144
Film: Derek Malcolm
TV: Sue Summers
Aimed at women aged 18–35
Lead time: 12 weeks
Circulation: 387,090

Creative Review
(monthly)
50 Poland Street
London W1V 4AX
Tel: 01 439 4222
Editor: Lewis Blackwell
Deputy editor: Lyndy Stout
Publisher: Annie Swift
Trade paper for creative people covering film, advertising and design. Film reviews, profiles and technical features
Lead time: 4 weeks
Circulation: 20,000

Daily Express
245 Blackfriars Road
London SE1 9UX
Tel: 01 928 8000
Film: Ian Christie, David Wigg
TV: Louise Court
Media: Mary Corbett
National daily newspaper
Circulation: 1,700,000

Daily Mail
Northcliffe House
London EC4Y 0JA
Tel: 01 353 6000
Film: Shaun Usher
TV: Corinna Honan
National daily newspaper
Circulation: 2,000,000

Daily Mirror
Holborn Circus
London EC1P 1DQ
Tel: 01 353 0246
Film: Pauline McLeod

TV: Hilary Kingsley
National daily newspaper
Circulation: 3,250,000

Daily Telegraph
Peterborough Court
at South Quay
181 Marsh Wall
London E14 9SR
Tel: 01 538 5000
Arts: Miriam Gross
Film: Victoria Mather
TV: Richard Last
National daily newspaper
Circulation: 1,200,000

The Economist
(weekly)
25 St James's Street
London SW1A 1HG
Tel: 01 839 7000
Film/video: Ann Wroe
TV: Anthony Gottlieb
International coverage of
major political, social and
business developments
with arts section
Press day: Wed
Circulation: 349,030

Elle (monthly)
Rex House
4–12 Lower Regent
Street
London SW1Y 4PE
Tel: 01 930 9050
Editor: Sally Brampton
Features editor: Jane
McCarthy
Glossy magazine aimed at
18–35 year old working
women
Lead time: 8 weeks

Evening Standard
(Mon–Fri)
New Northcliffe House
2 Derry Street
London W8 5SE
Tel: 01 938 6000
Editor: John Leese
Arts: Brian Sewell
Film: Alexander Walker
TV: Jaci Stephen
London weekday evening
newspaper

Everywoman
(monthly)
34a Islington Green
London N1 8DU
Tel: 01 359 5496
Editor: Barbara Rogers
Film: Jane Ehrlich
A magazine for women
interested in politics,
current affairs, arts etc
Lead time: 6 weeks
Circulation: 15,000

The Face (monthly)
The Old Laundry
Ossington Buildings

Moxon Street
London W1
Tel: 01 935 8232
Film: Ian Penman, Dylan
Jones
Visual-orientated youth
culture magazine:
emphasis on music,
fashion and films
Lead time: 4 weeks
Circulation: 94,000

Film (10 issues a year)
Film Society Unit
BFI, 21 Stephen Street
London W1P 1PL
Tel: 01 255 1444
Editor: Peter Cargin
Non-commercial aspects
of film
Lead time: 2 weeks

Film and Television Technician
(10 issues a year)
111 Wardour Street
London W1
Tel: 01 437 8506
Editor: Peter Avis
ACTT members' journal
Circulation: 28,000

Film Review
(monthly)
Spotlight Publications
Greater London House
Hampstead Road
London NW1 7QZ
Tel: 01 387 6611
Editor: David Aldridge
Reviews of new films, star
interviews and profiles

Films and Filming
(monthly)
Orpheus Publications
4th floor Centro House
Mandela Street
London NW1 0DU
Editor: John Russell
Taylor
Deputy editor: Kathryn
Kirby
Reviews of films on
cinema screen and video:
articles, interviews, book
reviews
Lead time: 8 weeks
Circulation: 10,000

Financial Times
1 Southwark Bridge
London SE1 9HL
Tel: 01 873 3000
Arts: J D F Jones
Film: Nigel Andrews
TV: Chris Dunkley
National daily newspaper
Circulation: 300,000

The Glasgow Herald
1 Jerome Street
London E1 6NJ
Tel: 01 377 0890
London editor/film critic:
William Russell
Scottish daily newspaper
Circulation: 122,030

The Guardian
119 Farringdon Road
London EC1R 3ER
Tel: 01 278 2332
Arts: Roger Alton
Film: Derek Malcolm
TV: Nancy Banks-Smith
Media editor: Georgina
Henry
National daily newspaper
Circulation: 438,000

Harpers & Queen
(monthly)
National Magazine House
72 Broadwick Street
London W1V 2BP
Tel: 01 439 7144
Art/reviews: Julie
Kavanagh
Glossy magazine for
women
Lead time: 10 weeks
Circulation: 102,000

The Hollywood Reporter
(daily; weekly
international, Tues)
71 Beak Street
London W1R 3LF
Tel: 01 629 6765
European bureau chief:
Paul Mungo
TV/video: Neil Watson
Showbusiness trade paper

i-D Magazine
(monthly)
27–29 Macklin Street
London WC2B 5LX
Tel: 01 430 0871
Film: John Godfrey
Fashion/style magazine
with items on film
Lead time: 8 weeks
Circulation: 45,000

Illustrated London News
(6 issues per year)
Lawrence House
91–93 Southwark Street
London SE1 9PF
Tel: 01 928 6969
Editor: James Bishop
Film listings: Roger
Sabin
News, pictorial record and
commentary, and a guide
to coming events
Lead time: 8–10 weeks
Circulation: 65,000

The Independent
40 City Road
London EC1Y 2DB
Tel: 01 253 1222
Arts: Thomas Sutcliffe
Film: Sheila Johnston
Media: Maggie Brown
National daily newspaper
with arts listings
Circulation: 400,000

The Jewish Chronicle (weekly)
25 Furnival Street
London EC4A 1JT
Tel: 01 405 9252
Editor: Geoffrey Paul
Press day: Fri
Circulation: 50,000

The List (fortnightly, Thur)
14 High Street
Edinburgh EH1 1TE
Tel: 031 558 1191
Editors: Sarah Hemming,
Nigel Billen
Film/video: Trevor
Johnston
TV: Nigel Billen
Edinburgh and Glasgow
events guide
Lead time: 1 week
Circulation: 10,000

The Listener (weekly, Thur)
Listener Publications Ltd
199 Old Marylebone Road
London NW1 5QS
Tel: 01 258 3581
Editor: Peter Fiddick
Broadcasting weekly with
current affairs and arts
slant. Covers the whole
broadcasting spectrum.
Extensive programme
preview section
Lead time: 3 weeks
Circulation: 36,500

London Weekly Diary of Social Events (weekly, Sun)
25 Park Row
Greenwich
London SE10 9NL
Tel: 01 305 1274/1419
Editor/film critic:
Denise Silvester-Carr
Arts-oriented
subscription magazine
with weekly film column

Mail on Sunday
(weekly, Sun)
Northcliffe House
Tudor Street
London EC4Y 0JA
Tel: 01 353 6000
Film: Tom Hutchinson
TV: Alan Coren
TV/video: Liz Cowley

Press day: Wed
Circulation: 2,030,000

Marie Claire
(monthly)
2 Hatfields
London SE1 9LF
Tel: 01 261 7152
Film/TV: Sean French
Features: Beverley Perry

Marxism Today
(monthly)
16 St John Street
London EC1M 4AY
Tel: 01 608 0265
Arts: Chris Granlund
Lively current affairs and
cultural magazine
Lead time: 8 weeks
Circulation: 17,500

Media Week (weekly,
Thur)
20–22 Wellington Street
London WC2E 7DD
Tel: 01 379 5155
Editor: Steven Buckley
News Editor: Liz Roberts
Broadcast Reporter:
Richard Gold
News magazine aimed at
the advertising and media
industries
Press day: Wed
Circulation: 17,766

Melody Maker
(weekly, Tues)
King's Reach Tower
Stamford Street
London SE1 9LF
Tel: 01 261 6228
Film: Ted Mico
Rock music newspaper
Press day: Thur
Circulation: 57,146

Midweek (weekly,
Thur)
7–9 Rathbone Street
London W1P 1AF
Tel: 01 636 6651
Arts/Film: Bill
Williamson
Free magazine with film
section
Press day: Tues
Circulation: 125,000

Morning Star
74 Luke Street
London EC2A 4PY
Tel: 01 739 6166
Film: Jeff Sawtell
TV: Jeffrey James
The only national daily
owned by its readers as a
co-operative. Weekly film
and TV reviews
Circulation: 28,000

Ms London (weekly,
Mon)
7–9 Rathbone Street
London W1P 1AF
Tel: 01 636 6651
Arts: Juliet Avis
Film: Jane Bartlett
Free magazine with film
section
Press day: Fri
Circulation: 138,238

New Musical Express
(weekly, Wed)
25th Floor
King's Reach Tower
Stamford Street
London SE1 9LS
Tel: 01 261 5000
Film/TV: Gavin Martin
Rock music newspaper
Press day: Mon
Circulation: 100,000

New Scientist
(weekly, Thur)
King's Reach Tower
Stamford Street
London SE1 9LS
Tel: 01 261 5000
Editor: Michael Kenward
Audio-visual: Barry Fox
Contains articles and
reports on the progress of
science and technology in
terms which the non-
specialist can understand
Press day: Mon
Circulation: 97,000

New Socialist
(monthly)
150 Walworth Road
London SE17 1JT
Tel: 01 703 5298
Editors: Nigel Williamson
and John Willman
Film/TV: Nigel
Williamson and John
Willman
Political magazine with
coverage of a wide range
of cultural activities
Lead time: 4 weeks
Circulation: 16,000

New Statesman and Society (weekly,
Thur)
Foundation House
Perseverance Works
38 Kingsland Road
London E2 8DQ
Tel: 01 739 3211
Editor: Tony Gould
Film: Suzanne Moore
Arts editor: Sally
Townsend
Independent radical
journal of investigation,
revelation and comment

Press day: Mon
Circulation: 40,000

News of the World
(weekly, Sun)
News International
1 Pennington Street
London E1 9BD
Tel: 01 782 4000
Editor: Patsy Chapman
Film: Ivan Waterman
TV: Charles Catchpole
National Sunday
newspaper
Press day: Sat
Circulation: 5,360,000

Nine to Five (weekly)
9a Margaret Street
London W1
Tel: 01 637 1377
Editor: John Symes
Film/entertainments
editor: Debbie Smithers
Free magazine
Press day: Wed
Circulation: 325,000

19 (monthly)
IPC Magazines
King's Reach Tower
London SE1 9LS
Tel: 01 261 6360
Film: Minty Clinch,
Maureen Rice
Arts: Maureen Rice
Magazine for young
women

The Observer
(weekly, Sun)
Chelsea Bridge House
Queenstown Road
London SW8 4NN
Tel: 01 627 0700
Arts editor: Gillian
Widdicombe
Film: Philip French
TV: John Naughton
National Sunday
newspaper
Press day: Fri

Observer Magazine
(Sun)
Editor: Jo Foley
Supplement to 'The
Observer'

Options (monthly)
IPC
King's Reach Tower
Stamford Street
London SE1 9LS
Tel: 01 261 5000
Film: Dave Pirie
TV: Jennifer Selway
Magazine for women
Lead time: 12 weeks
Circulation: 240,000

The People
Orbit House

9 New Fetter Lane
London EC4A 1AR
Tel: 01 353 0246
Film: Peter Bishop
TV: Margaret Forwood
National Sunday
newspaper
Press day: Fri

Punch (weekly, Wed)
23–27 Tudor Street
London EC4Y 0HR
Tel: 01 583 9199
Features editor: Jan
Abrams
Film: Dilys Powell
TV: Sally Vincent
A combination of topical
satire, comment and
wide-ranging arts
coverage
Lead time: 10 days
Circulation: 58,250

Q (monthly)
42 Great Portland Street
London W1N 5AH
Tel: 01 436 5430
Editor: Mark Ellen
Specialist music
magazine for 18–45 year
olds. Includes reviews of
new albums, films and
books
Lead time: 14 days
Circulation: 117,359

Sanity (monthly)
22–24 Underwood Street
London N1 7JG
Tel: 01 250 4010
Editor: Ben Webb
Film: David Collier
CND's magazine,
covering film, TV and
video. Reviews cover a
wide range of political/
environmental topics as
well as general interest
Lead time: 3 weeks
Circulation: 30,000

The Scotsman
20 North Bridge
Edinburgh EH1 1YT
Tel: 031 225 2468
Arts/film/TV: Allen
Wright
National daily newspaper

Screen Digest
(monthly)
37 Gower Street
London WC1E 6HH
Tel: 01 580 2842
Editorial chairman:
John Chittock
Editor: David Fisher
News editor: Ben Keen
An industry news digest
covering film, TV, cable,
satellite, video and other
multimedia information.

Has a centre page reference system every month on subjects like law, statistics or sales. Now also available on a computer data base via fax at 01 580 0060 under the name Screenfax
Lead time: 2 weeks

Screenfax (database)
see entry under Screen Digest

Screen International
(weekly, Fri)
King Publications
6–7 Great Chapel Street
London W1V 4BR
Tel: 01 734 9452
Editor: Nick Roddick
Deputy editor: John Hazelton
International trade magazine for the film, TV, video, cable and satellite industries. Regular news, features, production information from around the world
Press day: Thur
Circulation: 10,000

Spare Rib (monthly)
27 Clerkenwell Close
London EC1R 0AT
Tel: 01 253 9792
TV: Esther Bailey
Women's liberation magazine produced by an editorial collective
Lead time: 3–6 weeks
Circulation: 26,000

The Spectator
(weekly, Thur)
56 Doughty Street
London WC1N 2LL
Tel: 01 405 1706
Arts editor: Jenny Naipaul
Film: Hilary Mantel
TV: Wendy Cope
Independent review of politics, current affairs, literature and the arts
Press day: Wed
Circulation: 40,000

The Star
Ludgate House
245 Blackfriars Road
London SE1 9UX
Tel: 01 928 8000
Film: Liz Phillips, Pat Codd
TV: Geoff Baker, Michael Burke
National daily newspaper

The Sun
PO Box 481
1 Virginia Street
London E1 9BD
Tel: 01 782 4000
Film: Garry Bushell
TV: Jim Taylor
National daily newspaper
Circulation: 4,226,278

Sunday Express
Ludgate House
245 Blackfriars Road
London SE1 9UX
Tel: 01 928 8000
Film/TV: Clive Hirschhorn
National Sunday newspaper
Circulation: 2,300,000

Sunday Express Magazine
Ludgate House
245 Blackfriars Road
London SE1 9UX
Tel: 01 928 8000
Editor: Dee Nolan
Deputy editor: Sue Peart
Associate editor: Keith Turner
Film/TV: Paul Kerton
Supplement to 'Sunday Express' newspaper
Lead time: 4 weeks

Sunday Magazine
214 Gray's Inn Road
London WC1X 8EZ
Tel: 01 782 7000
Editor: Colin Jenkins
Features editor: Pete Picton
Supplement to 'News of the World'
Lead time: 8 weeks

Sunday Mirror
33 Holborn Circus
London EC1P 1DQ
Tel: 01 353 0246
Film: Madeleine Harmsworth
TV: Keith Richmond
Showbusiness: Gordon Blair
National Sunday newspaper
Circulation: 3,045,502

Sunday Telegraph
Peterborough Court at South Quay
181 Marsh Wall
London E14 9SR
Tel: 01 538 5000
Arts: Michael Shepherd
Film: Richard Mayne
TV: Christopher Tookey
National Sunday newspaper
Circulation: 695,299

Sunday Times
News International
1 Pennington Street
London E1 9BD
Tel: 01 481 4100
Screen Media Correspondent: Alex Sutherland
Film Reviews: Iain Johnstone
TV Reviews: Patrick Stoddart
National Sunday newspaper
Press day: Fri

Sunday Times Magazine
214 Gray's Inn Road
London WC1X 8EZ
Tel: 01 481 4100
Editor: Philip Clarke
Film: George Perry
Supplement to 'Sunday Times'
Lead time: 6 weeks
Circulation: 1,310,000

TV Times (weekly, Tues)
ITV Publications
247 Tottenham Court Road
London W1P 0AU
Tel: 01 323 3222
Guide to ITV and Channel 4 TV programmes
Circulation: c 3,000,000

TV World (monthly)
100 Avenue Road
London NW3 3TP
Tel: 01 935 6611
Editor: Ross Welford
Covers the international television and video programme businesses
Lead time: 5 days
Circulation: 12,488

The Tatler (10 issues a year)
Vogue House
1–2 Hanover Square
London W1R 0AD
Tel: 01 499 9080
Arts: Eve MacSweeney
Smart society magazine favouring profiles, fashion and the arts
Lead time: 12 weeks
Circulation: 56,000

The Teacher – Voice of The Profession Magazine (weekly, Mon)
Hamilton House
Mabledon Place
London WC1H 9BS

Tel: 01 388 1952
Editor: Nathan Goldberg
Media: Dorothy Stefanczyk
Weekly newspaper of the National Union of Teachers. Carries special film and video supplements 3 times a year
Press day: Wed
Circulation: 35,000

Telegraph Weekend Magazine
Editor: Nigel Horne
Supplement to Saturday edition of the 'Daily Telegraph'
Lead time: 6 weeks

Television Today
(weekly, Thur)
47 Bermondsey Street
London SE1 3XT
Tel: 01 403 1818
Editor: Peter Hepple
'Television Today' constitutes the middle section of 'The Stage' and is a weekly trade paper

Television Week
Meed House
21 John Street
London WC1N 2BP
Tel: 01 404 5513
Editor: Peter Montief

Televisual (monthly)
50 Poland Street
London W1V 4AX
Tel: 01 439 4222
Editor: Mundy Ellis
Monthly business magazine for production professionals in the business of moving pictures

Time Out (weekly, Wed)
Tower House
Southampton Street
London WC2E 7HD
Tel: 01 836 4411
Film: Geoff Andrew
Film listings: Wally Hammond
Films on TV: Nigel Floyd
TV: Alkarim Jivani
London listings magazine with cinema and TV sections
Listings lead time: 8 days
Features lead time: 1 week
Circulation: 76,000

The Times
News International
1 Pennington Street
London E1 9BD

Tel: 01 782 5000
Film: David Robinson
Video: Peter Waymark
Arts (TV): Chris
Peachment
Saturday editor: Mark
Law
National daily newspaper
Circulation: 449,000

The Times Educational Supplement (weekly, Fri)
Priory House
St John's Lane
London EC1M 4BX
Tel: 01 253 3000
Arts: Heather Neill
Film critic: Robin Buss
Video/film/broadcasting:
Gillian Macdonald
Press day: Wed
Circulation: 116,833

The Times Higher Education Supplement (weekly, Fri)
Priory House
St John's Lane
London EC1M 4BX
Tel: 01 253 3000
Arts: Anne-Marie
Conway
Features: Peter Aspden
Press day: Wed
Circulation: 15,000

The Times Literary Supplement (weekly, Fri)
Priory House
St John's Lane
London EC1M 4BX
Tel: 01 253 3000
Commentary editor:
Lindsay Duguid
Press day: Tues
Circulation: 30,000

The Times Scottish Education Supplement
(weekly, Fri)
37 George Street
Edinburgh EH2 2HN
Tel: 031 220 1100
Editor: Willis Pickard
Press day: Wed

Today
70 Vauxhall Bridge Road
London SW1V 2RP
Tel: 01 630 1300
Film: Sue Heal
TV: Lester Middlehurst
Showbusiness editor:
June Walton
National daily newspaper
(Sundays inclusive)

Tribune (weekly, Fri)
308 Gray's Inn Road
London WC1X 8DY
Tel: 01 278 0911
Reviews editor: Paul
Anderson
Political, literary
newspaper with socialist
and feminist approach

20/20 (monthly)
Tower House
Southampton Street
London WC2E 7HD
Tel: 01 836 4411
Film: Geoff Andrew
Film listings: Rupert
Smith
TV: Alkarim Jivani
National arts and
entertainment magazine
with extensive film
coverage
Listings lead time: 1
month
Features lead time: 5
weeks

Variety (weekly, Wed)
34–35 Newman Street
London W1P 3PD
Tel: 01 637 3663
London editor: Jack
Pitman
International
showbusiness newspaper
Press day: Tues

Vogue (monthly)
Vogue House
Hanover Square
London W1R 0AD
Tel: 01 499 9080
Editor: Elizabeth Tiberis
Features: Alex Shulman,
Kathy O'Shaughnessy,
Lisa Armstrong
Glossy magazine for
women
Lead time: 12 weeks

The Voice (weekly)
370 Coldharbour Lane
London SW9 8PL
Tel: 01 737 7377
Editor: Steve Pope
Film: Lorraine Griffiths
Britain's leading black
newspaper with mainly
18–35 age group
readership. Regular film,
TV and video coverage
Press day: Fri
Circulation: 45,000

Western Mail
Thomson House
Cardiff CF1 1WR
Tel: 0222 33022
Features editor: Gareth
Jenkins
Film: Mario Basini
TV: Gethyn Stoodley

Thomas
National daily of Wales
Circulation: 78,407

What's On in London (weekly, Tues)
182 Pentonville Road
London N1 9LB
Tel: 01 278 4393
Editor: David Parkes-
Bristow
Film editor: Michael
Darvell
Film correspondent:
Phillip Bergson
London based weekly
covering cinema, theatre,
music, arts,
entertainment, books and
fashion
Press day: Mon
Lead time: 10 days
Circulation: 50,000

Yorkshire Post
Wellington Street
Leeds
West Yorkshire LS1 1RF
Tel: 0532 432701
Regional daily morning
newspaper
Deadline: 10.00 pm
Circulation: 94,000

NEWS AND PHOTO AGENCIES

Associated Press
12 Norwich Street
London EC4
Tel: 01 353 1515

Central Office of Information
Hercules Road SE1
Tel: 01 928 2345

Central Press Features
131 Aldersgate Street
London EC1A 4JA
Tel: 01 600 4502

Fleet Street News Agency
68 Exmouth Market
London EC1R 4RA
Tel: 01 278 5661

More News
Dalling House
132 Dalling Road
London W6 0EP
Tel: 01 741 7000

Press Association
85 Fleet Street
London EC4P 4BE
Tel: 01 353 7440

Reuters
85 Fleet Street
London EC4P 4AJ
Tel: 01 250 1122

Unicom News Service
72 Fleet Street
London EC4Y 1HY
Tel: 01 353 4861

United Press International
Meridian House
2 Greenwich View
Millharbour
London E14 9NN
Tel: 01 538 5310

BBC TELEVISION

BBC
Television Centre
Wood Lane
London W12 7RJ
Tel: 01 743 8000
BBC1
*Omnibus; Film '89;
Breakfast Time*
BBC2
Arena; The Late Show

INDEPENDENT TELEVISION

Anglia Television
Anglia House
Norwich NR1 3JG
Tel: 0603 615151
About Anglia; WideAngle

Border Television
Television Centre
Carlisle CA1 3NT
Tel: 0228 25101
Lookaround

Central Independent Television
Central House
Broad Street
Birmingham B1 2JP
Tel: 021 643 9898
East Midlands Television
Centre
Nottingham NG7 2NA
Tel: 0602 863322
Unit 9, Windrush Court
Abingdon Business Park
Abingdon
Oxon OX14 1SA
Tel: 0235 554123
*Here and Now; Central
News; Central Lobby;
Central Weekend;
Contrasts*

**Channel 4
Television**
60 Charlotte Street
London W1P 2AX
Tel: 01 631 4444
*Channel 4 News c/o ITN;
Right to Reply*

Channel Television
The Television Centre
La Pouquelaye
St Helier
Jersey
Channel Islands
Tel: 0534 68999
Television Centre
St George's Place
St Peter Port
Guernsey
Channel Islands
Tel: 0481 23451
Channel Report

**Grampian
Television**
Queen's Cross
Aberdeen AB9 2XJ
Tel: 0224 646464
*North Tonight; Crossfire;
Crann Tara*

Granada Television
Quay Street
Manchester M60 9EA
Tel: 061 832 7211
Bridgegate House
5 Bridge Place
Lower Bridge Street
Chester CH1 1SA
Tel: 0244 313966
White Cross
Lancaster LA1 4XQ
Tel: 0524 60688
Albert Dock
Liverpool L3 4BA
Tel: 051 709 9393
Granada Reports

HTV Wales
Television Centre
Culverhouse Cross
Cardiff CF5 6XJ
Tel: 0222 590590
Scene at Six

HTV West
Television Centre
Bath Road
Bristol BS4 3HG
Tel: 0272 778366
*Scene 1989; HTV News;
The West This Week;
What's On*

**Independent
Television News**
ITN House
48 Wells Street
London W1P 4DE
Tel: 01 637 2424
*News at One, 5.40, 10;
The World This Week;*

ITN's *Channel 4 News,*
includes items of film
news

**London Weekend
Television**
South Bank Television
Centre
London SE1 9LT
Tel: 01 261 3434
South Bank Show

Scottish Television
Cowcaddens
Glasgow G2 3PR
Tel: 041 332 9999
The Gateway
Edinburgh EH7 4AH
Tel: 031 557 4554
Scotland Today

TV-am
Hawley Crescent
London NW1 8EF
Tel: 01 267 4300/4377
*Good Morning Britain;
After Nine; Saturday
Sports Show; Wideawake;
Anne Diamond on
Sunday*

Television South
Television Centre
Vinters Park
Maidstone
Kent ME14 5NZ
Tel: 0622 691111
Television Centre
Northam
Southampton SO9 5HZ
Tel: 0703 634211
Art Beat

**Television South
West**
Derry's Cross
Plymouth
Devon PL1 2SP
Tel: 0752 663322
*Today; Newsview;
Consumer File; Business
South West*

Thames Television
306–316 Euston Road
London NW1 3BB
Tel: 01 387 9494

**Tyne Tees
Television**
The Television Centre
City Road
Newcastle upon Tyne
NE1 2AL
Tel: 091 261 0181
Northern Life

Ulster Television
Havelock House
Ormeau Road
Belfast BT7 1EB
Tel: 0232 328122
Six Tonight; Spectrum

**Yorkshire
Television**
The Television Centre
Leeds LS3 1JS
Tel: 0532 438283
Calendar

BBC RADIO

BBC
Broadcasting House
London W1A lAA
Tel: 01 580 4468
RADIO 1
Steve Wright, Mark
Goodier
RADIO 2
*Cinema 2; Round
Midnight; Gloria
Hunniford Show*
RADIO 3
Critics' Forum; Third Ear
RADIO 4
Kaleidoscope
WORLD SERVICE
Bush House
Strand
London WC2B 4PH
Tel: 01 257 2775
Meridian

BBC LOCAL RADIO STATIONS

**Greater London
Radio (BBC)**
35a Marylebone High
Street
London W1A 4LG
Tel: 01 224 2424
Big City

**Greater
Manchester Radio
(GMR)**
PO Box 90
New Broadcasting House
Oxford Road
Manchester M60 1SJ
Tel: 061 228 3434
What's On

Radio Bristol
PO Box 194
Bristol BS99 7QT
Tel: 0272 741111
*What's On; Events West;
Tea-Time Show*

**Radio
Cambridgeshire**
104 Hills Road
Cambridge CB2 1LD
Tel: 0223 315970
Bill Dod

Radio Cleveland
PO Box 1548
Broadcasting House
Newport Road
Middlesbrough TS1 5DG
Tel: 0642 225211
Ann Davies, Peter Hedley

Radio Cornwall
Phoenix Wharf
Truro TR1 1UA
Tel: 0872 75421
*Seen and Heard;
Cornwall Daily*

Radio Cumbria
Hilltop Heights
London Road
Carlisle CA1 2NA
Tel: 0228 31661
*What's On; Cumbria
Today*

Radio Derby
PO Box 269
Derby DE1 3HL
Tel: 0332 361111
*269 Tonight; Weekender;
Sunday Best;
Springboard; Film Guide*

Radio Devon
PO Box 100
Exeter EX4 4DB
Tel: 0392 215651
*Countysound; The Arts
Programme*

Radio Foyle
PO Box 927
8 Northland Road
Londonderry BT48 7NE
Tel: 0504 262244
Afternoon Delight

Radio Humberside
63 Jameson Street
Hull HU1 3NU
Tel: 0482 23232
Steve Massam

Radio Kent
Sun Pier
Chatham
Kent ME4 4EZ
Tel: 0634 830505
Soundtrack

Radio Lancashire
Darwin Street
Blackburn
Lancs BB2 2EA
Tel: 0254 62411
Arts producer: Joe Wilson
Film specialist: Wendy
Howard

Radio Leeds
Broadcasting House
Woodhouse Lane
Leeds LS2 9PN
Tel: 0532 442131

Alison Lister (films),
Tony Fisher (TV)

Radio Leicester
Epic House
Charles Street
Leicester LE1 3SH
Tel: 0533 516688
*The Light Programme;
Prime Time; Listening In*

Radio Lincolnshire
PO Box 219
Newport
Lincoln LN1 3XY
Tel: 0522 511411
Arts producer: Alan
Stennett
What's On Diary; Gallery

Radio Merseyside
55 Paradise Street
Liverpool L1 3BP
Tel: 051 708 5500
Film critic: Ramsey
Campbell

Radio Newcastle
Broadcasting Centre
Fenham
Newcastle upon Tyne
NE99 1RN
Tel: 091 232 4141
Arts producer: Ian
MaCrae

Radio Norfolk
Norfolk Tower
Surrey Street
Norwich NR1 3PA
Tel: 0603 617411
Arts producer: Stewart
Orr

**Radio
Northampton**
PO Box 1107
Northampton NN1 2BE
Tel: 0604 239100
Arts producer: David
Saint

Radio Nottingham
PO Box 222
Nottingham NG1 3NZ
Tel: 0602 415161
Programme organiser:
Nick Brunger

Radio Oxford
269 Banbury Road
Oxford OX2 7DW
Tel: 0865 311444
David Freeman

Radio Sheffield
Ashdell Grove
60 Westbourne Road
Sheffield S10 2QU
Tel: 0742 686185
Programme organiser:
Frank Mansfield

Radio Solent
South Western House
Canute Road
Southampton SO9 4PJ
Tel: 0703 631311
Arts producer: Mike Gray

Radio Stoke
Cheapside
Hanley
Stoke-on-Trent ST1 1JJ
Tel: 0782 208080
First Edition

Radio Sussex
Marlborough Place
Brighton BN1 1TU
Tel: 0273 680231
Arts producer: Jim
Beaman

Radio WM
PO Box 206
Birmingham B5 7SD
Tel: 021 414 8484
Entertainment WM

INDEPENDENT LOCAL RADIO

BRMB Radio
Radio House
PO Box 555
Aston Road North
Birmingham B6 4BX
Tel: 021 359 4481
Features producer: Kate
Pugh

Beacon Radio
267 Tettenhall Road
Wolverhampton
WV6 0DQ
Tel: 0902 757211
Programme manager:
Pete Wagstaff

Beacon Shropshire
Thorn's Hall
28 Castle Street
Shrewsbury SY1 2BQ
Tel: 0743 232271

CN.FM 103
PO Box 1000
The Vision Park
Chivers Way
Histon
Cambridge CB4 4WW
Tel: 0223 235255
Programme controller:
Andy Gillies

Capital Radio
Euston Tower
Euston Road
London NW1 3DR
Tel: 01 388 1288
David Castell

*In Focus; The Way It Is;
The David Jensen Show*

Chiltern Radio
Chiltern Road
Dunstable LU6 1HQ
Tel: 0582 666001
Programme controller:
Paul Robinson

City FM
PO Box 96.7
Liverpool L69 1TQ
Tel: 051 227 5100
Senior producer: Brian
Harvey
Film reviews: Mark Jones

County Sound
The Friary
Guildford
Surrey GU1 4YX
Tel: 0483 505566
Paul Owen

DevonAir Radio
35–37 St David's Hill
Exeter EX4 4DA
Tel: 0392 430703

Downtown Radio
Newtownards BT23 4ES
Tel: 0247 815555
Flm/video: John Daly

Essex Radio
Radio House
Clifftown Road
Southend-on-Sea SS1 1SX
Tel: 0702 333711
Programme manager

GWR
Lime Kiln Studios
Wootton Bassett
Swindon
Wilts SN4 7EX
Tel: 0793 853222
Arts producer: Simon
Cooper

Hereward Radio
PO Box 225
Queensgate Centre
Peterborough PE1 1XJ
Tel: 0733 46225
Programme controller:
Andy Gillies

LBC News Radio
Communications House
Gough Square
London EC4P 4LP
Tel: 01 353 1010
Film/TV: Carol Allen

Leicester Sound
Granville House
Granville Road
Leicester LE1 7RW
Tel: 0533 551616
Programme controller:

Chris Hughes
Film and media
programmes: Guy Morris

**Mercia Sound
24-hour Radio**
Hertford Place
Coventry CV1 3TT
Tel: 0203 633933
Managing director/
programme controller:
Stuart Linnell
Head of news: Colin
Palmer

Metro Radio
Newcastle upon Tyne
NE99 1BB
Tel: 091 488 3131
Programme controller:
Giles Squire

Moray Firth Radio
PO Box 271
Inverness IV3 6SF
Tel: 0463 224433
Music Box

Northsound Radio
45 King's Gate
Aberdeen AB2 6BL
Tel: 0224 632234
Head of news: Andy
Stenton

Ocean Sound
Whittle Avenue
Segensworth-West
Fareham
Hants PO15 5PA
Tel: 04895 89911
Film reviews: Cheryl
Phillips

Pennine Radio
Bradford
W Yorks BD1 5NP
Tel: 0274 731521
Dee Marshall

Piccadilly Radio
127–131 The Piazza
Piccadilly Plaza
Manchester M1 4AW
Tel: 061 236 9913
Programme controller:
Mike Briscoe

Plymouth Sound
Earl's Acre
Alma Road
Plymouth PL3 4HX
Tel: 0752 227272
Programme controller:
Louise Churchill

Radio Aire
PO Box 362
Leeds LS3 1LR
Tel: 0532 452299
Programme controller:
Christa Ackroyd

Radio Broadland
47–49 St Georges Plain
Colegate
Norwich NR3 1DB
Tel: 0603 630621
Arts producers: Steve
Allen, Mike Stewart
6.20pm Review

Radio Clyde
Clydebank Business Park
Glasgow G81 2RX
Tel: 041 941 1111
Mike Riddoch, Andy
Dougan

Radio Forth
PO Box 4000
Forth House
Forth Street
Edinburgh EH1 3LF
Tel: 031 556 9255

Radio Hallam
PO Box 194
Hartshead
Sheffield S1 1GP
Tel: 0742 766766
Presentation controller:
Dean Petall

Radio Orwell
Electric House
Lloyds Avenue
Ipswich IP1 3HZ
Tel: 0473 216971
Screenguide

Radio Tay
PO Box 123
Dundee DD1 9UF
Tel: 0382 200800
Station manager: A J
Wilkie

Radio Trent
29–31 Castle Gate
Nottingham NG1 7AP
Tel: 0602 581731
Market Place
Derby DE1 3AA
Tel: 0332 292945
Programme controller:
Chris Hughes

Radio 210
PO Box 210
Reading RG3 5RZ
Tel: 0734 413131
Programme controller:
Phil Coope

Radio Wyvern
5–6 Barbourne Terrace
Worcester WR1 3JZ
Tel: 0905 612212
Programme controller:
Norman Bilton

Red Dragon Radio
Radio House
West Canal Wharf

Cardiff CF1 5XJ
Tel: 0222 384041
Programme controller:
Peter Milburn
Film/video: John Dash

Red Rose Radio
PO Box 301
St Paul's Square
Preston PR1 1YE
Tel: 0772 556301
Programme controller:
Dave Lincoln

Saxon Radio
Long Brackland
Bury St Edmunds
Suffolk IP33 1JY
Tel: 0284 701511
Screenguide

Severn Sound
PO Box 388
67 Southgate Street
Gloucester GL1 2DQ
Tel: 0452 423791
Arts producer: Tony
Wickham

Signal Radio
Studio 257
Stoke Road
Stoke-on-Trent ST4 2SR
Tel: 0782 747047
John Evington

Southern Sound
Radio House
PO Box 2000
Brighton BN4 2SS
Tel: 0273 43011
Tim Locke

Southern Sound FM
Radio House
PO Box 2000
Eastbourne BN21 4ZZ
Tel: 0323 430111
Paul Chantler

Swansea Sound
Victoria Road
Gowerton
Swansea SA4 3AB
Tel: 0792 893751
Programme controller:
David Thomas

TFM 96.60
74 Dovecot Street
Stockton-on-Tees
Cleveland TS18 1HB
Tel: 0642 615111
Heather Raw

Two Counties Radio
5–7 Southcote Road
Bournemouth BH1 3LR
Tel: 0202 294881
Programme controller:

Stan Horobin
News editor: Chris Kelly

West Sound
Radio House
54 Holmston Road
Ayr KA7 3BE
Tel: 0292 283662
Programme controller:
John McCauley
*Kenny Campbell Show;
John McCauley's Show;
Artyfax*

PREVIEW THEATRES

Alva Films
16 Brook Street
Alva
Clackmannanshire FK12
5JL
Tel: 0259 60936
Formats: 16mm double-head, U-Matic, VHS
Seats: 24

BAFTA
195 Piccadilly
London W1V 9LG
Tel: 01 734 0022
Formats: Twin 16mm and
Super 16mm double-head
stereo, 35mm double-head
Dolby Stereo at all aspect
ratios, U-Matic and VHS
stereo
Seats: 213 (Princess
Anne),
30 (Run Run Shaw)

Baronet Theatre
84 Wardour Street
London W1
Tel: 01 437 2233
Formats: 16mm and
35mm double-head,
U-Matic, VHS
Seats: 25

Bijou Theatre
113 Wardour Street
London W1
Tel: 01 437 2233
Formats: 16mm and
35mm double-head, Dolby
Stereo
Seats: 70

British Universities
Film and Video
Council (BUFVC)
55 Greek Street
London W1V 5LR
Tel: 01 734 3687
Formats: 16mm double-head, VHS, U-Matic
Seats: 15-20

CFS Conference
Centre
22 Portman Close
London W1A 4BE
Tel: 01 486 2881
Formats: 16mm and
35mm film projection.
Full in-house and outside
catering
Seats: 110

Cannon Cinemas
Preview Theatre
Ground Floor
Pathé House
76 Hammersmith Road
London W14 9YR

Tel: 01 603 4555
Formats: 16mm and
35mm double-head,
U-Matic, VHS triple
standard
Seats: 36

Century Preview
Theatre
31–32 Soho Square
London W1V 6AP
Tel: 01 437 7766
Formats: 35mm Dolby
optical and magnetic
stereo, 2000′ double-head
projection, mono and
Dolby. Reception room
available
Seats: 61

Chapter Cinema
Market Road
Canton
Cardiff CF5 1QE
Tel: 0222 396061
Formats: 35mm optical,
16mm double-head, high
quality video projection,
U-Matic/VHS. Reception
space and restaurant
Seats: 78

Columbia Tri-Star
Films UK
19–23 Wells Street
London W1P 3FP
Tel: 01 580 2090
Formats: 16mm, 35mm
double-head Dolby Stereo
Seats: 34

Coronet Theatre
84 Wardour Street
London W1
Tel: 01 437 2233
Formats: 35mm double-head, U-Matic, VHS
Seats: 15

Crawford Preview
Theatre
15–17 Old Compton
Street
London W1V 6JR
Tel: 01 734 5298
Formats: 16mm, 35mm.
Triple standard U-Matic,
VHS, Beta
Seats: 1 (film):15,
2 (video):15

Cygnet Preview
Theatre
Bilton Centre Studios
Coronation Road
High Wycombe
Bucks HP12 3TA
Tel: 0494 450541
Formats: 16mm double
head, all video systems
Seats: 10–12

De Lane Lea
75 Dean Street
London W1V 5HA
Tel: 01 439 1721
Formats: 35mm and
16mm, Dolby stereo
Seats: 25

Edinburgh Film
Studios
Nine Mile Burn
Penicuik EH26 9LT
Tel: 0968 72131
Formats: 16mm and
35mm double-head,
U-Matic, VHS
Seats: 100

The Gem
86 Wardour Street
London W1V 3LF
Tel: 01 437 2233
Video theatre
Seats: 15

Goldcrest Elstree
Studios
Shenley Road
Borehamwood
Herts WD6 1JG
Tel: 01 953 1600
Formats: 16mm, 35mm
Seats: 1:102, 2:17, 3:18

Grip House Preview
Theatre
5–11 Taunton Road
Metropolitan Centre
Greenford
Middx UB6 8UQ
Tel: 01 578 2382
Formats: 16mm and
35mm, optical and
magnetic double-head
projection
Seats: 40

King's Lynn Centre
for the Arts
27 King Street
King's Lynn
Norfolk PE30 1HA
Tel: 0553 774725
Formats: 16mm, 35mm
Seats: 359

Malvern Cinema
Grange Road
Malvern
Worcestershire
WR14 3HB
Tel: 0684 892279
Format: 35mm
Seats: 407

The Metro
11 Rupert Street
London W1V 7FS
Tel: 01 434 3357/734 1506
Formats: 16mm and
35mm double-head,
U-Matic
Seats: 195

The Minema
45 Knightsbridge
London SW1X 7NL
Tel: 01 235 4225
Formats: 35mm and
16mm, full AV systems
Seats: 68

Mr Young's
First Floor
1–6 Falconberg Court
London W1V 5FG
Tel: 01 437 1771/734 4520
Formats: 16mm, Super
16mm, 35mm, U-Matic,
VHS, Betamax, Dolby
stereo double-head optical
and magnetic Dolby SR
Seats: 35 (extended to 40
on request)

**New Crown
Theatre**
86 Wardour Street
London W1V 3LF
Tel: 01 437 2233
Formats: 16mm and
35mm double-head, Dolby
Stereo
Seats: 40

Pinewood Studios
Iver
Bucks SL0 0NH

Tel: 0753 656296
Formats: 16mm, 35mm,
70mm, U-Matic
Seats: Five theatres with
12 to 115 seats

**Rank Preview
Theatre**
127 Wardour Street
London W1V 4AD
Tel: 01 437 9020 x211
Formats: 16mm, 35mm
double-head, Dolby
stereo, VHS, U-Matic,
Betamax, slides
Seats: 58

**Scottish Council for
Educational
Technology**
Dowanhill
74 Victoria Crescent Road
Glasgow G12 9JN
Tel: 041 334 9314
Formats: 16mm, 35mm
double-head and 8mm
Seats: 173

**Shepperton
Studios**
Shepperton
Middx TW17 0RD
Tel: 09328 62611

Formats: 35mm, 16mm
Seats: 1 (35mm):40, 2
(16mm):20

Sherman Theatre
Senghenydd Road
Cardiff CF2 4YE
Tel: 0222 396844
Formats: 16mm, 35mm,
Dolby stereo, U-Matic
Seats: 474

**Twickenham
Studios**
St Margaret's
Twickenham
Middx TW1 2LT
Tel: 01 892 4477
Formats: 16mm, 35mm
Seats: 31

**Warner Bros
Preview Theatre**
135 Wardour Street
London W1V 3TD
Tel: 01 734 8400
Formats: 16mm, 35mm
double-head, Dolby Stereo
Seats: 32

**Watershed Media
Centre**
1 Canons Road
Bristol BS1 5TX
Tel: 0272 276444
Formats: Super 8mm,
16mm double-head,
35mm, U-Matic, VHS
Seats: 1:(200), 2:(50)

**Weintraub House
Preview Theatre**
167–169 Wardour Street
London W1V 3TA
Tel: 01 439 1790
Formats: 35mm Dolby
stereo, U-Matic, VHS

**Whitgift Film
Theatre**
Humberside County
Council
Crosland Road
Willows
Grimsby
South Humberside
DN37 9EH
Tel: 0472 240410
Formats: 8mm, 16mm,
35mm Dolby stereo
Seats: 206

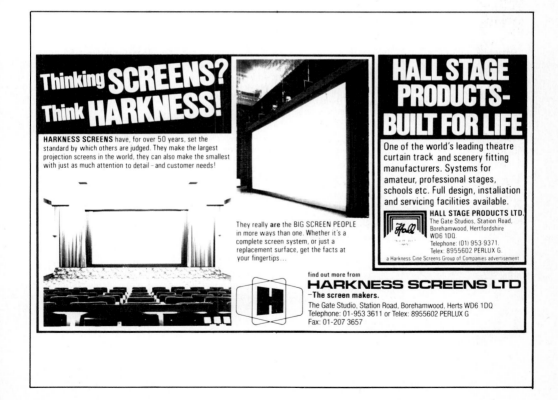

PRODUCTION COMPANIES

These are UK companies which are currently active in financing and/or making audiovisual product for UK and international media markets. Also making audiovisual product are film and video workshops (see p260). Not listed below are the numerous companies making TV commercials, educational and other non-broadcast material, nor those companies set up to facilitate the production of particular films (see Facilities p122)

A-Side Concepts
239 High Holborn
London WC1
Tel: 01 405 1843
Marsha R Levine
Rock programmes

Aardman Animations
14 Wetherell Place
Clifton
Bristol BS8 1AR
Tel: 0272 744802
Peter Lord
David Sproxton
Specialists in claymation and model animation

Abracadabra Productions
Hillgate House
13 Hillgate Street
London W8 7SP
Tel: 01 727 8747
Jan Silchenstedt
Michelle Silchenstedt
Producers of children's drama

Acacia Productions
80 Weston Park
London N8 9TB
Tel: 01 340 2619/341 9392
J Edward Milner
Nikki Nagasiri
In 1988 the company produced *Vietnam: After the Fire*, a feature documentary for Channel 4 *True Stories* series about the long-term human and environmental effects of the Vietnam war; *Young Vietnam*, a documentary film for BBC Schools about young people in Vietnam today; *Sharing the Burden*, a short documentary for Africapix and UNICEF Kenya. Films in production include *Storm on the Mountain* for Grampian TV and Channel 4, a documentary film about the Cairngorm Mountains in Scotland

Action Time
22 Woodstock Street
London W1R 1HF
Tel: 01 409 3421
Jeremy Fox
Producers of *Solid Soul, Revid, Catch Phrase, Beadle's About, Chain Letters, Cross Wits, Pass the Buck, Show Me* and *Frame Game*

After Image
32 Acre Lane
London SW2 5SG
Tel: 01 737 7300
Jane Thorburn
Mark Lucas
Alex Graham
After Image is best known for the long-running arts series *Alter Image* featuring artists and performers. Other productions include *The Alternative Miss World*, a series of musical comedies, *Map of Dreams* and three programmes featuring new circus acts from all over the world. Currently pursuing dramatic/fiction projects

After Words Pictures
5 Brewer Street
London W1R 3FN
Tel: 01 439 1984
Bruce Hyman
Harvey Kass

Albany Video
The Albany
Douglas Way
London SE8 4AG
Tel: 01 692 6322
Malcolm Dowmunt

Allied Stars
55 Park Lane
London W1Y 3DH
Tel: 01 493 1050
Dodi Fayed
Luke Randolph
Made *Breaking Glass*, co-financed *Chariots of Fire* and produced *F/X* for Orion

Anglia Films
48 Leicester Square
London WC2H 7FB
Tel: 01 321 0101
Graeme McDonald
Brenda Reid
John Rosenberg
David FitzGerald
The filmmaking and drama production arm of Anglia TV. Current projects include *A Quiet Conspiracy, Anything More Would Be Greedy, Goldeneye, The Chief* and *Soft Targets*

Animation City
69 Well Street
London W1P 3RB
Tel: 01 494 3084
Maddy Sparrow
Company currently producing a series of animated films scripted by well-known writers for Channel 4. Also produces animated and live action commercials, designs and produces TV and film titles and optical effects

Antelope Films
3 Fitzroy Square
London W1P 5AH
Tel: 01 387 4454
Clive Syddall
Productions undertaken for various broadcast

television companies including BBC TV and Channel 4 in 1988/89: *Portrait of the Soviet Union, Testament, Global Rivals, Margot Fonteyn Story, The Midas Touch, Pasternak.* In development: *Inside the Kremlin, Great Women Explorers,* and *Childhood.* Drama: *The Russian Album* from a book by Michael Ignatieff, and *True Blue,* a feature film based on the book by Daniel Topolski and Patrick Robinson

Antonine Productions

Blackcat Studios
830 Springfield Road
Glasgow G31 4HG
Tel: 041 554 4667/2742
Paddy Higson
In production *Silent Scream,* a Channel 4/BFI co-production for completion in 1990

Ariel Productions

162–170 Wardour Street
London W1
Tel: 01 437 7700
Otto Plaschkes
Produced *Shadey,* written by Snoo Wilson, directed by Philip Saville and starring Anthony Sher, for Film Four International. In development are *Changing Places,* scripted by Peter Nichols, and *The Double Helix,* by James Watson

Artifax

17 Clifford Street
London W1X 1RG
Tel: 01 734 4584
Elizabeth Queenan
Documentaries, arts, music, drama and light entertainment. Produced the 1987 Prix Italia prize-winning *Behind the Mask – Perspectives on the Music of Harrison Birtwistle.* In production: *Keep It Country,* a six-part series on country music with Hank Wangford. In development: a second series of *The Secret Life of Machines,* with Tim Hunkin and a film on the Russian composer, Alfred Schnittke

Aspect Film and Television Production

36 Percy Street
London W1P 9FG
Tel: 01 636 5303
Mark Chapman
Producers of documentaries, current affairs and children's programmes

Associates Film Productions (AFP)

60 Farringdon Road
London EC1R 3BP
Tel: 01 251 3885
Christian Wangler
Mike Dodds
Offshoot of the AKA film facility company

Astramead

38 Gloucester Mews
London W2 3HE
Tel: 01 723 4678
Mark Shivas
Following *The Price* and *Kipling* for Channel 4, Astramead has plans for a series with the BBC. Shivas is planning to produce Bernard McLaverty's *Perugia* and an adaptation of a major novel for Granada in 1988/9. TV productions of *The Petition* and *Sassoon,* which Astramead presented on stage in the West End, are in discussion

Avatar Film Corporation World Sales

Unit 5
Imperial Studios
Imperial Road
London SW6 2AG
Tel: 01 384 1366
Jon Brewer
Robert Patterson

BFI Production

21 Stephen Street
London W1P 1PL
Tel: 01 636 5783
Ben Gibson
Recent productions include Terence Davies' award-winning *Distant Voices, Still Lives.* For further information, see p00

BJE

Home Farm
Church Hill
High Littleton
Bristol BS18 5HF
Tel: 0761 71055

John King
Laurie Lee's *As I Walked Out One Midsummer Morning* and *A Rose For Winter, Telly Addicts, King and Company.* Animal dramas include: *Priddy The Hedgehog* and *Carna The Otter,* and in 1989, *The Swan*

Peter Batty Productions

Claremont House
Renfrew Road
Kingston
Surrey KT2 7NT
Tel: 01 942 6304
Peter Batty
Recent Channel 4 productions include *The Divided Union, Fonteyn and Nureyev, The Algerian War, Swindle* and *Il Poverello.* Previous independent productions include *The Story of Wine, Battle for Warsaw, Battle for Dien Bien Phu, Birth of the Bomb, Search for the Super, Superspy, Battle for the Bulge, Battle for Cassino, Operation Barbarossa* and *Farouk: Last of the Pharaohs*

Bedford Productions

Canalot Production Studios
222 Kensal Road
London W10 5BN
Tel: 01 960 5798
Mike Dineen
Francis Megahy
Television, documentary, drama production, and business to business programming

Bevanfield Films

22 Soho Square
London W1V 5FJ
Tel: 01 287 0628
Producers of animated and feature films

Bordeaux Films International

22 Soho Square
London W1V 5FJ
Tel: 01 434 3459
Recent projects include *Caravans, Double Jeopardy, Giselle, Guns and the Fury, Laura, Mr Wrong* and *The Witch*

Boyd's Co Film Productions

40–44 Clipstone Street
London W1P 7EA
Tel: 01 323 3220

Don Boyd
Continuing in the eclectic tradition established with such films as *The Tempest, The Great Rock'n'Roll Swindle, An Unsuitable Job for a Woman, Scum, Honky Tonk Freeway* and *Captive,* Boyd co-produced Derek Jarman's *The Last of England* in 1986/7 and produced *Aria* with segments directed by Altman, Beresford, Bryden, Godard, Jarman, Roddam, Roeg, Russell, Sturridge and Temple. He is currently in the final development stages of three features for 1988/9

Britannia Entertainment

Pinewood Studios
Iver
Bucks SL0 0NH
Tel: 0753 651700
David Nicholas Wilkinson
Robin Edwards
Carol Riley
Long established independent production company specialising in international co-production. Also raises finance for and acts as consultant to other independent producers

British Lion

Pinewood Studios
Iver Heath
Bucks SL0 0NH
Tel: 0753 651700
Peter Snell
As Britannic Films, first project was the telemovie *Squaring the Circle,* co-financed with TVS and Metromedia Producers Associates. Also *Lady Jane* for Paramount Pictures and *Turtle Diary,* in association with United British Artists. Most recent production is *A Prayer for the Dying* for Samuel Goldwyn Company

Broadcast Communications (Corporate)

14 King Street
London WC2E 8HN
Tel: 01 240 6941
Stephen Chambers
Michael Braham
Michael Braham is

currently executive producer of the Channel 4 *Business Programme* and *Business Daily*

Brook Productions
21–24 Bruges Place
Randolph Street
London NW1 0TF
Tel: 01 482 6111
Udi Eichler
Philip Whitehead
Produced *Late Great Britains* for BBC and the following for Channel 4: *Voices; A Week in Politics; Shape of the World; Enoch: A Life in Politics; The Writing on the Wall; All the Prime Minister's Men.* Works in progress for Channel 4 include: *A Vote for Hitler* (docu-drama); *1968: A Spectre Haunts Europe; Prisoners of Childhood* (docu-drama). Works in progress for Thames TV: *A Matter of Life and Debt; The Paper Peace*

Burrill Productions
19 Cranbury Road
London SW6 2NS
Tel: 01 736 8673
Timothy Burrill
Produced *Tess, Pirates of Penzance, Supergirl, The Fourth Protocol* and *To Kill a Priest. Challenge* and *Princess of Siberia* are in development

Cadogan Communications
PO Box 758
London NW6 1EQ
Tel: 01 794 5552
Noel Fox
L V R Chiappini

Camden Productions
20 Jeffreys Street
London NW1 9PR
Tel: 01 482 0527
Theresa FitzGerald
Small company developing own projects for film and TV

Cartwn Cymru
Model House
Bull Ring
Llantrisant
Mid Glamorgan
Tel: 0443 237758
Naomi Jones
Animation production

Castle Productions
22A Ainslie Place
Edinburgh

EH3 6AJ
Tel: 031 220 3711
Malcolm Fane
Producers of documentaries and drama projects for broadcast/satellite TV

Celador Productions
39 Long Acre
London WC2E 9JT
Tel: 01 240 8101
Bob Louis
Television: primarily entertainment programming for all broadcast channels. Includes factual entertainment, game shows, variety, with selected documentary and drama output including *Delorean* and *Don't cry for me, Sergeant Major*

Celtic Films
1–2 Bromley Place
London W1
Tel: 01 637 7651
Muir Sutherland

Centre Films
118 Cleveland Street
London W1P 5DN
Tel: 01 387 4045
Jeffrey Taylor
Derek Granger
Kent Walwin
Eddie Leahy

Champion Television
TWI House
23 Eyot Gardens
London W6
Tel: 01 994 1444
Bryan Cowgill
Founded in 1989 by Mark McCormack's International Management Group to run the BSB Sports Channel as appointed television sports contractor to the British Satellite Broadcasting Co. From October 1989, will present over 12 hours of British and international sports programming and news every day of the year on the BSB direct broadcast satellite

Charisma Films
4th Floor
Russell Chambers
London WC2E 8AA
Tel: 01 379 4267
David Gideon Thomson

Chatsworth Television
97–99 Dean Street
London W1V 5RA
Tel: 01 734 4302
Malcolm Heyworth
Sister company to the Chatsworth distribution outfit and producer of light entertainment and drama programming, including *Treasure Hunt* and *Interceptor* for Thames, *Bullseye* darts quiz for Central and *Operation Julie* for Tyne Tees

Cheerleader Productions
The Trocadero
19 Rupert Street
London W1V 7FS
Tel: 01 287 3333
Charles Balchin
Producers of sports programmes for Channel 4 (American football, sumo, baseball, rowing, etc), BBC and Sky Channel

Chrysalis Visual Programming
4th Floor
Threeways House
40–44 Clipstone Street
London W1P 7EA
Tel: 01 436 3933
Shelley Miller
Producers of *The Max Headroom Show*

Cinema Verity
The Mill House
Millers Way
1a Shepherds Bush Road
London W6 7NA
Tel: 01 749 8485
Verity Lambert
Ann Weir
In 1988, Verity Lambert produced *A Cry in the Dark* in Australia, starring Meryl Streep, Sam Neill and directed by Fred Schepisi. She also recently executive produced the sitcom *May to December* for the BBC

Colstar Communications and Entertainment
1 Wardour Mews
D'Arblay Street
London W1V 3FF
Tel: 01 437 5725
Producers of art, history, sport, biography and wildlife documentaries for video sale

Columbia Pictures
19–23 Wells Street
London W1P 3FP
Tel: 01 580 2090
Arthur Leese

The Comic Strip
43a Berwick Street
London W1V 3RE
Tel: 01 439 9509
Peter Richardson

Compact Yellowbill Group
118 Cleveland Street
London W1P 5DN
Tel: 387 4045
Kent Walwin
Pom Oliver
Eddie Leahy

Compass Film Productions
3rd Floor
18–19 Warwick Street
London W1R 5RB
Tel: 01 439 6456
Simon Heaven
Involved since 1974 in cultural, educational and sponsored programmes for television. 1988 work includes *Concerning Cancer ... The Nature of the Problem* for Channel 4

Consolidated Productions (UK)
5 Jubilee Place
London SW3 3TD
Tel: 01 376 5151
Stephen Smallwood
Producer of films and television programmes

Creative Law
Media Legal Services
Burbank House
75 Clarendon Road
Sevenoaks
Kent TN13 1ET
Tel: 0732 460592
John Wheller
Production arm of Media Legal Services developing legal projects for film and TV, including series centred on The Inns of Court

Crossbow Films
2/2a Drayson Mews
Kensington
London W8 4LY
Tel: 01 376 2755
Simon Oakes
Mark Grenside
Recent projects: 72 half-hour TV shows of William Tell. In production: 12 one-hour shows, based on Patricia Highsmith's mystery

stories, with plans for a TV movie based on the life of Ian Fleming

Csaky
32 Willow Road
London NW3 1TL
Tel: 01 794 1574
Mick Csaky
Produces international documentary and drama productions for TV. Recent productions include the International Emmy Award winning *Chasing A Rainbow – The Life of Josephine Baker* and a six-part documentary series *The Midas Touch* with Anthony Sampson

Cue Film and Video Productions
33 Gloucester Avenue
London NW1 7TJ
Tel: 01 485 6049
Maureen McCue
Television and low-budget features

DBA Television
21 Ormeau Avenue
Belfast BT2 8HD
Tel: 0232 231197
David Barker
Northern Ireland's leading production and facilities company. Wide range of documentary programmes for Channel 4 and BBC. In production/development: *Singing Cowboys, Dust on the Bible, ABTOCTPADA – Highway Through Russia, War Without End* and projects on Jim Larkin and Maria Jolas

Debonair Production Co
74 Newman Street
London W1P 3LA
Tel: 01 323 3220
Toni Strasburg
Michael Rossiter
Chris Menges
Recent productions 1988/89 include: *Frontline Southern Africa – Destructive Engagement* (award-winning documentary), *The Other Bomb*, a documentary about German scientists working on Soviet atomic bomb, and *Chain of Tears*, a documentary about child war victims in Southern Africa

Deptford Beach Productions
79 Wardour Street
London W1V 3TH
Tel: 01 734 8508
Tony Kirkhope

Walt Disney Company
31–32 Soho Square
London W1V 6AP
Tel: 01 734 8111
Etienne De Villiers
UK arm of major US production company

Diverse Production
6–12 Gorleston Street
London W14 8XS
Tel: 01 603 4567
Frank Dynes
Company with commitment to innovative television. Producers of *Diverse Reports, The New Enlightenment, Uncertainties, 9-11-5* and a number of other broadcast series

Domino Films
8 Stockwell Terrace
Stockwell London
SW9 0QD
Tel: 01 582 0393
Joanne Mack
Steve Humphries
Century of Childhood, a major eight-part series for Channel 4 on childhood in the twentieth century; and *Lost Children of the Empire*, a major 90-minute documentary filmed in Australia, Canada and Zimbabwe for Granada TV. In development and production: major series on the Soviet Union; *Secret World of Sex; Faces of Freedom*, a series on independence leaders; *Breadline Britain – in the Nineties*

Dramatis Personae
122 Kennington Road
London SE11 6RE
Tel: 01 735 0831
Maria Aitken
Nathan Silver
In production with second TV series on *Acting*, co-produced with the BBC. Series *Boom Architecture* in preparation. This company is concerned with features on artistic skills and human

development having broad cultural or social interest

Edinburgh Film and Video Productions
Edinburgh Film and TV Studios
Nine Mile Burn by Penicuik
Midlothian EH26 9LT
Tel: 0968 72131
Robin Crichton
Major Scottish production company. Currently in production *The Stamp of Greatness* TV series and *Silent Mouse*, a TV Christmas special

Endboard Productions
Zair Works
111–119 Bishop Street
Birmingham B5 6JL
Tel: 021 622 1325
Yugesh Walia
Sunandan Walia
Producers of TV programmes and information videos. In 1988, produced *Sikh Festivals* for Channel 4, *Silver Shine* for Central TV and the Arts Council, *Road Safety Video* in six languages for Birmingham City Council

Equal Time
Heath Lodge
Heathside
London NW3 1BL
Tel: 01 431 1927
Martin Minns
Produces broadcast documentaries on music, the arts and current affairs

Euston Films
365 Euston Road
London NW1 3AR
Tel: 01 387 0911
John Hambley
Andrew Brown
The filmmaking subsidiary of Thames TV. Recent projects include: *Minder, Dealers, Capital City, The Fear*, and *Bellman and True*

Eye Film and Television
The Guildhall
Church Street
Eye
Suffolk IP23 7BD
Tel: 0379 870083

Fairwater Films
68 Vista Rise

Llandaff
Cardiff CF5 2SD
Tel: 0222 554416
Tony Barnes
Producers of *The Shoe People*, an animated cartoon series for TV-am

Falkman Communications
33 Gresse Street
London W1P 1PN
Tel: 01 636 1371
Bernard Falk
Independent television production company set up by BBC presenter Falk. Produced *Thank Heaven for Little Girls* documentary on the Walton sextuplets for ITV, *Sand and Land Yachting* for Channel 4, and *Eating Out with Tovey* for BBC2

FilmFair
1–4 Jacobs Well Mews
London W1
Tel: 01 935 1596
Lewis Rudd
Prolific producers of cartoon and puppet animation series for children, including *Huxley Pig, Bangers and Mash, Paddington Bear*, and *The Wombles*

The Filmworks
65 Brackenbury Road
Hammersmith
London W6 0BG
Tel: 01 741 5631
Recent productions: *Struggle for the Pole – In the Footsteps of Scott, Body and Soul, On the Trail of Yen Ren, Antarctic Challenge* and *Anything's Possible*

Flamingo Pictures
47 Lonsdale Square
London N1 1EW
Tel: 01 607 9958
Christine Oestreicher
James Scott
Produced *Loser Takes All*, based on Graham Greene's novel. Plans for 1989 include *Dibs*, based on a true story by Virginia M Axlune

Flashback Productions
22 Kildare Terrace
London W2 5LX
Tel: 01 727 9904
Victoria Wegg – Prosser
Producers of *Flashback*, a 20-part series for

Channel 4 which won a BFI Award. Makers of documentaries for Channel 4 on the Olympic Games (sold to 15 countries), the Palestinians, *Orphans of Minsk* and *Tales Out of School* and 60 programmes on *The March of Time*, recently sold in the USA. Many sports and documentary projects in development

Flashback Television
125 Tottenham Court Road
London W1P 9HN
Tel: 01 387 1246
Taylor Downing
See previous entry for details of product

Flickers Productions
10 Chesilton Road
London SW6 5AB
Tel: 01 731 0505
Martin Proctor
Neil Zeiger
Produced award-winning feature *Lamb*, written by Bernard McClaverty and directed by Colin Gregg. *Reasonable Force* by P G Duggan, a co-production with BBC TV and International Contracts, directed by John Goddard, was broadcast in 1988. Film projects in development include *The Eleventh Crushing* by Howard Brenton, *The China Egg* by Julian Bond, *Promising Material* by John Foster, *Secret Americans* by Jeff Povey, and *Weatherman* by Peter Berry

Focus Films
Rotunda Studio
R/O 116–118 Finchley Road
London NW3 5HT
Tel: 01 435 9004/5
David Pupkewitz
Marsha Levin
Louise Whitby
Glen Morris
Documentaries, drama, features. Produced *Othello*, directed by Janet Suzman for Channel 4. Currently in production, *Aphrodite*, a feature film directed by Gad Hollander

Forever Films
7a–9 Earlham Street

London WC2H 9LL
Tel: 01 836 5105
Clare Downs
In development: *Buster's Bedroom, Berlin in the Eye of The Storm, A Very Private Island* and *Nisanit*

Mark Forstater Productions
8A Trebeck Street
London W1Y 7RL
Tel: 01 408 0733
Mark Forstater
Nicola Lund
Produced *Wherever You Are* by Krzysztof Zanussi, *The Wolves of Willoughby Chase* for Zenith Productions, *Streets of Yesterday* directed by Judd Ne'eman and *Painted It Black* directed by Tim Hunter. Productions for 1989 include *The Touch* directed by Krzysztof Zanussi, *The Shadowland* directed by Harry Bromley Davenport, *Lycanthrope* written by Des Adams, *The Foundling* to be directed by Witold Starecki, *Blighton Lock* directed by Paul Morris, and *In Cahoots* directed by Chris Fallon

Freeway Films
31 Albany Street
Edinburgh EH1 3QN
Tel: 031 253200
John McGrath
Susie Brown

Frontroom Productions
79 Wardour Street
London W1V 3TH
Tel: 01 734 4603
John Davies
Robert Smith
Chris Harvey
Now involved in the production of drama and commercials. Produced the 1983 feature *Acceptable Levels* directed by John Davies. Short features include: *Intimate Strangers* directed by Robert Smith, and *Ursula and Glenys* devised and directed by John Davies in 1985. 1987 feature *The Love Child* directed by Robert Smith. Planned for 1989: drama *Wild Flowers* by Sharman Macdonald, directed by Robert Smith. Five feature projects in development

David Furnham Films
39 Hove Park Road
Hove
East Sussex BN3 6LH
Tel: 0273 559731
New developments: *Harriet and Her Harmonium*, a new musical; *South Coast Jazz*, a series; *The David Heneker Collection*, a performance documentary; and *Our Lady of Good Counsel* for BBC TV

Gatetarn Productions
9 Little Common
Stanmore Hill
Stanmore
Middx
Tel: 01 437 8696
Paul Knight

John Gau Video
Burston House
1 Burston Road
London SW15 6AR
Tel: 01 788 8811
John Gau
Ivan Rendall
Anne Munyard
Television documentary production

Noel Gay Television
24 Denmark Street
London WC2H 8NJ
Tel: 01 379 5953
Bill Cotton
Paul Jackson
Light entertainment/ documentaries, including: *Morris Minor, Red Dwarf* and *Scruples*

Genesis Project
Pinewood Studios
Iver Heath
Bucks SL0 0NH
Tel: 0753 651700
John Heyman

Gibb Rose Organisation (GRO)
Pinewood Studios
Pinewood Road
Iver Heath
Bucks SL0 0HN
Tel: 0753 651700
Sydney Rose
Company formed by Sydney Rose and Bee Gee Maurice Gibb to make international film and TV productions

Nick Gifford
Street Farmhouse
Woodnesborough
Nr Sandwich
Kent CT13 ONF
Tel: 0304 612631
Nick Gifford
c/o Hope and Lyne
Gifford is starting a third film about Sid in Bristol (a black family) for Channel 4. Shot a feature in 1988. In development, script for a feature film with BBC Wales

Bob Godfrey Films
119 Kings Cross Road
London WC1X 9DB
Tel: 01 278 5711
Bob Godfrey
Mike Hayes
Children's programmes, entertainments, promos, audiovisual and educational films

Goldcrest Films and Television
36–44 Brewer Street
London W1R 3HP
Tel: 01 437 8696
Major feature film, sales and finance company. Recent films include *The Mission, A Room with a View, The Name of the Rose, A Man in Love, Hope and Glory, Maurice* and *Fire and Ice*

The Grade Company
Embassy House
3 Audley Square
London W1
Tel: 01 409 1925
Lord Grade
Company currently producing TV films based on Barbara Cartland novels and developing other potential film projects

Grasshopper Productions
50 Peel Street
London W8 7PD
Tel: 01 229 1181
Joy Whitby
Company set up by Joy Whitby. Productions to date: for children *Grasshopper Island* and *Emma and Grandpa* (in conjunction with Griffin Productions); *East of the Moon*, film series based on the Terry Jones fairy tales with music by Neil Innes; and telefilm *A Pattern of Roses*, based on

the supernatural novel by K M Peyton

Greenpoint Films
5a Noel Street
London W1V 3RB
Tel: 01 437 6492
Ann Scott
Patrick Cassavetti
A loose association of nine filmmakers: Simon Relph, David Hare, Christopher Morahan, Ann Scott, Richard Eyre, Stephen Frears, Patrick Cassavetti, John Mackenzie and Mike Newell.
Projects have included Eyre's *The Ploughman's Lunch* and *Laughterhouse*, Morahan's *In The Secret State*, Hare's *Wetherby* and *Paris by Night*, Newell's *The Good Father*, and *Giles Foster's Tree of Hands*

Colin Gregg Films
Floor 2
1–6 Falconberg Court
London W1V 5FG
Tel: 01 439 0257
Colin Gregg
Gregg directed *Lamb* for Flickers-Limehouse Productions. Completed third feature *We Think the World of You* in 1988, followed by current projects *Genoa* for the BBC and *Earthly Powers*, an eight-part drama series

Griffin Productions
Balfour House
46–54 Great Titchfield Street
London W1P 7AE
Tel: 01 636 5066
Adam Clapham
Documentary, drama. Produced *Act of Betrayal* mini-series with Elliot Gould and Lisa Harrow, *Dispatches* for Channel 4. Co-productions: *Captain James Cook* with Revcom for ITV, *Club X* with Screenwish for Channel 4, *Maharajas* with BBC TV

Hammer Film Productions
Goldcrest Elstree Studios
Borehamwood
Herts WD6 1JG
Tel: 01 953 1600
Roy Skeggs
The company responsible for many classic British horror films was revived under new management in 1983 to start work on 13 films under the title *Hammer House of Mystery and Suspense*, to be released worldwide by 20th Century Fox. A second series is in development. Also purchased rights in 1985 to six novels with a view to feature film production

HandMade Films (Productions)
26 Cadogan Square
London SW1X 0JP
Tel: 01 584 8345
George Harrison
Denis O'Brien
Ray Cooper
Producers of *Monty Python's Life of Brian*, *The Long Good Friday*, *Time Bandits*, *Privates on Parade*, *The Missionary*, *Scrubbers*, *A Private Function*, *Mona Lisa*, *Withnail and I*, *Five Corners*, *Bellman and True*, *Track 29*, *The Lonely Passion of Judith Hearne*, and *Raggedy Rawney*. Current releases include *Powwow Highway*, *Checking Out* and *How to Get Ahead in Advertising*. Filming in 1989 *Cold Dog Soup*, *Nuns on the Run* and *Breakfast of Champions*

Harcourt Films
77 Camden Mews
London NW1 9BU
Tel: 01 267 0882
Jeremy Marre
Producer and director of documentaries for Channel 4, BBC and ITV. Also many overseas co-productions. Most recent productions include: 14-part music series *Beats of the Heart*; 7-part series for Channel 4 *Chasing Rainbows*; 12-part wildlife series *Ourselves and Other Animals* with Gerald Durrell; and *Nature of Music* – three films produced for Channel 4 and R M Arts

Hemdale Holdings
21 Albion Street
London W2
Tel: 01 724 1010
George Miller
Produced *Terminator*, *Return of the Living Dead*, *Falcon and the Snowman*, *Salvador*, *At Close Range*, *Platoon*, *Hoosiers* and *Hotel Colonial*. All production activities currently based in US. UK office, sales outfit only

Jim Henson Productions
2 Old Brewery Mews
Hampstead High Street
London NW3 1PZ
Tel: 01 435 7121
Duncan Kenworthy
Martin Baker
Jim Henson's UK-based film and TV production company. Recently produced two one-hour films for TVS, *Living with Dinosaurs* and *Monster Maker*, to be shown on Channel 4 as part of *The Jim Henson Hour* series. Producers of the BAFTA-nominated series *The Storyteller*, and a feature film based on Roald Dahl's novel 'Labyrinth'. Producers of international adaptations of *The Muppet Show*, *Fraggle Rock* and *Muppet Babies*, and of holiday specials and series for children such as *The Tale of the Bunny Picnic* with the BBC, *Mother Goose* with TSW, and *The Ghost of Faffner Hall* with Tyne Tees

Jim Henson's Creature Shop
1b Downshire Hill
Hampstead
London NW3
Tel: 01 431 2818
John Stephenson
William Plant
Animatronics, puppets and prosthetics designers and creators for feature films, television and commercials.
Made creatures for films such as *The Dark Crystal*, *Labyrinth*, *Dreamchild*, *The Bear* and most recently Nic Roeg's *The Witches*. Currently working on *Teenage Mutant Ninja Turtles*. Television work includes Emmy Award winning series *The Storyteller* and other projects for Jim Henson Productions

Hightimes Productions
7 Garrick Street
London WC2E 9AR
Tel: 01 240 1128

Tony Humphreys
Al Mitchell
Production and packaging company which set up the Anglia quiz show *The Zodiac Game* and packaged the *Me and My Girl* situation comedy for LWT (five completed series). Drama series, situation comedy and game shows in development for 1989/90

Holmes Associates
10–16 Rathbone Street
London W1P 1AH
Tel: 01 637 8251
Andrew Holmes
Robert Eagle
Adrian Bate
Stephen Taylor

ILEA Learning Resources Branch
Television and Publishing Centre
Thackeray Road
London SW8 3TB
Tel: 01 622 9966
The Inner London Education Authority develops and produces materials, including videocassettes, aimed at supporting educational developments in schools and colleges. The videocassettes are available within ILEA, nationally and internationally. Produced *Women in Engineering*, shown by the BBC

ITC Productions
45 Seymour Street
London W1A 1AG
Tel: 01 262 3262
The newly formed UK-based production arm of ITC Entertainment Group, which successfully completed a management buy-out in November 1988. Concentrates on major international TV and feature co-productions. Currently working on a range of projects with producers and broadcasters in France, Germany, Italy, Holland, Australia, US, UK and Hong Kong

Illuminations
16 Newman Passage
London W1P 3PE
Tel: 01 580 7877
Diane Large
Geoff Dunlop
John Wyver
Linda Zuck

Producers of cultural programmes for Channel 4 and others. Recent projects include *Ghosts in the Machine II*, a 20-part series featuring video art, *Campaign!*, a 2-hour documentary about the relationship between TV and US presidential politics, and *Shock of the Neo* for Channel 4's *Signals*, an exploration of originality and authenticity in art. In development, *The New Museum*, a programme on how we make sense of the visual environment

Illustra Communications
13–14 Bateman Street
London W1V 6EB
Tel: 01 437 9611
Douglas Kentish

Independent Film Production Associates (IFPA)
87 Dean Street
London W1V 5AA
Tel: 01 734 3847/439 3795
Charles Thompson
Aileen McCracken
Film, video, TV production in the areas of documentary, light entertainment, music and the arts. Recent work comprises *Crossing the Line*, *Disciples of Chaos* and *Royal Ellington* for Channel 4

Independent Producers
65 Shelton Street
London WC2H 9HE
Tel: 01 240 3742
Jan Martin

Infovision
63 White Lion Street
London N1 9PP
Tel: 01 837 0012
Helen McCrorie

Initial Film and Television
22 Golden Square
London W1R 3PA
Tel: 01 439 8994
Malcolm Gerrie
Eric Fellner

Insight Productions
Gidleigh Studio
Gidleigh
Chagford
Newton Abbot
Devon TQ13 8HP
Tel: 06473 2686

Brian Skilton
TV production in arts, drama, entertainment, environment and documentary. Recent work includes the documentary series *Taming the Flood*, a three-part series on Britain's rivers and wetlands. In pre-production: *Camargue*, environment documentary and *Landscape and Poetry* with Ted Hughes

International Broadcasting Trust
2 Ferdinand Place
London NW1 8EE
Tel: 01 482 2847
Anthony Isaacs
A consortium of some 80 organisations, including development agencies, churches and trade unions, formed to make television programmes about the Third World and its relationship with developed countries. Recent productions include *AIDS – An African Perspective* for Channel 4 and *War Generation – Beirut* for BBC1

Interprom
7a Tythings Court
Minehead
Somerset TA24 5NT
Tel: 0643 6774
Clive Woods
Producers and distributors of various music programmes, specialising in jazz and blues

Island Films
22 St Peter's Square
London W6 9NW
Tel: 01 741 1511
John Mills

Isolde Films
4 Kensington Park Gardens
London W11 3HB
Tel: 01 727 3541
Tony Palmer
Maureen Murray
Recent productions include *Testimony* starring Ben Kingsley. Feature film *The Children* in development

Jennie & Co
3 Duck Lane
London W1V 1FL

Tel: 01 437 0600
Chris Richmond
Terry Bedford
Barry Lategan
Steve Hilliker

Kai Productions
1 Ravenslea Road
London SW12 8SA
Tel: 01 673 4550
George Haggerty
Marie Kodani
Channel 4 productions:
Malltime (1987), *Voice Trip* (1988), *Robotopia* (1989), *Tomorrow's Eve* (1989)

Kestrel Films
45 Walham Grove
London SW6 1QR
Tel: 01 385 5577
Bill Shapter
Currently developing TV drama and feature scripts. Linked to Kestrel Films Incorporated, Tony Garnett's LA-based production company, associated with Warner Bros

Kestrel II
23 Hamilton Gardens
London NW8 9PU
Tel: 01 286 8602
Irving Teitelbaum
Ken Loach
Kestrel II produced *Fatherland*, a feature film directed by Ken Loach. The company was also responsible for the TV documentary series *About Men* for Channel 4

King Rollo Films
17 Wigmore Street
London W1H 9LA
Tel: 01 580 5816
Clive Juster
Producers and distributors of the animated series:
Mr Benn, King Rollo, Victor and Maria, Towser, Watt the Devil and *The Adventures of Spot and Ric*

Kinmonth
c/o Foxtrot Films
45 Elgin Crescent
London W11
Tel: 01 229 1322
Margy Kinmonth
Drama productions include *Baker's Dozen* and *To the Western World*

Koninck
175 Wardour Street
London W1V 3AB

Tel: 01 734 4943
Keith Griffiths and The Brothers Quay. Specialists in puppet animation. Producers of arts documentaries and fiction.
Latest projects include: *Rehearsals for Extinct Anatomies; Doodlin', Impressions of Len Lye; The Land of Counterpane; Hilda at Darjeeling;* and *Japan Live Performance* all for Channel 4. Jan Švankmajer completed his first feature, *Alice,* and is currently developing his second *Faust.* The Brothers Quay are developing *Sketch for Troubled Sleep* and a first feature *The Institute Benjamenta.* Koninck celebrates its tenth birthday in 1989

Landseer Film and Television Productions
140 Royal College Street
London NW1 0TA
Tel: 01 485 7333
Documentary, drama, music and arts.
Productions include: *A Penny For Your Dreams, Peter Hall – Work in Progress, Sinfonietta Series II,* and two *South Bank Shows: Two Women in Three Dimensions* and *From the New World*

Helen Langridge Associates of London
75 Kenton Street
London WC1N 1NN
Tel: 01 833 2955
Helen Langridge
Juliet Naylor
Producers of TV programming, including productions for Channel 4, commercials, and music videos including Tanita Tikaram's 'Cathedral Song'

Brian Lapping Associates
21–24 Bruges Place
Randolph Street
London NW1 0TF
Tel: 01 482 5855
Producers of TV programming, incl. a current drama project for Granada TV

Large Door

41–45 Beak Street
London W1R 3LE
Tel: 01 439 1381
John Ellis
Simon Hartog
Producers of
documentaries on the
media and related topics,
including *New Chinese
Cinema, Charlie Chaplin*
and the *Visions* series
(1982–85). Projects in
development include
series on food, heritage,
and TV in Brazil

Lazer
Entertainments
(UK)

118 Cleveland Street
London W1P 5DN
Tel: 01 388 2323
Feature production
company. Editing and
other post-production
facilities

Limehouse
Productions

The Trocadero
19 Rupert Street
London W1V 7FS
Tel: 01 287 3333
Iain Bruce
Richard Key
Currently producing the
daily and weekly
Business Programme
through Business
Television, and sports
programmes on Channel
4 and other channels
through Cheerleader
Productions. A major
single production in 1988
was Mozart's opera *Don
Giovanni*, live from the
Royal Opera House,
Covent Garden, for
Channel 4

Limelight Films

3 Bromley Place
London W1P 5HB
Tel: 01 255 3939
Steve Barron
Simon Fields
Producers of pop promos,
TV commercials, TV
programming and feature
films, with offices in
London and LA

Little Bird Co

91 Regent Street
London W1R 7TA
Tel: 01 434 1131
James Mitchell
Jeffrey Rosenblatt
Company has made three
series of *The Irish RM*
drama. Partners for the

first series were
Rediffusion Films, Ulster
TV and RTE. Second and
third series were in
association with Channel
4 and Ulster TV

Living Tape
Productions

Ramillies House
1–2 Ramillies Street
London W1V 1DF
Tel: 01 439 6301
Nick Freethy
Stephen Bond
Producers of educational
and documentary
programmes for TV and
video distribution.
Currently in production
with major new TV series
Oceans of Wealth

Euan Lloyd
Productions

Pinewood Studios
Iver Heath
Bucks SL0 0NH
Tel: 0753 651700
Euan Lloyd
Chris Chrisafis
Since 1968, Lloyd has
made nine major action
adventures including *The
Wild Geese, Who Dares
Wins* and *The Sea Wolves.*
In development are
Centrifuge and *Okavango*

London Film
Productions

44a Floral Street
London WC2E 9DA
Tel: 01 379 3366
Mark Shelmerdine
Rosie Bunting
Founded in 1932 by
Alexander Korda. Many
co-productions with the
BBC, including *I,
Claudius, Poldark* and
Testament of Youth.
Produced *The Country
Girls* for Channel 4. In
receipt of a direct drama
commission from a US
network for *Scarlet
Pimpernel* and *Kim.*
Renowned for productions
of classics, now
developing more
contemporary fiction
work

Lusia Films

7–9 Earlham Street
London WC2
Tel: 01 240 2350
Mark Karlin
Karlin made *For Memory,*
a BFI/BBC co-production,
and a four-part series of
documentaries on
Nicaragua. Also a two-

hour film called *Utopias*
for Channel 4

Jo Lustig

PO Box 472
London SW7 4NL
Tel: 01 937 6614
Jo Lustig
Represents Mel Brooks
and Managing Director of
Brooksfilms (UK).
Co-producer *84 Charing
Cross Road* (Brooksfilms
and Columbia), producer
of TV documentaries:
*Maria Callas – Life and
Art* (Channel 4); *The
Unforgettable Nat 'King'
Cole* (BBC TV); *John
Cassavetes* (BBC TV)

MGM-UA
Communications
Co

UIP House
45 Beadon Road
Hammersmith
London W6 OEG
Tel: 01 741 9041

MPC Television

20 St Anne's Court
London W1V 3AW
Tel: 01 494 2967/8/9
Avie Littler
Ted Barnes
TV production arm of
Carlton Communications.
Recent TV productions
include *Beyond
Timbuktu,* a natural
history programme filmed
in West Africa, a BBC/
WNET co-production; *The
Stars,* a six-part
astronomy series with
Heather Couper for
Channel 4; series 3 of
Smith's Superchamps, a
children's sports series for
Channel 4; *A to Z,* a film
essay on typography for
Signals, Channel 4

Magic Hour Films/
Magic Hour
Productions

143 Chatsworth Road
London NW2 5QT
Tel: 01 459 3074
Bianka Ford
Production company
making films, dramas,
documentaries and series
for TV. Also provides
research and packaging
for film and television
projects

Malachite

Malachite Associate
Productions
East Kirkby House

Spilsby
Lincolnshire PE23 4BX
Tel: 01 487 5451/07903
538
Charles Mapleston
Hugh Newsam
Nancy Thomas
Specialists in arts, music
and documentary
programming

Malone Gill
Productions

16 Newman Passage
London W1P 3PE
Tel: 01 580 6594
Michael Gill
Georgina Denison
Mandy Field
Lita Yong
Hugh Newsam
Recent productions
include *Vintage: A
History of Wine* (1989) for
Channel 4 and PBS, and
*Paul Gauguin: The
Savage Dream* broadcast
on PBS in 1989. In pre-
production is *Monet* for
WGBH; *Straws in the
Wind* with Pacem
Productions, Los Angeles;
Music on Earth with
Mainman SAAG; *Nomads*
with ITEL; *Masters of Art*
with Sir Lawrence
Gowing and Christie's
International; *The
Garden* with WETA and
Channel 4; and *The
Buried Mirror* with
Carlos Fuentes and the
Smithsonian Institution

Mike Mansfield
Television

5–7 Carnaby Street
London W1V 1PG
Tel: 01 494 3061
Mike Mansfield
Producing light
entertainment and music
promos

Medialab

Unit 8 Chelsea Wharf
15 Lots Road
London SW10 0QH
Tel: 01 351 5814
John Gaydon
Kevin Godley
Lol Creme
Lexi Godfrey
Producers of pop promos,
videolas, documentaries
and features. Also run
Exposed Films and The
Videolabel

Meditel
Productions

Bedford Chambers
The Piazza

Covent Garden
London WC2 8HA
Tel: 01 836 9216/9364
Joan Shenton
Provides medical and
science-based
documentaries for TV.
Productions: *Food – Fad
or Fact?* for TSW (two six-
part series), *For What It's
Worth Special on NSAIDs*
for Thames TV, and
Impotence, a documentary
for Channel 4

Bill Melendez
Productions
32–34 Great
Marlborough Street
London W1
Tel: 01 439 4411
Steve Melendez
Graeme Spurway

Mendoza
Productions
22 Soho Square
London W1V 5FJ
Tel: 01 434 9641
Debby Mendoza
Oscar Moore

Merchant Ivory
Productions
46 Lexington Street
London W1
Tel: 01 437 1200
Ismail Merchant
Paul Bradley
Producer Ismail
Merchant and director
James Ivory together
made *Heat and Dust, The
Bostonians, A Room with
a View, Maurice* and
*Slaves of New York.
Mr and Mrs Bridge* will
be completed during 1989
followed by E M Forster's
Howards End

Mersey Television
18 Rodney Street
Liverpool L1 2TQ
Tel: 051 250 1602
Phil Redmond
Operates Brookside
Productions, which has a
Channel 4 contract to
produce the twice-weekly
drama series *Brookside*.
Mersey Music and Mersey
Casting are subsidiary
companies of Mersey
Television

Mersham
Productions
41 Montpellier Walk
London SW7 1JH
Tel: 01 589 8829
Lord Brabourne
Lord Brabourne, a Fellow

and a Governor of the
BFI, is a director of
Thames Television.
Amongst other films, he
has produced in
conjunction with Richard
Goodwin four films based
on stories by Agatha
Christie and *A Passage to
India* directed by David
Lean. During 1986,
co-produced *Little Dorrit*.
In 1988/9, co-produced
the TV series *Leontyne*

Metropolis Pictures
147 Crouch Hill
London N8 9QH
Tel: 01 340 4649
Elizabeth Taylor-Mead
Nicholas Dubrule
TV documentaries and
cinema features. Recent
productions for Channel 4
include *My Mama Done
Told Me* and *Pottery
Ladies*

Midnight Films
26 Soho Square
London W1V 5FJ
Tel: 01 434 0011
Michael Hamlyn
Features, promos and
television
(1987/8). Produced the
full-length feature film
U2 Rattle and Hum –
part concert film, part
cinema verité
documentary. Currently
developing future feature
projects

Milesian Film
Productions
10 Selwood Place
London SW7
Tel: 01 373 8858
Christopher Miles

Millaney, Grant,
Mallet, Mulcahy
22 Golden Square
London W1R 3PA
Tel: 01 439 9527
Scott Millaney
Pop promos, live concerts
and shorts

Mirus Productions
2nd Floor
9 Carnaby Street
London W1V 1PG
Tel: 01 439 7113/494 2399
Howard Johnson
Mike Wallington
Produced *Songs of
Freedom; CLR James* in
1986. *Colonial Madness;
This Joint is Jumpin'* in
1987. *One Love* and *Art
Tatum* in 1988. Current
productions: *Family Saga*
and *Black Faith*

NAAS Film and
Video Production
49 Goodge Street
London W1P 1FB
Tel: 01 580 7448
Christopher Mould
NAAS has been
producing
international
documentaries and
current affairs
programmes for TV since
1977. Clients include:
Channel 4, Central TV
and KRO-Holland

NVC Arts
Liberty House
222 Regent Street
London W1R 5DE
Tel: 01 434 9571
Produces recordings of
live opera and ballet from
the world's leading
international venues and
companies. Recent
recordings include *Opera
Stories,* a series of 10
programmes in which
Charlton Heston narrates
the stories of the operas
with extensive
performance extracts; *La
Sylphide* from Royal
Danish Ballet; and *Le
Corsaire* from the Kirov
Ballet

New Era
Productions
First Floor
113 Wardour Street
London W1V 3TD
Tel: 01 439 6889
Marc Samuelson
Jane Bird

New Media
12 Oval Road
London NW1 7DH
Tel: 01 482 5258
Dick Fletcher
Interactive videodiscs and
CD-I for a wide range of
applications. TV series
include *What a Picture*

New World
Pictures (UK)
27 Soho Square
London W1V 5FL
Tel: 01 434 0497
Martin Goldthorpe
In 1987 New World
financed their first
British ventures,
Hellraiser, produced by
Christopher Figg and
directed by Clive Barker;
and *Queenie*, a television
mini – series produced in
association with LWT and
directed by Larry Peerce.
1988 productions included

the sequel to *Hellraiser
(Hellbound: Hellraiser 2),*
and the TV mini-series
Shadow on the Sun in
association with LWT

Nordfeld
Animation
77 Kingshurst Road
Northfield
Birmingham B31 2LJ
Tel: 021 476 3552
Dale Hemenway
Kevan Goode
Produced animation for
the BBC TV series
Hartbeat. Other projects
include a pilot for an
animated TV series

North South
Productions
Woburn Buildings
1 Woburn Walk
London WC1H 0JJ
Tel: 01 388 0351
Richard Keefe
Stephen Bottomore
Company set up to make
films on third world
issues and international
themes. Recent
productions include *Only
One Earth*, a major
12-part co-production
with BBC on environment
and development

Ocean Pictures
25 Melody Road
London SW18 2QW
Tel: 01 870 5345
Lucinda Sturgis
Roger Brown
John D Eberts

Opix Films
Pinewood Studios
Pinewood Road
Iver Heath
Bucks SL0 0NH
Tel: 0753 651700
Terry Ryan
Productions include a
four-part series *Boyce
Goes West*, co-produced
with Brent Walker for the
BBC, *American Carrott*,
made for Channel 4 and
HBO, *Dash*, a one-hour
entertainment with
Wayne Sleep, and *Max
Boyce in Kathmandu* for
BBC1. Also two films for
TV, *Going Home* and
Heaven on Earth,
co-produced with
Primedia (Canada), BBC
and CBC. In production
Witness to War, a series
of seven one-hour
drama/documentaries and
two features, *The Boxty
Chronicle* and *East Coast,
West Coast*

Orion Pictures Corporation

31–32 Soho Square
London W1V 6AP
Tel: 01 437 7766
Stuart Salter
Company was involved with various films during 1987 including Paul Verhoeven's *Robocop* and Woody Allen's *Radio Days,* and in 1988/89, *Mississippi Burning, Dirty Rotten Scoundrels* and *Another Woman*

Oxford Scientific Films

Long Hanborough
Oxford OX7 2LD
Tel: 0993 881881
OSF productions due for 1989 transmission include two one-hour films for Channel 4: *To Be a Butterfly* and *Enemies of the Oak*. Additional OSF productions scheduled for 1989 include two one-hour films for Anglia TV *Great Wood of Caledon* and *Hunters of the Skies*

Pacesetter Enterprises

1 Wardour Mews
D'Arblay Street
London W1V 3FF
Tel: 01 437 5725
Production, co-production of international broadcast programming. A wholly-owned subsidiary of Colstar Communications and Entertainment. Credits include *The Wandering Company,* and *In Search of Wildlife*. In development: *Brabant Antartica – A Survey;* and *In Search of Wildlife,* second and third series. Currently looking for new co-production properties in drama, documentary, the arts, sciences and nature

Pacesetter Productions

New Barn House
Leith Hill Lane
Ockley
Surrey RH5 5PH
Tel: 0306 70433
Adele Spencer
Anglo/Soviet feature co-production in preparation for shooting in 1989. On-going documentary and sponsored production

Palace Productions, Pictures, Video

16–17 Wardour Mews
London W1V 3FF
Tel: 01 734 7060
Nik Powell
Stephen Woolley
Daniel Battsek
Robert Jones

Panoptic Productions

73 Great Titchfield Street
London W1P 7FN
Tel: 01 636 9626
Nicholas Fraser
Michael Jones
Jean Newington
Producer of *Opinions, My Britain, The Other Europe, The Big Company* and *American Power,* all for Channel 4, and *Bookmark* for the US

Paramount Pictures

UIP House
45 Beadon Road
London W6 0EG
Tel: 01 741 9041
Michael O'Sullivan

Partridge Films

38 Mill Lane
London NW6 1NR
Tel: 01 435 1182
Michael Rosenberg
Makers of the award-winning wildlife series *Path of the Rain God* for Channel 4; and *Okavango: Jewel of the Kalahari* for the BBC

Partridge Productions

38 Mill Lane
London NW6 1NR
Tel: 01 435 1182
Michael Rosenberg
Makers of the award-winning wildlife documentaries *Fragile Earth* series, *Stolen River* and *Lords of Hokkaido* for Channel 4

Pelicula Films

7 Queen Margaret Road
Glasgow G20 6DP
Tel: 041 945 3333
Mike Alexander
Producer of programmes for TV, including Channel 4 and BBC TV

Pennies from Heaven

83 Eastbourne Mews
London W2
Tel: 01 402 0051/576 1197
Kenith Trodd
Trodd is a prolific

producer of films for the BBC and others. Recent work includes *After Pilkington, The Singing Detective, Christabel* and *Here is The News,* all for the BBC. He also produced the feature *Dreamchild* for Thorn EMI and *A Month in the Country* for Film Four International. Much of this work has been from screenplays by Dennis Potter, the company's other principal director

Persistent Vision Productions

133 Ravenslea Road
London SW12 8RT
Tel: 01 673 7924
John Stewart
Carol Lemon
Following the award-winning short film *Crash,* the company completed *The Gaol,* a 25-minute drama. Currently in pre-production are a 35mm short film *A Murder of Crows* (working title), and a half-hour drama *The Interrogation*

Picture Palace Productions

65–69 Beak Street
London W1R 3LF
Tel: 01 439 9882
Malcolm Craddock
Firing the Bullets, the second English episode of the *Eurocops* drama series was completed and broadcast in 1988. A third episode will be shot in late 1989. Currently in pre-production: *When Love Dies* for Channel 4. In development: Po Chih Leong's *Passage to Heaven* and Gillies MacKinnon's *French Kisses*

Picture Partnership Productions

73 Newman Street
London W1
Tel: 01 637 8056
Brian Eastman
Recently completed the feature film *Wilt,* the TV series *Forever Green* and *Agatha Christie's Poirot* both for LWT and *Traffik* for Channel 4. Previously made *Words of Love* (shown in the BBC Screen 2 slot), *Porterhouse Blue* (Channel 4) and *Blott on the Landscape* (BBC)

PolyGram Musicvideo

1 Rockley Road
London W14 0DL
Tel: 01 743 3474
A division of PolyGram Records, making music programming for video release, featuring such bands as Dire Straits, Level 42, The Mission, Curiosity Killed the Cat, Bananarama, Tears for Fears and Style Council

Portman Productions

159–165 Great Portland Street
London W1N 6NR
Tel: 01 637 4041
Ian R Warren
Tom Donald
Victor Glynn
The production arm of Global Television sales company

Portobello Productions

42 Tavistock Road
London W11 1AW
Tel: 01 221 2426
Eric Abraham
Specialize in drama, documentary, music and arts programming. First feature: Roald Dahl's *Danny The Champion Of The World* went into production in 1988. Other productions include: *Bartok's Last Years, Solti Conducts Bartok,* and *Claudio Arrau's 85th Birthday Concert*. Projects planned for 1989 include: *Still Life At The Penguin Cafe, Murray Perahia,* and *The Jacqueline Du Pre Fund Concert*

Poseidon Productions

1st Floor
Hammer House
113 Wardour Street
London W1V 3TD
Tel: 01 734 4441/5140
Frixos Constantine
Productions include: *Tomorrow There Was A War, Ashik Kerib, The Stain, Little Vera, Solovetskaya Power, The Return*, and *The Rape Of Aphrodite*

Primetime Television

Seymour Mews House
Seymour Mews
Wigmore Street

London W1H 9PE
Tel: 01 935 9000
Deidre Simms
Independent TV
production company,
associated with TV
distributor RPTA and
specialising in
international
co-productions. Recent
projects include *Great
Expectations* (six hours for
HTV/Disney), *John
Silver's Return to
Treasure Island* with
HTV/Disney, *Fortunes of
War* (seven hours with the
BBC), *Lost Belongings*
(six hours with Euston
Films and Channel 4),
Always Afternoon (four
hours with Henry
Crawford for SBS
Australia and
Multimedia Hamburg),
Waltz Through the Hill
(five half-hours with
Barron Films and
Wonderworks/PBS) and
several Gerald Durrell
natural history
documentaries with
Channel 4 and Primedia,
Canada

Prominent Features
68a Delancey Street
London NW1 7RY
Tel: 01 284 0242
Steve Abbott
Anne James
Company formed by Steve
Abbott, John Cleese,
Terry Gilliam, Eric Idle,
Anne James, Terry Jones
and Michael Palin to
produce in-house
features. Produced *The
Adventures of Baron
Munchausen*, *Erik The
Viking* and *A Fish Called
Wanda*. In development:
American Friends

Quanta
12 Wicks Drive
Chippenham
Wiltshire FN15 3ES
Tel: 0249 660599
Glyn Jones
Nicholas Jones
Specialists in TV
programmes on science,
technology and
engineering. Most recent
productions are mainly
for Channel 4, including
Equinox series

RM Arts
44 Great Marlborough
Street
London W1V 1DB
Tel: 01 439 2637

RM Arts produces music
and arts programming
and co-produces on an
international basis with
major broadcasters
including BBC, LWT,
Channel 4, ARD and ZDF
in Germany, NOS-TV in
Holland, Danmarks Radio
and TV2/Denmark, ORF
in Austria, SVT in
Sweden, RTVE in Spain
and La Sept in France.
Recent work includes *The
Nature of Music*,
co-produced with Channel
4; a 6-part series on
design; a drama series for
the bicentenary of the
French Revolution, *Les
Nuits Revolutionnaires;*
ballet productions from
London Festival Ballet,
Swedish Royal Opera
Ballet, The Nederlands
Dance Theatre and
Carolyn Carlson and
opera recordings
including productions
from San Francisco
Opera, Vienna State
Opera, Drottningholm
Court Theatre and
English National Opera

RSPB Film and Video Unit
The Lodge
Sandy
Bedfordshire SG19 2DL
Tel: 0767 80551
Jeffery Boswall
In-house unit making
at least three 30-minute
16mm films a year, most
recently *Eagles
International, Northern
Flights*, and *For Love of
Birds*. The unit also acts
as an independant
producer of
environmental films and
videos. The RSPB
stockshot library holds
one million feet of film

Ragdoll Productions
34 Harborne Road
Edgbaston
Birmingham B15 3AA
Tel: 021 454 5453/4344
Anne Wood
Specialist children's TV
producer of live action
and animation. *Pob* for
Channel 4, *Playbox* for
Central TV, *Storytime* for
BBC TV

Recorded Development
8–12 Broadwick Street
London W1V 1FH
Tel: 01 439 0607
A subsidiary of Recorded
Picture Co set up to bring
projects to pre-production
stage. In development are
Jonathan Demme's *King
of the Cannibal Islands*,
Marek Kanievska's
Passion Play, David
Cronenberg's *The Naked
Lunch* and a project with
Nagisa Oshima

Recorded Picture Co
8–12 Broadwick Street
London W1V 1FH
Tel: 01 439 0607
Jeremy Thomas
Thomas produced Nagisa
Oshima's *Merry
Christmas, Mr Lawrence*,
Stephen Frears' *The Hit*,
Nicolas Roeg's
Insignificance and *The
Last Emperor*, directed by
Bernardo Bertolucci. In
production in 1989:
Everybody Wins directed
by Karel Reisz

Red Rooster Films
11–13 Macklin Street
London WC2B 5NH
Tel: 01 405 8147
Stephen Bayly
Linda James
Christian Routh
Carolyn Parry-Jones
Jenny Matheson
Stephen Bayly directed
and Linda James
produced the feature *Just
Ask For Diamond* by
Anthony Horowitz. Linda
James co-produced a
documentary special
Letters For My Children
for HTV with David Jones
directing. Christian
Routh is developing
several feature films and
drama series

Rediffusion Films
c/o Buxton Films
5 The Square
Buxton
Derbyshire SK17 6AZ
Tel: 0298 77623
Jette Bonneure
The production finance
arm of a diversified
communications
company. In the past has
provided finance for TV
productions and feature
films. Most recent
involvements include a
13-part athletic coaching

series financed in
conjunction with the
International Athletic
Federation

Regent Production
Brander House
Broomhill Road
London SW18 4JG
Tel: 01 877 1444
William Stewart
Productions for 1989
include an 80-part series
of *Fifteen to One* (third
series), Channel 4's
daytime quiz show, and a
new comedy series, *The
Nineteenth Hole* for
Central TV

Revere Entertainment Company
24 D'Arblay Street
London W1V 3FH
Tel: 01 437 4551
John Goldstone
Goldstone produced
*Monty Python's The
Meaning of Life* and *Erik
the Viking*

Rhode Island Films
Suite 413
29 Great Pulteney Street
London W1R 3DD
Tel: 01 434 3861
Philip Lowrey
Jon Scoffield
Barbara Coles
Producers of
documentaries,
commercials, and pop
promos

Rite Films
20 Bouverie Road West
Folkestone
Kent CT20 2SZ
Tel: 0303 52335
George Wright
Mainly engaged in
corporate videos,
documentary film
productions, and TV news
gathering

Riverfront Pictures
Dock Cottages
Peartree Lane
Glamis Road
Wapping
London E1 9SR
Tel: 01 481 2939
Jeff Perks
Tony Freeth
Specialise in music, arts
and drama–
documentaries. New
productions include *Raag
Rang*, a series on Indian
classical music and a
major programme on the
Maniput Chorus

Theatre's production of *Chakravyuha*, both for Channel 4. In development, a programme on art fraud for Thames TV

Sandfire Productions
Pinewood Studios
Iver Heath
Bucks SL0 0NH
Tel: 0753 651700
Anthony Williams
Feature film producers.
Projects include *Messiah* and *Chameleon*

Sands Films
119 Rotherhithe Street
London SE16 4NF
Tel: 01 231 2209
Richard Goodwin
Goodwin produced *Stories From A Flying Trunk;* the puppet animation short *The Nightingale;* and features *Biddy* and the six-hour feature *Little Dorrit* both directed by Christine Edzard at the company's Rotherhithe Studios base

Scimitar Films
6–8 Sackville Street
London W1X 1DD
Tel: 01 734 8385
Michael Winner
Winner has produced and directed many films, including *Death Wish 3, Appointment with Death* and *A Chorus of Disapproval*

Scope Films
Flat 3
38 Canfield Gardens
London NW6
Tel: 01 624 5571
Michael Grigsby
Chris Menges
Ivan Strasburg
Toni Strasburg
Scope was established in 1980 by documentarist Grigsby and three cameramen. Productions include the *Picture of Health* series for Channel 4 and the *People of the Islands* documentary on the Inuit people

Scotquest
38 Chalton Road
Bridge of Allan
Stirling PK9 4EF
Tel: 0786 832168
Alastair Hetherington
Makers of Channel 4 series *Columba, Great Walks, Scottish View* and *Down the Line*

Screen Ventures
49 Goodge Street
London W1P 1FB
Tel: 01 580 7448
Christopher Mould
Screen Ventures is a production company specialising in documentaries and current affairs.
Productions include:
Afghanistan, Iran The Revolution, Refugees in Africa, Desert Island, Tayarra – A Racing Legend, Burma – A Special Report and *Dhows of the Arabian Sea* for Channel 4, BBC TV, Central TV, KRO-Holland, and others

Secker Walker
Suite 101
The Colosseum
Production Centre
Portland Gate
Leeds LS2 3AW
Tel: 0532 461311
David Secker
Stan Walker
Producer of light entertainment programmes *Bands of Gold, International Ballroom Dancing* and *The Tony Capstick Show*

Seventh Art Productions (UK)
129 Queen's Crescent
London NW5 4HE
Tel: 01 485 7132
Phil Grabsky
Mike Whiteley
Documentary-makers for UK and international TV. Currently working on a four-part series *The New Spain*

Siriol Productions
Phoenix Buildings
3 Mount Stuart Square
Butetown
Cardiff CF1 6RW
Tel: 0222 488400
Robin Lyons
Formerly Siriol Animation. Producers of high quality animation for television and the cinema

Skreba Films
5a Noel Street
London W1V 3RB
Tel: 01 437 6492
Ann Skinner
Simon Relph
Produced *Return of the Soldier* and *Secret Places*, directed by Zelda Barron. Other projects include

Bad Hats, A Profile of Arthur J Mason, Honour, Profit and Pleasure and *The Gourmet*. Relph produced the Bill Douglas-directed *Comrades* and Skinner was executive producer on *Heavenly Pursuits* and produced *The Kitchen Toto* and *A Very British Coup* for Channel 4

Skyline Film and TV Productions
4 Picardy Place
Edinburgh EH1 3JT
Tel: 031 557 4580
24 Scala Street
London W1P 1LU
Tel: 01 631 4649
Steve Clark-Hall
Producers of *Years Ahead, International Volleyball, Down the Line* and *Pioneers of Socialism* for Channel 4

Span Pictures
12 St Vincent Street
London W1M 3HA
Tel: 01 487 3188
Phillip Goodhand-Tait
Steve Webber
Independent production company for TV and video. Rock and classical music, documentaries, children's programmes.
Productions include: *An Evening with Placido, The Story of Steam 1989,* and *Live On Stage* – a series of 13 rock music concerts recorded In the USA

Spectre Productions
41–45 Beak Street
London W1R 3LE
Tel: 01 439 1381
Simon Hartog
Michael Whyte
Spectre is a co-operative of nine filmmakers which also includes the Large Door production company. Productions include Stephen Dwoskin's *Further and Particular;* Philip Mullay's *The Return;* Vera Neubaver's animation series *World of Children; Mid-Air;* and *End of a Journey.* Other films include: Michael Whyte's *The Gourmet,* and Anna Ambrose's film about Handel *Honour, Profit and Pleasure* – both made in association with Skreba

Speedy Films
8 Royalty Mews
Dean Street
London W1V 5AW
Tel: 01 437 9313/494 4043
Paul Vester
Bobbie Clennell
Barry Baker
Producers of shorts *Sunbeam* and *Picnic*

Spitting Image Productions
17–19 Plumbers Row
Aldgate
London E1 1EQ
Tel: 01 375 1561

Stagescreen Productions
118 Cleveland Street
London W1P 5DN
Tel: 01 437 7525
Jeffrey Taylor
Derek Granger
Film, television and theatre company whose work includes *A Handful of Dust,* and *Death of a Son* (for BBC TV)

Robert Stigwood Organisation
118–120 Wardour Street
London W1V 4BT
Tel: 01 437 2512
David Land
David Herring
Theatre and film producer Stigwood is currently involved in the film of *Evita* and several other projects with Jerry Weintraub and the WEG group of companies

TV Cartoons
70 Charlotte Street
London W1P 1LR
Tel: 01 637 4727
John Coates
Wendy Saunders
Gail Wright
TVC produced the Academy Award-nominated film *The Snowman,* and the feature *When The Wind Blows,* both adaptations from books by Raymond Briggs. Production was completed in May 1989 of *Granpa,* a ½-hour television special for Channel 4 and TVS.
Currently in pre-production with the feature-length film – *The Adventures of Peter Rabbit* from the Beatrix Potter books

Target International Pictures
Avon House
360 Oxford Street
London W1N 9HA
Produced *The Naked Cell*, directed by John Crome.
See also under International Sales, and Distributors (Premier Releasing)

Tartan Television
35 Piccadilly
London W1V 9PB
Tel: 01 439 8985
Norrie Maclaren
Christopher Mitchell
Producing for both TV and film

Richard Taylor Cartoon Films
76 Dukes Avenue
London N10 2QA
Tel: 01 444 7547
Richard Taylor
Catherine Taylor
Currently producing a 72-minute all animation video for BBC English by Television for world wide distribution

Television History Workshop
42 Queen Square
London WC1N 3AJ
Tel: 01 405 6627
Sharon Goulds
Marilyn Wheatcroft
Greg Lanning
Productions include: *In the Club – Birth Control This Century,* a three-part series transmitted on Channel 4 in 1988. In development *Rumours from School* for Channel 4. Programmes distributed via Television History Centre (see under Distributors)

Tempest Films
33 Brookfield
Highgate West Hill
London N6 6AT
Tel: 01 340 0877
Jacky Stoller
Produced *An Affair in Mind* from the Ruth Rendell novel 'Face of Trespass' for the BBC. Also produced the five-part drama series *The Fear* for Euston Films. Projects for 1989: in production, three Dick Francis movies of the week; in development, two feature films and two drama series for the BBC

TV and Anglia TV

Third Eye Productions
Unit 210 Canalot Studios
222 Kensal Road
London W10 5BN
Tel: 01 969 8211
Geoffrey Haydon
Peter West
David Collison
TV productions covering the worlds of arts, music, ethnography and developing world culture

Timeless Films
134 Royal College Street
London NW1 6TA
Tel: 01 267 7625
Ian Emes has directed cinema shorts *French Windows, The Beard, The Oriental Nightfish, The Tent, The Magic Shop,* Paramount's Academy Award-winning *Goody Two Shoes,* his first feature for Enigma, *Knights and Emeralds, The Yob* for Channel 4, *How To Be Cool* for GTV and more recently *Streetwise* for TVS

Tiny Epic Video Co
138–140 Wardour Street
London W1V 3AU
Tel: 01 437 2854
Luke Jeans
Roger Thomas
Credits include *The Gong Show, The Business Programme, ITN News* and promos for Elton John's 'Flash' album

Trans World International
The Pier House
Strand on the Green
London W4 3NN
Tel: 01 994 1444
Eric Drossart
Buzz Hornett
Bill Sinrich
Founded in 1968.
TV sports production and rights representation branch of Mark McCormack's International Management Group. Product ranges from made-for-TV events (*Superstars, World's Strongest Man, Tennis Legends* and *Conquer the Arctic*) and sports documentaries to event highlights and live coverage. The company represents the television rights to over 70

international sports worldwide.

Transatlantic Films
100 Blythe Road
London W14 OHE
Tel: 01 727 0132
Revel Guest
Recent productions include a 13-part series, *In Search of Paradise;* a four-part series directed by Peter Greenaway, *Four American Composers; Placido – A Year in the Life of Placido Domingo;* and an eight-part series *The Horse in Sport* with Channel 4 and ABC Australia. Currently in production, a 10-part documentary series on the legacy of Ancient Greece in the modern world, *Greek Fire*

Triple Vision
11 Great Russell Street
London WC1B 3NH
Tel: 01 323 2881
Terry Flaxton
Penny Dedman
Have been producing social documentaries, drama and arts programmes since 1982 for various sponsors including Channel 4 and the BBC and for non-broadcast purposes. Recent productions include: 1988: *The Cold War Game: The USA and USSR* for Channel 4, and *The Lift* for the London Housing Unit; 1989: *Intensive Care* for Channel 4

Try Again
74 Newman Street
London W1P 3LA
Tel: 01 323 3220
Michael Darlow
Rod Taylor
Produces documentary, drama, light entertainment, arts, music

Turner Holberton Films
9–12 St Anne's Court
London W1V 3AX
Tel: 01 439 0489
Ken Turner
Glenn Holberton
Producers of TV programmes and promos

Twentieth Century Fox
31–32 Soho Square
London W1V 6AP
Tel: 01 437 7766

Twenty Twenty Television
10 Stucley Place
London NW1 8NS
Tel: 01 284 1979
Claudia Milne
Mike Whittaker
The company continues to produce programmes exclusively for broadcast television, specialising in worldwide investigative journalism, current affairs, factually-based drama and science. Recent productions include: *Turkey-Trading with Torture* and *The Copper 7 Story* for the Channel 4 series *Dispatches, Burma's Forgotten War* and *The Mormon Murders* for the BBC series *Everyman,* and a six-part series *Inside The Brotherhood* for Granada TV

Ty Gwyn Films
Y Ty Gwyn
Llanllyfni
Caernarfon
Gwynedd LL54 6DG
Tel: 0286 881235
Gareth Wynn Jones

Tyburn Productions
Pinewood Studios
Iver Heath
Bucks SL0 0NH
Tel: 0753 651700
Kevin Francis
Gillian Garrow
Long-established independent TV production company

Uden Associates
Chelsea Wharf
Lots Road
London SW10 0QJ
Tel: 01 351 1255
Adam De Wan

Umbrella Entertainment Productions
25 Denmark Street
London WC2H 8NJ
Tel: 01 379 6145
Sandy Lieberson
Formed in 1977. First production was *Jabberwocky,* and since then has produced a number of films, including *Finding Maubee* starring Denzel Washington for MGM, *Stars and Bars* starring Daniel Day Lewis and directed by Pat O'Connor

for Columbia, and *Rita, Sue and Bob Too* for Channel 4

Umbrella Films

31 Percy Street
London W1P 9FG
Tel: 01 637 1169
Simon Perry
Stacy Bell
Made Michael Radford's *Another Time, Another Place, 1984* and *White Mischief*, Richard Eyre's *Loose Connections, Nanou*, from writer-director Conny Templeman and Jana Bokova's *Hotel du Paradis*. In development is a feature to be directed by Mike Radford *Slow Train to Milan* and *The Playboys*, written by Kerry Crabbe and Shane Connaughton. Other projects also in development

Unicorn Organisation

Pottery Lane Studios
34a Pottery Lane
Holland Park
London W11 4LZ
Tel: 01 229 5131
Michael Seligman
Julian Roberts

United British Artists (UBA)

Monro House
40–42 King Street
London WC2E 8JS
Tel: 01 240 9891
Peter Shaw
Richard Johnson
Brian Morgan
Production company for cinema, and TV projects. Produced feature films *Turtle Diary* for the Samuel Goldwyn Company, *Castaway* for Cannon and *The Lonely Passion of Judith Hearne* for Handmade Films

VATV

17–19 Foley Street
London W1P 7LB
Tel: 01 636 9421
Jane Lighting
Mike Latham
Most recent productions include a two-part programme for BBC's *QED* series: *An Everyday Miracle*, a film report for *Eye Witness* on LWT, and home video *7lbs In 7 Days*. VATV

distributes for 22 independent companies, the BBC and is one of Channel 4's approved distributors

Verronmead

30 Swinton Street
London WC1X 9NX
Tel: 01 278 5523/8476
Maureen Harter
David Wood
Produced *Assert Yourself* series and *Old Man of Lochnagar*. Currently in production with TVS and Disney on *Back Home*, a TV film drama

The Video Connection

68–70 Wardour Street
London W1V 3HP
Tel: 01 734 0101
Nicholas de Rothschild
Produced a documentary *Glory of the Gardens*. Most recently has produced a film *A Vision of Paradise* for SCETV in the USA

Videotel Productions

Ramillies House
1/2 Ramillies Street
London W1V 1DF
Tel: 01 439 6301
Nick Freethy
Stephen Bond
Producers of educational and training packages for TV and video distribution including the series *Catering With Care, Working With Care, Tourism: The Welcome Business*, and the award-winning *Role and Duties of the Bellman* amongst others

Vivid

1st Floor
Centro House
Mandela Street
London NW1
Tel: 01 388 4559
Luc Roeg

Vulgar Productions

3–5 St John Street
London EC1M 4AE
Tel: 01 608 2131
Sue Hayes
Flora Gregory
Developing drama and documentary projects for Channel 4, Granada TV and the BBC

WKBC-TV

1 St Andrew's Road
London W14 9SX
Tel: 01 385 1907
George Snow
Angie Daniell
A video production company. Past productions include drama for the BFI and Channel 4, and music promos. Offer an integrated audio/video studio facility

WTTV

10 Livonia Street
London W1V 3PH
Tel: 01 439 2424
Tim Bevan
Sarah Radclyffe
Antony Root
Alison Jackson
Julia Duff
Television programmes, single drama and mini-series. A subsidiary of Working Title

Wall To Wall TV

The Elephant House
35 Hawley Crescent
London NW1 8NP
Tel: 01 485 7424
Alex Graham
Andy Lipman
Jane Root
Producers of *The Media Show* and other TV arts documentaries for Channel 4

Walnut Production Partnership

Crown House
Armley Road
Leeds LS12 2EJ
Tel: 0532 456913
Geoff Penn
Television, film and video production company

Wardour Motion Pictures

11 Wardour Mews
London W1
Tel: 01 439 4313/437 2388
Mike Sutton
Produced *A Garden For Chelsea* for BBC 2. Post-production on *California Cowboys* and *Soweto*

Warner Sisters

21 Russell Street
London WC2
Tel: 01 836 0134
Lavinia Warner
Jane Wellesley
Producer of drama and documentary

programmes, the company was founded by Warner, following the success of *Tenko* which she created. Productions include *Jailed by the British*, and award-winning *GI Brides* for Channel 4; *Lizzie – An Amazon Adventure* with the BBC; *Wish Me Luck* an eight-part drama with LWT; and currently mini-series co-production with Euston Films on the Hitler diaries scandal. In development – series of plays for Channel 4

Waterloo Films

Silver House
31–35 Beak Street
London W1R 3LD
Tel: 01 494 4060
Dennis Woolf
Ray Davies
Producer of *Return to Waterloo*, a fantasy film for Channel 4 written and directed by Ray Davies of The Kinks, which was co-financed by Channel 4 and RCA Video Productions. Other projects in development

Watershed Television

53 Queen Square
Bristol BS1 4LH
Tel: 0272 276864
Video and film production. Broadcast as well as corporate and commercials

Michael White Productions

13 Duke Street
St James's
London SW1Y 6DB
Tel: 01 839 3971
Michael White
Trade product. Film and theatre producer. Recent films include *High Season, Eat the Rich*, and *White Mischief*. In production: *Nuns on the Run*

White City Films

79 Sutton Court Road
London W4 3EQ
Tel: 01 994 6795
Aubrey Singer
Current affairs and documentary productions

David Wickes Productions

169 Queen's Gate

London SW7 5HE
Tel: 01 225 1382
David Wickes
Joanna Elferink
Produced two series of
Marlowe Private Eye, a
drama series for HBO and
LWT

Witzend Productions

3 Derby Street
Mayfair
London W1Y 7HD
Tel: 01 355 2868
Allan McKeown
Producers of comedy
programming and films
for US and UK outlets.
Projects include *Auf
Wiedersehen, Pet; Shine
on Harvey Moon; Roll
Over Beethoven; Mog* and
Girls on Top for Central
TV, and *Lovejoy* for the
BBC

Woodfilm

61a Great Titchfield
Street
London W1P 7FL
Tel: 01 631 5429
Elizabeth Wood
Producers of arts and
features programmes:
*The Pantomime Game,
The Future of Things
Past, Stairs, In Praise of
Folly, Go For It* – a series
of six half-hour
documentaries about
children with special
needs, and *By Herself –
Sophie*, a half-hour drama
for C4

Working Title

10 Livonia Street
London W1V 3PH
Tel: 01 439 2424
Sarah Radclyffe
Tim Bevan
Responsible for *My
Beautiful Laundrette,*

*Personal Services,
Caravaggio* (in
association with the BFI),
*Wish You Were Here,
Sammy and Rosie Get
Laid, Paperhouse, For
Queen and Country, The
Tall Guy* and *Diamond
Skulls*. Productions for
Channel 4 include *Tears,
Laughter, Fear and Rage;
Elphida* and *Echoes*. See
also WTTV

Works On Screen

24 Scala Street
London W1P 1LV
Tel: 01 631 4649
Sue Eatwell-Conte
Alison Joseph
Recent productions
include: *Through the
Devil's Gateway* (1989)
presented by Helen
Mirren for Channel 4.
Documentaries in
development cover the
environment, women's
issues and European
personalities

World Wide International Television

21–25 St Anne's Court
London W1V 3AW
Tel: 01 343 1121
Ray Marshall
The company's main
interest is in family
drama and children's
programmes, but it also
produces light
entertainment,
documentary and current
affairs programmes.
Recent productions
include Catherine
Cookson's *The Fifteen
Streets*, a two-hour TV
feature for Tyne Tees, and
Kappatoo, a six-part
children's series for the
ITV network. The

company also produces
Channel 4's weekly
religious magazine
programme *Not on
Sunday*

Worldmark Productions

The Old Studio
18 Middle Row
London W10 5AT
Tel: 01 960 3251
Drummond Challis
Productions include
Olympic Experience with
Charlton Heston; *Tor!
Total Football; A Fast
Drive in the Country* with
James Coburn; *That's
Incredible – Snow and
Ice;* and *Golden Moments*,
the official Olympic
highlights from Seoul. In
production: *Soccer
Sensation*, a 13-part TV
series leading into the
1990 World Cup; and *The
Official Film of the World
Cup in Rome*

Wot Music

Room 607
Linen Hall
162 Regent Street
London W1R 7FB
Tel: 01 439 8504
George Pavlou
Jay Williams
Patrick Kelly
Producers of light
entertainment
programmes and pop
promos

Yorkshire Film Co

Tong Hall
Tong
Bradford BD4 0RR
Tel: 0532 853113
Producers of satellite/
broadcast sports
documentaries, news
coverage, and corporate
and commercial work

Zed

KJP House
11 Great Marlborough
Street
London W1V 1BE
Tel: 01 494 3181
Sophie Balhetchet
Glenn Wilhide
Completed productions
for transmission in 1989
include *The Road Home*, a
feature co-production
with film Polski directed
by Jerzy Kaszubowski;
and *The Manageress*, a
major six-part drama
series directed by
Christopher King,

starring Cherie Lunghi
for Channel 4 and the
ECA. In pre-production, a
second series of *The
Manageress*

Zenith Productions

15 St George Street
London W1R 9DE
Tel: 01 499 8006
Charles Denton
Margaret Matheson
Film and TV production
subsidiary of Carlton
Communications. Recent
feature films include *The
Dead, Milk and Honey,
Soursweet, For Queen and
Country, The Wolves of
Willoughby Chase*. Recent
TV productions include
*Conspiracy: The Trial of
the Chicago 8, Closing
Ranks, Tales from the
Hollywood Hills, Fields of
Fire II* and *Inspector
Morse II*. Recent music
specials include
*Graceland: The African
Concert, Island 25,
Prince's Trust Rock Gala*
and *Terence Trent D'Arby
in Munich*

Zero One (Z1)

10 Martello Street
London E8 3PE
Tel: 01 249 8269
Mark Nash
James Swinson
Producers of various short
documentary and fiction
pieces

Zooid Pictures

63–67 Hargrave Park
London N19 5JW
Tel: 01 272 9115
Richard Philpott
Jasmine Nancholas
Founded by Philpott in
1984 after producing
feature documentary
Road Movie. Producers of
experimental and
television documentaries
such as *Spirit of Albion*
and shorts, including *The
Messiah in the Shadow of
Death, Dead Pigeon* and
Stones Off Holland. Also
produces promos and
campaign films, and
operates 'The Art of Film'
scheme, programming
and promoting new
British experimental
cinema internationally
(festivals, cinémathèques,
TV, etc). Zooid provides
specialist technical
services to independent
filmmakers

**The Canadian
Connection**

Telefilm
Canada's
London office
can put you
in touch with
the key
professionals
in Canada's
rapidly
expanding
film and
television
industry.

Phone us at
01 437 8308
for information
and advice on
· **Co-production**
· **Financing**
· **Shooting
locations**

Telefilm Canada
in London
55/59
Oxford Street
Fourth Floor
London
W1R 1RD

Telefilm Canada

MAJOR REFERENCE BOOKS

The BFI Library (see p9) currently holds some 35,000 books in many languages. Below is a selection of its general cinema and TV reference books in English. The Library produces bibliographies on specific subjects and a list of these is obtainable from the Librarian

CINEMA

ACTT Directory of Members
London: PEAR Books, 1985–86. Ed Peter Avis
Contact information, credits

Academy Awards
New York: Frederick Ungar, 1982. Compiled by Richard Shale. 2nd ed
For 1927–1977, full lists of nominations organised by category and by year. With a supplement containing a chronological listing for 1978–1981. Cross-indexed by name and title

The American Film Institute Catalog of Motion Pictures Produced in the United States
Feature Films 1911–1920
Berkeley, Ca: University of California Press, 1988. 2 vols
Feature Films 1921–1930
New York: R R Bowker, 1971. 2 vols
Feature films 1961–1970
New York: R R Bowker, 1976. 2 vols
Alphabetical listing of US features released during these decades, with credits and plot synopses. Credit and subject indices

A Biographical Dictionary of the Cinema
London: Secker & Warburg, 1975 (revised 1980). By David Thomson
Over 800 entries on directors, actors, producers. Described by its author as 'personal, opinionated and obsessive'

British Film Catalogue, 1895–1985
Newton Abbott: David & Charles, 1986. Ed Denis Gifford. 2nd ed
Basic reference work on British cinema, listing films by month and year of release. Includes footage or r/t, cast, basic technical credits and category

British Films 1927–1939
London: BFI, 1986. Ed Linda Wood
Concise survey of the period followed by annual 'in production' charts, and comprehensive statistics for the British film industry 1927–1939

British Films 1971–1981
London: BFI, 1983. Ed Linda Wood
Concise survey of the period followed by lists, with basic credits, of commercial features made and/or released in Britain between 1971 and 1981

Broadcast Production Guide 1988/89
London: International Thomson, 1988
Comprehensive directory of companies involved in film and broadcasting in Britain

Catalog of Copyright Entries: Motion Pictures, 1894–1981 (various vols)
Washington: Library of Congress
Entries give copyright date and owner, production company, sound, colour, r/t, director, writer, editor and where appropriate, author and title of original story and composer. Indices of series, authors and organisations

Cinema. A Critical Dictionary
London: Secker & Warburg, 1980. Ed Richard Roud. 2 vols
Biographical and critical entries on over 200 major filmmakers in world cinema

Directors Guild of Great Britain Directory of Members 1988/89
London: Directors Guild of Great Britain, 1988.
Type of work, credits, contact addresses

Directory of International Film and Video Festivals 1987–88
London: British Council; BFI, 1986
Film, television and video festivals, contact addresses, coverage and requirements for awards

Encore Directory 1988
Darlinghurst, NSW: Trade News Corporation, 1987
Australian directory of film, video and television companies, technicians and services

50 Golden Years of Oscar
California: ESE, 1979
The official history of the Academy Awards, with full lists of nominations and awards. Index by name and title

The Great Movie Stars: The Golden Years
London: Hamlyn, 1979. By David Shipman
Entries for 200 stars, tracing their lives and careers during the peak years of Hollywood and mentioning all their films

The Great Movie Stars: The International Years

London: Angus and Robertson, 1980. By David Shipman
Life and career entries for over 230 stars who have become known in the post-war years

The Guinness Book of Film Facts and Feats

London: Guinness Superlatives, 1985. By Patrick Robertson. 2nd ed
Illustrated compendium of facts and figures on cinema

Halliwell's Film Guide

St Albans: Granada, 1987. By Leslie Halliwell. 6th ed
Alphabetical listing of over 10,000 film titles with main credits, brief summary of plot and evaluation

Halliwell's Filmgoer's and Video Viewer's Companion

London: Granada, 1988. By Leslie Halliwell. 9th ed
Biographical dictionary with entries also on subjects and fictional characters

The Illustrated Guide to Film Directors

London: Batsford, 1983. By David Quinlan
Career studies and full filmographies for 550 directors

The Illustrated Who's Who in British Films

London: B T Batsford, 1978. By Denis Gifford
Outline biographical entries with lists of credits for 1,000 British actors and directors

The International Directory of Films and Filmmakers

London: St James Press, 1984–87. 5 vols
Dictionary of world cinema

The International Encyclopedia of Film

London: Michael Joseph, 1972. Ed Roger Manvell and others
Articles on national cinema, technical developments, genre and other topics as well as entries for individuals

The International Film Encyclopedia

London: Macmillan, 1980. By Ephraim Katz
More than 7,000 entries mainly biographical but including industry and technical processes

International Film Guide 1989

London: Tantivy Press, 1988. Ed Peter Cowie
Regular features include film books and magazines, film schools, art cinemas and festivals. Also special features and studies of directors

International Motion Picture Almanac 1988

New York: Quigley, 1987
Yearbook of the US industry, including who's who section, running index of releases from 1955, market analyses from some 50 countries, awards and top US box-office films

Kay's Database: video, film, television

London: B L Kay Publishing Co, 1987
Annual UK directory of film, video and television companies and services

Kay's International Production Manual 1987

London: B L Kay Publishing Co
International directory of film, video and television companies and technicians organised by country (and state for USA, Canada and Australia), then by activity

Kemp's International Film and Television Yearbook 1988/89

London: Kemp's Printing and Publishing Co
Information on a wide range of companies and technical services in the UK plus directory entries for the industry abroad

The Knowledge 1989

London: PA Publishing Co, 1989
Annual directory of British film and TV companies and services

The Motion Picture Guide 1927–1988

Evanston, Ill: Cinebooks, 1985 to date. 12 vols plus annual updates
A listing of 50,000 English and notable foreign film titles with credits and synopses

Movies on TV: 1988/89

New York: Bantam Books, 1987. Ed Stephen H Scheuer
Alphabetical listing, with brief notes on films available on TV in USA

New York Times Encyclopedia of Film

New York: Times Books, 1984. Ed Gene Brown. 13 vols
A collection of articles on film from the New York Times 1896–1979, arranged chronologically with an index

The Oxford Companion to Film

London: OUP, 1976. Ed Liz-Anne Bawden
3,000 entries on all aspects of world cinema

Quinlan's Illustrated Directory of Film Stars

London: B T Batsford, 1986. By David Quinlan
1,700 brief career studies of top players and full lists of credits

Reel Facts: The Movie Book of Records

London: Penguin Books, 1981. New York: Vintage Books, 1982 (revised ed). By Cobbett Steinberg
Lists of awards and prize winners, top box office films, most successful stars etc

Researcher's Guide to British Film and Television Collections

London: British Universities Film and Video Council, 1985 (revised ed). Ed Elizabeth Oliver
Combines guidance for researchers with information about collections of film, video and relevant documentation and how to access them

Researcher's Guide to British Newsreels

London: British Universities Film and Video Council, 1983. Ed James Ballantyne
Full abstracts of writing published between 1901 and 1982 provide a history of British newsreels. Additional information includes lists of newsreel company staff and details of relevant film libraries and documentation centres, their holdings and policies. vol II, 1988

Screen International Film and TV Yearbook 1988/89

London: King Publications. Ed Peter Noble
A who's who of British film and TV with directory information on cinemas, studios, companies etc, with a foreign section

Screen World 1987

London: Frederick Muller, 1987. Ed John Willis
Pictorial and statistical record of the movie season

The Studio Blu-Book: 1987 Directory
Hollywood: Hollywood Reporter, 1986
Directory of California film and TV specialist services

Variety Film Reviews 1907–1984
New York, London: Garland Publications, 1983–86. 18 vols
Chronologically arranged collection of 'Variety' film reviews, with a title index

Variety International Show Business Reference
New York, London: Garland Publications, 1983. Ed Mike Kaplan
Includes career biographies, credits for films and TV programmes released 1976–1980, major awards

Who Played Who on the Screen
London: B T Batsford, 1988. By Roy Pickard
An A–Z guide to film portrayals of famous figures of fact and fiction

Who Was Who on the Screen
New York: R R Bowker, 1983. By Evelyn Mack Truitt. 3rd ed
Biographical dictionary of over 9,000 screen personalities who died between 1905 and 1975

Who Wrote the Movie, and What Else Did He Write?
Los Angeles: Academy of Motion Picture Arts and Sciences, 1970
An index of American screenwriters and their works, 1936–1969, compiled from Academy publications

Who's Who in the Motion Picture Industry 1986/87
Hollywood: RG Publishing, 1986. Ed Rodman Gregg
A–Z of directors, producers, writers and executives with credits, addresses, agents

A Who's Who of British Film Actors
New Jersey: The Scarecrow Press, 1981. By Scott Palmer
Short career sketches with lists of films

The World Encyclopedia of the Film
London: Studio Vista, 1972. Ed John M Smith and Tim Cawkwell
Biographical entries with filmographies and a film index of 22,000 titles

TV/VIDEO

Actors' Television Credits 1950–1972
Metuchen, NJ: Scarecrow Press, 1973. Supplement 1 (1973–1976), 1978. Supplement 2 (1977–1981), 1982. Supplement 3 (1982–85), 1986. By James Robert Parish
Each name is followed by a list of titles with transmission date and US TV company

The American Vein; Directors and Directions in Television
London: Talisman Books, 1979. By Christopher Wicking and Tise Vahimagi
Critical evaluation and credits for American TV directors

BBC Annual Report and Accounts 1986/87
London: BBC, 1987
The Corporation's annual report and accounts

BBC Annual Report and Handbook 1987
London: BBC, 1987
The Corporation's annual report and accounts with details of organisation, programmes, etc

Broadcast Yearbook and Diary 1986
London: International Thomson, 1986. Ed Nick Radlo
Diary containing

information on British television industry and services

The Complete Directory of Prime Time Network TV Shows
New York: Ballantine Books, 1985. By Tim Brooks and Earle Marsh. 3rd ed
The detailed information, from 1946 to the present, includes broadcasting history, front of camera credits and descriptive and evaluative comment

Halliwell's Television Companion
London: Granada, 1986. By Leslie Halliwell with Philip Purser. 3rd ed
Revision of Halliwell's Teleguide. An A–Z of programmes and personalities in UK television with critical comment

International TV and Video Guide 1987
London: Tantivy Press, 1986. Ed Richard Paterson
The TV and video companion volume to the International Film Guide

International Television and Video Almanac 1988
New York: Quigley, 1987
Record of US television industry and its personalities. UK and World Market sections

Leonard Maltin's TV Movies and Video Guide, 1989
New York: New American Library, 1988. Ed Leonard Maltin
Brief credits and plot synopses for 15,000 films appearing on US television

Les Brown's Encyclopedia of Television
New York: Zoetrope, 1982. By Les Brown
A–Z guide to

programmes, people, history, and business of American television

Professional Video International Yearbook 1987–88
Croyden Link House, 1985
Directory of technical information for the TV and video industries

TV Facts
New York: Facts on File, 1980. By Cobbett S Steinberg
'50,000 facts about American TV.' Ratings, awards, revenues, prime-time schedules, etc

TV Feature Film Sourcebook
New York: Broadcast Information Bureau, 1988
Annual listing with supplements including all feature films and TV series currently available to American TV companies or which have already been televised. Includes brief technical and credit information with a plot synopsis and names of export and domestic sales agents

TV Guide Almanac
New York: Ballantine Books, 1980. Ed Craig T and Peter G Norback
Encyclopedia of information on television in the US

Television and Radio 1988
London: IBA, 1987
Annual IBA guide to independent broadcasting

Television Drama Series Programming: Comprehensive Chronicle 1959–1975
Metuchen, NJ: Scarecrow Press, 1978. Supplements (1975–1980), 1981. (1980–1982), 1983. By Larry James Gianakos
Provides a season by season breakdown of American TV drama series. Gives title of each episode, date of first transmission, series stars and guest stars

Who's Who on Television

London: Independent
Television Publications,
1985
Alphabetical listing of
information on over 1,000
personalities in British
television

PUBLICATIONS AVAILABLE FROM THE INTERNATIONAL FEDERATION OF FILM ARCHIVES

The International
Federation of Film
Archives (FIAF) was
founded in 1938 to
encourage the
establishment of film
archives throughout
the world. Its specialist
publications are often
the only detailed
research works
available in this field.
All the titles below can
be ordered from: FIAF,
Room 113, Canalot
Studios, 222 Kensal
Road, London
W10 5BN. (Prices
include p & p)

Bibliography of National Filmographies

Compiled by Dorothea
Gebauer. Edited by
Harriet W Harrison, 1985
80pp, £7.00

Cinema 1900–1906: An Analytical Study

Proceedings of the FIAF
Symposium at Brighton
1978. Vol I contains
transcriptions of the
papers, Vol II contains an
analytical filmography of
550 films of the period.
Prepared by the National
Film Archive, London,
1982
373pp and 392pp, £17.00

FIAF Technical Manual 1987

Loose leaf in lever arch
file £5.00

Glossary of Filmographic Terms

Compiled by Jon
Gartenberg, 1985. Lists
and defines English,
French, German, Spanish
and Russian terms
141pp, £13.00

A Handbook for Film Archives

Basic manual on the
functioning of a film
archive edited by Eileen
Bowser and John Kuiper,
1980
151pp with illustrations,
£25.00. (Also available in
French, £20.00). New
edition to be published
shortly

International Index to Film Periodicals

Published since 1972, this
indexes literature on film
in over 100 of the world's
most important film
magazines under general
subjects, film and
personalities
Available as: microfiches
cumulating 15 years,
1972–86, including
directors index at £280.
1987–88 cumulation at
£15. 1989 cumulating
microfiche service (6
despatches per year) £445
Annual published
volumes from 1974–87
(£52.00), 1988 (£56.00)

International Index to Television Periodicals

Published since 1979, this
indexes literature on
television in over 40
media journals under
general subjects,
television programmes
and personalities.
Available as: microfiches
cumulating 1979–86,
including directors index
at £75, 1987–88
cumulation at £10. 1989
cumulating microfiche
service (6 despatches per
year) at £200
Annual published
volumes cumulated as
1979–80, 1981–82
(£25.00 each), 1983–86
(£48.00)

Preservation and Restoration of Moving Images and Sound

1986. £15.00

Study on the Usage of Computers for Film Cataloguing

A survey and analysis on
the usage of computers for
the cataloguing of
material in film and
television archives.
Edited by Roger Smither,
1985
275pp, £15.00

ENGLISH LANGUAGE FILM, TV, VIDEO AND CABLE PERIODICALS

A select list of film,
television, video and
cable journals, most of
which can be studied in
the BFI Library (see
p9)

f Afterimage

(irregular)
1 Birnham Road
London N4
Each issue deals with a
specific area of film and/or
critical theory

American Cinematographer

(monthly)
ASC Holding Corporation
PO Box 2230
Hollywood
California 90028
USA
International journal of
film and video production
techniques. Published by
the American Society of
Cinematographers

American Film

(10 pa)
Membership Services
PO Box 2046
Marion OH 43305
USA
Journal of the AFI. A
magazine of the Film and
Television Arts

Animator (quarterly)

13 Ringway Road
Park Street
St Albans
Herts AL2 2RE
Intended for all levels of
animators and animation
fans

Ariel (weekly)

BBC
Room G1
12 Cavendish Place
London W1A 1AA
The BBC staff magazine.
Contains articles of
general interest about the
BBC

Audio Visual

(monthly)
PO Box 109
Maclaren House
Scarbrook Road
Croydon
Surrey CR9 1QH
Tel: 01 688 7788
Aimed at management
and businesses which use
audio-visual materials

Audiovisual Librarian (quarterly)

Library Association
Publishing
7 Ridgmount Street
London WC1E 7AE
Tel: 01 636 7543
The official organ of the
audio-visual groups
Aslib and the LA.
Includes articles, book
reviews and a
bibliographic update

Australian Journal of Screen Theory

(irregular)
Department of Drama
University of New South
Wales
PO Box 1
Kensington
NSW 2033
Australia
Scholarly articles on film
studies

BBC Record (2 or 3 pa)

Printed Documents BBC
Broadcasting House
London W1A 1AA
Tel: 01 580 4468
News-sheet on major
BBC events and policy

BETA News

(irregular)
Broadcasting and
Entertainment Trades
Alliance
181–185 Wardour Street
London W1V 3AA
Tel: 01 439 7585
The official journal of the
Broadcasting and
Entertainment Trades
Alliance

BUFVC Newsletter

(3 pa)
British Universities Film

and Video Council
55 Greek Street
London W1V 5LR
Tel: 01 734 3687
News and reviews of new
productions available to
workers in higher
education, articles on, for
example, storing and
handling videotape.
Includes some book
reviews

 **British National
Film and Video
Catalogue** (quarterly)
British Film Institute
21 Stephen Street
London W1P 1PL
Tel: 01 255 1444
Details of films and
videocassettes made
available for non-
theatrical use in the UK,
classified by subject.
Cumulates annually

Broadcast (weekly)
International Thomson
Publishing
23–29 Emerald Street
London WC1N 3QJ
Television industry news
magazine. Regular
sections devoted to video,
cable and industry news.
Now incorporates
Television Weekly

Broadcasting
(weekly)
Broadcasting
Publications Inc
1735 DeSales Street
NW Washington DC
20036
USA
America's main
broadcasting trade
weekly

Bulgarian Films
(8 pa)
Bulgarian
Cinematography State
Corporation
96 Rakovski Street
Sofia
Bulgaria
News of the Bulgarian
cinema in English

**Bulletin of the
Royal Television
Society** (monthly)
Royal Television Society
Tavistock House East
Tavistock Square
London WC1H 9HR
Tel: 01 387 1970
Bulletin of RTS events

and members, with
relevant television
industry news items

**The Business of
Film** (monthly)
4 Conduit Street
London W1R 9TG
Tel: 01 499 9933/491 3777
Aimed at film industry
professionals –
producers, distributors,
exhibitors, investors,
financiers

**Cable and Satellite
Europe** (monthly)
533 Kings Road
London SW10 0BR
Journal covering the
European cable and
satellite industry

Cineaste (quarterly)
419 Park Avenue South
New York NY 10016
USA
Reviews, interviews,
articles on the art and
politics of cinema.
International in scope

Cinema Papers (6 pa)
644 Victoria Street
North Melbourne 3051
Australia
Australia's leading film
journal

Combroad (quarterly)
Commonwealth
Broadcasting Association
Broadcasting House
London W1A 1AA
Tel: 01 580 4468
Articles on
Commonwealth
television, radio and
broadcasting in general

**Communication
Research
Trends** (quarterly)
Centre for the Study of
Communication and
Culture
221 Goldhurst Terrace
London NW6 3EP
Tel: 01 637 9005
Information on
international
communications research

Czechoslovak Film
(quarterly)
Czechoslovak Filmexport
Press Department
Praha 1
Vaclavske Namesti '28
Czechoslovakia
News from the Czech
cinema in English

Direct (8 pa)
Directors' Guild of Great
Britain
Lyndhurst Hall
Lyndhurst Road
London NW3 5NG
Tel: 01 431 1800
Journal of Directors'
Guild of Great Britain

EMMY (6 pa)
4605 Lankershim
Boulevard
North Hollywood
CA 91602
USA
Published by the
Academy of Television
Arts and Sciences

Encore (fortnightly)
1st Floor
41a The Corso
Manly
NSW 2095
Australia
Entertainments
magazine now
incorporating The
Australian Film Review

 Film (monthly)
British Federation of
Film Societies
Film Society Unit
BFI
21 Stephen Street
London W1P 1PL
Tel: 01 255 1444
Non-commercial
aspects of film. See also
p14

**Film and Television
Technician** (monthly)
ACTT
111 Wardour Street
London W1V 4AY
Tel: 01 437 8506
ACTT members' journal

Film Comment
(bi-monthly)
140 West 65th Street
New York
NY 10023
USA
Published by the Film
Society of Lincoln Center.
Aimed at intelligent
American filmgoers

Film Dope
(irregular)
40 Willifield Way
London NW11 7XT
Mainly an A–Z of
international film
personalities but also
includes some long
interviews

Film Monthly
1 Golden Square
London W1R 3AB
Tel: 01 437 0626
Film-fan magazine
incorporating Photoplay

Film Quarterly
University of California
Berkeley
California 94720
USA
International critical
journal with particular
emphasis on film
literature and book
reviews

Film Reader
(irregular)
Film Division
Northwestern University
1905 Sheridan Road
Evanston
Illinois 60201
USA
Substantial journal of
film and cultural studies

Film Review
(monthly)
Spotlight Publications
Greater London House
Hampstead Road
London NW1 7QZ
Tel: 01 387 6611
All English-speaking
films on release and in
production covered in
reviews, interviews,
articles and pictures, book
and record reviews

Films and Filming
(monthly)
Subscription Department
Cloister Court
22–26 Farringdon Lane
London EC1R 3AU
Tel: 01 253 3135
Reviews of films on
cinema screen and video:
articles, interviews, book
reviews

Films in Review
(10 pa)
PO Box 589
Lennox Hill Station
New York NY 10021
USA
Popular magazine aimed
at 'film buffs'. Notable for
career articles and
historical information

Framework
(irregular)
Comedia
9 Poland Street
London W1V 3DG
Tel: 01 439 2059

Historical Journal of Film, Radio and Television

(bi-annual)
Carfax Publishing
PO Box 25
Abingdon
Oxfordshire OX14 1RW
Academic journal founded
by IAMHIST in 1981.
Articles, book reviews,
archival reports and
reviews of film, television
and radio programmes of
historical or educational
importance

The Hollywood Reporter (daily)

6715 Sunset Boulevard
Hollywood
California 90028
USA
International
showbusiness trade paper

Hungarofilm Bulletin (5 pa)

Bathori utca 10
Budapest V
Hungary
News on Hungarian films
and filmmakers in
English

IPPA Bulletin

(irregular)
Independent Programme
Producers Association
3 Fitzroy Square
London W1P 5AH
Tel: 01 388 1234
The journal of the
Independent Programme
Producers Association

Independent Media

(monthly)
The Media Centre
South Hill Park
Bracknell
Berks RG12 4PA
Tel: 0344 427272
A broadsheet designed for
those working outside the
broadcast or mainstream
video production
industries. Mixture of
news and information and
articles on cable, Channel
4 and so on

Intermedia

(bi-monthly)
International Institute of
Communications
Tavistock House South
Tavistock Square
London WC1H 9LF
Tel: 01 388 0671
Articles on international
communications and
broadcasting

International Broadcasting Systems and Operation (monthly)

3–5 St John Street
London EC1 4AE
Tel: 01 253 7174
Articles, news and other
information on mainly
technical and engineering
topics

International Media Law (monthly)

21–27 Lamb's Conduit
Street
London WC1N 3NJ
A monthly bulletin on
rights clearances and
legal practice. Includes a
regular update section

Journal of Broadcasting

(quarterly)
Broadcast Education
Association
1771 N Street
NW Washington DC
20036
USA
Articles on current
research mainly in the
US; book reviews

Journal of Communication

(quarterly)
PO Box 13358
Philadelphia PA 19101
USA
Published by the
Annenberg School of
Communications.
Theoretical and research
articles and book reviews

Journal of Film and Video (quarterly)

Division of Mass
Communication
Emerson College
100 Beacon Street
Boston MA 02116
USA
Articles on current
academic research in film
and television, as well as
film and video practices,
book reviews, video and
film reviews

The Journal of Media Law and Practice (3 pa)

Frank Cass
11 Gainsborough Road
London E11 1RS
Tel: 01 530 4226
Covers media law
relating to copyright and

video recording. Includes
articles, news and book
reviews

The Journal of Popular Film and Television (quarterly)

Popular Culture Center
Bowling Green State
University
Bowling Green
Ohio 43403
USA
Dedicated to popular film
and television in the
broadest sense.
Concentration on
commercial cinema and
TV

Jump Cut (quarterly)

PO Box 865
Berkeley
California 94701
USA
Radical critical journal
with a special interest in
politics of cinema

Kino (irregular)

Dina Lom
German Film Board
113–117 Wardour Street
London W1V 3TB
Tel: 01 439 9129
Official publication in
English on the West
German cinema

The Listener (weekly)

BBC Publications
35 Marylebone High
Street
London W1M 4AA
Tel: 01 580 4468/5577
Reviews, discussion and
transcripts of BBC
television and radio
programmes

Making Better Movies (monthly)

Henry Greenwood and
Company
28 Great James Street
London WC1N 3NL
Tel: 01 404 4202
Amateur cine and video
monthly incorporating
'Movie Maker'

Media, Culture and Society

(quarterly)
Sage Publications
28 Banner Street
London EC1Y 8QE
Articles on the mass
media in their political,
cultural and historical
contexts

Media Report to Women (bi-monthly)

3306 Ross Place
NW Washington DC
20008
USA
Published by the
Women's Institute for
Freedom of the Press, this
journal deals with what
women are thinking and
doing to change the
communications media

Monthly Film Bulletin

(monthly)
British Film Institute
21 Stephen Street
London W1P 1PL
Tel: 01 255 1444
Full credits, synopses and
reviews of all UK
theatrical releases, and
some video releases, along
with articles and
interviews. See also p10

Movie (irregular)

2a Roman Way
London N7 8XG
Tel: 01 609 4019/4010
Journal of theory and
criticism with special
emphasis on American
cinema

Movie Scene

(monthly)
Robud Productions
61 Woodmere Avenue
Shirley
Croydon
Surrey
Tel: 01 654 2791
Popular journal dealing
mainly with current
cinema. Includes pictorial
reviews and previews

Moviegoer (monthly)

13–30 Corporation
505 Market Street
Knoxville
Tenn 37902
USA
Illustrated feature film
magazine for the popular
market

On Air/Off Air

(bi-monthly)
The Volunteer Centre
29 Lower King's Road
Berkhamsted
Herts HP4 2AB
Tel: 04427 73311
The magazine of the
Media Project at the
Volunteer Centre, giving
news about nationwide
projects, for example,
community broadcasting

Onfilm (bi-monthly)
PO Box 6374
Wellington
New Zealand
The magazine of the NZ
picture industry

Picture House
(irregular)
123b Central Road
Worcester Park
Surrey KT4 8DU
The magazine of the
Cinema Theatre
Association, presenting
historical articles on
cinema buildings,
circuits, architects and
so on

Post Script (3 pa)
Jacksonville University
2800 University
Boulevard N
Jacksonville FL 32211
USA
Journal of essays in film
and the humanities

Primetime
(quarterly)
Wider TV Access
11 Grape Street
London WC2
Primetime is published by
WTVA, a society devoted
to the wider circulation of,
and discussion about, old
TV programmes, with
reviews of TV material
available on video

Producer (monthly)
Association of
Independent Producers
17 Great Pulteney Street
London W1
Tel: 01 434 0181
The journal of the
Association of
Independent Producers

**Quarterly Review
of Film Studies**
Redgrave Publishing
Company
PO Box 67
South Salem
New York NY 10590
USA
Academic journal dealing
with cinema in context of
larger aesthetic or
sociopolitical issues

Radio Times (weekly)
BBC
35 Marylebone High
Street
London W1M 4AA
Tel: 01 580 5577
Guide to BBC
programmes

Screen
(quarterly)
(incorporating Screen
Education)
29 Old Compton Street
London W1V 5PL
Tel: 01 734 5455
Journal of the Society for
Education in Film and
Television. Aimed at
teachers/lecturers in film
theory

Screen (weekly)
Express Towers
Nariman Point
Bombay 400 021
India
Trade journal

Screen Digest
(monthly)
37 Gower Street
London WC1E 6HH
Tel: 01 580 2842
An industry news digest
covering film, TV, cable,
satellite, video and other
multimedia
presentations. Has a
centre page reference
section every month on
subjects like law,
statistics or sales

Screen Finance
Financial Times Business
Information
Tower House
Southampton Street
London WC2E 7HA
Tel: 01 240 9391
International financial
news for the film and
television industry

**Screen
International**
(weekly)
King Publications
6–7 Great Chapel Street
London W1
Tel: 01 734 9452
Cinema industry
magazine mainly focussed
on the cinema, with a
regular section which has
industry news and
information about
upcoming productions for
TV and video

**Sight and
Sound** (quarterly)
British Film Institute
21 Stephen Street
London W1P 1PL
Tel: 01 255 1444
International critical
journal of film and
television now in its 55th
year. See also p10

Soviet Film (monthly)
9b Gnezdnikovsky
Pereulok
Moscow 103009
USSR
News in English of Soviet
films and filmmakers

**Stage and
Television Today,
The** (weekly)
47 Bermondsey Street
London SE1 3XT
Tel: 01 403 1818
'Television Today'
constitutes the middle
section of 'The Stage' and
is a weekly trade paper

TV Times (weekly)
Independent Television
Publications
247 Tottenham Court
Road
London W1P 0AU
Tel: 01 636 3666
Guide to ITV and
Channel 4 TV
programmes

TV World (monthly)
27 Wilfred Street
London SW1E 6PR
Tel: 01 828 6107

Television
(bi-monthly)
The Royal Television
Society
Tavistock House East
Tavistock Square
London WC1H 9HR
Tel: 01 387 1970
Articles on the television
industry, technical and
general

Television Week
Reader Applications
EMAP Maclaren Group II
PO Box 109
Croydon CR9 9ET
News magazine for the
television industry

Televisual (monthly)
The Communications
60 Kingly Street
London W1R 5LH
Glossy publication aimed
at the industrial and
business user of video.
Features, details of shows
and exhibitions, a
hardware catalogue and
new programmes of
interest to the industrial
user

Trade Guide (weekly)
Monek Chambers
Lamington Road
Bombay 400 004
India
Trade journal

Variety (weekly)
154 West 46th Street
New York
NY 10036
USA
The American showbiz
journal including
worldwide coverage of
cinema and other media

**The Velvet Light
Trap** (irregular)
PO Box 9240
Madison
Wisconsin 53715
USA
Critical journal in which
each issue addresses a
particular aspect of film
theory or culture

Video (monthly)
Box 118
Dover
NY 07801
USA
Home video magazine
with reviews of new
releases and equipment

Video Business
(weekly)
Record Business
Publications
Hyde House
13 Langley Street
London WC2H 9JG
Tel: 01 836 9311
A dealers' magazine
concerned mostly with
software and distribution.
Lists Top 40s for rental
and sales, news items, a
features and a software
suppliers' directory

Video Review
(monthly)
PO Box 919
Farmingdale
New York 11737
USA
Consumer orientated
home video magazine
with sections on computer
software, tape and disc
reviews, video tests of
new hardware and
articles

Video Today
(monthly)
Argus Specialist Press
1 Golden Square
London W1R 3AB
Tel: 01 437 0626
Consumer-orientated
magazine with short
reviews of new releases. It
also includes readers'
problems, hardware tests,
articles, with information
on London and regional
dealers

Video Trade Weekly
20 Bowling Green Lane
London EC1R 0BD
Weekly newspaper aimed at the retail trade, with news about the distribution industry, new products, festivals, awards and so on

Views (quarterly)
79 Wardour Street
London W1V 3PH
Magazine of the Independent Film, Video and Photography Association

Wide Angle
(irregular)
Ohio University Press
Box 388
Athens
Ohio 45701
USA
Academic journal with each issue concentrating on a single aspect of film culture

Zerb (2 pa)
The Guild of TV Cameramen
c/o Andy Hall
St Anne's House
Hessenford
Torpoint
Cornwall PL11 3HR
Tel: 05034 668
The journal for the Guild of TV Cameramen

FOREIGN LANGUAGE FILM PERIODICALS

L'Avant-Scène Cinéma (monthly)
16 rue des Quatre Vents
75006 Paris
France
Articles, reviews, interviews, often complete scripts

Bianco e Nero
(quarterly)
Via Tuscolana 1524
00173 Roma
Italy
The leading Italian critical journal. Film and book reviews. articles

Cahiers de la Cinémathèque
(irregular)
Palais des Congrés
66000 Perpignan
France
Published with the Cinémathèque de Toulouse. Each issue treats one subject

Cahiers du Cinéma
(monthly)
9 Passage de la Boule Blanche
75012 Paris
France
Leading critical journal with a special interest in US cinema

Chaplin (bi-monthly)
Filmhuset
Box 27 126
102 52 Stockholm
Sweden
Journal of the Swedish Film Institute

Cine Cubano
(irregular)
Calle 23 no 1155
Havana
Cuba
Critical journal mainly concerned with the Latin-American cinema

Cineinforme
(bi-monthly)
Gran Via 62–90–1
Madrid 13
Spain
Trade magazine on Spanish and Latin-American cinema

Cinema e Cinema
(quarterly)
Matsilio Editori
Fondamenta S Chiara
Santa Croce 518/A
Venezia 30125
Italy
Critical journal with a special interest in Italian cinema

Cinema Novo
(irregular)
Rua de Cedofeito 455–4
Sala 40
Porto
Portugal
Magazine aimed at Portuguese film buffs

Cinema Nuovo
(bi-monthly)
Casello Postale 362
70100 Bari
Italy
Serious critical journal – features many book reviews

Cinéma 88/89
(weekly)
49 rue Faubourg
Poissonniere
75009 Paris
France
This journal, previously monthly, is now published weekly and in tabloid form. Reviews of current releases in France, articles, interviews, book reviews are included plus a section on films on television

Cinématographe
(bi-monthly)
14 rue du Cherch-Midi
75006 Paris
France
International review aimed at the serious French filmgoer

Film (monthly)
Friedrichstrasse 2–6
6000 Frankfurt 17
West Germany
Authoritative film journal featuring articles and criticism

Film a Doba (monthly)
Václavské nam 43
Praha 1
Czechoslovakia
International film journal with emphasis on eastern European cinema

Film Echange
(quarterly)
50 avenue Marceau
75008 Paris
France
Substantial journal of information on international law, economics and sociology of the audio-visual media

Film Echo/Film Woche (72 pa)
Wilhelmstrasse 42
6200 Wiesbaden
West Germany
West German trade magazine

Film Français
(weekly)
90 rue de Flandre
75943 Paris
France
Trade paper for French cinema professionals. Includes video information

Filmowy Serwis Prasowy (2 per month)
ul Mazawiecka 6/8
00–950 Warszawa
Poland
Official journal of Polish film contains information on films and filmmakers

Frauen und Film
(irregular)
Verlag Stoemfeld/Roter Stern
Postfach 180147
6000 Frankfurt am Main
West Germany
Concentrates on German and foreign issues concerning women and film

Iskusstvo Kino
(monthly)
Moscou Smalenskaja – Sennaja
32/34 V/O
Mezadunarodnaja Kniga
USSR
Leading Soviet journal concentrating on national cinema with credits

Kosmorama
(quarterly)
Det Danske Filmmuseum
Store Søndervoldstraede
1419 København K
Denmark
Leading Danish periodical containing essays, credits and film and book reviews

Positif (monthly)
Nouvelles Editions Opta
1 Quai Conti
75006 Paris
France
International critical journal with wide festival coverage

Revue du Cinéma/ Image et Son
(monthly)
3 rue Recamier
75341 Paris 07
France
Reviews of films, television and video. Aimed at cine-club audience

Skoop (10 pa)
Postbus 18277
1001 2D Amsterdam
Netherlands

1988 PERIODICALS

The following journals were added to the BFI Library collection during 1988

Black Film Review (USA)
Blimp (Austria)
Bulletin of the British Vintage Wireless Association (GB)
CNCL Lettre d'Information (France)
Cine-Bulletin (Switzerland)
Continuum (Australia)
Dia Logas de la Communication (Peru)
Filmograf (Yugoslavia)
Free Press (GB)
National Cable Guide (GB)
Nouvel Observateur (USA)
Screen Finance (GB)
Talkback (GB)
Television Week (GB)
Yorkshire Television News (GB)

INDEXES TO FILM AND TV PERIODICALS

BFI Library Services (see p9) maintains three indexes to articles and information published in periodicals – indexes to film and TV programme titles (including information about the individual titles), to personalities and to other subjects. Eventually this information will be available on-line. In the meantime it can be purchased on roll microfilm from World Microfilms Ltd, 62 Queen's Grove, London NW8 6ER.

Unique in the extent of its coverage, the indexing is a much-prized resource; inevitably though it is not complete. Some periodicals are not indexed, others not indexed fully.

Listed below is a selection of publications, held by BFI Library Services, which usefully complements its periodical indexes

The Critical Index: A Bibliography of Articles on Film in English, 1946–1973
By John C Gerlach and Lana Gerlach. New York; London: Teachers College Press, 1974

The Film Index: A Bibliography
Vol 1 The Film as Art: compiled by Workers of the Writers' Program of the Work Projects Administration in the City of New York. New York: Museum of Modern Art Film Library; HW Wilson, 1941. Vol 2 The Film as Industry. White Plains, NY: Kraus, 1985.

The Film Literature Index
Quarterly Author-Subject Periodical Index to the International Literature of Film 1973 to date. Albany, NY; Filmdex, 1975 to date. Quarterly issues with annual cumulations

Index to Critical Film Reviews in British and American Film Periodicals
Compiled by Stephen E Bowles. New York: Burt Franklin, 1974

Index to Motion Pictures Reviewed by Variety, 1907–1980
By Max Joseph Alvarez. Metuchen, NJ; London: Scarecrow Press, 1982

International Index to Film Periodicals 1972 to date
International Index to Television Periodicals 1979 to date
These annotated guides are published as monthly cumulative microfiche and annual volumes. Over 100 journals from over 20 countries are indexed to include general subjects, reviews and personalities together with author and director indexes. London: International Federation of Film Archives

Motion Picture Directors: A Bibliography of Magazine and Periodical Articles, 1900–1972
Compiled by Mel Schuster. Metuchen, NJ: Scarecrow Press, 1973

Motion Picture Performers: A Bibliography of Magazine and Periodical Articles, 1900–1969
Compiled by Mel Schuster. Metuchen, NJ: Scarecrow Press, 1973. Supplement 1 (1970–74), 1976

The New Film Index: A Bibliography of Magazine Articles in English, 1930–1970
By Richard Dyer MacCann and Edward S Perry. New York: EP Dutton, 1975

Performing Arts Biography Master Index
Ed Barbara McNeil and Miranda C Herbert. 2nd ed Detroit: Gale Research Co, 1981

Retrospective Index to Film Periodicals 1930–1971
By Linda Batty. New York; London: RR Bowker, 1975

 – BFI publications

 – Supported by the BFI

INTERNATIONAL VISUAL COMMUNICATIONS ASSOCIATION

THE PROFESSIONAL ASSOCIATION
FOR VISUAL COMMUNICATIONS

Royal Patron: HRH Duke of Gloucester · *Honorary President:* Sir Terence Beckett KBE

IVCA is the professional association representing the interests and needs of the visual communications user or supplier. In particular, the Association represents those organisations involved in the non-broadcast commissioned film, video and av market. The Association strives to advance the standing and recognition of the industry and its practitioners, and markets visual communications to potential users.

IVCA is a non-profit making Association and is the only British association whose membership and interests span film, video, live events and audio-visual communications. The Association offers a professional network, information and advice services, special interest groups, insurance and other membership services, a monthly magazine, national and regional events and produces publications on a wide range of subjects. The Association also organises the UK's premier film and video communications festival and a residential Convention.

MEMBERS OF THE IVCA INCLUDE:

■ Production companies providing programmes to meet a wide range of applications

■ Businesses and organisations using or commissioning film, video and av programmes to enhance their communications activities

■ Suppliers of facilities to the production industry

■ In-house production units in both the corporate and institutional sectors

■ Suppliers of hardware to the production and visual communications industry

■ Live Event and Multi-Image suppliers

■ Companies providing miscellaneous services to the production and visual communications industry

■ Freelance individuals and sole traders servicing the production and visual communications industry

■ Companies and institutions who need to be kept informed about activities and developments within the visual communications industry

■ Students in recognised full or part-time courses

For a membership prospectus and application form, please contact

THE MEMBERSHIP SECRETARY
IVCA · BOLSOVER HOUSE · 5/6 CLIPSTONE STREET · LONDON W1P 7EB
Tel 01-580 0962 · Fax 01-436 2606

Listed here are films of 40 minutes and over, both British and foreign, which had a theatrical release in the UK during 1988 and the first quarter of 1989. Entries quote the Monthly Film Bulletin reference. Back issues of MFB are available for reference from BFI Library Services

Above the Law see **Nico**

Accused, The (18) USA Dir Jonathan Kaplan with Kelly McGillis, Jodie Foster, Bernie Coulson. UIP. 111 mins. MFB Feb 1989 p35

Action Jackson (18) USA Dir Craig R Baxley with Carl Weathers, Craig T Nelson, Vanity. Guild. 96 mins. MFB Aug 1988 p225

Adventures in Babysitting see **Night on the Town, A**

Adventures of Baron Munchausen, The (PG) UK/W Germany Dir Terry Gilliam with John Neville, Sarah Polley, Eric Idle. Columbia-Tri-Star. 126 mins. MFB March 1989 p71

Alice (Neco z Alenky) (PG) Switzerland Dir Jan Švankmajer with Kristyna Kohoutova, Camilla Power. Animation combined with live action. ICA Projects. 85 mins. MFB Nov 1988 p319

Allan Quatermain and the Lost City of Gold (PG) USA Dir Gary Nelson with Richard Chamberlain, Sharon Stone, James Earl Jones. Cannon. 99 mins. MFB June 1988 p164

Amazing Grace and Chuck see **Silent Voice**

Amazing Stories (15) USA Dirs Steven Spielberg, William Dear,

The Accused

Bagdad Cafe

Robert Zemeckis with Kevin Costner, Christopher Lloyd, Kiefer Sutherland. UIP. 110 mins. MFB Jan 1988 p11

Ami de mon amie, L' (My Girlfriend's Boyfriend) (PG) France Dir Eric Rohmer with Emmanuelle Chaulet, Sophie Renoir, Anne-Laure Meury. Artificial Eye. 103 mins. Subtitles. MFB July 1988 p198

And God Created Woman (18) USA Dir Roger Vadim with Rebecca De Mornay, Vincent Spano, Frank Langella. Vestron. 98 mins. MFB Sept 1988 p263

Angel Dust see **Poussière d'ange**

Anna (15) USA Dir Yurek Bogayevicz with Sally Kirkland, Robert Fields, Paulina Porizkova. Vestron. 100 mins. MFB Aug 1988 p226

Appointment With Death (PG) USA Dir Michael Winner with Peter Ustinov, Lauren Bacall, Carrie Fisher. Cannon. 102 mins. MFB May 1988 p135

April Fool's Day (18) USA Dir Fred Walton with Deborah Foreman, Deborah Goodrich, Griffin O'Neal. UIP. 89 mins. MFB May 1988 p135

Arthur 2: On the Rocks (PG) USA Dir Bud Yorkin with Dudley Moore, Liza Minnelli, John Gielgud. Warner Bros. 113 mins. MFB March 1989 p72

Astérix chez les Brétons (Asterix in Britain) (U) France Dir Pino Van Lamsweerde. Palace Pictures. 89 mins. English version. MFB April 1988 p103

Au revoir les enfants (PG) France/W Germany Dir Louis Malle with Gaspard Manesse, Raphael Fejtö, Francine Racette. Curzon. 104 mins. Subtitles. MFB Oct 1988 p296

Babette's Feast see **Babettes Gaestebud**

Babettes Gaestebud (Babette's Feast) (U) Denmark Dir Gabriel Axel with Stéphane Audran, Jean-Philippe Lafont, Bibi Andersson. Artificial Eye. 103 mins. Subtitles. MFB March 1988 p74

Baby Boom (PG) USA Dir Charles Shyer with Diane Keaton, Harold Ramis, Sam Shepard. UIP. 111 mins. MFB March 1988 p71

Backfire (18) USA Dir Gilbert Cates with Karen Allen, Keith Carradine, Jeff Fahey. Virgin. 91 mins. MFB Oct 1988 p297

Backlash Australia Dir Bill Bennett with David Argue, Gia Carides, Lydia Miller. Blue Dolphin. 90 mins. MFB Oct 1988 p298

Bagdad Café (Out of Rosenheim) (PG) W Germany Dir Percy Adlon with Marianne Sägebrecht, C C H Pounder, Jack Palance. Mainline. 91 mins. Filmed in English. MFB Oct 1988 p307

Barfly (18) USA Dir Barbet Schroeder with Mickey Rourke, Faye Dunaway, Alice Krige. Cannon Releasing. 100 mins. MFB March 1988 p75

BAT 21 (15) USA Dir Peter Markle with Gene Hackman, Danny Glover, Jerry Reed. Guild. 105 mins. MFB Dec 1988 p357

*batteries not included (PG) USA Dir Matthew Robbins with Hume Cronyn, Jessica Tandy, Frank McRae. UIP. 106 mins. MFB April 1988 p104

Bedroom Window, The (15) USA Dir Curtis Hanson with Elizabeth McGovern, Steve Guttenberg, Isabelle Huppert. UKFD (20th Century Fox). 113 mins. MFB Dec 1988 p357

Bee Keeper, The see **Melissokomos, O**

Beetlejuice (15) USA Dir Tim Burton with Alec Baldwin, Geena Davis, Michael Keaton. Warner Bros. 92 mins. MFB Aug 1988 p227

Believers, The (18) USA Dir John Schlesinger with Martin Sheen, Helen Shaver, Harley Cross. Rank. 114 mins. MFB April 1988 p105

Bernadette (U) France Dir Jean Delannoy with Sydney Penny, Jean-Marc Bory, Jean-Marie Bernicat. Cannon. 119 mins. Subtitles. MFB May 1988 p136

Bez Końca (No End) (18) Poland Dir Krzysztof Kieslowski with Grażyna Szapolowska, Maria Pakulnis, Aleksander Bardini. Artificial Eye. 107 mins. Subtitles. MFB March 1988 p76

Big (PG) USA Dir Penny Marshall with Tom Hanks, Elizabeth Perkins, Robert Loggia. 20th Century Fox. 104 mins. MFB Oct 1988 p298

Big

209

The Big Blue

Big Blue, The (15)
USA/France Dir Luc
Besson with Rosanna
Arquette, Jean-Marc
Barr, Jean Reno. 20th
Century Fox. 119 mins.
MFB March 1989 p73

Big Business (PG)
USA Dir Jim Abrahams
with Bette Midler, Lily
Tomlin, Fred Ward.
Warner Bros. 98 mins.
MFB Sept 1988 p264

Big Parade, The see
Da Yuebing

Big Time (PG) USA Dir
Chris Blum with Tom
Waits. Recorded
Releasing. 87 mins. MFB
Nov 1988 p324

Biloxi Blues (15) USA
Dir Mike Nichols with
Matthew Broderick,
Christopher Walken,
Matt Mulhern. UIP. 107
mins. MFB Sept 1988
p256

Bird (15) USA Dir Clint
Eastwood with Forest
Whitaker, Diane Venora,
Michael Zelniker. Warner
Bros. 160 mins. MFB Nov
1988 p325

Black Eagle (15) USA
Dir Eric Karson with Sho
Kosugi, Jean-Claude Van
Damme, Doran Clark.
VPD/Winstone. 104 mins.
MFB Dec 1988 p358

Bloodsport (18) USA
Dir Newt Arnold with
Jean-Claude Van
Damme, Donald Gibb,
Leah Ayres. Cannon. 92
mins. MFB Aug 1988
p228

Blue Jean Cop (18)
USA Dir James
Glickenhaus with Peter
Weller, Sam Elliott,
Patricia Charbonneau.
Rank. 96 mins. MFB Dec
1988 p359

Bohème, La (U)
France/Italy Dir Luigi
Comencini with Barbara
Hendricks, José Carreras,
Luca Canonici. Electric
Pictures. Subtitles. 107
mins. MFB Jan 1989 p11

**Braddock: Missing
in Action III** (18) USA
Dir Aaron Norris with
Chuck Norris, Aki
Aleong, Roland Harrah
III. Cannon. 103 mins.
MFB Sept 1988 p265

Brain Damage (18)
USA Dir Frank
Henenlotter with Rick
Herbst, Gordon
MacDonald, Jennifer
Lowry. Palace Pictures.
85 mins. MFB April 1988
p106

**Bright Lights, Big
City** (18) USA Dir James
Bridges with Michael J
Fox, Kiefer Sutherland,
Phoebe Cates. UIP. 107
mins. MFB June 1988
p165

Broadcast News (15)
USA Dir James L Brooks
with William Hurt,
Albert Brooks, Holly
Hunter. UKFD (20th
Century Fox). 132 mins.
MFB April 1988 p107

Bulletproof (15) USA
Dir Steve Carver with
Gary Busey, Darlanne
Fluegel, Henry Silva.
Virgin. 94 mins. MFB Jan
1988 p12

Buster (15) GB Dir
David Green with Phil
Collins, Julie Walters,
Larry Lamb. Vestron. 102
mins. MFB Sept 1988
p266

Call Me (18) USA Dir
Sollace Mitchell with
Patricia Charbonneau,
Stephen McHattie, Boyd
Gaines. Vestron. 93 mins.
MFB Dec 1988 p360

Cameron's Closet
(18) USA Dir Armand
Mastroianni with Cotter
Smith, Mel Harris, Scott
Curtis. Medusa. 87 mins.
MFB Jan 1989 p12

Can't Buy Me Love
(PG) USA Dir Steve Rash
with Patrick Dempsey,
Amanda Peterson,
Courtney Gains. Warner
Bros. 93 mins. MFB June
1988 p166

**Cane Toads – An
Unnatural History**
Australia Dir Mark
Lewis. Ritzy Distribution.
46 mins. 16mm. MFB Dec
1988 p361

**Care Bears
Adventure in
Wonderland, The**
(U) Canada Dir Raymond
Jafelice. Virgin/UKFD
(20th Century Fox). 75
mins. MFB April 1988
p108

China Girl (18) USA
Dir Abel Ferrara with
James Russo, Richard
Panebianco, Sari Chang.
Vestron. 90 mins. MFB
Jan 1988 p12

**Chinese Ghost
Story, A** see *Qian Nü
Youhun*

**Chuck Berry Hail!
Hail! Rock 'n' Roll**
(PG) USA Dir Taylor
Hackford with Chuck
Berry, Eric Clapton, Etta
James. UIP. 121 mins.
MFB April 1988 p109

bfi **Circle of Gold**
GB Dir Uday
Bhattacharya. BFI
Production. 52 mins.
16mm. MFB June 1988
p167

Cobra Verde (PG) W
Germany Dir Werner
Herzog with Klaus
Kinski, King Ampaw,
José Lewgoy. Palace
Pictures. 111 mins.
Subtitles. MFB May 1988
p131

Cobra Verde

210

Cocktail (15) USA Dir Roger Donaldson with Tom Cruise, Bryan Brown, Elisabeth Shue. Warner Bros. 103 mins. MFB Jan 1989 p13

Colors (18) USA Dir Dennis Hopper with Sean Penn, Robert Duvall, Maria Conchita Alonso. Rank. 121 mins. MFB Nov 1988 p326

Coming to America (15) USA Dir John Landis with Eddie Murphy, James Earl Jones, Arsenio Hall. UIP. 117 mins. MFB Aug 1988 p229

Consuming Passions (15) GB/USA Dir Giles Foster with Vanessa Redgrave, Jonathan Pryce, Tyler Butterworth. Vestron. 98 mins. MFB Nov 1988 p328

Cop (18) USA Dir James B Harris with James Woods, Lesley Ann Warren, Charles Durning. Entertainment. 110 mins. MFB June 1988 p159

Couch Trip, The (15) USA Dir Michael Ritchie with Dan Aykroyd, Walter Matthau, Charles Grodin. Rank. 98 mins. MFB July 1988 p199

Courier, The (15) Eire Dirs Joe Lee, Frank Deasy with Gabriel Byrne, Ian Bannen, Cait O'Riordan. Palace Pictures. 85 mins. MFB Feb 1988 p41

Crazy Love (18) Belgium Dir Dominique Deruddere with Josse De Pauw, Geert Hunaerts, Michaël Pas. Mainline. 87 mins. Subtitles. MFB Mar 1989 p75

Creepshow 2 (18) USA Dir Michael Gornick with George Kennedy, Dorothy Lamour, Tom Savini. Entertainment. 90 mins. MFB Jan 1988 p13

Crocodile Dundee II (PG) Australia Dir John Cornell with Paul Hogan, Linda Kozlowski, Mark Blum. UIP. 111 mins. MFB July 1988 p200

DOA (15) USA Dirs Rocky Morton, Annabel Jankel with Dennis Quaid, Meg Ryan, Charlotte Rampling. Warner Bros. 97 mins. MFB March 1989 p77

Da Yuebing (The Big Parade) China Dir Chen Kaige with Wang Xueqi, Sun Chun, Lu Lei. ICA Projects. 103 mins. Subtitles. MFB March 1988 p67

Dangerous Liaisons (15) USA Dir Stephen Frears with Glenn Close, John Malkovich, Michelle Pfeiffer. Warner Bros. 120 mins. MFB March 1989 p76

Dark Eyes see **Oci Ciornie**

Dark Side of the Moon, The see **Manden I Månen**

Dawandeh (The Runner) Iran Dir Amir Naderi with Majid Nirumand, Musa Torkizadeh, A Gholamzadeh. Electric Pictures. 94 mins. Subtitles. MFB Aug 1988 p230

Dangerous Liaisons

Dawning, The (PG) GB Dir Robert Knights with Anthony Hopkins, Rebecca Pidgeon, Jean Simmons. Enterprise. 97 mins. MFB Nov 1988 p329

Dead Can't Lie, The (15) USA Dir Lloyd Fonvielle with Tommy Lee Jones, Virginia Madsen, Colin Bruce. Cannon. 98 mins. MFB Feb 1989 p44

Dead of Winter (15) USA Dir Arthur Penn with Mary Steenburgen, Roddy McDowall, Jan Rubeš. UIP. 100 mins. MFB Feb 1988 p42

Dead Ringers (18) Canada Dir David Cronenberg with Jeremy Irons, Genevieve Bujold, Heidi Von Palleske. Rank. 115 mins. MFB Jan 1989 p113

Deadly Pursuit (15) USA Dir Roger Spottiswoode with Sidney Poitier, Tom Berenger, Kirstie Alley. Warner Bros. 110 mins. MFB July 1988 p201

Death of a Salesman (PG) USA Dir Volker Schlöndorff with Dustin Hoffman, Kate Reid, John Malkovich. Artificial Eye. 136 mins. MFB Aug 1988 p231

Death Wish 4: The Crackdown (18) USA Dir J Lee Thompson with Charles Bronson, Kay Lenz, John P Ryan. Cannon Releasing. 98 mins. MFB April 1988 p110

Death Wish 4: The Crackdown

Deceivers, The (15) GB Dir Nicholas Meyer with Pierce Brosnan, Saeed Jaffrey, Shashi Kapoor. Enterprise. 103 mins. MFB Sept 1988 p267

Deuda Interna, La see **Veronico Cruz**

Die Hard (18) USA Dir John McTiernan with Bruce Willis, Bonnie Bedelia, Reginald Veljohnson. 20th Century Fox. 132 mins. MFB Feb 1989 p45

bfi **Distant Voices, Still Lives** (15) GB Dir Terence Davies with Freda Dowie, Pete Postlethwaite, Angela Walsh. BFI Production. 84 mins. MFB Oct 1988 p293

Dogs in Space (18)
Australia Dir Richard
Lowenstein with Michael
Hutchence, Saskia Post,
Nique Needles. Recorded
Releasing. 109 mins.
MFB May 1988 p137

**Drachenfutter
(Spicy Rice)** (PG) W
Germany/Switzerland Dir
Jan Schütte with
Bhasker, Ric Young,
Buddy Uzzaman. Cannon.
72 mins. Subtitles. MFB
Aug 1988 p232

Dragnet (PG) USA Dir
Tom Mankiewicz with
Dan Aykroyd, Tom
Hanks, Christopher
Plummer. UIP. 106 mins.
MFB March 1988 p77

Dream Demon (18)
GB Dir Harley Cokliss
with Jemma Redgrave,
Kathleen Wilhoite,
Timothy Spall. Palace
Pictures. 89 mins. MFB
Nov 1988 p321

Dressmaker, The
(15) GB Dir Jim O'Brien
with Joan Plowright,
Billie Whitelaw, Jane
Horrocks. Rank. 91 mins.
MFB Jan 1989 p14

**Drowning by
Numbers** (18) GB Dir
Peter Greenaway with
Bernard Hill, Joan
Plowright, Juliet
Stevenson. Recorded
Releasing. 119 mins.
MFB Oct 1988 p288

Dudes (15) USA Dir
Penelope Spheeris with
Jon Cryer, Catherine
Mary Stewart, Daniel
Roebuck. Recorded
Releasing. 97 mins. MFB
May 1988 p138

Eddie Murphy Raw
(18) USA Dir Robert
Townsend with Tatyana
Ali, Billy Allen, Eddie
Murphy. UIP. 90 mins.
MFB March 1988 p79

18 Again! (PG) USA
Dir Paul Flaherty with
George Burns, Charlie
Schlatter, Tony Roberts.
Entertainment. 100 mins.
MFB Nov 1988 p329

**Elvira, Mistress Of
the Dark** (15) USA Dir
James Signorelli with
Cassandra Peterson, W
Morgan Sheppard, Daniel
Greene. Entertainment.
96 mins. MFB March
1989 p78

Drowning by Numbers

Empire of the Sun ▶
(PG) USA Dir Steven
Spielberg with Christian
Bale, John Malkovich,
Miranda Richardson.
Warner Bros. 152 mins.
70 mm. MFB April 1988
p95

**Everlasting Secret
Family, The** (18)
Australia Dir Michael
Thornhill with Arthur
Dignam, Mark Lee,
Heather Mitchell.
Cannon. 93 mins. MFB
Dec 1988 p362

Family Viewing (18)
Canada Dir Atom Egoyan
with David Hemblen,
Aidan Tierney, Gabrielle
Rose. The Other Cinema.
86 mins. 16mm. MFB Oct
1988 p299

Fatal Attraction (18)
USA Dir Adrian Lyne
with Michael Douglas,
Glenn Close, Anne
Archer. UIP. 120 mins.
MFB Jan 1988 p14

Fatal Beauty (18)
USA Dir Tom Holland
with Whoopi Goldberg,
Sam Elliott, Ruben

Blades. Enterprise. 104
mins. March 1989 p79

**Fish Called Wanda,
A** (15) GB Dir Charles
Crichton with John
Cleese, Jamie Lee Curtis,
Kevin Kline. UIP. 108
mins. MFB Oct 1988 p300

Five Corners (15)
USA Dir Tony Bill with
Jodie Foster, Tim
Robbins, Todd Graff.
Recorded Releasing. 94
mins. MFB May 1988
p139

**Flame in My Heart,
A** see **Flamme dans
mon coeur, Une**

**Flamme dans mon
coeur, Une (A
Flame in My Heart)**
(18) France/Switzerland
Dir Alain Tanner with
Myriam Mézières, Benoît
Régent, Aziz Kabouche.
Mainline. 110 mins.
Subtitles. MFB March
1988 p79

Flowers in the Attic
(15) USA Dir Jeffrey

**Drachenfutter
(Spicy Rice)**

Bloom with Louise
Fletcher, Victoria
Tennant, Kristy
Swanson. Entertainment.
92 mins. MFB April 1988
p111

For Queen and
Country
(15) GB/USA
Dir Martin Stellman with
Denzel Washington,
Dorian Healy, Amanda
Redman. UIP. 106 mins.
MFB Jan 1989 p15

4 Adventures of
Reinette and
Mirabelle
see
4(Quatre)
aventures de
Reinette et
Mirabelle

Frantic
(15) USA Dir
Roman Polanski with
Harrison Ford, Betty
Buckley, Emmanuelle
Seigner. Warner Bros.
120 mins. MFB Sept 1988
p268

Friday the 13th Part
VI: Jason Lives
see
Jason Lives: Friday
the 13 Part VI

Fruit Machine, The
(15) GB Dir Philip Saville
with Emile Charles, Tony
Forsyth, Robert Stephens.
Vestron. 108 mins. MFB
Nov 1988 p330

Furong Zhen
(Hibiscus Town)
China Dir Xie Jin with
Liu Xiaoqing, Jiang Wen,
Zheng Zaishi. ICA
Projects. 135 mins.
Subtitles. MFB July 1988
p195

Gaby – A True
Story
(15) USA Dir Luis
Mandoki with Liv
Ullmann, Norma
Aleandro, Robert Loggia.
Columbia. 114 mins. MFB
July 1988 p201

Gardens of Stone
(15) USA Dir Francis
Coppola with James
Caan, Anjelica Huston,
James Earl Jones.
Columbia. 112 mins. MFB
Feb 1988 p43

Hanna's War USA Dir Menahem Golan with Ellen Burstyn, Maruschka Detmers, Anthony Andrews. Cannon. 148 mins. MFB Oct 1988 p303

Hawks (15) GB Dir Robert Ellis Miller with Timothy Dalton, Anthony Edwards, Janet McTeer. Rank. 109 mins. MFB Aug 1988 p233

Heart of Midnight (18) USA Dir Matthew Chapman with Jennifer Jason Leigh, Denise Dummont, Gale Mayron. Vestron. 105 mins. MFB Feb 1989 p50

Hello Again (PG) USA Dir Frank Perry with Shelley Long, Judith Ivey, Gabriel Byrne. Warner Bros. 96 mins. MFB June 1988 p168

bfi George Kuchar: The Comedy of the Underground USA Dirs Gustavo Vazquez O, David Hallinger with George Kuchar, Stella Kuchar, Mike Kuchar. BFI. 60 mins. 16mm. MFB Sept 1988 p269

Ghost Chase (PG) W Germany Dir Roland Emmerich with Jason Lively, Jill Whitlow, Tim McDaniel. Medusa. 89 mins. Filmed in English. MFB Feb 1989 p46

Glass Menagerie, The (PG) USA Dir Paul Newman with Joanne Woodward, John Malkovich, Karen Allen. Columbia. 135 mins. MFB Jan 1988 p15

Good Morning, Vietnam (15) USA Dir Barry Levinson with Robin Williams, Forest Whitaker, Tung Thanh Tran. Warner Bros. 108 mins. MFB Oct 1988 p301

Good Mother, The USA Dir Leonard Nimoy with Diane Keaton, Liam Neeson, Jason Robards. Warner Bros. 103 mins. MFB Feb 1989 p47

Gorillas in the Mist (15) USA Dir Michael Apted with Sigourney Weaver, Bryan Brown, John Omirah Miluwi. Warner Bros/Universal. 129 mins. MFB Feb 1989 p48

Grand Chemin, Le (15) France Dir Jean-Loup Hubert with Anemone, Richard Bohringer, Antoine Hubert. Warner Bros. 107 mins. Subtitles. MFB Feb 1989 p49

Hairspray (PG) USA Dir John Waters with Divine, Ricki Lake, Debbie Harry. Palace Pictures. 92 mins. MFB July 1988 p202

Haizi Wang (King of the Children) (15) China Dir Chen Kaige with Xie Yuan, Yang Xuewen, Chen Shaohua. ICA Projects. 106 mins. Subtitles. MFB Sept 1988 p260

Handful of Dust, A (PG) GB Dir Charles Sturridge with James Wilby, Kristin Scott Thomas, Alec Guinness. Premier Releasing. 118 mins. MFB June 1988 p167

A Handful of Dust

Hairspray

Hibiscus Town see **Furong Zhen**

Hidden, The (18) USA Dir Jack Sholder with Kyle MacLachlan, Michael Nouri, Claudia Christian. Palace Pictures. 97 mins. MFB Jan 1989 p16

Hidden City (15) GB Dir Stephen Poliakoff with Charles Dance, Cassie Stuart, Bill Paterson. The Other Cinema. 108 mins. MFB June 1988 p169

High Hopes (15) GB Dir Mike Leigh with Philip Davis, Ruth Sheen, Edna Doré. Palace Pictures. 112 mins. MFB Jan 1989 p9

High Spirits (15) USA Dir Neil Jordan with Peter O'Toole, Daryl Hannah, Steve Guttenberg. Palace Pictures. 96 mins. MFB Dec 1988 p362

High Tide Australia Dir Gillian Armstrong with Judy Davis, Jan Adele, Claudia Karvan. Ritzy Distribution. 104 mins. MFB Dec 1988 p364

Himmel über Berlin, Der (Wings of Desire) (15) West Germany/France Dir Wim Wenders with Bruno Ganz, Solveig Dommartin, Otto Sander. Recorded Releasing. 128 mins. Subtitles. MFB July 1988 p203

High Spirits

Hollywood Shuffle (15) USA Dir Robert Townsend with Robert Townsend, Anne-Marie Johnson, Starletta Dupois. Virgin. 81 mins. MFB April 1988 p99

Homme amoureux, Un (A Man in Love) (18) France Dir Diane Kurys with Peter Coyote, Greta Scacchi, Jamie Lee Curtis. Virgin. 111 mins. Filmed in English. MFB May 1988 p140

Hong Gaoliang (Red Sorghum) (15) China Dir Zhang Yimou with Gong Li, Jiang Wen. Teng Rujun. Palace Pictures. 92 mins. Subtitles. MFB March 1989 p79

House on Carroll Street, The (PG) USA Dir Peter Yates with Kelly McGillis, Jeff Daniels, Mandy Patinkin. Rank. 101 mins. MFB Nov 1988 p331

Housekeeping (PG) USA Dir Bill Forsyth with Christine Lahti, Sara Walker, Andrea Burchill. Columbia. 116 mins. MFB Jan 1988 p16

Imagine (15) USA Dir Andrew Solt. Documentary. Warner Bros. 106 mins. MFB Nov 1988 p332

Invocation Maya Deren GB Dir Jo Ann Kaplan with Hella Hammid, Stan Brakhage, Amos Vogel. Arts Council of Great Britain. 53 mins. 16mm. MFB June 1988 p170

Ironweed (15) USA Dir Hector Babenco with Jack Nicholson, Meryl Streep, Carroll Baker. Palace Pictures. 143 mins. MFB May 1988 p141

It Couldn't Happen Here (15) GB Dir Jack Bond with Neil Tennant, Chris Lowe, Joss Ackland. Entertainment. 86 mins. MFB Aug 1988 p234

Der Himmel über Berlin (Wings of Desire)

I've Heard the ▲ Mermaids Singing
(15) Canada Dir Patricia Rozema with Sheila McCarthy, Paule Baillargeon, Ann-Marie MacDonald. Electric Pictures/Contemporary. 83 mins. MFB March 1988 p81

Jane and the Lost City

Jane and the Lost City (PG) GB Dir Terry Marcel with Sam Jones, Maud Adams, Jasper Carrott. Blue Dolphin. 92 mins. MFB May 1988 p142

Jason Lives: Friday the 13th Part VI (18) USA Dir Tom McLoughlin with Thom Mathews, Jennifer Cooke, David Kagen. UIP. 87 mins. MFB April 1988 p112

Jimmy Reardon (15) USA Dir William Richert with River Phoenix, Ann Magnuson, Meredith Salenger. Enterprise. 93 mins. MFB Sept 1988 p270

Juexiang (Swan Song) China Dir Zhang Zeming with Kong Xianzhu, Chen Rui, Mo Shaoying. ICA Projects. 100 mins. Subtitles. MFB June 1988 p171

Just Ask For Diamond (U) GB Dir Stephen Bayly with Susannah York, Colin Dale, Dursley McLinden. 20th Century Fox. 94 mins. MFB Dec 1988 p365

Kansas (15) USA Dir David Stevens with Matt Dillon, Andrew McCarthy, Leslie Hope. Entertainment. 113 mins. MFB Dec 1988 p365

King Lear (15) USA Dir Jean-Luc Godard with Burgess Meredith, Peter Sellars, Molly Ringwald. Cannon. 90 mins. MFB Feb 1988 p38

King Lear

Kreitzerova Sonata (The Kreutzer Sonata)

King of the Children
see **Haizi Wang**

Kongbufenzi (The Terroriser) (15)
Taiwan/Hong Kong Dir
Edward Yang (Yang
Dechang) with Cora Miao,
Li Liqun, Jin Shijie. ICA
Projects. 109 mins.
Subtitles. MFB March
1989 p69

**Kreitzerova Sonata
(The Kreutzer
Sonata)** (15) USSR
Dirs Mikhail Schweitzer,
Sofia Milkina with Oleg
Yankovsky, Aleksandr
Trofimov, Irina
Seleznyova. Cannon. 135
mins. Subtitles. MFB Jan
1989 p17

Last Emperor, The
(15) China/Italy Dir
Bernardo Bertolucci with
John Lone, Joan Chen,
Peter O'Toole. Columbia.
163 mins. Filmed in
English; some subtitles.
MFB March 1988 p82

**Last Temptation of
Christ, The** (18) USA/
Canada Dir Martin
Scorsese with Willem
Dafoe, Harvey Keitel,
Paul Greco. UIP. 163
mins. MFB Oct 1988 p287

Law of Desire, The
see **Ley del Deseo,
La**

Lectrice, La (18)
France Dir Michel Deville
with Miou-Miou, Régis
Royer, Christian
Ruché. Curzon. 98
mins. Subtitles. MFB
March 1989 p81

**Les Patterson
Saves the World** (15)
Australia Dir George
Miller with Barry
Humphries, Pamela
Stephenson, Thaao
Penghlis. Recorded
Releasing. 90 mins. MFB
Nov 1988 p333

**Ley del Deseo, La
(The Law of Desire)**
Spain Dir Pedro
Almodóvar with Eusebio
Poncela, Carmen Maura,
Antonio Benderas. The
Other Cinema. 100 mins.
Subtitles. MFB Nov 1988
p334

La Ley del Deseo
(The Law of
Desire)

217

The Lighthorsemen

Light of Day (PG)
USA Dir Paul Schrader
with Michael J Fox, Gena
Rowlands, Joan Jett.
Rank. 107 mins. MFB
Aug 1988 p234

**Lighthorsemen,
The** (PG) Australia Dir
Simon Wincer with Peter
Phelps, Tony Bonner,
Gary Sweet. Medusa. 115
mins. MFB Nov 1988
p335

**Like Father, Like
Son** (PG) USA Dir Rod
Daniel with Dudley
Moore, Kirk Cameron,
Margaret Colin.
Columbia-Tri-Star. MFB
Jan 1989 p18

**Lonely Passion of
Judith Hearne, The**
(15) GB Dir Jack Clayton
with Maggie Smith, Bob
Hoskins, Wendy Hiller.

Recorded Releasing. 116
mins. MFB May 1988
p143

Long Live the Lady!
see **Lunga Vita alla
Signora**

Lost Boys, The (15)
USA Dir Joel
Schumacher with Jason
Patric, Corey Haim,
Dianne Wiest. Warner
Bros. 97 mins. MFB Jan
1988 p4

**Lunga Vita alla
Signora! (Long Live
the Lady!)** (15) Italy
Dir Ermanno Olmi with
Marco Esposito, Simona
Brandalise, Stefania
Busarello. Artificial Eye.
106 mins. Subtitles. MFB
Sept 1988 p271

Macbeth (PG) France/
W Germany Dir Claude

D'Anna with Leo Nucci,
Johan Leysen, Shirley
Verrett. Curzon. 136
mins. Subtitles. MFB
March 1988 p83

Madame Sousatzka
UK Dir John Schlesinger
with Shirley MacLaine,
Peggy Ashcroft, Twiggy.
Curzon. 122 mins. MFB
Mar 1989 p82

Making Mr Right
(15) USA Dir Susan
Seidelman with John
Malkovich, Ann
Magnuson, Glenne
Headly. Rank. 98 mins.
MFB May 1988 p144

Man on Fire (18)
France/Italy Dir Elie
Chouraqui with Scott
Glenn, Jade Malle, Joe
Pesci. Rank. 92 mins.
Filmed in English. MFB
June 1988 p173

**Manden I Månen
(The Dark Side of
the Moon)** (15)
Denmark Dir Erik
Clausen with Peter Thiel,
Catherine Poul Jupont,
Christina Bengtsson.
Cannon. 94 mins.
Subtitles. MFB April
1988 p113

Manhunter (18) USA
Dir Michael Mann with
William Peterson, Kim
Greist, Joan Allen.
Recorded Releasing. 120
mins. MFB Feb 1989 p51

Maniac Cop (18) USA
Dir William Lustig with
Tom Atkins, Bruce
Campbell, Laurene
Landon. Medusa. 85 mins.
MFB Feb 1989 p53

Manifesto (18) USA ▶
Dir Dušan Makavejev
with Camilla Søeberg,
Alfred Molina, Simon
Callow. Cannon. 96 mins.
MFB Sept 1988 p272

Mapantsula (15)
South Africa Dir Oliver
Schmitz with Thomas
Mogotlane, Marcel Van
Heerden, Thembi
Mtshali. Electric
Pictures. 104 mins.
Subtitles. MFB Jan 1989
p19

**Marusa no Onna (A
Taxing Woman** (18)
Japan Dir Juzo Itami
with Nobuko Miyamoto,
Tsutomu Yamazaki,
Masahiko Tsugawa.
Artificial Eye. 127 mins.
Subtitles. MFB Dec 1988
p366

Masquerade (18)
USA Dir Bob Swaim with
Rob Lowe, Meg Tilly, Kim
Cattrall. UIP. 91 mins.
MFB Oct 1988 p303

Maybe Baby (15)
USA Dir John G Avildsen
with Molly Ringwald,
Randall Batinkoff,
Kenneth Mars. Columbia.
98 mins. MFB June 1988
p174

**Melissokomos, O
(The Bee Keeper)**
(18) Greece/France Dir
Thodorus Angelopoulos
with Marcello
Mastroianni, Nadia
Mourouzi, Serge
Reggiani. Artificial Eye.
122 mins. Subtitles. MFB
Jan 1988 p17

Midnight Crossing
(18) USA Dir Roger
Holzberg with Faye
Dunaway, Daniel J
Travanti, Kim Cattrall.
Vestron. 96 mins. MFB
Nov 1988 p336

Midnight Run (15)
USA Dir Martin Brest
with Robert De Niro,
Charles Grodin, Yaphet
Kotto. UIP. 126 mins.
MFB Oct 1988 p304

**Milagro Beanfield
War, The** (15) USA Dir
Robert Redford with
Ruben Blades, Richard
Bradford, Sonia Braga.

UIP. 118 mins. MFB Aug
1988 p236

Moderns, The (15)
USA Dir Alan Rudolph
with Keith Carradine,
Linda Fiorentino,
Genevieve Bujold. Rank.
126 mins. MFB March
1989 p67

**Monanieba
(Repentance)** (PG)
USSR Dir Tengiz
Abuladze with Avtandil
Makharadze, Iya Ninidze,
Merab Ninidze. Cannon.
150 mins. Subtitles. MFB
March 1988 p84

**Monster Squad,
The** (15) USA Dir Fred
Dekker with André
Gower, Robby Kiger,
Stephen Macht. Rank. 82
mins. MFB July 1988
p205

Moonstruck (PG)
USA Dir Norman Jewison
with Cher, Nicolas Cage,
Vincent Gardenia. UIP.
102 mins. MFB April
1988 p114

Moonwalker (PG)
USA Dirs Colin Chilvers,
Jerry Kramer with
Michael Jackson, Joe
Pesci, Sean Lennon.
Warner Bros. 93 mins.
MFB Jan 1989 p20

▼ Mapantsula

Mr North (PG) USA Dir Danny Huston with Anthony Edwards, Robert Mitchum, Lauren Bacall. Columbia-Tri-Star. 93 mins. MFB Feb 1989 p54

My Demon Lover (15) USA Dir Charlie Loventhal with Scott Valentine, Michelle Little, Robert Trebor. Palace Pictures. 87 mins. MFB Oct 1988 p305

My Girlfriend's Boyfriend see **Ami de mon amie, L'**

My Little Girl (15) USA Dir Connie Kaiserman with James Earl Jones, Geraldine Page, Mary Stuart Masterson. Enterprise. 117 mins. MFB Sept 1988 p273

My Sweet Little Village see **Vesničko Má Středisková**

Nadine (PG) USA Dir Robert Benton with Jeff Bridges, Kim Basinger, Rip Torn. Columbia. 83 mins. MFB Feb 1988 p44

Naked Cell, The (18) GB Dir John Crome with Vicky Jeffrey, Richard Fallon, Jacquetta May. Premier Releasing. 90 mins. MFB June 1988 p175

Naked Gun: From the Files of Police Squad!, The (15) USA Dir David Zucker with Leslie Nielsen, Priscilla Presley, Ricardo Montalban. UIP. 85 mins. MFB Feb 1989 p55

Napló Szerelmeimnek (Diary for My Loves) (PG) Dir Márta Mészáros with Zsuzsa Czinkóczi, Anna Polony, Jan Nowicki. Artificial Eye. 130 mins. Subtitles. MFB March 1989 p83

Nature of the Beast, The (PG) Great Britain Dir Franco Rosso with Lynton Dearden,

The Naked Gun

Paul Simpson, Tony Melody. Cannon. 96 mins. MFB Dec 1988 p367

Near Dark (18) USA Dir Kathryn Bigelow with Adrian Pasdar, Jenny Wright, Lance Henriksen. Entertainment. 94 mins. MFB Jan 1988 p3

Neco z Alenky see **Alice**

Nico (Above the Law) (18) USA Dir Andrew Davis with Steven Seagal, Pam Grier, Henry Silva. Warner Bros. 99 mins. MFB Nov 1988 p336

Night on the Town, A (Adventures in Babysitting) (PG) USA Dir Chris Columbus with Elisabeth Shue, Maia Brewton, Keith Coogan. Warner Bros. 102 mins. MFB Feb 1988 p45

976-EVIL (18) USA Dir Robert Englund with Stephen Geoffreys, Patrick O'Bryan, Sandy Dennis. Medusa. 100 mins. MFB Jan 1989 p22

90 Days (15) Canada Dir Giles Walker with Stefan Wodoslawsky, Christine Pak, Sam Grana. The Other Cinema. 99 mins. 16mm. MFB Feb 1988 p46

No End see **Bez Końca**

No Man's Land (15) USA Dir Peter Werner with D B Sweeney, Charlie Sheen, Lara Harris. Rank. 106 mins. MFB Oct 1988 p306

No Way Out (15) USA Dir Roger Donaldson with Kevin Costner, Gene Hackman, Sean Young. Rank. 115 mins. MFB Feb 1988 p47

Noir et Blanc France Dir Claire Devers with Francis Frappat, Jacques Martial, Joséphine Fresson. Electric Pictures. 80 mins. Subtitles. MFB April 1988 p115

The Nature of the Beast

Nutcracker – The Motion Picture (U) USA Dir Carroll Ballard with Hugh Bigney, Vanessa Sharp, Patricia Barker. Entertainment. 85 mins. MFB April 1988 p116

Nuts (18) USA Dir Martin Ritt with Barbra Streisand, Richard Dreyfuss, Maureen Stapleton. Warner Bros. 116 mins. MFB Feb 1988 p48

Oci Ciornie (Dark Eyes) (PG) Italy Dir Nikita Mikhalkov with Marcello Mastroianni, Silvana Mangano, Marthe Keller. Curzon. 118 mins. Subtitles. MFB Aug 1988 p237

bfi On the Black Hill (15) GB Dir Andrew Grieve with Mike Gwilym, Robert Gwilym, Bob Peck. BFI. 117 mins. MFB May 1988 p145

Orphans (15) USA Dir Alan J Pakula with Albert Finney, Matthew Modine, Kevin Anderson. UKFD (20th Century Fox). 115 mins. MFB March 1988 p86

Ososhiki (Death Japanese Style) (18) Japan Dir Juzo Itami with Tsutomu Yamazaki, Nobuko Miyamoto, Kin Sugai. Electric Pictures. 124 mins. MFB Nov 1988 p337

bfi Out of Order (15) GB Dir Jonnie Turpie with Sharon Fryer, Gary Webster, Pete Lee-Wilson. BFI Production. 98 mins. 16mm; shot on video. MFB Aug 1988 p223

Out of Rosenheim see **Bagdad Café**

Overboard (PG) USA Dir Garry Marshall with Goldie Hawn, Kurt Russell, Roddy McDowall. UIP. 112 mins. MFB June 1988 p175

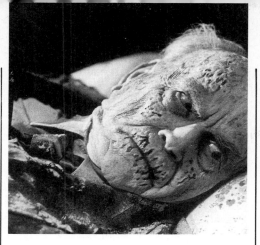

Pascali's Island (15) GB Dir James Dearden with Ben Kingsley, Charles Dance, Helen Mirren. Virgin. 104 mins. MFB Jan 1989 p23

Pathfinder (Veiviseren) (15) Norway Dir Nils Gaup with Mikkel Gaup, Ingvald Guttorm, Ellen Anne Buljo. Guild. 86 mins. Subtitles. MFB Sept 1988 p278

Perfect Murder, The (PG) India Dir Zafar Hai with Naseeruddin Shah, Stellan Skarsgard, Amjad

Phantasm II

Khan. Enterprise. 93 mins. Filmed in English. MFB July 1988 p206

Phantasm II (18) USA Dir Don Coscarelli with James Le Gros, Reggie Bannister, Angus Scrimm. Guild. 97 mins. MFB Jan 1989 p24

Planes, Trains and Automobiles (15) USA Dir John Hughes with Steve Martin, John Candy, Laila Robbins. UIP. 92 mins. MFB June 1988 p176

Pointsman, The see **Wisselwachter, De**

Police Academy 5: Assignment Miami Beach (PG) USA Dir Alan Myerson with Bubba Smith, David Graf, Michael Winslow. Warner Bros. 90 mins. MFB Aug 1988 p238

Poltergeist III (15) USA Dir Gary Sherman with Tom Skeritt, Nancy Allen, Heather O'Rourke. UIP. 98 mins. MFB Oct 1988 p309

Poussière d'ange (Angel Dust) (15) France Dir Edouard Niermans with Bernard Giraudeau, Fanny Bastien, Fanny Cottençon. Palace Pictures. 95 mins. Subtitles. MFB Jan 1988 p18

Powaqqatsi (U) USA Dir Godfrey Reggio. Documentary. Cannon. 99 mins. MFB Aug 1988 p239

Planes, Trains and Automobiles

Prayer For the Dying, A (15) GB Dir Mike Hodges with Mickey Rourke, Bob Hoskins, Alan Bates. Guild. 108 mins. MFB May 1988 p146

Predator (18) USA Dir John McTiernan with Arnold Schwarzenegger, Carl Weathers Elpidia Carrillo. UKFD (20th Century Fox). 106 mins. MFB Jan 1988 p19

Presidio, The (15) USA Dir Peter Hyams with Sean Connery, Mark Harmon, Meg Ryan. UIP. 98 mins. MFB Jan 1989 p25

Prince – Sign o' the Times (15) USA Dir Prince with Prince, Cat, Sheena Easton. Palace Pictures. 85 mins. MFB Aug 1988 p240

Prince of Darkness (18) USA Dir John Carpenter with Donald Pleasence, Jameson Parker, Victor Wong. Guild. 101 mins. MFB May 1988 p147

Prince of Pennsylvania, The (15) USA Dir Ron Nyswaner with Fred Ward, Keanu Reeves, Bonnie Bedelia. Palace Pictures. 93 mins. MFB Feb 1989 p56

Princess Bride, The (PG) USA Dir Rob Reiner with Cary Elwes, Mandy Patinkin, Chris Sarandon. Vestron. 98 mins. MFB March 1988 p87

Principal, The (18) USA Dir Christopher Cain with James Belushi, Louis Gossett Jr, Rae Dawn Chong. Columbia-Tri-Star. 110 mins. MFB Oct 1988 p310

Prison (18) USA Dir Renny Harlin with Viggo Mortensen, Chelsea Field,

Lane Smith. Entertainment. 103 mins. MFB June 1988 p178

Prisoner of Rio (15) Brazil Dir Lech Majewski with Steven Berkoff, Paul Freeman, Peter Firth. Palace. 105 mins. Filmed in English. MFB Jan 1989 p26

Promised Land (15) USA Dir Michael Hoffman with Jason Gedrick, Tracy Pollan, Kiefer Sutherland. Vestron. 102 mins. MFB May 1988 p148

4 aventures de Reinette et Mirabelle (4

Adventures of Reinette and Mirabelle) (U) France Dir Eric Rohmer with Joëlle Miquel, Jessica Forde, Philippe Laudenbach. 99 mins. Subtitles. MFB Feb 1988 p49

Qian Nü Youhun (A Chinese Ghost Story) (15) Hong Kong Dir Ching Siu-Tung with Leslie Cheung, Wang Zuxian, Wu Ma. The Other Cinema. 95 mins. Subtitles. MFB March 1988 p88

Qingchun Ji (Sacrificed Youth) (PG) China Dir Zhang

Nuanxin with Li Fengxu, Feng Yuanzheng, Song Tao. Artificial Eye. 96 mins. Subtitles. MFB Dec 1988 p368

Rain Man (15) USA Dir Barry Levinson with Dustin Hoffman, Tom Cruise, Valeria Golino. UIP. 133 mins. MFB March 1989 p84

Rambo III (18) USA Dir Peter MacDonald with Sylvester Stallone, Richard Crenna, Marc de Jonge. Columbia-Tri-Star. 100 mins. MFB Sept 1988 p274

Red Heat (18) USA Dir Walter Hill with Arnold Schwarzenegger, James

Rain Man

Belushi, Peter Boyle. Columbia-Tri-Star. 104 mins. MFB Jan 1989 p27

Red Sorghum see **Hong Gaoliang**

Repentance see **Monanieba**

Retribution (18) USA Dir Guy Magar with Dennis Lipscomb, Leslie Wing, Suzanne Snyder. Premier Releasing/ Medusa. 109 mins. MFB May 1988 p149

Return of the Living Dead Part II (18) USA Dir Ken Wiederhorn with James Karen, Thom Mathews, Dana Ashbrook. Guild. 89 mins. MFB March 1989 p85

Robocop (18) USA Dir Paul Verhoeven with Peter Weller, Nancy Allen, Daniel O'Herlihy. Rank. 102 mins. MFB Feb 1988 p35

Yaphet Kotto. Rank. 101 mins. MFB Oct 1988 p311

Sacrificed Youth see **Qingchun Ji**

Saigon (18) USA Dir Christopher Crowe with Willem Dafoe, Gregory Hines, Fred Ward. UKFD (20th Century Fox). 102 mins. MFB July 1988 p207

Salaam Bombay! (15) India/France/GB Dir Mira Nair with Shafiq Syed, Raghubir Yadav, Aneeta Kanwar. Mainline. 114 mins. Subtitles. MFB Feb 1989 p42

Salome's Last Dance (18) GB Dir Ken Russell with Glenda Jackson, Stratford Johns, Nickolas Grace. Vestron. 89 mins. MFB July 1988 p209

Rouge Baiser

Roger Milo, Féodor Atkine. ICA Projects. 121 mins. Subtitles. MFB Jan 1988 p8

Scandal (18) UK Dir Michael Caton-Jones with John Hurt, Joanne Whalley-Kilmer, Bridget Fonda. Palace Pictures. 115 mins. MFB March 1989 p87

School Daze (18) USA Dir Spike Lee with Giancarlo Esposito, Tisha Campbell, Spike Lee. Columbia-Tri-Star Films. 120 mins. MFB Aug 1988 p241

Scrooged (PG) USA Dir Richard Donner with Bill Murray, Karen Allen, John Forsythe. UIP. 101 mins. MFB Dec 1988 p369

September (PG) USA Dir Woody Allen with Denholm Elliott, Dianne Wiest, Mia Farrow. Rank. 83 mins. MFB July 1988 p210

Victor Schonfeld. Blue Dolphin. 173 mins. 16mm. Partly subtitled. MFB Feb 1988 p50

She Must Be Seeing Things USA Dir Sheila McLaughlin with Sheila Dabney, Lois Weaver, Kyle DiCamp. The Other Cinema. 91 mins. MFB Sept 1988 p276

Sherman's March (15) USA Dir Ross McElwee. Artificial Eye. 160 mins. 16mm. MFB July 1988 p211

Short Circuit 2 (PG) USA Dir Kenneth Johnson with Fisher Stevens, Michael McKean, Cynthia Gibb. Columbia-Tri-Star. 110 mins. MFB Feb 1989 p57

Shy People (15) USA Dir Andrei Konchalovsky with Jill Clayburgh, Barbara Hershey, Martha

Rouge baiser France/ W Germany Dir Véra Belmont with Charlotte Valandrey, Lambert Wilson, Marthe Keller. The Other Cinema. 112 mins. Subtitles. MFB April 1988 p117

Runner, The see **Dawandeh**

Running Man, The (18) USA Dir Paul Michael Glaser with Arnold Schwarzenegger, Maria Conchita Alonso,

Salsa (PG) USA Dir Boaz Davidson with Robby Rosa, Rodney Harvey, Magali Alvarado. Cannon. 97 mins. MFB Aug 1988 p240

Sammy and Rosie Get Laid (18) GB Dir Stephen Frears with Shashi Kapoor, Frances Barber, Claire Bloom. Palace Pictures. 101 mins. MFB Jan 1988 p20

Sarraounia (15) France Dir Med Hondo with Aï Keïta, Jean-

Seventh Sign, The (15) USA Dir Carl Schultz with Demi Moore, Michael Biehn, Jurgen Prochnow. Columbia-Tri-Star. 97 mins. MFB Nov 1988 p339

Shag (15) USA Dir Zelda Barron with Phoebe Cates, Scott Coffey, Bridget Fonda. Palace Pictures. 98 mins. MFB Sept 1988 p275

Shattered Dreams – Picking Up the Pieces (PG) GB Dir

Plimpton. Cannon. 119 mins. MFB June 1988 p179

Sicilian, The (15) USA Dir Michael Cimino with Christopher Lambert, Terence Stamp, Joss Ackland. 20th Century Fox. 146 mins. MFB Oct 1988 p312

Siesta (18) USA Dir Mary Lambert with Ellen Barkin, Jodie Foster, Gabriel Byrne. Palace Pictures. 97 mins. MFB May 1988 p150

**Silent Voice
(Amazing Grace
and Chuck)** (PG) USA
Dir Mike Newell with
Alex English, Joshua
Zuehlke, Gregory Peck.
Columbia. 115 mins. MFB
March 1988 p89

'68 (15) USA Dir Steven
Kovacs with Eric Larson,
Robert Locke, Sandor
Tecsi. Entertainment. 98
mins. MFB Oct 1988 p314

Slipstream (PG) GB
Dir Steven M Lisberger
with Mark Hamill, Bob
Peck, Bill Paxton.
Entertainment. 102 mins.
MFB Feb 1989 p36

Someone to Love ▲
USA Dir Henry Jaglom
with Orson Welles, Henry
Jaglom, Andrea
Marcovicci. ICA Projects.
105 mins. MFB Jan 1989
p28

**Someone to Watch
Over Me** (15) USA Dir
Ridley Scott with Tom
Berenger, Mimi Rogers,
Lorraine Bracco.
Columbia. 106 mins. MFB
April 1988 p118

**Sous le soleil de
Satan (Under
Satan's Sun)** (15)
France Dir Maurice
Pialat with Gérard
Depardieu, Sandrine

Bonnaire, Maurice Pialat.
Cannon. 98 mins.
Subtitles. MFB June 1988
p180

Souvenir (15) GB Dir
Geoffrey Reeve with
Christopher Plummer,
Catherine Hicks, Michael
Lonsdale. Curzon. 93
mins. MFB Jan 1989 p29

Spicy Rice see
Drachenfutter

Squeeze, The (15)
USA Dir Roger Young
with Michael Keaton, Rae
Dawn Chong, Joe
Pantoliano. Columbia.
102 mins. MFB March
1988 p90

Stakeout (15) USA Dir
John Badham with
Richard Dreyfuss, Emilio
Estevez, Madeleine
Stowe. Warner Bros. 117
mins. MFB April 1988
p119

Stand and Deliver
(15) USA Dir Ramon
Menendez with Edward
James Olmos, Lou
Diamond Phillips, Rosana
De Soto. Warner Bros.
103 mins. MFB Dec 1988
p371

Starlight Hotel (PG)
New Zealand Dir Sam
Pillsbury with Greer
Robson, Peter Phelps,

Marshall Napier.
Recorded Releasing. 94
mins. MFB July 1988
p212

Stars and Bars (15)
USA Dir Pat O'Connor
with Daniel Day Lewis,
Harry Dean Stanton,
Kent Broadhurst.
Columbia-Tri-Star. 94
mins. MFB Sept 1988
p255

Stepfather, The (18)
USA Dir Joseph Ruben
with Terry O'Quinn, Jill
Schoelen, Shelley Hack.
Virgin. 89 mins. MFB Jan
1988 p21

Sticky Fingers (15)
USA Dir Catlin Adams
with Helen Slater,
Melanie Mayron, Eileen
Brennan. Virgin. 88 mins.
MFB Sept 1988 p277

Stormy Monday (15)
GB Dir Mike Figgis with
Melanie Griffith, Tommy
Lee Jones, Sting. Palace
Pictures. 93 mins. MFB
Feb 1989 p58

Strike, The GB Dir
Peter Richardson with
Peter Richardson,
Jennifer Saunders, Alexei
Sayle. Palace Pictures. 53
mins. MFB Feb 1988 p51

Summer Story, A
(15) GB Dir Piers
Haggard with Imogen
Stubbs, James Wilby,
Ken Colley. Warner Bros.
96 mins. MFB Nov 1988
p340

Tampopo

Sunset (15) USA Dir
Blake Edwards with
Bruce Willis, James
Garner, Malcolm
McDowell. Columbia-Tri-
Star. 107 mins. MFB Dec
1988 p372

Suspect (15) USA Dir
Peter Yates with Cher,
Dennis Quaid, Liam
Neeson. Columbia. 121
mins. MFB July 1988
p213

Swan Song see
Juexiang

**Sweet Hearts
Dance** (15) USA Dir
Robert Greenwald with
Don Johnson, Susan
Sarandon, Jeff Daniels.
Columbia-Tri-Star. 101
mins. MFB March 1989
p88

**Switching
Channels** (PG) USA
Dir Ted Kotcheff with
Kathleen Turner, Burt
Reynolds, Christopher
Reeve. Rank. 105 mins.
MFB Aug 1988 p243

Taffin (18) GB/USA Dir
Francis Megahy with
Pierce Brosnan, Ray
McAnally, Alison Doody.
Vestron. 96 mins. MFB
Nov 1988 p340

Tampopo (18) Japan
Dir Juzo Itami with
Tsutomu Yamazaki,
Nobuko Miyamoto, Koji
Yakusho. Electric
Pictures/Contemporary.
114 mins. Subtitles. MFB
April 1988 p101

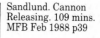

Taxing Woman, A
see **Marusa no Onna**

Teen Wolf Too (PG)
USA Dir Christopher
Leitch with Jason
Bateman, Kim Darby,
John Astin.
Entertainment. 94 mins.
MFB Feb 1988 p52

Terminus (15) France/
W Germany Dir Pierre-
William Glenn with
Johnny Hallyday, Karen
Allen, Jurgen Prochnow.
UKFD (20th Century
Fox). 83 mins. Subtitles.
MFB Feb 1988 p52

Terroriser, The see
Kongbufenzi

**Three Men and a
Baby** (PG) USA Dir
Leonard Nimoy with Tom
Selleck, Steve
Guttenberg, Ted Danson.
Warner Bros. 102 mins.
MFB April 1988 p120

**Throw Momma
From the Train** (15)
USA Dir Danny DeVito
with Danny DeVito, Billy
Crystal, Anne Ramsey.
Rank. 88 mins. MFB
April 1988 p121

**Tiempo de Morir
(Time to Die)** (15)
Colombia/Cuba Dir Jorge
Alí Triana with Gustavo
Angarita, Sebastian
Ospina, Jorge Emilio

Durning. Entertainment.
97 mins. MFB May 1988
p151

Time to Die see
Tiempo de Morir

**Time to Live and
the Time to Die,
The** see **Tongnian
Wangshi**

To Kill a Priest USA/
France Dir Agnieszka
Holland with Christopher
Lambert, Ed Harris, Joss
Ackland. Columbia-Tri-
Star. 117 mins. MFB Nov
1988 p342

Testimony

Sandlund. Cannon
Releasing. 109 mins.
MFB Feb 1988 p39

Track 29 (18) GB Dir
Nicolas Roeg with
Theresa Russell, Gary
Oldman, Christopher
Lloyd. Recorded
Releasing. 90 mins. MFB
July 1988 p191

Travelling North (15)
Australia Dir Carl
Schultz with Leo McKern,
Julia Blake, Graham
Kennedy. Recorded
Releasing. 97 mins. MFB
May 1988 p152

36 fillette (Virgin)
France Dir Catherine
Breillat with Delphine
Zentout, Etienne Chicot,
Olivier Parnière. Electric
Pictures. 88 mins.
Subtitles. MFB Feb 1989
p40

**Tucker: The Man
and His Dream** (PG)
USA Dir Francis Ford
Coppola with Jeff
Bridges, Joan Allen,
Martin Landau. UIP. 111
mins. MFB Dec 1988 p351

Twins (PG) USA Dir
Ivan Reitman with
Arnold Schwarzenegger,
Danny DeVito, Kelly
Preston. UIP. 107 mins.
MFB Mar 1989 p88

**Unbearable
Lightness of Being,
The** (18) USA Dir Philip
Kaufman with Daniel
Day Lewis, Juliette
Binoche, Lena Olin. UIP.
172 mins. MFB April
1988 p122

Under Satan's Sun
see **Sous le soleil de
Satan**

U2 Rattle and Hum
(15) USA Dir Phil Joanou.
UIP. 99 mins. MFB Dec
1988 p354

Veiviseren see
Pathfinder

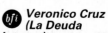 **Veronico Cruz
(La Deuda
Interna)** Argentina/GB
Dir Miguel Pereira with
Juan José Camero,
Gonzalo Morales, René
Olaguivel. Recorded

Testimony (PG) GB
Dir Tony Palmer with
Ben Kingsley, Sherry
Baines, Magdalen
Asquith. Enterprise. 157
mins. MFB June 1988
p181

Things Change (PG)
USA Dir David Mamet
with Don Ameche, Joe
Mantegna, Robert
Prosky. Columbia-Tri-
Star. 100 mins. MFB Feb
1989 p59

Salazar. Artificial Eye. 98
mins. Subtitles. MFB
March 1988 p90

Tiger Warsaw (15)
USA Dir Amin Q
Chaudhri with Patrick
Swayze, Piper Laurie, Lee
Richardson. Recorded
Releasing. 93 mins. MFB
Nov 1988 p341

Tiger's Tale, A (15)
USA Dir Peter Douglas
with Ann Margret, C
Thomas Howell, Charles

**Tongnian Wangshi
(The Time to Live
and the Time to
Die)** (PG) Taiwan Dir
Hou Hsiao-hsien with
You Anshun, Tian Feng,
Mei Fang. ICA Projects.
137 mins. Subtitles. MFB
June 1988 p161

**Tough Guys Don't
Dance** (18) USA Dir
Norman Mailer with
Ryan O'Neal, Isabella
Rossellini, Debra

Releasing. 96 mins. Subtitles. MFB Nov 1988 p343

Vesničko Má Středisková (My Sweet Little Village) (PG) Czechoslovakia Dir Jiří Menzel with János Bán, Marian Labuda, Rudolf Hrušínský. Cannon. 100 mins. Subtitles. MFB Jan 1988 p22

Vice Versa (PG) USA Dir Brian Gilbert with Judge Reinhold, Fred Savage, Corinne Bohrer. Columbia. 98 mins. MFB July 1988 p214

Vincent: The Life and Death of Vincent Van Gogh (PG) Australia Dir Paul Cox with John Hurt, Gabi Trsek, Sky Bilu. Artificial Eye. 99 mins. MFB Sept 1988 p278

Virgin see **36 fillette**

Vita Futurista: Italian Futurism 1909-44 GB Dir Lutz Becker. Arts Council of Great Britain. 52 mins. 16mm. MFB Feb 1988 p53

Vroom (15) GB Dir Beeban Kidron with Clive Owen, Diana Quick, David Thewlis. Enterprise Pictures. 89 mins

Wall Street (15) USA Dir Oliver Stone with Michael Douglas, Charlie Sheen, Daryl Hannah. UKFD (20th Century Fox). 126 mins. MFB April 1988 p123

War Requiem (PG) GB Dir Derek Jarman with Nathaniel Parker, Tilda Swinton, Laurence Olivier. Anglo International Films. 93 mins. MFB Feb 1989 p60

We Are the Elephant GB Dir Glenn Ujebe Masokoane with Burt Caesar, Margaret Williams, Thulani Sifeni. Ceddo. 54 mins. 16mm. MFB May 1988 p153

Whales of August, The (U) USA Dir Lindsay Anderson with Bette Davis, Lillian Gish, Vincent Price. Curzon. 91 mins. MFB May 1988 p154

White Mischief (18) GB Dir Michael Radford with Charles Dance, Greta Scacchi, Joss Ackland. Columbia. 107 mins. MFB Feb 1988 p54

Who Framed Roger Rabbit? (PG) USA Dir Robert Zemeckis with Bob Hoskins, Christopher Lloyd, Joanna Cassidy. Warner Bros. 104 mins. MFB Dec 1988 p373

Willow (PG) USA Dir Ron Howard with Val Kilmer, Joanne Whalley, Warwick Davies. UIP. 125 mins. MFB Dec 1988 p375

Wings of Desire see **Himmel über Berlin, Der**

Wisselwachter, De (The Pointsman) (15) Netherlands Dir Jos Stelling with Jim Van Der Woude, Stéphane Excoffier, John Kraaykamp. Vestron. 96 mins. Subtitles. MFB July 1988 p214

Withnail and I (15) GB Dir Bruce Robinson with Richard E Grant, Paul McGann, Richard Griffiths. Recorded Releasing. 107 mins. MFB Feb 1988 p55

Wizard of Speed and Time, The (PG) USA Dir Mike Jittlov with Mike Jittlov, Richard Kaye, Paige Moore. Medusa. 98 mins. MFB Oct 1988 p314

Woo Woo Kid, The (PG) USA Dir Phil Alden Robinson with Patrick Dempsey, Talia Balsam, Beverly D'Angelo. Guild. 98 mins. MFB Jan 1988 p23

World Apart, A (PG) GB Dir Chris Menges with Jodhi May, Barbara Hershey, Jeroen Krabbé. Palace Pictures. 113 mins. MFB Aug 1988 p244

Yeelen (The Light) (PG) Mali Dir Souleymane Cissé with Issiaka Kane, Aoua

A World Apart

Sangare, Niamanto Sanogo. Artificial Eye. 104 mins. Subtitles. MFB Nov 1988 p343

Yob, The GB Dir Ian Emes with Keith Allen, Betsy Brantley, Adrian Edmondson. Palace Pictures. 53 mins. MFB Feb 1988 p56

Young Guns (18) USA Dir Christopher Cain with Emilio Estevez, Kiefer Sutherland, Charlie Sheen. Vestron. 107 mins. MFB Jan 1989 p6

Zoo la Nuit, Un (Night Zoo) (18) Canada Dir Jean-Claude Lauzon with Gilles Maheu, Roger Le Bel, Lynne Adams. Hendring. 115 mins. Subtitles. MFB March 1989 p89

bfi – **Produced or distributed by the BFI**

Wall Street

Scene of Europe's leading media centre • Featuring IMAX: Britain's largest cinema screen • Winner of the Museum of the Year 1988* • "The World's Top Photo Museum" International Herald Tribune • Soon to do for film and television what we've done for photography.

NATIONAL MUSEUM OF
PHOTOGRAPHY
FILM AND TELEVISION

*WE WOULD LIKE TO THANK THE FOLLOWING PEOPLE WITHOUT WHOM WINNING THIS MUCH COVETED AWARD WOULD NOT HAVE ETC. ETC.

STARTS

Across the Lake
BBC TV/Challenger
Locations: Coniston/
Windermere
Producer: Innes Lloyd
Associate producer: Derek
Nelson
Director: Tony Maylam
Screenwriter: Roger
Milner
Camera: Andrew Dunn
Editor: Ray Wingrove
Cast: Anthony Hopkins,
Ewan Hooper, Angela
Richards, Julia Watson,
Rosemary Leach

And a Nightingale Sang
Portman/Tyne Tees TV
Location: north-east
England
Executive producer:
Victor Glynn
Producer: Philip
Hinchcliffe
Director: Robert Knights
Screenwriter: Jack
Rosenthal, from the play
by C P Taylor
Camera: Norman Langley
Editor: Chris Wimble
Cast: Phyllis Logan, Tom
Watt, Joan Plowright,
John Woodvine, Pippa
Hinchley

Barracuda
Barracuda Films/
Amalgamated/Portman
Productions/7 Network
Location: Australia
Executive producer: Tom
Donald
Producers: Alan
Bateman, Victor Glynn
Director: Pino Amenta
Screenwriter: Philip
Ryall, Keith Thompson
Camera: Dave Connell
Editor: Richard Francis-
Bruce
Cast: Dennis Miller,
Andrew McFarlane,
Shane Briant, Graham
Rouse, John O'Brien

Batman
Guber-Peters/Warner
Bros
Studio: Pinewood
Location: UK
Producers: Jon Peters,
Peter Guber, Chris Kenny
Director: Tim Burton
Screenwriter: Sam
Hamm, Warren Skaaren
Camera: Roger Pratt
Editor: Ray Lovejoy
Cast: Jack Nicholson,
Michael Keaton, Kim
Basinger, Jack Palance,
Robert Wuhl ▼

Bulldance

Filmscreen Productions/
Marlborough Productions
Location: Yugoslavia
Executive producers:
Timothy Woolford, Robin
Hardy
Producer: Peter Watson-Wood
Director: Zelda Barron
Screenwriters: Robin
Hardy, Jesse Lasky, Pat
Silver
Camera: Richard
Greatrex
Editor: George Akers
Cast: Lauren Hutton,
Cliff de Young, Robert
Beltran, Viveka Davis,
Renee Estevez

Burning Secret

NFH/B A Produkion/
Burning Secret
Productions
Location: Czechoslovakia
Producers: Norma
Heyman, Carol Lynn
Greene, Eberhardt
Junkersdorf
Director/screenwriter:
Andrew Birkin
Camera: Ernest Day
Editor: Paul Green
Cast: Faye Dunaway,
Klaus Maria Brandauer,
David Eberts, John
Nettleton, Eva Roth

Bye Bye Baby

BBC TV
Location: London
Producer: Richard Broke
Director: Robert Young
Screenwriter: Mick Ford
Camera: John McGlashan
Editor: Tariq Anwar

Choice, The

Pelt/Pelt SA
Locations: Gstaad, Swiss
Alps/New York
Executive producer:
Frederic Kuffer
Producer: Peter R Ensor
Associate producer: Pam
Bernard
Director/screenwriter:
Robert Paget
Camera: Nick Tebbet
Editor: Steve Bache
Cast: Deborah Shelton,
Ferdinand Mayne, Jay
Benedict, Moira Lister,
Felix Howard

Choirboys

BBC TV
Locations: Halifax/
Blackpool
Producer: Andree
Molyneux
Director: Michael Darlow

Screenwriter: Stephen
Wakelam
Camera: Barry McCann
Editor: Masahiro
Hirakubo
Cast: Michael Williams,
Brian Shelley, Alan
Rothwell, Ruth
Whitehead, Raymond
Wallbank

Chorus of Disapproval, A

Palisades Entertainment/
Cinema Seven/Andre
Blay-Elliott Kastner
Location: Scarborough,
North Yorkshire
Producer/director:
Michael Winner
Associate producer: Ron
Purdie
Screenwriters: Alan
Ayckbourn, Michael
Winner
Camera: Alan Jones
Editor: Chris Barnes
Cast: Anthony Hopkins,
Jeremy Irons, Richard
Briers, Barbara Ferris,
Gareth Hunt

Coded Hostile

(working title: Flight 007)
Darlow Smithson
Production/Granada TV/
Home Box
Office
Studio: Twickenham
Studios
Location: Washington
DC/London
Executive producer:
Leslie Woodhead
Producer: John Smithson
Director: David Darlow
Camera: Rodrigo
Gutierrez
Editor: Chris Gill
Cast: Michael Moriarty,
Michael Murphy, Chris
Sarandon, Harris Yulin,
Jay Patterson

Conquest of the South Pole

Jam Jar Films
Location: Edinburgh/
Leith Docks
Producer: Gareth Wardell
Associate producer:
Penny Thomson
Director: Gillies
MacKinnon
Screenwriter: Gareth
Wardell
Camera: Sean Van Hales
Editor: Steve Singleton
Cast: Stevan Rimkus,
Leonard O'Malley,
Gordon Cameron, Ewen
Bremner, Alastair
Galbraith

Cook, The Thief, His Wife and Her Love, The

Allarts Cook/Erato Films/
Films Inc
Studio: Goldcrest Elstree
Producers: Kees
Kasander, Dennis
Wigman, Pascal Dauman,
Daniel Toscan du Plantier
Director/screenwriter:
Peter Greenaway
Camera: Sacha Vierny
Editor: John Wilson
Cast: Michael Gambon,
Richard Bohringer, Helen
Mirren, Alan Howard,
Ciaran Hinds

Danny the Champion of the World

Portobello Productions/
Disney Channel/Thames
TV/Wonderworks (PBS)/
British Screen/Children's
Film and Television
Foundation
Location: Oxford
Producers: Eric Abraham,
Robin Douet

Director: Gavin Millar
Screenwriter: John
Goldsmith
Camera: Oliver Stapleton
Editor: Peter Tanner
Cast: Jeremy Irons, Sam
Irons, Cyril Cusack,
Robbie Coltrane, Lionel
Jeffries

Dealers

Euston Films
Studio: Pinewood
Location: London
Executive producer:
Andrew Brown
Producer: Bill Cartlidge
Director: Colin Bucksey
Screenwriter: Andrew
Maclear
Camera: Peter Sinclair
Editor: Jon Costelloe
Cast: Paul McGann,
Rebecca De Mornay,
Derrick O'Connor,
Rosalind Bennett, John
Castle

Coded Hostile

Death of a Son
Centre Films/BBC TV
Locations: Oxford/London
Executive producers:
Jeffrey Taylor, Kent
Walwin
Producers: Martin
Thompson, Derek
Granger
Director: Ross Devenish
Screenwriter: Tony
Marchant
Camera: Nigel Walters
Editor: John Stothart
Cast: Lynn Redgrave,
Malcolm Storry, Jay
Simpson, Mark Anstee,
Ross Boatman

Death of a Son

Defrosting the Fridge
BBC TV/Contracts
International
Locations: Norfolk/
Suffolk
Executive producer:
James Reeve
Producer: Terry Coles
Director: Sandy Johnson
Screenwriter: Ray
Connolly
Camera: Andrew Dunn
Editor: Kate Evans
Cast: Joe Don Baker,
Phyllis Logan, William
Armstrong, Togo Igawa,
Emma Wray

Diamond Skulls
Working Title/Film Four
International/British
Screen
Locations: Yorkshire/
London
Producer: Tim Bevan
Associate producer: Jane
Frazer
Director: Nick Broomfield
Screenwriter: Tim Rose
Price
Camera: Michael Coulter
Editor: Rodney Holland
Cast: Gabriel Byrne,
Amanda Donohoe, Sir
Michael Hordern, Judy
Parfitt, Douglas Hodge

Dog It Was That Died, The
Granada TV
Locations: Manchester/
Bridlington/London
Producer: Roy Roberts
Director: Peter Wood
Screenwriter: Tom
Stoppard
Camera: Ken Morgan
Editor: Anthony Ham
Cast: Alan Bates, Alan
Howard, Simon Cadell,
Geoffrey Chater, Maurice
Denham

Dr Jekyll and Mr Hyde – a Journey into Fear
Allied Vision
Location: Budapest,
Hungary
Executive producer: Peter
McRae
Producers: Edward
Simons, H A Towers
Director: Gerard Kikoine
Camera: Tony Spratling
Editor: Malcolm Cooke
Cast: Anthony Perkins,
Glynis Barber, David
Lodge, Sarah Maur
Thorpe, Ben Cole

Dream Baby
BBC Plays Dept
Producer: David M
Thompson
Director: Angela Pope
Screenwriter: David Kane
Camera: Remi Aderafasin
Editor: Sue Wyatt
Cast: Jenny McCrindle,
Mandy Matthews, Kevin
McNally, Peter Capaldi,
Billy McElhaney

Dry White Season, A
Davros/MGM
Location: Harare,
Zimbabwe
Executive producer: Tim
Hampton
Producer: Paula
Weinstein
Director/screenwriter:
Euzhan Palcy
Camera: Roger Deakins
Editor: Francoise Bonnot
Cast: Marlon Brando,
Donald Sutherland,
Susan Sarandon, Janet
Suzman, Zakes Mokae

Diamond Skulls *(below)*

Duck
Tandemdock/Film Four
International/British
Screen
Location: London
Executive producer:
Therese Pickard
Producer: Paul Bradley
Director: Simon Shore
Screenwriter: David
Ashton
Camera: Clive Tickner
Editor: Bill Shapter
Cast: Frances Barber, Jim
Carter, Denica Fairman,
Marissa Dunlop

Ending Up
Thames TV
Studio: Twickenham
Location: Oxfordshire
Executive producer: Lloyd
Shirley
Producer/Director: Peter
Sasdy
Screenwriter: Douglas
Livingstone
Camera: Simon Kossoff
Editor: Bob Dearberg

Erik the Viking ▲
Prominent Viking
Studio: Lee International,
Shepperton
Location: Malta
Producer: John Goldstone
Director/screenwriter:
Terry Jones
Camera: Ian Wilson
Editor: George Akers
Cast: Tim Robbins, Terry
Jones, Eartha Kitt,
Mickey Rooney, Tsutomu
Sekine

Everybody Wins
Recorded Picture Co
Location: Wilmington,
North Carolina/
Connecticut
Executive producers:
Terry Glinwood, Linda
Yellen
Producers: Jeremy
Thomas, Ezra Swerdlow
Director: Karel Reisz

Screenwriter: Arthur Miller
Editor: John Bloom
Cast: Debra Winger, Nick Nolte, Jack Warden, Will Patton, Judith Ivey

Flying in the Branches

BBC TV
Locations: London/Dover
Executive producer: Barry Hanson
Producer: Martyn Auty
Director: Eva Kolouchova
Screenwriter: Anna Fodorova
Camera: Elmer Cossey
Editor: Sue Wyatt
Cast: Edita Brychta, Susan Fleetwood, Ralph Bates, Matthew Marsh, Donald Gee

Getting It Right

Evenaction/Management Company Entertainment Group
Location: London
Executive producer: Rusty Lemorande
Producer: Jonathon Krane
Director: Randal Kleiser
Screenwriter: Elizabeth Jane Howard
Camera: Clive Tickner
Editor: Chris Kelly
Cast: Jesse Birdsall, Helena Bonham-Carter, Kevin Drinkwater, Shirley Anne Field, Sir John Gielgud

Great Diamond Robbery, The

HTV/Jay Bernstein Productions/Columbia Pictures Television
Locations: Bristol/London/New York/Los Angeles
Executive producers: Patrick Dromgoole, Johnny Goodman, Jay Bernstein
Producer: N T Maffeo
Director: Don Taylor
Camera: B Edwards
Cast: Howard Hesseman, Ed Marinaro, Brooke Shields, Twiggy

Great Expectations

Prime Time Television/Disney Channel/HTV
Studio: Pinewood
Locations: Chatham/Rochester/Dorney/Eton
Producer: Greg Smith
Director: Kevin Connor
Screenwriter: John Goldsmith

Camera: Doug Milsome
Editor: Barry Peters
Cast: Jean Simmons, John Rhys Davies, Ray McAnally, Anthony Calf, Anthony Hopkins

Heartland

(working title: Face of the Earth)
BBC Wales
Locations: Preseli Hills/Cardiff
Executive producer: Keith Williams
Producer: Christine Benson
Director: Kevin Billington
Screenwriter: Steve Gough
Camera: Russ Walker
Editor: Tim Kruydenberg
Cast: Anthony Hopkins, Lynn Farleigh, Mark Lewis Jones, Martin Glyn Murray, Jane Horrocks

Heat of the Day, The

Granada TV
Locations: Cheshire/Sussex/Kent/London/Shropshire/Liverpool/Manchester
Executive producer: Steve Hawes
Producer: June Wyndham Davies
Director: Christopher Morahan
Screenwriter: Harold Pinter, from the novel by Elizabeth Bowen
Camera: Jon Woods
Editor: Andy Sumner
Cast: Michael Gambon, Patricia Hodge, Michael York, Peggy Ashcroft, Imelda Staunton

Hellbound: Hellraiser II

Film Futures/New World International
Studio: Pinewood
Executive producers: Clive Barker, Christopher Webster
Producer: Christopher Figg
Director: Tony Randel
Screenwriter: Peter Atkins
Camera: Robin Vidgeon
Editor: Richard Marden
Cast: Clare Higgins, Ashley Laurence, Kenneth Cranham, Imogen Boorman, Sean Chapman

Hellbound: Hellraiser II

Helpline
Independent Feature
Film Production/Silent
Fiction Films
Distribution
Location: London
Executive producer:
Anders Palm, John de
Borman
Producer: James Ewart
Director/screenwriter:
Anders Palm
Editor: Paul Endacott
Cast: Emma Jacobs, Peter
Blake, Andrew Wilde,
Allen Surtees, Simon
Shepherd

Henry V
Renaissance Films
Studio: Lee International,
Shepperton
Executive producer:
Stephen Evans
Producer: Bruce Sharman
Director: Kenneth
Branagh
Camera: Ken MacMillan
Editor: Michael Bradsell
Cast: Kenneth Branagh,
Derek Jacobi, Simon
Shepherd, James Larkin,
Brian Blessed

Home
BBC TV
Location: UK
Producer: Graham
Massey
Director: Penny Cherns
Screenwriter: Nick
McCarthy
Camera: Colin Munn
Editor: Frances Parker

Cast: Nick Stringer,
Stephen McGann, Jan
Ruppe, Wilbert Johnson,
Jason Cunliffe

Honor Bound
Michel Roy/FilmAccord
Locations: Berlin/
Yugoslavia
Executive producers:
Michel Roy, Jean Gontier
Producers: Tim Van
Rellim, Eric Weymueller
Director: Jeannot Szwarc
Screenwriters: Terrell
Tannen, Melissa Ford
Camera: Bobby Stevens
Editor: John Jympson
Cast: John Philbin,
Gabrielle Lazure, Tom
Skerrit, George Dzundza,
Lawrence Pressman

Hound of the Baskervilles, The
Granada TV
Locations: Manchester/
Liverpool/Yorkshire/
Cheshire/Derbyshire/
Staffordshire
Executive producer:
Michael Cox
Producer: June Wyndham
Davies
Director: Brian Mills
Screenwriter: Trevor
Bowen
Camera: Michael B
Popley
Editor: Alan Ringland
Cast: Jeremy Brett,
Edward Hardwicke, Neil
Duncan, James Faulkner,
Fiona Gillies

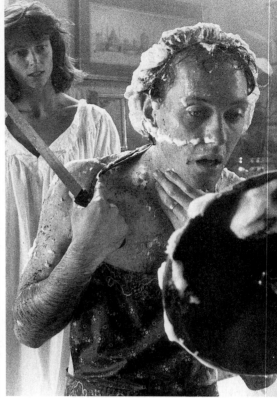

How to Get Ahead in Advertising
HandMade Films
(Productions)
Studio: Lee International,
Shepperton
Executive producers:
George Harrison, Denis
O'Brien
Producers: David
Wimbury, Ray Cooper
Director/screenwriter:
Bruce Robinson
Camera: Peter Hannan
Editor: Alan Strachan
Cast: Richard E Grant,
Rachel Ward, Richard
Wilson, Jacqueline Tong,
Susan Wooldridge

Indiana Jones and the Last Crusade
Lucasfilm
Studio: Goldcrest Elstree
Locations: Spain/Italy/
Jordan/US
Executive producers:
George Lucas, Frank
Marshall
Producer: Robert Watts
Director: Steven
Spielberg
Camera: Douglas
Slocombe
Editor: Colin Wilson
Cast: Harrison Ford, Sean
Connery, Denholm
Elliott, Alison Doody,
John Rhys-Davies

How to Get Ahead in
Advertising

Indiscreet
HTV/Republic Pictures
Locations: London/Bath/
Bristol
Executive producers:
Patrick Dromgoole,
Johnny Goodman, Karen
Mack
Producer: John Davies
Director: Richard
Michaels
Screenwriters: Walter
Lockwood, Sally Robinson
Camera: Bob Edwards
Editor: Terry Maisey
Cast: Robert Wagner,
Lesley-Anne Down,
Maggie Henderson,
Robert McBain, Fanny
Carby

Island Gardens
BBC TV
Locations: London
Docklands/Greenwich
Producer: David Snodin
Director: Nick Renton
Screenwriter: Andy
Armitage
Camera: Philip Bonham-
Carter
Editor: Ian Pitch
Cast: Michael Kitchen,
Corinne Dacla, Keith
Barron, Tom Georgeson,
Anne Carroll

The Hound of the
Baskervilles

Joyriders

Little Bird/Granada TV/
British Screen
Location: Dublin
Producer: Emma Hayter
Associate producer:
Jonathan Cavendish
Director: Aisling Walsh
Screenwriter: Andy
Smith
Camera: Gabriel
Beristain
Editor: Tom Schwalm
Cast: Patricia Kerrigan,
Andrew Connolly, Billie
Whitelaw, Deirdre
Donoghue, Tracey
Peacock

Killing Dad

Applecross Berg
Studio: Lee International,
Shepperton
Location: Southend-On-
Sea
Producer: Iain Smith
Director/screenwriter:
Michael Austin
Camera: Jamie Harcourt
Editor: Edward Marnier
Cast: Denholm Elliott,
Julie Walters, Richard E
Grant, Anna Massey,
Tom Radcliffe

Kitchen Child, The

Techniques of Persuasion/
British Screen/Channel 4
Location:
Northumberland
Executive producer: Ann
Wingate
Producer: Peter Jaques
Director: Joy Perino
Screenwriter: Susan
Campbell
Camera: David Tattersall
Editor: Justin Krish
Cast: Annette Badland,
Paul Brooke, Garry
Halliday, Janet Henfrey,
Jill Barker

Ladder of Swords

Magna Serve/Film Four
International/British
Screen
Location: north-east
England
Producer: Jennifer
Howarth
Director: Norman Hull
Screenwriter: Neil Clarke
Camera: Thaddeus
O'Sullivan
Editor: Scott Thomas
Cast: Martin Shaw, Bob
Peck, Juliet Stevenson,
Eleanor David

Lady and the Highwayman, The

(working title: Dangerous
Love)
Lord Grade/Gainsborough
Pictures
Studio: Pinewood
Locations: Lincolnshire/
Derbyshire/Dover Castle/
Surrey/Dorset/Windsor
Executive producers:
John Hough, Laurie
Johnson
Producer: Peter Manley
Director: John Hough
Screenwriter: Terence
Feely
Camera: Terry Cole
Editor: Peter Weatherley
Cast: Emma Sams, Oliver
Reed, Claire Bloom,
Michael York,
Christopher Cazenove

Lair of the White Worm, The

White Lair/Vestron
Pictures
Studio: Goldcrest Elstree
Locations: Hertfordshire/
Derbyshire
Producer/director: Ken
Russell
Camera: Dick Bush
Editor: Peter Davies
Cast: Amanda Donohoe,
Hugh Grant, Peter
Capaldi, Sammi Davis,
Catherine Oxenberg

Lenny Live

Palace/Sleeping Partners
Location: Hackney
Empire, London
Executive producers: Nik
Powell, Stephen Woolley
Producers: Martin Auty,
Andy Harries
Associate producer:
Raymond Morris
Director: Andy Harries
Screenwriter: Lenny
Henry, Kim Fuller

Lenny Live

The Lair of the White
Worm

Editor: Gerry Hambling
Cast: Lenny Henry,
Robbie Coltrane

Living Doll

Spectacular Film
Location: London/New
York
Producer: Dick Randall
Associate producer:
Frank Green
Directors: Peter Litten,
George Dugdale
Screenwriter: Mark Ezra
Editor: Jim Connock
Cast: Mark Jax, Gary
Martin, Katie Orgill,
Freddie Earlie, Marcel
Grant

Living with Dinosaurs

TVS Films/Jim Henson
Productions
Studio: Lee International,
Wembley
Location: Suffolk coast
Executive producer: Jim
Henson
Producer: Duncan
Kenworthy
Associate producer:
Alexander De Grunwald
Director: Paul Weiland
Screenwriter: Anthony
Minghella
Camera: Peter Hannan
Editor: Henry Richardson
Cast: Michael Maloney,
Juliet Stevenson, Patrick
Malahide, Brian Henson,
Gregory Chisholm

Loser Takes All
British Screen/BBC TV
Studio: Pinewood
Location: south of France
Producers: Christine
Oestreicher, Graham
Easton
Director: James Scott
Screenwriter: James
Scott, from the novel by
Graham Greene
Camera: Robert Paynter
Editor: Thomas Schwalm
Cast: Robert Lindsay,
Molly Ringwald, Sir John
Gielgud, Frances De La
Tour, Max Wall

Magic Moments
Arena Films/Yorkshire
TV/Atlantic
VideoVentures
Studio: Twickenham
Locations: London/
Madrid
Producer: David Conroy
Associate producer: Eric
Rattray
Director: Lawrence
Gordon Clark
Camera: Ken Westbury
Editor: John S Smith
Cast: John Shea, Jenny
Seagrove, Paul Freeman,
Debora Weston, Sam
Douglas

Man for All Seasons, A
Agamemnon/British
Lion/Turner Network
Television
Studio: Pinewood
Executive producer: Peter
Snell
Producer: Fraser Heston
Associate producer: Ted
Lloyd
Director: Charlton Heston
Screenwriter: Robert Bolt
Camera: Denis Lewiston
Editor: Eric Boyd-Perkins

Melancholia

Monster Maker

Cast: Charlton Heston,
Vanessa Redgrave, John
Gielgud, Richard
Johnson, Roy Kinnear

Melancholia
BFI
Locations: London/
Hamburg/Florence
Executive producer: Jill
Pack
Producers: Colin
MacCabe, Helga Bahr
Associate producer: Katy
Radford
Director: Andi Engel
Camera: Denis Crossan
Cast: Jeroen Krabbe,
Ulrich Wildgruber,
Susannah York, Kate
Hardie, Jane Gurnett

Monster Maker
TVS/Jim Henson
Productions
Studio: Lee International,
Wembley
Location: London
Executive producer: Jim
Henson
Producer: Duncan
Kenworthy
Associate producer:
Alexander De Grunwald
Director: Giles Foster
Screenwriter: Matthew
Jacobs, from the novel by
Nicholas Fisk
Camera: Nat Crosby
Editor: Robin Sales
Cast: Harry Dean
Stanton, Kieran O'Brien,
George Costigan

Monster Maker

Mountain and the Molehill, The
BBC TV
Location: Hampshire
Producers: Ruth Caleb,
Graham Massey
Director: Moira
Armstrong
Screenwriter: David Reid
Camera: Philip Bonham-
Carter
Editor: Tariq Anwar
Cast: Michael Quill,
Demetri Jagger, Jacob
Krichefski, Michael
Gough, John Carson

Mountains of the Moon
IndieProd Company
Studio: Lee International,
Shepperton
Locations: UK/Kenya
Executive producers:
Mario Kassar, Andrew
Vajna
Producer: Daniel Melnick
Director: Bob Rafelson
Screenwriter: Bob
Rafelson, William
Harrison
Camera: Roger Deakins
Editor: Thom Noble
Cast: Patrick Bergin, Iain
Glenn, Fiona Shaw, Omar
Sharif, John Savident

Melancholia

Murder on the Moon

Murder on the Moon
Productions/Tamara
Asseyev Productions/
CBS/LWT
Studio: Bray
Location: London
Producer: Tamara
Asseyev
Director: Michael
Lindsay-Hogg
Screenwriter: Carla
Wagner
Camera: Derek Browne
Cast: Brigitte Nielsen,
Julian Sands, Gerald
Mcraney, Jane Lapotaire,
Brian Cox

Murder Story

Murder Story BV/
Contracts International/
Elsevier Vendex Film
Beheer
Location: Holland
Producer: Tom Reeve
Director/screenwriter:
Eddie Arno Markus
Innocenti
Camera: Mark Felperlaan
Editor: Rodney Holland
Cast: Christopher Lee,
Alexis Denisof, Stacia
Burton, Bruce Boa, Kate
Harper

Mwg Glas, Lleuad Waed (Blue Smoke, Red Moon)

Ffilm Cymru/Lluniau
Lliw
Locations: Cardiff/Vale of
Glamorgan
Producer/director: Peter
Edwards
Screenwriter: Sion Eirian
Camera: Ray Orton
Editor: Mali Evans
Cast: Jeff Thomas, John
Woodvine, Lowri Glain,
Dyfed Thomas, Greg
Evans

My Kingdom for a Horse

BBC Drama
Locations: Barnsley/
Yorkshire/Warwickshire
Producer: Chris Parr
Director: Barbara Rennie
Camera: David Feig
Editor: Kate Evans
Cast: Nicholas Woodeson,
Sean Bean, Andrew
Livingston, Sheila
Hancock, Bryan Pringle

My Left Foot

Granada International/
Ferndale Films
Studio: Ardmore

Locations: Dublin/
Wicklow
Executive producers: Paul
Heller, Steve Morrison
Producer: Noel Pearson
Director: Jim Sheridan
Screenwriters: Jim
Sheridan, Shane
Connaughton
Camera: Jack Conroy
Editor: J Patrick Duffner
Cast: Daniel Day Lewis,
Hugh O'Connor, Ray
McAnally, Brenda
Fricker, Fiona Shaw

Nightbreed

Morgan Creek/Film
Futures
Studio: Pinewood
Executive producers:
James G Robinson, Joe
Roth
Producer: Christopher
Figg
Director/screenwriter:
Clive Barker
Camera: Robin Vidgeon
Editor: Richard Marden
Cast: Craig Sheffer, Anne
Bobby, David
Cronenberg, Charles
Haid, Hugh Quarshie

Number 27

BBC TV
Location: London
Producer: Innes Lloyd
Director: Tristram Powell
Screenwriter: Michael
Palin
Camera: Philip Bonham-
Carter
Editor: Mark Day
Cast: Joyce Carey, Nigel
Planer, Helena Michell,
Alun Armstrong, Philip
McGough

Out of Time

Alexander's Treasure
Project/Tamido Film
Productions
Locations: Athens/Egypt
Producer/director: Anwar
Kawadri
Screenwriter: Jesse
Graham
Camera: Fred Tammes
Editor: John Shirley
Cast: Jeff Fahey, Camilla
More, Spiros Focas,
Michael Gothard, Michel
Russo

Person to Person

BBC TV
Location: London
Producer: Kenith Trodd
Director: Witold Starecki
Screenwriter: Boleslaw
Sulik

Camera: Kevin Rowley
Editor: Ardan Fisher
Cast: Maggie O'Neill,
David Threlfall, Thorley
Walters

Poliakoff Film

BBC TV/BBC Enterprises
Location: London
Producer: Kenith Trodd
Director: Peter Hall
Camera: Philip Bonham-
Carter
Editor: Arden Fisher
Cast: Peggy Ashcroft,
Geraldine James, James
Fox, Rebecca Pidgeon,
Rosalie Crutchley

Precious Bane

BBC TV/WGBH Boston/
BBC Enterprises
Location: Shropshire
Producer: Louis Marks
Associate producer: Alex
Gohar
Director: Chris Menaul
Screenwriter: Maggie
Wadey
Camera: Colin Munn
Editor: Dave King
Cast: Janet McTeer, Clive
Owen, John Bowe, Emily
Morgan, John McEnery

Precious Bane

The Real Eddy English

Pursuit
HTV/Columbia Pictures
Television
Location: Yugoslavia
Executive producers:
Patrick Dromgoole,
Johnny Goodman
Producer: Larry White
Director: Ian Sharp
Camera: Bob Edwards
Cast: Ben Cross, Veronica
Hamel, Bruce Greenwood,
Nikolas Grace, Ian
Richardson

Queen of Hearts
Enterprise Pictures/TVS/
Nelson Entertainment
Locations: London/Italy
Executive producer:
Graham Benson
Producer: John Hardy
Director: Jon Amiel
Screenwriter: Tony
Grisoni
Camera: Mike Southon
Editor: Peter Boyle
Cast: Joseph Long, Anita
Zagaria, Eileen Way,
Vittorio Duse, Vittorio
Amandola

Rachel Papers, The
Initial Film and
Television
Studio: JDC, Stonebridge
Park
Location: London
Executive producer: Eric
Fellner
Producers: Andrew
Karsch, Paul Raphael
Director/screenwriter:
Damian Harris
Camera: Alex Thomson
Editor: David Martin
Cast: Dexter Fletcher,
Ione Skye, Jonathan
Pryce, James Spader, Bill
Paterson

Rainbow, The
Rainbow Films/Vestron
Pictures
Studio: Pinewood
Locations: Oxfordshire/
London/Cumbria
Producer/director: Ken
Russell
Editor: Peter Davies
Cast: Sammi Davis, Paul
McGann, Amanda
Donohoe, Elton John,
Glenda Jackson

Real Eddy English,
The
(working title: English)
North and South
Partnership/Channel 4
Location: Oxford
Producers: Colin
McKeown, Martin

Tempia
Director: David Attwood
Screenwriter: Frank
Cottrell Boyce
Camera: Peter Fearon
Cast: Stephen Persaud,
Dona Croll, Helen
Cotterill

Resurrected
Film Four International/
British Screen/St Pancras
Locations: Manchester/
Huddersfield/
Saddleworth Moor
Producers: Adrian
Hughes, Tara Prem
Director: Paul Greengrass
Screenwriter: Martin
Allen
Camera: Ivan Strasburg
Editor: Dan Rea
Cast: David Thewlis, Tom
Bell, Rita Tushingham,
Michael Pollitt, Rudi
Davies

Return from the
River Kwai
Screenlife Establishment/
Leisure Time Productions
BV
Location: Manila
Executive producer:
Daniel Unger
Producer: Kurt Unger
Director: Andrew
McLaglen
Screenwriter: Sargon
Tamimi, Paul
Mayersberg
Camera: Arthur Wooster
Editor: Alan Strachan
Cast: Denholm Elliott,
Edward Fox, Christopher
Penn, Timothy Bottoms,
George Takei

Return of the
Musketeers, The
Timothy Burrill
Productions/Fildebroc/Cia

The Rainbow

Ibero Americana
Locations: Madrid/Spain
Producer: Pierre Spengler
Director: Richard Lester
Camera: Bernard Lutic
Cast: Michael York,
Oliver Reed, Frank
Finlay, C Thomas Howell,
Kim Cattrall

Rockula

Cannon Films
Location: Los Angeles
Executive producers:
Menahem Golam, Yoram
Globus
Producer: Jefery Levy
Director: Luca Bercovici
Screenwriters: Jefery
Levy, Luca Bercovici,
Christopher Verwiel
Camera: John
Schwartzman
Cast: Dean Cameron,
Toni Basil, Thomas
Dolby, Bo Diddley,
Tawney Fere

Scandal

Palace/British Screen
Studio: Lee International,
Wembley
Location: UK
Executive producers: Nik
Powell, Joe Boyd, Harvey
Weinstein, Bob Weinstein
Producer: Stephen
Woolley
Associate producer:
Redmond Morris
Director: Michael Caton-
Jones
Screenwriter: Michael
Thomas
Camera: Mike Molloy
Editor: Angus Newton
Cast: John Hurt, Joanne
Whalley, Ian McKellan,
Bridget Fonda, Britt
Eckland

Shirley Valentine

Lewis Gilbert/Willy
Russell/Paramount
Pictures
Studio: Twickenham
Locations: Greece/UK
Executive producer: John
Dark
Producer/director: Lewis
Gilbert
Screenwriter: Willy
Russell
Camera: Alan Hume
Editor: Lesley Walker
Cast: Pauline Collins,
Tom Conti, Julia
McKenzie, Alison
Steadman, Joanna
Lumley

Simon Wiesenthal Story, The

TVS Films/Robert Cooper
Entertainment/HBO
Enterprises/MTV
Hungary
Location: Budapest,
Hungary
Executive producers:
Graham Benson, Abby
Mann
Producers: Robert Cooper
John Kemeny
Director: Brian Gibson
Screenwriters: Abby
Mann, Lane Slate, Ron
Hutchinson
Camera: Elemer Ragalyi
Editor: Chris Wimble
Cast: Ben Kingsley, Rene
Soutendyk, Craig T
Nelson, Louisa Haigh,
Anton Lesser

Scandal

Slipstream

Entertainment Film
Productions
Studio: Pinewood
Locations: Turkey/
Yorkshire
Executive producers:
Nigel Green, William
Braunstein, Arthur
Maslansky
Producers: Gary Kurtz,
Steve Lanning
Director: Steven
Lisberger
Screenwriters: Charles
Pogue, Tony Kayden,
Steven Lisberger
Camera: Frank Tidy
Editor: Terry Rawlings
Cast: Mark Hamill, Bob
Peck, Bill Paxton, Kitty
Aldridge, Eleanor David

Small Zones

BBC TV
Locations: Hull/Bradford
Producer: Terry Coles
Director: Michael Whyte
Screenwriter: Jim
Hawkins

Shirley Valentine

Camera: Kevin Rowley
Editor: Ardan Fisher
Cast: Catherine Neilson,
Sean Bean, Angela
Walsh, William Ilkley,
Barrie Houghton

Some Other Spring

HTV/Hamster Films,
Paris
Locations: Istanbul/
Bristol/Somerset
Executive producer:
Patrick Dromgoole
Producer: Peter Graham
Scott
Director: Peter Duffell
Screenwriter: Peter
Duffell, from a story by
Francis King
Camera: Dave Hillier
Editor: Lyndon Matthews
Cast: Jenny Seagrove,
Dinsdale Landen, David
Robb, Judy Campbell,
Bud Breckon

Spirit
Elephant Rock
Locations: Siena, Italy/
London
Producer/director:
Jonathan Ripley
Associate producer: Paul
Tucker
Screenwriters: Jonathan
Ripley, Bev Doyle
Camera: Ivan Bartos
Editor: John Gregory
Cast: Paul Rhys, Russell
Irwin, Amelda Brown,
Brian Gwaspari, Richard
Lynch

Star Trap
Zenith/LWT Location:
Cotswolds
Executive producer: Nick
Elliott
Producer: Nigel Stafford
Clark
Associate producer: David
Lascelles
Director/screenwriter:
Tony Bicat

Star Trap

Camera: Witold Stok
Editor: Bill Shapter
Cast: Nicky Henson,
Frances Tomelty, Philip
Sayer, Jeananne Crowley,
Jim Carter

Strapless
Granada Studio: Lee
International, Shepperton
Location: Lisbon
Producers: Rick
McCallum, Patsy Pollock
Director/screenwriter:
David Hare
Camera: Andrew Dunn
Editor: Edward Marnier
Cast: Blair Brown, Bruno
Ganz, Bridget Fonda,
Constantin Alexandrov,
Dana Gillespie

Streets of Yesterday
Channel 4/Mark
Forstater Productions/
Allianz Filmproduktion
(Berlin)
Locations: Israel/Berlin
Producers: Mark
Forstater, Yeud Lavanon,
Wolfgang Tumler
Associate producer: Dov
Maoz
Director: Judd Ne'eman
Screenwriters: Judd
Ne'eman, David Lan
Camera: Miklos Janeso Jr
Editor: Graham Walker
Cast: Paul McGann, Jon
Finch, Suzan Sylvester,
Nadim Sawalha, Alon
Abutbul

Tall Guy, The
(working title: Camden
Town Boy)
Working Title/LWT/
Virgin Vision
Location: London
Executive producer: Tim
Bevan
Producer: Paul Webster
Director: Mel Smith
Screenwriter: Richard
Curtis
Camera: Adrian Biddle
Editor: Dan Rae
Cast: Jeff Goldblum,
Rowan Atkinson, Emma
Thompson, Geraldine
James, Emil Wolk

The Tall Guy

Tank Malling
Pointlane Films
Location: London
Producers: Jamie
Foreman, Glen Murphy
Associate producer:
Terence Murphy
Director: James Marcus
Screenwriters: James
Marcus, Micky South
Camera: Jason Lehel
Editor: David de Wilde
Cast: Ray Winstone, Glen
Murphy, Amanda
Donohoe, Marsha Hunt,
Jason Connery

Tears in the Rain
British Lion/Yorkshire
Television
Studio: Pinewood
Producer: Peter Snell
Associate producer: Ted
Lloyd
Director: Don Sharp
Screenwriter: Fred
Kelsall
Camera: Ken Westbury
Editor: Teddy Darvas
Cast: Sharon Stone,
Christopher Cazenove,
Paul Daneman, Anna
Massey, Leigh Lawson

Testimony of a Child
BBC Screenplay
Location: London
Producers: Ruth Caleb,
Louise Panton
Associate producer: Peter
Wolfes
Director: Peter Smith
Camera: Remi Adefarasin
Editor: John Stothart
Cast: John Bowe, Jill
Baker, Jonathan Leigh,
Victoria Shalet, Heather
Tobias

Thomas and Ruth
BBC TV
Location: north Wales
Executive producer:
Graham Massey
Producer: Ruth Caleb
Associate producer: Peter
Wolfes
Director: Michael
Houldey
Screenwriter: Tom Clark
Camera: John Else
Editor: Jerry Leon
Cast: Emrys James,
Daffyd Hywell, Juliet
Stevenson, Cadfan
Roberts, Eluned Jones

Threepenny Opera, The
Cannon Screen
Entertainment

Tree of Hands

Location: Budapest,
Hungary
Executive producers:
Menahem Golan, Yoram
Globus
Producer: Stanley Chase
Director: Menahem Golan
Screenwriter: Joseph
Goldman
Camera: Elemer Ragalyi
Editor: Tova Neeman
Cast: Raul Julia, Richard
Harris, Julia Migenes,
Julie Walters, Roger
Daltrey

Tree of Hands
Greenpoint/Granada Film
Productions/British
Screen
Studio: Goldcrest Elstree
Location: London
Producer: Ann Scott
Associate producer: Ann
Wingate
Director: Giles Foster
Screenwriter: Gordon
Williams
Camera: Kenneth
MacMillan
Editor: David Martin
Cast: Helen Shaver,
Lauren Bacall,
Peter Firth, Paul
McGann, Malcolm
Stoddard

Unexplained Laughter
BBC Wales/Cornerstone
Films
Location: Brecon Beacons
Executive producer: John
Hefin
Producer: Tom
Kinninmont
Associate producers: Jane
Cussons, Phyllida Nash
Director: Gareth Davies
Screenwriter: Alun Owen
Camera: Ashley Rowe
Editor: John Gillanders
Cast: Diana Rigg, Elaine
Paige, Joanna David, Jon
Finch, Robert Gwilym

Unexplained Laughter

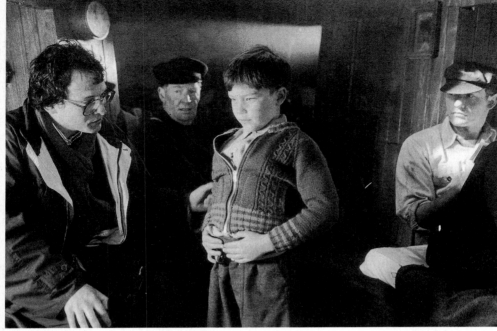

Venus Peter
BFI/Christopher Young
Films/British Screen/
Film Four International/
Scottish Film Production
Fund/Orkney Islands
Council
Location: Orkney
Executive producer: Colin
McCabe
Producer: Christopher
Young
Director: Ian Sellar
Screenwriters: Ian Sellar,
Christopher Rush
Camera: Gabriel
Beristain
Editor: David Spiers
Cast: Ray McAnally,
Caroline Paterson, Peter
Caffrey, Sinead Cusack,
Louise Breslan

View of Harry
Clark, A
BBC Scotland
Locations: Glasgow/
Liverpool
Producer: Tom
Kinninmont
Director: Alastair Reid
Screenwriter: Daniel
Boyle
Camera: Charlie
Ringland
Editor: Graham
Greenhorn
Cast: Griff Rhys Jones,
Elaine Paige, Laura
Claire Duerden, Benjie

Lawrence, Charlotte
Coleman

Virtuoso
Ideal Communications
Films and Television
Location: London
Executive producers:
Graham Massey, Kevin
Christie
Producer: Philip
Hinchcliffe
Associate producer: Peter
Wolfes
Director: Tony Smith
Screenwriter: William
Humble
Camera: John McGlashan
Editor: Dick Allen
Cast: Alfred Molina,
Alison Steadman, Sverre
Anker Ousdal, Jane
Booker, Philip Lock

Vote for Hitler, A
Brook Productions
Location: Oxford
Executive producer: Anne
Lapping
Associate producer: Rob
Shepherd
Director: Paul Bryers
Screenwriter: Paul Bryers
Camera: Michael Coulter
Editor: Andy Page
Cast: Owen Brenman,
Elizabeth Carling, Peter
Cellier, James Coombes,
Barry Crane

War and
Remembrance
Circle Location Services/
ABC Entertainment
Studio: Pinewood
Executive producer: Dan
Curtis
Producer: Barbara Steele
Director: Dan Curtis
Camera: Egil Woxholt
Editor: Peter Zinner,
Gary Smith, Peter Boita
Cast: Jane Seymour,
Michael Woods, Earl
Hindman, Michael
Lemon, Richard Lineback

War Requiem
Anglo International
Films
Location: London
Producer: Don Boyd
Associate producer:
Christopher Harrison
Director: Derek Jarman
Camera: Richard Greatex
Editor: Rick Elgood
Cast: Laurence Olivier,
Nathaniel Parker, Tilda
Swinton, Owen Teale,
Patricia Hayes

We Think the World
of You
British Screen/Film Four
International/Cinecom
Entertainment Group/
Gold Screen Production
Location: London
Producer: Tommaso

Venus Peter

Jandelli, Paul Cowen
Director: Colin Gregg
Screenwriter: Hugh
Stoddart
Camera: Mike Garfath
Editor: Peter Delfgou
Cast: Alan Bates, Gary
Oldman, Frances Barber,
Liz Smith, Max Wall

White Roses
Amy International/
Jadran
Location: Yugoslavia
Executive producer:
Susan George
Producers: Simon
MacCorkindale, Zdravko
Mihalic
Director: Rajko Grlic
Screenwriters: Borislav
Pecic, Rajko Grlic, Simon
MacCorkindale
Camera: Tomislav Pinter
Editor: Damir German
Cast: Tom Conti, Susan
George, Rod Steiger, Alun
Armstrong, Vanya Drach

**We Think the World
of You**

Why the Whales Came

Cygnet Films/Golden Swan Films
Location: Scilly Isles
Executive producer: Geoffrey Wansell
Producer: Simon Channing Williams
Director: Clive Rees
Screenwriter: Michael Morpurgo
Camera: Robert Paynter
Editor: Andrew Boulton
Cast: Helen Mirren, Paul Scofield, David Suchet, Barbara Jefford, David Threlfall

Winter

Film Four International/British Screen/Portman
Location: London
Executive producer: Tom Donald
Producers: Victor Glynn, Simon Channing-Williams
Director/screenwriter: Mike Leigh
Camera: Roger Pratt
Editor: Jon Gregory
Cast: David Bamber, Philip Davis, Edna Dore, Yvonne French, Philip Jackson

Witches, The

Jim Henson Productions
Studio: Bray
Locations: Norway/Cornwall
Executive producer: Jim Henson
Producer: Mark Shivas
Director: Nicolas Roeg
Screenwriter: Allan Scott
Camera: Harvey Harrison
Editor: Tony Lawson
Cast: Mai Zetterling, Anjelica Huston, Ann Lambton, Rowan Atkinson, Sukie Smith

Wolves of Willoughby Chase, The

Atlantic/Zenith
Location: Czechoslovakia
Producer: Mark Forstater
Associate producer: Raymond Day
Director: Stuart Orme
Camera: Paul Beeson
Editor: Martin Walsh
Cast: Stephanie Beacham, Mel Smith, Geraldine James, Emily Hudson, Alex Darowska

Woman In Black, The

Central Films
Locations: Essex/Wiltshire/Norfolk/Berkshire/London
Executive producer: Ted Childs
Producer: Chris Burt
Director: Herbert Wise
Screenwriter: Nigel Kneale
Camera: Michael Davis

The Wolves of Willoughby Chase

Editor: Laurence Mery-Clark
Cast: Adrian Rawlins, Bernard Hepton, David Daker, Pauline Moran, David Ryall

Yellow Wallpaper, The

BBC TV
Location: Ipswich
Producer: Sarah Curtis
Director: John Clive
Screenwriter: Maggie Wadey, from the novella by Charlotte Perkins Gilman
Camera: John Hooper
Editor: Sue Wyatt
Cast: Julia Watson, Stephen Dillon, Carolyn Pickles, Dorothy Tutin, James Faulkner

STUDIOS

Bray Studios
Down Place
Windsor Road
Water Oakley
Berks SL4 5UG
Tel: 0628 22111
STAGES

1	952 sq metres
2	948 sq metres
3	279 sq metres
4	175 sq metres

FILMS
Dark of the Moon for
Viacom International
The Manageress for Zed
Saracen for Central TV
The Witches for Henson
Organisation

Goldcrest Elstree Studios
Borehamwood
Herts WD6 1JG
Tel: 01 953 1600
STAGES

1	1350 sq metres
2	1350 sq metres
3	1350 sq metres
4	1350 sq metres
5	1470 sq metres
6	2787 sq metres
7	480 sq metres
8	720 sq metres
9	720 sq metres
10	720 sq metres

FILMS
Behaving Badly, for
Channel 4
*Indiana Jones and the
Last Crusade,* starring
Harrison Ford; director
Steven Spielberg;
producer Robert Watts;
executive producers
George Lucas and Frank
Marshall
Lair of the White Worm,
starring Amanda
Donohoe; director Ken
Russell; producers Ken
Russell and Ronaldo
Vasconcellos
Piece of Cake series, for
LWT
The Storyteller series for
Henson Organisation
The Tree of Hands,
director Giles Foster;
producer Ann Scott

Halliford Studios
Manygate Lane
Shepperton
Middx TW17 9EG
Tel: 0932 226341
STAGES

A	334 sq metres
B	223 sq metres

Isleworth Studios
Studio Parade
484 London Road

Isleworth
Middx TW7 4DE
Tel: 01 568 3511
STAGES

A	292 sq metres
B	152 sq metres
C	152 sq metres
D	152 sq metres
Packshot stage	141 sq metres

Lee International Film Studios
128 Wembley Park Drive
Wembley
Middlesex HA9 8JE
Tel: 01 902 1262
STAGES

A	613 sq metres
B	613 sq metres
C	401 sq metres
D	297 sq metres
E	293 sq metres
F	93 sq metres

Lee International Studios Shepperton
Studios Road
Shepperton
Middx TW17 0QD
Tel: 0932 562611
STAGES

A	1674 sq metres
B	1116 sq metres
C	1674 sq metres
D	1116 sq metres
H	2790 sq metres
I	657 sq metres
J	284 sq metres
K	120 sq metres
L	604 sq metres
M	260 sq metres
T	261 sq metres

FILMS
Cry Freedom starring
Kevin Kline, Denzel
Washington and Penelope
Wilton; producer/director
Sir Richard Attenborough
Gorillas in the Mist
starring Sigourney
Weaver, Brian Brown and
Julie Harris; director
Michael Apted; producer
Terry Clegg
Handful of Dust starring
James Wilby and Kristin
Scott Thomas; director
Charles Sturridge;
producer Derek Granger
*Lonely Passion of Judith
Hearne, The* for
HandMade: starring
Maggie Smith and Bob
Hoskins; director Jack
Clayton
Poor Little Rich Girl
starring Farrah Fawcett:
director Charles Jarrott;
producer Nick Gillott
Raggedy Rawney for

HandMade: starring Bob
Hoskins; director Bob
Hoskins
Stealing Heaven starring
Denholm Elliott and
Bernard Hepton; director
Clive Donner; producers
Simon MacCorkindale
and Susan George
White Mischief starring
Joss Ackland, Charles
Dance, Greta Scacchi,
Sarah Miles and John
Hurt; director Michael
Radford; producer Simon
Perry
You Bet series for LWT:
starring Bruce Forsyth;
directors Noel D Greene,
John Birkin; producer
Richard Hearsey

Pinewood Studios
Pinewood Road
Iver
Bucks SL0 0NH
Tel: 0753 651700
STAGES

A	1685 sq metres
B	827 sq metres
C	827 sq metres
D	1685 sq metres
E	1685 sq metres
F	700 sq metres
G	247 sq metres
H	300 sq metres
J	825 sq metres
K	825 sq metres
L	880 sq metres
M	880 sq metres
007 (silent)	4350 sq metres
South Dock (silent)	1548 sq metres
North Dock (silent)	628 sq metres
Special FX (silent)	658 sq metres
Large Process	439 sq metres
Small Process	226 sq metres

FILMS
Batman, starring Michael
Keaton, Jack Nicholson,
Kim Basinger; director
Tim Burton
Dangerous Love, starring
Emma Sams, Oliver Reed
Dry White Season, A,
starring Marlon Brando,
Donald Sutherland;
director Euzhan Palcy
Great Expectations
Hellbound: Hellraiser II
Jack the Ripper
Man for All Seasons, A,
starring Charlton Heston,
Vanessa Redgrave, John
Gielgud; director
Charlton Heston
Nightbreed

Slipstream, starring
Mark Hamill, Bob Peck
Without a Clue

**The Production
Village**
100 Cricklewood Lane
London NW2
Tel: 01 450 9361
STAGES
A   1116 sq metres
B   360 sq metres

**Twickenham Film
Studios**
St Margaret's
Twickenham

Middx TW1 2AW
Tel: 01 892 4477
STAGES
1   702 sq metres
2   186 sq metres
3   519 sq metres

Westway Studios
Olaf Street
London W11 4BE
Tel: 01 221 9041
STAGES
1   602 sq metres
2   520 sq metres
3   169 sq metres
4   242 sq metres
5   70 sq metres

Below are listed all British television companies, with a selection of their key personnel and programmes. The titles listed are a cross-section of productions initiated (but not necessarily broadcast) during 1988 and the first quarter of 1989. 'F' and 'V' indicate whether productions were shot on film or video. For details of feature films made for television, see Starts (p228)

INDEPENDENT TELEVISION

ANGLIA
Television Limited

Anglia Television
Anglia House
Norwich NR1 3JG
Tel: 0603 615151
Chairman: Sir Peter Gibbings
Chief Executive: David McCall
Managing Director, Broadcasting Division: Philip Garner

Antarctica – the Last Frontier
Production company: Anglia/Survival
Producer/Director: Graham Creelman
Scriptwriters: Graham Creelman, and David Hickman
Editor: Alan Newton
3 × 1 hour F
Network documentary on the threat to the world's last great wilderness from commercial exploitation and political pressures

Anything Goes
Presenter: Paul Barnes
6 × 30 mins V
Second series of network holiday and leisure programme concentrating on Britain

A Place in the Sun
Producer/Director: Ron Trickett
Camera: David Jones
Editor: Keith Judge
6 × 30 mins V
ITV network series on Britons with second homes abroad

Border Television
The Television Centre
Carlisle CA1 3NT
Tel: 0228 25101
Chairman: The Earl of Lonsdale
Managing Director: James Graham
Director of Programmes: Paul Corley

Ghost Train
Executive producer: Harry King
Producer: Tony Nicholson
The Ghost Train arrives every Sunday at Border TV

Hills are Alive
Executive producer: Paul Corley
Producer: Clem Shaw
Director: Nick May
One hour documentary for Channel 4 shot over twelve months tracing the effects of Chernobyl on Lake District shepherds

The Joke Machine
Executive producer: Paul Corley
Producer/Director: Harry King
Jimmy Cricket presents the fourth series of this ITV network children's programme

Jools Holland – The Groovy Fellers
Executive producer: Paul Corley
Producer: John Gwyn
Director: Tim Pope
Jools Holland and The Martian embark on a series of zany adventures in search of the truth about the world

Jung, Wisdom of the Dream
Executive producer: Paul Corley
Producer/Director: Steven Segaller
3 × 1 hour documentary on the life and ideas of Carl Jung

KTV Krankies Television
Executive producer: Paul Corley
Producer/Director: Harry King
The Krankies set up their own satellite TV station

The Wool Strand
Executive producer: Lis Howell
Producer: Lis Bloor
More than 25,000 information packs have been distributed in connection with this knitting strand in Daytime Live

CENTRAL

Central Independent Television
Central House
Broad Street
Birmingham B1 2JP
Tel: 021 643 9898
East Midlands Television Centre
Nottingham NG7 2NA
Tel: 0602 863322
35–38 Portman Square
London W1A 2HZ
Tel: 01 486 6688
Hesketh House
43–45 Portman Square
London W1H 9FG
Central South
Television House
23–25 Commercial Road
Gloucester GL1

Chairman: David
Justham
Managing Director:
Leslie Hill
Director of Programmes:
Andy Allan
General Manager,
Programme Production:
Philip Gilbert
Controller, Drama: Ted
Childs
Controller, Network
Features: Richard
Creasey
Controller,
Entertainment: Tony
Wolfe
Controller, Young
People's Programmes:
Lewis Rudd
Controller, Regional
Programmes: Robert
Southgate

Boon
Executive producer:
William Smethurst
Series producer: Esta
Charkham
Directors: L Moody, Bren
Simson, B MacDonald,
G Husson, Baz Taylor,
Sarah Hellings, A Kirby
Cast: Michael Elphick,
David Daker, Amanda
Burton
13 × 1 hour
Weekly drama series
centred around ex-
fireman turned private
detective

The Cook Report
Executive producer: Bob
Southgate
Series producer: Mike
Townson
Presenter: Roger Cook
8 × 30 mins
Roger Cook returns to
expose more criminals in
the third series of the no-
holds-barred
investigative programme

A Kind of Living
Producer: Glen Cardno
Director: Paul Harrison
Scriptwriter: Paul Makin
Cast: Frances de la Tour,
Richard Griffiths, Tim
Healy
6 × 30 mins
Situation comedy
following the life and
times of a school teacher
as he struggles with the
80s while constantly
reliving the past

New Faces
Producer: Richard
Holloway
Director: David G Hillier,

Peter Harris
Presenter: Marti Caine
12 × 1 hour, Final 1 × 90
mins
Nationwide talent contest
to find stars of the future

The Nuclear Age
Executive producers:
Richard Creasey, Zvi
Dorner
A Central production in
association with WGBH
Boston and NHK Japan
12 × 1 hour
An authoritative
documentary series traces
40 years of international
nuclear strategy

Woof
Executive producer:
Lewis Rudd
Producer/Director: David
Cobham
Scriptwriters: Richard
Fegen, Andrew Norris
Cast: Lisa Goddard, John
Ringham, Thomas
Aldwinckle, Edward
Fidoe, Pippin the Dog
Lighthearted four-part
family series about a boy
who changes into a dog

Channel Television
Television Centre
St Helier
Jersey
Tel: 0534 73999
Television Centre
St George's Place
St Peter Port
Guernsey
Tel: 0481 23451
Chairman: Major J R
Riley
Managing Director: John
Henwood

Bertie the Bat
Producer: Jane Bayer
Animator: Julia
Coutanche
Scriptwriter: Lisa
Beresford
Creator: Jane Aireton
Narrator: Bernard
Cribbins
4 mins 20 secs V
A new character to
children's television,
Bertie the Bat longs to be
different and with the
help of his friend the
Skypainter, he achieves
his dream.

Channel Report
Producer/Director: Paul
Brown
News Editor: Martyn
Farley
Presenter: Russell Labey
24 mins V
Half-hour news magazine
broadcast Monday to
Friday jointly presented
from Channel's Jersey
and Guernsey news
studios but also featuring
live or taped inserts from
the smaller islands

The Dodo Club
Producer/Director: Bob
Evans
Scriptwriter: Bob Evans
Camera: Tim Ringsdore
Presenters: Michael
Bassett, Sue Robbie
7 × 20 mins V
A look at wildlife in
danger including the
work of Jersey Zoo and
organisations looking
after the animals and
countryside of Britain

Highway
Producer/Director: Bob
Evans
Scriptwriter: Bob Evans
Camera: Tim Ringsdore
Editor: Garry Knight
Presenter: Sir Harry
Secombe
3 × 30 mins 35 secs V
Sir Harry Secombe
presents programmes
from the Channel Islands
and Malta

Ready Aye Ready
Producer/Director: Bill
Brown
Scriptwriter: Bill Brown
Camera: Richard Hall,
Tim Ringsdore, Kevin
Banner
Editor: Garry Knight
25 mins, 5 secs V
The history of the Jersey
Fire Brigade provides a
fascinating foil to the
drama of modern fire
fighting. A week in the
life of white watch

Wildlife – On the Edge
Producer: Bob Evans
Director/Scriptwriter:
Jane Bayer
Camera: Tim Ringsdore,
Roy Manning
Editor: Jim Best
5 × 25 mins V
A look at the world of
Jersey's Wildlife
Preservation Trust

CHANNEL FOUR TELEVISION

**Channel Four
Television**
60 Charlotte Street
London W1P 2AX
Tel: 01 631 4444
Chairman: Sir Richard
Attenborough
Chief Executive: Michael
Grade
Director of Programmes:
Liz Forgan
Director of Programme
Acquisitions & Sales:
Colin Leventhal
Deputy Director of
Programmes &
Controller, Arts &
Entertainment: Mike
Bolland
Head of Drama: David
Rose
Commissioning Editors:
David Lloyd (Senior
Commissioning Editor,
News & Current Affairs);
Gwynn Pritchard (Senior
Commissioning Editor,
Education); Peter
Ansorge (Drama Series &
Serials); Seamus Cassidy
(Entertainment);
Farrukh Dhondy
(Multicultural
Programmes); Alan
Fountain (Independent
Film and Video); Stephen
Garrett (Youth); (Arts
vacant); Caroline
Thomson (Finance,
Industry and Science);
Bob Towler (Education
and Religion); Avril
MacRory (Music); Mike
Miller (Sport); Peter
Moore (Documentaries);
Michael Attwell (Talk &
Features); Karin
Bamborough (Single
Drama)
Chief Film Buyer: Mairi
Macdonald

**Art of the Western
World**
Production company: TVS
Executive producer:
Andrew Snell
Presenter: Michael Wood
18 × 30 mins
Major series looking at
the history of Western art
from the clasical period to
the 20th century

**In the Shadow of the
Sun**
Production company:

Seventh Art Productions
Producer: Pere Roca
Writer/Director: Phil
Grabsky
6 × 60 mins
Documentary series
looking at modern Spain
through the lives of
individual Spaniards and
assessing the results of
the recent years of change
and modernisation

Mahabharata
Production company: RM
Associates
Director: Peter Brook
360 mins
Peter Brook's own version
of his acclaimed theatre
production based on the
classic Indian epic. The
central story tells of a
protracted struggle
between the two wings of
a royal family

The Manageress
Production company: Zed
Productions
Producers: Sophie
Balhetchet, Glenn
Wilhide
Director: Christopher
King
Writers: Stan Hey,
Neville Smith
6 × 60 mins
A woman takes over as
manager of an ailing
second division football
club and attempts to take
them to the top

Signals
Production company:
Holmes Associates
Series editor: Roger Graef
24 × 45 mins
Channel 4's weekly arts
magazine programme
exploring and questioning
how the arts reflect and
affect all our lives

Skyscraper
Production company: Inca
Producer: Karl Sabbagh
5 × 60 mins
The story behind the
building of a modern
skyscraper in Madison
Square Gardens showing
the technology of a
skyscraper construction,
the decision-making
process of those involved
and the effects on the
local community

Other programmes
include:
Equinox
A Very British Coup

GRAMPIAN TELEVISION

Grampian Television
Queen's Cross
Aberdeen AB9 2XJ
Tel: 0224 646464
Chairman: Douglas
Hardie CBE
Chief Executive: Donald
H Waters
Director of Television:
Robert L Christie
Director of Finance:
Graham Good

The Big Break
Executive producer:
Robert L Christie
Producer/Director:
Graeme Matthews
5 × 30 mins V
A series of variety
contests featuring new
Scottish entertainers
hosted by comedian
George Duffus

**Celebrity Shoot at
Gleneagles**
Executive producer: John
Hughes
Director: Alan Franchi
1 × 54 mins F
A charity clay pigeon
shoot by celebrities
including a team from the
Royal Family

Home at Last
Producer: Ted
Brocklebank
Director: Graham
McLeish
1 × 27 mins F
Story of the sinking of
HM Yacht Iolaire and the
drowning of more than
200 men in 1919

**On the Road with Art
Sutter**
Production company:
Creative Production
Associates
Commissioning Editor:
Ted Brocklebank
Director: Brian Freeston
6 × 27 mins V
Broadcaster Art Sutter
takes to the road to profile
towns in North Scotland

Sea Farmers
Executive producer: Ted
Brocklebank
Director: Michael Steele
1 × 54 mins

A sequel to Grampian's
Last of the Hunters
programme on fish
catching, this
documentary examines
progress in fish farming

Storm On the Mountain
Production company:
Acacia Productions
Executive producer: Ted
Brocklebank
Director: Ed Milner
1 × 54 mins F
A year in the life of the
Cairngorms and the
controversy raging there
between conservationists
and developers

Granada Television
Granada Television
Centre
Manchester M60 9EA
Tel: 061 832 7211
Granada News Centre
Albert Dock
Liverpool L3 4BA
Tel: 051 709 9393
Granada News Centre
White Cross
South Road
Lancaster LA1 4XH
Tel: 0524 60688
Granada News Centre
Bridgegate House
5 Bridge Place
Lower Bridge Street
Chester CH1 15A
Tel: 0244 313966
Chairman: David
Plowright
Managing Director:
Andrew Quinn
Director of Programmes:
Steve Morrison
Programme Board: David
Boulton, Rod Caird,
Michael Cox, Paul
Doherty, Ray Fitzwalter,
Steve Hawes, David
Liddiment, Andrew
McLaughlin

After the War
Producer: Michael Cox,
Sita Williams
Directors: John Glenister,
John Madden
Scriptwriter: Frederick
Raphael
Cast: Adrien Lukis,
Robert Reynolds
10 part series F
Story of two ambitious
Jewish men pursuing
with single-minded

determination the fallible
rewards of post-war
success

Capstick's Law
Production company:
Messenger Television
Producer: Roderick
Graham
Directors: Richard
Martin, John Michael
Phillips
Scriptwriters: John
Finch, John Stevenson
Cast: Robin Ellis, William
Gaunt, Christopher
Villiers, Vanda Wentham
6 × 1 hour F
The life of a country
solicitor practice in a
North Yorkshire market
town in the early 1950s

Confessional
Production company:
Granada/Harmony Gold
USA/Rete Europa
Producers: David
Plowright, Bill
McCutchen
Director: Gordon
Flemyng
Scriptwriter: James
Mitchell
Cast: Keith Carradine,
Anthony Higgins
4 × 1 hour F
Based on Jack Higgins'
best seller, Confessional
follows the turbulent
friendship of two young
men

Game Set and Match
Producer: Brian
Armstrong
Director: Patrick Lau
Scriptwriter: Len
Deighton
Cast: Ian Holm, Mel
Martin
13 × 1 hour F
Len Deighton's epic
trilogy of deceit and
treachery in a world of
espionage, filmed on
location in Berlin, Mexico
and London

Surgical Spirit
Production company:
Humphrey Barclay
Productions
Producer: Humphrey
Barclay
Scriptwriter: Peter
Learmouth
Cast: Nichola McAuliffe,
Duncan Preston
6 × 30 mins V
Sheila Sabatini is a
surgeon in a male
dominated world who

gives as good as she gets. Her caustic wit becomes legendary everywhere from the operating theatre to the sluice room

A Tale of Two Cities
Production company: Granada/Dune Productions
Producer: Roy Roberts
Director: Philippe Monnier
Scriptwriter: Arthur Hopcraft
Cast: Jean Pierre Aumont, Xavier Deluc, Serena Gordon, Alfred Lynch, Anna Massey, Sir John Mills, James Wilby
2 × 2 hour F
Adaptation of Charles Dickens' epic love story played out against the turbulent background of the French Revolution

HTV
Television Centre
Culverhouse Cross
Cardiff CF5 6XJ
Tel: 0222 590590
HTV Ltd
99 Baker St
London W1M 2AJ
Tel: 01 486 4311
HTV Group
Chairman: Sir Melvyn Rosser
Chief Executive: Patrick Dromgoole
Deputy Chief Executive and Director Television Group: H H Davies
Director Finance and Administration: Alan Burton
HTV Cymru/Wales Ltd
Chairman: I E Symonds
Managing Director: H H Davies
Director of Programmes: Emyr Daniel

Ballroom
Producer/Director: Alan Clayton
Scriptwriter: Robert Pugh
Cast: Glyn Houston, Beth Morris, William Thomas, Hannah Roberts, Stevie Parry
1 × 90 mins F
Actor/Playwright Robert Pugh's recollections of a South Wales Valleys character he knew as a youngster

Better Days
Producer/Director: Alan Clayton
Scriptwriter: Robert Pugh
Cast: Glyn Houston, Gareth Thomas, Christina Greatrex, Robert Pugh, Beth Morris, Michael Quill, Dicken Ashworth, Ivor Roberts
1 × 90 mins F
Edgar, a valleys widower, goes to live in a posh Cardiff suburb with his eldest son Gwilym, a successful but emotionless barrister who has become a slave to success

The Snow Spider
Producer/Director: Pennant Roberts
Writer: Julia Jones, from a story by Jenny Nimmo
Cast: Sian Phillips, Osian Roberts, Sharon Morgan, Robert Blythe, Rosslyn Killick, Gareth Pritchard
4 × 30 mins
Set in the present day, a story of magic and fantasy using devices and ideas from the Celtic legends, 'The Mabinogion'

We are Seven
Production company: HTV/TV60
Producer/Director: Alan Clayton
Writer: Robert Pugh, from a novel by Una Troy
Cast: Helen Roberts, Dafydd Hywel, Elizabeth Morgan, Huw Ceredig, William Thomas, Beth Morris
6 × 1 hour F
Story about Bridget Morgan, her seven illegitimate children and their various fathers. Set in rural West Wales in the 1930s

HTV West
Television Centre
Bath Road
Bristol BS4 3HG
Tel: 0272 778366
Chairman: Colin Atkinson
Managing Director: Ron Evans
Director of Programmes: Derek Clark
Head of News: Steve Matthews

All Muck and Magic
At Home

The Bubblegum Brigade
Dors, The Other Diana
HTV News
Keynotes
Rolf's Cartoon Club
Scene
West Country Farming
The West This Week

Independent Television News
ITN House
48 Wells Street
London W1P 4DE
Tel: 01 637 2424
Chairman and Chief Executive: David Nicholas
Editor: Stewart Purvis

Independent Television News provides programmes of national and international news for the independent television network. It also produces the award-winning Channel Four News each weekday evening and since March 1989 has produced the World News for the Channel Four Daily. ITN also operates the first international English language news programme. ITN World News is a daily programme specifically designed for a worldwide audience and is now seen on four continents. Other programmes for the other ITV companies include *The World This Week* and *The Parliament Programme* for Channel Four; elections at home and abroad, the budget, royal tours, state visits, overseas events and special celebrations. ITN also provides general, sport and business news for Oracle

Channel Four News
5am Morning News
ITN World News
Morning Bulletins
News at One

News at 5.40
News at Ten
Night Time Bulletins
Oracle
The Parliament Programme
Special Programmes
The World This Week
World News on Channel Four Daily

London Weekend Television
South Bank Television Centre
London SE1 9LT
Tel: 01 261 3434
Chairman and Managing Director: Brian Tesler
Deputy Managing Director and Director of Programmes: Greg Dyke
Director of Corporate Affairs: Barry Cox
Controller of Drama and Arts: Nick Elliott
Head of Arts: Melvyn Bragg
Controller of Entertainment: Marcus Plantin
Controller of Features and Current Affairs: Jane Hewland
Deputy Controller of Features and Current Affairs: Robin Paxton
Controller of Sport: John Bromley
Deputy Controller of Sport: Stuart McConachie

Eyewitness
Executive producer: Jane Hewland
Editor: Simon Shaps
32 × 50 mins live + V
Reporters: Jan Rowland, Paul Ross, Carson Black, Sebastian Scott, Trevor Phillips, Michael Elliott
First major new weekly current affairs programme on the ITV network for 16 years, reporting on important stories worldwide

Floyd on TV
Executive producer: Marcus Plantin
Producer: Nick Barrett
Director: Nick Vaughan-Barratt
6 × 30 mins V
The television cook turns

his attention to other programmes on the small screen, uncovering buried treasures from archive material around the world

Forever Green
Production company: Picture Partnership Production
Executive producer: Nick Elliott
Producer: Brian Eastman
Director: David Giles
6 × 60 mins F
This drama series stars John Alderton and Pauline Collins as a city couple moving to the country

Hale & Pace
Executive producer: Marcus Plantin
Producer: Alan Nixon
Director: Vic Finch
7 × 30 mins V
Anarchic comedy duo whose first series was chosen as the ITV entry for the Golden Rose of Montreux

Piece of Cake
Production company: Holmes Associates
Executive producer: Linda Agran
Producer: Andrew Holmes
Director: Ian Toynton
6 × 60 mins F

The Walden Interview
Executive producer: Hugh Pile
Series producer: John Wakefield
11 × 60 mins live
Brian Walden returns to television with a series of major one-to-one interviews with national and international figures

S4C

S4C
Sophia Close
Cardiff CF1 9XY
Tel: 0222 343421
Chairman: John Howard Davies CBE DL
Chief Executive: Geraint Stanley Jones
Programme Controller: Euryn Ogwen Williams
Controller of Planning

and Marketing: Christopher Grace

C'mon Midfield
Production company: Ffilmiau'r Nant
Producer/Director: Alun Ffred Jones
Scriptwriters: Mei Jones, Alun Ffred Jones
Cast: John Pierce Jones, Mei Jones, Bryn Fon, Llion Williams, Sian Wheldon
6 × 30 mins
Comedy series about a small football club with big or biggish ideas – Bryncoch United, the world's most unlikely football team

Fideo 9
Production company: Criw Byw
Production Team: Dafydd Rhys, Geraint Jarman, Andy Brice
Presenter: Eddie Ladd
16 × 40 mins
Series of contemporary music featuring Welsh rock and international music combined with features and items on people in the arts

Jabas
Production company: Ffilmiau Eryri
Producer: Norman Williams
Directors: Gwennan Sage, Emlyn Williams
Script: Penri Jones
Camera: Ray Orton
Editor: Richard Bradley
Cast: Owain Gwilym, Buddug Povey, Harri Pritchard, Eleri Vaughan Williams, Lowri Mererid
12 × 30 mins
Adventure series set in North Wales featuring the trials and tribulations of Jabas and his friends

Satellite City
Production company: Fairwater Films
Producer: Mike Young
Director: Clennell Rawson
Scriptwriter: Nia Ceidiog
12 × 6 mins
Children's animation series highlighting a topical issue as the inhabitants of Satellite City battle against the evil forces of Acid Rain, Slime and Toxin

SCOTTISH TELEVISION

Scottish Television
Cowcaddens
Glasgow G2 3PR
Tel: 041 332 9999
114 St Martin's Lane
London WC2N 4AZ
Tel: 01 836 1500
Chairman: Sir Campbell Fraser
Deputy Chairman and Managing Director: William Brown CBE
Director of Programmes: Gus Macdonald
Controller of Drama: Robert Love
Controller of Education, Religion and Children's Programmes: Robert McPherson
Controller of Entertainment: Sandy Ross
Controller of News, Sport and Current Affairs: David Scott

Rescue
Producer: Paul Berriff
Network documentary series on the Air Sea rescue services

Scotsport
Producer: David Scott
60 mins
Weekly sports magazine

Scottish Women
Producer: David Scott
30 mins
Discussion forum for 100 Scottish women

Taggart
Producer: Robert Love
3 × 60 mins
Detective series set in Glasgow

Take the High Road
Producer: Brian Mahoney
30 mins
Network drama serial

Winners and Losers
Producer: Robert Love
3 × 60 mins
Fast moving drama set in the boxing world

TSW – Television South West
Derry's Cross
Plymouth
Devon PL1 2SP
Tel: 0752 663322
Chairman: Sir Brian Bailey OBE
Managing Director: Harry Turner
Controller of Programmes: Paul Stewart Laing
Head of News: Richard Myers
Head of Current Affairs: Tom Keene
Head of Education and Religion: Thomas Goodison
Head of Documentaries: Frank Wintle
Head of Programme Planning: Elizabeth Mahoney

Food – Fad or Fact?
Joan Shenton returns with a second series which separates the myths from the realities of healthy eating habits

The Man Who Went Mad On Paper
This programme counterpoints the hilarity of the work that won cartoonist H M Bateman fame with the sombre obsessions which destroyed his marriage and turned him into a dour recluse

Mother Goose Stories
A series of pre-school programmes based on well-known nursery rhymes, made in association with Henson International
13 × 8 mins

Sounds Like Music
Bobby Crush returns to the small screen to compere a musical quiz testing knowledge of film and musicals

Tube Mice
Animation series, about four mice who live in the London Underground, using voices of George

Cole and Dennis
Waterman
26 × 5 mins

White Knights, Fiery Steeds
The RAF's low-flying
exercises over the British
countryside are the
subject of this hour long
documentary

TV-am

TV-am
Breakfast Television
Centre
Hawley Crescent
London NW1 8EF
Tel: 01 267 4300
Chairman: Ian Irvine
Managing Director/
Director of Programmes:
Bruce Gyngell
Director of News and
Current Affairs: Bill
Ludford
Director of Technical
Operations and
Production: David
Davidovitz
Controller, News and
Current Affairs: Jeff
Berliner

**The Morning
Programme/Good
Morning Britain/After
Nine**
Presenters: Anne
Diamond, Mike Morris,
Richard Keys, Jayne
Irving, Kathy Tayler,
Lisa Aziz, Lizzie Webb,
Geoff Clark, Carol Dooley
News, current affairs,
weather, sport and
features on a wide range
of topics

TVS

TVS
Television Centre
Vinters Park
Maidstone Kent
ME14 5NZ
Tel: 0622 691111
Television Centre
Southampton SO9 5HZ
Tel: 0703 634211
60 Buckingham Gate
London SW1
Tel: 01 828 9898
Chairman: Lord Boston of

Faversham
Chief Executive: James
Gatward
Director of Programmes:
Alan Boyd
Deputy Director of
Programmes: Clive Jones
Controller of Factual
Programmes: Peter
Williams
Controller of Drama:
Graham Benson
Controller of Children's
Programmes: Nigel
Pickard
Controller of
Entertainment: Gill
Stribling-Wright
Head of Sport: Gary
Lovejoy

Bismarck
Executive producer: Peter
Williams
Producer/Director:
Gordon Hurley
The man who found the
Titanic, Dr Robert
Ballard, going in search of
the German battleship,
Bismarck

Dial-a-Hymn
Executive producer: Peter
Williams
Producer/Director:
Andrew Barr
25 mins
Viewers request hymns
by telephone, the
congregation sings them

**John Gielgud – an
Actor's Life**
Producer: Jonathan
Miller
Director: David Heather
Scriptwriter: John Miller
Camera: Ron Dallinger
Editor: Robin Stokes, Vic
Mabey
Cast: Sir John Gielgud,
John Miller
2 × 1 hour V
John Gielgud talks about
his life, work and great
contemporaries to John
Miller

Kat'A Kabanova
Producer: John Miller
Directors: Nikolaus
Lehnhoff, Derek Bailey
Cast: Ryland Davies,
Nancy Gustafson, Barry
MacCauley, Felicity
Palmer

Native Land
Executive producer: Peter
Williams
Producer/Director: Tim
Rayner

Presenter: Nigel Barley
Six parts
Who are the English?
Nigel Barley travels the
length and breadth of the
land in search of quirks
and characters

Paradise on Earth
Executive producer: John
Miller
Producer/Director:
Christopher Swann
Presenter: Edwin Mullins
Six-part series
Our visions of paradise

Thames Television
Thames Television House
306–316 Euston Road
London NW1 3BB
Tel: 01 387 9494
149 Tottenham Court
Road
London W1P 9LL
Tel: 01 387 9494
Teddington Lock
Teddington
Middlesex TW11 9NT
Tel: 01 977 3252
Mobile Division
Twickenham Road
Hanworth
Middlesex
Tel: 01 898 0011
Regional Sales
Norfolk House
Smallbrook Queensway
Birmingham B5 4LJ
Tel: 021 643 9151
Chairman: Sir Ian
Trethowan
Deputy Chairman: John
Davey
Managing Director:
Richard Dunn
Director of Programmes:
David Elstein
Controller of Sport and
Outside Broadcasts: Bob
Burrows
Controller of Features:
Catherine Freeman
Head of Variety: John
Fisher
Controller of Children's
and Education
Department: Allan
Horrox
Controller of Light
Entertainment: John
Howard Davies
Head of Music and Arts:
Ian Martin
Deputy Director of
Programmes: Barrie
Sales

Director of Drama: Lloyd
Shirley
Director of Corporate
Affairs: Ron Allison
Director of Production:
Tim Riordan

Capital City
Production company:
Euston Films
Producer: Irving
Teitelbaum
Directors: Paul Seed,
Sarah Hellings, Mike
Vardy
Scriptwriter: Andrew
Maclear
Camera: Terry Cole
Editor: Andrew Nelson
Cast: William Armstrong,
John Bowe, Dorian Healy,
Douglas Hodge, Jason
Isaacs
13 × 1 hour
Set in a London-based
international bank and
centred on eight young
high-flying dealers from
Britain, Europe and
America

Ending Up
Producer/Director: Peter
Sasdy
Scriptwriter: Douglas
Livingstone
Camera: Simon Kossoff
Editor: Bob Dearberg
Cast: Dame Wendy
Hiller, Sir Michael
Hordern, Lionel Jeffries,
Sir John Mills, Googie
Withers
90 mins F
Based on the book by
Kingsley Amis

Flying Squad
Production company:
Argo Productions
Producer/Director: Robert
Fleming
Scriptwriter: Robert
Fleming
Camera: Paul Williams
Editor: Roger
Shufflebottom
8 × 30 mins F
Fly on the wall
documentary series
following the operations
of the Metropolitan Police
Flying Squad team based
at Tower Bridge

French Fields
Producer: James Gilbert
Director: Derrick
Goodwin
Scriptwriter: John
Chapman, Ian Davidson
Cast: Anton Rodgers,
Julia McKenzie

6 × 30 mins
Moves the action of the successful Fresh Fields to France

Führer
Production company: Brook Productions
Producer: Stephen White
Camera: Steve Albins
1 hour 5 mins
Documentary re-examining the Hitler phenomenon with the insight of modern psychiatric knowledge and the techniques of modern media management.

Young Charlie Chaplin
Production company: Thames Television/PBS/Wonderworks
Producer: Colin Shindler
Director: Baz Taylor
Scriptwriter: Colin Shindler
Camera: Simon Kossof
Editor: Trevor Waite
Cast: Joe Geary, Ian McShane, Twiggy, Lee Whitlock
6 × 30 mins F
Chronicles Charlie Chaplin's extraordinary childhood, encompassing his poverty-stricken family and his slow but sure progress as actor and comedian

TYNE TEES

Tyne Tees Television
Television Centre
City Road
Newcastle upon Tyne
NE1 2AL
Tel: 091 2610181
Chairman: Sir Ralph Carr-Ellison TD
Deputy Chairman: R H Dickinson
Managing Director: David Reay
Director of Programmes: Geraint Davies
Controller, Entertainment: Trish Kinane
Controller, Factual: Jim Manson
Controller of Public Affairs: Peter Moth
Assistant Programme Controller: Michael Partington

Education Officer: Andrea Kinghorn

And a Nightingale Sang
Production company: Portman Productions/Tyne Tees
Producer: Philip Hinchcliffe
Director: Robert Knights
Scriptwriter: Jack Rosenthal
Camera: Dave Dixon
Editor: Chris Wimble
Cast: Tom Watt, Phyllis Logan, Joan Plowright, John Woodvine, Pippa Hinchley, Stephen Tomkinson, Des Young
1 × 100 mins F
Adapted from C P Taylor's drama of wartime romance. The story of two sisters – Helen who is resigned to being left on the shelf and Joyce who has a pair of nylons from every Yank in town

Chain Letters
Producer: Christine Williams
Director: Michael Metcalf
Presenter: Andrew O'Connor
24 × 30 mins V
Word game with cash prizes

Crying in the Dark
Producer/Director: Graeme Duckham
Camera: Andy Greenwood
Editor: John Louvre
Reporter: Luke Casey
1 hour F
Documentary looking at the facts behind the crusade against sex abuse

The Ghost of Faffner Hall
Production company: Tyne Tees/Jim Henson Organisation
Producer/Writer: Jocelyn Stevenson
Director: Tony Kysh
Camera: David Petrie
Editor: Ed Quigley
13 × 30 mins V
A fun show and an educational tool. Each episode handles a specific theme, from hearing and listening to using instruments, from music round the world to using individual sounds

Voices of War
Producer: Heather Ging

Director: Barry Crosier
Camera: David Petrie
Editor: Robin Sinton
Associate Producer: Derek Smith
6 × 30 mins V
Reveals the personal experiences of men and women during the First World War in their own words

Ulster Television
Havelock House
Ormeau Road
Belfast BT7 1EB
Tel: 0232 328122
Chairman: R B Henderson CBE
Managing Director: J D Smyth
Assistant Managing Director: J A Creagh
General Manager: J McCann
Controller of Programmes: M M Sinnerton
Assistant Controller of Programmes: A Crockart
Assistant Controller of Programmes (News and Current Affairs): M Beattie
Archive Manager: D G Hannon

A Bunch of Time
Producer: John Anderson
Director: Robert Lamrock
Special prepared for St Patrick's Day 1988 featuring James Ellis in both contemplative and entertaining mood with traditional thoughts from Belfast mixed with music from several Irish traditions

Dancing
Director: Bruce Milliard
Writer/Presenter: Professor John Blacking
Series reflecting the development and the impact of dance on our society
6 × 30 mins

God's Frontiersmen
Producer/Writer: Rory Fitzpatrick
Drama-documentary mini series reflecting the impact of the Scots/Irish who moved from

Northern Ireland to the United States
4 × 60 mins

Kitchen Garden
Director: Ruth Johnston
A series of short programmes in which advice on the growing of vegetables is co-ordinated with additional material on how best to prepare them for the table

Shamrock, Rose and Thistle
Director: David Donaghy
Light entertainment programmes reflecting the best of Irish, Scottish, and English folk music, recorded on location in one of Ulster's singing pubs
6 × 30 mins

Van Morrison and the Chieftains
Director: Bruce Milliard
In concert performance, recorded at the Belfast folk festival

YORKSHIRE TELEVISION

Yorkshire Television
The Television Centre
Leeds LS3 1JS
Tel: 0532 438283
Television House
32 Bedford Row
London WC1R 4HE
Tel: 01 242 1666
Chairman: Sir Derek Palmar
Managing Director: Clive Leach
Director of Programmes: John Fairley
Controller of Drama: Keith Richardson
Controller of Entertainment: Vernon Lawrence
Head of Documentaries and Current Affairs: Grant McKee
Head of Science and Features: Duncan Dallas
Head of Education, Children's Programmes and Religion: Chris Jelley
Head of Local Programmes and Sport: Graham Ironside

A Bit of a Do
Producer: David Reynolds

Director: David Reynolds, Ronnie Baxter, Les Chatfield
Writer: David Nobbs
Cast: David Jason, Nicola Pagett, Gwen Taylor, Michael Jayston, Paul Chapman
A conventional white wedding in a small North Yorkshire town leads to an unconventional tangle of love, lusts, jealousies and ambitions
6 × 51 mins VTR

A Day in Summer
Producer: Keith Richardson
Director: Bob Mahoney
Writer: Alan Plater from the novel by J L Carr
Camera: Peter Jackson
Editor: Terry Warwick
Cast: Peter Egan, Jack Shepherd, John Sessions, Jill Bennett, Ian Carmichael
104 mins F
A stranger with a murderous mission arrives in a country town on the first train of the day. By the end of the dramatic day of the annual feast, the lives of many of the inhabitants will never be the same again

First Tuesday
Series editor: Grant McKee
Directors: Various, including Peter Kosminsky, Nick Gray, Mike Cocker, Ian McFarlane, Chris Bryer
Presenter: Olivia O'Leary
Documentary showcase, launched in 1983 and consistently praised and honoured around the world. Afghansti which for the first time revealed the depth of self-criticism of the Soviety army in Afghanistan has emerged as the documentary of the year, already honoured with the Golden Nymph at Monte Carlo, the critic's award and an RTS accolade
12 × 1 hour F

The New Statesman
Producer: Tony Charles
Director: Geoffrey Sax
Writers: Laurence Marks, Maurice Gran
Cast: Rik Mayall, Michael Troughton, Marsha

Fitzalan
7 × 26 mins V
Rik Mayall as one of television's most outrageous characters, the loathsome Alan B'Stard, a Conservative MP who will stop at nothing to achieve his ends. A remarkably popular anti-hero deservedly gunned down in the final episode of the second series

Singles
Producer/Director: Vernon Lawrence
Scriptwriters: Eric Chappell, Jean Warr
Cast: Roger Rees, Judy Loe, Eamon Boland, Susie Blake
7 × 30 mins V
Four very different, unattached people meet up in a singles bar. The series follows their developing – and often turbulent – relationships as they encounter mistaken identities, financial hardship and meetings with former loves. A bitter-sweet comedy from the writers of YTV's successful series Duty Free

Stay Lucky
Producer/Director: David Reynolds
Writer: Geoff McQueen
Camera: Allan Pyrah
Editor: David Aspinall
Cast: Dennis Waterman, Jan Francis
A cockney wideboy, forced to flee from London to escape the clutches of the Chinese mafia, encounters a lively young lady with whom he gets involved in a succession of hairy adventures until the mysteries surrounding her late husband's business affairs are finally unravelled
4 × 51 mins F

BBC TELEVISION

British Broadcasting Corporation
Television Centre

Wood Lane
London W12 7RJ
Tel: 01 743 8000
Broadcasting House
Portland Place
London W1A 1AA
Tel: 01 580 4468
Chairman: Marmaduke Hussey
Director-General: Michael Checkland
Deputy Director-General: John Birt
Managing Director Network Television and Chairman BBC Enterprises: Paul Fox CBE
Managing Director, Regional Broadcasting: Ron Neil
Assistant Managing Director, Network Television: Will Wyatt
Controller of BBC1: Jonathan Powell
Controller of BBC2: Alan Yentob

BBC TV Children's Programmes
Television Centre
Wood Lane
London W12 7RJ
Head: Anna Home
Tel: 01 743 8000

Blue Peter
Programme editor: Lewis Bronze
Presenters: Yvette Fielding, Caron Keating, Mark Curry, John Leslie
Continuing × 25 mins F and live V
Blue Peter began on October 1958. The programme is named after the blue and white flag which is raised within 24 hours of a ship leaving harbour: the idea is that the programme is like a ship setting out on a voyage, having new adventures and discovering new things

Going Live
Programme editor: Chris Bellinger
Cast: Sarah Greene, Phillip Schofield
Continuing × 3 hrs F and live V
A mixture of cartoons, live music, videos, competitions and the chance to speak to famous guests on the telephone

Grange Hill
Producer: Albert Barber

Script Editor: Leigh Jackson
Writers: Barry Purchess, David Angus, Margaret Simpson, Chris Ellis
20 × 25 mins V
Fictional characters face true-to-life situations at a large comprehensive school

BBC Community Programme Unit
Television Centre
Wood Lane
London W12 7RJ
Tel: 01 743 8000
Editor: Tony Laryea
This Unit is responsible for programmes made by and with the general public, usually as a direct response to public request. A voice is given to those who feel that the media distorts or ignores their point of view, and so offers viewers new perspectives on issues of social concern they would not expect to find aired elswhere on television. Currently the Unit's output is presented under three main titles, *Open Space*, *Split Screen* and *Network*

Open Space
Contributors make their own programme on their chosen subjects with production help from the Unit but keeping full editorial control, or in 'partnership' with the Unit if they prefer. Alternatively members of the public can simply suggest programme ideas

Going Home
Producer/Director: Rosalind Erskine
Accessees: Nafiz Bostanci
Camera: Laurie Rush
Editor: Gabe Soloman
40 mins
Followed Turkish Exile Nafiz Bostanci as he made a courageous journey back to Turkey where previously he had been tortured and criminalised under Turkish law

Inside Out. Open Space specials: The Prisoners Film, The Prison Officers Film
Producer/Director: Paul Pierrot
Accessees: Prisoners and prison officers

Camera: David Swan
Editor: Denise Perrin
2 × 50 mins
Two films offering unique
access to those who face
day-to-day life inside the
walls of Swansea jail: the
prisoners and the prison
officers, both in different
ways complaining of the
overcrowded conditions
they must endure and
portraying the futility of a
system that offers little
chance of rehabilitation.

Licence to Kill
Producer: Sue Davidson
Director: Carole
Daughtrey
Accessees: Campaign
Against Drunken Driving
Camera: John Baker
Editor: Jackie Powell
30 mins F
A powerful indictment of
current practice and
legislation as it applies to
those guilty of causing
death by drunken driving

Network
A peak time monthly
show which offers a studio
audience the opportunity
to confront executives,
producers and performers
with their views about
BBC programmes and
policies

Rights not Charity
Producer: Jeremy Gibson
Director: Gerry Pomeroy
Accessees: Colin Low,
Patricia Rock
Camera: John Record
Editor: Kevin Hinchey
50 mins F
Made by Colin Low who is
totally blind and
wheelchair user Patricia
Rock, this programme
reflected the poor
conditions of life
experienced by many of
this country's disabled
and compared their
experiences with those of
people in Europe and
America

A State of Danger
Producer/Directors:
Jenny Morgan, Haim
Brasheeth
Editor: Lois Davies
30 mins V
Filmed in Israel and the
Occupied Territories, this
programme, made by the
Committee for the
Freedom of Expression of
Palestinians and Israelis

charted the development
of the Palestinian
Intifada (uprising) and
followed the efforts of the
tiny minority of Jewish
people campaigning for a
peaceful solution to the
Palestinian struggle for
self-determination

Split Screen
The holders of opposing
views on a controversial
subject each make a short
film presenting their case
with production help from
the Unit. Subjects covered
include new music,
offensive self defence for
women, segregated
schools and prostitution

Video Diaries
A unique series of
programmes giving
people self-operated video
cameras to record the
unfolding events of their
lives

Water Down the Drain
Producer: Giles Oakley
Director: Paul O'Connor
Accessees: Joint Action
for Water Services
Camera: Graham Smith
Editor: Peter Clarke
30 mins
Presented the fears of
environmentalists, health
specialists and water
industry workers about
the government's
controversial
privatisation of water
supply

BBC TV Continuing Education
Villiers House
The Broadway
London W5 2PA
Tel: 01 743 8000

Advice Shop
Series Editor: Chris Lent
Presenters: Hugh Scully,
Helen Madden
Advice on a wide range of
topics taking into account
the problems of
unemployed people and
helping viewers to pursue
solutions through the
appropriate
organisations. Areas
covered include social
security, housing debt,
credit and pensions
20 × 25 mins

Business Matters
Editor: Brian Davies

Techniques, ideas and
approaches to problems
and opportunities in the
world of business. The
series is aimed at anyone
at work in a responsible
position and at a general
audience. It contains a
mixture of presentations
from management gurus
and instructive case
studies
18 × 25 mins BBC1
20 × 25 mins BBC2
Bryn Brooks

**The Education
Programme**
Editors: Sally Kirkwood,
(Bernard Adams,
November 1989 onwards)
A regular weekly insight
into the world of
education ranging from
nurseries to the
University of the Third
Age. Aimed at the general
public but of particular
interest to both the
providers and consumers
of education

Having a Baby
Producer: Anna Jackson
Presenter: Sue Cook
Honest realistic
information from women
and their partners about
what having a baby is
really like. Experts also
provide information about
how to manage and enjoy
pregnancy
6 × 30 mins BBC1

Police Powers
Producer: John Twitchen,
Chris Lent
Up-to-date information on
recent changes in the law
and how they affect the
relationship between the
police and the public,
especially in relation to
the police and Criminal
Evidence Act 1984 and
the Public Order Act 1986

Spelling it Out
Producer: Charles Pascoe
Strategies for tackling
common difficulties,
aimed at anyone whose
spelling could be
improved. With Don
Henderson
8 × 10 BBC1

BBC TV Documentary Features
Kensington House
Richmond Way
London W14 0AX

Tel: 01 895 6227
Head: Colin Cameron

40 Minutes
Series Editor: Edward
Mirzoeff
A series of documentary
films about the way we
live now. Major films this
series include
Dolebusters, The
Kingdom of Fun, Our
Darren, Gerald Scarfe's
and Knickerbockers in
Knightsbridge
26 × 40 mins F

Holiday 89
Series Producer: Patricia
Houlihan
Directors: Richard
Lightbody, Clare Riley,
Bruce Thompson, Prue
Geary
Camera: Chris Sadler and
others
14 × 29 mins approx F,V
After 21 years, the
original holiday
programme is back with a
new presenter, Desmond
Lynam, and a new look

Inside Story
Executive producer: Paul
Hamann
14 × 50/60 mins F
A series of powerful single
documentaries ont he
world today. Executive
producer Paul Hamann is
the maker of the award
winning series *The Duty
Men* and *Fourteen Days In
May*. He hopes *Inside
Story* will be a platform
for major hard-hitting
contemporary
documentaries

Missionaries
Series Editor: Tim Slessor
Producer/Directors: Alan
Bookbinder, Sue Bourne,
Jean-Paul Davidson,
Richard Bradley
Scriptwriter: Julian
Pettifer
Camera: Various
Editor: Various
Cast: Missionaries in
South America, Africa,
Middle and Far East,
Papua New Guinea,
Europe
6 × 55 mins F
Today's missionaries are
highly sophisticated,
heavily funded and armed
with the latest in hard
and software. This
programme travels the
globe to see how mission
has changed and find out

what drives these armies of evangelists

Saturday Night Clive
Producer: Beatrice Ballard
Executive producer: Richard Drewett
Presenter: Clive James
45 mins V
Clive James attempts to make some sense of the new and de-regulated universe of ever expanding media

Taking Liberties
Series producer: Elizabeth Clough
Director: Various
Scriptwriter/Presenter: David Jessel
Camera: Chris Hartley
Exposes cases of natural injustice through the eyes of individual victims, for example racial bullying in the army, how British judges sent a Jamaican prisoner to the gallows, the agony of anaesthetic awareness and why so many deaths in prison receive a verdict of lack of care

BBC TV Light Entertainment Comedy Programmes
Television Centre
Wood Lane
London W12 7RJ
Tel: 01 743 8000
Head: Gareth Gwenlan

Alas Smith & Jones
Producers: John Kilby, Jamie Rix
Director: John Kilby
Cast: Mel Smith, Griff Rhys Jones
Sketch show
7 × 30 mins

'Allo 'Allo
Producer: David Croft
Directors: Martin Dennis, Susan Belbin, Richard Boden
Scriptwriters: David Croft, Jeremy Lloyd
Cast: Gorden Kaye, Carmen Silver
26 × 25 mins
This popular comedy made for the first time in a run of 26 weekly episodes continues the improbable story of cafe owner and reluctant French resistance hero, René, the problems and loves of his life

Black Adder
Producer: John Lloyd
Director: Mandie Fletcher
Scriptwriters: Ben Elton, Richard Curtis
Cast: Rowan Atkinson, Tony Robinson, Hugh Laurie
6 × 30 mins
Rowan Atkinson rises phoenix-like from his Elizabethan ashes to preen and scheme in Regency England as butler to mad George III

Bread
Producer/Director: Robin Nash
Scriptwriter: Carla Lane
Cast: Peter Howitt, Jean Boht, Nick Conway, Jonathan Morris, Gilly Coman, Ronald Forfar, Kenneth Waller, Hilary Crowson
13 × 30 mins
Comedy about a very close family living in Liverpool who all have personal problems and are good at swindling the DHSS

Last of the Summer Wine
Producer/Director: Alan Bell
Scriptwriter: Roy Clarke
Cast: Bill Owen, Peter Sallis, Michael Aldridge, Kathy Staff, Thora Hird
6 × 30 mins
Comedy classic about a lovable trio of pensioners who prove you are as young as you feel

Only Fools and Horses
Producer: Gareth Gwenlan
Director: Tony Dow
Scriptwriter: John Sullivan
Cast: David Jason, Nicholas Lyndhurst, Buster Merryfield
6 × 50 mins
The ever popular comedy about two London street-trading brothers and the day-to-day problems they encounter making a living

BBC TV Light Entertainment Variety Programmes
Television Centre
Wood Lane
London W12 7RJ
Tel: 01 743 8000
Head: Jim Moir

Bob Says Opportunity Knocks
Producer: Stewart Morris
Scriptwriters: Colin Edmonds, John Junkin, Gavin Osbon
Musical Director: John Coleman
Presenter: Bob Monkhouse
13 × 50 mins

Carrott Confidential
Producer: Bill Wilson
Director: Geoff Miles
Script Associate: Neil Shand
Scriptwriters: Paul Alexander, Dick Hills, Steve Punt
8 × 35 mins
Live topical sketches and music starring Jasper Carrott

French and Saunders
Producer: Geoff Posner
Scriptwriters: Dawn French, Jennifer Saunders
Cast: Jennifer Saunders, Dawn French, with the backing orchestra Raw Sex
6 × 30 mins

The Paul Daniels Magic Show
Producer/director: Geoff Miles
Cast: Paul Daniels and guests
8 × 30 mins V
Magician Paul Daniels and speciality act guests

The Rory Bremner Show
Producer/Director: Marcus Mortimer
Script Editors: Barry Cryer, John Langdon
Cast: Rory Bremner, Jim Sweeney, Sara Crowe, Steve Steen
6 × 30 mins

The Russ Abbot Show
Producer/Director: John Bishop
Script Associate: Barry Cryer
Cast: Russ Abbott, Les Dennis, Bella Emberg, Sherrie Hewson, Tom Bright
7 × 30 mins
Zany comedy and music show

BBC TV Music and Arts
Kensington House
Richmond Way

London W14 0AX
Tel: 01 743 1272
Head: Leslie Megahey

The Artist's Eye
Executive producer: Rosemary Bowen-Jones
Five contemporary artists, including Paula Rego and Carel Weight RA, in autobiographical films about their work, lives and inspiration

British Art Week
Editor: John Archer
A week of programmes, films, profiles, discussions and events, reflecting the variety and preoccupations of contemporary British painting and sculpture

Duke Bluebeard's Castle
Director: Leslie Megahey
Original production on film of Bartok's opera, starring Robert Lloyd and Elizabeth Laurence

Exiles
Executive producer: Diana Lashmore
Series of profiles of major writers, musicians, artists who live and work in exile from their own countries

The Late Show
Editor: Michael Jackson
Arts and media programme running nightly on BBC2

Rhythms of the World
Producers: Frank Hanly, Tim May
World music performed by leading groups and soloists of the African, American and Asian continents

A Vision of Britain
Producer: Christopher Martin
Omnibus special written and presented by HRH the Prince of Wales, outlining his views on contemporary architecture and planning

BBC TV News and Current Affairs
Television Centre
Wood Lane
London W12 7RJ
Tel 01 743 8000
Editor, News and Current Affairs, Television: Tony Hall

253

Main news programmes:
BBC1 1.00pm, 6.00pm,
9.00pm; hourly
summaries
Breakfast Time 7.00am–
9.00am
BBC2 10.30pm
Newsnight (Saturdays)

Other programmes
include:
**The Money Programme
On The Record
Panorama
Question Time**

BBC TV Plays
Television Centre
Wood Lane
London W12 7RJ
Tel: 01 743 8000
Head: Peter Goodchild

Screenplay
A mixture of short films
and studio plays, united
by a concern to present
challenging drama both
in terms of technique and
subject metter. *The
Interrogation of John,
Cariani and the
Courtesans, Land* and
Road were among the
year's titles

Screen Two
The BBC's original
feature-length film
strand. Highlights of the
1987 season include *After
Pilkington, East of
Ipswich, Northanger
Abbey, Coast to Coast,
Inappropriate Behaviour*
and *Will You Still Love
Me Tomorrow?*

Sunday Premiere
An annual series of
popular feature-length
films for television. Those
broadcast in 1987 include
*The Happy Valley, Love
After Lunch* and *Harry's
Kingdom*

Theatre Night
Original productions of
internationally-renowned
theatre plays, both classic
and contemporary,
including *The Devil's
Disciple, What the Butler
Saw, The Birthday Party*
and *Ghosts*

BBC TV Programme Acquisition
Centre House
56 Wood Lane
London W12 7RJ
Tel: 01 743 8000

General Manager: Alan
Howden

Purchased Programmes
Head: Barry Brown
Selects and presents BBC
TV's output of feature
films and series on both
channels

Business Unit
Business Manager:
Felicity Irlam
Contact for commissioned
material and acquisition
of completed programmes,
film material and
sequences for all other
programme departments

BBC TV Religious Programmes
Television Centre
Wood Lane
London W12 7RJ
Tel: 01 743 8000
Head: John Whale

Everyman
Editor: Jane Drabble
20 × 40 mins F
Reflective religious
documentary series

Heart of the Matter
Producer: Olga Edridge
12 × 35 mins F
Immediate and topical
religious documentary
series

Songs of Praise
Editor: Stephen Whittle
39 × 35 mins V
Community hymn-
singing

This is the Day
Editor: Stephen Whittle
34 × 30 mins live and V
Morning worship from a
viewer's home, with the
viewing audience itself
making up the
congregation

When I Get to Heaven
Producer: Jim Murray
6 × 30 mins V
Interviews on ultimate
belief

BBC TV Schools Broadcasting
Villiers House
The Broadway
London W5 2PA
Tel: 01 743 8000
Head: Alan Rogers

Artwork
Producer: Edward
Hayward
Directors: Edward

Hayward, Judy Brooks,
Wanda Petrusewicz
Scriptwriters: Edward
Hayward, Judy Brooks
Camera: Alan Stevens,
Vicky Parnall
Editor: John Delfgon,
Peter Clarke
Commentary: Anthony
Daniels
5 × 19 mins approx V
Looks at the work of a
number of young
professionals who follow
the approach advocated
by the GCSE Art and
Design syllabus. Painters,
sculptors, environmental
and performance artists,
interior and graphic
designers talk about ideas
and their development
into finished projects

English Time: Handles
Producer: Morton Suguy
Director: Chris Ellis
Scriptwriter: Michael
Robson
Camera: Godfrey Johnson
Cast: Tim Charrington,
Mary Elliott-Nelson,
Natasha Jones, Holly de
Jong, Jason Kercher,
Patrick Monckton, Steven
O'Donnell
3 × 20 mins F,V
A three-part
dramatisation of the
novel by Jan Mark.
Eleven year old city girl
Erica finds herself on an
arranged holiday deep in
the country with boring
Auntie Joan and Uncle
Peter but then she
discovers Elsie
Wainwright's motor cycle
repair shop

**English Time: Tea-leaf
on the Roof**
Producer: Morton Suguy
Director: Chris Ellis
Scriptwriter: Stephen
Wakelam
Camera: Tony Mayne
Editor: Roland Tongue
Cast: Nick Bartlett,
Rochelle Gadd, Ben
Griffith, Naomie Harris,
Robin Hayter, Valerie
Holliman, Shvetu Manek,
Jean Marc Perret, David
Troughton
2 × 20 mins F, V
A two-part dramatisation
of the novel by Jean Ure.
William wishes life in
Tettiscombe terrace was
as exciting as the 'silly'
children's adventure
stories his father writes –
then someone starts
nicking lead from the roof

**Look and Read Geordie
Racer**
Producer/Director: Sue
Weeks
Scriptwriter: Christopher
Russell
Camera: Colin Munn
Editors: Ian McKendrick,
David Painter, Steve
Knattress
Cast: Leon Armstrong,
Lesley Casey, Charles
Collingwood, Michael
Heath
10 × 20 mins F,V
An exciting story set
against a background of
preparations for a road
race in Newcastle

Quinze Minutes
Producer/ Director/
Scriptwriter: Caroline
Godley
Camera: Henry Farrar
Editor: John Dinwoodie
Presenter: Nicholas Mead
10 × 15 mins V
Lively beginner's French
magazine series featuring
simple language
structures and functions

Tutorial Topic
Producer: Len Brown
Director: Various
Scriptwriter: Various
Camera: Various
18 × 10 mins V
The series offers
provocative topics for
discussion and classwork
to lower secondary pupils
taking part in weekly
tutorial sessions.
Programmes are drama,
documentary and
improvised drama. All are
led by children of the
audience's age range

Words Into Action
Producer: John Forrest
Editor: Tony Kovacs
Presenter: Simon Mayo
5 × 20 mins F,V
A fast moving teenage
magazine introduction to
Christianity

BBC TV Science and Features
Kensington House
Richmond Way
London W14 0AX
Tel: 01 895 6611
Head: Mick Rhodes
Manager: Maggie
Bebbington

Horizon
BBC2
Executive producer:
Robin Brightwell

24 × 50 mins
Single subject
documentaries presenting
science to the general
public and analysing the
implications of new
discoveries

QED
Executive producer:
David Filkin
14 × 30 mins F
Documentary films, each
on a single subject. Topics
vary enormously, using a
very broad interpretation
of science

Tomorrow's World
BBC1
Executive producer:
Richard Reisz
Presenters: Judith Hann,
Peter Macann, Maggie
Philbin, Howard
Stableford
Continuing × 30 mins
live
Studio-based programme
which includes filmed
items investigating and
demonstrating the latest
in science and technology

**Your Life In Their
Hands**
BBC2
Executive producer:
David Paterson
5 × 40 mins
Series about medicine

**BBC TV Series and
Serials**
Television Centre

Wood Lane
London W12 7RJ
Tel: 01 743 8000
Head of Drama: Mark
Shivas
Head of Series: Peter
Cregeen
Head of Serials: Michael
Wearing

A Sense of Guilt
Producer: Simon
Passmore
Director: Bruce
MacDonald
Scriptwriter: Andrea
Newman
Cast: Trevor Eve, Rudi
Davies
7 × 50 mins V
A man returns to London
after years abroad and at
once his charm, his
selfishness and his
appetite for pleasure
upset the precariously
balanced lives of those
around him

Mother Love
Producer: Ken Riddington
Director: Simon Langton
Scriptwriter: Andrew
Davies from the novel by
Domini Taylor
Cast: Diana Rigg, James
Wilby
4 × 52 mins F
A rejected woman takes
revenge on her husband's
second spouse, then goes
to work on her son's wife

Never Come Back
Producer: Joe Waters

Director: Ben Bolt
Scriptwriter: David Pirie
from the novel by John
Mair
3 × 50 mins F
A fatal sexual attraction
involves a journalist in
political conspiracy and
murder at the start of the
Second World War

**Oranges Are Not the
Only Fruit**
Producer: Philippa Giles
Director: Beeban Kidron
Scriptwriter: Jeanette
Winterson
3 × 50 mins F
Jeanette Winterson's
mordantly funny
reworking of the rites of
passage genre

Portrait of a Marriage
Producer: Colin Tucker
Director: Stephen
Whittaker
Scriptwriter: Penelope
Mortimer
4 × 50 mins F
Story of the extraordinary
relationship between Vita
Sackville-West and
Harold Nicolson

Summer's Lease
Producer: Colin Rogers
Director: Martyn Friend
Scriptwriter: John
Mortimer
Cast: John Gielgud,
Susan Fleetwood,
Rosemary Leach, Leslie
Phillips
4 × 55 F
An unwilling family and

all too willing father
holiday in a Tuscan villa
where bizarre events start
to take place

**BBC TV Sport and
Events**
Kensington House
Richmond Way
London W14 0AX
Tel: 01 895 6611
Head: Jonathan Martin
Assistant Head: Nick
Hunter

Ceremonial Occasions
Producer: Tim Marshall

Football
Editor: Brian Barwick
Producer: John
Shrewsbury
Director: Charles Balchin
Presenter: Desmond
Lynam/Jimmy Hill

Grandstand
Editor: John Philips
Producer/director: Martin
Hopkins
Presenter: Desmond
Lynam

One Man and His Dog
Producer: Ian Smith
Presenter: Phil Drabble

Royal Tournament
Producer/director: Peter
Hylton Cleaver
Presenter: Mike Smith

Sportsnight
Editor: John Rowlinson
Producer/director:
Charles Balchin
Presenter: Steve Rider

These companies acquire the UK rights to all forms of audiovisual product and arrange for its distribution on videodisc or cassette at a retail level (see also Distributors p116). Listed is a selection of titles released on each label

A & M Sound Pictures
136–140 New King's Road
London SW6 4LZ
Tel: 01 736 3311
Joan Armatrading, Track Record
Chris de Burgh, The Video
Sting, Bring on the Night
Suzanne Vega, Live at the Royal Albert Hall

Albany Video
The Albany
Douglas Way
London SE8 4AG
Tel: 01 692 6322
Coffee Coloured Children
Framed Use
Jean Genet is Dead
Looking for Langston
Ostia
Passion of Remembrance, The
Perfect Image
Territories
Two in Twenty

Ariel Films
Film and Video
Distributors
3 High Street
Christchurch
Dorset BH23 1AB
Tel: 0202 479868
Being, The
Hell Raiders
Hometown USA
Judgement, The
Macon County Line

Avatar Film Corporation
Unit 5
Imperial Studios
Imperial Road
London SW6
Tel: 01 384 1366
Demons
Hamburger
Lost
Mission Kill
Strike Command
Tainted
Trap

BBC Video
Woodlands
80 Wood Lane
London W12 0TT
Tel: 01 576 2610
Distributed by MGM/UA and Pickwick International
After Pilkington
Aliens from Inner Space
Ashes '72, The
Fast and Furious
BBC Shakespeare: various
Bill and Ben, Flowerpot Men
Birds for All Seasons
Camberwick Green
Dr Who: various
Okavango
Victoria Wood As Seen on TV
Young Ones, The

Buena Vista Home Video
3 Centaurs Business Park
Grant Way
Off Syon Lane
Isleworth
Middx TW7 5QD
Tel: 01 569 8080
Can't Buy Me Love
Pinocchio
Stakeout
Three Men and a Baby

CBS/Fox Video UK
Unit 1
Perivale Industrial Park
Greenford
Middx UB6 7RU
Tel: 01 997 2552
Crocodile Dundee
Flight of the Navigator
Fly, The
Jumpin' Jack Flash
No Mercy
Peggy Sue Got Married
Raising Arizona
Raw Deal
Short Circuit
Space Camp

CIC Video
4th Floor
Glenthorne House
5–17 Hammersmith Grove
London W6 0ND
Tel: 01 846 9433
The Accused
The 'Burbs
Cousins
Fletch Lives
The Naked Gun
Scrooged
Serpent and the Rainbow, The
Twins

Capital Home Video
Unit 10
Brunswick Industrial Park
Waterfall Road
New Southgate
London N11 1JL
Club Med
Murder by the Book
Underground Aces

Castle Communications
15–16 Northfields Prospect
Putney Bridge Road
London SW18 1PE
Tel: 01 877 0922
Major distribution company which licenses product from UK TV companies such as Channel 4, Granada and Yorkshire, and independents such as Itel and NVC. Also licenses US product from companies such as Hanna-Barbera, NBC and Worldvision. Specialists in children's programmes, documentary, comedy and sport
American Carrott
Falklands War, The
Mandela
Men of Our Time
Poirot
Tugs
Viv Richards – The King of Cricket

Castle Home Video
Unit 5
Ripon House
35–37 Station Lane
Hornchurch
Essex RM12 6JL
Tel: 04024 57025
Body Slam
Deadly Vows
Freddy's Nightmares
Handful of Dust, A
Invisible Kid, The
Naked Cell

Night At the Magic Castle, A
Rejuvenator
Witchcraft

Channel 5 Video Distribution
1 Rockley Road
London W14 0DL
Tel: 01 743 3474
Barbie – Rockin Back to Earth
Bridget Woods – Complete Workout
Elvis Presley Movie Series, The
Hill Street Blues (TV Series)
INXS – Kick the Video Flick
Level 42 – Fait Accomplis
Ratties, The (TV Series)
Room with a View, A
Thunderbirds (TV Series)
Wet Wet Wet – Videosingles

Chrysalis Records
12 Stratford Place
London W1N 9AF
Tel: 01 408 2355
Distributed by
Pickwick Video
Billy Connolly – Bites Yer Bum
Billy Connolly – Hand Picked
Billy Idol – More Vital Idol
Blondie – Best of
Dance Craze
Housemartins – Now That's What I Call Quite Good
Huey Lewis – Video Hits
Pat Benatar – Best Shots
Proclaimers, The
Spandau Ballet – Over Britain

Colstar Home Video
1 Wardour Mews
D'Arblay Street
London W1V 3FF
Tel: 01 437 5725
Distributed through
Odyssey Video, Start
Records and others
Daley Thompson's Body Shop
In Search of Wildlife with David Shepherd
Kenneth Clark's Romantic versus Classic Art
Life and Times of Lord Mountbatten, The
Man Who Loves Giants, The
Most Dangerous Animal, The
National Gallery, The A Private View

Walt Disney Productions
31–32 Soho Square
London W1V 6AP
Tel: 01 734 8111
Distributed by Buena
Vista Home Video

Entertainment in Video
27 Soho Square
London W1V 5FL
Tel: 01 439 1979
Cop
Full Moon in Blue Water
Kansas
Killer Klowns from Outer Space
Near Dark
Prison
Summer Heat
Teen Wolf Too
Tiger's Tale, A
Wiseguy

Goldcrest Films
36–44 Brewer Street
London W1R 3HP
Tel: 01 437 8696
Georgian State Dance Company, The
Mountbatten: The Last Viceroy

Guild Home Video
Crown House
2 Church Street
Walton-on-Thames
Surrey KT12 2QS
Tel: 01 546 3377
Action Jackson
Angel Heart
Bat-21
Cohen and Tate
Moonwalker
Prince of Darkness
Rambo III
Time Guardian, The

Hendring
20A Eccleston Street
London SW1W 9LT
Tel: 01 730 8691
Damned, The
Eisenstein Catalogue – including Battleship Potemkin
Freedom Beat
Grateful Dead, The
Jazz at Ronnie Scott's series – including Nina Simone
My Life as a Dog
Sherlock Holmes
Stevie Nicks – At Red Rock

Ideal Opix Video
26 Soho Square
London W1V 5FJ
Tel: 01 434 0011
Dash with Wayne Sleep

Focus on Rugby
Focus on Soccer
No Second Prize – The Pat Cash Story

Island Visual Arts
334–336 King Street
London W6
Tel: 01 846 9141
Distributed by PolyGram
Record Operations

Jettisoundz
28–30 The Square
St Annes-on-Sea
Lancashire FY8 1RF
Tel: 0253 712453
Alien Sex Fiend
Atom Kraft
Exploited Sexual Favours
Rose of Avalanche
War Force – Concept of Hatred

Jubilee Film and Video
Egret Mill
162 Old Street
Ashton-under-Lyne
Manchester
Lancashire OL6 7ST
Tel: 061 330 9555

London Weekend Television
South Bank Television
Centre
London SE1 9LT
Tel: 01 261 3434
Agatha Christie's Poirot
Dame Edna Experience, The
Piece of Cake, A
Upstairs, Downstairs

MGM/UA
Hammer House
113 – 117 Wardour Street
London W1V 3TD
Tel: 01 439 9932
America 3000
Fatal Beauty
Hazard of Hearts, A
Munchies
Spaceballs
Walk Like a Man

Media Releasing Distributors
27 Soho Square
London W1V 5FL
Tel: 01 437 2341
Day of the Dead
Eddie and the Cruisers
Kentucky Fried Movie
Return of Captain Invincible

Medusa Communications
Home Video Division
Regal Chambers
51 Bancroft
Hitchin
Herts SG5 1LL
Tel: 0462 421818
Cameron's Closet
976-EVIL
Wizard of Speed and Time, The
For further product, see
Medusa Pictures in
Distributors

Mogul Communications
35–37 Wardour Street
London W1A 4BT
Tel: 01 734 7195
Devil in the Flesh
No Sweat
Shout

Nelson Entertainment International
8 Queen Street
Mayfair
London W1X 7PH
Tel: 01 493 3362
Destiny
Labyrinth
Name of the Rose, The
Room with a View, A
Sammy and Rosie Get Laid
Whales of August, The
Whistle Blower, The

New World Video
27 Soho Square
London W1V 5FL
Tel: 01 434 0497
Angel III
Beyond Therapy
Bliff
Creepshow III
Flowers in the Attic
Hell Comes to Frog Town
Hellraiser
Pin
Tour of Duty

Odyssey Video
15 Dufours Place
London W1V 1FE
Tel: 01 437 8251
Bill
Just Dennis
Romantic Englishwoman
Too Young the Hero
Woman Of Substance, A

Palace Video
16–17 Wardour Mews
London W1V 3FF
Tel: 01 734 7060
Angel Dust
Drowning by Numbers
High Spirits

Jean de Florette
Manon des sources
Shag
World Apart, A

Pickwick Video
Hyde Industrial Estate
The Hyde
London NW9 6JU
Tel: 01 200 7000
Fawlty Towers
Gregory's Girl
Mary Poppins
Nursery Rhymes
Out of Africa
Thomas, Percy and
  Harold
Watch with Mother
Water Babies

Picture Music International
20 Manchester Square
London W1A 1ES
Tel: 01 486 4488
Cliff Richard – Private
  Collection
Live and Guaranteed
  1988!
Climie Fisher – Best of
  Everything
Duran Duran – 6ix
  By 3hree
Kate Bush – The Whole
  Story
Nat King Cole – The

Unforgettable Nat King
  Cole
Paul McCartney – Once
  Upon a Video
Pet Shop Boys –
  Showbusiness

PolyGram Music Video
1 Rockley Road
London W14 0DL
Tel: 01 743 3474
A subsidiary of PolyGram
International making
music programming for
video release with such
bands as Bananarama,
Bon Jovi, Def Leppard,
Dire Straits, Level 42,
Style Council, Tears for
Fears

Quadrant Video
37a High Street
Carshalton
Surrey SM5 3BB
Tel: 01 669 1114
Sports video cassettes

RCA/Columbia Pictures Video (UK)
Metropolis House
22 Percy Street
London W1P 9FF
Tel: 01 636 8373
Last Emperor, The

Little Nikita
Monster Squad
My Demon Lover
Running Man
Suspect
Vice Versa

Shiva Video
Unit 3 Pop In Building
South Way
Wembley
Middx HA9 0AJ
Tel: 01 903 6957
Indian videos

Sony Video Software Europe
41–42 Berners Street
London W1P 3AA
Tel: 01 631 4000
Bay Cove
Code Name: Dancer
Contagion
Death Games
Hollow Point
Jimmy Reardon
Last Fling, The
Love and War
Nightmare in Bitter Creek
Shadow of Death

Thames Video Collection
149 Tottenham Court
Road
London W1P 9LL
Tel: 01 387 9494
Benny Hill
Count Duckula
Jack the Ripper
Wind in the Willows
World War, The

Vestron Video International
69 New Oxford Street
London WC1A 1DG
Tel: 01 379 0406/528 7767
Backtrack
Blue Steel
Buster
Cannonball Fever
Jacknife

The Video Collection
Prestwich House
Caxton Way
Watford
Herts WD1 8UF
Count Duckula
George Best Story, The
Jack Nicklaus – Golf My
  Way
Jane Fonda's Workouts
Liverpool – Greavsie's Six
  of the Best Games of
  the 80's
Michael Jackson – The
  Legend Continues
Quiet Man, The
10 to Midnight
Thomas The Tank Engine
Thundercats Ho!

Video Gems
1st Floor
Acorn House
Victoria Road
London W3 6UL
Tel: 01 993 7705
Best of Treasure Hunt,
  The
Black Beauty
Cabaret
Defenders of the Earth
Guys and Dolls
Joan of Arc
Lizzie Webb Body
  Programme, The
Transformers
Visionaries
Wuthering Heights

Video Programme Distributors (VPD)
Building No 1
GEC Estate
East Lane
Wembley
Middx HA9 7FF
Tel: 01 904 0921
Distributors for VPD,
Rogue and American
Imperial
Above the Law
Black Eagle
Dragons Forever
Police Story 2

Virgin Video
328 Kensal Road
London W10 5XJ
Tel: 01 968 8888
Distributed by Virgin/
PVG
Depeche Mode 101
Erasure – Innocence
Eurythmics – Savage
Harry Enfield Live in
  Concert
Olympic Games – The
  Golden Moments
Pascali's Island
Robocop
Seven Pounds in 7 Days
Terminator, The

Warner Home Video
135 Wardour Street
London W1
Tel: 01 437 5600
Warner distributes
certain UIP and
Weintraub
Entertainment products
as well as films from
Warner subsidiaries
Castaway
Color Purple, The
Deadly Friend
Heartbreak Ridge
Lethal Weapon
Little Shop of Horrors
Mannequin
Mission, The
Pirates
Who's That Girl

GRANADA
We make television
worth watching

The film and video workshops listed below are non-profit-distributing and subsidised organisations. Some workshops are also active in making audiovisual product for UK and international media markets

A19 Film and Video
21 Foyle Street
Sunderland SR1 1LE
Tel: 091 565 5709
Mick Catmull
Nick Oldham
Alan Carter
Video production, distribution and exhibition. A19 makes films and videotapes which reflect the needs, concerns and aspirations of people on Wearside. Also offers production facilities, training and advice to schools, community groups and institutions

APHRA Workshops for Women
99 Leighton Road
London NW5
Tel: 01 485 2105
Jo Neylin
Rebecca Maguire
Scriptwriting and pre-production workshops for women – in particular, black and ethnic minorities – through which skills for employment in the film, television and satellite broadcasting industries can be developed. Basic introductory workshops, intermediate and specialised theme based workshops and seminars. Access includes community and commercial hire of VHS off-line edit suite and U-matic CCD camera kit

AVA (Audio Visual Arts)
110 Mansfield Road
Nottingham NG1 3HL
Tel: 0602 483684
Chris Ledger
Madeline Holmes
Women's film/video production co-operative, specialising in art and education work. Commissioned tapes for galleries, museums, arts and education organisations including a 'Video Showcase' series on contemporary craftspeople. Grant-aided production of *Wedding Album*/*Great Expectations*, a video installation funded by East Midlands Arts. Work in progress includes *Pretty Women*, and *Where the Blarney Roses Grow* . . .

Aberystwyth Media Group
See Ceredigion Media Association

Activision Studios
Unit 20
St James Wharf
All Saints Street
London N1 9RL
Tel: 01 833 4488
Karen Knaggs
Francis Martin
Rod Iverson
Film/video production, exhibitions and tape archive.
Offers all these facilities to others. Output includes innovative documentary work including *Clause 28 – An Unnatural Act, Torch of Resistance, Agent Orange – Policy of Poison, In Search of the Griot.* Other productions: *Activision Pop Compilation* (including promos with Head, 23 Skidoo and Easterhouse) and art-fiction *Time and Motion.* Other services include video animation and 3 machine off-line editing

Alva Films
Island House
16 Brook Street
Alva
Clackmannanshire
FK12 5JP
Tel: 0259 60936
Russell Fenton
Bill Borrows
Brian Kelly
Film/video production, distribution and exhibition. Offers production, post-production and exhibition facilities to others.
Scottish Working Class History Unit

F Amber Side Workshop
5 Side
Newcastle upon Tyne
NE1 3JE
Tel: 091 232 2000
Murray Martin
Film/video production, distribution and exhibition. Offers exhibition facilities to others

Avid Productions
Keswick House
30 Peacock Lane
Leicester LE1 5NY
Tel: 0533 539733
Laura McGregor
Video production mainly for local authorities and the voluntary sector. Training, promo, education, public information, with back-up publications where required. Training in video/photography within the community, particularly gay groups, women's and special needs groups

Banner Film and TV
11 Swaledale Road
Sheffield S7 2BY
Tel: 0742 556875
David Rea
Community programmes and drama

Bath Community Television
7 Barton Buildings
Bath
Avon BA1 7JR
Tel: 0225 314480
Ray Brooking

Belfast Film Workshop
37 Queen Street
Belfast BT1 6EA
Tel: 0232 326661
Alastair Herron
Kate McManus
Only film co-operative in Northern Ireland offering

film/video/animation production and exhibition. Offers both these facilities to others. Made *Acceptable Levels* (with Frontroom), *Thunder Without Rain* and various youth animation pieces

Belfast Independent Video
9 Winetavern Street
Belfast BT1 1JQ
Tel: 0232 245495
Co-operative providing video production, distribution and exhibition. Offers hi/low band recording, editing and 16 track sound recording. Productions include 1987 *Our Words Jump to Life*, and 1988 *Moving Myths*. Training/ education courses for community, women's unemployment and campaign groups and organisations

Benchmark Video Workshop
11a Forth Street
Edinburgh EH1 3LE
Tel: 031 557 2721
Co-operative which runs 'Tapefinder', a free information service for educational users of AV resources. The database holds information on films and videos for social, cultural and arts education from distributors, film and video workshops and other independent producers

Birmingham Film and Video Workshop
2nd Floor
Pitman Buildings
161 Corporation Street
Birmingham B4 6PT
Tel: 021 233 3423
Rob Burkitt
Film/video production, distribution and exhibition. Offers production facilities with reduced rates for grant-aided work. Recent productions include *The Black and White Pirate Show*, *Out of Order* and *Paradise Circus*. Catalogue of productions and accompanying education packs available on request

Black Audio Film Collective
89 Ridley Road
London E8 2NH
Tel: 01 254 9527/9536
Lina Gopaul
Avril Johnson
Film/video production, distribution, exhibition and consultancy in the field of black filmmaking. Produced *Handsworth Songs*, *Testament*, and *Twilight City*

Black Film and Video Workshop in Wales
1st Floor
4 Dock Chambers
Bute Road
Butetown
Cardiff
Tel: 0222 499835
Charles Thompson

Black Vision
649 High Road
London N17 8AA
Tel: 01 801 8896
Low-band U-Matic recording and editing facilities. Productions include *Taste of Carnival*, *Reggae Starwars*, *Beach Bash*, *Sister Angela*, *Tiger Spectacular*, *Drug Video* and *Alan Boesak Speaks*

Bristol Asian Video Association
114 St Mark's Road
Easton
Bristol BS5 6JD
Tel: 0272 521318
Gurmit Singh

Bristol Film Workshop
37–39 Jamaica Street
Bristol BS2 8JP
Tel: 0272 426199
Mike Leggett
Frank Passingham

Cambridge Video Unit
6 William Smith Close
Cambridge CB1 3QF
Tel: 0223 241030
Anna Kronschnabl
Tom Drummond
Andy Lomas
Video production co-operative. Production of experimental, community and commercial videos. Workshops in video production using low-band U-Matic and VHS equipment

Cambridge Women's Resource Centre
Hooper Street
Cambridge CB1 2NZ
Tel: 0223 321148
Ila Chandavarkar
Mary Knox
Video classes for women include scriptwriting, basic camera techniques, lighting, production and editing using U-Matic equipment

Ceddo Film and Video Workshop
First Floor
South Tottenham Education and Training Centre
Braemar Road
London N15 5EU
Tel: 01 802 9034
June Reid
Dennis Davis
Ujebe Masokoane
Film/video production, distribution and exhibition. Offers all these facilities to others. Provides training workshops in film and video, organises screenings and discussions and is currently establishing an archive. Productions include *Street Warriors*, *The People's Account*, *Time and Judgement – A Diary of a 400 Year Exile*, *Omega Rising: Woman of Rastafari* and *We Are the Elephant*

Ceredigion Media Association
(formerly Aberystwyth Media Group)
Blwch Post 54
Aberystwyth
Dyfed
Wales SY23 1LN
Tel: 0970 624001
Catrin M S Davies
Media education for all ages and interests with specific reference to Welsh speakers and to rural themes and issues. Comprises training, teaching and development of photography, audio work, basic S8 film and VHS video. Runs lectures, seminars, workshops, courses as well as longer term practical projects

Chapter Film and Animation Workshop
Chapter Arts Centre
Market Road
Canton
Cardiff CF5 1QE
Tel: 0222 396061
Christine Wilks
Carol Salter
Film production, training and distribution. Offers production and exhibition facilities to others. Provides training courses in 16mm and Super 8 film and animation. Organises screenings, discussions and seminars

Chapter Video Workshop
Chapter Arts Centre
Market Road
Canton
Cardiff CF5 1QE
Tel: 0222 396061
Babs Williams
Video production, distribution and exhibition. Offers production facilities to others. Working with community organisations and trades unions on social, political and cultural issues

Cinema Action
27 Winchester Road
London NW3
Tel: 01 586 2762
Gustav Lamche
Film/video production, distribution and exhibition. Offers all these facilities to others. Productions include *Rocking the Boat*, *So That You Can Live*, *The Miners' Film*, *People of Ireland*, *Film from the Clyde* and *Rocinante*

Cinestra Pictures
The Co-op Centre
11 Mowll Street
London SW9 6BG
Tel: 01 793 0157
Women's video production and training company. Aim to promote an alternative women's cinema and TV culture through training and production. U-Matic video courses from beginners to specialist advanced

Clio Co-op
91c Mildmay Road
London N1
Tel: 01 249 2551

Ros Pearson
Produce documentaries
about women's history

Colchester Film and Video Workshop
21 St Peters Street
Colchester CO1 1EW
Tel: 0206 560255
Paul Pelowski
Film/video resource for
local community. Services
in training, media
education, equipment
hire and production. and
exhibition. Operates
outreach service for
north-east Essex

Community Productions Merseyside
Merseyside Innovation
Centre
131 Mount Pleasant
Liverpool L3 5TF
Tel: 051 708 5767/0123
x225
Offers production,
training, distribution and
exhibition to enable
voluntary groups and
organisations in the
Merseyside area to
undertake video projects
of specific benefit to their
local communities and
also to enable
traditionally
disadvantaged groups and
individuals to represent
themselves, primarily
through the medium of
video

Connections
Palingswick House
241 King Street
London W6 9LP
Tel: 01 741 1766/7
Paul Jones
David Barnard
Shabnam Grewal
Video project provides:
training from basic VHS
to advanced U-Matic, hire
of VHS, Video 8, U-Matic
production equipment,
VHS editing, 3 machine
U-Matic switchable to hi-
band; script to screen
production; distribution
and media education

Connexions
Third Floor
9–15 Blackett Street
Newcastle upon Tyne
NE1 5BS
Tel: 091 261 7002
Clare Segal
Video production and
distribution. Offers

production and
distribution facilities to
others. Concentrates on
producing promotional
and training videos and
accompanying written
material for public and
voluntary sector.
Undertakes commissions
or works alongside client.
Productions include
community video *Girls Talk*

Converse Pictures
Bon Marche Building
444 Brixton Road
London SW9 8EJ
Tel: 01 274 4000
Film/video/photography
production, distribution
and exhibition.
Specialises in work on
equality, sexuality,
identity and
representation. Also acts
as an information/contact
resource for those
working on these issues
and for lesbians and gay
men working in film/
video/photography

Co-option Women's Film and Video Group
27 Clemence Street
London E14
Tel: 01 987 3224
Jeanette Iljon

Counter Image
19 Whitworth Street West
Manchester M1 5WG
Tel: 061 228 3551
Ivor Frankell
Independent media
charity. Film/video
production, distribution
and exhibition. Offers
production and exhibition
facilities to
independent film and
video makers and
photographers.
Productions include
Fever House and *Land of Colagne*

Cutting Edge Video Unit
4 Compass Court
Norfolk Street
Spon End
Coventry CV1 3LL
Tel: 0203 229660
Glenn Harvey

F Derry Film and Video
1 Westend Park
Derry City

N Ireland BT48 9JF
Tel: 0504 260326/260128
Brendan McMenamin
Film/video production
and distribution. Offers
training to local
community. Aims to
contribute to an
indigenous view of
Ireland in the media and
a positive representation
of women and women's
issues in its productions.
Titles include *Stop Strip Searching, Planning, Hush-a-Bye Baby* and *Mother Ireland*

Despite TV
178 Whitechapel Road
London E1
Tel: 01 377 0737
Mark Saunders

Doncaster Film Group
Walney House
Greengate
Epworth
Doncaster DN9 1EZ
Tel: 0427 342982
Rodney Challis
Film/video production.
Offers production/editing
facilities on U-Matic/VHS
suite. Emphasis on
productions of a
collaborative nature and
on training

East Anglian Film Makers
22–24 Colegate
Norwich NR3 1BQ
Tel: 0603 622313
Alistair Reid
Grant-aided film
workshop, revenue
funded by Eastern Arts
and Norwich City
Council. Film/video
distribution, exhibition
and some production
facilities. Offers periodic
training courses and
production and exhibition
facilities to others

F Edinburgh Film Workshop Trust
29 Albany Street
Edinburgh EH1 3QN
Tel: 031 557 5242
Cassandra McGrogan
Robin MacPherson
Facilities include VHS
and low-band U-Matic
production equipment,
low-band edit suite with
TBC, caption camera,
waveform monitor and

VHS edit suite.
Animation facililties
include Nelson Hordell
rostrum, 16mm and
Super 8

Edinburgh Film Workshop Trust Animation Workshop
address as above
Edward O'Donnelly

Exeter Film and Video Workshop
c/o Exeter and Devon Arts
Centre
Gandy Street
Exeter EX4 3LS
Tel: 0392 218928
Joyce McCarthy
Film/video production,
distribution and
exhibition. Offers all
these facilities to others.
Holds training courses in
film and video production
as well as teaching in
schools

Eye to Eye
6 Fore Street
Gold Sithney
Penzance TR20 9HD
Tel: 0736 710797
Lynn Aubrey

Faction Films
28–29 Great Sutton
Street
London EC1
Tel: 01 608 0654
Sylvia Stevens
Group of socialist
filmmakers, offering
production facilities to
others. Equipment
includes a 6-plate
Steenbeck, 16mm edit
suite, VHS off-line edit
suite, sound recording
and transferring
facilities. Titles include
Irish News: British Stories, Year of the Beaver, Picturing Derry and *Past Decisions: Future Choices*

Falmouth Film and Video Workshop
Bank House
Bank Place
Falmouth
Cornwall
Tel: 0326 316104
Lee Berry

Film Form Productions
64 Fitzjohn's Avenue
London NW3 5LT

Tel: 01 794 6967
Susi Oldroyd
Tony Harrild
Film/video production,
drama and documentary
for television and video
distribution. We offer full
crewing, writers,
producers and directors

Film Work Group
Top Floor
79–89 Lots Road
London SW10 0RN
Tel: 01 352 0538
Film/video production.
Offers 6-plate Steenbeck
cutting room, 3-machine
low-band edit suite and
telecine to others with
special rates for grant-
aided and non-profit
groups

Filmshed
9 Mill Lane
Canterbury
Kent
Tel: 0227 69415
Tim Reed
Open-access collective for
the promotion and
production of independent
film. Film production and
exhibition. Offers
exhibition facilities to
others; filmmakers on
tour and regular
screenings of political/
workshop films

Forum Television
11 Regent Street
Bristol BS8 4HW
Tel: 0272 741490
David Parker
Co-operative with
emphasis on South West.
Film/video production,
distribution and
exhibition. Offers film/
video editing suites.
Recent work has involved
social and political issues
around work,
unemployment, the police
and judiciary, racism and
community education.
Titles for Channel 4
include: *Lands at the
Margin, A Question of
Cornwall, A Gilded
Cage?, Like Mothers, Like
Daughters*. For the BBC:
*The School Belongs to All
of Us, Dying for a Job*. For
HTV: *Hurried Orders*

F Four Corners
Film Workshop
113–115 Roman Road
London E2 0HU
Tel: 01 981 4243/6111

Clare Palmer
Provides access to Super 8
and 16mm film
production and post-
production facilities, and
exhibition and provides
technical training
courses. Special rates for
grant-aid/low budget.
Past productions include:
*Bred and Born, Is That
It?, Hang on a Minute*.
Recent work around
issues specific to women
includes *Tiger's Milk:
Women of Nicaragua*

Fradharc Ur
11 Scotland Street
Stornoway
Isle of Lewis PA87
Tel: 0851 5766
Mairead Nicdhomhnuill
Tormod Macilleathainn
The first Gaelic film and
video workshop, offering
VHS and hi-band editing
and shooting facilities.
Production and training
in Gaelic for community
groups. Productions
include *Under the
Surface, Na Deilbh Bheo,
The Weaver* and *As an
Fhearran*

Free Focus
The Old School
Beauley Road
Southville Bristol
BS3 1QG
Tel: 0272 634443
Sue Robinson
Adrian Jones

F Frontroom
Productions
79 Wardour Street
London W1V 3TH
Tel: 01 734 4603
Robert Smith
Film production and
distribution. Offers
production and editing
facilities to others.
Productions (16mm)
include *Acceptable Levels,
Intimate Strangers,
Ursula and Glenys, The
Love Child* (35mm), and
Wild Flowers

Glasgow Film and
Video Workshop
Dolphin Arts Centre
7 James Street
Glasgow G40 1BZ
Tel: 041 554 6502
Ken Gill
GFVW is a film/video
resource for independent
producers in Scotland.
Runs basic video

familiarisation courses
and provides advanced
specialist courses in low-
and hi-band video, 16mm
and Super 8. Occasionally
offers bursaries to artist
filmmakers and continues
to programme showings of
independent film and
video work in the city

Gog Theatre Co
Assembly Rooms
High Street
Glastonbury
Somerset BA6 9DU
Tel: 0458 34252
Stephen Clarke

Grapevine
Television
Second Floor
Robinson Building
Norfolk Place
Bedminster
Bristol BS3 4NQ
Tel: 0272 637973
Adrian Mack
Lynne Harwood

Guildford Video
Workshop
c/o The Guildford
Institute
Ward Street
Guildford
Surrey
Michael Aslin
Video production and
training facilities

F Gweithdy Fidio
Cydweithredol
Scrin Cyf
(Community
Screen Film and
Video Workshop)
12 Palace Street
Caernarvon
Gwynedd LL55 1RR
Tel: 0286 4545

Hull Community
Artworks
(formerly Outreach
Community Arts)
Northumberland Avenue
Hull HU2 0LN
Tel: 0482 226420
Tony Hales
Film/video production,
distribution and
exhibition. Offers
production and exhibition
facilities to others. Holds
regular training
workshops

Hull Time Based
Arts
6 Posterngate
Hull HU1 2JN

Tel: 0482 216446
Mike Stubbs
Film/video production
and exhibition. Offers
exhibition facilities to
others. Works with
experimental film, video,
performance and music.
Intends to provide
equipment, workshop
facilities and exhibition
space

Intermedia Film
and Video
(Nottingham)
(formerly New Cinema
Workshop and
Nottingham Video
Project)
110 Mansfield Road
Nottingham NG1 3HL
Tel: 0602 505434
Roger Suckling
Pat Silburn
Malcolm Leick
Offers film and video
production, distribution
and exhibition facilities to
others. Runs training
courses on VHS recording
and editing and U-Matic
production. Offers
training workshops and
information to
independent film and
videomakers

Ipswich Media
Project
202 Brunswick Road
Ipswich
Suffolk
Tel: 0473 716609
Mike O'Sullivan
Super 8 film and VHS
video production
equipment.
Familiarisation training
and media work

Island Arts Centre
Tiller Road
Isle of Dogs
London E14 8PX
Tel: 01 987 7925
Namita Chakrabarty
Facilities for local groups
and individuals; video
workshops and
productions

Jubilee Community
Arts
84 High Street West
Bromwich
West Midlands
Tel: 021 553 6862
Multi-media team
working in Sandwell and
West Midlands, using
video, photography,

music, drama and visual art. Working in partnership with community groups

Lambeth Video
Unit 7
245a Coldharbour Lane
London SW9 8RR
Tel: 01 737 5903
Video production, access (with preferential rates) and training, hire of production and post-production equipment and advice to tapemakers

Latin American Independent Film/ Video Association
Latin American House
Kingsgate Place
London NW6 4TA
Tel: 01 372 6442
Offers 16mm film and VHS equipment (production and post-production) for hire. Film and video courses, workshops and exhibitions

F Leeds Animation Workshop
45 Bayswater Row
Leeds LS8 5LF
Tel: 0532 484997
Janis Goodman
A women's collective working in animation, distribution and exhibition. Offers distribution, rostrum and line-testing facilities to others. Productions include *Risky Business, Pretend You'll Survive, Give Us a Smile, Council Matters, Crops and Robbers, Home and Dry* and *Out to Lunch*. Free catalogue available on request

Leicester Independent Film and Video Association
11 Newarke Street
Leicester LE1 5SS
Tel: 0533 559711
Malcolm Ellis
Film/video production, distribution and exhibition. Offers production and exhibition facilities to others. Holds annual international Super 8 film festival on new British and international Super 8

films with workshops and seminars

Light House Media Centre
Art Gallery
Lichfield Street
Wolverhampton
WV1 1DU
Tel: 0902 312033
Frank Challenger
Krysia Rozanska
Lewis Frost
Kate Child
Video production with 3-machine edit, computer graphics/animation; cinema and galleries. Training includes a two-year full-time course. Films, conferences, events, courses and exhibitions. Joint Wolverhampton Borough Council/Wolverhampton Polytechnic development with Arts Council and West Midlands Arts support

Liverpool Black Media Group
64 Mount Pleasant
Liverpool L3 5SH
Tel: 051 709 2321
Michael Greenidge

London Fields Film and Video
10 Martello Street
London E8 3PE
Tel: 01 249 8269
Low-band production and editing facilities, computer graphics. Special rates for artists and community use

London Film Makers' Co-op
42 Gloucester Avenue
London NW1
Tel: 01 586 4806
Abina Manning
Film production, distribution and exhibition workshop with full range of S8 and 16mm filmmaking equipment. Distribution library available to hirers with over 1400 films. Cinema screenings twice weekly. Accent on experimental and art-based film

London Video Access
23 Frith Street
London W1V 5TS
Tel: 01 437 2786/734 7410

Peter Harvey
Alison Malone
Marion Urch
Video production, editing and post-production facilities. Distribution library of video art; promotion and exhibition of artists' videos. Training courses in production and post-production. Art-based works for library and promotion

Macro Films
Macro House
180 Soho Hill
Handsworth
Birmingham B19 1AG
Tel: 021 523 8272
Don Shaw
Video production, distribution and exhibition. Production and distribution facilities offered to others. Two-year video production course run in conjunction with local colleges and mainstream TV companies

Media Arts
Town Hall Studios
Regents Circus
Swindon SN1 1QF
Tel: 0793 26161 x3140
Carol Comely
Martin Parry
Production, distribution, exhibition, education and training. Well-equipped studios in film, video, photography and sound. Small media library, viewing facilities, multimedia events, archive. Productions include *On Behalf of the People, Melting into the Countryside, View from the Sink, Stories From the First Estate* and *Dyslexia Rules KO*

The Media Centre
South Hill Park
Bracknell
Berks RG12 4PA
Tel: 0344 427272
Bob Gibbs
Kim Clancy
Isla Hyslop
Training, video production, distribution, exhibition and media education. Offers all these facilities to others. Runs national video courses for independent videomakers and general training in arts administration

Media Education Centre
Leigh College
Railway Road
Leigh WN7 4AH
Tel: 0942 608811 x301
Julie Cox
Carol Dahl
Provides video production and exhibition facilities for schools, colleges and local community groups. Facilities include community cinema/small TV studio, teachers resource material and advisor team with technical support

Midnight Time Productions
46 Salisbury Gardens
Newcastle upon Tyne
NE2 1HP
Tel: 091 281 3031
Mark Lavender
Grant-aided voluntary organisation. Film/video production, distribution and exhibition. Offers all these facilities to others. Gives amateurs the opportunity to work with film and video professionals

Moonshine Community Arts Workshop
1090 Harrow Road
London NW10 5XQ
Tel: 01 960 0055
Jeff Lee
Offers video production facilities to others. Provides training in production and post-production with U-Matic and VHS edit suites and special effects. Also has 16 track recording studio with effects, and silk screen and offset litho printing facilities. Works with Brent-based groups and individuals with emphasis on young people and black community groups producing work including documentaries, music videos and video art

New Cinema Workshop
(see Intermedia)

Nottingham Video Project
(see Intermedia)

F Open Eye Film and Video and Animation

90–92 Whitechapel
Liverpool L1 6EN
Tel: 051 709 9460
Strinda Davies
Greg Dropkin
Film/video/animation
production and post-
production, distribution
and exhibition. Offers
production, education and
exhibition facilities
primarily to community
groups, grant-aided and
independent producers.
Some basic and
specialised training
courses according to
demand. ACTT
franchised workshop

Outline Arts Trust

69 Rothbury Terrace
Heaton
Newcastle upon Tyne
NE6 5XJ
Tel: 091 276 3207
Kate Hancock
A community arts trust
using video mostly for
very specific and local use

Oxford Film and Video Makers

The Stables
North Place
Headington
Oxford OX3 9HY
Tel: 0865 60074
Anne-Marie Sweeney
Film/video production,
distribution and
exhibition. Offers
production facilities and
film/video training to
others

Oxford Independent Video

Pegasus Theatre
Magdalen Road
Oxford OX4 1RE
Tel: 0865 250150
Maddie Shepherd
Educational, community
and arts video project
working with
disadvantaged and under-
represented groups in
Oxfordshire

Picture 5 Women

3 Lescudjack Road
Penzance TR18 3AD
Tel: 0736 67164/67581
Lally Henty

Pictures of Women

The Pavement
London SW4
Tel: 01 720 2240

Pimlico Arts and Media Scheme

St James the Less School
Moreton Street
London SW1 2PT
Tel: 01 630 6409
David Drake
One of the biggest media
training centres in
London, running courses
in video, photography and
graphic design
exclusively for
unemployed people to
give them a grounding in
these three areas and
prepare them for
employment. Offers
graphics studio, VHS,
U-Matic equipment, fully-
equipped darkroom and
exhibition space, and can
accommodate 165
trainees

Platform Films

13 Tankerton House
Tankerton Street
London WC1
Tel: 01 278 8394
Chris Reeves
Film/video production
and distribution. Work
aims to reflect issues
within the labour and
trade union movement

Plymouth Film and Video Workshop

Plymouth Arts Centre
38 Looe Street
Plymouth
Tel: 0752 660060

Powys Video Project

Drama Centre
Tremont Road
Llandridnod Wells
Powys
Tel: 0597 4444
Paul Brown
Uses S-VHS equipment in
schools on residential
basis. Plans projects on
wider basis within the
community

Praxis Films

14 Manor Drive
Binbrook
Lincoln LN3 6BX
Tel: 0472 83547
John Goddard
Mike Thomson
Chris Bryer
Film and video production
– documentaries, current
affairs, educational and
drama. Specialise in
rural, industrial and sea
themes nationally and
internationally, and films

for and about Eastern and
Northern England. Runs
'The Visual Archive of
Eastern England'

Projects UK

1 Black Swan Court
Westgate Road
Newcastle upon Tyne
NE1 1SG
Tel: 091 232 2410
Caroline Taylor
Experimental arts and
media. Offers education
and training, product
work and production and
distribution of a range of
art and media products

Real Time Video

Newtown Community
House
117 Cumberland Road
Reading RG1 3JY
Tel: 0734 351023
Jackie Shaw
Clive Robertson
Debbi O'Brien
Process-based community
access video workshop.
Video production,
distribution and
exhibition. Offers
exhibition facilities to
others. Runs courses and
workshops, organises
screenings and projects

F Red Flannel Films

Maritime Offices
Woodland Terrace
Pontypridd
Mid Glamorgan
Tel: 0443 401743/480564
Red Flannel is a women's
collective working on film
and video production,
distribution, exhibition,
education, training,
archive and video library.
Productions include Mam
on 16mm and video

F Retake Film and Video Collective

19 Liddell Road
London NW6 2EW
Tel: 01 328 4676
Mahmood Jamal
Seema Gill
Sebastian Shah
Ahmed Jamal
Film/video production,
distribution and training.
Organising screenings
and discussions around
the history of Indian
cinema. Productions
include two feature
dramas, Majdhar and
Hotel London and

documentaries Living in
Danger, Environment of
Dignity, Who Will Cast
the First Stone?, and
Sanctuary Challenge

F Sankofa Film and Video

Unit K 32–34 Gordon
House Road
London NW5 1LP
Tel: 01 485 0848
Maureen Blackwood
Robert Crusz
Isaac Julien
Nadine Marsh-Edwards
Film/video production
and distribution. Offers
production facilities to
others, runs training
workshops in film and
video. Organises
screenings and
discussions. Productions
include The Passion of
Remembrance, Perfect
Image, Dreaming Rivers
and Looking for Langston

Screenworks – Portsmouth Media Trust

The Hornpipe
143 Kingston Road
Portsmouth PO2 7EB
Tel: 0705 861851
Steve Jackman
Dave Allen
Margaret O'Connor
Film/video production,
training workshops.
Regular exhibition of
independent film, video
and photography in
Rendezvous cinema and
Screenworks gallery

Second Sight

Zair Works
111 Bishop Street
Birmingham B5 6JL
Tel: 021 622 4223
(productions),
021 622 5750 (training)
Dylis Pugh
Glynis Powell
Claire Hodson
Video production
company specialising in
arts, social issues and
training programmes.
Runs practical training
courses for women from
beginners level to low-
band production. Provides
an information resource
on all aspects of AV media

F Sheffield Film Co-op

Brown Street
Sheffield S1 2BS
Tel: 0742 727170
Chrissie Stansfield
Women's film and video
production workshop
reflecting women's views
on a wide range of issues.
Distribute work on
film/tape including
*Red Skirts on Clydeside,
Changing Our Lives,
Women of Steel, Let Our
Children Grow Tall!,
Bringing It All Back
Home, Diamonds in
Brown Paper,* and *For a
Living Wage*

Sheffield Independent Film

Avec
Brown Street
Sheffield S1 2BS
Tel: 0742 720304
Colin Pons
A resource base for
independent film and
videomakers in the
Sheffield region. Regular
training workshops;
access to a range of film
and video equipment;
technical and
administrative backup;
and regular screenings of
independent film and
video

Sheffield Media Unit

Central Library
Surrey Street
Sheffield S1 1XZ
Tel: 0742 734746
Georgia Stone
Andy Stamp
Gaining international
recognition for developing
practical media
techniques, particularly
for educationalists. Offers
training in media and
communication skills.
Produced 'The Television
Programme' workbook in
1987

Silver Valley Video

The Old Cottage
Trebullet
Launceston
Cornwall PL15 9QA
Tel: 0566 82501
John Sheppard

Siren Film and Video Co-op

Customs House
St Hilda's
Middlesbrough

Cleveland
Tel: 0642 221298
Dave Eadington
Wendy Critchley
Pete Woodhouse
Sarah Shaw
Film/video production,
distribution and
exhibition. Offers
production facilities to
others. Workers' co-
operative producing for
community groups and
television. Recent titles
include *All Things Being
Equal* and *Neutralism*
(working title)

South Wales Women's Film Group (Grwp Ffilmiau Menywod De Cymru)

c/o Chapter Arts Centre
Market Road
Canton
Cardiff
Tel: 0222 396061
Sol Jorgenson
Andrea Williams
Helen Catermole
Twenty women actively
concerned with issues of
representation of women
via low-budget film and
video production,
screenings and
discussions. Work
includes producing
miniatures through
training

Sprockettes (York Film Workshop/ Women's Group)

8 The Crescent
Blossom Street
York YO2 2AW
Tel: 0904 641394
Penny Florence
Film/video production.
Basic training and
education courses. Films
and videos (mainly short
fiction and documentary)
for hire

Star Productions

61 Thistlewaite Road
London E5 0QG
Studio: 1 Cornthwaite
Road
London E5
Tel: 01 986 4470
Raj Patel
Film/video production
company working from an
Asian perspective. Multi-
lingual productions.
Offers production and
exhibition facilities and

studio for hire. Output
includes community
documentaries, video
films of stage plays and
feature films

F Steel Bank Film Co-op

Brown Street
Sheffield S1 2BS
Tel: 0742 721235
Susie Field
Jessica York
Simon Reynell
Dinah Ward
Noemie Mendelle
Film/video production
and distribution. Channel
4 funded. Work includes
documentaries, art
programmes, campaign
tapes and fiction films.
Productions include
*Winnie, Security, Clocks
of the Midnight Hours,
Great Noises that Fill the
Air, For Your Own Good*
and *Tales from Two New
Towns*

Studio Nine, The Video Production House

Monyhull Hall Road
Kings Norton
Birmingham B30 3QB
Tel: 021 444 4750
Alison Richards
Gary Liszewski
Michael Smyth
Two or three machine
low-band edit suite
available for hire with or
without editor. On and
off-line editing. Script to
screen productions in
training, documentary,
information and
promotional films. Also
caters for pop promos and
entertainment. Freelance
ENG crew, photographic
stills.

Studio One Video

Peterborough Arts Centre
Media Department
Orton Goldhay
Peterborough PE2 OJQ
Tel: 0733 237073
Satinder Sohal
Video and photography
productions, workshops
and exhibitions. Offers
U-Matic and VHS
production/edit facilities,
dark room and gallery
space. Committed to
equal access for all
sections of the community

Sutton Community Video

28 Lucknow Drive

Sutton-in-Ashfield
Notts NG17 4LS
Tel: 0623 558415
Clem Turff

Swingbridge Video

Norden House
41 Stowell Street
Newcastle upon Tyne
NE1 4YB
Steve Colton
Hugh Kelly
Sarah McCarthy
Gev Pringle
A community video
project making tapes with
and on behalf of
community and campaign
groups in the North East.
Video production,
distribution and training

TURC Video

7 Frederick Street
Birmingham B1 3HE
Tel: 021 233 4061
Marian Hall
Video production,
distribution and
exhibition. 3 machine
editing. Offers all these
facilities to others. Works
mainly on trade union
and campaign issues,
locally and nationally.
Productions include
*Rights Wot Rights,
P & O . . . Profit before
People* and *The
Journalist's Tale*

The Television Co-operative

100 Fawnbrake Avenue
London SE24 OBZ
Tel: 01 738 7789
John Underwood
Ron Stoneman

33 Video Co-operative

33–35 Guildford Street
Luton
Beds
Tel: 0582 21448
Dermot Byrne
Gary Whiteley
Three machine lo-band,
time-code. 2 machine
S-VHS. Computer
graphics, Chromakey

F Trade Films

36 Bottle Bank
Gateshead
Tyne and Wear NE8 2AR
Tel: 091 477 5532
Derek Stubbs
Film/video production,
distribution and
exhibition. Offers
production facilities to
others. Workshop

comprises Trade Films (fiction/documentary) and Northern Newsreel (current affairs), together with the Northern Film and Television Archive

Trilith Video
Corner Cottage
Brickyard Lane
Bourton
Gillingham
Dorset SP8 5PJ
Tel: 0747 840750/840727
Trevor Bailey
John Holman
Sue Holman
Specialises in rural video on community action, rural issues and the outlook and experience of country-born people. Produces tapes, undertakes commissions and gathers archive film in order to make it publicly available on video. Distributes own work nationally

F 20th Century Vixen
50 Brunswick Street West

Hove
Sussex BN3 1EL
Tel: 0273 735594/21149
Trudi Davies
Claire Hunt
Kim Longinotto
Film/video production, training, distribution and screening. Offers these facilities to local groups. Prioritises women. Programmes available for hire/sale include *Fireraiser* (winner of Pascoe McFarlane Memorial Award 1988), *Eat the Kimono* (1989), *Clause and Effect, Between Ourselves, Save Our Village Schools* and *I'm a Loudmouth*

Valley and Vale Community Arts
Blaengarw Workmen's Hall
Blaengarw
Mid Glamorgan
Tel: 0656 871911
Justine Ennion
The Holm View Centre
Skomer Road
Gibbonsdown

Barry
South Glamorgan
Tel: 0446 742289
Jerry Rothwell
Video production, distribution and exhibition. Open-access workshop offering training to community groups in VHS and low-band U-Matic

Vera Productions
PO Box HP5
Leeds LS6 2ED
Tel: 0532 428646
Al Garthwaite
Catherine Mitchell
Hilary Readman
Film/video production, training, exhibition and distribution. Offers production and consultancy on commission. Runs training courses for women in 16mm, VHS and low-band. Information network and resource for women

Video in Pilton
30 Ferry Road Avenue

West Pilton
Edinburgh EH4 3BA
Tel: 031 332 5764
Joel Venet
Barbara Orton
Hugh Farrell
Community-based training facilities; production work for national campaigning groups, trades unions and local authority; exhibition at the Edinburgh Film Festival

Vokani
c/o Wolverhampton Art Gallery
Litchfield Street
Wolverhampton
Tel: 0902 24549
Tony Small
Exhibition, distribution and information network working in black film and video culture

WITCH (Women's Independent Cinema House)
c/o Open Eye
90–92 Whitechapel
Liverpool L1 6EN

051 709 9460
Judy Mason Seal
Ann Carney
Barbara Phillips
Film/video production,
distribution and
exhibition. Workshops in
film, video, photography,
animation, sound. Has a
Black women's section.
Offers advice and some
screenings

Watershed Media Centre
1 Canon's Road
Bristol BS1 5TX
Tel: 0272 276444
Shafeeq Vellani

Welfare State International
PO Box 9
Ulverston
Cumbria LA12 1AA
Tel: 0229 57146
A consortium of artists,
musicians, technicians
and performers. Film/
video production,
distribution and
exhibition. Output
includes community
feature films and work for
television

West Glamorgan Video and Film Workshop
F6–7–10, Burrows
Chambers
East Burrows Road
Swansea SA1 1RQ
Tel: 0792 476441
Lynfa Protheroe
Rob Watling
Community co-operative
dedicated to increasing
the use and
understanding of video,
film and photography
amongst all sections of
the local community in
England and Wales. VHS,
low-band, 8mm,
darkroom and sound
facilities. Regular
training courses,
production groups and
screenings (brochure and
rate card available).
Supported by Welsh Arts
Council

West London Media Workshop
118 Talbot Road
London W11
Tel: 01 221 1859
Ka Choi
John Goff
Yvonne Jones

Video production,
distribution and
exhibition. Offers
production facilities to
others. WLMW runs a
bursary scheme aimed to
encourage new makers to
debate various cultural/
social issues

Wide Angle Film Video and Photography Workshop
c/o Birmingham
Community Association
Jenkins Street
Small Heath
Birmingham B10 0HQ
Tel: 021 772 2889
Hossein Mirshahi
Pauline Walton
Video production and
exhibition. Open-access
workshop offering
training in video and
photography. Offers
production facilities

Women in Moving Pictures
Unit 3a
Central Trading Estate
Bath Road
Brislington
Bristol BS4 0TG
Tel: 0272 712529
Pauline Battson
Jane Roberts
Penni Russell
Specialises in working
with young women and
women with physical
disabilities or learning
difficulties. Organises
workshops, tailored to the
needs of particular
groups, on all aspects of
video production. Runs
sessions on scripting and
fundraising for video.
Offers support for others
wishing to make or
distribute material.
Videos on local and
national issues,
documentary and fiction

Women in Sync
Units 5 and 6
Wharfdale Projects
47–51 Wharfdale Road
London N1
Tel: 01 278 2215
Eleesha
Pelin
Dorothy
Women's video workshop
offering facilities,
production, post-
production, screenings,
training and advice

Women's Audio-Visual Resource
(formerly Women's Film
Consortium)
Devonshire House
High Street
Digbeth B12 0LP
Tel: 021 773 9306
Patsy Davis
Exhibits film/video for
women's and girls' groups
and other groups
undertaking anti-sexist
and anti-racist work.
Video library. Arranges
screening days

Women's Media Resource Project (WMRP)
85 Kingsland High Street
London E8 2PB
Tel: 01 254 6536
Offers sound engineering
courses, video exhibition
equipment, hire of
equipment and studio,
women only screenings
and discussion

Workers' Film Association
Media and Cultural
Centre
9 Lucy Street
Manchester M15 4BX
Tel: 061 848 9785
Wowo Wauters
Rosemary Orr
Main areas of work
include media access and
training with a full range
of production, post-
production and exhibition
equipment and facilities
for community, semi-
professional and
professional standards.
Video production unit
(ACTT). Distribution and
sale of 16mm films and
videos, booking and
advice service, video
access library. Cultural
work, mixed media
events. Bookshop/
outreach work

Worthing Film and Video Workshop
Connaught Theatre
Union Place
Worthing
West Sussex BN11 1LG
Tel: 0903 200647/35334
Howard Johnson

Wrexham Community Video
The Place in the Park
Bellevue Road

Wrexham
Clwyd
Tel: 0978 358522
Eddie Meek
Video production,
distribution and
exhibition. Offers
production and exhibition
facilities to others. Runs
short training courses in
video production

Wyeside Arts Centre
Castle Street
Builth Wells
Powys LD2 3BN
Tel: 0982 552555/553668
Chris Senett
Video production,
distribution and
exhibition. Offers all
facilities to others. Runs
workshops with local
schools and organisations.

York Film Workshop
The Old Dairy Studios
156b Haxby Road
York YO3 7JN
Tel: 0904 641394
William Lawrence
Film/video production,
distribution and
exhibition, 8-track sound
recording studio and a
darkroom equipped for
full disabled access.
Courses are held in
production, sound
recording and
photography

Yorkshire Film and Video Centre
Hall Place Studios
4 Hall Place
Leeds LS9 8JD
Tel: 0532 405553
Alf Bower
Mick Houlder
Sara Worrall
Anna Zaluczkowska
Jan Wells
Facility and training
centre offering film/video
production facilities on
site and for hire on sliding
scale. Also offers
programme of training
and events, membership
scheme and community
outreach programme

F – Supported by the
BFI through finance

INDEX

INDEX TO ADVERTISERS